Testing Macroeconometric Models

Testing Macroeconometric Models

Ray C. Fair

Harvard University Press

Cambridge, Massachusetts

London, England

1994

This book is printed on acid-free paper, and its binding materials
have been chosen for strength and durability.

Library of Congress Cataloging-in-Publication Data
Fair, Ray C.
    Testing macroeconometric models / Ray C. Fair.
      p.   cm.
    Includes bibliographical references and index.
    ISBN 0-674-87503-6 (acid-free paper)
    1. United States—Economic conditions—1945– —Econometric models.
2. Econometric models. I. Title
HC106.5.F32 1994
330.973—dc20

94-13914
CIP

*To my son, John, who wasn't born in time to
make the dedication of the previous book*

Contents

List of Tables

List of Figures

Preface

This book brings together my macroeconometric research of roughly the last decade. It is a sequel to my previous book, Fair (1984), which brought together my macroeconometric research through the early 1980s. It presents the current version of my multicountry econometric model, including my U.S. model, and it discusses and applies various econometric techniques to it. All the empirical work using the model has been updated for this book.

I have indicated in a footnote at the beginning of each relevant section the article upon which the material in the section is based. Some of the articles are joint. The coauthors are Donald W. K. Andrews, Kathryn M. Dominguez, William R. Parke, Robert J. Shiller, and John B. Taylor. Some of the work is new for this book and has not been published elsewhere.

Chapter 1 gives a general view of where I think my work fits into the literature. It is a rallying cry for the Cowles Commission approach, an approach I feel too many academic researchers abandoned in the 1970s. This book is in large part an application of the Cowles Commission approach to current macro data, with particular emphasis on testing.

Ray C. Fair
March 1994

Testing Macroeconometric Models

1

Introduction

1.1 Background[1]

Interest in research topics in different fields fluctuates over time, and the field of macroeconomics is no exception. From Tinbergen's (1939) model building in the late 1930s through the 1960s, there was considerable interest in the construction of structural macroeconomic models. The dominant methodology of this period was what I will call the "Cowles Commission" approach.[2] Structural econometric models were specified, estimated, and then analyzed and tested in various ways. One of the major macroeconometric efforts of the 1960s, building on the earlier work of Klein (1950) and Klein and Goldberger (1955), was the Brookings model [Duesenberry, Fromm, Klein, and Kuh (1965, 1969)]. This model was a joint effort of many individuals, and at its peak it contained nearly 400 equations. Although much was learned from this exercise, the model never achieved the success that was initially expected, and it was laid to rest around 1972.

Two important events in the 1970s contributed to the decline in popularity of the Cowles Commission approach. The first was the commercialization of macroeconometric models. This changed the focus of research on the models. Basic research gave way to the day to day needs of keeping the models up to date, of subjectively adjusting the forecasts to make them "reasonable," and of meeting the special needs of clients.[3] The second event was Lucas's (1976)

---

[1]The discussion in this section and some of the discussion in the rest of this chapter is taken from Fair (1993d), which has the same title as this book

[2]See Arrow (1991) and Malinvaud (1991) for interesting historical discussions of econometric research at the Cowles Commission (later Cowles Foundation) and its antecedents.

[3]The commercialization of models has been less of a problem in the United Kingdom than

1

critique, which argued that the models are not likely to be useful for policy purposes. The Lucas critique led to a line of research that culminated in real business cycle (RBC) theories, which in turn generated a counter response in the form of new Keynesian economics More will be said about these latter two areas later in this chapter.

My interest in structural macroeconomic model building began as a graduate student at M.I.T. in the mid 1960s. This was a period in which there was still interest in the Brookings model project and in which intensive work was being carried out on the MPS (M.I.T.–Penn–SSRC) model. Many hours were spent by many students in the basement of the Sloan building at M.I.T. working on various macroeconometric equations using an IBM 1620 computer (punch cards and all). This was also the beginning of the development of TSP (Time Series Processor), a computer program that provided an easy way of using various econometric techniques. The program was initiated by Robert Hall, and it soon attracted many others to help in its development. I played a minor role in this development.

Perhaps because of fond memories of my time in the basement of Sloan, I have never lost interest in structural models. I continue to believe that the Cowles Commission approach is the best way of trying to learn how the macroeconomy works, and I have continued to try to make progress using this approach. This book brings together my macroeconometric research of roughly the last decade. It presents the current version of my multicountry econometric model, including my U.S. model, and it discusses various econometric techniques. The book is a sequel to Fair (1984), which brought together my macroeconometric research through the early 1980s.

The theory behind the econometric model has changed very little from that described in the earlier book, and so the theory is only briefly reviewed in the present book. On the other hand, all the empirical work is new (because there is nearly a decade's worth of new data), and all of this work is discussed. In the choice of econometric techniques to discuss, I have been idiosyncratic in the present book, as I was in the earlier book. I have chosen techniques that I think are important for macroeconometric work, but these by no means exhaust all relevant techniques. Most of the techniques that are discussed are new since the earlier book was written.

Advances in computer hardware have considerably lessened the computa-

in the United States. In 1983 the Macroeconomic Modelling Bureau of the Economic and Social Research Council was established at the University of Warwick under the direction of Kenneth F. Wallis. Various U.K. models and their associated databases are made available to academic researchers through the Bureau.

tional burden of working with large scale models. In particular, the availability of fast, inexpensive computers has made stochastic simulation routine, and this has greatly expanded the ways in which models can be tested and analyzed. Many of the techniques discussed in this book require the use of stochastic simulation.

All the techniques discussed in the earlier book and in the present book are programmed into the Fair-Parke (FP) program. This program is joint work with William R. Parke. The FP program expands on TSP in an important way. Whereas TSP was designed with single equation estimation in mind, FP was designed to treat all equations of a model at the same time. System wide techniques, such as FIML estimation, 3SLS estimation, deterministic and stochastic simulation, optimal control techniques, and techniques for rational expectations models, are much more straightforward to use in FP than they are in programs like TSP. The FP program is discussed in Fair and Parke (1993), and this discussion is not repeated in the present book.

There is considerable stress in this book on testing (hence the title of the book), both the testing of single equations and the testing of overall models. Much of my work in macroeconomics has been concerned with testing, and this is reflected in the current book. My primary aim in macroeconomics is to develop a model that is a good approximation of how the macroeconomy works, and testing is clearly an essential ingredient in this process.

The complete multicountry econometric model will be called the "MC" model. This model consists of estimated structural equations for 33 countries. There are also estimated trade share equations for 44 countries plus an "all other" category, labelled "AO." The trade share matrix is thus 45×45. The United States part of the MC model will be called the "US" model. It consists of estimated equations for the United States only, and it does not include the trade share equations. The non United States part of the MC model will be called the "ROW" (rest of world) model. Some of the more advanced techniques are applied only to the US model.

The rest of this chapter is a discussion and defense of the Cowles Commission approach and a criticism of the alternative approaches of real business cycle theorists and new Keynesian economists. It also partly serves as an outline of the book.

1.2   The Cowles Commission Approach[4]

Specification

Some of the early macroeconometric models were linear, but this soon gave
way to the specification of nonlinear models. Consequently, only the nonlinear
case will be considered here. The model will be written as

$$f_i(y_t, x_t, \alpha_i) = u_{it}, \quad (i = 1, \ldots, n), \quad (t = 1, \ldots, T) \quad (1.1)$$

where y_t is an n–dimensional vector of endogenous variables, x_t is a vector
of predetermined variables (including lagged endogenous variables), α_i is a
vector of unknown coefficients, and u_{it} is the error term for equation i for
observation t. For equations that are identities, u_{it} is identically zero for all t.

Specification consists of choosing 1) the variables that appear in each
equation with nonzero coefficients, 2) the functional form of each equation,
and 3) the probability structure for u_{it}.[5] Economic theory is used to guide the
choice of variables. In most cases there is an obvious left hand side variable
for the equation, where the normalization used is to set the coefficient of this
variable equal to minus one. This is the variable considered to be "explained"
by the equation.

Chapters 2, 5, and 6 form an example of the use of theory in the specification of an econometric model. The theory is discussed in Chapter 2, and
the specification of the stochastic equations is discussed in Chapters 5 and 6.
Before moving to the theory in Chapter 2, however, it will be useful to consider
a simpler example.

---

[4]Part of material in this section and in Sections 1.3–1.5 is taken from Fair (1992). It
should be noted that I am using the phrase "Cowles Commission approach" in a much
broader way than it is sometimes used. Heckman (1992), for example, uses the phrase
to mean the procedure of forming a hypothesis (from some theory), testing it, and then
stopping. Heckman argues (correctly in my view) that this is a very rigid way of doing
empirical work. I am using the phrase to mean the actual approach used by structural macro
model builders, where there is much back and forth movement between specification and
empirical results. Perhaps a better phrase would have been "traditional model building
approach," but this is awkward. I will thus use "Cowles Commission approach" in a general
way, but it should be kept in mind that there are narrower definitions in use.

[5]In modern times one has to make sufficient stationarity assumptions about the variables
to make time series econometricians happy. The assumption, either explicit or implicit, of
most macroeconometric model building work is that the variables are trend stationary. If
in fact some variables are not stationary, this may make the asymptotic distributions that
are used for hypothesis testing inaccurate. Fortunately, the accuracy of the asymptotic
distributions that are used in macroeconometric work can be examined, and this is done in
Section 7.5. It will be seen that the asymptotic distributions appear fairly accurate.

Consider the following maximization problem for a representative household. Maximize

$$E_0 U(C_1, \ldots, C_T, L_1, \ldots, L_T) \tag{1.2}$$

subject to

$$
\begin{aligned}
S_t &= W_t(H - L_t) + r_t A_{t-1} - P_t C_t \\
A_t &= A_{t-1} + S_t \\
A_T &= \bar{A}
\end{aligned}
\tag{1.3}
$$

where C is consumption, L is leisure, S is saving, W is the wage rate, H is the total number of hours in the period, r is the one period interest rate, A is the level of assets, P is the price level, $\bar{A}$ is the terminal value of assets, and $t = 1, \ldots, T$. E_0 is the expectations operator conditional on information available through time 0. Given A_0 and the conditional distributions of the future values of W, P, and r, it is possible in principle to solve for the optimal values of C and L for period 1, denoted C_1^* and L_1^*. In general, however, this problem is not analytically tractable. In other words, it is not generally possible to find analytic expressions for C_1^* and L_1^*.

The approach that I am calling the Cowles Commission approach can be thought of as specifying and estimating *approximations* of the decision equations. This approach in the context of the present example is the following. First, the random variables, W_t, P_t, and r_t, $t = 1, \ldots, T$, are replaced by their expected values, $E_0 W_t$, $E_0 P_t$, and $E_0 r_t$, $t = 1, \ldots, T$. Given this replacement, one can write the expressions for C_1^* and L_1^* as

$$C_1^* = g_1(A_0, \bar{A}, E_0 W_1, \cdots, E_0 W_T, E_0 P_1, \cdots, E_0 P_T, E_0 r_1, \cdots, E_0 r_T, \beta) \tag{1.4}$$

$$L_1^* = g_2(A_0, \bar{A}, E_0 W_1, \cdots, E_0 W_T, E_0 P_1, \cdots E_0 P_T, E_0 r_1, \cdots, E_0 r_T, \beta) \tag{1.5}$$

where β is the vector of parameters of the utility function. Equations 1.4 and 1.5 simply state that the optimal values for the first period are a function of 1) the initial and terminal values of assets, 2) the expected future values of the wage rate, the price level, and the interest rate, and 3) the parameters of the utility function.[6]

The functional forms of equations 1.4 and 1.5 are not in general known. The aim of the empirical work is to try to estimate equations that are approximations of equations 1.4 and 1.5. Experimentation consists in trying different

---

[6]If information for period 1 is available at the time the decisions are made, then $E_0 W_1$, $E_0 P_1$, and $E_0 r_1$ should be replaced by their actual values in equations 1.4 and 1.5.

functional forms and in trying different assumptions about how expectations are formed. Because of the large number of expected values in equations 1.4 and 1.5, the expectational assumptions usually restrict the number of free parameters to be estimated. For example, the parameters for $E_0 W_1, \ldots, E_0 W_T$ might be assumed to lie on a low order polynomial or to be geometrically declining. The error terms are usually assumed to be additive, as specified in equation 1.1, and they can be interpreted as approximation errors.

It is often the case when equations like 1.4 and 1.5 are estimated that lagged dependent variables are used as explanatory variables. Since C_0 and L_0 do not appear in 1.4 and 1.5, how can one justify the use of lagged dependent variables? A common procedure is to assume that C_1^* in 1.4 and L_1^* in 1.5 are long run "desired" values. It is then assumed that because of adjustment costs, there is only a partial adjustment of actual to desired values. The usual adjustment equation for consumption would be

$$C_1 - C_0 = \lambda(C_1^* - C_0), \quad 0 < \lambda < 1 \tag{1.6}$$

which adds C_0 to the estimated equation. This procedure is ad hoc in the sense that the adjustment equation is not explicitly derived from utility maximization. One can, however, assume that there are utility costs to large changes in consumption and leisure and thus put terms like $(C_1 - C_0)^2$, $(C_2 - C_1)^2$, $(L_1 - L_0)^2$, $(L_2 - L_1)^2$, $\ldots$ in the utility function 1.2. This would add the variables C_0 and L_0 to the right hand side of equations 1.4 and 1.5, which would justify the use of lagged dependent variables in the empirical approximating equations for 1.4 and 1.5.

This setup can handle the assumption of rational expectations in the following sense. Let $E_{t-1} y_{2t+1}$ denote the expected value of y_{2t+1}, where the expectation is based on information through period $t - 1$, and assume that $E_{t-1} y_{2t+1}$ appears as an explanatory variable in equation i in 1.1. (This equation might be an equation explaining consumption, and y might be the wage rate.) If expectations are assumed to be rational, this equation and equations like it can be estimated by either a limited information or a full information technique. In the limited information case, $E_{t-1} y_{2t+1}$ is replaced by y_{2t+1}, and the equation is estimated by Hansen's (1982) generalized method of moments (GMM) procedure. In the full information case, the entire model is estimated at the same time by full information maximum likelihood, where the restriction is imposed that the expectations of future values of variables are equal to the model's predictions of the future values. Again, the parameters of the expected future values might be restricted in order to lessen the number of free parameters to be estimated.

The specification that has just been outlined does not allow the estimation of "deep structural parameters," such as the parameters of utility functions, even under the assumption of rational expectations. Only approximations of the decision equations are being estimated. The specification is thus subject to the Lucas (1976) critique. More will be said about this below. The specification also uses the certainty equivalence procedure, which is strictly valid only in the linear quadratic setup.

Estimation

A typical macroeconometric model is dynamic, nonlinear, simultaneous, and has error terms that may be correlated across equations and with their lagged values. A number of techniques have been developed for the estimation of such models. Techniques that do not take account of the correlation of the error terms across equations (limited information techniques) include two stage least squares (2SLS) and two stage least absolute deviations (2SLAD). Techniques that do account for this correlation (full information techniques) include full information maximum likelihood (FIML) and three stage least squares (3SLS). These techniques are discussed in Fair (1984), including their modifications to handle the case in which the error terms follow autoregressive processes. They are used in the current book, although they are only briefly discussed here. 2SLS is discussed in Section 4.2, 2SLAD in Section 4.4, and 3SLS and FIML in Section 7.2.

As noted above, estimation techniques are available that handle the assumption of rational expectations. Hansen's method is discussed in Section 4.3, and FIML is discussed in Section 7.10. It will be seen in Section 7.10 that computational advances have made even the estimation of models with rational expectations by FIML computationally feasible. It is also possible, as discussed in Section 7.4, to obtain median unbiased (MU) estimates of the coefficients of macroeconometric models, and these estimates are also computed in this book.

Finally, it is now possible using stochastic simulation and reestimation to compute "exact" distributions of estimators that are used for macroeconometric models. These distributions can then be compared to the asymptotic distributions that are typically used for hypothesis testing. If some variables are not stationary, the asymptotic distributions may not be good approximations. The procedure for computing exact distributions is explained in Section 7.5 and applied to the 2SLS estimates of the US model in Section 8.4.

Testing

Testing has always played a major role in applied econometrics. When an equation is estimated, one examines how well it fits the data, if its coefficient estimates are significant and of the expected sign, if the properties of the estimated residuals are as expected, and so on. Equations are discarded or modified if they do not seem to approximate the process that generated the data very well. Sections 4.5–4.7 discuss the methods used in this book to test the individual equations, and Chapters 5 and 6 present the results of the tests.

Complete models can also be tested, but here things are more complicated. Before a complete model is tested, it must be solved. Given 1) a set of coefficient estimates, 2) values of the exogenous variables, 3) values of the error terms, and 4) lagged values of the endogenous variables, a model can be solved for the endogenous variables. If the solution (simulation) is "static," the actual values of the lagged endogenous variables are used for each period solved, and if the solution is "dynamic," the values of the lagged endogenous variables are taken to be the predicted values of the endogenous variables from the previous periods. If one set of values of the error terms is used, the simulation is said to be "deterministic." The expected values of the error terms are usually assumed to be zero, and so in most cases the error terms are set to zero for a deterministic solution. A "stochastic" simulation is one in which 1) the error terms are drawn from an estimated distribution, 2) the model is solved for each set of draws, and 3) the predicted value of each endogenous variable is taken to be the average of the solution values.

A standard procedure for evaluating how well a model fits the data is to solve the model by performing a dynamic, deterministic simulation and then to compare the predicted values of the endogenous variables with the actual values using the root mean squared error (RMSE) criterion. Other criteria include mean absolute error and Theil's inequality coefficient. If two models are being compared and model A has lower RMSEs for most of the variables than model B, this is evidence in favor of model A over model B.

There is always a danger in this business of "data mining," which means specifying and estimating different versions of a model until a good fit has been achieved (say in terms of the RMSE criterion). The danger with this type of searching is that one finds a model that fits well within the estimation period that is in fact a poor approximation of the economy. To guard against this, predictions are many times taken to be outside of the estimation period. If a model is poorly specified, it should not predict well outside the period for which it was estimated, even though it may fit well within the period.[7]

One problem with the RMSE criterion (even if the predictions are outside of the estimation period) is that it does not take account of the fact that forecast error variances vary across time. Forecast error variances vary across time because of nonlinearities in the model, because of variation in the exogenous variables, and because of variation in the initial conditions. Although RMSEs are in some loose sense estimates of the averages of the variances across time, no rigorous statistical interpretation can be placed on them: they are not estimates of any parameters of a model.

A more serious problem with the RMSE criterion as a means of comparing models is that models may be based on different sets of exogenous variables. If, for example, one model takes investment as exogenous and a second does not, the first model has an unfair advantage when computing RMSEs.

I have developed a method, which uses stochastic simulation, that accounts for these RMSE difficulties. The method accounts for the four main sources of uncertainty of a forecast from a model: uncertainty due to 1) the error terms, 2) the coefficient estimates, 3) the exogenous variables, and 4) the possible misspecification of the model. The forecast error variance for each variable and each period that is estimated by the method accounts for all four sources of uncertainty, and so it can be compared across models. The estimated variances from different structural models can be compared, or the estimated variances from one structural model can be compared to those from an autoregressive or vector autoregressive model. If a particular model's estimated variances are in general smaller than estimated variances from other models, this is evidence in favor of the particular model.

A by-product of the method is an estimate of the degree of misspecification of a model for each endogenous variable. Any model is likely to be somewhat misspecified, and the method can estimate the quantitative importance of the misspecification.

The method can handle a variety of assumptions about exogenous variable uncertainty. One polar assumption is that there is no uncertainty attached to

---

[7]This is assuming that one does not search by 1) estimating a model up to a certain point, 2) solving the model for a period beyond this point, and 3) choosing the version that best fits the period beyond the point. This type of searching may lead to a model that predicts well *outside* the estimation period even though it is in fact a poor approximation. If this type of searching is done, then one has to wait for more observations to provide a good test of the model. Even if this type of searching is not formally done, it may be that information beyond the estimation period has been implicitly used in specifying a model. This might then lead to a better fitting model beyond the estimation period than is warranted. In this case, one would also have to wait for more observations to see how accurate the model is.

the exogenous variables. This might be true, for example, of some policy variables. The other polar assumption is that the exogenous variables are in some sense as uncertain as the endogenous variables. One can, for example, estimate autoregressive equations for each exogenous variable and add these equations to the model. This would produce a model with no exogenous variables, which could then be tested. An in between case is to estimate the variance of an exogenous variable forecast error from actual forecasting errors made by a forecasting service—say the errors made by a commercial forecasting service in forecasting defense spending.

This method was developed in Fair (1980), and it is also discussed in Fair (1984). It is briefly reviewed in Section 7.7 of the current book and then used in Section 8.6 to compare the US model to other models.

Another method of comparing complete models is to regress the actual value of an endogenous variable on a constant and forecasts of the variable from two or more models. This method, developed in Fair and Shiller (1990), is discussed in Section 7.8 and applied in Section 8.7. It is related to the literature on encompassing tests—see, for example, Davidson and MacKinnon (1981), Hendry and Richard (1982), and Chong and Hendry (1986).

Another test, developed in Fair (1993c), is discussed in Section 7.9 and applied in Section 8.8. It examines how well a model predicts various economic events, such as a recession or severe inflation. This test uses stochastic simulation to estimate event probabilities from macroeconometric models, where the estimated probabilities are then compared to the actual outcomes.

Tests of the sort just described seem clearly in the spirit of the Cowles Commission approach. A model to the Cowles Commission was a null hypothesis to be tested.

Analysis

Once a model has been estimated, there are a variety of ways in which it can be analyzed. Methods for analyzing the properties of models are discussed in Chapter 10. Again, stochastic simulation is used for many of these methods. The methods include computing multipliers and their standard errors, examining the sources of economic fluctuations, examining the optimal choice of monetary-policy instruments, and solving optimal control problems.

It is sometimes felt that analyzing the properties of a model is a way of testing it, but one must be very careful here. A model may be specified and constrained in ways that lead it to have "reasonable" properties from the point of view of the model builder, but this does not necessarily mean that it is a good approximation of the economy. Unless a model tests well, it is not likely to be a good approximation even if it has reasonable properties. If, on the other hand, a model has what seem to be bizarre properties, this may mean that the model is not a good approximation even if it has done well in the tests. This may indicate that the tests that were performed have low power.

In practice there is considerable movement back and forth from analysis to specification. If a model's properties do not seem reasonable, the model may be changed and then analyzed again. This procedure usually results in a model with "reasonable" properties, but again this is not a substitute for testing the model.

Use of the Cowles Commission Approach for the MC Model

To review, the use of the Cowles Commission approach for the MC model is as follows. The theory that has been used to guide the empirical specifications is discussed in Chapter 2. Chapter 3 presents the data to which the specifications are to be applied. It also briefly discusses the transition from theory to empirical specifications. Chapters 5 and 6 combine elements of specification, estimation, and testing. The individual stochastic equations are specified, estimated, and tested in these two chapters—Chapter 5 for the US model and Chapter 6 for the ROW model. Because specification, estimation, and testing are so closely linked, it is generally useful to discuss these together, and this is what is done in Chapters 5 and 6. The complete models are then tested in Chapters 8 and 9—the US model in Chapter 8 and the entire MC model in Chapter 9. There is no further specification in these two chapters. Finally, Chapters 11 and 12 examine the properties of the models. This is the analysis part of the Cowles Commission approach.

Before proceeding to a discussion of the theory, it will be useful to consider the real business cycle approach and the approach of new Keynesian economists from the perspective of the Cowles Commission approach, and this is the subject matter for the rest of this chapter.

1.3   The Real Business Cycle Approach

As noted in Section 1.1, the RBC approach is a culmination of a line of research that was motivated by the Lucas critique. In discussing this approach, it will be useful to begin with the utility maximization model in Section 1.2. The RBC approach to this model would be to specify a particular functional form for the utility function in equation 1.2. The parameters of this function would then be either estimated or simply chosen ("calibrated") to be in line with parameters estimated in the literature. Although there is some parameter estimation in the RBC literature, most of the studies calibrate rather than estimate, in the spirit of the seminal article by Kydland and Prescott (1982). If the parameters are estimated, they are estimated from the first order conditions. A recent example is Christiano and Eichenbaum (1990), where the parameters of their model are estimated using Hansen's (1982) GMM procedure. Altug (1989) estimates the parameters of her model using a likelihood procedure. Chow (1991) and Canova, Finn, and Pagan (1991) contain interesting discussions of the estimation of RBC models. There is also a slightly earlier literature in which the parameters of a utility function like the one in equation 1.2 are estimated from the first order conditions—see, for example, Hall (1978), Hansen and Singleton (1982), and Mankiw, Rotemberg, and Summers (1985).

The RBC approach meets the Lucas critique in the sense that, given the various assumptions, deep structural parameters are being estimated (or calibrated). It is hard to overestimate the appeal this has to many people. Anyone who doubts this appeal should read Lucas' 1985 Jahnsson lectures [Lucas (1987)], which are an elegant argument for dynamic economic theory. The tone of these lectures is that there is an exciting sense of progress in macroeconomics and that there is hope that in the end there will be essentially no distinction between microeconomics and macroeconomics. There will simply be economic theory applied to different problems.

Once the coefficients are chosen, by whatever means, the overall model is solved. In the example in Section 1.2, one would solve the utility maximization problem for the optimal consumption and leisure paths. The properties of the computed paths of the decision variables are then compared to the properties of the actual paths of the variables. If the computed paths have similar properties to the actual paths (e.g., similar variances, covariances, and autocovariances), this is judged to be a positive sign for the model. If the parameters are chosen by calibration, there is usually some searching over parameters to find that set that gives good results in matching the computed paths to the actual paths in terms of the particular criterion used. In this sense the calibrated parameters are also estimated.

Is the RBC approach a good way of testing models? At first glance it might seem so, since computed paths are being compared to actual paths. But the paths are being compared in a very limited way from the way that the Cowles Commission approach would compare them. Take the simple RMSE procedure. This procedure would compute a prediction error for a given variable for *each* period and then calculate the RMSE from these prediction errors. This RMSE might then be compared to the RMSE from another structural model or from an autoregressive or vector autoregressive model.

I have never seen this type of comparison done for a RBC model. How would, say, the currently best fitting RBC model compare to a simple first order autoregressive equation for real GDP in terms of the RMSE criterion? Probably very poorly. Having the computed path mimic the actual path for a few selected moments is a far cry from beating even a first order autoregressive equation (let alone a structural model) in terms of fitting the observations well according to the RMSE criterion. The disturbing feature of the RBC literature is there seems to be no interest in computing RMSEs and the like. People generally seem to realize that the RBC models do not fit well in this sense, but they proceed anyway.

If this literature proceeds anyway, it has in my view dropped out of the race for the model that best approximates the economy. The literature may take a long time to play itself out, but it will eventually reach a dead end unless it comes around to developing models that can compete with other models in explaining the economy *observation by observation*.

One of the main reasons people proceed anyway is undoubtedly the Lucas critique and the general excitement about deep structural parameters. Why waste one's time in working with models whose coefficients change over time as policy rules and other things change? The logic of the Lucas critique is certainly correct, but the key question for empirical work is the quantitative importance of this critique. Even the best econometric model is only an approximation of how the economy works. Another potential source of coefficient change is the use of aggregate data. As the age and income distributions of the population change, the coefficients in aggregate equations are likely to change, and this is a source of error in the estimated equations. This problem may be quantitatively much more important than the problem raised by Lucas. Put another way, the representative agent model that is used so much in macroeconomics has serious problems of its own, and these problems may swamp the problem of coefficients changing when policy rules change. The RBC literature has focused so much on solving one problem that it may have exacerbated the effects of a number of others. In what sense, for example, is the RBC literature estimating deep structural parameters if a representative agent utility function is postulated and used that is independent of demographic changes over time? (A way of examining the possible problem of coefficients in macroeconomic equations changing as the age distribution changes is discussed in Section 4.7 and applied in Chapter 5.)

When deep structural parameters have been estimated from the first order conditions, the results have not always been very good even when judged by themselves. The results in Mankiw, Rotemberg, and Summers (1985) for the utility parameters are not supportive of the approach. In a completely different literature—the estimation of production smoothing equations—Krane and Braun (1989), whose study uses quite good data, report that their attempts to estimate first order conditions were unsuccessful. It may simply not be sensible to use aggregate data to estimate utility function parameters and the like.

Finally, one encouraging feature regarding the Lucas critique is that it can be tested. Assume that for an equation or set of equations the parameters change considerably when a given policy variable changes. Assume also that the policy variable changes frequently. In this case the model is obviously misspecified, and so methods like those mentioned in Section 1.2 should be able to pick up this misspecification if the policy variable has changed frequently. If the policy variable has not changed or changed very little, then the model will be misspecified, but the misspecification will not have been given a chance to be picked up in the data. But otherwise, models that suffer in an important way from the Lucas critique ought to be weeded out by various tests.

1.4   The New Keynesian Economics

I come away from reading new Keynesian articles feeling uneasy. It's like coming out of a play that many of your friends liked and feeling that you did not really like it, but not knowing quite why. Given my views of how the economy works, many of the results of the new Keynesian literature seem reasonable, but something seems missing. One problem is that it is hard to get a big picture. There are many small stories, and it's hard to remember each one. In addition, many of the conclusions do not seem robust to small changes in the models.

Upon further reflection, however, I do not think this is my main source of uneasiness. The main problem is that this literature is not really empirical in the Cowles Commission sense. *This literature has moved macroeconomics away from its econometric base.* Consider, for example, the articles in the two volumes of *New Keynesian Economics*, edited by Mankiw and Romer (1991). By my count, of the 34 papers in these two volumes, only eight have anything

to do with data.[8] Of these eight, one (Carlton, "The Rigidity of Prices")
is more industrial organization than macro and one (Krueger and Summers,
"Efficiency Wages and the Interindustry Wage Structure") is more labor than
macro. These two studies provide some interesting insights that might be of
help to macroeconomists, but they are not really empirical macroeconomics.

It has been pointed out to me[9] that the Mankiw and Romer volumes may
be biased against empirical papers because of space constraints imposed by
the publisher. Nevertheless, it seems clear that there is very little in the new
Keynesian literature similar to the structural modeling outlined in Section 1.2.
As is also true in the RBC literature of RBC models, one does not see, say,
predictions of real GDP from some new Keynesian model compared to predictions of real GDP from an autoregressive equation using a criterion like the
RMSE criterion. But here one does not see it because no econometric models
of real GDP are constructed! So this literature is in danger of dropping out of
the race not because it is necessarily uninterested in serious tests but because
it is uninterested in constructing econometric models.

I should hasten to add that I do not mean by the above criticisms that there is
no interesting empirical work going on in macroeconomics. For example, the
literature on production smoothing, which is largely empirical, has produced
some important results and insights. It is simply that literature of this type is
not generally classified as new Keynesian. Even if one wanted to be generous
and put some of this empirical work in the new Keynesian literature, it is surely
not the essence of new Keynesian economics.

One might argue that new Keynesian economics is just getting started and
that the big picture (model) will eventually emerge to rival existing models of
the economy. This is probably an excessively generous interpretation, given
the focus of this literature on small theoretical models, but unless the literature
does move in a more econometric and larger model direction, it is not likely
to have much long run impact.

1.5 Looking Ahead

So I see the RBC and new Keynesian literatures passing each other like two
runners in the night, both having left the original path laid out by the Cowles
Commission and its predecessors. The RBC literature is only interested in test-

---

[8]One might argue nine. Okun's article "Inflation: Its Mechanics and Welfare Costs,"
which I did not count in the eight, presents and briefly discusses data in one figure.

[9]By Olivier Blanchard.

ing in a very limited way, and the new Keynesian literature is not econometric enough to even talk about serious testing.

But I argue there is hope. Models can be tested, and there are procedures for weeding out inferior models. Even the quantitative importance of the Lucas critique can be tested. The RBC literature should entertain the possibility of testing models based on estimating deep structural parameters against models based on estimating approximations of decision equations. Also, the tests should be more than just observing whether a computed path mimics the actual path in a few ways. The new Keynesian literature should entertain the possibility of putting its various ideas together to specify, estimate, and test structural macroeconometric models.

Finally, both literatures ought to consider bigger models. I have always thought it ironic that one of the consequences of the Lucas critique was to narrow the number of endogenous variables in a model from many (say a hundred or more) to generally no more than three or four. If one is worried about coefficients in structural equations changing, it seems unlikely that getting rid of the structural detail in large scale models is going to get one closer to deep structural parameters.

At any rate, what follows is an application of the Cowles Commission approach. A structural macroeconomic model is specified, estimated, tested, and analyzed.

2

Theory

2.1 One Country

2.1.1 Background

The theory that has guided the specification of the US model was first presented in Fair (1974) and then in Chapter 3 in Fair (1984). This work stresses three ideas: 1) basing macroeconomics on solid microeconomic foundations, 2) allowing for the possibility of disequilibrium in some markets, and 3) accounting for all balance-sheet and flow of funds constraints. The implications of the first two ideas were first worked on by Patinkin (1956), Chapter 13, and Clower (1965). This was followed by the work of Barro and Grossman (1971). By requiring that the decisions of agents be "choice theoretic" (i.e., based on the maximizing postulates of microeconomics) and by relaxing the assumption that markets are always in equilibrium, this work provided a more solid theoretical basis for the existence of the Keynesian consumption function and for the existence of unemployment. The existence of excess supply in the labor market is a justification for including income as an explanatory variable in the consumption function, and the existence of excess supply in the goods market is a justification for the existence of unemployment.

The problem with these early disequilibrium studies is that they did not provide an explanation of why prices and wages may not always clear markets. Prices and wages were either taken to be exogenous or determined in an ad hoc manner. This was also true of the related literature on fixed price equilibria (see Grandmont (1977) for a survey of this literature). The treatment of prices and wages as exogenous or in an ad hoc manner is particularly restrictive in a disequilibrium context because disequilibrium questions are inherently

17

concerned with whether prices always get set in such a way as to clear markets.

The theoretical work in Fair (1974) and Fair (1984), Chapter 3, provides an explanation of disequilibrium. This explanation draws heavily on the studies in Phelps et al. (1970), which in turn were influenced by Stigler's classic article (1961) on imperfect information and search. In these studies prices and wages are part of the decision variables of firms. If a firm raises its price above prices of other firms, this does not result in an immediate loss of all its customers, and if a firm lowers its price below prices of other firms, this does not result in an immediate gain of everyone else's customers. There is, however, a tendency for high price firms to lose customers over time and for low price firms to gain customers. A similar statement holds for wages. This feature is likely to be true if customers and workers have imperfect information about prices and wages, hence the relevance of Stigler's article.

If a firm's market share is a function of its price relative to the prices of other firms, then a firm's optimal price strategy is a function of this relationship. Models of this type are in Phelps and Winter (1970) for prices and in Phelps (1970) and Mortensen (1970) for wages. Disequilibrium can occur in models of this type. In the Phelps and Winter model, for example, disequilibrium occurs if the average price set by firms differs from the expected average price (1970, p. 335).

In the model in Fair (1974) and Fair (1984), Chapter 3, prices and wages are decision variables of firms, along with investment, employment, and output. Firms choose these variables in a multiperiod profit maximization context. The maximization problems require that firms form expectations of various variables before the problems are solved, and expectation errors may lead to the setting of prices and wages that do not clear markets. In other words, disequilibrium can occur because of expectation errors. Errors can occur if firms do not know the exact processes that generate the variables for which they must form expectations, and these errors can persist for more than one period.

This model thus expands on the fixed price disequilibrium studies by adding prices and wages as decision variables, and it expands on the studies in Phelps et al. (1970) by adding investment, employment, and output as decision variables. The model is also more general in its treatment of household behavior and the behavior of financial markets. Also, as noted above, the model accounts for all balance-sheet and flow of funds constraints among the sectors. This means that the government budget constraint is automatically accounted for. Christ (1968) was one of the first to emphasize the government budget constraint.

The properties of the theoretical model were analyzed in Fair (1974) and Fair (1984), Chapter 3, using simulation techniques. The following is a brief outline of the model and the simulation results. Regarding the use of simulation techniques in this context, note that the simulation of theoretical models is not a test of the models in any way. This is in contrast to the stochastic simulation of econometric models, which, as discussed in Chapter 7, can be used in the testing of models. Simulating a theoretical model is simply a way of learning about its properties for the particular set of parameters used.

2.1.2 Household Behavior

The household maximization problem is similar to the example presented in Section 1.2. Taxes and transfers have been added to the problem, and a relationship has been added between the level of money holdings and time spent taking care of these holdings. There are thus three things a household can do with its time: work, take care of money holdings, and engage in leisure. The treatment of money holdings provides a choice theoretic explanation of the interest sensitivity of the demand for money. There is also a possible labor constraint on a household, which is that it may not be able to work as many hours as it would like (i.e., as much as the solution of its maximization problem implies).

The variables that influence how much a household consumes and works include current and expected future values of 1) the wage rate, 2) the price level, 3) the interest rate, 4) the tax rate, and 5) the level of transfer payments. The initial and terminal values of wealth also affect these decisions. If the substitution effect dominates the income effect, which it does in the simulation runs, then an increase in the after tax wage rate relative to the price level leads a household to work and consume more. An increase in transfer payments or in the initial value of wealth leads it to work less and consume more. An increase in the interest rate, other things being equal, has a positive effect on the household's saving rate at the beginning of the horizon and a negative effect near the end.

The possible labor constraint can also affect household behavior. If the labor constraint is binding after the household has solved its maximization problem ignoring the constraint, the household reoptimizes subject to the constraint.[1] This leads the household to consume less than it otherwise would. It works as much as the labor constraint allows. A household's "unconstrained"

---

[1]It was assumed for the simulation exercises that households do not expect the labor constraint to be binding in future periods.

decision is defined to be the decision it would make if the labor constraint were not binding, and a household's "constrained" decision is defined to be the decision it actually makes taking into account the possible labor constraint. If the labor constraint is not binding, then the unconstrained and constrained decisions are the same.

Regarding money demand, time spent taking care of money holdings responds negatively to the wage rate and positively to the interest rate. In other words, a household spends more time keeping money balances low when the wage rate is low or the interest rate is high. The demand for money is also a function of the level of transactions.

Note that *real* interest rate effects on household behavior are accounted for in the model. A household solves its multiperiod optimization problem based on expectations of future prices and wages (as well as of nominal interest rates), and so future inflation effects are captured.

2.1.3 Firm Behavior

As noted above, firms solve profit maximization problems in which prices, wages, investment, employment, and output are decision variables. The technology of a firm is assumed to be of a "putty-clay" type, where at any one time there are a number of different types of machines that can be purchased. The machines differ in price, in the number of workers that must be used per machine per unit of time, and in the amount of output that can be produced per machine per unit of time. The worker-machine ratio is assumed to be fixed for each type of machine.

There are assumed to be costs involved in changing the size of the work force and the size of the capital stock. Because of these adjustment costs, it may be optimal for a firm to operate some of the time below capacity and "off" its production function. This means that some of the time the number of worker hours paid for may be greater than the number of hours that the workers are effectively working. Similarly, some of the time the number of machine hours available for use may be greater than the number of machine hours actually used. The difference between hours paid for by a firm and hours worked is "excess labor," and the difference between the number of machines on hand and the number of machines required to produce the output is "excess capital."

A firm expects that it will gain customers by lowering its price relative to the expected prices of other firms. The main expected costs from doing this, aside from the lower price it is charging per good, are the adjustment costs.

The firm also expects that other firms over time will follow it if it lowers its price, and so it does not expect to be able to capture an ever increasing share of the market with its lower price. Conversely, a firm expects that it will lose customers by raising its price relative to the expected prices of other firms. The main costs from doing this, aside from the lost customers, are again the adjustment costs. On the plus side, the firm expects that other firms over time will follow it if it raises its price, and so it does not expect to lose an ever increasing share of the market with its higher price.

Similar reasoning holds for wages. A firm expects that it will gain (lose) workers if it raises (lowers) its wage rate relative to the expected wage rates of other firms. The firm also expects that other firms will follow it if it raises (lowers) its wage rate, and so it does not expect to capture (lose) an ever increasing share of the market with its wage rate increase (decrease).

Because of the adjustment costs, a firm, if it chooses to lower output, may choose in the current period not to lower its employment and capital stock to the minimum levels required. In other words, it may be optimal for the firm to hold either excess labor or excess capital or both during certain periods.

Some of the main properties of the model of firm behavior that result from the simulation runs are the following. 1) A change in the expected prices (wages) of other firms leads the given firm to changes its own price (wage) in the same direction. 2) Excess labor on hand has a negative effect on current employment decisions, and excess capital on hand has a negative effect on current investment decisions. 3) An increase (decrease) in the interest rate leads to a substitution away from (toward) less labor intensive machines and a decrease (increase) in investment expenditures. 4) A firm responds to a decrease in demand by lowering its price and contracting, and it responds to an increase in demand by raising its price and expanding.

Similar to household behavior, *real* interest rate effects on firm behavior are accounted for in the model through the multiperiod optimization problem of a firm.

2.1.4 Bank and Government Behavior

The model in Fair (1974) allowed for the possible existence of credit rationing, and so both labor and *loan* constraints were considered. I did not find in the empirical work much evidence of the effects of loan constraints on the economy, and so in presenting the model in Fair (1984), Chapter 3, the possible existence of loan constraints was dropped. This considerably simplifies the model. The household and firm maximization problems are easier to specify, and it no longer necessary to specify a maximization problem for banks. This simpler model of bank behavior is outlined here.

Banks receive money from households and firms in the form of demand deposits. They must hold a certain portion of these deposits in the form of bank reserves, and they are assumed never to hold excess reserves. The percent of bank reserves borrowed from the monetary authority is a function of the spread between the bank loan rate and the discount rate. Banks loan money to households, firms, and the government.

The fiscal authority in the government sets the tax rates and collects taxes from households, firms, and banks. It chooses its spending for goods and labor, and it pays interest on its debt. The monetary authority earns interest on its loans to the banks. It sets the reserve requirement ratio and the discount rate. It can also engage in open market operations by buying and selling government securities.[2] In Fair (1974) the amount of government securities outstanding was taken as exogenous, i.e., as a policy variable of the monetary authority. In Fair (1984), Chapter 3, on the other hand, an interest rate reaction function was postulated for the monetary authority, where the interest rate implied by the reaction function was attained through open market operations. In this version the amount of government securities outstanding is endogenous—the amount is whatever is needed to have the interest rate value from the reaction function be met. The addition of an interest rate reaction function to the theoretical model grew out of empirical work I had done in estimating a reaction function of the Federal Reserve [Fair (1978)]. As will be seen in Chapter 4, an estimated reaction function is part of the US model.

All the flows of funds among the sectors are accounted for, and so the government budget constraint is met. The constraint states that any nonzero level of saving of the government must result in the change in non borrowed reserves or the amount of government securities outstanding.

2.1.5   The Complete Model

The complete model consists of the maximization problems of households and firms and the specification of how households, firms, banks, and the government interact. Some of the main properties of the complete model as gleaned from the simulation results are the following.

---

[2]The phrase "government securities" is used for convenience here and in what follows even though there is no distinction in the model between government securities and other types of securities.

1. If the quantity of labor demanded from firms and the government (banks do not demand labor) is less than the quantity of labor that households want to supply from their unconstrained maximization problems, the labor constraint is binding on households. When households reoptimize subject to the labor constraint, they consume less than they otherwise would. This lowers firms' sales, and firms respond in the next period by lowering output and their demand for labor. This further constrains the households, which leads them to consume even less, and so on. A multiplier reaction can thus get started from an initial labor constraint on households. Unemployment in the model can be thought of as the difference between the unconstrained and constrained supply of labor from the households.

2. Disequilibrium of the kind just described can occur because firms do not necessarily set the correct prices and wages, which comes about from expectation errors. In order for a firm to form correct expectations, it would have to know the maximization problems of all the other firms and of the households. It would also have to know the exact way that transactions take place once the decisions have been solved for. Firms are not assumed to have this much knowledge, and so they can make expectation errors. Note that this explanation of disequilibrium does not rely on price and wage rigidities, although if there are such rigidities, this is another reason for the existence of disequilibrium.

3. Once the economy begins to contract, the interest rate is one of the key variables that prevents it from contracting indefinitely. As unemployment increases, the interest rate is lowered by the reaction function of the monetary authority. A fall in the interest rate results in a capital gain on stocks. Both the lower interest rate and the higher wealth have a positive effect on consumption. The lower interest rate may also lead firms to switch to more expensive, less labor intensive machines, which increases investment expenditures.

4. The unemployment rate is a positive function of the supply of labor, which in turn is a function of such variables as the after tax real wage and the level of transfer payments. The effects of a policy change on the unemployment rate thus depend in part on the labor supply response to the policy change. For example, increasing the income tax rate lowers labor supply (assuming the substitution effect dominates), whereas decreasing the level of transfer payments raises it. Given the many fac-

tors that affect labor supply, there is no stable relationship in the model between the unemployment rate and real output and between the unemployment rate and the rate of inflation. There is, in other words, no stable Okun's law and no stable Phillips curve in the model.

This completes the outline of the single country theoretical model. Simulation results for the model can be found in Fair (1984), Chapter 3. To complete the theory, the model needs to be opened to the outside world. A straightforward way of doing this is to link one single country model to another, and this will now be done. The two country model that is developed is sufficient to capture the main links among the countries that exist in the MC model. It accounts for the trade, price, interest rate, and exchange rate links among the countries.

2.2   Two Countries

2.2.1   Background

The theoretical two country model that has guided the specification of the MC model was first presented in Fair (1979). This model was in part a response to the considerable discussion in the literature that had taken place in the 1970s as to whether the exchange rate is determined in a stock market or in a flow market. [See, for example, Frenkel and Rodriguez (1975), Frenkel and Johnson (1976), Dornbusch (1976), Kouri (1976), and the survey by Myhrman (1976).] The monetary approach to the balance of payments stressed the stock market determination of the exchange rate, which was contrasted with "the popular notion that the exchange rate is determined in the flow market so as to assure a balanced balance of payments" [Frenkel and Rodriguez (1975, p. 686)]. In the model in Fair (1979), on the other hand, there is no natural distinction between stock market and flow market determination of the exchange rate. The exchange rate is merely one endogenous variable out of many, and in no rigorous sense can it be said to be *the* variable that clears a particular market. In other words, there is no need for a stock-flow distinction in the model; stock and flow effects are completely integrated. [Other studies in the 1970s in which the stock-flow distinction was important included Allen (1973), Black (1973), Branson (1974), and Girton and Henderson (1976).] The reason there is no stock-flow distinction in the model is the accounting for all flow of funds and balance-sheet constraints. These constraints are accounted for in the single country model, and they are also accounted for when two single country models are put together to form a two country model.

The main features of the model in Fair (1979) that are relevant for the construction of the MC model were discussed in Fair (1984), Section 3.2. Contrary to the case for the single country theoretical model, however, the two country theoretical model was not analyzed by simulation techniques in Fair (1984). In this section a version of the two country model is presented that will be analyzed by simulation techniques. This should help in understanding the properties of the theoretical model before it is used to guide the specification of the MC model. Again, the simulation of the theoretical model is not meant to be a test of the model in any sense.

2.2.2 Notation

In what follows capital letters denote variables for country 1, lower case letters denote variables for country 2, and an asterisk (*) on a variable denotes the other country's holdings or purchase of the variable. There are three sectors per country: private non financial (h), financial (b), and government (g). The private non financial sector includes both households and firms. It will be called the "private sector." Members of the financial sector will be called "banks." Each country specializes in the production of one good (X, x). Each country has its own money (M, m) and its own bond (B, b). Only the private sector of the given country holds the money of the country. The bonds are one period securities. If a sector is a debtor with respect to a bond (i.e., a supplier of the bond), then the value of B or b for that sector is negative. The interest rate on B is R and on b is r. The price of X is P and of x is p. e is the price of country 1's currency in terms of country 2's currency, so that, for example, and increase in e is a depreciation of country 1's currency. The government of each country holds a positive amount of the international reserve (Q, q), which is denominated in the units of country 1's currency, and collects taxes (T, t) as a proportion of income (Y, y). The government of a country does not hold the bond of the other country and does not buy the good of the other country. f_{ij} is the derivative of f_i with respect to argument j.

2.2.3 Equations

There are 17 equations per country and one redundant equation. The equations for country 1 are as follows. (The derivative indicates the expected effect of the particular variable on the left hand side variable.) The demands for the two goods by the private sector of country 1 are

$$X_h = f_1(P, e \cdot p, R', Y - T), \quad f_{11} < 0, f_{12} > 0, f_{13} < 0, f_{14} > 0 \quad (2.1)$$

$$x_h^* = f_2(P, e \cdot p, R', Y - T), \quad f_{21} > 0, f_{22} < 0, f_{23} < 0, f_{24} > 0 \quad (2.2)$$

R' is the real interest rate, $R - (EP_{+1} - P)$, where EP_{+1} is the expected value of P for the next period based on current period information. The equations state that the demands are a function of the two prices, the real interest rate, and after tax income. X_h is the purchase of country 1's good by the private sector of country 1, and x_h^* is the purchase of country 2's good by the private sector of country 1. The domestic price level is assumed to be a function of demand pressure as measured by Y and of the level of import prices, $e \cdot p$:

$$P = f_3(Y, e \cdot p), \quad f_{31} > 0, f_{32} > 0 \qquad (2.3)$$

There is assumed to be no inventory investment, so that production is equal to sales:

$$Y = X_h + X_g + X_h^* \qquad (2.4)$$

where X_g is the purchase of country 1's good by its government and X_h^* is the purchase of country 1's good by country 2. Taxes paid to the government are

$$T = TX \cdot Y \qquad (2.5)$$

where TX is the tax rate.

The demand for real balances is assumed to be a function of the interest rate and income:

$$\frac{M_h}{P} = f_6(R, Y), \quad f_{61} < 0, f_{62} > 0 \qquad (2.6)$$

Borrowing by the banks from the monetary authority (BO) is assumed to be a function of R and of the discount rate RD:

$$BO = f_7(R, RD), \quad f_{71} > 0, f_{72} < 0 \qquad (2.7)$$

Since the private sector is assumed to be the only sector holding money,

$$M_b = M_h \qquad (2.8)$$

where M_b is the money held in banks. Equation 2.8 simply says that all money is held in banks. Banks are assumed to hold no excess reserves, so that

$$BR = RR \cdot M_b \qquad (2.9)$$

where BR is the level of bank reserves and RR is the reserve requirement rate.

Let Ee_{+1} be the expected exchange rate for the next period based on information available in the current period. Then from country 1's perspective, the expected (one period) return on the bond of country 2, denoted Er, is $\frac{Ee_{+1}}{e}(1+r) - 1$, where r is the interest rate on the bond of country 2. The demand for country 2's bond is assumed to be a function of R and Er :

$$b_h^* = f_{10}(R, Er), \quad f_{10,1} < 0, f_{10,2} > 0 \tag{2.10}$$

b_h^* is the amount of country 2's bond held by country 1. Equation 2.10 and the equivalent equation for country 2 are important in the model. If capital mobility is such as to lead to uncovered interest parity almost holding (i.e., R almost equal to Er), then large changes in b_h^* will result from small changes in the difference between R and Er. If uncovered interest parity holds exactly, which is not assumed here,[3] then equation 2.10 and the equivalent equation for country 2 drop out, and there is effectively only one interest rate in the model.

The next three equations determine the financial saving of each sector:

$$S_h = P \cdot X_g + P \cdot X_h^* - e \cdot p \cdot x_h^* - T + R \cdot B_h + e \cdot r \cdot b_h^* \tag{2.11}$$

$$S_b = R \cdot B_b - RD \cdot BO \tag{2.12}$$

$$S_g = T - P \cdot X_g + R \cdot B_g + RD \cdot BO \tag{2.13}$$

Equation 2.11 states that the saving of the private sector is equal to revenue from the sale of goods to the government, plus export revenue, minus import costs, minus taxes paid, plus interest received (or minus interest paid) on the holdings of country 1's bond, and plus interest received on the holdings of country 2's

---

[3]It was incorrectly stated in Fair (1984), pp. 154–155, that the version of the model that is used to guide the specification of the MC model is based on the assumption of perfect substitution of the two bonds. The correct assumption is that uncovered interest parity does not hold. As will be seen in Chapter 6, the MC model consists of estimated interest rate and exchange rate equations (reaction functions) for a number of countries (all exchange rates are relative to the U.S. dollar). If there were uncovered interest parity between, say, the bonds of countries A and B, it would not be possible to estimate interest rate equations for countries A and B plus an exchange rate equation. There is an exact relationship between the expected future exchange rate, the two interest rates, and the spot exchange rate if uncovered interest parity holds, and so given a value of the expected future exchange rate, only two of the other three values are left to be determined. It would not make sense in this case to estimate three equations. Covered interest parity, on the other hand, does roughly hold in the data used here. This will be seen in Chapter 6 in the estimation of the forward rate equations.

bond. If the private sector is a net debtor with respect to the bond of country 1, then B_h is negative and $R \cdot B_h$ measures interest payments. Remember that the private sector (h) is a combination of households and firms, and so transactions between households and firms net out of equation 2.11. Equation 2.12 states that the saving of banks is equal to interest revenue on bond holdings (assuming B_b is positive) minus interest payments on borrowings from the monetary authority. Equation 2.13 determines the government's surplus or deficit. It states that the saving of the government is equal to tax revenue, minus expenditures on goods, minus interest costs (assuming B_g is negative), and plus interest received on loans to banks.

The next three equations are the budget constraints facing each sector:

$$0 = S_h - \Delta M_h - \Delta B_h - e \cdot \Delta b_h^* \tag{2.14}$$

$$0 = S_b - \Delta B_b + \Delta M_b - \Delta(BR - BO) \tag{2.15}$$

$$0 = S_g - \Delta B_g + \Delta(BR - BO) - \Delta Q \tag{2.16}$$

Equation 2.14 states that any nonzero value of saving of the private sector must result in the change in its money or bond holdings. Equation 2.15 states that any nonzero value of saving of the financial sector must result in the change in bond holdings, money deposits (which are a liability to banks), or nonborrowed reserves. Equation 2.16 states that any nonzero value of saving of the government must result in the change in bond holdings, nonborrowed reserves (which are a liability to the government), or international reserve holdings.

There is also a constraint across all sectors, which says that someone's asset is someone else's liability with respect to the bond of country 1:

$$0 = B_h + B_b + B_g + B_h^* \tag{2.17}$$

These same 17 equations are assumed to hold for country 2, with lower case and upper case letters reversed except for Q and with $1/e$ replacing e. Q is replaced by q/e. (Remember that Q and q are in the units of country 1's currency.) The last equation of the model is

$$0 = \Delta Q + \Delta q$$

which says that the change in reserves across countries is zero. This equation is implied by equations 2.11–2.17 and the equivalent equations for country 2, and so it is redundant. There are thus 34 independent equations in the model.

It will be useful in what follows to consider two equations that can be derived from the others. First, let S denote the financial saving of country 1, which is the sum of the saving of the three sectors:

$$S = S_h + S_b + S_g$$

S is the balance of payments on current account of country 1. Summing equations 2.14–2.16 and using 2.17 yields the first derived equation:

$$0 = S + \Delta B_h^* - e \cdot \Delta b_h^* - \Delta Q \qquad (i)$$

This equation simply says that any nonzero value of saving of country 1 must result in the change in at least one of the following three: country 2's holdings of country 1's bond, country 1's holding of country 2's bond, and country 1's holding of the international reserve. The second derived equation is obtained by summing equations 2.11–2.13 and using 2.17:

$$S = P \cdot X_h^* - e \cdot p \cdot x_h^* - R \cdot B_h^* + e \cdot r \cdot b_h^* \qquad (ii)$$

This equation says that the saving of country 1 is equal to export revenue, minus import costs, minus interest paid to country 2, and plus interest received from country 2.

2.2.4   Closing the Model

The exogenous government policy variables are: X_g, government purchases of goods; TX, the tax rate; RD, the discount rate; RR, the reserve requirement rate; and the same variables for country 2. Not counting these variables, there are 40 variables in the model: B_b, B_g, B_h, B_h^*, BO, BR, M_b, M_h, P, Q, R, S_b, S_g, S_h, T, X_h, X_h^*, Y, these same 18 variables for country 2, e, Ee_{+1}, EP_{+1}, and Ep_{+1}. In order to close the model one needs to make an assumption about how the three expectations are determined and to take three other variables as exogenous. (Remember there are 34 independent equations in the model.)

Assume for now that exchange rate expectations are static in the sense that $Ee_{+1} = e$ always. (This implies that $Er = r$ and $ER = R$. Remember that R does not necessarily equal r since uncovered interest parity is not necessarily assumed to hold.) Assume also that the two price expectations are static, $EP_{+1} = P$ and $Ep_{+1} = p$. The model can then be closed by taking B_g, b_g, and Q as exogenous. These are the three main tools of the monetary authorities. Taking these three tools of the monetary authorities as exogenous thus closes the model.

Instead of taking the three tools to be exogenous, however, one can assume that the monetary authorities use the tools to manipulate R, r, and e. If reaction functions for these three variables are used (or the three variables are taken to be exogenous), then B_g, b_g, and Q must be taken to be endogenous. The solution values of B_g, b_g, and Q are whatever is needed to have the target values of R, r, and e met.

Note that in closing the model no mention was made of stock versus flow effects. The exchange rate e is just one of the many endogenous variables, and it is determined, along with the other endogenous variables, by the overall solution of the model.

2.2.5 Links in the Model

The trade links in the model are standard. Country 1 buys country 2's good (x_h^*), and country 2 buys country 1's good (X_h^*). The price links come through equation 2.3 and the equivalent equation for country 2. Country 2's price affects country 1's price, and vice versa. The interest rate and exchange rate links are less straightforward, and these will be discussed next in the context of the overall properties of the model.

2.2.6 Properties of the Model

As will be discussed in the next section, the exchange rate and interest rate equations in the MC model are based on the assumption that the monetary authorities manipulate R, r, and e. (Thus, from above, B_g, b_g, and Q are endogenous in the MC model.) The interest rate and exchange rate equations are interpreted as reaction functions, where the explanatory variables in the equations are assumed to be variables that affect the monetary authorities' decisions. The key question in this work is what variables affect the monetary authorities' decisions. If capital mobility is high in the sense that uncovered interest parity almost holds, it will take large changes in the three tools to achieve values of R, r, and e much different from what the market would otherwise achieve. Since the monetary authorities are likely to want to avoid large changes in the tools, they are likely to be sensitive to and influenced by market forces. In other words, they are likely to take market forces into account in setting their target values of R, r, and e. Therefore, one needs to know the market forces that affect R, r, and e in the theoretical model in order to guide the choice of explanatory variables in the estimated reaction functions in the MC model.

In order to examine the market forces on R, r, and e in the theoretical model, a simulation version has been analyzed. Particular functional forms and coefficients have been chosen for equations 2.1, 2.2, 2.3, 2.6, 2.7, and 2.10 and the equivalent equations for country 2. The five equations for country 1 are:

$$\log X_h = a_1 - .25 \cdot \log P + .25 \cdot \log e \cdot p - 1.0 \cdot R' + .75 \cdot \log(Y - T) \quad (2.1)'$$

$$\log x_h^* = a_2 + 1.0 \cdot \log P - 1.0 \cdot \log e \cdot p - 1.0 \cdot R' + .75 \cdot \log(Y - T) \quad (2.2)'$$

$$\log P = a_3 + .1 \cdot \log e \cdot p + .1 \cdot \log Y \quad (2.3)'$$

$$\log \frac{M_h}{P} = a_6 - 1.0 \cdot R + .5 \cdot \log Y \quad (2.6)'$$

$$BO = a_7 + 50 \cdot R - 50 \cdot RD \quad (2.7)'$$

$$b_h^* = a_{10} - 100 \cdot R + 100 \cdot Er \quad (2.10)'$$

The same functional forms and coefficients were used for country 2. The a_i coefficients were chosen so that when the model was solved using the base values of all the variables, the solution values were the base values.[4] The model was solved using the Gauss-Seidel technique.[5]

The properties of the model can be examined by changing one or more exogenous variables, solving the model, and comparing the solution values to the base values. The following experiments were chosen with the aim of learning about the market forces affecting R, r, and e in the model. Unless otherwise noted, the experiments are based on the assumption that $Ee_{+1} = e$. This means from equation 2.10 and the equivalent equation for country 2 that b_h^* and B_h^* are simply a function of R and r. The experiments are also based on the assumptions that $EP_{+1} = P$ and $Ep_{+1} = p$.

In all but the last experiment, e is endogenous and Q is exogenous. Taking Q to be exogenous means that the monetary authorities are not manipulating e. This is a way of examining the market forces on e without intervention. The solution value of e for each experiment is the value that would pertain if the monetary authorities did not intervene at all in the foreign exchange market in response to whatever change was made for the experiment. B_g and b_g are always endogenous for the experiments because all the experiments

---

[4]The base values were $X_h = x_h = 60$, $X_h^* = x_h^* = 20$, $X_g = x_g = 20$, $Y = y = 100$, $TX = tx = .2$, $T = t = 20$, $M_h = M_b = m_h = m_b = 100$, $RR = rr = .2$, $BR = br = 20$, $e = 1$, all prices $= 1$, all interest rates $= .07$, and all other variables, including lagged values when appropriate, equal to zero.

[5]See Fair (1984), Section 7.2, for a discussion of the Gauss-Seidel technique.

either have R and r exogenous or M_b and m_b exogenous. In other words, it is always assumed that the monetary authorities either keep interest rates or money supplies unchanged in response to whatever change was made for the experiment. When R and r are exogenous, M_b and m_b are endogenous, and vice versa. All shocks in the experiments are for country 1.

The results of all the experiments are reported in Table 2.1, and the following discussion of the experiments relies on this table. Only signs are presented in the table because the magnitudes mean very little given that the coefficients and base values are not empirically based. The simulation experiments are simply meant to be used to help in understanding the qualitative effects on various variables. Even the qualitative results, however, are not necessarily robust to alternative choices of the coefficients. At least some of the signs in Table 2.1 may be reversed with different coefficients. The simulation work is meant to help in understanding the theoretical model, but the results from this work should not be taken as evidence that all the signs in the table hold for all possible coefficient values. In two cases it is necessary to know which interest rate (R or r) changed the most, and these cases are noted in Table 2.1 and discussed below.

Experiment 1: R decreased, r unchanged

For this experiment the interest rate for country 1 was lowered (from its base value) and the interest rate for country 2 was assumed to remain unchanged. (Both interest rates are exogenous in this experiment.) This change resulted in a depreciation of country 1's currency.[6] The fall in R relative to r led to an increase in the demand for the bond of country 2 by country 1 (b_h^* increased) and a decrease in the demand for the bond of country 1 by country 2 (B_h^* decreased). From equation i in Section 2.2.3 it can be seen that this must result in an increase in S, country 1's balance of payments, since Q is exogenous and unchanged. S is increased by increasing country 1's exports and decreasing its imports—equation ii—which is accomplished by a depreciation. Another way of looking at this is that the fall in R relative to r led to a decreased demand for country 1's currency because of the capital outflow, which resulted in a depreciation of country 1's currency. Output for country 1 (Y) increased because of the lower interest rate and the depreciation, and the demand for money increased because of the lower interest rate and the higher level of in-

---

[6]Remember that a rise in e is a depreciation of country 1's currency. The $+$ in Table 2.1 for e for experiment 1 thus means that country 1's currency depreciated.

Table 2.1
Simulation Results for the Two Country Model

	Experiment					
	1	2	3	4	5	6
	$R(-)$	$M_b(+)$	Eq2.3(+)	Eq2.3(+)	Eq2.2(+)	$R(-)$
e	+	+	+	+	+	0
R	−	−[a]	0	+[b]	+	−
r	0	−	0	+	−	0
S	+	+	0	−	−	−
s	−	−	0	+	+	+
b_h^*	+	+	0	−	−	+
B_h^*	−	−	0	+	+	−
x_h^*	−	−	0	+	−	+
X_h^*	+	+	0	−	+	+
Y	+	+	0	−	+	+
y	−	−	0	+	−	+
P	+	+	+	+	+	+
p	−	−	0	+	−	+
M_h	+	+	+	0	0	+
m_h	−	0	0	0	0	+
Q	0	0	0	0	0	−
q	0	0	0	0	0	+
B_g	+	+	0	−	+	+
b_g	−	−	0	+	−	−

Q is exogenous exept for experiment 6.
Size of changes:
   1. R lowered by .001, r exogenous
   2. M_b raised by 1.0, m_b exogenous
   3. Equation 2.3 shocked by .10, R and r exogenous
   4. Equation 2.3 shocked by .10, M_b and m_b exogenous
   5. Equation 2.2 shocked by .10, M_b and m_b exogenous
   6. R lowered by .001, r and e exogenous
[a] R decreased more than did r.
[b] R increased more than did r.

come. The monetary authority of country 1 bought bonds to achieve the reduction in R (B_g increased).

Although not shown in Table 2.1, experiments with alternative coefficients in the equations explaining b_h^* and B_h^*—equation 2.10 and the equivalent equation for country 2—showed that the more sensitive are the demands for the foreign bonds to the interest rate differential, the larger is the depreciation of the exchange rate and the larger is the increase in B_g for the same drop in R. In other words, the higher is the degree of capital mobility, the larger is the size of open market operations that is needed to achieve a given target value of the interest rate.

Remember that the above experiment is for the case in which exchange rate expectations are static, i.e. where $Ee_{+1} = e$. If instead expectations are formed in such a way that Ee_{+1} turns out to be less than e, which means that the exchange rate is expected to appreciate in the next period relative to the value in the current period (i.e., reverse at least some of the depreciation in the current period), then the depreciation in the current period is less. This is because if Ee_{+1} is less than e, the expected return on country 2's bond (Er) falls. The differential between R and Er thus falls less as a result of the decrease in R, which leads to a smaller increase in b_h^* and a smaller decrease in B_h^*. There is thus less downward pressure on country 1's currency and thus a smaller depreciation. If expectations are formed in such a way that Ee_{+1} turns out to be greater than e, which means that the exchange rate is expected to depreciate further in the next period, there is more of a depreciation in the current period. The expected return on country 2's bond rises, which leads to greater downward pressure on country 1's exchange rate.

Experiment 2: M_b increased, m_b unchanged

For this experiment the monetary authorities are assumed to target the money supplies (M_b and m_b are exogenous), and the money supply of country 1 was increased. The increase in M_b led to a decrease in R, both absolutely and relative to r, which led to a depreciation of country 1's currency. The results of this experiment are similar to those of experiment 1. The monetary authority of country 1 bought bonds to increase the money supply (B_g increased). Country 1's output increased as a result of the depreciation and the fall in R. Note that the effect of a change in the money supply on the exchange rate works through the change in relative interest rates. The interest rate of country 1 falls relative to that of country 2, which decreases the demand for country 1's bond and increases the demand for country 2's bond, which leads to a depreciation of country 1's exchange rate.

Experiment 3: Positive price shock, R and r unchanged

For this experiment the price equation for country 1 was shocked positively. The monetary authorities were assumed to respond to this by keeping interest rates unchanged. The positive price shock resulted in a depreciation of country 1's currency. Given the coefficients and base values that are used for the simulation model, the exchange rate depreciated by the same percent that P increased, and there was no change in any real magnitudes. The reason for the exchange rate depreciation is the following. Other things being equal, a positive price shock leads to a decrease in the demand for exports and an increase in the demand for imports, which puts downward pressure on S. If, however, interest rates are unchanged, then b_h^* and B_h^* do not change, which means from equation i that S cannot change. Therefore, a depreciation must take place to decrease export demand and increase import demand enough to offset the effects of the price shock.

Experiment 4: Positive price shock, M_b and m_b unchanged

This experiment is the same as experiment 3 except that the money supplies rather than the interest rates are kept unchanged. The positive price shock with the money supplies unchanged led to an increase in R. Even though R increased relative to r, country 1's currency depreciated. The negative effects of the price shock offset the positive effects of the interest rate changes.

Experiment 5: Positive import demand shock, M_b and m_b unchanged

For this experiment the import demand equation of country 1 was shocked positively. The increased demand for imports led to a depreciation of country 1's currency, since there was an increased demand for country 2's currency. The depreciation led to an increase in Y and P, which with an unchanged money supply, led to an increase in R. R also increased relative to r, which increased B_h^* and decreased b_h^*. The balance of payments, S, worsened. It may at first glance seem odd that a positive import shock would lead to an increase in Y, but remember that the shock does not correspond to any shock to the demand for the domestic good. The experiment is not a substitution away from the domestic good to the imported good, but merely an increase in demand for the imported good. The latter results in an increase in Y because of the stimulus from the depreciation.

Experiment 6: R decreased, r unchanged, e unchanged

This experiment is the same as experiment 1 except that e rather than Q is exogenous. In this case the monetary authorities choose B_g, b_g, and Q so as to lower R and keep r and e unchanged. One of the key differences between the results for this experiment and the results for experiment 1 is that the

Table 2.2
Summary of the Experiments

| Experiment | Effect on: | |
	Domestic Interest Rate	Exchange Rate
1. Interest rate lowered	—	Depreciation
2. Money supply raised	Lowered	Depreciation
3. Positive price shock; interest rates unchanged	—	Depreciation
4. Positive price shock; money supply unchanged	Raised	Depreciation
5. Positive import shock; money supply unchanged	Raised	Depreciation

balance of payments, S, decreases rather than increases. In experiment 1 S had to increase because of the increase in the demand for country 2's bond by country 1 and the decrease in the demand for country 1's bond by country 2. In experiment 1 S must increase because Q is exogenous—equation i. The increase in S is accomplished by a depreciation. In the present experiment there is still an increase in the demand for country 2's bond and a decrease in the demand for country 1's bond—because R falls relative to r—but S does not necessarily have to increase because Q can change. The net effect is that S decreases (and thus Q decreases). The reason for the decrease in S is fairly simple. The decrease in R is an expansionary action in country 1, and among other things it increases the country's demand for imports. This then worsens the balance of payments. There is no offsetting effect from a depreciation of the currency to reverse this movement.

This completes the discussion of the experiments. They should give one a fairly good idea of the properties of the model. Of main concern here are the effects of the various changes on the domestic interest rate and the exchange rate. Table 2.2 presents a summary of these effects in the model (experiment 6 is not included in the table because both R and e are exogenous in it).

2.2.7 The Use of Reaction Functions

As noted in the previous section, reaction functions for interest rates and exchange rates have been estimated in the MC model. To put this approach in perspective, it will help to consider an alternative approach that in principle could have been followed. If equations 2.1, 2.2, 2.3, 2.6, 2.7, 2.10, and the equivalent equations for country 2 were estimated, one could solve the model for R, r, and e (and the other endogenous variables) by taking B_g, b_g, and Q as exogenous. R, r, and e would thus be determined without having to estimate any direct equations for them. Their values would be whatever is needed to clear the two bond markets and the market for foreign exchange. In doing this, however, one would be making the rather extreme assumption that the monetary authorities' choices of B_g, b_g, and Q are never influenced by the state of the economy, i.e. are always exogenous.

If one believes that monetary authorities intervene at least somewhat, there are essentially two options open. One is to estimate equations with B_g, b_g, and Q on the left hand side, and the other is to estimate equations with R, r, and e on the left hand side. If the first option is followed, then the B_g, b_g, and Q equations are added to the model and the model is solved for R, r, and e. If the second option is followed, the R, r, and e equations are added to the model and the model is solved for B_g, b_g, and Q. The first option is awkward because one does not typically think of the monetary authorities having target values of the instruments themselves. It is more natural to think of them having target values of interest rates (or money supplies[7]) and exchange rates, and this is the assumption made for the MC model.

There is also a practical reason for taking the present approach. If B_g, b_g, and Q are taken to be exogenous or equations estimated for them, equations like 2.10, which determine the bilateral demands for securities, must be estimated. In practice it is very difficult to estimate such equations. One of the main problems is that data on bilateral holdings of securities either do not exist or are not very good. If instead equations for interest rates and exchange rates are estimated, one can avoid estimating equations like 2.10 in order to determine interest rates and exchange rates if one is willing to give up determining B_g, b_g, and Q. For many applications one can get by without knowing the amounts

---

[7]It is in the spirit of the present approach to estimate money supply reaction functions rather than interest rate reaction functions. In either case B_g is endogenous. No attempt has been made in the construction of the MC model to try to estimate money supply reaction functions. The present work is based on the implicit assumption that interest rate reaction functions provide a better approximation of the way monetary authorities behave than do money supply reaction functions.

of government bonds outstanding and government reserve holdings. One can simply keep in mind that the values of these variables are whatever is needed to have the interest rate and exchange rate values be met.

2.2.8   Further Aggregation

Data on bilateral security holdings were not collected for the MC model, and so data on variables like B_h^* and b_h^* are not available. Instead, a net asset variable, denoted A in the MC model, was constructed for each country. In terms of the variables in the theoretical model, $\Delta A = -\Delta B_h^* + e \cdot \Delta b_h^* + \Delta Q$. Equation i thus becomes

$$0 = S - \Delta A \qquad\qquad (i)'$$

Data on S are available for each country, and A was constructed as $A_{-1} + S$, where an initial value for A for each country was first chosen.

   This aggregation is very convenient because it allows A to be easily constructed. The cost of doing this is that capital gains and losses on bonds from exchange rate changes are not accounted for. Given the current data, there is little that can be done about this limitation.

3

The Data, Variables, and Equations

3.1 Transition from Theory to Empirical Specifications

The transition from theory to empirical work in macroeconomics is not always straightforward. The quality of the data are never as good as one might like, so compromises have to be made in moving from theory to empirical specifications. Also, extra assumptions usually have to be made, in particular about unobserved variables like expectations and about dynamics. There usually is, in other words, considerable "theorizing" involved in this transition process.[1]

The first step in the transition, which is taken in this chapter, is to choose the data and variables. All the data and variables in the US and ROW models are presented in this chapter. The second step, also taken in this chapter, is to choose which variables are to be treated as exogenous, which are to be determined by stochastic (estimated) equations, and which are to be determined by identities. All the equations in the two models are listed in this chapter. The third step, which is where most of the theory is used, is to choose the explanatory variables in the stochastic equations and the functional forms of the equations. This is the task of Chapters 5 and 6. The discussion in the present chapter relies heavily on the tables in Appendices A and B.

As noted in Section 1.1, the overall MC model consists of estimated structural equations for 33 countries. There are 30 stochastic equations for the United States and up to 15 each for each of the other countries. There are 101 identities for the United States and up to 19 each for each of the others. There are 44 countries in the trade share matrix plus an all other category called "all other" (AO). The trade share matrix is thus 45×45. The countries are listed

---

[1]This transition is discussed in detail in Fair (1984), Section 2.2.

in Table B.1. The data for the United States begin in 1952:1, and the data for
the other countries begin in 1960:1. As will be discussed, some of the country
models are annual rather than quarterly.

3.2 The US Model

The data, variables, and equations for the US model are discussed in this
section. The relevant tables are Tables A.1–A.9 in Appendix A, and these will
be briefly outlined first.

3.2.1 The Tables (Tables A.1–A.9)

Table A.1 presents the six sectors in the US model: household (h), firm (f),
financial (b), foreign (r), federal government (g), and state and local government (s). In order to account for the flow of funds among these sectors and
for their balance-sheet constraints, the U.S. Flow of Funds Accounts (FFA)
and the U.S. National Income and Product Accounts (NIPA) must be linked.
Many of the 101 identities in the US model are concerned with this linkage.
Table A.1 shows how the six sectors in the US model are related to the sectors
in the FFA. The notation on the right side of this table (H1,FA, etc.) is used in
Table A.4 in the description of the FFA data.

Table A.2 lists all the variables in the US model in alphabetical order, and
Table A.3 lists all the stochastic equations and identities. The functional forms
of the stochastic equations are given, but not the coefficient estimates. The
coefficient estimates are presented in Tables 5.1–5.30 in Chapter 5. Tables
A.2 and A.3 are the main reference tables for the US model. Of the remaining
tables, Tables A.4–A.6 show how the variables were constructed from the raw
data, Table A.7 lists the first stage regressors that were used for the 2SLS and
3SLS estimates, and Table A.8 shows how the model is solved under various
assumptions about monetary policy. Finally, Table A.9 shows which variables
appear in which equations. It will be useful to begin with Tables A.4–A.6
before turning to Tables A.2 and A.3.

3.2.2 The Raw Data

The NIPA Data

Table A.4 lists all the raw data variables. The variables from the NIPA are
presented first, in the order in which they appear in the *Survey of Current*

Business, August 1993. In early 1992 the NIPA data were revised, with the benchmark year changed from 1982 to 1987. At the same time the Bureau of Economic Analysis began publishing quantity and price indices based on other than fixed weights. The alternatives to the "fixed 1987 weights" are "chain type annual weights" and "benchmark year weights." There are a number of problems with using the fixed 1987 weights over a period as long as that used in this study (1952:1–1993:2),[2] and so the alternative weights have considerable appeal for present purposes. One of the alternative set of weights—the chain type annual weights—was thus used in the construction of the data for the model.

At the time of this writing the alternative weights are not available before 1959 and after 1987. The procedure that was followed to create the real variables from the NIPA data is a follows. First, the regular data from 1988 on were used (based on fixed 1987 weights). Second, the pre-revised data (based on 1982 weights) were used between 1952 and 1958. In the absence of alternative weights for this period, the 1982 weights seemed a better choice than the 1987 weights, since they are closer to the period. The old data for this period that were in units of 1982 dollars were multiplied up to be in units of 1987 dollars, and the old price indices that were 100 in 1982 were multiplied up to be 100 in 1987. Third, the chain type weights were used for the data between 1959 and 1987. Table A.4 shows how this was done. The chain type price indices were taken from NIPA Table 7.1 (variables R84–R93), and the nominal variables were deflated by these indices (see variables R11–R16, R19–R22).

The use of the chain type price indices in this way means that between 1959 and 1987 real GDP is not the sum of its real components. Consequently, a discrepancy variable, denoted $STATP$, was created, which is the difference between real GDP and the sum of its real components. ($STATP$ is constructed using equation 83 in Table A.3.) $STATP$ is, of course, zero before 1959 and after 1987. Between 1959 and 1987 it is a fairly smoothly trending variable, slowly decreasing in absolute value during the period. $STATP$ is taken to be exogenous in the model.

The Other Data

The variables from the FFA are presented next in Table A.4, ordered by their code numbers. Some of these variables are NIPA variables that are not pub-

---

[2]See Young (1992) and Triplett (1992) for a good discussion of these problems and of the proposed alternative weights.

lished in the *Survey* but that are needed to link the two accounts. Interest rate variables are presented next in the table, followed by employment and population variables. The source for the interest rate data is the *Federal Reserve Bulletin*, denoted FRB in the table. The main source for the employment and population data is *Employment and Earnings*, denoted EE in the table. Some of these data are unpublished data from the Bureau of Labor Statistics (BLS), and these are indicated as such in the table.

Some adjustments that were made to the raw data are presented next in Table A.4. These are explained beginning in the next paragraph. Finally, all the raw data variables are presented at the end of Table A.4 in alphabetical order along with their numbers. This allows one to find a raw data variable quickly. Otherwise, one has to search through the entire table looking for the particular variable. All the raw data variables are numbered with an "R" in front of the number to distinguish them from the variables in the model.

The adjustments that were made to the raw data are as follows. The quarterly social insurance variables R195–R200 were constructed from the annual variables R78–R83 and the quarterly variables R38, R60, and R71. Only annual data are available on the breakdown of social insurance contributions between the federal and the state and local governments with respect to the categories "personal," "government employer," and "other employer." It is thus necessary to construct the quarterly variables using the annual data. It is implicitly assumed in this construction that as employers, state and local governments do not contribute to the federal government and vice versa.

The constructed tax variables R201 and R202 pertain to the breakdown of corporate profit taxes of the financial sector between federal and state and local. Data on this breakdown do not exist. It is implicitly assumed in this construction that the breakdown is the same as it is for the total corporate sector.

The quarterly variable R203, $INTROW$, which is the level of net interest receipts of the rest of the world, is constructed from the annual variable R96 and the quarterly and annual data on the $INTF$ and $INTG$ variables, R45 and R65. Quarterly data on net interest receipts of the rest of the world do not exist. It is implicitly assumed in the construction of the quarterly data that the quarterly pattern of the level of interest receipts of the rest of the world is the same as the quarterly pattern of the level of net interest payments of the firm and federal government sectors. Note that $INTROW$ is the level of net *receipts*, not payments. The other interest variables in the model are net payments.

The tax variables R57 and R62 were adjusted to account for the tax surcharge of 1968:3–1970:3 and the tax rebate of 1975:2. The tax surcharge and the tax rebate were taken out of personal income taxes (TPG) and put into personal transfer payments ($TRGH$). The tax surcharge numbers were taken from Okun (1971), Table 1, p. 171. The tax rebate was 7.8 billion dollars at a quarterly rate.

The multiplication factors in Table A.4 pertain to the population, labor force, and employment variables. Official adjustments to the data on POP, $POP1$, $POP2$, $CL1$, $CL2$, and CE were made a few times, and these must be accounted for. The multiplication factors are designed to make the old data consistent with the new data. For further discussion, see Fair (1984), pp. 414–415.

Table A.5 presents the balance-sheet constraints that the data satisfy. The variables in this table are raw data variables. The equations in the table provide the main checks on the collection of the data. If any of the checks are not met, one or more errors have been made in the collection process. Although the checks in Table A.5 may look easy, considerable work is involved in having them met. All the receipts from sector i to sector j must be determined for all i and j (i and j run from 1 through 6).

3.2.3   Variable Construction

Table A.6 explains the construction of the variables in the model (i.e., the variables in Table A.2) from the raw data variables (i.e., the variables in Table A.4). With a few exceptions, the variables in the model are either constructed in terms of the raw data variables in Table A.4 or are constructed by identities. If the variable is constructed by an identity, the notation "Def., Eq." appears, where the equation number is the identity in Table A.2 that constructs the variable. In a few cases the identity that constructs an endogenous variable is not the equation that determines it in the model. For example, equation 85 constructs LM, whereas stochastic equation 8 determines LM in the model. Equation 85 instead determines E, E being constructed directly from raw data variables. Also, some of the identities construct exogenous variables. For example, the exogenous variables $D2G$ is constructed by equation 49. In the model equation 49 determines TFG, TFG being constructed directly from raw data variables. If a variable in the model is the same as a raw data variable, the same notation is used for both. For example, CD, consumption expenditures on durable goods, is both a variable in the model and a raw data variable.

The financial stock variables in the model that are constructed from flow identities need a base quarter and a base quarter starting value. The base quarter values are indicated in Table A.6. The base quarter was taken to be 1971:4, and the stock values for this quarter were taken from the FFA stock values.

There are also a few internal checks on the data in Table A.6 (aside from the balance-sheet checks in Table A.5). The variables for which there are both raw data and an identity available are GDP, MB, $PIEF$, PUG, and PUS. In addition, the saving variables in Table A.5 (SH, SF, and so on) must match the saving variables of the same name in Table A.6. There is also one redundant equation in the model, equation 80, which the variables must satisfy.

There are a few variables in Table A.6 whose construction needs some explanation.

HFS: **Peak to Peak Interpolation of HF**

HFS is a peak to peak interpolation of HF, hours per job. The peaks are listed in Table A.6. The deviation of HF from HFS, which is variable HFF in the model, is used in equation 15, which explains overtime hours.

HO: **Overtime Hours**

Data are not available for HO for the first 16 quarters of the sample period (1952:1–1955:4). The equation that explains HO in the model has $\log HO$ on the left hand side and a constant, HFF, and HFF lagged once on the right hand side. The equation is also estimated under the assumption of a first order autoregressive error term. The missing data for HO were constructed by estimating the $\log HO$ equation for the 1956:1–1993:2 period and using the predicted values from this regression for the (outside sample) 1952:3–1955:4 period as the actual data. The values for 1952:1 and 1952:2 were taken to be the 1952:3 predicted value.

$TAUS$: **Progressivity Tax Parameter—s**

$TAUS$ is the progressivity tax parameter in the personal income tax equation for state and local governments (equation 48). It was obtained as follows. The sample period 1952:1–1993:2 was divided into three subperiods, 1952:1–1970:4, 1971:1–1971:4, and 1972:1–1993:2. These were judged from a plot of THS/YT, the ratio of state and local personal income taxes to taxable income, to be periods of no large tax law changes. Two assumptions were then made about the relationship between THS and YT. The first is that within a subperiod THS/POP equals $[D1 + TAUS(YT/POP)](YT/POP)$ plus a random error term, where $D1$ and $TAUS$ are constants. The second is that changes in the tax laws affect $D1$ but not $TAUS$. These two assumptions led to the estimation of an equation with THS/POP on the left hand side and a constant, $DUM1(YT/POP)$, $DUM2(YT/POP)$, $DUM3(YT/POP)$, and $(YT/POP)^2$ on the right hand side, where $DUMi$ is a dummy variable that takes on a value of one in subperiod i and zero otherwise. (The estimation period was 1952:1–1993:2 excluding 1987:2. The observation for 1987:2 was excluded because it corresponded to a large outlier.) The estimate of the coefficient of $DUMi(YT/POP)$ is an estimate of $D1$ for subperiod i. The estimate of the coefficient of $(YT/POP)^2$ is the estimate of $TAUS$. The estimate of $TAUS$ was .00111, with a t-statistic of 11.34. This procedure is, of course, crude, but at least it provides a rough estimate of the progressivity of the state and local personal income tax system.

Given $TAUS$, $D1S$ is defined to be $THS/YT - (TAUS \cdot YT)/POP$ (see Table A.6). In the model $D1S$ is taken to be exogenous, and THS is explained by equation 48 as $[D1S + (TAUS \cdot YT)/POP]YT$. This treatment allows a state and local marginal tax rate to be defined in equation 91: $D1SM = D1S + (2 \cdot TAUS \cdot YT)/POP$.

$TAUG$: **Progressivity Tax Parameter—g**

$TAUG$ is the progressivity tax parameter in the personal income tax equation for the federal government (equation 47). A similar estimation procedure was followed for $TAUG$ as was followed above for $TAUS$, where 27 subperiods where chosen. The 27 subperiods are: 1952:1–1953:4, 1954:1–1963:4, 1964:1–1964:4, 1965:1–1965:4, 1966:1–1967:4, 1968:1–1970:4, 1971:1–1971:4, 1972:1–1972:4, 1973:1–1973:4, 1974:1–1975:1, 1975:2–1976:4, 1977:1–1977:1, 1977:2–1978:2, 1978:3–1981:3, 1981:4–1982:2, 1982:3–1983:2, 1983:3–1984:4, 1985:1–1985:1, 1985:2–1985:2, 1985:3–1987:1, 1987:2–1987:2, 1987:3–1987:4, 1988:1–1988:4, 1989:1–1989:4, 1990:1–1990:4, 1991:1–1991:4, and 1992:1–1993:2. The estimate of $TAUG$ was .00270, with a t-statistic of 1.84. Again, this procedure is crude, but it provides a rough estimate of the progressivity of the federal personal income tax system.

Given $TAUG$, $D1G$ is defined to be $THG/YT - (TAUG \cdot YT)/POP$ (see Table A.6). In the model $D1G$ is taken to be exogenous, and THG is explained by equation 47 as $[D1G + (TAUG \cdot YT)/POP]YT$. This treatment allows a federal marginal tax rate to be defined in equation 90: $D1GM = D1G + (2 \cdot TAUG \cdot YT)/POP$.

KD: Stock of Durable Goods

KD is an estimate of the stock of durable goods. It is defined by equation 58:

$$KD = (1 - DELD)KD_{-1} + CD \qquad (58)$$

Given quarterly observations for CD, which are available from the NIPA, quarterly observations for KD can be constructed once a base quarter value and a value for the depreciation rate $DELD$ are chosen. End of year estimates of the stock of durable goods are available from 1925 through 1990 from the *Survey of Current Business*, January 1992, Table 4, p. 137. Given the value of KD at, say, the end of 1952 and given a value of $DELD$, a quarterly series for KD can be constructed using the above equation and the quarterly series for CD. This was done for different values of $DELD$ to see how close the constructed end of year (i.e., fourth quarter) values of KD could be matched to the values published in the *Survey*. The value of $DELD$ that was chosen as achieving a good match is .049511. A quarterly series for KD was then constructed using this value and a base quarter value of 313.7 in 1952:4, which is the value published in the *Survey* for 1952.

KH: Stock of Housing

KH is an estimate of the stock of housing of the household sector. It is defined by equation 59:

$$KH = (1 - DELH)KH_{-1} + IHH \qquad (59)$$

A similar procedure was followed for estimating $DELH$ as was followed for estimating $DELD$. The value of $DELH$ that was chosen as achieving a good match of the created stock data to the published stock data is .006716. (The housing stock data are also in Table 4 in the January 1992 issue of the *Survey*.) The residential stock data that is published in the *Survey* is for total residential investment, which in the model is $IHH + IHK + IHB$, whereas equation 59 pertains only to the residential investment of the household sector. The procedure that was used for dealing with this difference is as follows. First, the value for $DELH$ was chosen using total residential investment as the investment series, since this series matched the published stock data. Second, once $DELH$ was chosen, KH was constructed using IHH (not total residential investment). A base quarter value of 1270.276 in 1952:4 was used, which is .98 times the value published in the *Survey* for 1952. The value .98 is the average of $IHH/(IHH + IHK + IHB)$ over the sample period.

KK: Stock of Capital

KK is an estimate of the stock of capital of the firm sector. It is determined by equation 92:

$$KK = (1 - DELK)KK_{-1} + IKF \qquad (92)$$

A similar procedure was followed for estimating $DELK$ as was followed for estimating $DELD$ and $DELH$. (Again, the stock data are in Table 4 in the January 1992 issue of the *Survey*.) It turned out in this case that three values of $DELK$ were needed to achieve a good match, one (.014574) for the 1952:1–1970:4 period, one (.018428) for the 1971:1–1980:4 period, and one (.023068) for the 1981:1–1993:2 period. The nonresidential stock data that is published in the *Survey* is for total fixed nonresidential investment, which in the model is $IKF + IKH + IKB + IKG$, whereas equation 92 pertains only to the fixed nonresidential investment of the firm sector. A similar procedure was followed here as was followed for residential investment above. First, the values for $DELK$ were chosen using total fixed nonresidential investment as the investment series, since this series matched the published stock data. Second, once the values for $DELK$ were chosen, KK was constructed using IKF (not total fixed nonresidential investment). A base quarter value of 887.571 in 1952:4 was used, which is .71 times the value published in the *Survey* for 1952. The value .71 is the average of $IKF/(IKF + IKH + IKB + IKG)$ over the sample period.

V: Stock of Inventories

V is the stock of inventories of the firm sector (i.e., the nonfarm stock). By definition, inventory investment (IVF) is equal to the change in the stock, which is equation 117:

$$IVF = V - V_{-1} \qquad (117)$$

Both data on V and IVF are published in the *Survey*, the data on V in Table 5.13. For present purposes V was constructed from the formula $V = V_{-1} + IVF$ using the IVF series and base quarter value of 870.0 in 1988:4. The

base quarter value was taken from Table 5.13 in the July 1992 issue of the *Survey*.

Excess Labor and Excess Capital

In the theoretical model the amounts of excess labor and excess capital on hand affect the decisions of firms. In order to test for this in the empirical work, one needs to estimate the amounts of excess labor and capital on hand in each period. This in turn requires an estimate of the technology of the firm sector.

The measurement of the capital stock KK is discussed above. The production function of the firm sector for empirical purposes is postulated to be

$$Y = \min[\lambda(JF \cdot HF^a), \mu(KK \cdot HK^a)] \tag{3.1}$$

where Y is production, JF is the number of workers employed, HF^a is the number of hours worked per worker, KK is the capital stock discussed above, HK^a is the number of hours each unit of KK is utilized, and λ and μ are coefficients that may change over time due to technical progress. The variables Y, JF, and KK are observed; the others are not. For example, data on the number of hours paid for per worker exist (HF in the model), but not on the number of hours actually worked per worker (HF^a).

Equation 92 for KK and the production function 3.1 are not consistent with the putty-clay technology of the theoretical model. To be precise with this technology one has to keep track of the purchase date of each machine and its technological coefficients. This kind of detail is not possible with aggregate data, and one must resort to simpler specifications.

Given the production function 3.1, excess labor was measured as follows.[3] Output per paid for worker hour, $Y/(JF \cdot HF)$, was plotted for the 1952:1– 1993:2 period. The peaks of this series were assumed to correspond to cases in which the number of hours worked equals the number of hours paid for, which implies that the values of λ in equation 3.1 are observed at the peaks. The values of λ other than those at the peaks were assumed to lie on straight lines between the peaks. This gives an estimate of λ for each quarter.

Given an estimate of λ for a particular quarter and given equation 3.1, the estimate of the number of worker hours required to produce the output of the quarter, denoted $JHMIN$ in the model, is simply Y/λ. In the model, λ is

---

[3] The estimation of excess labor in the following way was first done in Fair (1969) using three digit industry data.

denoted LAM, and the equation determining $JHMIN$ is equation 94 in Table A.3. The actual number of workers hours paid for ($JF \cdot HF$) can be compared to $JHMIN$ to measure the amount of excess labor on hand. The peaks that were used for the interpolations are listed in Table A.6 in the description of LAM.[4]

For the measurement of excess capital there are no data on hours paid for or worked per unit of KK, and thus one must be content with plotting Y/KK. This is, from the production function 3.1, a plot of $\mu \cdot HK^a$, where HK^a is the average number of hours that each machine is utilized. If it is assumed that at each peak of this series HK^a is equal to the same constant, say $\bar{H}$, then one observes at the peaks $\mu \cdot \bar{H}$. Interpolation between peaks can then produce a complete series on $\mu \cdot \bar{H}$. If, finally, $\bar{H}$ is assumed to be the maximum number of hours per quarter that each unit of KK can be utilized, then $Y/(\mu \cdot \bar{H})$ is the minimum amount of capital required to produce Y (denoted $KKMIN$). In the model, $\mu \cdot \bar{H}$ is denoted MUH, and the equation determining $KKMIN$ is equation 93 in Table A.3. The actual capital stock (KK) can be compared to $KKMIN$ to measure the amount of excess capital on hand. The peaks that were used for the interpolations are listed in Table A.6 in the description of MUH.

The estimated percentages of excess labor and capital by quarter are presented in Table 3.1. For labor each figure in the table is 100 times $[(JF \cdot HF)/JHMIN - 1.0]$, and for capital each figure is 100 times $(KK/KKMIN - 1.0)$. The table shows that in the most recent recession both excess labor and capital peaked at 3.6 percent in 1991:1. The largest value for excess labor during the entire 1952:1–1993:2 period was 4.9 percent in 1960:4. The largest value for excess capital was 10.5 percent in 1982:4.[5]

---

[4]The values of LAM before the first peak were assumed to lie on the backward extension of the line connecting the first and second peaks. Similarly, the values of LAM after the last peak were assumed to lie on the forward extension of the line connecting the second to last and last peak. Contrary to the case for LAM, for some of the peak to peak interpolations in this study the values before the first peak were taken to be the value at the first peak. This is denoted "flat beginning" in Table A.6. Also, for some of the interpolations the values after the last peak were taken to be the value at the last peak. This is denoted "flat end" in Table A.6.

[5]A few values in Table 3.1 are negative. A negative value occurs when the actual value of output per paid for worker hour or output per capital is above the interpolation line. The peak to peak interpolation lines were not always drawn so that every point between the peaks lay on or below the line.

Table 3.1
Estimated Percentages of Excess Labor and Capital

Quar.	ExL	ExK	Quar.	ExL	ExK	Quar.	ExL	ExK	Quar.	ExL	ExK
1952:1	1.0	1.9	1962:3	.1	.0	1973:1	-.8	-1.1	1983:3	1.7	4.7
1952:2	1.1	3.3	1962:4	.4	1.2	1973:2	.0	-.7	1983:4	1.5	3.1
1952:3	1.2	2.8	1963:1	.7	.7	1973:3	1.1	.3	1984:1	1.2	1.1
1952:4	1.4	1.2	1963:2	.7	.5	1973:4	.9	.2	1984:2	1.0	.0
1953:1	.6	.2	1963:3	-.4	-.3	1974:1	2.3	2.2	1984:3	.8	.1
1953:2	-.1	.0	1963:4	.1	.2	1974:2	2.5	3.2	1984:4	1.0	.6
1953:3	.5	1.3	1964:1	-1.5	-1.1	1974:3	3.3	4.9	1985:1	1.4	1.0
1953:4	.0	2.9	1964:2	-.7	-.8	1974:4	2.9	6.4	1985:2	1.2	1.6
1954:1	1.4	4.9	1964:3	-.4	-.4	1975:1	3.2	9.8	1985:3	.5	1.1
1954:2	1.2	5.8	1964:4	.8	.7	1975:2	1.1	8.6	1985:4	.8	1.5
1954:3	.2	4.9	1965:1	.5	.0	1975:3	.4	6.9	1986:1	-.3	1.1
1954:4	.0	3.6	1965:2	1.5	.6	1975:4	.6	6.0	1986:2	.0	2.1
1955:1	-.3	1.4	1965:3	.1	.3	1976:1	.0	4.2	1986:3	.2	2.0
1955:2	.2	.7	1965:4	.0	.0	1976:2	.3	4.3	1986:4	.7	2.4
1955:3	1.2	.0	1966:1	-.7	-1.3	1976:3	.4	4.7	1987:1	1.0	2.0
1955:4	2.3	-.2	1966:2	.2	-.2	1976:4	.0	4.0	1987:2	.9	1.4
1956:1	2.6	.7	1966:3	.6	.2	1977:1	-.1	3.2	1987:3	1.1	1.1
1956:2	3.0	1.1	1966:4	.5	.8	1977:2	.5	2.1	1987:4	.7	.2
1956:3	3.5	1.9	1967:1	1.0	1.2	1977:3	.0	1.2	1988:1	.5	.0
1956:4	2.3	1.3	1967:2	.1	1.5	1977:4	1.4	2.3	1988:2	1.2	-.1
1957:1	1.9	1.2	1967:3	.3	1.2	1978:1	1.7	2.6	1988:3	1.1	.1
1957:2	2.1	2.0	1967:4	.9	1.5	1978:2	1.0	.0	1988:4	1.4	-.2
1957:3	2.1	2.2	1968:1	.0	1.0	1978:3	1.0	.1	1989:1	2.1	-.2
1957:4	2.5	4.5	1968:2	.1	.3	1978:4	1.0	-.1	1989:2	2.0	.0
1958:1	2.2	7.0	1968:3	.3	.3	1979:1	2.1	1.0	1989:3	2.5	.3
1958:2	1.5	6.6	1968:4	1.1	1.0	1979:2	2.4	1.8	1989:4	2.4	.3
1958:3	.1	3.9	1969:1	1.6	.0	1979:3	2.4	2.0	1990:1	2.6	.0
1958:4	-.5	1.4	1969:2	2.3	1.3	1979:4	2.6	2.7	1990:2	2.4	.2
1959:1	1.0	1.6	1969:3	2.4	2.0	1980:1	2.2	3.4	1990:3	2.5	.9
1959:2	2.2	.0	1969:4	3.1	3.7	1980:2	3.4	6.9	1990:4	3.5	2.2
1959:3	3.0	1.9	1970:1	3.5	5.2	1980:3	3.1	7.4	1991:1	3.6	3.6
1959:4	2.8	2.1	1970:2	3.8	6.6	1980:4	2.2	5.8	1991:2	3.1	3.5
1960:1	1.8	1.3	1970:3	2.0	6.3	1981:1	1.8	4.9	1991:3	2.9	3.3
1960:2	3.9	2.9	1970:4	2.8	8.3	1981:2	1.7	5.4	1991:4	2.7	3.3
1960:3	4.2	3.3	1971:1	1.0	5.7	1981:3	1.4	5.3	1992:1	2.0	2.8
1960:4	4.9	5.2	1971:2	1.6	6.0	1981:4	2.6	7.2	1992:2	1.5	2.0
1961:1	4.0	5.1	1971:3	1.0	5.8	1982:1	3.3	9.1	1992:3	.0	.5
1961:2	1.3	3.9	1971:4	1.8	5.4	1982:2	2.6	9.1	1992:4	.0	.0
1961:3	.6	2.9	1972:1	1.5	3.9	1982:3	3.3	10.4	1993:1	.6	.6
1961:4	.0	1.4	1972:2	.9	2.6	1982:4	3.0	10.5	1993:2	1.2	.8
1962:1	.6	.7	1972:3	.3	1.8	1983:1	2.6	9.5			
1962:2	.7	.4	1972:4	.1	1.0	1983:2	1.2	6.4			

Comparisons to the Fay-Medoff Estimates[6]

It is of interest to compare the estimates of excess labor in Table 3.1 with
the survey results of Fay and Medoff (1985). Fay and Medoff surveyed 168
U.S. manufacturing plants to examine the magnitude of labor hoarding during
economic contractions. They found that during its most recent trough quarter,
the typical plant paid for about 8 percent more blue collar hours than were
needed for regular production work. Some of these hours were used for other
worthwhile work, usually maintenance work, and after taking account of this,
4 percent of the blue collar hours were estimated to be hoarded for the typical
plant.

The estimates of excess labor in Table 3.1 probably correspond more to the
concept behind the 8 percent number of Fay and Medoff than to the concept

---

[6]The following discussion is updated from Fair (1985).

behind the 4 percent number. If, for example, maintenance work is shifted from high to low output periods, then $JHMIN$ is a misleading estimate of worker hour requirements. In a long run sense, $JHMIN$ is too low because it has been based on the incorrect assumption that the peak productivity values could be sustained over the entire business cycle. This error is not a serious one from the point of estimating the labor demand equations in Chapter 5. If the same percentage error has been made at each peak, which is likely to be approximately the case, the error will merely be absorbed in the estimates of the constant terms in the equations. The error is also not serious for the Fay-Medoff comparisons as long as the Fay-Medoff concept behind the 8 percent number is used. This concept, like the concept behind the peak to peak interpolation work, does not account for maintenance that is shifted from high to low output periods.

There are two possible troughs that are relevant for the Fay-Medoff study, the one in mid 1980 and the one in early 1982. The first survey upon which the Fay-Medoff results are based was done in August 1981, and the second (larger) survey was done in April 1982. A follow up occurred in October 1982. The plant managers were asked to answer the questionnaire for the plant's most recent trough. For the last responses the trough might be in 1982, whereas for the earlier ones the trough is likely to be in 1980. Table 3.1 shows that the percentage of excess labor reached 3.4 percent in 1980:2 and 3.3 percent in 1982:1.[7]

The Fay-Medoff estimate of 8 percent is thus compared to the 3.4 and 3.3 percent values in Table 3.1. These two sets of results seem consistent in that there are at least two reasons for expecting the Fay-Medoff estimate to be somewhat higher. First, the trough in output for a given plant is on average likely to be deeper than the trough in aggregate output, since not all troughs are likely to occur in the same quarter across plants. Second, the manufacturing sector may on average face deeper troughs than do other sectors, and the aggregate estimates in Table 3.1 are for the total private sector, not just manufacturing. One would thus expect the Fay-Medoff estimate to be somewhat higher than the aggregate estimates, and 8 percent versus a number around 3 to 3.5 percent seems consistent with this.

The Fay-Medoff results appear to provide strong support for the excess labor hypothesis. At a micro level Fay and Medoff found labor hoarding and

---

[7]The estimates in Fair (1985) using earlier data were 4.5 percent in 1980:4 and 5.5 percent in 1982:1. The use of more recent data has thus lowered the excess labor estimates by a little over a percentage point. Also, the Fay-Medoff estimate of 4 percent hoarded labor cited above was 5 percent in an earlier version of the paper cited in Fair (1985).

of a magnitude that seems in line with aggregate estimates. This is one of the few examples in macroeconomics where a hypothesis has been so strongly confirmed using detailed micro data.

Labor Market Tightness: The Z Variable

An important feature of the theoretical model is the possibility that households may at times be constrained in how much they can work. In the empirical work one needs some way of measuring this constraint. The approach taken here is the following. The variable JJ in the model is the ratio of the total number of worker hours paid for in the economy to the total population 16 and over (equation 95). JJ was first plotted for the 1952:1–1993:2 period, and a peak to peak interpolation was made. The interpolation series is denoted JJP, and the peaks that were used for this interpolation are presented in Table A.6 in the description of JJP. A variable Z was then defined as $\min(0, 1 - JJP/JJ)$, where Z is called the "labor constraint variable." In the data Z is always nonpositive because JJP is constructed from the peak to peak interpolations and is always greater than or equal to JJ. In the solution of the model, however, the predicted value of JJ may be greater than JJP, in which case Z is taken to be zero. Z is a labor constraint variable in the sense that it is zero or close to zero when the worker hours-population ratio is at or near its peak and gets progressively larger in absolute value as the ratio moves below its peak. The exact use of Z is explained in Chapter 5.

YS: Potential Output of the Firm Sector

A measure of the potential output of the firm sector, YS, is used in the price equation (equation 10). YS is defined by equation 98:

$$YS = LAM(JJP \cdot POP - JG \cdot HG - JM \cdot HM - JS \cdot HS) \qquad (98)$$

JJP is the peak or potential ratio of worker hours to population (as constructed from the peak to peak interpolation of JJ), and so $JJP \cdot POP$ is the potential number of worker hours. The terms that are subtracted from $JJP \cdot POP$ in equation 98 are, in order, the number of federal civilian worker hours, the number of federal military worker hours, and the number of state and local government worker hours. The entire number in parentheses is thus the potential number of worker hours in the firm sector. LAM is the coefficient λ in the production function 3.1. Since YS in equation 98 is LAM times the potential number of workers in the firm sector, it can be interpreted as the potential output of the firm sector unless the capital input is insufficient to produce YS. This construction of YS is thus based on the assumption that there is always sufficient capital on hand to produce YS.

The Bond Variables BF and BG

BF is an estimate of the value of long term bonds issued by the firm sector in the current period. Similarly, BG is an estimate of the value of long term bonds issued by the federal government sector in the current period. These variables are determined by equations 55 and 56 respectively. They are used in the interest payments equations, 19 and 29. The construction of BF and BG is somewhat involved, and this discussion is presented in Chapter 5 in the context of the discussion of equations 19 and 29.

3.2.4   The Identities

The identities in Table A.3 are of two types. One type simply defines one variable in terms of others. These identities are equations 31, 33, 34, 43, 55, 56, 58–87, and 89–131. The other type defines one variable as a rate or ratio times another variable or set of variables, where the rate or ratio has been constructed to have the identity hold. These identities are equations 32, 35-42, 44-54, 57, and 88. Consider, for example, equation 50:

$$TFS = D2S \cdot PIEF \tag{50}$$

where TFS is the amount of corporate profit taxes paid from firms (sector f) to the state and local government sector (sector s), $PIEF$ is the level of corporate profits of the firm sector, and $D2S$ is the "tax rate." Data exist for TFS and $PIEF$, and $D2S$ was constructed as $TFS/PIEF$. The variable $D2S$ is then interpreted as a tax rate and is taken to be exogenous. This rate, of course, varies over time as tax laws and other things that affect the relationship between TFS and $PIEF$ change, but no attempt has been made to explain these changes. This general procedure was followed for the other identities involving tax rates.

A similar procedure was followed to handle relative price changes. Consider equation 38:

$$PIH = PSI5 \cdot PD \tag{38}$$

where PIH is the price deflator for housing investment, PD is the price deflator for total domestic sales, and $PSI5$ is a ratio. Data exist for PIH and PD, and $PSI5$ was constructed as PIH/PD. $PSI5$, which varies over time as the relationship between PIH and PD changes, is taken to be exogenous. This procedure was followed for the other identities involving prices and wages. This treatment means that relative prices and relative wages are exogenous in the model. (Prices relative to wages are not exogenous, however.) It is beyond the scope of the model to explain relative prices and wages, and the foregoing treatment is a simple way of handling these changes.

Another identity of the second type is equation 57:

$$BR = -G1 \cdot MB \tag{57}$$

where BR is the level of bank reserves, MB is the net value of demand deposits of the financial sector, and $G1$ is a "reserve requirement ratio." Data on BR and MB exist, and $G1$ was constructed as $-BR/MB$. (MB is negative, since the financial sector is a net debtor with respect to demand deposits, and so the minus sign makes $G1$ positive.) $G1$ is taken to be exogenous. It varies over time as actual reserve requirements and other features that affect the relationship between BR and MB change.

Many of the identities of the first type are concerned with linking the FFA data to the NIPA data. An identity like equation 66

$$0 = SH - \Delta AH - \Delta MH + CG - DISH \tag{66}$$

is concerned with this linkage. SH is from the NIPA, and the other variables are from the FFA. The discrepancy variable, $DISH$, which is from the FFA, reconciles the two data sets. Equation 66 states that any nonzero value of saving of the household sector must result in a change in AH or MH. There are equations like 66 for each of the other five sectors: equation 70 for the firm sector, 73 for the financial sector, 75 for the foreign sector, 77 for the federal government sector, and 79 for the state and local government sector. Equation 77, for example, is the budget constraint of the federal government sector. Note also from Table A.3 that the saving of each sector (SH, SF, etc.) is determined by an identity. The sum of the saving variables across the six sectors is zero, which is the reason that equation 80 is redundant.

3.2.5   The Stochastic Equations

A brief listing of the stochastic equations is presented in Table A.3. The left hand side and right hand side variables are listed for each equation. Chapter 5 discusses the specification, estimation, and testing of these equations. Of the thirty equations, the first nine pertain to the household sector, the next twelve to the firm sector, the next five to the financial sector, the next to the foreign sector, the next to the state and local government sector, and the final two to the federal government sector.

3.3 The ROW Model

The data, variables, and equations for the ROW model are discussed in this section. Remember that the ROW model includes structural models for 32 countries. The relevant tables for the model are Tables B.1–B.7 in Appendix B, and these will be outlined first.

3.3.1 The Tables (Tables B.1–B.7)

Table B.1 lists the countries in the model and provides a brief listing of the variables per country. The 32 countries for which structural equations are estimated are Canada (CA) through Thailand (TH), which are countries 2 through 33. Countries 34 through 45 are countries for which only trade share equations are estimated. A detailed description of the variables per country is presented in Table B.2, where the variables are listed in alphabetical order. Data permitting, each of the 32 countries has the same set of variables. Quarterly data were collected for countries 2 through 14, and annual data were collected for the others. Countries 2 through 14 will be referred to as "quarterly" countries, and the others will be referred to as "annual" countries. The way in which each variable was constructed is explained in brackets in Table B.2. All of the data with potential seasonal fluctuations have been seasonally adjusted. In some cases, quarterly data for a particular variable, such as a population variable, did not exist. When quarterly data were needed but only annual data were available, quarterly observations were interpolated from annual data using the procedure described in Table B.6.

Table B.3 lists the stochastic equations and the identities. The functional forms of the stochastic equations are given, but not the coefficient estimates. The coefficient estimates for all the countries are presented in Chapter 6. Table B.4 lists the equations that pertain to the trade and price links among the countries, and it explains the construction of the trade share variables—the α_{ij} variables. It also explains how the quarterly and annual data were linked for the trade share calculations. Table B.5 lists the links between the US and ROW models. Finally, Table B.7 explains the construction of the balance of payments data—data for variables S and TT.

It will be useful to begin with a discussion of the construction of some of the variables in Table B.2.

3.3.2   The Raw Data

The data sets for the countries other than the United States (i.e., the countries in the ROW model) begin in 1960. The sources of the data are the IMF and OECD. Data from the IMF are international financial statistics (IFS) data and direction of trade (DOT) data. Data from the OECD are quarterly national accounts data, annual national accounts data, quarterly labor force data, and annual labor force data. These are the "raw" data. As noted above, the way in which each variable was constructed is explained in brackets in Table B.2. When "IFS" precedes a number or letter in the table, this refers to the IFS variable number or letter. Some variables were constructed directly from IFS and OECD data (i.e., directly from the raw data), and some were constructed from other (already constructed) variables.

3.3.3   Variable Construction

S, TT, and A: Balance of Payments Variables

One important feature of the data collection is the linking of the balance of payments data to the other export and import data. The two key variables involved in this process are S, the balance of payments on current account, and TT, the value of net transfers. The construction of these variables and the linking of the two types of data are explained in Table B.7. Quarterly balance of payments data do not generally begin as early as the other data, and the procedure in Table B.7 allows quarterly data on S to be constructed as far back as the beginning of the quarterly data for merchandise imports and exports ($M\$$ and $X\$$).

The variable A is the net stock of foreign security and reserve holdings. It was constructed by summing past values of S from a base period value of zero. The summation begins in the first quarter for which data on S exist. This means that the A series is off by a constant amount each period (the difference between the true value of A in the base period and zero). In the estimation work the functional forms were chosen in such a way that this error was always absorbed in the estimate of the constant term. It is important to note that A measures only the net asset position of the country vis-à-vis the rest of the world. Domestic wealth, such as the domestically owned housing stock and plant and equipment stock, is not included.

K: The Capital Stock

If depreciation is proportional to the capital stock K, then $K = (1-\delta)K_{-1}+I$, where δ is the depreciation rate and I is gross investment. (See, for example, equation 92 for the US model.) Given 1) a value for δ, 2) a base value for K, and 3) data on I, K can be constructed from this formula. Although, as discussed in Section 3.2.3, data on both the capital stock and investment exist for the United States, only data on investment exist for most other countries. Therefore, some way must be found for constructing K for the other countries that does not require direct data on K. This was done as follows.

First, the U.S. data were used to compute an implicit depreciation rate. This rate is about .015 (1.5 percent) per quarter for fixed nonresidential and residential capital combined. (The data on I for the other countries includes both fixed nonresidential and residential investment, and so the appropriate depreciation rate is for the sum of the two.) This rate is the value that was used for δ in the construction of K for each of the other countries. (For countries with annual data, the value used for δ was .06.)

Second, a base value of K was constructed. A preliminary base value was chosen, and K was constructed for each period using this base value and the depreciation rate of .015 (.06 for the annual countries). The capital-output ratio (K/Y) was then computed for the first and last periods. If the ratios in the two periods were similar, the base value was used. Otherwise, the preliminary base value was changed, and the process was repeated. The process was stopped when the ratios in the first and last periods were similar. In other words, the base value was chosen so as to make the capital-output ratio have no long run trend.

This procedure for constructing data on K is obviously crude, but it is about the best that can be done given the available data. It provides at least a rough estimate of the capital stock of each country.

V: Stock of Inventories

Data on inventory investment, denoted $V1$ in the ROW model, are available for each country, but not data on the stock of inventories, denoted V. By definition $V = V_{-1} + V1$. (See, for example, equation 117 for the US model.) Given this equation and data for $V1$, V can be constructed once a base period and base period value are chosen. The base period was chosen for each country to be the quarter or year prior to the beginning of the data on $V1$, and the base period value was taken to be zero. This means that the constructed data for

V are off by a constant amount throughout the sample period (the difference between the true value in the base period and zero). This error is absorbed in the estimate of the constant term in the equation in which V appears as an explanatory variable, which is the production equation 4.

Excess Labor and Excess Capital

As was the case for the United States, the short run production function for each country is assumed to be one of fixed proportions:

$$Y = \min[\lambda(J \cdot HJ^a), \mu(K \cdot HK^a)] \tag{3.2}$$

where Y is production, J is the number of workers employed, HJ^a is the number of hours worked per worker, K is the capital stock discussed above, HK^a is the number of hours each unit of K is utilized, and λ and μ are coefficients that may change over time due to technical progress. The notation in equation (3.2) is changed slightly from that in (3.1) for the United States. J is used in place of JF because there is no disaggregation in the ROW model between the firm sector and other sectors. Similarly, HJ^a is used in place of HF^a. Finally, K is used in place of KK because there is no disaggregation in the ROW model between types of capital. Note also that Y refers here to the total output of the country (real GDP), not just the output of the firm sector. Data on Y, J, and K are observed (or, in the case of K, constructed); the others are not. Also, contrary to the case for the United States, data on the number of hours paid for per worker (denoted HF in the US model) are not available.

Given the production function 3.2, excess labor was measured as follows for each country. Y/J was plotted over the sample period, and peaks of this series were chosen. This is from 3.2 a plot of $\lambda \cdot HJ^a$. If it is assumed that at each peak HJ^a is equal to the same constant, say $\overline{HJ}$, then one observes at the peaks $\lambda \cdot \overline{HJ}$. Straight lines were drawn between the peaks (peak to peak interpolation), and $\lambda \cdot \overline{HJ}$ was assumed to lie on the lines. If, finally, $\overline{HJ}$ is assumed to be the maximum number of hours that each worker can work, then $Y/(\lambda \cdot \overline{HJ})$ is the minimum number of workers required to produce Y, which is denoted $JMIN$ in the ROW model. $\lambda \cdot \overline{HJ}$ is denoted LAM, and the equation determining $JMIN$ is equation I-13 in Table B.3. The actual number of workers on hand (J) can be compared to $JMIN$ to measure the amount of excess labor on hand.

A similar procedure was followed to measure excess capital. Y/K was plotted over the sample period, and peaks of this series were chosen. This is from 3.2 a plot of $\mu \cdot HK^a$. If it is assumed that at each peak HK^a is equal to the same constant, say $\overline{HK}$, then one observes at the peaks $\mu \cdot \overline{HK}$. Straight lines were drawn between the peaks, and $\mu \cdot \overline{HK}$ was assumed to lie on the lines. If, finally, $\overline{HK}$ is assumed to be the maximum number of hours that each machine can be utilized, then $Y/(\mu \cdot \overline{HK})$ is the minimum amount of capital required to produce Y, which is denoted $KMIN$ in the ROW model. $\mu \cdot \overline{HK}$ is denoted MUH, and the equation determining $KMIN$ is equation I-11 in Table B.3. The actual capital stock (K) can be compared to $KMIN$ to measure the amount of excess capital on hand.

Labor Market Tightness: The Z variable

A labor market tightness variable (the Z variable) was constructed for each country in the same manner as was done for the United States. For each country a peak to peak interpolation of JJ $(= J/POP)$ was made, and JJP (the peak to peak interpolation series) was constructed. Z is then equal to the minimum of 0 and $1 - JJP/JJ$, which is equation I-16 in Table B.3. See the discussion in Section 3.2.3 about the Z variable.

YS: Potential Output

A measure of potential output (YS) was constructed for each country in the same manner as was done for the United States. The only difference is that here output refers to the total output of the country rather than just the output of the firm sector. The equation for YS is $YS = LAM \cdot JJP \cdot POP$, which is equation I-17 in Table B.3. Given YS, a gap variable can be constructed as $(YS - Y)/YS$, which is denoted ZZ in the ROW model. ZZ is determined by equation I-18 in Table B.3.

3.3.4 The Identities

The identities for each country are listed in Table B.3. There are up to 19 identities per country. Equation I-1 links the non NIPA data on imports (i.e., data on M and MS) to the NIPA data (i.e., data on IM). The variable $IMDS$ in the equation picks up the discrepancy between the two data sets. It is exogenous in the model. Equation I-2 is a similar equation for exports. Equation I-3 is the income identity; equation I-4 defines inventory investment as the difference between production and sales; and equation I-5 defines the stock of inventories as the previous stock plus inventory investment. The income identity I-3 is the empirical version of equation 2.4 in Section 2.2.3 except that the level of imports (IM) has to be subtracted in I-3 because C, I, and G include imports.

Equation I-6 defines S, the balance of payments on current account, the saving of the country. This is the empirical version of equation ii in Section 2.2.3. Equation I-7 defines A, the net stock of foreign security and reserve holdings, as equal to last period's value plus S. (Remember that A is constructed by summing past values of S.) This is the empirical version of equation i′ in Section 2.2.8.

Equation I-8 links M, total merchandise imports in 85 lc, to $M85\$A$, merchandise imports from the countries in the trade share matrix in 85 $. The variable $M85\$B$ is the difference between total merchandise imports (in 85$) and merchandise imports (in 85$) from the countries in the trade share matrix. It is exogenous in the model.

Equation I-9 links E, the average exchange rate for the period, to EE, the end of period exchange rate. If the exchange rate changes fairly smoothly within the period, then E is approximately equal to $(EE + EE_{-1})/2$. A variable $PSI1$ was defined to make the equation $E = PSI1[(EE+EE_{-1})/2]$ exact, which is equation I-9. One would expect $PSI1$ to be approximately one and not to fluctuate much over time, which is generally the case in the data.

Equation I-10 defines the capital stock, and equation I-11 defines the minimum capital stock needed to produce the output. These two equations were discussed above. Equation I-12 defines the civilian unemployment rate, UR. $L1$ is the labor force of men, and $L2$ is the labor force of women. J is total employment, including the armed forces, and AF is the level of the armed forces. UR is equal to the number of people unemployed divided by the civilian labor force.

Equations I-13 through I-18 pertain to the measurement of excess labor, the labor constraint variable, and potential output. These have all been discussed above.

Finally, equation I-19 links PM, the import price index obtained from the IFS data, to PMP, the import price index computed from the trade share calculations. The variable that links the two, $PSI2$, is taken to be exogenous.

3.3.5   The Stochastic Equations

The stochastic equations for a given country are listed in Table B.3. There are up to 15 estimated equations per country. It will be useful to relate some of the equations in the table to those in the theoretical model in Chapter 2, Section 2.2.3. Chapter 6 discusses the specification, estimation, and testing of these equations. As will be discussed in Chapter 6, many of these equations are similar to the corresponding equations in the US model.

Equation 1 in Table B.3 explains the demand for imports. It is matched to equation 2.2 of the theoretical model. Equation 2 explains consumption. It is matched to equation 2.1 except that consumption for equation 2 includes consumption of imported goods. In the theoretical model X_h is only the value of domestically produced goods consumed. Equation 3 explains fixed investment, and equation 4 explains production with sales as an explanatory variable, which is in effect an inventory investment equation. Neither of these equations was included in the theoretical model. The price equation 5 is matched to equation 2.3.

Equation 6 explains the demand for money, and it is matched to equation 2.6. Equation 7 is an interest rate reaction function, explaining the short term interest rate RS. RS is equivalent to R in the theoretical model. (Interest rate reaction functions are discussed in Section 2.2.7.) Equation 8 is a term structure of interest rates equation, explaining the long term interest rate RB. The theoretical model does not contain a long term rate. Equation 9 is an exchange rate reaction function, explaining the exchange rate E. E is equivalent to e in the theoretical model. (Exchange rate reaction functions are also discussed in Section 2.2.7.) Equation 10 is an estimated arbitrage condition and explains the forward exchange rate. In the theoretical model this equation would be $F = e\frac{1+R}{1+r}$, where F is the forward rate.

Equation 11 explains the price of exports. In the theoretical model the price of exports is simply the price of domestic output, but this is not true in practice and an additional equation has to be introduced, which is equation 11. Equation 12 explains the wage rate; equation 13 explains the demand for employment; and equations 14 and 15 explain the labor force participation rates of men and women, respectively. These equations are not part of the theoretical model because it has no labor sector.

3.3.6 The Linking Equations

The equations that pertain to the trade and price links among countries are presented in Table B.4. (All imports and exports in what follows are merchandise imports and exports only.) The equations L-1 define the export price index for each country in U.S. dollars, $PX\$_i$. i runs from 1 through 44, and so there are 44 such equations. $PX\$_i$ depends on the country's exchange rate and on its export price index in local currency.

The equations L-2 are the trade link equations. The level of exports of country i in 85 \$, $X85\$_i$, is the sum of the amount that each of the other 44 countries imports from country i. For example, the amount that country j imports from country i is $\alpha_{ij} M85\$A_j$, where α_{ij} is the fraction of country i's exports imported by j and $M85\$A_j$ is the total imports of country j from the countries in the trade share matrix. There are 33 of these trade link equations. The α_{ij} values are determined from the trade share equations. These equations are discussed in Section 6.16, and the use of these equations in the solution of the model is discussed in Section 9.2.

The equations L-3 link export prices to import prices, and there are 33 such equations. The price of imports of country i, PMP_i, is a weighted average of the export prices of other countries (except for country 45, the "all other" category, where no data on export prices were collected). The weight for country j in calculating the price index for country i is the share of country j's exports imported by i.

The equations L-4 define a world price index for each country, which is a weighted average of the 33 countries' export prices except the prices of Saudi Arabia and Venezuela, the oil exporting countries. (As discussed in Section 6.12, the aim is to have the world price index not include oil prices.) The world price index differs slightly by country because the own country's price is not included in the calculations. The weight for each country is its share of total exports of the relevant countries.

Table B.5 explains how the US and ROW models are linked. When the two models are combined (into the MC model), the price of imports PIM in the US model is endogenous and the level of exports EX is endogenous.

4

Estimating and Testing
Single Equations

4.1 Notation

This chapter discusses the estimation and testing of single equations. The notation that will be used is the same as that used in Section 1.2. The model is written as

$$f_i(y_t, x_t, \alpha_i) = u_{it}, \quad (i = 1, \ldots, n), \quad (t = 1, \ldots, T) \qquad (4.1)$$

where y_t is an n–dimensional vector of endogenous variables, x_t is a vector of predetermined variables (including lagged endogenous variables), α_i is a vector of unknown coefficients, and u_{it} is the error term for equation i for observation t. It will be assumed that the first m equations are stochastic, with the remaining u_{it} $(i = m + 1, \ldots, n)$ identically zero for all t.

The following notation is also used. u_i denotes the T–dimensional vector $(u_{i1}, \ldots, u_{iT})'$. G_i' denotes the $k_i \times T$ matrix whose tth column is $\partial f_i(y_t, x_t, \alpha_i)/\partial \alpha_i$, where k_i is the dimension of α_i. α denotes the vector of all the unknown coefficients in the model: $\alpha = (\alpha_1', \ldots, \alpha_m')$. The dimension of α is k, where $k = \sum_{i=1}^{m} k_i$. Finally, Z_i denotes a $T \times K_i$ matrix of predetermined variables that are to be used as first stage regressors for the two stage least squares technique.

It will sometimes be useful to consider the case in which the equation to be estimated is linear in coefficients. In this case equation i in 4.1 will be written as

$$y_{it} = X_{it}\alpha_i + u_{it}, \quad (i = 1, \ldots, n), \quad (t = 1, \ldots, T) \qquad (4.2)$$

63

where y_{it} is the left hand side variable and X_{it} is a k_i–dimensional vector of explanatory variables in the equation. X_{it} includes both endogenous and predetermined variables. Both y_{it} and the variables in X_{it} can be nonlinear functions of other variables, and thus 4.2 is more general than the standard linear model. All that is required is that the equation be linear in α_i. Note from the definition of G'_i above that for equation 4.2 $G'_i = X'_i$, where X'_i is the $k_i \times T$ matrix whose tth column is X_{it}.

Each equation in 4.1 is assumed to have been transformed to eliminate any autoregressive properties of its error term. If the error term in the untransformed version, say w_{it} in equation i, follows a rth order autoregressive process, $w_{it} = \rho_{1i} w_{it-1} + \ldots + \rho_{ri} w_{it-r} + u_{it}$, where u_{it} is *iid*, then equation i is assumed to have been transformed into one with u_{it} on the right hand side. The autoregressive coefficients $\rho_{1i}, \ldots, \rho_{ri}$ are incorporated into the α_i coefficient vector, and the additional lagged values that are involved in the transformation are incorporated into the x_t vector. This transformation makes the equation nonlinear in coefficients if it were not otherwise, but this adds no further complications to the model because it is already allowed to be nonlinear. It does result in the "loss" of the first r observations, but this has no effect on the asymptotic properties of the estimators. u_{it} in 4.1 can thus be assumed to be *iid* even though the original error term may follow an autoregressive process.

Many nonlinear optimization problems in macroeconometrics can be solved by general purpose algorithms like the Davidon-Fletcher-Powell (DFP) algorithm. This algorithm is discussed in Fair (1984), Section 2.5, and this discussion will not be repeated here. Problems for which the algorithm seems to work well and those for which it does not are noted below.

Unless otherwise stated, the goodness of fit measures have not been adjusted for degrees of freedom. For the general model considered here (non-linear, simultaneous, dynamic) only asymptotic results are available, and so if any adjustments were made, they would have to be based on analogies to simpler models. In many cases there are no obvious analogies, and so no adjustments were made. Fortunately, in most cases the number of observations is fairly large relative to numbers that might be used in the subtraction, and so the results are not likely to be sensitive to the current treatment.

4.2 Two Stage Least Squares[1]

Probably the most widely used estimation technique for single equations that produces consistent estimates is two stage least squares (2SLS).[2] The 2SLS estimate of α_i (denoted $\hat{\alpha}_i$) is obtained by minimizing

$$S_i = u_i' Z_i (Z_i' Z_i)^{-1} Z_i' u_i = u_i' D_i u_i \tag{4.3}$$

with respect to α_i. Z_i can differ from equation to equation. An estimate of the covariance matrix of $\hat{\alpha}_i$ (denoted $\hat{V}_{2ii}$) is

$$\hat{V}_{2ii} = \hat{\sigma}_{ii} (\hat{G}_i' D_i \hat{G}_i)^{-1} \tag{4.4}$$

where $\hat{G}_i$ is G_i evaluated at $\hat{\alpha}_i$, $\hat{\sigma}_{ii} = T^{-1} \sum_{t=1}^{T} \hat{u}_{it}^2$, and $\hat{u}_{it} = f_i(y_t, x_t, \hat{\alpha}_i)$.

The 2SLS estimate of the $k \times k$ covariance matrix of all the coefficient estimates in the model (denoted $\hat{V}_2$) is

$$\hat{V}_2 = \begin{bmatrix} \hat{V}_{211} & \cdots & \hat{V}_{21m} \\ & & \\ & & \\ & & \\ \hat{V}_{2m1} & \cdots & \hat{V}_{2mm} \end{bmatrix} \tag{4.5}$$

where

$$\hat{V}_{2ij} = \hat{\sigma}_{ij} (\hat{G}_i' D_i \hat{G}_i')^{-1} (\hat{G}_i' D_i D_j \hat{G}_j')(\hat{G}_j' D_j \hat{G}_j')^{-1} \tag{4.6}$$

and $\hat{\sigma}_{ij} = T^{-1} \sum_{t=1}^{T} \hat{u}_{it} \hat{u}_{jt}$.

4.3 Estimation of Equations with Rational Expectations[3]

With only slight modifications, the 2SLS estimator can be used to estimate equations that contain expectational variables in which the expectations are formed rationally. As discussed later in this chapter, this estimation technique

---

[1]See Fair (1984), Section 6.3.2, for a more detailed discussion of the two stage least squares estimator, especially for the case in which the equation is linear in coefficients and has an autoregressive error.

[2]Ordinary least squares is used a lot in practice in the estimation of commercial models even when the estimator does not produce consistent estimates. This lack of care in the estimation of such models is undoubtedly one of the reasons there has been so little academic interest in them.

[3]The material in this section is taken from Fair (1993b), Section 3 and Appendix A.

can be used to test the rational expectations hypothesis against other alternatives. The modifications of the 2SLS estimator that are needed to handle the
rational expectations case are discussed in this section.

It will be useful to begin with an example. Assume that the equation to be
estimated is

$$y_{it} = X_{1it}\alpha_{1i} + E_{t-1}X_{2it+j}\alpha_{2i} + u_{it}, \quad (t = 1, \ldots, T) \tag{4.7}$$

where X_{1it} is a vector of explanatory variables and $E_{t-1}X_{2it+j}$ is the expectation of X_{2it+j} based on information through period $t - 1$. j is some fixed
positive integer. This example assumes that there is only one expectational
variable and only one value of j, but this is only for illustration. The more
general case will be considered shortly.

A traditional assumption about expectations is that the expected future
values of a variable are a function of its current and past values. One might
postulate, for example, that $E_{t-1}X_{2it+j}$ depends on X_{2it} and X_{2it-1}, where
it assumed that X_{2it} (as well as X_{2it-1}) is known at the time the expectation
is made. The equation could then be estimated with X_{2it} and X_{2it-1} replacing $E_{t-1}X_{2it+j}$ in 4.7. Note that this treatment, which is common to many
macroeconometric models, is not inconsistent with the view that agents are
"forward looking." Expected future values do affect current behavior. It's just
that the expectations are formed in fairly simply ways—say by looking only
at the current and lagged values of the variable itself.

Assume instead that $E_{t-1}X_{2it+j}$ is rational and assume that there is an
observed vector of variables (observed by the econometrician), denoted here as
Z_{it}, that is used in part by agents in forming their (rational) expectations. The
following method does not require for consistent estimates that Z_{it} include all
the variables used by agents in forming their expectations.

Let the expectation error for $E_{t-1}X_{2it+j}$ be

$$_{t-1}\epsilon_{it+j} = X_{2it+j} - E_{t-1}X_{2it+j} \quad (t = 1, \ldots, T) \tag{4.8}$$

where X_{2it+j} is the actual value of the variable. Substituting 4.8 into 4.7
yields

$$y_{it} = X_{1it}\alpha_{1i} + X_{2it+j}\alpha_{2i} + u_{it} -_{t-1}\epsilon_{it+j}\alpha_{2i}$$

$$= X_{it}\alpha_i + v_{it} \quad (t = 1, \ldots, T) \tag{4.9}$$

where $X_{it} = (X_{1it} \ X_{2it+j})$, $\alpha_i = (\alpha_{1i} \ \alpha_{2i})'$, and $v_{it} = u_{it} -_{t-1}\epsilon_{it+j}\alpha_{2i}$.

Consider now the 2SLS estimation of 4.9, where the vector of first stage
regressors is the vector Z_{it} used by agents in forming their expectations. A

necessary condition for consistency is that Z_{it} and v_{it} be uncorrelated. This will be true if both u_{it} and $_{t-1}\epsilon_{it+j}$ are uncorrelated with Z_{it}. The assumption that Z_{it} and u_{it} are uncorrelated is the usual 2SLS assumption. The assumption that Z_{it} and $_{t-1}\epsilon_{it+j}$ are uncorrelated is the rational expectations assumption. If expectations are formed rationally and if the variables in Z_{it} are used (perhaps along with others) in forming the expectation of X_{2it+j}, then Z_{it} and $_{t-1}\epsilon_{it+j}$ are uncorrelated. Given this assumption (and the other standard assumptions that are necessary for consistency), the 2SLS estimator of α_i in equation 4.9 is consistent.

The 2SLS estimator does not, however, account for the fact that v_{it} in 4.9 is a moving average error of order $j - 1$, and so it loses some efficiency for values of j greater than 1. The modification of the 2SLS estimator to account for the moving average process of v_{it} is Hansen's (1982) generalized method of moments (GMM) estimator, which will now be described.

Write 4.9 in matrix notation as

$$y_i = X_i\alpha_i + v_i \qquad (4.10)$$

where X_i is $T \times k_i$, α_i is $k_i \times 1$, and y_i and v_i are $T \times 1$. Also, let Z_i denote, as above, the $T \times K_i$ matrix of first stage regressors. The assumption in 4.9 that there is only one expectational variable and only one value of j can now be relaxed. The matrix X_i can include more than one expectational variable and more than one value of j per variable. In other words, there can be more than one led value in this matrix.

The 2SLS estimate of α_i in 4.10 is

$$\hat{\alpha}_i = [X_i'Z_i(Z_i'Z_i)^{-1}Z_i'X_i]^{-1}X_i'Z_i(Z_i'Z_i)^{-1}Z_i'y_i \qquad (4.11)$$

This use of the 2SLS estimator for models with rational expectations is due to McCallum (1976).

As just noted, this use of the 2SLS estimator does not account for the moving average process of v_{it}, and so it loses efficiency if there is at least one value of j greater than 1. Also, the standard formula for the covariance matrix of $\hat{\alpha}_i$ is not correct when at least one value of j is greater than 1. If, for example, j is 3 in 4.9, an unanticipated shock in period $t + 1$ will affect $_{t-1}\epsilon_{it+3}$, $_{t-2}\epsilon_{it+2}$, and $_{t-3}\epsilon_{it+1}$, and so v_{it} will be a second order moving average. Hansen's GMM estimator accounts for this moving average process. The GMM estimate in the present case (denoted $\tilde{\alpha}_i$) is

$$\tilde{\alpha}_i = (X_i'Z_iM_i^{-1}Z_i'X_i)^{-1}X_i'Z_iM_i^{-1}Z_i'y_i \qquad (4.12)$$

where M_i is some consistent estimate of $\lim T^{-1} E(Z_i' v_i v_i' Z_i)$. The estimated covariance matrix of $\tilde{\alpha}_i$ is

$$T(X_i' Z_i M_i^{-1} Z_i' X_i)^{-1} \tag{4.13}$$

There are different versions of $\tilde{\alpha}_i$ depending on how M_i is computed. To compute M_i, one first needs an estimate of the residual vector v_i. The residuals can be estimated using the 2SLS estimate $\hat{\alpha}_i$:

$$\hat{v}_i = y_i - X_i \hat{\alpha}_i \tag{4.14}$$

A general way of computing M_i is as follows. Let $f_{it} = \hat{v}_{it} \otimes Z_{it}$, where $\hat{v}_{it}$ is the tth element of $\hat{v}_i$. Let $R_{ip} = (T - p)^{-1} \sum_{t=p}^{T} f_{it} f_{it-p}'$, $p = 0, 1, \ldots, P$, where P is the order of the moving average. M_i is then $(R_{i0} + R_{i1} + R_{i1}' + \ldots + R_{iP} + R_{iP}')$. In many cases computing M_i in this way does not result in a positive definite matrix, and so $\tilde{\alpha}_i$ cannot be computed. I have never had much success in obtaining a positive definite matrix for M_i computed in this way.

There are, however, other ways of computing M_i. One way, which is discussed in Hansen (1982) and Cumby, Huizinga, and Obstfeld (1983) but is not pursued here, is to compute M_i based on an estimate of the spectral density matrix of $Z_{it}' v_{it}$ evaluated at frequency zero. An alternative way, which is pursued here, is to compute M_i under the following assumption:

$$E(v_{it} v_{is} \mid Z_{it}, Z_{it-1}, \ldots) = E(v_{is} v_{is}) \quad , \quad t \geq s \tag{4.15}$$

which says that the contemporaneous and serial correlations in v_i do not depend on Z_i. This assumption is implied by the assumption that $E(v_{it} v_{is}) = 0, t \geq s$, if normality is also assumed. Under this assumption M_i can be computed as follows. Let $a_{ip} = (T - p)^{-1} \sum_{t=p}^{T} \hat{v}_{it} \hat{v}_{it-p}$ and $B_{ip} = (T - p)^{-1} \sum_{t=p}^{T} Z_{it} Z_{it-p}'$, $p = 0, 1, \ldots, P$. M_i is then $(a_{i0} B_{i0} + a_{i1} B_{i1} + a_{i1} B_{i1}' + \ldots + a_{iP} B_{iP} + a_{iP} B_{iP}')$. In practice, this way of computing M_i usually results in a positive definite matrix.

The Case of an Autoregressive Structural Error

Since many macroeconometric equations have autoregressive error terms, it is useful to consider how the above estimator is modified to cover this case. Return for the moment to the example in 4.7 and assume that the error term u_{it} in the equation follows a first order autoregressive process:

$$u_{it} = \rho_{1i} u_{it-1} + \eta_{it} \tag{4.16}$$

Lagging equation 4.7 one period, multiplying through by ρ_{1i}, and subtracting the resulting expression from 4.7 yields

$$y_{it} = \rho_{1i} y_{it-1} + X_{1it}\alpha_{1i} - X_{1it-1}\alpha_{1i}\rho_{1i} + E_{t-1}X_{2it+j}\alpha_{2i}$$

$$- E_{t-2}X_{2it+j-1}\alpha_{2i}\rho_{1i} + \eta_{it} \qquad (4.17)$$

Note that this transformation yields a new viewpoint date, $t - 2$. Let the expectation error for $E_{t-2}X_{2it+j-1}$ be

$$_{t-2}\epsilon_{it+j-1} = X_{2it+j-1} - E_{t-2}X_{2it+j-1} \qquad (4.18)$$

Substituting 4.8 and 4.18 into 4.17 yields

$$y_{it} = \rho_{1i} y_{it-1} + X_{1it}\alpha_{1i} - X_{1it-1}\alpha_{1i}\rho_{1i} + X_{2it+j}\alpha_{2i} - X_{2it+j-1}\alpha_{2i}\rho_{1i}$$

$$+ \eta_{it} -_{t-1} \epsilon_{it+j}\alpha_{2i} +_{t-2} \epsilon_{it+j-1}\alpha_{2i}\rho_{1i}$$

$$= \rho_{1i} y_{it-1} + X_{it}\alpha_i - X_{it-1}\alpha_i\rho_{1i} + v_{it} \qquad (4.19)$$

where X_{it} and α_i are defined after 4.9 and now $v_{it} = \eta_{it} -_{t-1}\epsilon_{it+j}\alpha_{2i} +_{t-2}\epsilon_{it+j-1}\alpha_{2i}\rho_{1i}$. Equation 4.19 is nonlinear in coefficients because of the introduction of ρ_{1i}. Again, X_{it} can in general include more than one expectational variable and more than one value of j per variable.

Given a set of first stage regressors, equation 4.19 can be estimated by 2SLS. The estimates are obtained by minimizing

$$S_i = v_i' Z_i (Z_i' Z_i)^{-1} Z_i' v_i = v_i' D_i v_i \qquad (4.20)$$

4.20 is just 4.3 rewritten for the error term in 4.19. A necessary condition for consistency is that Z_{it} and v_{it} be uncorrelated, which means that Z_{it} must be uncorrelated with η_{it}, $_{t-1}\epsilon_{it+j}$, and $_{t-2}\epsilon_{it+j-1}$. In order to insure that Z_{it} and $_{t-2}\epsilon_{it+j-1}$ are uncorrelated, Z_{it} must not include any variables that are not known as of the beginning of period $t - 1$. This is an important additional restriction in the autoregressive case.[4]

In the general nonlinear case 4.20 (or 4.3) can be minimized using a general purpose optimization algorithm. In the particular case considered here, however, a simple iterative procedure can be used, where one iterates between

---

[4]There is a possibly confusing statement in Cumby, Huizinga, and Obstfeld (1983), p. 341, regarding the movement of the instrument set backward in time. The instrument set must be moved backward in time as the order of the autoregressive process increases. It need not be moved backward as the order of the moving average process increases due to an increase in j.

estimates of α_i and ρ_{1i}. Minimizing $v_i' D_i v_i$ with respect to α_i and ρ_{1i} results in the following first order conditions:

$$\hat{\alpha}_i = [(X_i - X_{i-1}\hat{\rho}_{1i})' D_i (X_i - X_{i-1}\hat{\rho}_{1i})]^{-1} (X_i - X_{i-1}\hat{\rho}_{1i})' D_i (y_i - y_{i-1}\hat{\rho}_{1i}) \tag{4.21}$$

$$\hat{\rho}_{1i} = \frac{(y_{i-1} - X_{i-1}\hat{\alpha}_i)' D_i (y_i - X_i \hat{\alpha}_i)}{(y_{i-1} - X_{i-1}\hat{\alpha}_i)' D_i (y_{i-1} - X_{i-1}\hat{\alpha}_i)} \tag{4.22}$$

where the -1 subscript denotes the vector or matrix of observations lagged one period. Equations 4.21 and 4.22 can easily be solved iteratively. Given the estimates $\hat{\alpha}_i$ and $\hat{\rho}_{1i}$ that solve 4.21 and 4.22, one can compute the 2SLS estimate of v_i, which is

$$\hat{v}_i = y_i - y_{i-1}\hat{\rho}_{1i} - X_i\hat{\alpha}_i + X_{i-1}\hat{\alpha}_i\hat{\rho}_{1i} \tag{4.23}$$

Regarding Hansen's estimator, given $\hat{v}_i$, one can compute M_i in one of the number of possible ways. These calculations simply involve $\hat{v}_i$ and Z_i. Given M_i, Hansen's estimates of α_i and ρ_{1i} are obtained by minimizing[5]

$$SS_i = v_i' Z_i M_i^{-1} Z_i' v_i = v_i' C_i v_i \tag{4.24}$$

Minimizing 4.24 with respect to α_i and ρ_{1i} results in the first order conditions 4.21 and 4.22 with C_i replacing D_i. The estimated covariance matrix is

$$T(G_i' C_i G_i)^{-1} \tag{4.25}$$

where $G = (X_i - X_{i-1}\hat{\rho}_{1i} \quad y_{i-1} - X_{i-1}\hat{\alpha}_i)$.

To summarize, Hansen's method in the case of a first order autoregressive structural error consists of: 1) choosing Z_{it} so that it does not include any variables not known as of the beginning of period $t - 1$, 2) solving 4.21 and 4.22, 3) computing $\hat{v}_i$ from 4.23, 4) computing M_i in one of the number of possible ways using $\hat{v}_i$ and Z_i, and 5) solving 4.21 and 4.22 with C_i replacing D_i.

4.4 Two Stage Least Absolute Deviations[6]

Another single equation estimator that is of interest to consider is two stage least absolute deviations (2SLAD). This estimator is used for comparison purposes in Chapter 8. The following is a brief review of it.

---

[5]The estimator that is based on the minimization of 4.24 is also the 2S2SLS estimator of Cumby, Huizinga, and Obstfeld (1983).

[6]See Fair (1984), Sections 6.3.6 and 6.5.4, for a more detailed discussion of the two stage least absolute deviations estimator.

It is assumed for the 2SLAD estimator that the model in 4.1 can be written:

$$y_{it} = h_i(y_t, x_t, \alpha_i) + u_{it}, \quad (i = 1, \ldots, n), \quad (t = 1, \ldots, T) \quad (4.26)$$

where in the ith equation y_{it} appears only on the left hand side.

Let $\hat{y}_i = D_i y_i$ and $\hat{h}_i = D_i h_i$, where, as above, $D_i = Z_i(Z_i'Z_i)^{-1}Z_i'$, where Z_i is a matrix of first stage regressors. There are two ways of looking at the 2SLAD estimator. One is that it minimizes

$$\sum_{t=1}^{T} \left| \hat{y}_{it} - \hat{h}_{it} \right| \quad (4.27)$$

and the other is that it minimizes

$$\sum_{t=1}^{T} \left| y_{it} - \hat{h}_{it} \right| \quad (4.28)$$

Amemiya (1982) has proposed minimizing

$$\sum_{t=1}^{T} \left| q y_{it} + (1 - q) \hat{y}_{it} - \hat{h}_{it} \right| \quad (4.29)$$

where q is chosen ahead of time by the investigator. The estimator that is based on minimizing 4.29 will be called the 2SLAD estimator. For the computational results in Chapter 8, $q = .5$ has been used.

The 2SLAD estimator weights large outliers less than does 2SLS, and so it is less sensitive to these outliers. It is a robust estimator in the sense that its properties are less sensitive to deviations of the distributions of the error terms from normality than are the properties of 2SLS.

4.5 Chi-Square Tests

Many single equation tests are simply of the form of adding a variable or a set of variables to an equation and testing whether the addition is statistically significant. Let S_i^{**} denote the value of the minimand before the addition, let S_i^{*} denote the value after the addition, and let $\hat{\sigma}_{ii}$ denote the estimated variance of the error term after the addition. Under fairly general conditions, as discussed in Andrews and Fair (1988), $(S_i^{**} - S_i^{*})/\hat{\sigma}_{ii}$ is distributed as χ^2 with k degrees of freedom, where k is the number of variables added. For the 2SLS estimator the minimand is defined in equation 4.3, i.e., $S_i = u_i' D_i u_i$.

For Hansen's estimator the minimand is defined in equation 4.24, i.e., $SS_i = v_i' C_i v_i$. In this case $(SS_i^{**} - SS_i^*)/T$ is distributed as χ^2, where T is the number of observations. When performing this test the M_i matrix that is used in the construction of C_i must be the same for both estimates. For the results in Chapter 5, M_i was always estimated using the residuals for the unrestricted case (i.e., using the residuals from the equation with the additions).

The following is a list of tests of single equations that can be made by adding various things to the equations and performing χ^2 tests.

Dynamic Specification

Many macroeconomic equations include the lagged dependent variable and other lagged endogenous variables among the explanatory variables. A test of the dynamic specification of a particular equation is to add *further* lagged values to the equation and see if they are significant. For equation 4.2, for example, one could add the lagged value of y_i if the lagged value is not already included in X_i and the lagged values of the variables in X_i. (If the lagged value of y_i is in X_i, then the value of y_i lagged twice would be added for the test.) Hendry, Pagan, and Sargan (1984) show that adding these lagged values is quite general in that it encompasses many different types of dynamic specifications. Therefore, adding the lagged values and testing for their significance is a test against a fairly general dynamic specification.

Time Trend

Long before units roots and cointegration became popular, model builders worried about picking up spurious correlation from common trending variables. One check on whether the correlation might be spurious is to add a time trend to the equation. If adding a time trend to the equation substantially changes some of the coefficient estimates, this is cause for concern. A simple test is to add the time trend to the equation and test if this addition is significant.

Serial Correlation of the Error Term

As noted in Section 4.1, if the error term in an equation follows an autoregressive process, the equation can be transformed and the coefficients of the autoregressive process can be estimated along with the structural coefficients. Even if, say, a first order process has been assumed and the first order coefficient estimated, it is still of interest to see if there is serial correlation of the (transformed) error term left. This can be done by assuming a more general process for the error term and testing its significance. For the results in Chapters 5 and 6 a fourth order process was used. If the addition of a fourth order process over, say, a first order process results in a significant increase in explanatory power, this is evidence that the serial correlation properties of the error term have not been properly accounted for.

Other Explanatory Variables

Variables can obviously be added to an equation and their statistical significance tested. This is done for the equations in the next two chapters. If a variable or set of variables that one does not expect from the theory to belong in the equation is significant, this is evidence against the theory.

Variables can also be added that others have found to be important explanatory variables in similar contexts. For example, Friedman and Kuttner (1992), (1993) have found the spread between the six month commercial paper rate and the six month Treasury bill rate is significant in explaining real GNP in a vector autoregressive system. If the spread is significant in explaining real GNP, then it should be in explaining some of the components of real GNP. It is thus of interest to add the spread to equations explaining consumption and investment to see if it has independent explanatory power. This is done in the next chapter for some of the equations in the US model.[7]

Leads[8]

Adding values led one or more periods and using Hansen's method for the estimation is a way of testing the hypothesis that expectations are rational. Consider the example in equation 4.7 above, and consider testing the RE hypothesis against the simpler alternative that $E_{t-1}X_{2it+j}$ is only a function of X_{2it} and X_{2it-1}, where both of these variables are assumed to be known at the time the expectation is made. Under the simpler alternative, X_{2it} and X_{2it-1} are added as explanatory variables to 4.7. Under the RE alternative, X_{2it+j} is added as an explanatory variable, and the equation is estimated using Hansen's method. A test of the RE hypothesis is thus to add X_{2it+j} to the equation with X_{2it} and X_{2it-1} included and test the hypothesis that

---

[7]The six month commercial paper rate and the six month Treasury bill rate are not variables in the US model, and they are not presented in Appendix A. The data are available from the Federal Reserve.

[8]The material in this subsection is taken from Fair (1993b), Section 3.

the coefficient of X_{2it+j} is zero. The Z_{it} vector used for Hansen's method should include the predetermined variables in X_{1it} in 4.7—including X_{2it} and X_{2it-1}—plus other variables assumed to be in the agents' information sets.[9] The test is really whether these other variables matter. If agents do not use more information than that contained in the predetermined variables in X_{1it} in forming their expectation of X_{2ti+j}, then the use of the variables in Z_{it} as first stage regressors for X_{2it+j} adds nothing not already contained in the predetermined variables in X_{1it}.

The test of the RE hypothesis is thus to add variable values led one or more periods to an equation with only current and lagged values and estimate the resulting equation using Hansen's method. If the led values are not significant, this is evidence against the RE hypothesis. It means essentially that the extra variables in Z_{it} do not contribute significantly to the explanatory power of the equation.

An implicit assumption behind this test is that Z_{it} contains variables other than the predetermined variables in X_{1it}. If, say, the optimal predictor of X_{2it+j} were solely a function of X_{2it} and X_{2it-1}, then the above test would not be appropriate. In this case the traditional approach is consistent with the RE hypothesis, and there is nothing to test. The assumption that Z_{it} contains many variables is consistent with the specification of most macroeconometric models, where the implicit reduced form equations for the endogenous variables contain a large number of variables. This assumption is in effect maintained throughout this book. The tests in Chapters 5 and 6 have nothing to say about cases in which there is a very small number of variables in Z_{it}.

As an example of the test, consider the wage variable W in the consumption equation 1.4 in Chapter 1. Assume that W_t is known, where t is period 1. The wage variables in equation 1.4 are then W_t, $E_{t-1}W_{t+1}$, $E_{t-1}W_{t+2}$, etc. If

---

[9]Remember that X_{2it} is assumed to be known at the time the expectations are made, which is the reason for treating it as predetermined. In practice, a variable like X_{2it} is sometimes taken to be endogenous, in which case it is not part of the Z_{it} vector. When a variable like X_{2it} is taken to be endogenous, an interesting question is whether one can test the hypothesis that agents know it at the time they make their expectations as opposed to having only a rational expectation of it. It is not possible to test this if the Z_{it} vector used for the 2SLS method is the same vector used by the agents in forming their expectations. It would, however, be possible to test this hypothesis if there were some contemporaneous exogenous variables in the model that agents forming rational expectations do not know at the time they make their forecasts. These variables are appropriate first stage regressors for 2SLS (since they are exogenous), but they are not used by agents. In practice, however, this is likely to be a small difference upon which to base a test, and no attempt is made here to do so. The focus here is on values dated $t+1$ and beyond.

agents use only current and lagged values of W in forming expectations of future values of W, then candidates for explanatory variables are W_t, W_{t-1}, W_{t-2}, etc. Under the RE hypothesis, on the other hand, agents use Z_{it} in forming their expectations for periods $t+1$ and beyond, and candidates for explanatory variables are W_{t+1}, W_{t+2}, etc., with Hansen's method used for the estimation. The test is to test for the joint significance of the led values.

The test proposed here is quite different from Hendry's (1988) test of expectational mechanisms. Hendry's test requires one to postulate the expectation generation process, which is then examined for its constancy across time. If the structural equation that contains the expectations is constant but the expectations equations are not, this refutes the expectations equations. As noted above, for the test proposed here Z_{it} need not contain all the variables used by agents in forming their expectations, and so the test does not require a complete specification of the expectations generation process. The two main requirements are only that Z_{it} be correlated with X_{2it+j} but not with $_{t-1}\epsilon_{it+j}$.

4.6   Stability Tests

One of the most important issues to examine about an equation is whether its coefficients change over time, i.e., whether the structure is stable over time. A common test of structural stability is to pick a date at which the structure is hypothesized to have changed and then test the hypothesis that a change occurred at this date. In the standard linear regression model this is an F test, usually called the Chow test. More general settings are considered in Andrews and Fair (1988).

One test in the more general setting is simply the χ^2 test discussed in the previous section, where S_i^{**} is the value of the minimand under the assumption of no structural change and S_i^* is the value of the minimand under the assumption that the change occurred at the specified date. Assume, for example, that the estimation period is from 1 through T and that the specified date of the structural change is T^*. Assume also that the equation is estimated by 2SLS. Computing the χ^2 value in this case requires estimating the equation for three periods: 1 through T^*, $T^* + 1$ through T, and 1 through T. Let $S_i^{(1)}$ be the value of the minimand in 4.3 for the first estimation period, and let $S_i^{(2)}$ be the value for the second estimation period. Then $S_i^* = S_i^{(1)} + S_i^{(2)}$. S_i^{**} is the value of the minimand in 4.3 that is obtained when the equation is estimated over the full estimation period. When estimating over the full period, the Z_i matrix used for the full period must be the union of the matrices used for the two subperiods in order to make S_i^{**} comparable to S_i^*. This means that for each first stage regressor Q_{it}, two variables must be used in Z_i for the full estimation period, one that is equal to Q_{it} for the first subperiod and zero otherwise and one that is equal to Q_{it} for the second subperiod and zero otherwise. If this is done, then the χ^2 value is $(S_i^{**} - S_i^*)/\hat{\sigma}_{ii}$, where $\hat{\sigma}_{ii}$ is equal to the sum of the sums of squared residuals from the first and second estimation periods divided by $T - 2k_i$, where k_i is the number of estimated coefficients in the equation.

Recently, Andrews and Ploberger (1994) have proposed a class of tests that does not require that the date of the structural change be chosen *a priori*. Let the overall sample period be 1 through T. The hypothesis tested is that a structural change occurred between observations T_1 and T_2, where T_1 is an observation close to 1 and T_2 is an observation close to T. If the time of the change (if there is one) is completely unknown, Andrews and Ploberger suggest taking T_1 very close to 1 and T_2 very close to T. This puts little restriction on the time of the change. If, on the other hand, the time of the change is known to lie in a narrower interval, the narrower interval should be used to maximize power. One of the main advantages of the Andrews-Ploberger tests is that they have nontrivial power asymptotically and have been designed to have certain optimality properties.

The particular Andrews-Ploberger test used here is easy to compute. The test is carried out as follows:

1. Compute the χ^2 value for the hypothesis that the change occurred at observation T_1. This requires estimating the equation three times— once each for the estimation periods 1 through $T_1 - 1$, T_1 through T, and 1 through T. Denote this value as $\chi^{2(1)}$.[10]

2. Repeat step 1 for the hypothesis that the change occurred at observation $T_1 + 1$. Denote this χ^2 value as $\chi^{2(2)}$. Keep doing this through the hypothesis that the change occurred at observation T_2. This results in $N = T_2 - T_1 + 1$ χ^2 values being computed—$\chi^{2(1)}, \ldots, \chi^{2(N)}$.

3. The Andrews-Ploberger test statistic (denoted AP) is

$$AP = \log[(e^{\frac{1}{2}\chi^{2(1)}} + \ldots + e^{\frac{1}{2}\chi^{2(N)}})/N] \qquad (4.30)$$

In words, the AP statistic is a weighted average of the χ^2 values, where there is one χ^2 value for each possible split in the sample period between observations T_1 and T_2.

---

[10]This χ^2 value is computed in the regular way as discussed above.

Table 4.1
Critical Values for the AP Statistic
for $\lambda = 2.75$

No.of coefs.	5%	1%	No.of coefs.	5%	1%
1	2.01	3.36	8	8.22	10.23
2	3.07	4.69	9	9.01	11.20
3	4.00	5.62	10	9.55	12.14
4	4.95	7.00	11	10.33	12.73
5	5.80	7.65	12	11.03	13.43
6	6.59	8.72	13	11.62	14.47
7	7.31	9.50	14	12.37	15.20

Asymptotic critical values for AP are presented in Tables I and II in Andrews and Ploberger (1994). The critical values depend on the number of coefficients in the equation and on a parameter λ, where in the present context $\lambda = [\pi_2(1 - \pi_1)]/[\pi_1(1 - \pi_2)]$, where $\pi_1 = (T_1 - .5)/T$ and $\pi_2 = (T_2 - .5)/T$.

If the AP value is significant, it may be of interest to examine the individual χ^2 values to see where the maximum value occurred. This is likely to give one a general idea of where the structural change occurred even though the AP test does not reveal this in any rigorous way.

Since the AP test is used in the next two chapters, it will be useful to give a few critical values. For the work in the next chapter the basic sample period is 1954:1–1993:2, and for the stability tests T_1 was taken to be 1970:1 and T_2 was taken to be 1979:4. This choice yields a value of λ of 2.75. Table 4.1 presents the 5 percent and 1 percent asymptotic critical values for this value of λ and various values of the number of estimated coefficients in the equations. These values are interpolated from Table I in Andrews and Ploberger (1994).

Although the values in Table 4.1 are for just one particular value of λ (namely, 2.75), Andrews and Ploberger's Table I shows that the critical values are not very sensitive to different values of λ. The above critical values are thus approximately correct for different choices of T_1 and T_2 than the one made here.

4.7   Tests of Age Distribution Effects[11]

A striking feature of post war U.S. society has been the baby boom of the late 1940s and the 1950s and the subsequent falling off of the birth rate in the 1960s. The number of births in the United States rose from 2.5 million in 1945 to 4.2 million in 1961 and then fell back to 3.1 million in 1974. This birth pattern implies large changes in the percentage of prime age (25–54) people in the working age (16+) population. In 1952 this percentage was 57.9, whereas by 1977 it had fallen to 49.5. Since 1980 the percentage of prime aged workers has risen sharply as the baby boomers have begun to pass the age of 25.

As noted in Chapter 1, an important issue in macroeconomics is whether the coefficients of macroeconomic equations change over time as other things change. The Lucas critique focuses on policy changes, but other possible changes are changes in the age distribution of the population. This section discusses a procedure for examining the effects of the changes in the U.S. population age distribution on macroeconomic equations. The procedure is as follows.

Divide the population into J age groups. Let $D1_{ht}$ be 1 if individual h is in age group 1 in period t and 0 otherwise; let $D2_{ht}$ be 1 if individual h is in age group 2 in period t and 0 otherwise; and so on through DJ_{ht}. Consider equation i in 4.2, an equation that is linear in coefficients. Let equation i for individual h be:

$$y_{hit} = X_{hit}\alpha_i + \beta_{0i} + \beta_{1i} D1_{ht} + \ldots + \beta_{Ji} DJ_{ht} + u_{hit}$$

$$(h = 1, \ldots, N_t), \quad (t = 1, \ldots, T) \tag{4.31}$$

where y_{hit} is the value of variable i in period t for individual h (e.g., consumption of individual h in period t), X_{hit} is a vector of explanatory variables excluding the constant, α_i is a vector of coefficients, and u_{hit} is the error term. The constant term in the equation is $\beta_{0i} + \beta_{ji}$ for an individual in age group j in period t. N_t is the total number of people in the population in period t.

Equation 4.31 is restrictive because it assumes that α_i is the same across all individuals, but it is less restrictive than a typical macroeconomic equation, which also assumes that the constant term is the same across individuals. Given X_{hit}, y_{hit} is allowed to vary across age groups in equation 4.31. Because most macroeconomic variables are not disaggregated by age groups, one cannot test for age sensitive α_i's. For example, suppose that one of the variables in X_{hit}

---

[11]The material in this section is taken from Fair and Dominguez (1991).

is Y_{ht}, the income of individual h in period t. If the coefficient of Y_{ht} is the same across individuals, say γ_{1i}, then $\gamma_{1i} Y_{ht}$ enters the equation, and it can be summed in the manner discussed in the next paragraph. If, on the other hand, the coefficient differs across age groups, then the term entering the equation is $\gamma_{11i} D1_{ht} Y_{ht} + \ldots + \gamma_{1Ji} DJ_{ht} Y_{ht}$. The sum of a variable like $D1_{ht} Y_{ht}$ across individuals is the total income of individuals in age group 1, for which data are not generally available. One is thus restricted to assuming that age group differences are reflected in different constant terms in equation 4.31.

Let N_{jt} be the total number of people in age group j in period t, let y_{it} be the sum of y_{hit}, let X_{it} be the vector whose elements are the sums of the corresponding elements in X_{hit}, and let u_{it} be the sum of u_{hit}. (All sums are for $h = 1, \ldots, N_t$.) Given this notation, summing equation 4.31 yields:

$$y_{it} = X_{it}\alpha_i + \beta_{0i} N_t + \beta_{1i} N_{1t} + \ldots + \beta_{Ji} N_{Jt} + u_{it}, \quad (t = 1, \ldots, T) \quad (4.32)$$

If equation 4.32 is divided through by N_t, it is converted into an equation in per capita terms. Let $p_{jt} = N_{jt}/N_t$, and reinterpret y_{it}, the variables in X_{it}, and u_{it} as being the original values divided by N_t. Equation 4.32 in per capita terms can then be written:

$$y_{it} = X_{it}\alpha_i + \beta_{0i} + \beta_{1i} p_{1t} + \ldots + \beta_{Ji} p_{Jt} + u_{it}, \quad (t = 1, \ldots, T) \quad (4.33)$$

A test of whether age distribution matters is simply a test of whether the $\beta_{1i}, \ldots, \beta_{Ji}$ coefficients in equation 4.33 are significantly different from zero.[12] If the coefficients are zero, one is back to a standard macroeconomic equation. Otherwise, given X_{it}, y_{it} varies as the age distribution varies. Since the sum of p_{jt} across j is one and there is a constant in the equation, a restriction on the β_{ji} coefficients must be imposed for estimation. In the estimation work below, the age group coefficients are restricted to sum to zero: $\sum_{j=1}^{J} \beta_{ji} = 0$. This means that if the distributional variables do not matter, then adding them to the equation will not affect the constant term.

The Age Distribution Data

The age distribution data that are used in the next chapter are from the U.S. Bureau of the Census, *Current Population Reports*, Series P-25. The data from

---

[12] Stoker (1986) characterizes this test (that all proportion coefficients are zero) as a test of microeconomic linearity or homogeneity (that all marginal reactions of individual agents are identical). He shows that individual differences or more general behavioral nonlinearities will coincide with the presence of distributional effects in macroeconomic equations.

the census surveys, which are taken every ten years, are updated yearly using data provided by the National Center for Health Statistics, the Department of Defense, and the Immigration and Naturalization Service. The data are estimates of the total population of the United States, including armed forces overseas, in each of 86 age groups. Age group 1 consists of individuals less than 1 year old, age group 2 consists of individuals between 1 and 2 years of age, and so on through age group 86, which consists of individuals 85 years old and over. The published data are annual (July 1 of each year). Because the equations estimated below are quarterly, quarterly population data have been constructed by linearly interpolating between the yearly points.

Fifty five age groups are considered: ages 16, 17, . . . , 69, and 70+. The "total" population, N_t, is taken to be the population 16+. In terms of the above notation, 55 p_{jt} variables ($j = 1, \ldots, 55$) have been constructed, where the 55 variables sum to one for a given t.

Constraints on the Age Coefficients

Since there are 55 β_{ji} coefficients to estimate, some constraints must be imposed on them if there is any hope of obtaining sensible estimates. One constraint is that the coefficients sum to zero. Another constraint, which was used in Fair and Dominguez (1991), is that the coefficients lie on a second degree polynomial. The second degree polynomial constraint allows enough flexibility to see if the prime age groups behave differently from the young and old groups while keeping the number of unconstrained coefficients small. A second degree polynomial in which the coefficients sum to zero is determined by two coefficients, and so there are two unconstrained coefficients to estimate per equation. The two variables that are associated with two unconstrained coefficients will be denoted AGE_{1t} and AGE_{2t}.

The variables AGE_{1t} and AGE_{2t} are as follows. First, the age variables enter equation i as $\sum_{j=1}^{55} \beta_{ji} p_{jt}$, where $\sum_{j=1}^{55} \beta_{ji} = 0$. The polynomial constraint is

$$\beta_{ji} = \gamma_0 + \gamma_1 j + \gamma_2 j^2 \quad , \quad (j = 1, \ldots, 55) \tag{4.34}$$

where γ_0, γ_1, and γ_2 are coefficients to be determined.[13] The zero sum constraint on the β_{ji}'s implies that

$$\gamma_0 = -\gamma_1 \frac{1}{55} \sum_{j=1}^{55} j - \gamma_2 \frac{1}{55} \sum_{j=1}^{55} j^2 \tag{4.35}$$

---

[13] For ease of notation, no i subscripts are used for the γ coefficients.

The way in which the age variables enter the estimated equation is then

$$\gamma_1 AGE_{1t} + \gamma_2 AGE_{2t}$$

where

$$AGE_{1t} = \sum_{j=1}^{55} j p_{jt} - \frac{1}{55}(\sum_{j=1}^{55} j)(\sum_{j=1}^{55} p_{jt}) \qquad (4.36)$$

and

$$AGE_{2t} = \sum_{j=1}^{55} j^2 p_{jt} - \frac{1}{55}(\sum_{j=1}^{55} j^2)(\sum_{j=1}^{55} p_{jt}) \qquad (4.37)$$

Given the estimates of γ_1 and γ_2, the 55 β_{ji} coefficients can be computed. This technique is simply Almon's (1965) polynomial distributed lag technique, where the coefficients that are constrained are the coefficients of the p_{jt} variables ($j = 1, \ldots, 55$) rather than coefficients of the lagged values of some variable.

One test of whether age distribution matters is thus to add AGE_{1t} and AGE_{2t} to the equation and test if the two variables are jointly significant.

For the work in the next chapter a different set of constraints was imposed on the β_{ji} coefficients. The population 16+ was divided into four groups (16–25, 26–55, 56–65, and 66+) and it was assumed that the coefficients are the same within each group. Given the constraint that the coefficients sum to zero, this leaves three unconstrained coefficients to estimate. Let $P1625$ denote the percent of the 16+ population aged 16–25, and similarly for $P2655$, $P5665$, and $P66+$. Let γ_0 denote the coefficient of $P1625$ in the estimated equation, γ_1 the coefficient of $P2655$, γ_2 the coefficient of $P5665$, and γ_3 the coefficient of $P66+$, where $\gamma_0 + \gamma_1 + \gamma_2 + \gamma_3 = 0$. The summation constraint can be imposed by entering three variables in the estimated equation: $AG1 = P2655 - P1625$, $AG2 = P5665 - P1625$, and $AG3 = (P66+) - P1625$. $AG1$, $AG2$, and $AG3$ are variables in the US model. The coefficient of $AG1$ in an equation is $\gamma_1 - \gamma_0$, the coefficient of $AG2$ is $\gamma_2 - \gamma_0$, and the coefficient of $AG3$ is $\gamma_3 - \gamma_0$. From the estimated coefficients for $AG1$, $AG2$, and $AG3$ and the summation constraint, one can calculate the four γ coefficients.

Imposing the constraints in the manner just described has an advantage over imposing the quadratic constraint of allowing more flexibility in the sense that three unconstrained coefficients are estimated instead of two. Also, I have found that the quadratic constraint sometimes leads to extreme values of β_{ji} for the very young and very old ages. The disadvantage of the present approach over the quadratic approach is that the coefficients are not allowed to change within the four age ranges.

5

The Stochastic Equations
of the US Model

5.1 Introduction

The stochastic equations of the US model are specified, estimated, and tested in this chapter. As noted at the beginning of Chapter 3, extra "theorizing" is involved in going from theory like that in Chapter 2 to empirical specifications. This chapter thus uses the theory in Chapter 2 plus additional theory in the specification of the stochastic equations.

The stochastic equations are listed in Table A.3 in Appendix A, and the variables are defined in Table A.2. The construction of the variables is discussed in Chapter 3. There are 30 stochastic equations in the US model. The empirical results for the equations are presented in Tables 5.1 through 5.30 in this chapter, one table per equation except for equations 19 and 29. (There are no tables for equations 19 and 29.) Each table gives the left hand side variable, the right hand side variables that were chosen for the "final" specification, and the results of the tests described in Chapter 4. The basic tests are 1) adding lagged values, 2) estimating the equation under the assumption of a fourth order autoregressive process for the error term, 3) adding a time trend, 4) adding values led one or more quarters, 5) adding additional variables, and 6) testing for structural stability. Also, the joint significance of the age distribution variables is examined in the household expenditure and money demand equations. Remember that "adding lagged values" means adding lagged values of all the variables in the equation (including the left hand side variable if the lagged dependent variable is not an explanatory variable). As discussed in Section 4.5, this is a test against a quite general dynamic specification. For the autoregressive test, the notation "RHO=4" will be used to denote the fact that a fourth order autoregressive process was used.

It will be seen that only a few of the equations pass all the tests. My experience is that it is hard to find macroeconomic equations that do. If an equation does not pass a test, it is not always clear what should be done. If, for example, the hypothesis of structural stability is rejected, one possibility is to divide the sample period into two parts and estimate two separate equations. If this is done, however, the resulting coefficient estimates are not always sensible in terms of what one would expect from theory. Similarly, when the additional lagged values are significant, the equation with the additional lagged values does not always have what one would consider sensible dynamic properties. In other words, when an equation fails a test, the change in the equation that the test results suggest may not produce what seem to be sensible results. In many cases, the best choice seems to be to stay with the original equation even though it failed the test. My feeling (being optimistic) is that much of this difficulty is due to small sample problems, which will lessen over time as sample sizes increase, but this is an important area for future work. Obviously less confidence should be placed on equations that fail a number of the tests than on those that do not.

The χ^2 value is presented for each test along with its degrees of freedom. Also presented for each test is the probability that the χ^2 value would be whatever it is if the null hypothesis that the additional variables do not belong in the equation is true. These probabilities are labeled "p-value" in the tables. A small p-value is evidence against the null hypothesis and thus evidence against the specification of the equation. In the following discussion of the results, a p-value of less than .01 will be taken as a rejection of the null hypothesis and thus as a rejection of the specification of the equation.[1]

It will be seen that lagged dependent variables are used as explanatory variables in many of the equations. They are generally highly significant, even after accounting for any autoregressive properties of the error terms. It is well known that they can be accounting for either partial adjustment effects or expectational effects and that it is difficult to identify the two effects separately.[2] For the most part no attempt is made in what follows to separate the two effects, although, as discussed in Chapter 4, the tests of the significance

---

[1]Using a value of .01 instead of, say, .05 gives the benefit of the doubt to the equations, but, as indicated above, the equations need all the help they can get.

[2]See Fair (1984), Section 2.2.2, for a discussion of this.

of the led values are tests of the rational expectations hypothesis.

In testing for the significance of nominal versus real interest rates, some measure of expected future inflation must be used in constructing real interest rate variables. Two measures were used in the following work: the actual rate of inflation in the past four quarters, denoted p_4^e, and the actual rate of inflation (at an annual rate) in the past eight quarters, denoted p_8^e. The price deflator used for this purpose is PD, the price deflator for domestic sales, and so $p_4^e = 100[(PD/PD_{-4}) - 1]$ and $p_8^e = 100[(PD/PD_{-8})^{.5} - 1]$.

The significance of nominal versus real interest rates was tested as follows. Consider RMA, the after tax mortgage rate, which is used in the model as the long term interest rate facing the household sector. Assume that p_8^e is an adequate proxy for inflation expectations of the household sector. If real interest rates affect household behavior, then $RMA - p_8^e$ should enter the household expenditure equations, and if nominal interest rates affect household behavior, then RMA alone should enter. The test of real versus nominal rates was first to estimate the equation with RMA included and then to add p_8^e and reestimate. If real rates instead of nominal rates matter and if p_8^e is a good proxy for actual inflation expectations, then p_8^e should be significant and have a coefficient estimate that equals (aside from sampling error) the negative of the coefficient estimate of RMA. The same reasoning holds for p_4^e.

As will be seen, the p_4^e and p_8^e variables were never significant when added to the household expenditure equations, whereas the nominal interest rate variables were, and so the data support the use of nominal over real interest rates. It could be, of course, that the inflation expectations variables are not good approximations of actual expectations and that if better expectations variables were used they would be significant. This is an open question and an area for future research. It will also be seen below that the real interest rate does affect nonresidential fixed investment, although the estimated effect is small and may be the result of data mining.

The basic estimation period was 1954:1–1993:2, for a total of 158 observations. For the AP stability tests, T_1, the first possible quarter for the break, was taken to be 1970:1 and T_2, the last possible quarter for the break, was taken to be 1979:4. The "break" quarter that is presented in the tables for the AP test is the quarter at which the break in the sample period corresponds to the largest χ^2 value. Although not shown in the tables, it was generally the case that the χ^2 values monotonically rose to the largest value and monotonically fell after that. A * after the AP value in the tables denotes that the value is significant at the one percent level. In other words, a * means that the hypothesis of no break is rejected at the one percent level: the equation fails the stability test.

Tests of the Leads

Three sets of led values were tried per equation. For the first set the values of
the relevant variables led once were added. For the second set the values led
one through four times were added. For the third set the values led one through
eight times were added, with the coefficients for each variable constrained to
lie on a second degree polynomial with an end point constraint of zero. To see
what was done for the third set, assume that one of the variables for which the
led values are used is X_{2i}. Then for the third set the term added is

$$\sum_{j=1}^{8} \beta_j X_{2it+j} \tag{5.1}$$

where $\beta_j = \gamma_0 + \gamma_1 j + \gamma_2 j^2$, $j = 1, \ldots, 8$, $\beta_9 = 0$. The end point constraint
of zero implies that $\gamma_0 = -9\gamma_1 - 81\gamma_2$. Given this constraint, the led values
enter the equation as

$$\gamma_1 F_{1t} + \gamma_2 F_{2t} \tag{5.2}$$

where

$$F_{1t} = \sum_{j=1}^{8} (j - 9) X_{2it+j} \tag{5.3}$$

$$F_{2t} = \sum_{j=1}^{8} (j^2 - 81) X_{2it+j} \tag{5.4}$$

There are thus two unconstrained coefficients to estimate for the third set. For
the second set the equation is estimated under the assumption of a moving
average error of order three, and for the third set the equation is estimated
under the assumption of a moving average error of order seven.

It may be helpful to review the exact procedure that was followed for the
leads test. First, the estimation period was taken to be shorter by one, four,
or eight observations. (When values led once are added the sample period
has to be shorter by one to allow for the led values; when the values led four
times are added the sample period has to be shorter by four; and so on.) The
equation with the led values added was then estimated using Hansen's GMM
estimator under the appropriate assumption about the moving average process
of the error term (zero for leads +1, three for leads +4, and seven for leads
+8). The M_i matrix discussed in Section 4.3 that results from this estimation
was then used in the estimation of the equation without the led values by
Hansen's method for the same (shorter) estimation period. The χ^2 value is
then $(SS_i^{**} - SS_i^*)/T$, as discussed at the beginning of Section 4.5.

The results of adding the led values to the stochastic equations are used in Chapter 11, Section 11.6, to examine the economic significance of the rational expectations assumption in the US model.[3] The question asked in Section 11.6 is: How much difference to the properties of the US model does the addition of the led values make? Two versions of the model are examined. The first consists of the "base" equations in Tables 5.1–5.30, which have no led values in them. This version is called Version 1. The second version consists of the equations with the third set of led values added (i.e., with F_{1t} and F_{2t} added). This version is called Version 2. The particular variables for which led values were used are mentioned in this chapter in the discussion of each equation. For some equations no led values were tried because none seemed appropriate, and so these equations are the same for both Versions 1 and 2.

First Stage Regressors

The first stage regressors (FSRs) that were used for each equation are listed in Table A.7 in Appendix A. The choice of FSRs for large scale models is discussed in Fair (1984), pp. 215–216, and this discussion will not be repeated here.

Autoregressive Errors

Each equation was first estimated under the assumption of a first order autoregressive error term, and the assumption was retained if the estimate of the autoregressive coefficient was significant. In one case (equation 4) a second order process was used in the final specification, and in one case (equation 11) a third order process was used. In the notation in the tables "RHO1" refers to the first order coefficient, "RHO2" to the second order coefficient, and "RHO3" to the third order coefficient.

Previous Version of the US Model

The previous version of the US model is presented in Fair (1984), Chapter 4. The present discussion of the model is self contained, and so this previous material does not have to be read. For the most part the current version of the model is quite similar to the previous version. Three of the main changes are 1) the use of disposable income in the household expenditure equations instead of the wage, price, nonlabor income, and labor constraint variables

---

[3]This work is an updated version of the material in Section 5 in Fair (1993b).

separately, 2) the use of the age distribution variables, and 3) the different treatment of the interest payment variables of the firm and federal government sectors (equations 19 and 29). In addition, a few more coefficient constraints have been imposed in the current version, and different functional forms have been used in a few cases.

5.2 Household Expenditure and Labor Supply Equations

The two main decision variables of a household in the theoretical model are consumption and labor supply. The determinants of these variables include the initial value of wealth and the current and expected future values of the wage rate, the price level, the interest rate, the tax rate, and the level of transfer payments. The labor constraint also affects the decisions if it is binding.

In the econometric model the expenditures of the household sector are disaggregated into four types: consumption of services (CS), consumption of nondurable goods (CN), consumption of durable goods (CD), and investment in housing (IHH). Four labor supply variables are used: the labor force of men 25–54 ($L1$), the labor force of women 25–54 ($L2$), the labor force of all others 16+ ($L3$), and the number of people holding more than one job, called "moonlighters" (LM). These eight variables are determined by eight estimated equations.

Consider first the four expenditure equations. The household wealth variable in the model is AA, and the lagged value of this variable was tried in each of the equations. The variable is expected to have a positive sign, and if it did not, which occurred in two of the four equations, it was dropped.

The household after tax interest rate variables in the model are RSA, a short term rate, and RMA, a long term rate. RSA was used in the CS equation, and RMA was used in the others. The CS and CN equations are in log form per capita, and the interest rates were entered additively in these equations. The means that, say, a one percentage point change in the interest rate has the same percent change over time in each of the two equations. The CD and IHH equations, on the other hand, are in per capita but not log form, and if the interest rates were entered additively in these equations, the effect of, say, a one percentage point change in the interest rate would have a smaller and smaller percent effect over time on per capita durable consumption and on per capita housing investment as both increase in size over time. Since this does not seem sensible, the interest rate in the CD equation was multiplied by CDA, which is a variable constructed from peak to peak interpolations of

CD/POP. Similarly, the interest rate in the IHH equation was multiplied by $IHHA$, which is a variable constructed from peak to peak interpolations of IHH/POP. Both CDA and $IHHA$ are merely scale variables, and they are taken to be exogenous.

These interest rate variables are nominal rates. As discussed above, the inflation expectations variables p_4^e and p_8^e were added in the testing of the equations to test for real interest rate effects, and the results of these tests are reported below.

The age distribution variables were tried in the four expenditure equations, and they were jointly significant at the five percent level in three of the four, the insignificant results occurring in the IHH equation. They were retained in the three equations in which they were significant. The lagged dependent variable and the constant term were included in each of the four expenditure equations.

Regarding the wage, price, and income variables, there are at least two basic approaches that can be taken in specifying the expenditure equations. The first is to add the wage, price, nonlabor income, and labor constraint variables separately to the equations. These variables in the model are as follows. The after tax nominal wage rate variable is WA, the price deflator for total household expenditures is PH, the after tax nonlabor income variable is YNL, and the labor constraint variable, discussed in Chapter 3, is Z. The price deflators for the four expenditure categories are PCS, PCN, PCD, and PIH.

Consider the CS equation. Under the first approach one might add WA/PH, PCS/PH, YNL/PH, and Z to the equation. The justification for including Z is the following. By construction, Z is zero or nearly zero in tight labor markets (i.e., when JJ is equal to or nearly equal to JJP, where JJ is the actual ratio of worker hours paid for to the total population and JJP is the potential ratio). In this case the labor constraint is not binding and Z has no effect or only a small effect in the equation. This is the "classical" case. As labor markets get looser (i.e., as JJ falls relative to JJP), on the other hand, Z falls and begins to have an effect in the equation. Loose labor markets, where Z is large in absolute value, correspond to the "Keynesian" case. Since Z is highly correlated with hours paid for in loose labor markets, having both WA and Z in the equation is similar to having a labor income variable in the equation in loose labor markets.

The second, more traditional, approach is to replace the above four variables with real disposable personal income, YD/PH. This approach in effect assumes that labor markets are always loose and that the responses to changes in labor and nonlabor income are the same. One can test whether the data support YD/PH over the other variables by including all the variables in the equation and examining their significance. The results of doing this in the four expenditure equations generally supported the use of YD/PH over the other variables, and so the equations reported below use YD/PH. This is a change from the version of the model in Fair (1984), where the first approach was used.

The dominance of YD/PH does not necessarily mean that the classical case never holds in practice. What it does suggest is that trying to capture the classical case through the use of Z does not work. An interesting question for future work is whether the classical case can be captured in some other way. It will be seen below that the Z variable does work in the labor supply equations, where it is picking up "discouraged worker" effects when labor markets are loose.

Some searching was done in arriving at the "final" equations presented below. Explanatory variables lagged once as well as unlagged were generally tried, and variables were dropped from the equation if they had coefficient estimates of the wrong expected sign in both the unlagged and lagged cases. Also, as noted above, each equation was estimated under the assumption of a first order autoregressive error term, and the assumption was retained if the estimate of the autoregressive coefficient was significant. All this searching was done using the 2SLS technique.

Equation 1. CS, consumer expenditures: services

The results of estimating equation 1 are presented in Table 5.1. The equation is in real, per capita terms and is in log form. The series for CS is quite smooth, and most of the explanatory power in equation 1 comes from the lagged dependent variable. The disposable income variable has a small short run coefficient (.0570) and a long run coefficient of roughly one [.991 $=$ .0570/(1 $-$ .9425)].[4] The short term interest rate is significant. The age variables are jointly significant at the five percent level (but not at the one percent level) according to the χ^2 value. Remember that the coefficient of $AG1$ is the coefficient for people 26–55 minus the coefficient for those 16–25.

---

[4]Since the equation is in log form, these coefficients are elasticities.

Table 5.1
Equation 1
LHS Variable is $\log(CS/POP)$

Equation				χ^2 Tests		
RHS Variable	Est.	t-stat.	Test	χ^2	df	p-value
cnst	.0870	2.17	Lags	8.53	3	.0362
$AG1$	-.2347	-2.86	$RHO = 4$	1.30	4	.8611
$AG2$	.2293	0.99	T	17.25	1	.0000
$AG3$	.2242	1.14	Leads +1	6.53	1	.0106
$\log(CS/POP)_{-1}$	.9425	29.58	Leads +4	25.60	4	.0000
$\log[YD/(POP \cdot PH)]$	.0570	1.88	Leads +8	28.92	2	.0000
RSA	-.0009	-3.93	P_4^e	3.30	1	.0692
			P_8^e	2.29	1	.1299
			Other[a]	22.63	5	.0004
			Spread	0.82	4	.9362
SE	.00412					
R^2	.999					
DW	2.01					

$\chi^2(AGE) = 10.47$ (df = 3, p-value = .0150)

Stability Test:

AP		T_1	T_2	λ		Break
14.49*		1970:1	1979:4	2.75		1971:4

Estimation period is 1954:1–1993:2.
[a] $\log(AA/POP)_{-1}$, $\log(WA/PH)$, $\log(PCS/PH)$, Z, $\log[YNL/(POP \cdot PH)]$.

Similarly, the coefficient of $AG2$ is the coefficient for people 56–65 minus the coefficient for those 16–25, and the coefficient of $AG3$ is the coefficient for people 66+ minus the coefficient for those 16–25. The age coefficient estimates for the CS equation suggest that, other things being equal, people 26–55 spend less than others (the coefficient estimate for $AG1$ is negative and the other two age coefficient estimates are positive), which is consistent with the life cycle idea that people in their prime working years spend less relative to their incomes than do others.

Consider now the test results in Table 5.1. (Remember that an equation will be said to have passed a test if the p-value is greater than .01.) Equation 1 passes the lags test[5] and the RHO=4 test. These results thus suggest that the dynamic specification of the equation is fairly accurate.

On the other hand, the equation dramatically fails the T test: the time trend is highly significant when it is added to equation 1. This suggests that

---

[5] Remember that for the lags test all the variables in the equation lagged once are added to the equation (except for the age variables). This means that for equation 1 three variables are added: $\log(CS/POP)_{-2}$, $\log[YD/(POP \cdot PH)]_{-1}$, and RSA_{-1}.

the trending nature of the CS series has not been adequately accounted for in the equation. None of the other specifications that were tried eliminated this problem, and it is an interesting area for future research.

Disposable income was the variable for which led values were tried—in the form $\log[YD/(POP \cdot PH)]$—and the test results show that leads +4 and leads +8 are highly significant. This is thus evidence in favor of the rational expectations assumption. The largest χ^2 value was for 8 leads. This is the equation that is used for Version 2 in Section 11.6 to examine the sensitivity of the model's properties to the use of the led values.

The inflation expectations variables are not significant, which is evidence against the use of real versus nominal interest rates. The additional variables ("Other"), which, as discussed above, are the variables that one might use in place of disposable income, are significant. However, although not shown in the table, the coefficient estimates for the variables are all of the wrong expected sign, and so the version of the equation with these variables added is not sensible. There appears to be too much collinearity among these variables to be able to get sensible estimates.

For the "spread" test in Table 5.1 and in the other relevant tables that follow, the current and first three lagged values of the spread between the commercial paper rate and the Treasury bill rate were added to the equation. For this test the estimation period began in 1960:2 rather than 1954:1 because data on the spread were only available from 1959:1 on.[6] As can be seen, the spread values are not close to being significant, with a p-value of .9362.

Finally, the equation fails the stability test. The AP value is 14.49, which compares with the one percent critical value in Chapter 4 (for 7 coefficients) of 9.50. The largest χ^2 value occurred for 1971:4, which is near the beginning of the test period of 1970:1–1979:4.

Equation 2. CN, consumer expenditures: nondurables

Equation 2 is also in real, per capita, and log terms. The results are presented in Table 5.2. The asset, disposable income, and interest rate variables are significant in this equation, along with the age variables and the lagged dependent variable. Both the level and change of the lagged dependent variable are significant in the equation, and so the dynamic specification is more complicated than that of equation 1. Again, the age coefficients show that people 26–55 spend less than others, other things being equal.

---

[6]Whenever an estimation period had to be changed for a test, the basic equation was always reestimated for this period in calculating the χ^2 value for the test.

Table 5.2
Equation 2
LHS Variable is $\log(CN/POP)$

	Equation			χ^2 Tests		
RHS Variable	Est.	t-stat.	Test	χ^2	df	p-value
cnst	-.1229	-1.41	Lags	9.43	4	.0511
$AG1$	-.4791	-4.14	$RHO = 4$	17.40	4	.0016
$AG2$	1.4067	4.58	T	0.07	1	.7983
$AG3$	-.3364	-1.99	Leads +1	9.16	1	.0025
$\log(CN/POP)_{-1}$	.6203	14.53	Leads +4	12.28	4	.0154
$\Delta \log(CN/POP)_{-1}$	.1374	2.17	Leads +8	11.54	2	.0031
$\log(AA/POP)_{-1}$	.0509	4.51	p_4^e	1.15	1	.2841
$\log[YD/(POP \cdot PH)]$	.2383	8.17	p_8^e	0.04	1	.8516
RMA	-.0019	-3.78	Other[a]	9.93	4	.0416
			Spread	10.02	4	.0400
SE	.00557					
R^2	.997					
DW	1.87					

$\chi^2(AGE) = 44.68$ (df = 3, p-value = .0000)

Stability Test:

AP		T_1	T_2	λ		Break
14.28*		1970:1	1979:4	2.75		1973:2

Estimation period is 1954:1–1993:2.
[a] $\log(WA/PH)$, $\log(PCN/PH)$, Z, $\log[YNL/(POP \cdot PH)]$.

The equation passes the lags test and the T test, but it fails the RHO=4 test. The variable for which led values were tried is again disposable income, and leads +1 and +8 are significant. The inflation expectations variables are not significant. The additional variables, representing the wage, price, nonlabor income, and labor constraint variables are not significant at the one percent level. Likewise, the spread values are not significant at the one percent level. The equation fails the stability test. The AP value is 14.28, which compares to the one percent critical value (for 9 coefficients) of 11.20. The maximum χ^2 value occurs for 1973:2.

Equation 3. CD, consumer expenditures: durables

Equation 3 is in real, per capital terms. One of the explanatory variables is the lagged stock of durable goods, and the justification for including this variable is as follows. Let KD^{**} denote the stock of durable goods that would be desired if there were no adjustment costs of any kind. If durable consumption is proportional to the stock of durables, then the determinants of consumption can be assumed to be the determinants of KD^{**}:

$$KD^{**} = f(\ldots) \tag{5.5}$$

where the arguments of f are the determinants of consumption. Two types of partial adjustment are then postulated. The first is an adjustment of the durable stock:

$$KD^* - KD_{-1} = \lambda(KD^{**} - KD_{-1}) \tag{5.6}$$

where KD^* is the stock of durable goods that would be desired if there were no costs of adjusting gross investment. Given KD^*, desired gross investment in durable goods is

$$CD^* = KD^* - (1 - DELD)KD_{-1} \tag{5.7}$$

where $DELD$ is the depreciation rate. By definition $CD = KD - (1 - DELD)KD_{-1}$, and equation 5.7 is merely the same equation for the desired values. The second type of adjustment is an adjustment of gross investment to its desired value:

$$CD - CD_{-1} = \gamma(CD^* - CD_{-1}) \tag{5.8}$$

Combining equations 5.5–5.8 yields:

$$CD = (1 - \gamma)CD_{-1} + \gamma(DELD - \lambda)KD_{-1} + \gamma\lambda f(\ldots) \tag{5.9}$$

The specification of the two types of adjustment is a way of adding to the durable expenditure equation both the lagged dependent variable and the lagged stock of durables. Otherwise, the explanatory variables are the same as they are in the other expenditure equations.[7]

The disposable income and interest rate variables are significant in Table 5.3. The coefficient of the lagged dependent variable is .5746, and so γ above is .4254. As discussed in Chapter 3, the depreciation rate, $DELD$, is equal to .049511. Given these two values and given the coefficient of the lagged stock variable in Table 5.3 of $-.0106$, the implied value of λ is .074. This implies an adjustment of the durable stock to its desired value of 7.4 percent per quarter.

---

[7]Note in equation 3 that CD is divided by POP and CD_{-1} and KD_{-1} are divided by POP_{-1}, where POP is population. If equations 5.5–5.8 are defined in per capita terms, where the current values are divided by POP and the lagged values are divided by POP_{-1}, then the present per capita treatment of equation 5.9 follows. The only problem with this is that the definition used to justify 5.7 does not hold if the lagged stock is divided by POP_{-1}. All variables must be divided by the same population variable for the definition to hold. This is, however, a minor problem, and it has been ignored here. The same holds for equation 4.

Table 5.3
Equation 3
LHS Variable is CD/POP

Equation				χ^2 Tests		
RHS Variable	Est.	t-stat.	Test	χ^2	df	p-value
cnst	-.5903	-3.24	Lags	2.49	3	.4769
$AG1$	.7377	2.25	$RHO = 4$	15.74	4	.0034
$AG2$	.2590	0.28	T	22.34	1	.0000
$AG3$	-1.0850	-2.65	Leads +1	18.35	1	.0000
$(CD/POP)_{-1}$	.5746	9.05	Leads +4	21.67	4	.0002
$(KD/POP)_{-1}$	-.0106	-1.78	Leads +8	21.96	2	.0000
$YD/(POP \cdot PH)$	.1709	6.93	$p_4^e \cdot CDA$	3.40	1	.0650
$RMA \cdot CDA$	-.0063	-3.14	$p_8^e \cdot CDA$	3.28	1	.0701
			Other[a]	14.97	5	.0105
			Spread	20.43	4	.0004
SE	.01105					
R^2	.993					
DW	2.00					

$\chi^2(AGE) = 35.12$ (df = 3, p-value = .0000)

Stability Test:

AP	T_1	T_2	λ	Break
28.57*	1970:1	1979:4	2.75	1977:1

Estimation period is 1954:1–1993:2.
[a]$(AA/POP)_{-1}, WA/PH, PCD/PH, Z, YNL/(POP \cdot PH)$.

The age variables are jointly highly significant. The age coefficients show people 26–55 spending more, other things being equal, than the others. The pattern here is thus different than the pattern for service and nondurable consumption.

Regarding the tests, equation 3 passes the lags test, but it fails the RHO=4 and T tests. The variable for which led values were tried is disposable income, and the led values are significant. The inflation expectations variables are not significant. The other variables, which are the asset, wage, price, nonlabor income, and labor constraint variables, are significant at the five percent level but not quite at the one percent level. The spread values are highly significant. The equation fails the stability test by a wide margin.

Equation 4. IHH, residential investment—h

The same partial adjustment model is used for housing investment than was used above for durable expenditures, which adds both the lagged dependent variable and the lagged stock of housing to the housing investment equation. For example, the coefficient of the lagged housing stock variable, KH_{-1},

Table 5.4
Equation 4
LHS Variable is IHH/POP

Equation			χ^2 Tests			
RHS Variable	Est.	t-stat.	Test	χ^2	df	p-value
cnst	1.8493	3.01	Lags	1.61	4	.8063
$(IHH/POP)_{-1}$	.5322	9.59	$RHO = 4$	0.19	2	.9101
$(KH/POP)_{-1}$	-.0809	-5.15	T	0.00	1	.9869
$(AA/POP)_{-1}$	.0026	2.92	Leads +1	3.53	1	.0603
$YD/(POP \cdot PH)$	.1124	4.06	Leads +4	7.78	4	.1001
$RMA_{-1} \cdot IHHA$	-.0267	-4.81	Leads +8	2.97	2	.2267
$RHO1$	.6394	7.55	$p^e_{4-1} \cdot IHHA$	0.39	1	.5349
$RHO2$	.3519	4.17	$p^e_{8-1} \cdot IHHA$	0.02	1	.8797
			Other[a]	11.85	4	.0185
			Spread	1.46	4	.8334
SE	.00855					
R^2	.957					
DW	1.99					

$\chi^2(AGE) = 0.94$ (df = 3, p-value = .8151)

Stability Test:

AP	T_1	T_2	λ	Break
3.47	1970:1	1979:4	2.75	1974:1

Estimation period is 1954:1–1993:2.
[a]$(WA/PH)_{-1}, (PIH/PH)_{-1}, Z_{-1}, [YNL/(POP \cdot PH)]_{-1}$.

is $\gamma(DELH - \lambda)$, where $DELH$ is the depreciation rate of the housing stock. The equation is estimated under the assumption of a second order autoregressive error term.

The asset, income, and interest rate variables are significant in Table 5.4, as are the lagged dependent variable and the lagged housing stock variable. The coefficient of the lagged dependent variable is .5322, and so γ is .4678. As discussed in Chapter 3, the depreciation rate for the housing stock, $DELH$, is .006716. Given these two values and given the coefficient of the lagged housing stock variable of $-.0809$, the implied value of λ is .180. The estimated adjustment speed of the housing stock to its desired value is thus greater than the estimated adjustment speed of the durable goods stock. This is not necessarily what one would expect, and it may suggest that the estimated speed for the durable goods stock is too low.

The χ^2 test for the age variables shows that the age variables are not jointly significant. This is the reason they were not included in the final specification of the equation. Equation 4 passes the lags, RHO=4, and T tests. The variable for which led values were tried is disposable income, and the led values are not significant. The inflation expectations variables are not significant; the "other" variables are not significant; and the spread values are not close to being significant. Equation 4 thus passes all the χ^2 tests, the only expenditure equation of the four to do so. It also passes the stability test, again the only expenditure equation to do so.

The next four equations of the household sector are the labor supply equations, which will now be discussed.

Equation 5. $L1$, labor force—men 25–54[8]

One would expect from the theory of household behavior for labor supply to depend, among other things, on the after tax wage rate, the price level, and wealth. In addition, if the labor constraint is at times binding on households, one would expect a labor constraint variable like Z to affect labor supply through the discouraged worker effect.

Equation 5 explains the labor force participation rate of men 25–54. It is in log form and includes as explanatory variables the real wage (WA/PH), the labor constraint variable (Z), a time trend, and the lagged dependent variable. The coefficient estimate for the real wage is negative, implying that the income effect dominates the substitution effect for men 25–54, although the estimate is not significant. The coefficient estimate of the labor constraint variable is positive, as expected, but it is also not significant. The coefficient estimate for the time trend is negative and significant. There is a slight negative trend in the labor force participation of men 25–54 that does not seem to be explained by other variables, and so the time trend was included in the equation.

Equation 5 passes the lags test, but fails the RHO=4 test. The variable for which led values were tried is the real wage $[\log(WA/PH)]$, and the led values are not significant. Another test reported in Table 5.5 has $\log PH$ added as an explanatory variable. This is a test of the use of the real wage in the equation. If $\log PH$ is significant, this is a rejection of the hypothesis that the

---

[8]In Section II in Fair and Dominguez (1991) the age distribution data discussed above were used to examine some of Easterlin's (1987) ideas regarding the effects of cohort size on wage rates. This was done in the context of specifying equations for $L1$ and $L2$. I now have, however, (for reasons that will not be pursued here) some reservations about the appropriateness of the specifications that were used, and in the present work the age distribution data have not been used in the specification of equations 5 and 6. This is an area of future research. I am indebted to Diane Macunovich for helpful discussions in this area.

Table 5.5
Equation 5
LHS Variable is $\log(L1/POP1)$

Equation			Test	χ^2 Tests χ^2	df	p-value
RHS Variable	Est.	t-stat.				
cnst	-.0060	-3.11	Lags	3.35	3	.3401
$\log(L1/POP1)_{-1}$	.7763	15.63	$RHO = 4$	39.86	4	.0000
$\log(WA/PH)$	-.0036	-1.30	Leads +1	1.59	1	.2067
Z	.0139	1.50	Leads +4	10.11	4	.0386
T	-.0001	-3.73	Leads +8	1.14	2	.5667
			$\log PH$	6.36	1	.0117
			Other[a]	5.93	2	.0515
SE	.00196					
R^2	.984					
DW	2.22					
Stability Test:						
AP	T_1	T_2	λ		Break	
17.34*	1970:1	1979:4	2.75		1970:3	

Estimation period is 1954:1–1993:2.
[a] $\log(AA/POP)_{-1}$, $\log[YNL/(POP \cdot PH)]_{-1}$.

coefficient of $\log WA$ is equal to the negative of the coefficient of $\log PH$, which is implied by the use of the real wage. As can be seen, $\log PH$ is significant at the five percent level but not the one percent level. The final χ^2 test in Table 5.5 has asset and nonlabor income variables added to the equation. These variables are not significant at the five percent level. Equation 5 fails the stability test, with the maximum χ^2 value occurring for 1970:3.

Equation 6. $L2$, labor force—women 25–54

Equation 6 explains the labor force participation rate of women 25–54. It is also in log form and includes as explanatory variables the real wage, the labor constraint variable, and the lagged dependent variable. The coefficient estimate for the real wage is positive, implying that the substitution effect dominates the income effect for women 25–54. This is contrary to the case for men 25–54, where the income effect dominates. The coefficient estimate for the labor constraint is positive but not significant. The coefficient estimate for the lagged dependent variable is quite high (.9872).

Regarding the tests, the equation passes the lags test, the RHO=4 test, and the T test. The variable for which led values were tried is the real wage ($\log(WA/PH)$), and the led values are not significant. The equation thus

Table 5.6
Equation 6
LHS Variable is $\log(L2/POP2)$

Equation				χ^2 Tests		
RHS Variable	Est.	t-stat.	Test	χ^2	df	p-value
cnst	.0022	1.26	Lags	9.29	3	.0257
$\log(L2/POP2)_{-1}$	.9872	192.74	$RHO = 4$	5.77	4	.2170
$\log(WA/PH)$	.0177	2.43	T	0.49	1	.4816
Z	.0403	1.51	Leads +1	2.97	1	.0849
			Leads +4	7.21	4	.1251
			Leads +8	2.01	2	.3652
			$\log PH$	11.27	1	.0008
			Other[a]	12.15	2	.0023
SE	.00615					
R^2	.999					
DW	2.15					
Stability Test:						

AP	T_1	T_2	λ	Break
11.20*	1970:1	1979:4	2.75	1973:4

Estimation period is 1954:1–1993:2.
[a] $\log(AA/POP)_{-1}, \log[YNL/(POP \cdot PH)]_{-1}$.

does well on these tests. However, when $\log PH$ is added to the equation, it is highly significant, thus rejecting the real wage constraint. Although not shown in the table, when $\log PH$ is added to the equation, the coefficient for $\log WA$ is .0610 and the coefficient for $\log PH$ is $-.0087$. (The coefficient estimate for the lagged dependent variable is noticeably smaller—.828—when $\log PH$ is added.) It thus appears that it is primarily the nominal wage that is affecting participation. This is, of course, contrary to what one expects from most theories, and it certainly does not seem sensible that in the long run participation rises simply from an overall rise in prices and wages. Therefore, the real wage constraint was imposed on the equation, even though it is strongly rejected by the data.

For a final χ^2 test, asset and nonlabor income variables were added to the equation. These variables are significant, but (although not shown in the table) the coefficient estimates were of the wrong expected sign. One expects the level of assets and nonlabor income to have a negative effect on participation, but the coefficient estimates were positive.

The equation fails the stability test. The AP value is 11.20, which compares to the critical one percent value for 4 coefficients of 7.00.

Table 5.7
Equation 7
LHS Variable is $\log(L3/POP3)$

Equation				χ^2 Tests		
RHS Variable	Est.	t-stat.	Test	χ^2	df	p-value
cnst	.0162	0.66	Lags	3.29	4	.5110
$\log(L3/POP3)_{-1}$	.8896	24.73	$RHO = 4$	0.94	4	.9180
$\log(WA/PH)$	.0477	3.58	Leads +1	2.48	1	.1153
Z	.0663	2.36	Leads +4	14.58	4	.0057
$\log(AA/POP)_{-1}$	-.0158	-1.74	Leads +8	9.78	2	.0075
T	-.0002	-3.63	$\log PH$	0.11	1	.7428
			Other[a]	3.91	1	.0481
SE	.00533					
R^2	.981					
DW	1.88					
Stability Test:						
AP	T_1	T_2	λ		Break	
3.80	1970:1	1979:4	2.75		1979:2	

Estimation period is 1954:1–1993:2.
[a] $\log[YNL/(POP \cdot PH)]_{-1}$.

Equation 7. $L3$, labor force—all others 16+

Equation 7 explains the labor force participation rate of all others 16+. It is also in log form and includes as explanatory variables the real wage, the labor constraint variable, an asset variable, the time trend, and the lagged dependent variable. The coefficient estimate for the real wage is positive, implying that the substitution effect dominates the income effect for all others 16+. The asset variable has a negative coefficient estimate and the labor market tightness variable has a positive one, as expected. The coefficient estimate for the time trend is negative and significant, and so, like $L1$, $L3$ appears to have a negative trend that is not explained by other variables.

Equation 7 passes the lags test and the RHO=4 test. The variable for which led values were tried is the real wage, and the values led 4 and 8 are significant. When $\log PH$ is added to the equation, it is insignificant. The "other" variable that is added is the lagged value of nonlabor income, and it is not significant at the one percent level. The equation passes the stability test.

Equation 8. LM, number of moonlighters

Equation 8 determines the number of moonlighters. It is in log form and includes as explanatory variables the real wage, the labor constraint variable,

Table 5.8
Equation 8
LHS Variable is $\log(LM/POP)$

Equation				χ^2 Tests		
RHS Variable	Est.	t-stat.	Test	χ^2	df	p-value
cnst	-.4584	-3.92	Lags	4.00	3	.2618
$\log(LM/POP)_{-1}$	.8634	25.97	$RHO = 4$	2.54	4	.6380
$\log(WA/PH)$	.0185	0.62	T	0.02	1	.8919
Z	1.0396	3.87	Leads +1	0.05	1	.8164
			Leads +4	7.47	4	.1128
			Leads +8	3.04	2	.2185
			$\log PH$	0.07	1	.7920
			Other[a]	6.42	2	.0403
SE	.05647					
R^2	.858					
DW	1.98					
Stability Test:						
AP	T_1	T_2	λ		Break	
3.32	1970:1	1979:4	2.75		1973:2	

Estimation period is 1954:1–1993:2.
[a] $\log(AA/POP)_{-1}$, $\log[YNL/(POP \cdot PH)]_{-1}$.

and the lagged dependent variable. The coefficient estimate for the real wage is positive, suggesting that the substitution effect dominates for moonlighters, although the variable is not significant. The coefficient estimate for the labor constraint variable is positive and significant. The larger is the labor constraint, the fewer are the number of people holding two jobs.

Equation 8 does brilliantly in the tests. It passes the lags test, the RHO=4 test, and the T test. The variable for which led values were tried is the real wage, and the led values are not significant. When $\log PH$ is added to the equation, it is not significant, and so the real wage constraint is supported. The "other" variables that were added are the lagged value of wealth and the lagged value of nonlabor income, and they are not significant at the one percent level. Finally, the equation passes the stability test.

–This completes the discussion of the household expenditure and labor supply equations. A summary of some of the general results across the equations is in Section 5.10.

5.3   Money Demand Equations[9]

In the theoretical model a household's demand for money depends on the level of transactions, the interest rate, and the household's wage rate. High wage rate households spend less time taking care of money holdings than do low wage rate households and thus on average hold more money. With aggregate data it is not possible to estimate this wage rate effect on the demand for money, and in the empirical work the demand for money has simply been taken to be a function of the interest rate and a transactions variable. However, the age distribution variables have been added to the household money demand equation, and, as discussed below, this may pick up a wage rate effect.

The model contains three demand for money equations: one for the household sector, one for the firm sector, and a demand for currency equation. Before presenting these equations it will be useful to discuss how the dynamics were handled. The key question about the dynamics is whether the adjustment of actual to desired values is in nominal or real terms.

Let M_t^*/P_t denote the desired level of real money balances, let y_t denote a measure of real transactions, and let r_t denote a short term interest rate. Assume that the equation determining desired money balances is in log form and write

$$\log(M_t^*/P_t) = \alpha + \beta \log y_t + \gamma r_t \qquad (5.10)$$

Note that the log form has not been used for the interest rate. Interest rates can at times be quite low, and it may not be sensible to take the log of the interest rate. If, for example, the interest rate rises from .02 to .03, the log of the rate rises from -3.91 to -3.51, a change of .40. If, on the other hand, the interest rate rises from .10 to .11, the log of the rate rises from -2.30 to -2.21, a change of only .09. One does not necessarily expect a one percentage point rise in the interest rate to have four times the effect on the log of desired money holdings when the change is from a base of .02 rather than .10. In practice the results of estimating money demand equations do not seem to be very sensitive to whether the level or the log of the interest rate is used. For the work in this book the level of the interest rate has been used.

If the adjustment of actual to desired money holdings is in real terms, the

---

[9]The material in this section on the test of real versus nominal adjustment is taken from Fair (1987). The use of the age distribution variables in equation 9 is taken from Fair and Dominguez (1991).

adjustment equation is

$$\log(M_t/P_t) - \log(M_{t-1}/P_{t-1}) = \lambda[\log(M_t^*/P_t) - \log(M_{t-1}/P_{t-1})] + \epsilon_t$$
$$(5.11)$$

If the adjustment is in nominal terms, the adjustment equation is

$$\log M_t - \log M_{t-1} = \lambda(\log M_t^* - \log M_{t-1}) + \mu_t \qquad (5.12)$$

Combining 5.10 and 5.11 yields

$$\log(M_t/P_t) = \lambda\alpha + \lambda\beta \log y_t + \lambda\gamma r_t + (1-\lambda)\log(M_{t-1}/P_{t-1}) + \epsilon_t \quad (5.13)$$

Combining 5.10 and 5.12 yields

$$\log(M_t/P_t) = \lambda\alpha + \lambda\beta \log y_t + \lambda\gamma r_t + (1-\lambda)\log(M_{t-1}/P_t) + \mu_t \quad (5.14)$$

Equations 5.13 and 5.14 differ in the lagged money term. In 5.13, which is the real adjustment specification, M_{t-1} is divided by P_{t-1}, whereas in 5.14, which is the nominal adjustment specification, M_{t-1} is divided by P_t.

A test of the two hypotheses is simply to put both lagged money variables in the equation and see which one dominates. If the real adjustment specification is correct, $\log(M_{t-1}/P_{t-1})$ should be significant and $\log(M_{t-1}/P_t)$ should not, and vice versa if the nominal adjustment specification is correct. This test may, of course, be inconclusive in that both terms may be significant or insignificant, but I have found that this is rarely the case. This test was performed on the three demand for money equations, and in each case the nominal adjustment specification won. The nominal adjustment specification has thus been used in the model.[10]

Equation 9. MH, demand deposits and currency—h

Equation 9 is the demand for money equation of the household sector. It is in per capita terms and is in log form. Disposable income is used as the transactions variable, and the after tax three month Treasury bill rate is used

---

[10]The nominal adjustment hypothesis is also supported in Fair (1987), where demand for money equations were estimated for 27 countries. Three equations were estimated for the United States (versions of equations 9, 17, and 26) and one for each of the other 26 countries. Of the 29 estimated equations, the nominal adjustment dominated for 25, the real adjustment dominated for 3, and there was 1 tie. The nominal adjustment hypothesis is also supported in Chapter 6. Of the 19 countries for which the demand for money equation (equation 6) is estimated, the nominal adjustment hypothesis dominates in 13.

Table 5.9
Equation 9
LHS Variable is $\log[MH/(POP \cdot PH)]$

Equation				χ^2 Tests		
RHS Variable	Est.	t-stat.	Test	χ^2	df	p-value
cnst	-.2929	-1.59	$\log(\frac{MH}{POP \cdot PH})_{-1}$	0.05	1	.8164
$AG1$	.6533	1.78	Lags	5.91	3	.1159
$AG2$	-.5728	-0.65	$RHO = 4$	19.66	3	.0002
$AG3$	-.7462	-1.22	T	0.06	1	.8141
$\log \frac{MH_{-1}}{POP_{-1} \cdot PH}$	.8962	22.88				
$\log[YD/(POP \cdot PH)]$	.0796	1.72				
RSA	-.0035	-3.17				
$RHO1$	-.2677	-3.23				
SE	.02318					
R^2	.902					
DW	1.94					

$\chi^2(AGE) = 3.87$ (df = 3, p-value = .2763)

Stability Test:

AP	T_1	T_2	λ	Break
16.67*	1970:1	1979:4	2.75	1975:3

Estimation period is 1954:1–1993:2.

as the interest rate. The age distribution variables are included in the equation to pick up possible differences in the demand for money by age. The equation is estimated under the assumption of a first order autoregressive error term.

The short run income elasticity of the demand for money in Table 5.9 is .0796, and the long run elasticity is .767 = .0796/(1.0 − .8962). The coefficients for the age variables show that people 26–55 hold more money, other things being equal, than do others, which is as expected if people 26–55 have on average higher wage rates than the others. The age variables are not, however, jointly significant at the five percent level, and so not much confidence should be placed on this result.[11]

The test results show that the lagged dependent variable that pertains to the real adjustment specification—$\log[MH/(POP \cdot PH)]_{-1}$—is insignificant. As discussed above, this supports the nominal adjustment hypothesis. Equation 9 passes the lags and T tests, but it fails the RHO=4 and stability tests. For the stability test the largest χ^2 value occurred for 1975:3.

---

[11] A similar result was obtained in Fair and Dominguez (1991), Table 3. The sign pattern was as expected, but the χ^2 value of 4.92 was less than the five percent critical value.

Table 5.17
Equation 17
LHS Variable is $\log(MF/PF)$

Equation				χ^2 Tests		
RHS Variable	Est.	t-stat.	Test	χ^2	df	p-value
cnst	.1784	2.01	$\log(MF/PF)_{-1}$	0.57	1	.4511
$\log(MF_{-1}/PF)$	.9038	30.89	Lags	7.74	3	.0518
$\log(X - FA)$	.0552	3.00	$RHO = 4$	25.79	4	.0000
$RS(1 - D2G - D2S)$	-.0073	-2.42	T	3.41	1	.0648
SE	.03776					
R^2	.956					
DW	2.21					
Stability Test:						
AP	T_1	T_2	λ		Break	
1.77	1970:1	1979:4	2.75		1974:4	

Estimation period is 1954:1–1993:2.

Equation 17. MF, demand deposits and currency—f

Equation 17 is the demand for money equation of the firm sector. The results for this equation are presented in Table 5.17. The equation is in log form. The transactions variable is the level of nonfarm firm sales, $X - FA$, and the interest rate variable is the after tax three month Treasury bill rate. The tax rates used in this equation are the corporate tax rates, $D2G$ and $D2S$, not the personal tax rates used for RSA in equation 9.

All the variables in the equation are significant. Again, the test results show that the lagged dependent variable that pertains to the real adjustment specification $[\log(MF/PF)_{-1}]$ is insignificant. The equation passes the lags test, the T test, and the stability test. It fails the RHO=4 test.

Equation 26. CUR, currency held outside banks

Equation 26 is the demand for currency equation. It is in per capita terms and is in log form. The transactions variable that is used is the level of nonfarm firm sales. The interest rate variable used is RSA, and the equation is estimated under the assumption of a first order autoregressive error term.

The results are presented in Table 5.26. All the variables in the equation are significant. The test results show that the lagged dependent variable that pertains to the real adjustment specification—$\log[CUR/(POP \cdot PF)]_{-1}$—is insignificant at the one percent level. The equation passes all the tests.

Table 5.26
Equation 26
LHS Variable is $\log[CUR/(POP \cdot PF)]$

Equation				χ^2 Tests		
RHS Variable	Est.	t-stat.	Test	χ^2	df	p-value
cnst	-.0529	-7.67	$\log(\frac{CUR}{POP \cdot PF})_{-1}$	6.25	1	.0124
$\log \frac{CUR_{-1}}{POP_{-1} \cdot PF}$	.9572	86.21	Lags	5.02	3	.1702
$\log[(X - FA)/POP]$	.0499	7.95	$RHO = 4$	6.06	3	.1085
RSA	-.0009	-2.10	T	0.67	1	.4122
$RHO1$	-.3262	-4.32				
SE	.00966					
R^2	.989					
DW	2.02					
Stability Test:						
AP	T_1	T_2	λ		Break	
5.91	1970:1	1979:4	2.75		1977:3	

Estimation period is 1954:1–1993:2.

5.4 The Main Firm Sector Equations

In the maximization problem of a firm in the theoretical model there are five main decision variables: the firm's price, production, investment, demand for employment, and wage rate. These five decision variables are determined jointly in that they are the result of solving one maximization problem. The variables that affect this solution include 1) the initial stocks of excess capital, excess labor, and inventories, 2) the current and expected future values of the interest rate, 3) the current and expected future demand schedules for the firm's output, 4) the current and expected future supply schedules of labor facing the firm, and 5) the firm's expectations of other firms' future price and wage decisions.

In the econometric model seven variables were chosen to represent the five decisions: 1) the price level of the firm sector, PF, 2) production, Y, 3) investment in nonresidential plant and equipment, IKF, 4) the number of jobs in the firm sector, JF, 5) the average number of hours paid per job, HF, 6) the average number of overtime hours paid per job, HO, and 7) the wage rate of the firm sector, WF. Each of these variables is determined by a stochastic equation, and these are the main stochastic equations of the firm sector.

Moving from the theoretical model of firm behavior to the econometric specifications is not straightforward, and a number of approximations have to

be made. One of the key approximations is that the econometric specifications in effect assume that the five decisions of a firm are made sequentially
rather than jointly. The sequence is from the price decision, to the production
decision, to the investment and employment decisions, and to the wage rate
decision. In this way of looking at the problem, the firm first chooses its optimal price path. This path implies a certain expected sales path, from which
the optimal production path is chosen. Given the optimal production path, the
optimal paths of investment and employment are chosen. Finally, given the
optimal employment path, the optimal wage path is chosen.

Equation 10. PF, price deflator for $X - FA$[12]

Equation 10 is the key price equation in the model, and the results for this
equation are in Table 5.10. The equation is in log form. The price level is
a function of the lagged price level, the wage rate inclusive of the employer
social security tax rate, the price of imports, and a demand pressure variable.
The equation is estimated under the assumption of a first order autoregressive
error term. The lagged price level is meant to pick up expectational effects,
and the wage rate and import price variables are meant to pick up cost effects.
The demand pressure variable, $\log[(YS_{-1} - Y_{-1})/YS_{-1} + .04]$, is the log of
the percentage gap between potential and actual output plus .04. (Remember
that YS is the potential value of Y.) This functional form implies that as actual
output approaches four percent more than potential, the demand pressure variable approaches minus infinity, which implies that the price level approaches
plus infinity. This functional form effectively prevents actual output from ever
exceeding potential output by more than four percent. The demand pressure
variable is lagged one quarter in equation 10 because this gave slightly better
results than did the use of the variable unlagged.

   An important feature of the price equation is that the price *level* is explained
by the equation, not the price *change*. This treatment is contrary to the standard
Phillips-curve treatment, where the price (or wage) change is explained by the
equation. Given the theory outlined in Chapter 2, the natural decision variables
of a firm would seem to be the levels of prices and wages. For example, the
market share equations in the theoretical model have a firm's market share as
a function of the ratio of the firm's price to the average price of other firms.
These are price levels, and the objective of the firm is to choose the price level
path (along with the paths of the other decision variables) that maximizes the

---

[12]The material on the level versus change specification in this section is taken from Fair
(1993a).

Table 5.10
Equation 10
LHS Variable is log PF

Equation				χ^2 Tests		
RHS Variable	Est.	t-stat.	Test	χ^2	df	p-value
log PF_{-1}	.9194	155.61	Level form[a]	3.94	2	.1395
log$[WF(1 + D5G)]$	.0294	7.68	Lags	8.09	4	.0885
cnst	.1142	6.97	$RHO = 4$	10.67	3	.0137
log PIM	.0361	12.12	T	0.04	1	.8499
log$[(\frac{YS-Y}{YS})_{-1} + .04]$	-.0051	-3.78	Leads +1	0.06	1	.8150
$RHO1$	.1418	1.83	Leads +4	6.39	4	.1719
			Leads +8	2.98	2	.2253
			UR_{-1}	17.46	1	.0000
			$(\frac{YS-Y}{YS})_{-1}$	6.67	1	.0098
			Change form[b]	92.30	3	.0000
SE	.00400					
R^2	.999					
DW	1.96					
Stability Test:						
AP	T_1	T_2	λ		Break	
12.28*	1970:1	1979:4	2.75		1972:2	

Estimation period is 1954:1–1993:2.
[a] log$[WF(1 + D5G)]_{-1}$ and log PIM_{-1} added to the equation.
[b] log PF_{-1}, log$[WF(1 + D5G)]_{-1}$, and log PIM_{-1} added to the equation with
Δ log PF on the left hand side and a constant, Δ log$[WF(1 + D5G)]$, Δ log PIM,
and log$[((YS - Y)/YS)_{-1} + .04]$ on the right hand side (with the RHO1 assumption).

multiperiod objective function. A firm decides what its price *level* should be
relative to the price *levels* of other firms.

Fortunately, it is possible to test whether the price level or price change
specification is better. Let p denote the log of the price level, let w denote
the log of the wage rate, and let D denote the level of some demand pressure
variable. The price equation in level form is

$$p = \beta_0 + \beta_1 p_{-1} + \beta_2 w + \beta_3 D \tag{5.15}$$

and the equation in change form is

$$\Delta p = \eta_0 + \eta_1 \Delta w + \eta_2 D \tag{5.16}$$

The key difference between 5.15 and 5.16 is that D and not ΔD is in 5.16. If
β_1 in 5.15 is less than one, a permanent change in D results in a permanent
change in the level of P but not in the change in P. In 5.16, on the other
hand, a permanent change in D results in a permanent change in the change

in P. The constant term η_0 in 5.16 accounts for any trend in the level of P not captured by the other variables.

It is not possible to nest 5.15 into 5.16 or vice versa, but they can each be nested in a more general equation. This equation is

$$p = \delta_0 + \delta_1 p_{-1} + \delta_2 w + \delta_3 w_{-1} + \delta_4 D \qquad (5.17)$$

The restriction in 5.17 implied by the level specification in 5.15 is $\delta_3 = 0$. The restrictions in 5.17 implied by the change specification in 5.16 are $\delta_1 = 1$ and $\delta_2 = -\delta_3$. These restrictions can be tested. If both sets of restrictions are accepted, then the test has not discriminated between the two specifications. If neither set is accepted, then neither specification is supported by the data. Otherwise, one specification will be selected over the other.

Equation 10 in the model is like equation 5.15 above except that the price of imports is also an explanatory variable. This is a variable like w in that it is assumed to pick up cost effects. The results in Table 5.10 show that all the explanatory variables are significant.

The test results are as follows. First, to test the level specification, the lagged values of the wage rate and price of imports—$\log[WF(1 + D5G)]_{-1}$ and $\log PIM_{-1}$—are added. As can be seen, these two variables are not significant, and so the level specification is supported over the more general specification. The change specification, on the other hand, is not supported, as can be seen in the last χ^2 test in Table 5.10. When the lagged values of the price level, the wage rate, and the price of imports are added to the change form of the price equation, they are highly significant, with a χ^2 value of 92.30. The change form is thus strongly rejected.[13]

Equation 10 passes the lags test, the RHO=4 test, and the T test. The variable for which led values were tried is the wage rate, and the led values are not significant.

The test results next show that the unemployment rate lagged once is significant when added to the equation. Although not shown in the table, the addition of the unemployment rate makes the demand pressure variable insignificant. The next test shows that the simple percentage gap variable

---

[13]The level versus change specification was also tested in Fair (1993a) for 40 disaggregate price equations. The results were somewhat mixed, but overall slightly favored the level specification. The disaggregate results thus provide some support for the current aggregate estimates. Also, as will be seen, the results in Chapter 6 of estimating price equations for different countries strongly support the level specification over the change specification. As discussed later in this chapter, the result that the level specification is supported over the change specification has important implications for the long run properties of the economy.

lagged once, $[(YS - Y)/YS]_{-1}$, is significant. Although not shown in the table, the addition of this variable also makes the demand pressure variable insignificant. The functional form chosen for the demand pressure variable is thus not supported by the data. The best results (e.g., best fit) are obtained when no nonlinearity is introduced. This situation is unsatisfactory from a theoretical perspective in that one expects that there is some degree of demand pressure beyond which prices rise faster for a further increase in demand pressure than they did before this degree was reached. The problem is that the U.S. economy has not experienced enough periods in which demand pressure was very high to allow one to estimate adequately how prices behave in these extreme periods. The large price increases in the 1970s were primarily cost driven, and so they are of no help for this problem. The way that this problem has been handled in the model is simply to use the nonlinear functional form described above even though simpler forms do somewhat better. This problem is, of course, an important area for future work, and it suggests that any policy experiments with the model that push the economy to very high levels of activity should be interpreted with considerable caution. The behavior of prices at very high activity levels has probably not been very accurately estimated.

Finally, the price equation fails the stability test. The largest χ^2 value occurs for 1972:2, near the beginning of the first oil price shock.

Equation 11. Y, production—f

The specification of the production equation is where the assumption that a firm's decisions are made sequentially begins to be used. The equation is based on the assumption that the firm sector first sets it price, then knows what its sales for the current period will be, and from this latter information decides on what its production for the current period will be.

In the theoretical model production is smoothed relative to sales. The reason for this is various costs of adjustment, which include costs of changing employment, costs of changing the capital stock, and costs of having the stock of inventories deviate from some proportion of sales. If a firm were only interested in minimizing inventory costs, it would produce according to the following equation (assuming that sales for the current period are known):

$$Y = X + \beta X - V_{-1} \qquad (5.18)$$

where Y is the level of production, X is the level of sales, V_{-1} is the stock of inventories at the beginning of the period, and β is the inventory-sales ratio that minimizes inventory costs. Since by definition, $V - V_{-1} = Y - X$, producing according to 5.18 would ensure that $V = \beta X$. Because of the other adjustment costs, it is generally not optimal for a firm to produce according to 5.18. In the theoretical model there was no need to postulate explicitly how a firm's production plan deviated from 5.18 because its optimal production plan just resulted, along with the other optimal paths, from the direct solution of its maximization problem. For the empirical work, however, it is necessary to make further assumptions.

The estimated production equation is based on the following three assumptions:

$$V^* = \beta X \tag{5.19}$$

$$Y^* = X + \alpha(V^* - V_{-1}) \tag{5.20}$$

$$Y - Y_{-1} = \lambda(Y^* - Y_{-1}) \tag{5.21}$$

where $*$ denotes a desired value. Equation 5.19 states that the desired stock of inventories is proportional to current sales. Equation 5.20 states that the desired level of production is equal to sales plus some fraction of the difference between the desired stock of inventories and the stock on hand at the end of the previous period. Equation 5.21 states that actual production partially adjusts to desired production each period. Combining the three equations yields

$$Y = (1 - \lambda)Y_{-1} + \lambda(1 + \alpha\beta)X - \lambda\alpha V_{-1} \tag{5.22}$$

Equation 11 in Table 5.11 is the estimated version of equation 5.22. The equation is estimated under the assumption of a third order autoregressive process of the error term. The implied value of λ is $.7074 = 1.0 - .2926$, which means that actual production adjusts 70.74 percent of the way to desired production in the current quarter. The implied value of α is $.4727 = .3344/.7074$, which means that desired production is equal to sales plus 47.27 percent of the desired change in inventories. The implied value of β is $.7629$, which means that the desired stock of inventories is estimated to equal 76.29 percent of the (quarterly) level of sales.

Equation 11 passes all of the tests except the stability test. The variable for which led values were used is the level of sales, X, and it is interesting that the led values are not significant.[14] The hypothesis that firms have rational expectations regarding future values of sales is rejected. Note also that the spread values are not significant.

The estimates of equation 11 are consistent with the view that firms smooth production relative to sales. The view that production is smoothed relative to

---

[14]Collinearity problems prevented Leads +4 from being calculated for equation 11.

Table 5.11
Equation 11
LHS Variable is Y

Equation				χ^2 Tests		
RHS Variable	Est.	t-stat.	Test	χ^2	df	p-value
cnst	28.0418	1.85	Lags	1.24	2	.5392
Y_{-1}	.2926	6.50	$RHO = 4$	0.25	1	.6189
X	.9625	19.84	T	0.06	1	.8033
V_{-1}	-.3344	-8.26	Leads +1	4.58	1	.0323
$RHO1$	.3906	4.69	Leads +8	1.49	2	.4753
$RHO2$	.2788	3.41	Spread	5.45	4	.2442
$RHO3$	.2585	3.25				
SE	3.05348					
R^2	.999					
DW	1.98					
Stability Test:						
AP	T_1	T_2	λ		Break	
13.79*	1970:1	1979:4	2.75		1979:3	

Estimation period is 1954:1–1993:2.

sales has been challenged by Blinder (1981) and others, and this work has in turn been challenged in Fair (1989) as being based on faulty data. The results in Fair (1989) using physical units data for specific industries suggests that production is smoothed relative to sales. The results using the physical units data thus provide some support for the current aggregate estimates.

Equation 12. IKF, nonresidential fixed investment—f

Equation 12 explains nonresidential fixed investment of the firm sector. It is based on the assumption that the production decision has already been made. In the theoretical model, because of costs of changing the capital stock, it may sometimes be optimal for a firm to hold excess capital. If there were no such costs, investment each period would merely be the amount needed to have enough capital to produce the output of the period. In the theoretical model there was no need to postulate explicitly how investment deviates from this amount, but for the empirical work this must be done.

The estimated investment equation is based on the following three equations:

$$(KK - KK_{-1})^* = \alpha_0(KK_{-1} - KKMIN_{-1}) + \alpha_1 \Delta Y + \alpha_2 \Delta Y_{-1}$$

$$+ \alpha_3 \Delta Y_{-2} + \alpha_4 \Delta Y_{-3} + \alpha_5 \Delta Y_{-4} \qquad (5.23)$$

$$IKF^* = (KK - KK_{-1})^* + DELK \cdot KK_{-1} \qquad (5.24)$$

$$\Delta IKF = \lambda(IKF^* - IKF_{-1}) \qquad (5.25)$$

where again $*$ denotes a desired value. IKF is gross investment of the firm sector, KK is the capital stock, and $KKMIN$ is the minimum amount of capital needed to produce the output of the period. $(KK - KK_{-1})^*$ is desired net investment, and IKF^* is desired gross investment. Equation 5.23 states that desired net investment is a function of the amount of excess capital on hand and of five change in output terms. If output has not changed for four periods and if there is no excess capital, then desired net investment is zero. The change in output terms are meant to be proxies for expected future output changes. Equation 5.24 relates desired gross investment to desired net investment. $DELK \cdot KK_{-1}$ is the depreciation of the capital stock during period $t - 1$. By definition, $IKF = KK - KK_{-1} + DELK \cdot KK_{-1}$, and 5.24 is merely this same equation for the desired values. Equation 5.25 is a partial adjustment equation relating the desired change in gross investment to the actual change. It is meant to approximate cost of adjustment effects. Combining 5.23–5.25 yields

$$\Delta IKF = \lambda\alpha_0(KK_{-1} - KKMIN_{-1}) + \lambda\alpha_1\Delta Y + \lambda\alpha_2\Delta Y_{-1}$$

$$+\lambda\alpha_3\Delta Y_{-2} + \lambda\alpha_4\Delta Y_{-3} + \lambda\alpha_5\Delta Y_{-4}$$

$$- \lambda(IKF_{-1} - DELK \cdot KK_{-1}) \qquad (5.26)$$

Equation 12 in Table 5.12 is the estimated version of 5.26 with two additions. The two additional variables in Table 5.12 are cost of capital variables: an investment tax credit dummy variable, $TXCR$, and the real bond rate lagged three quarters, RB'_{-3}.[15] Both of these variables are multiplied by $IKFA$, which is a variable constructed by peak to peak interpolations of IKF. Since IKF has a trend and $TXCR$ and RB' do not, one would expect a given change in $TXCR$ or RB' to have an effect on IKF that increases over time, and multiplying both variables by $IKFA$ is a way of accounting for this. $IKFA$ is exogenous; it is merely a scale variable.

How can the use of the cost of capital variables be justified? In the theoretical model the cost of capital affects investment by affecting the kinds of machines that are purchased. If the cost of capital falls, more capital intensive

---

[15] RB' is equal to the after tax bond rate, $RB(1 - D2G - D2S)$, minus p_4^e, one of the measures of inflation expectations. Remember from Section 5.1 that p_4^e equals $100[(PD/PD_{-4}) - 1]$.

Table 5.12
Equation 12
LHS Variable is ΔIKF

Equation			χ^2 Tests			
RHS Variable	Est.	t-stat.	Test	χ^2	df	p-value
$(KK - KKMIN)_{-1}$	-.0013	-0.51	Lags	19.19	5	.0018
$IKF_{-1} - DELK \cdot KK_{-1}$	-.0396	-2.99	$RHO = 4$	7.31	4	.1203
ΔY	.0616	2.80	T	2.24	1	.1341
ΔY_{-1}	.0660	3.83	Leads +1	0.20	1	.6559
ΔY_{-2}	.0308	1.83	Leads +4	6.59	4	.1592
ΔY_{-3}	.0515	3.04	Leads +8	6.30	2	.0428
ΔY_{-4}	.0346	2.00	cnst	0.14	1	.7039
$TXCR \cdot IKFA$	.0013	0.45	Spread	1.19	4	.8792
$RB'_{-3} \cdot IKFA$	-.0016	-2.52				
SE	1.23863					
R^2	.436					
DW	1.99					
Stability Test:						
AP	T_1	T_2	λ		Break	
2.76	1970:1	1979:4	2.75		1978:2	

Estimation period is 1954:1–1993:2.

machines are purchased and investment expenditures increase. For the empirical work, data are not available by types of machines, and approximations have to be made. The key approximation is the postulation of the production function 3.1 in Chapter 3. This production function is one of fixed proportions in the short run. Technical change and changes in the cost of capital relative to the cost of labor affect over time the λ and μ coefficients in the equation, and these are accounted for through the peak to peak interpolations discussed in Chapter 3. $KKMIN$ in equation 93 in the model is determined using MUH, the peak to peak interpolation of $\mu \cdot \bar{H}$.

If, as seems quite likely, the effects of cost of capital changes on firms' decisions are not completely captured through the peak to peak interpolations, then adding cost of capital variables to equation 5.23 (and thus equation 5.26) may be warranted. For example, when the cost of capital falls, $KKMIN$ may underestimate the desired amount of capital, and at least part of this error may be picked up by adding cost of capital variables to the equation.

The estimate of λ in equation 12 is .0396, which says that gross investment adjusts 3.96 percent to its desired value each quarter. The implied value of α_0 is $-.0328 = -.0013/.0396$, which says that 3.28 percent of the amount of excess capital on hand is desired to be eliminated each quarter. The change in output terms have t-statistics greater than or equal to two except for the change lagged twice, which has a t-statistic of 1.83. The tax credit variable has a t-statistic of 0.45, and the real bond rate lagged three times has a t-statistic of -2.52. The tax credit variable is thus not significant, although its coefficient estimate is of the expected sign, and the bond rate is significant. I have found it very difficult over the years to obtain significant cost of capital effects in equation 12, and the current results are probably the best that I have ever done. Even here the lag of three quarters for the bond rate seems a little long, but shorter lags gave poorer results. The results may thus be spurious and merely the result of data mining, but they are retained because it is embarrassing not to have cost of capital effects in the investment equation.

Equation 12 fails the lags test, but it passes all the others, including the stability test. The variable used for the led values was the change in output, and it is interesting to see that the future output changes are not significant. This is evidence against the hypothesis that firms have rational expectations with respect to future values of output. Note also in Table 5.12 that the constant term is not significant. According to equation 5.26 there should be no constant term in the equation, and the results bear this out. The χ^2 test for the addition of the constant term is not significant. The spread values are also not significant.

Equation 13. JF, number of jobs—f

The employment equation 13 and the hours equation 14 are similar in spirit to the investment equation 12. They are also based on the assumption that the production decision is made first. Because of adjustment costs, it is sometimes optimal in the theoretical model for firms to hold excess labor. Were it not for the costs of changing employment, the optimal level of employment would merely be the amount needed to produce the output of the period. In the theoretical model there was no need to postulate explicitly how employment deviates from this amount, but this must be done for the empirical work.

The estimated employment equation is based on the following three equations:

$$\Delta \log JF = \alpha_0 \log(JF_{-1}/JF_{-1}^*) + \alpha_1 \Delta \log Y \qquad (5.27)$$

$$JF_{-1}^* = JHMIN_{-1}/HF_{-1}^* \qquad (5.28)$$

$$HF_{-1}^* = \bar{H}e^{\delta t} \qquad (5.29)$$

where $JHMIN$ is the number of worker hours required to produce the output of the period, HF^* is the average number of hours per job that the firm would like to be worked if there were no adjustment costs, and JF^* is the number of workers the firm would like to employ if there were no adjustment costs. The term $\log(JF_{-1}/JF^*_{-1})$ in 5.27 will be referred to as the "amount of excess labor on hand." Equation 5.27 states that the change in employment is a function of the amount of excess labor on hand and the change in output (all changes are in logs). If there is no change in output and if there is no excess labor on hand, the change in employment is zero. Equation 5.28 defines the desired number of jobs, which is simply the required number of worker hours divided by the desired number of hours worked per job. Equation 5.29 postulates that the desired number of hours worked is a smoothly trending variable, where $\bar{H}$ and δ are constants. Combining 5.27–5.29 yields

$$\Delta \log JF = \alpha_0 \log \bar{H} + \alpha_0 \log(JF_{-1}/JHMIN_{-1})$$

$$+ \alpha_0 \delta t + \alpha_1 \Delta \log Y \tag{5.30}$$

Equation 13 in Table 5.13 is the estimated version of equation 5.30 with two additions. The first addition is the use of the lagged dependent variable, $\Delta \log JF_{-1}$. This was added to pick up dynamic effects that did not seem to be captured by the original specification.

The second addition is accounting for what seemed to be a structural break in the mid 1970s. When testing the equation for structural stability, there was evidence of a structural break in the middle of the sample period, with the largest χ^2 value occurring in 1977:2. Contrary to the case for most equations that fail the stability test, the results for equation 13 suggested that the break could be modeled fairly simply. In particular, the coefficient of the change in output did not appear to change, but the others did. This was modeled by creating a dummy variable, $DD772$, that is one from 1977:2 on and zero otherwise and adding to the equation all the explanatory variables in the equation (except the change in output) multiplied by $DD772$ as additional explanatory variables.

The results in Table 5.13 show that the estimate of α_0, the coefficient of the excess labor variable, is $-.0867$ for the period before 1977:2 and $-.1843 = -.0867 - .0976$ after that. This means that in the latter period 18.43 percent of the amount of excess labor on hand is eliminated each quarter, up substantially from the earlier period.

Equation 13 does not pass the lags test, where the χ^2 value is quite large. Experimenting with various specifications of this equation reveals that it is very fragile with respect to adding lagged values in that adding these values changes the values of the other coefficient estimates substantially and in ways that do not seem sensible. The equation also fails the RHO=4 test. The variable

Table 5.13
Equation 13
LHS Variable is $\Delta \log JF$

Equation			χ^2 Tests			
RHS Variable	Est.	t-stat.	Test	χ^2	df	p-value
cnst	-.5418	-3.66	Lags	38.03	5	.0000
$DD772$	-.5775	-1.69	$RHO = 4$	14.07	4	.0071
$\log(\frac{JF}{JHMIN})_{-1}$	-.0867	-3.65	Leads +1	4.46	1	.0348
$DD772 \cdot \log(\frac{JF}{JHMIN})_{-1}$	-.0976	-1.75	Leads +4	20.18	4	.0005
$\Delta \log JF_{-1}$	.4233	7.48	Leads +8	6.31	2	.0427
$DD772 \cdot \Delta \log JF_{-1}$	-.2634	-1.93				
T	.0001	3.56				
$DD772 \cdot T$	-.0001	-2.28				
$\Delta \log Y$	.3037	9.34				
SE	.00329					
R^2	.755					
DW	2.07					

Estimation period is 1954:1–1993:2.

for which led values were tried is the change in output variable, and the values led four quarters (but not one and eight) are significant at the one percent level.

Equation 14. HF, average number of hours paid per job—f

The hours equation is based on equations 5.28 and 5.29 and the following equation:

$$\Delta \log HF = \lambda \log(HF_{-1}/HF^*_{-1}) + \alpha_0 \log(JF_{-1}/JF^*_{-1}) + \alpha_1 \Delta \log Y \tag{5.31}$$

The first term on the right hand side of 5.31 is the (logarithmic) difference between the actual number of hours paid for in the previous period and the desired number. The reason for the inclusion of this term in the hours equation but not in the employment equation is that, unlike JF, HF fluctuates around a slowly trending level of hours. This restriction is captured by the first term in 5.31. The other two terms are the amount of excess labor on hand and the current change in output. Both of these terms affect the employment decision, and they should also affect the hours decision since the two are closely related. Combining 5.28, 5.29, and 5.31 yields

$$\Delta \log HF = (\alpha_0 - \lambda) \log \bar{H} + \lambda \log HF_{-1} + \alpha_0 \log(JF_{-1}/JHMIN_{-1})$$

$$+ (\alpha_0 - \lambda)\delta t + \alpha_1 \Delta \log Y \tag{5.32}$$

Table 5.14
Equation 14
LHS Variable is $\Delta \log HF$

Equation			χ^2 Tests			
RHS Variable	Est.	t-stat.	Test	χ^2	df	p-value
cnst	.7219	4.64	Lags	3.11	4	.5394
$DD772$	.3034	2.10	$RHO = 4$	3.40	3	.3345
$\log HF_{-1}$	-.1837	-5.19	Leads +1	2.27	1	.1323
$\log(\frac{JF}{JHMIN})_{-1}$	-.0681	-3.50	Leads +4	2.07	4	.7236
$DD772 \cdot \log(\frac{JF}{JHMIN})_{-1}$	.0521	2.22	Leads +8	3.32	2	.1899
T	-.0002	-5.03				
$DD772 \cdot T$	.0001	4.02				
$\Delta \log Y$	.1694	7.30				
$RHO1$	-.2402	2.85				
SE	.00257					
R^2	.466					
DW	1.97					

Estimation period is 1954:1–1993:2.

Equation 14 in Table 5.14 is the estimated version of 5.32 with the addition of the terms multiplied by $DD772$ to pick up the structural break. The equation is estimated under the assumption of a first order autoregressive error term. The estimated value of λ is $-.1837$, which means that, other things being equal, actual hours are adjusted toward desired hours by 18.37 percent per quarter. The excess labor variable is significant in the equation, as are the time trend and the change in output.

Equation 14 passes the lags and RHO=4 tests. The variable for which led values were tried is the change in output variable, and the led values are not significant. This is contrary to the case for equation 13, where the values led four quarters are significant.

Equation 15. HO, average number of overtime hours paid per job—f

Equation 15 explains overtime hours, HO. One would expect HO to be close to zero for low values of total hours, HF, and to increase roughly one for one for high values of HF. An approximation to this relationship is

$$HO = e^{\alpha_1 + \alpha_2 HF} \tag{5.33}$$

which in log form is

$$\log HO = \alpha_1 + \alpha_2 HF \tag{5.34}$$

Table 5.15
Equation 15
LHS Variable is $\log HO$

Equation				χ^2 Tests			
RHS Variable	Est.	t-stat.	Test	χ^2	df	p-value
cnst	3.8834	78.31	Lags	4.99	2	.0825
HFF	.0201	8.08	$RHO = 4$	4.00	3	.2611
HFF_{-1}	.0122	4.91	T	3.92	1	.0476
$RHO1$	.9159	25.83				
SE	.04761					
R^2	.930					
DW	1.76					
Stability Test:						

AP	T_1	T_2	λ	Break
1.40	1970:1	1979:4	2.90	1975:3

Estimation period is 1956:1–1993:2.

Two modifications were made in going from equation 5.34 to equation 15 in Table 5.15. First, HF was detrended before being used in 5.34. HF has a negative trend over the sample period, although the trend appears somewhat irregular. To account for the irregular trend, a variable HFS was constructed from peak to peak interpolations of HF, and then $HF - HFS$, which is denoted HFF in the model, was included in equation 15. (The peak quarters used for the interpolation are presented in Table A.6.) HFF is defined by equation 100 in Table A.3. It is the deviation of HF from its peak to peak interpolations. Second, both HFF and HFF_{-1} were included in the equation, which appeared to capture the dynamics better. The equation is estimated under the assumption of a first order autoregressive error term.

The coefficient estimates are significant in equation 15. The equation passes the lags, RHO=4, and T tests. It also passes the stability test. The equation thus seems to be a reasonable approximation to the way that HO is determined, although the estimate of the autoregressive coefficient of the error term is quite high.

Equation 16. WF, average hourly earnings excluding overtime—f

Equation 16 is the wage rate equation. It is in log form. In the final specification, WF was simply taken to be a function of a constant, time, the current value of the price level, and the first four lagged values of the price level and the wage rate. Labor market tightness variables like the unemployment rate were not significant in the equation. The time trend is added to account for trend changes in the wage rate relative to the price level. Its inclusion is important, since it along with some of the lags identifies the price equation, equation 10. Equation 16 is estimated under the assumption of a first order autoregressive error.

Constraints were imposed on the coefficients in the wage equation to ensure that the determination of the real wage implied by equations 10 and 16 is sensible. Let $p = \log PF$ and $w = \log WF$. The relevant parts of the price and wage equations regarding the constraints are

$$p = \beta_1 p_{-1} + \beta_2 w + \ldots \tag{5.35}$$

$$w = \gamma_1 w_{-1} + \gamma_2 p + \gamma_3 p_{-1} + \gamma_4 w_{-2} + \gamma_5 p_{-2} + \gamma_6 w_{-3}$$
$$+ \gamma_7 p_{-3} + \gamma_8 w_{-4} + \gamma_9 p_{-4} + \ldots \tag{5.36}$$

The implied real wage equation from these two equations should not have $w - p$ as a function of either w or p separately, since one does not expect the real wage to grow simply because the level of w and p are growing. The desired form of the real wage equation is thus

$$w - p = \delta_1(w_{-1} - p_{-1}) + \delta_2(w_{-2} - p_{-2}) + \delta_3(w_{-3} - p_{-3})$$
$$+ \delta_4(w_{-4} - p_{-4}) + \ldots \tag{5.37}$$

which says that the real wage is a function of its own lagged values plus other terms. The real wage in 5.37 is *not* a function of the level of w or p separately. The constraints on the coefficients in equations 5.35 and 5.36 that impose this restriction are:

$$\gamma_3 = [\beta_1/(1 - \beta_2)](1 - \gamma_2) - \gamma_1$$

$$\gamma_5 = -\gamma_4$$

$$\gamma_7 = -\gamma_6$$

$$\gamma_9 = -\gamma_8$$

When using 2SLS or 2SLAD, these constraints were imposed by first estimating the price equation to get estimates of β_1 and β_2 and then using these estimates to impose the constraint on γ_3 in the wage equation. No sequential procedure is needed to impose the constraints when using 3SLS and FIML, since all the equations are estimated together.

The results for equation 16 (using 2SLS) are presented in Table 5.16. The wage rate lagged four times is significant, and this is the reason for the use

Table 5.16
Equation 16
LHS Variable is $\log WF$

Equation				χ^2 Tests			
RHS Variable	Est.	t-stat.	Test	χ^2	df	p-value
$\log WF_{-1}$	.6637	5.92	Real Wage Restr.[b]	6.54	4	.1625
$\log PF$	.2843	2.49	Lags	1.35	1	.2444
$\log WF_{-2}$	-.0038	-0.04	$RHO = 4$	7.34	3	.0619
$\log WF_{-3}$	.1506	1.96	UR_{-1}	0.00	1	.9863
$\log WF_{-4}$	.1757	2.18				
cnst	-.1180	-1.90				
T	.0005	5.05				
$RHO1$	.3269	2.33				
$\log PF_{-1}$ [a]	.0142	–				
$\log PF_{-2}$ [a]	.0038	–				
$\log PF_{-3}$ [a]	-.1506	–				
$\log PF_{-4}$ [a]	-.1757	–				
SE	.00628					
R^2	.999					
DW	1.91					

Stability Test:

AP	T_1	T_2	λ	Break
6.13	1970:1	1979:4	2.75	1972:3

Estimation period is 1954:1–1993:2
[a] Coefficient constrained; see the discussion in the text.
[b] Equation estimated with no restrictions on the coefficients.

of four lags even though lag 2 is not significant. The time trend is highly significant, which is picking up a trend in the real wage.

The χ^2 test results show that the real wage restrictions discussed above are not rejected by the data. The equation also passes the lags and RHO=4 tests. The final χ^2 test in the table has the unemployment rate lagged once added as an explanatory variable, and it is not significant. As noted above, no demand pressure variables were found to be significant in the wage equation. Finally, the equation passes the stability test.

5.5 Other Firm Sector Equations

Equation 18. DF, dividends paid—f

Let π denote after tax profits. If in the long run firms desire to pay out all of their after tax profits in dividends, then one can write $DF^* = \pi$, where DF^*

Table 5.18
Equation 18
LHS Variable is $\Delta \log DF$

Equation				χ^2 Tests		
RHS Variable	Est.	t-stat.	Test	χ^2	df	p-value
$\log \frac{PIEF-TFG-TFS}{DF_{-1}}$	.0251	9.30	Restriction	0.14	1	.7065
			Lags	10.29	2	.0058
			$RHO = 4$	31.66	4	.0000
			T	0.42	1	.5175
			cnst	1.25	1	.2636
SE	.02616					
R^2	.080					
DW	1.48					
Stability Test:						
AP	T_1	T_2	λ		Break	
1.65	1970:1	1979:4	2.75		1976:1	

Estimation period is 1954:1–1993:2.

is the long run desired value of dividends for profit level π. If it is assumed that actual dividends are partially adjusted to desired dividends each period as

$$DF/DF_{-1} = (DF^*/DF_{-1})^\lambda \qquad (5.38)$$

then the equation to be estimated is

$$\log(DF/DF_{-1}) = \lambda \log(\pi/DF_{-1}) \qquad (5.39)$$

Equation 18 in Table 5.18 is the estimated version of equation 5.39. The level of after tax profits in the notation of the model is $PIEF - TFG - TFS$. The estimate of λ is .0251, which implies a fairly slow adjustment of actual to desired dividends.

Because of the assumption that $DF^* = \pi$, the coefficient of $\log(PIEF - TFG - TFS)$ is restricted to be the negative of the coefficient of $\log DF_{-1}$ in equation 18. If instead $DF^* = \pi^\gamma$, where γ is not equal to one, then the restriction does not hold. The first test in Table 5.18 is a test of the restriction (i.e., a test that $\gamma = 1$), and the test is passed. The equation fails the lags and RHO=4 tests, and it passes the T and stability tests. The test results also show that the constant term is not significant. The above specification does not call for a constant term, and this is supported by the data.

Table 5.20
Equation 20
LHS Variable is IVA

Equation				χ^2 Tests			
RHS Variable	Est.	t-stat.	Test	χ^2	df	p-value
cnst	-1.2649	-1.75	Lags	4.05	2	.1316
$(PX - PX_{-1})V_{-1}$	-.2757	-3.04	$RHO = 4$	17.49	3	.0006
$RHO1$	.7687	14.37	T	0.33	1	.5664
SE	1.80039					
R^2	.711					
DW	2.03					
Stability Test:						
AP	T_1	T_2	λ		Break	
3.59	1970:1	1979:4	2.75		1974:4	

Estimation period is 1954:1–1993:2.

Equation 20. IVA, inventory valuation adjustment

In theory $IVA = -(P - P_{-1})V_{-1}$, where P is the price of the good and V is the stock of inventories of the good. Equation 20 in Table 5.20 is meant to approximate this. IVA is regressed on a constant and $(PX - PX_{-1})V_{-1}$, where PX is the price deflator for the sales of the firm sector. The equation is estimated under the assumption of a first order autoregressive error term. As an approximation, the equation seems fairly good. It passes all but RHO=4 test, including the stability test.

Equation 21. CCF, capital consumption—f

In practice capital consumption allowances of a firm depend on tax laws and on current and past values of its investment. Equation 21 in Table 5.21 is an attempt to approximate this for the firm sector. $PIK \cdot IKF$ is the current value of investment. The use of the lagged dependent variable in the equation is meant to approximate the dependence of capital consumption allowances on past values of investment. This specification implies that the lag structure is geometrically declining. The restriction is also imposed that the sum of the lag coefficients is one, which means that capital consumption allowances are assumed to be taken on all investment in the long run.

There are two periods, 1981:1–1982:4 and 1983:1–1983:4, in which CCF is noticeably higher than would be predicted by the equation with only $\log[(PIK \cdot IKF)/CCF_{-1}]$ in it, and two dummy variables, $D811824$ and

Table 5.21
Equation 21
LHS Variable is $\Delta \log CCF$

Equation				χ^2 Tests		
RHS Variable	Est.	t-stat.	Test	χ^2	df	p-value
$\log[(PIK \cdot IKF)/CCF_{-1}]$	.0568	16.43	Restriction	4.22	1	.0398
$D811824$	.0174	3.15	Lags	5.89	2	.0525
$D831834$	.0346	4.59	$RHO = 4$	6.02	4	.1976
			T	4.50	1	.0339
			cnst	3.04	1	.0812
SE	.01505					
R^2	.271					
DW	1.87					

Estimation period is 1954:1–1993:2.

$D831834$, have been added to the equation to account for this. This is, of course, a crude procedure, but the equation itself is only a rough approximation to the way that capital consumption allowances are actually determined each period. Tax law changes have effects on CCF that are not captured in the equation.

Regarding the use of the two dummy variables, if CCF is larger than usual in the two subperiods, which the coefficient estimates for the two dummy variables suggest, then one might expect CCF to be lower at some later point (since capital consumption allowances can be taken on only 100 percent of investment in the long run). No attempt, however, was made to try to account for this in equation 21.

The coefficient estimate of .0568 in Table 5.21 says that capital consumption allowances are taken on 5.68 percent of new investment in the current quarter, then 5.36 percent [.0568(1 − .0568)] of this investment in the next quarter, then 5.05 percent [.0568(1 − .0568)^2] in the next quarter, and so on.

The first χ^2 test in Table 5.21 is a test of the restriction that the sum of the lag coefficients is one. This is done by adding $\log CCF_{-1}$ to the equation. The results show that the restriction is not rejected at the one percent level. The equation passes the lags, RHO=4, and T tests. The results of the last χ^2 test in the table show that the constant term is not significant in the equation. This is as expected since the above specification does not call for a constant term. The stability test was not performed because of the use of the dummy variables.

Table 5.22
Equation 22
LHS Variable is BO/BR

Equation				χ^2 Tests			
RHS Variable	Est.	t-stat.	Test	χ^2	df	p-value
cnst	.0034	0.99	Lags	6.01	3	.1111
$(BO/BR)_{-1}$	.3170	4.23	$RHO = 4$	26.69	4	.0000
RS	.0062	2.05	T	0.80	1	.3698
RD	-.0039	-1.37				
SE	.01989					
R^2	.332					
DW	2.06					

Stability Test:

AP	T_1	T_2	λ	Break
6.19	1970:1	1979:4	2.75	1972:4

Estimation period is 1954:1–1993:2.

5.6 Financial Sector Equations

The stochastic equations for the financial sector consist of an equation explaining member bank borrowing from the Federal Reserve, two term structure equations, and an equation explaining the change in stock prices.

Equation 22. BO, bank borrowing from the Fed

The variable BO/BR is the ratio of borrowed reserves to total reserves. This ratio is assumed to be a positive function of the three month Treasury bill rate, RS, and a negative function of the discount rate, RD. The estimated equation also includes a constant term and the lagged dependent variable.

The coefficient estimates of RS and RD in Table 5.22 are positive and negative, respectively, as expected. The equation passes the lags, T, and stability tests, and it fails the RHO=4 test.

Equation 23. RB, bond rate; Equation 24. RM, mortgage rate

The expectations theory of the term structure of interest rates states that long term rates are a function of the current and expected future short term rates. The two long term interest rates in the model are the bond rate, RB, and the mortgage rate, RM. These rates are assumed to be determined according to the expectations theory, where the current and past values of the short term

Table 5.23
Equation 23
LHS Variable is $RB - RS_{-2}$

Equation			χ^2 Tests			
RHS Variable	Est.	t-stat.	Test	χ^2	df	p-value
cnst	.2438	5.34	Restriction	1.89	1	.1688
$RB_{-1} - RS_{-2}$	.8813	42.95	Lags	2.51	2	.2856
$RS - RS_{-2}$	.2963	8.78	$RHO = 4$	7.93	3	.0474
$RS_{-1} - RS_{-2}$	-.2180	-5.04	T	4.62	1	.0316
$RHO1$	.2019	2.47	Leads +1	0.33	1	.5658
			Leads +4	2.23	4	.6939
			p_4^e	3.33	1	.0682
			p_8^e	3.85	1	.0499
SE	.25359					
R^2	.958					
DW	2.04					
Stability Test:						
AP	T_1	T_2	λ		Break	
6.25	1970:1	1979:4	2.75		1979:4	

Estimation period is 1954:1–1993:2.

interest rate (the three month bill rate, RS) are used as proxies for expected future values. Equations 23 and 24 are the two estimated equations. The lagged dependent variable is used in each of these equations, which implies a fairly complicated lag structure relating each long term rate to the past values of the short term rate. In addition, a constraint has been imposed on the coefficient estimates. The sum of the coefficients of the current and lagged values of the short term rate has been constrained to be equal to one minus the coefficient of the lagged long term rate. This means that, for example, a sustained one percentage point increase in the short term rate eventually results in a one percentage point increase in the long term rate. (This restriction is imposed by subtracting RS_{-2} from each of the other interest rates in the equations.) Equation 23 (but not 24) is estimated under the assumption of a first order autoregressive error term.

The results for equations 23 and 24 are presented in Tables 5.23 and 5.24, respectively. The short rates are significant except for RS_{-1} in equation 24. The test results show that the coefficient restriction is not rejected for either equation. Both equations pass the lags, RHO=4, T, and stability tests. The results for both term structure equations are thus strong. My experience with these equations over the years is that they are quite stable and reliable. During most periods they provide a very accurate link from short rates to long rates.

Table 5.24
Equation 24
LHS Variable is $RM - RS_{-2}$

Equation			χ^2 Tests			
RHS Variable	Est.	t-stat.	Test	χ^2	df	p-value
cnst	.4749	6.03	Restriction	2.71	1	.0995
$RM_{-1} - RS_{-2}$	.8418	33.24	Lags	2.92	2	.2322
$RS - RS_{-2}$	.2597	5.72	$RHO = 4$	4.79	4	.3093
$RS_{-1} - RS_{-2}$	-.0169	-0.27	T	2.65	1	.1039
			Leads +1	2.12	1	.1457
			Leads +4	12.70	4	.0128
			Leads +8	7.20	2	.0273
			p_4^e	1.77	1	.1835
			p_8^e	2.29	1	.1298
SE	.34387					
R^2	.897					
DW	2.02					
Stability Test:						
AP	T_1	T_2	λ		Break	
5.72	1970:1	1979:4	2.75		1979:4	

Estimation period is 1954:1–1993:2.

The variable for which led values were tried was the short term interest rate (RS), and the χ^2 tests show that the led values are not significant at the one percent level.[16] This is thus at least slight evidence against the bond market having rational expectations with respect to the short term interest rate. The test results also show that the inflation expectations variables, p_4^e and p_8^e, are not significant in the equations.

Equation 25. CG, capital gains or losses on corporate stocks held by h

The variable CG is the change in the market value of stocks held by the household sector. In the theoretical model the aggregate value of stocks is determined as the present discounted value of expected future after tax cash flow, the discount rates being the current and expected future short term interest rates. The theoretical model thus implies that CG should be a function of changes in expected future after tax cash flow and of changes in the current and expected future interest rates. In the empirical work the change in the bond rate, ΔRB, was used as a proxy for changes in expected future interest rates, and the change in after tax cash flow, $\Delta(CF - TFG - TFS)$, was used

---

[16]Collinearity problems prevented Leads +8 from being calculated for equation 23.

Table 5.25
Equation 25
LHS Variable is CG

Equation			χ^2 Tests			
RHS Variable	Est.	t-stat.	Test	χ^2	df	p-value
cnst	23.1530	3.22	Lags	2.26	3	.5204
ΔRB	-68.1158	-2.47	$RHO = 4$	19.63	4	.0006
$\Delta(CF - TFG - TFS)$	1.5451	0.60	T	4.79	1	.0286
			Leads +1	0.12	2	.9413
			Leads +4	9.31	8	.3172
			Leads +8	13.92	4	.0076
			ΔRS	0.73	1	.3942
SE	89.27602					
R^2	.147					
DW	1.96					
Stability Test:						
AP	T_1	T_2	λ		Break	
2.22	1970:1	1979:4	2.75		1979:1	

Estimation period is 1954:1–1993:2.

as a proxy for changes in expected future after tax cash flow. Equation 25 in Table 5.25 is the estimated equation.

The fit of equation 25 is not very good, and the cash flow variable is not significant. The change in the bond rate is significant, however, which provides some link from interest rates to stock prices in the model. The equation passes the lags, T, and stability tests, and it fails the RHO=4 test. The variables for which led values were tried are the change in the bond rate and the change in after tax cash flow. The values led one and four quarters are not significant, but the values led eight quarters are. This is thus slight evidence in favor of there being rational expectations in the stock market. For the final χ^2 test ΔRS, the change in the short term rate, was added under the view that it might also be a proxy for expected future interest rate changes, and it is not significant.

5.7   The Import Equation

Equation 27. IM, Imports

The import equation is in per capita terms and is in log form. The explanatory variables are 1) per capita real disposable income, 2) the private, nonfarm price deflator (a price deflator for domestically produced goods) relative to the import price deflator, 3) the long term after tax interest rate lagged one

Table 5.27
Equation 27
LHS Variable is $\log(IM/POP)$

Equation			χ^2 Tests			
RHS Variable	Est.	t-stat.	Test	χ^2	df	p-value
cnst	-.4533	-4.00	Lags	9.21	4	.0561
$\log(IM/POP)_{-1}$	.8716	26.77	$RHO = 4$	24.08	4	.0001
$\log[YD/(POP \cdot PH)]$	.3172	4.19	T	9.12	1	.0025
$\log(PF/PIM)$	.0365	1.50	Leads +1	0.58	1	.4447
RMA_{-1}	-.0027	-1.32	Leads +4	10.90	4	.0277
D691	-.1183	-3.64	Leads +8	0.17	2	.9171
D692	.1478	4.52	p_4^e	22.44	1	.0000
D714	-.0871	-2.68	p_8^e	14.99	1	.0001
D721	.0943	2.91	$\log PF$	24.49	1	.0000
			$\log[(X - FA)/POP]$	2.94	1	.0863
			Other[a]	30.55	4	.0000
			Spread	35.07	4	.0000
SE	.03204					
R^2	.995					
DW	1.80					

Estimation period is 1954:1–1993:2.
[a] $\log(AA/POP)_{-1}$, $\log(WA/PH)$, Z, $\log[YNL/(POP \cdot PH)]$.

quarter, 4) the lagged dependent variable, and 5) four dummy variables to account for two dock strikes.

The results are in Table 5.27. The short run income elasticity of imports is .3172, and the long run elasticity is 2.47 [.3127/(1 − .8716)], both fairly high. The coefficient estimate for the relative price term is positive as expected, although it is not significant. The coefficient estimate for the long term interest rate is negative as expected, but it also is not significant.

Many χ^2 tests were performed for the import equation. It passes the lags test, but fails the RHO=4 and T tests. The variable for which led values were tried is disposable income, and the led values are not significant. The inflationary expectations variables, p_4^e and p_8^e, are highly significant, but (although not shown in the table) their coefficient estimates are of the wrong expected sign.

The next test in the table adds $\log PF$ to the equation, which is a test of the restriction that the coefficient of $\log PF$ is equal to the negative of the coefficient of $\log PIM$. The $\log PF$ variable is highly significant, and so the restriction is rejected. Although not shown in the table, when $\log PF$ is added to the equation, the coefficient for $\log PIM$ is −.0890 and the coefficient for $\log PF$ is .1844. The results thus suggest that the level of imports responds more to the domestic price deflator than to the import price deflator. As was the case for equation 6, this is contrary to what one expects from theory. It does not seem sensible that in the long run the level of imports rises simply from an overall rise in prices. Therefore, the relative price constraint was imposed on the equation, even though it is strongly rejected by the data.

The next test adds the level of per capita nonfarm firm sales—$\log[(X - FA)/POP]$—to the equation to see if it better explains imports than does disposable income. The χ^2 values is not significant, and so on this score the sales variable does not have independent explanatory power. On the other hand (not shown in the table), the t-statistic on the sales variable was higher (1.77) than the t-statistic on the disposable income variable (0.35). The sales variable thus dominates the disposable income variable in this sense. The consequences of using the sales variable in place of the disposable income variable are examined in Section 11.3.4.

The "other" variables that were added for the next test, which are asset, real wage, labor constraint, and nonlabor income variables, are highly significant, but (not shown in the table) they all have coefficient estimates of the wrong expected sign. Finally, the spread values are highly significant. The stability test was not performed for the import equation because of the use of the dummy variables.

Experimenting with the import equation reveals that it does much better in the tests if the relative price restriction is not imposed. In other words, when $\log PF$ is added, the equation does much better. So in summary, the import equation passes the lags and leads tests, but it fails the others. It is clearly an equation in which future research is needed.

5.8   Government Sector Equations

There is one stochastic equation for the state and local government sector, explaining unemployment insurance benefits, UB. There are two stochastic equations for the federal government sector, one explaining interest payments, $INTG$, and one explaining the three month Treasury bill rate, RS. The equation explaining RS is interpreted as an interest rate reaction function of the Federal Reserve. The equations for UB and RS are discussed in this section, and the equation for $INTG$ is discussed in the next section.

Table 5.28
Equation 28
LHS Variable is $\log U B$

Equation				χ^2 Tests			
RHS Variable	Est.	t-stat.	Test	χ^2	df	p-value
cnst	.1220	0.27	Lags	8.68	3	.0339
$\log U B_{-1}$	.2349	3.57	$RHO = 4$	5.89	3	.1168
$\log U$	1.2565	10.71	T	1.84	1	.1751
$\log W F$	.3459	4.57				
$RHO1$	.8164	14.71				
SE	.06586					
R^2	.995					
DW	2.19					
Stability Test:						
AP	T_1	T_2	λ		Break	
12.25*	1970:1	1979:4	2.75		1975:1	

Estimation period is 1954:1–1993:2.

Equation 28. $U B$, unemployment insurance benefits

Equation 28 is in log form and contains as explanatory variables the level of unemployment, the nominal wage rate, and the lagged dependent variable. The inclusion of the nominal wage rate is designed to pick up the effects of increases in wages and prices on legislated benefits per unemployed worker. The equation is estimated under the assumption of a first order autoregressive error term.

The results in Table 5.28 show that the coefficient estimates are significant except for the estimate of the constant term. The equation passes the lags, RHO=4, and T tests, and it fails the stability test.

Equation 30. $R S$, three month Treasury bill rate

A key question in any macro model is what one assumes about monetary policy. In the theoretical model monetary policy is determined by an interest rate reaction function, and in the empirical work an equation like this is estimated. This equation is interpreted as an equation explaining the behavior of the Federal Reserve (Fed).

In one respect, trying to explain Fed behavior is more difficult than, say, trying to explain the behavior of the household or firm sectors. Since the Fed is run by a relatively small number of people, there can be fairly abrupt changes in behavior if the people with influence change their minds or are replaced by others with different views. Abrupt changes are less likely to happen for the household and firm sectors because of the large number of decision makers in each sector. Having said this, however, only one abrupt change in behavior appeared evident in the data, which was between 1979:4 and 1982:3, and, as will be seen, even this change appears capable of being modeled.

Equation 30 is the estimated interest rate reaction function It has on the left hand side RS. This treatment is based on the assumption that the Fed has a target bill rate each quarter and achieves this target through manipulation of its policy instruments. The right hand side variables in this equation are variables that seem likely to affect the target rate. The variables that were chosen are 1) the rate of inflation, 2) the degree of labor market tightness, 3) the percentage change in real GDP, and 4) the percentage change in the money supply lagged one quarter. What seemed to happen between 1979:4 and 1982:3 was that the size of the coefficient of the lagged money supply growth increased substantially. This was modeled by adding the variable $D794823 \cdot PCM1_{-1}$ to the equation, where $D794823$ is a dummy variable that is 1 between 1979:4 and 1982:3 and 0 otherwise. The estimated equation also includes the lagged dependent variable and two lagged bill rate changes to pick up the dynamics.

The signs of the coefficient estimates in Table 5.30 are as expected, and the equation passes all of the tests. The results thus seem good for this equation. The stability test was not run because of the use of the dummy variable. The variables for which led values were tried are the inflation variable, the labor market tightness variable, and the percentage change in real GDP, and the led values are not significant.

Equation 30 is a "leaning against the wind" equation in the sense that the Fed is predicted to allow the bill rate to rise in response to increases in inflation, labor market tightness, real growth, and money supply growth. As just noted, the results show that the weight given to money supply growth in the setting of the bill rate target was much greater in the 1979:4–1982:3 period than either before or after.

Table 5.30
Equation 30
LHS Variable is RS

Equation				χ^2 Tests		
RHS Variable	Est.	t-stat.	Test	χ^2	df	p-value
cnst	-15.5116	-5.87	Lags	9.34	6	.1552
RS_{-1}	.8923	47.76	$RHO = 4$	3.01	4	.5565
$100[(PD/PD_{-1})^4 - 1]$	.0684	3.50	T	0.07	1	.7861
JJS	15.7411	5.91	Leads +1	1.96	3	.5806
$PCGDPR$	.0777	5.14	Leads +4	10.07	12	.6098
$PCM1_{-1}$	.0196	3.08	Leads +8	5.28	6	.5085
$D794823 \cdot PCM1_{-1}$	.2245	9.26	p_4^e	0.44	1	.5074
ΔRS_{-1}	.2033	3.36	p_8^e	0.43	1	.5096
ΔRS_{-2}	-.2964	-5.25				
SE	.50945					
R^2	.970					
DW	2.01					

Estimation period is 1954:1–1993:2.

5.9 Interest Payments Equations

Equation 19. $INTF$, interest payments—f; Equation 29. $INTG$, interest payments—g

$INTF$ is the level of net interest payments of the firm sector, and $INTG$ is the same for the federal government. Data on both of these variables are NIPA data. AF is the level of net financial assets of the firm sector, and AG is the same for the federal government. Data on both of these variables are FFA data. AF and AG are negative because the firm sector and the federal government are net debtors, and they consist of both short term and long term securities.

The current level of interest payments depends on the amount of existing securities issued at each date in the past and on the relevant interest rate prevailing at each date. The link from AF to $INTF$ (and from AG to $INTG$) is thus complicated. It depends on past issues and the interest rates paid on these issues. A number of approximations have to be made in trying to model this link, and the following is a discussion of the procedure used here.

Consider the federal government variables first. The difference $|AG| - |AG_{-1}|$ is the net change in the value of securities of the federal government between the end of the previous quarter and the end of the current quarter. The value of new securities issued by the federal government during the current quarter is this difference *plus* the value of old securities that came due during the current quarter. It is first assumed that the government issues two kinds of securities, a "short term" security, where the short term is defined to be one quarter, and a "long term" security, which is taken to be of length k quarters, where k is to be estimated. It is next assumed that λ percent of the net change in the value of securities in a quarter (i.e., of $|AG| - |AG_{-1}|$) consist of long term issues, with the rest consisting of short term issues. In addition, it is assumed that the long term securities that expire during the quarter are replaced with new long term securities. Let BG denote the value of long term securities issued during the current quarter by the federal government. Then the above assumptions imply that :

$$BG = \lambda(|AG| - |AG_{-1}|) + BG_{-k} \qquad (5.40)$$

λ is assumed to remain constant over time.

It is next assumed that the government pays an interest rate RS on its short term securities, where RS is the three month Treasury bill rate, and an interest rate $RB - \eta$ on its long term securities, where RB is the AAA bond rate and η is a constant parameter to be estimated. η is subtracted from RB because the government generally pays less than the AAA bond rate on its bonds. Given these assumptions, the interest payments of the federal government are:[17]

$$INTG = \sum_{i=-k}^{0} \frac{1}{400}(RB_i - \eta)BG_i + \frac{1}{400}RS(1 - \lambda)|AG| \qquad (5.41)$$

The interest rates are divided by 400 in this equation because they are at annual rates in percentage points and they need to be at quarterly rates in percents. ($INTG$ is at a quarterly rate.) Given the above assumptions, the value of short term securities is $(1 - \lambda)|AG|$, and so RS multiplies this. The other securities have the relevant bond rate multiplying them. For example, BG_{-1} is the value of long term securities issued last quarter, and the relevant interest rate for these securities is $RB_{-1} - \eta$. $(RB_{-1} - \eta)BG_{-1}$ is thus part of $INTG$ until the securities expire after k quarters.

Using equations 5.40 and 5.41, the aim of the estimation work is to find values of k, λ, η that lead to a good fit, i.e., that lead to the predicted values of $INTG$ from equation 5.41 being close to the actual values. This work takes as given the actual values of RS, RB, and AG. The estimation period was 1952:1–1993:2, which is the period for which data on AG exist. The

---

[17]In the notation in this equation BG_0 is the same as BG. Similarly, for the firm sector BF_0 is the same as BF.

estimation procedure was as follows. First, given a value for k and a value for λ, the value of BG for 1952:1 was taken to be equal to $(1/k)\lambda |AG_{1952:1}|$. In addition, the $k - 1$ values of BG before 1952:1 were taken to be equal to this value. Given these values, values of BG for 1952:2 through 1993:2 can be generated using equation 5.40 and the given values of k and λ. Second, if values of RB for the computations in equation 5.41 were needed before 1947:1, which is the first quarter for which data on RB exist, they were taken to be equal to the 1947:1 value. (Values before 1947:1 are needed if k is greater than 20 quarters.) Third, given the values of k and λ and the above computations and given a value for η, equation 5.41 can be used to obtain predicted values of $INTG$ for the 1952:1–1993:2 period, from which a root mean squared error (RMSE) can be computed. The entire procedure can then be repeated for a different set of values of k, λ, and η, and another RMSE computed.

A program was written to search over different sets of values of k, λ, and η and print out the RMSE for each set. The set that gave the smallest RMSE was $k = 10$, $\lambda = .72$, and $\eta = .5$, which produced a RMSE of .836. The objective function was, however, fairly flat over a number of values, and the set that was chosen for the model is $k = 16$, $\lambda = .66$, and $\eta = .4$, which produced a RMSE of .964. For the first set of values, a value of k of only 10 quarters seemed small, and so k was increased somewhat for the final set even though this resulted in some increase in RMSE.

Equation 5.40 above is equation 56 in the model, and equation 5.41 is equation 29. These two equations are presented in Table A.3 in Appendix A using the values of k, λ, and η chosen.

A similar procedure was followed for the interest payments of the firm sector, $INTF$, with two differences. First, η was taken to be zero, which means that firms are assumed to pay interest rate RB on their long term securities. Second, between 1981:3 and 1991:2 $INTF$ grew faster than seemed consistent with the values of the interest rates and AF. No values of k and λ could be found that gave sensible fits for this period. To account for this unexplained growth, a dummy variable, TI, was constructed that was 0 through 1981:2, 1 in 1981:3, 2 in 1981:4, ..., 40 in 1991:2, and 40 after 1991:2. The term γTI was then added to the equivalent of equation 5.41 for the firm sector, where γ is a coefficient to be estimated. The searching procedure for the firm sector thus consisted in searching over values of k, λ, and γ.

The set of values that gave the smallest RMSE was $k = 52$, $\lambda = .43$, and $\gamma = .40$, which produced a RMSE of 1.063. Again, the objective function was fairly flat over a number of values, and the set that was chosen for the model is $k = 40$, $\lambda = .40$, and $\gamma = .41$, which produced a RMSE of 1.144. A value of k of 52 quarters seemed large, and so k was decreased somewhat for the final set even though this resulted in some increase in RMSE.

Equation 5.40 above for the firm sector is equation 55 in the model, and equation 5.41 for the firm sector is equation 19. These two equations are also presented in Table A.3 using the values of k, λ, and γ chosen.

Although the above specification is obviously only a rough approximation of the links from interest rates, AG, and AF to interest payments, it does tie changes in these variables to changes in interest payments in a way that is not likely to deviate substantially in the long run from the true relationship. In other words, interest payments change as interest rates change and as AG and AF change in a way that seems unlikely to drift too far from the truth.[18]

It will be seen in Section 11.7 that equation 29 has an effect on the effectiveness of monetary policy in the model. As the size of the federal government debt ($|AG|$) increases, the change in interest payments of the federal government for a given change in interest rates increases in absolute value. Since households hold much of the debt, the change in interest revenue of the household sector for a given change in interest rates is getting larger in absolute value as the size of the debt increases. This income effect on households is thus increasing over time and, as will be seen, is now offsetting more of the substitution effect of a change in interest rates than it did earlier.

Finally, although equations 19 and 29 have not been estimated in a usual way, they are still stochastic equations in the sense that the predicted values from the equations do not in general equal the actual values. (Equations 55 and 56 are, however, identities because BF and BG have simply been constructed using the equations.) With respect to the notation for the model in equation 4.1 in Chapter 4, both equations 19 and 29 have in general nonzero values of u_{it}. For 3SLS and FIML estimation and the stochastic simulation work below, where an estimate of the covariance matrix of all the errors in the model is needed, the error terms for equations 19 and 29 have been used after adjusting for heteroskedasticity. The variance of the error term in equation 19

---

[18]In previous specifications of equations 19 and 29 the interest payments variables were regressed on interest rates and the value of securities. The equations were usually in log form and usually included the lagged dependent variable. For example, one version of equation 29 had log $INTG$ regressed on a constant, log $INTG_{-1}$, log$(-AG)$, log RS, and log RB. These types of equations provide a slightly better fit than the procedure discussed above, but they have poor dynamic properties. With no restrictions imposed, the predicted interest payments from the equations tend to drift away from sensible values, sensible in the sense of being consistent with the predicted values of interest rates and security issues.

was assumed to be proportional to $(AF + 10)^2$, and the variance of the error term in equation 29 was assumed to be proportional to AG^2. This means that equation 19 is divided through by $|AF + 10|$ and that equation 29 is divided through by $|AG|$ before computing the error terms to be used in estimating the covariance matrix.[19] This means that uncertainty from equations 19 and 29 is taken into account in 3SLS and FIML estimation and in the stochastic simulation work even though they are not estimated in a traditional way.

5.10 Additional Comments

The following is a discussion of some of the results that pertain to sets of equations.

1. The age variables are jointly significant at the five percent level in three of the four household expenditure equations, and the sign patterns are generally as expected. This is thus evidence that the U.S. age distribution has an effect on U.S. macroeconomic equations.[20]

2. The wealth variable is significant in two of the four household expenditure equations. Changes in stock prices thus affect expenditures in the model through their effect on household wealth.

3. At least some of the led values are significant in three of the four household expenditure equations and in one of the four labor supply equation. They are not significant at the one percent level in any of the other equations in which they were tried except for Leads +4 in the employment equation 13 and for Leads +8 in the capital gains equation 25. They are significant at the five percent level in eight other cases: 1) Leads +4 in equation 5, 2) Leads +1 in equation 11, 3) Leads +8 in equation 12, 4) Leads +1 in equation 13, 5) Leads +8 in equation 13, 6) Leads +4 in equation 24, 7) Leads +8 in equation 24, and 8) Leads +4 in equation 27. There is thus some evidence that the rational expectations assumption is helpful in explaining household behavior, but only slight evidence

---

[19] AF is close to zero for the first few quarters of the estimation period, and this is the reason for adding 10 to it.

[20] This same conclusion was also reached in Fair and Dominguez (1991). In Fair and Dominguez (1991), contrary to the case here, the age variables were also significant in the equation explaining IHH.

that it is helpful in explaining other behavior.[21] As noted previously, the economic consequences of the rational expectations assumption are examined in Section 11.6.

4. The evidence suggests that nominal interest rates rather than real interest rates affect household expenditures and imports. The inflation expectations variables are not significant in the four expenditure equations, and their coefficient estimates have the wrong expected sign in the import equation.

5. In all three of the money demand equations the nominal adjustment specification dominates the real adjustment specification. The nominal adjustment specification is equation 5.12.

6. All but 3 of 28 equations passed the lags test; all but 3 of 23 passed the T test; 18 of 28 passed the RHO=4 test; and 14 of 23 passed the stability test. The overall results thus suggest that the specifications of the equations are fairly accurate regarding dynamic and trend effects, but less so regarding the serial correlation properties of the error terms and stability. Given the number of equations that failed the stability test, it may be useful in future work to break some of the estimation periods in parts, but in general it seems that more observations are needed before this might be a sensible strategy.

7. The labor constraint variable (Z) is significant or close to significant in the four labor supply equations, suggesting that there is a discouraged worker effect in operation.

8. The excess labor variable is significant in the employment and hours equations, 13 and 14, but the excess capital variable is not significant in the investment equation 12.

9. Either the short term or long term interest rate is significant in the four household expenditure equations. Also, interest income is part of disposable personal income (YD), which is significant or nearly significant in the four equations. Therefore, an increase in interest rates has a negative effect on household expenditures through the interest rate variables

---

[21] This general conclusion is consistent with the results in Fair (1993b), Table 1, where led values were significant in three of the four household expenditure equations and in two of the four labor supply equations, but in almost none of the other equations.

and a positive effect through the disposable personal income variable. More will be said about this in Chapter 11.

10. There is a fairly small use of dummy variables in the equations. One appears in equations 13 and 14 to pick up a structural break; two appear in equation 21 to pick up an unexplained increase in capital consumption; four appear in equation 27 to pick up the effects of two dock strikes; one appears in equation 30 to pick up a shift of Fed behavior between 1979:4 and 1982:3; and one appears in equation 19 to pick up an unexplained increase in interest payments of the firm sector.

11. The level form of the price equation is not rejected, and the change form is strongly rejected. This result is consistent with the results of estimating highly disaggregate price equations in Fair (1993a), where the level form gave somewhat better results. The acceptance of the level form over the change form has important implications for the long run properties of the model. A permanent change in demand in the model does not have a permanent effect on the rate of inflation, only on the price level. The real wage constraint in the wage equation is not rejected, and so the data suggest that the real wage rate is not a function of the level of prices or nominal wage rates, which is as expected. On the other hand, the data have little to say about the behavior of prices in very high activity periods. One would expect there to be important nonlinearities in the behavior of prices as the economy moves into very high activity levels (and very low levels of unemployment), but this effect cannot be picked up in the data.

12. The spread values are highly significant in the consumption of durables and import equations. They are significant at the five but not one percent level in the consumption of nondurables equation. They are not significant in the housing investment equation 4, the production equation 11, and the investment equation 12. The evidence is thus mixed. If there is an effect of the spread values on the economy, it appears to come through the effects on household behavior rather than on firm behavior. This is not necessarily what one would expect from the discussion in Friedman and Kuttner (1993), where the stress is on the effects of the spread on investment behavior. This is perhaps an area for future research.

13. Four of the most serious negative test results are the highly significant time trends in equations 1 and 3, the significance of log PH in equation

6, and the significance of $\log PF$ in equation 27. Future work is needed on these equations.

6

The Stochastic Equations
of the ROW Model

6.1 Introduction

The stochastic equations of the ROW model are specified, estimated, and tested in this chapter. This chapter does for the ROW model what Chapter 5 did for the US model. Stochastic equations are estimated for 32 countries, with up to 15 equations estimated per country. The equations are listed in Table B.3, and they were briefly discussed in Section 3.3.5. The empirical results are presented in Tables 6.1a and 6.1b through 6.15a and 6.15b, one pair of tables per equation. The "a" part of each table presents the estimates of the "final" specification, and the "b" part presents the results of the tests.

The 2SLS technique was used for the quarterly countries and for equations 1, 2, and 3 for the annual countries. The OLS technique was used for the other equations for the annual countries. The 2SLS technique had to be used sparingly for the annual countries because of the limited number of observations. The selection criterion for the first stage regressors for each equation was the same as that used for the US model. Briefly, the main predetermined variables in each country's model were chosen to constitute a "basic" set, and other variables were added to this set for each individual equation. As noted in Chapter 5, the choice of first stage regressors for large scale models is discussed in Fair (1984), pp. 215–216.

The estimation periods were chosen based on data availability. With three exceptions, the periods were chosen to use all the available data. The three exceptions are the interest rate, exchange rate, and forward rate equations, where the estimation periods were chosen to begin after the advent of floating exchange rates. The earliest starting quarter (year) for these periods was 1972:2 (1972).

The tests are similar to those done for the US equations. To repeat from Chapter 5, the basic tests are 1) adding lagged values, 2) estimating the equation under the assumption of a fourth order autoregressive process for the error term, 3) adding a time trend, 4) adding values led one or more periods, 5) adding additional variables, and 6) testing for structural stability. For the annual countries the autoregressive process for the error term was taken to be third order rather than fourth order. Because of this, the notation "RHO+" instead of "RHO=4" is used in the tables in this chapter to denote the autoregressive test. The led values were one quarter ahead for the quarterly countries and one year ahead for the annual countries. This means that no moving average process of the error term has to be accounted for since the leads are only one period. The estimation periods used for the leads test were one period shorter than the regular periods because of the need to make room at the end of the sample for the led values.

One of the additional variables added, where appropriate, was the expected rate of inflation. As discussed in Chapter 5, this is a test of the nominal versus real interest rate specification. For the quarterly countries the expected rate of inflation was taken to be the actual rate of inflation during the past four quarters, and for the annual countries it was taken to be the inflation rate (at an annual rate) during the past two years. This measure of the expected rate of inflation will be denoted p^e. This variable was only added to the equations in which an interest rate was included as an explanatory variable in the final specification.

Specification

In Section 3.3.5 the equations of the econometric model were matched to the equations of the theoretical model of Section 2.2. This is a guide for the theory behind the model and in particular for the theory behind the linking together of the countries. Also, subject to data limitations, the specification of the ROW equations follows fairly closely the specification of the US equations, and so the theory in Section 2.1 that is behind the specification of the US model is relevant here.

The extra theorizing that is discussed at the beginning of Chapter 5 is also relevant here. For example, the searching procedure was the same as that used for the US equations. Lagged dependent variables were used extensively to try to account for expectational and lagged adjustment effects, and explanatory variables were dropped from the equations if they had coefficient estimates of the wrong expected sign. Both current and one quarter lagged values were generally tried for the price and interest rate variables for the quarterly countries, and the values that gave the best results were used. The equations were initially estimated under the assumption of a first order autoregressive error term, and the autoregressive assumption was retained if the estimate of the autoregressive coefficient was significant.

Data limitations prevented all 15 equations from being estimated for all 32 countries. Also, some equations for some countries were initially estimated and then rejected for giving what seemed to be poor results. For example, as will be seen, the rejection rate was high for the investment equation (equation 3), where many of the coefficient estimates of the output term seemed too large.

One difference between the US and ROW models to be aware of is that the asset variable A for each country in the ROW model measures only the net asset position of the country vis-à-vis the rest of the world; it does not include the domestic wealth of the country. Also, the asset variable has been divided by $PY \cdot YS$ before it was entered as an explanatory variable in the equations. (PY is the GDP deflator and YS is potential GDP.) This was done even for equations that were otherwise in log form. As discussed in Section 3.3.3, the asset variable is off by a constant amount, and so taking logs of the variable is not appropriate. Entering the variable in ratio form in the equations allows the error to be approximately[1] absorbed in the estimate of the constant term. This procedure is, of course, crude, but at least it somewhat responds to the problem caused by the level error in A.

Because much of the specification of the ROW equations is close to that of the US equations, the specification discussion in this chapter is brief. Only the differences are emphasized, and the reader is referred to Chapter 5 for more detail regarding the basic specifications.

The Tables

The construction of the tables in this chapter is as follows. All the coefficient estimates in an equation are presented in a table if there is room. If there is

---

[1]If the level error, say $\bar{A}$, is in A and not in $A/(PY \cdot YS)$, then including the latter variable in the equation means that it is not $\bar{A}$ but $\bar{A}/(PY \cdot YS)$ that is part of the equation, and $\bar{A}/(PY \cdot YS)$ is not constant. This is what is meant by the error being only approximately absorbed in the estimate of the constant term.

a space constraint, the estimate of the constant term is not presented. The R^2 values is also not presented if there is limited space. In a few cases other coefficient estimates are also not presented because of space limitations, and when this happens it is discussed in the text. The sample period that was used for the estimation of each equation is presented in the b tables except for equation 10, where the sample periods are presented in the a table. (There is no b table for equation 10.)

To save space, only the p-values are presented in the b tables for the χ^2 tests. As in Chapter 5, an equation will be said to pass a test if the p-value is greater than .01. For the stability test the AP value is presented along with the degrees of freedom and the value of λ. Many of the values of λ for the annual countries are 1.0, which means that only one possible break point was specified. This was done because of the short sample periods. The AP value has a * in front of it if it is significant at the one percent level, which means that the equation fails the stability test.

There are obviously a lot of estimates and test results in this chapter, and it is not feasible to discuss each estimate and test result in detail. The following discussion tries to give a general idea of the results, but the reader is left to pour over the tables in more detail if desired.

Previous Version of the ROW Model

The previous version of the ROW model is presented in Fair (1984), Chapter 4. Again, as with the US model, the present discussion of the model is self contained, and so this previous material does not have to be read. More changes have been made to the ROW model since 1984 than have been made to the US model. Some of the main changes are the following. First, the number of countries (not counting the United States) for which structural equations are estimated is now 32 rather than 42, and the trade share matrix is now 45×45 rather than 65×65. The model was cut in size to lessen problems caused by poor data. Second, OECD data were used whenever possible rather than IFS data. The OECD has better NIPA and labor data than is available from the IFS data. Third, annual data were used for countries in which only annual NIPA data existed. In the previous version, quarterly data were constructed for all the countries by interpolating the annual data. Fourth, wage, employment, and labor force equations were added to the model (equations 12–15). Fifth, estimates of the capital stock of each country were made, and the capital stock variable was used in the investment equation. Finally, as for the US model, a few more coefficient constraints were imposed.

The basic structure of the ROW model has, however, remained the same between the previous version and the current version, and some of the discussion in the following sections is similar to the discussion of the previous version in Sections 4.2.5 and 4.2.6 in Fair (1984).

6.2 Equation 1. *M*: Merchandise Imports

Equation 1 explains the real per capita merchandise imports of the country. The explanatory variables include price of domestic goods relative to the price of imports, the short term or long term interest rate, per capita income, the lagged value of real per capita assets, and the lagged dependent variable. The variables are in logs except for the interest rates and the asset variable. Equation 1 is similar to equation 27 in the US model. The three main differences between the equations are 1) the U.S. asset variable was not significant in equation 27 and so was dropped from the equation, 2) the import variable includes all imports in equation 27 but only merchandise imports in equation 1, and 3) the income variable is disposable personal income in equation 27 and total GDP in equation 1.

To save space, Table 6.1a does not include the estimate of the constant term. The results in Tables 6.1a and 6.1b show that reasonable import equations seem capable of being estimated for most countries. Only for Switzerland (ST) is the coefficient estimate for income of the wrong expected sign, although it is not significant. Four of the 32 equations fail the lags test (at the one percent level), 5 fail the RHO+ test, 9 fail the T test, and 14 fail the stability test. The led value of the income variable was used for the leads test, and it is significant at the one percent level in only 1 case. The expected inflation variable is relevant for 9 countries,[2] and it is only significant for 1. For the countries in which the relative price variable was used, the log of the domestic price level was added to test the relative price constraint. The constraint was rejected (i.e., log PY was significant) in 7 of the 23 cases.

6.3 Equation 2: *C*: Consumption

Equation 2 explains real per capita consumption. The explanatory variables include the short term or long term interest rate, per capita income, the lagged

---

[2]Remember that the expected inflation variable is relevant if an interest rate appears as an explanatory variable in the equation.

Table 6.1a

$$\log(M/POP) = a_1 + a_2 \log(M/POP)_{-1} + a_3 \log(PY/PM) + a_4(RS or RB)$$
$$+ a_5 \log(Y/POP) + a_6[A/(PY \cdot YS)]_{-1}$$

	a_2	a_3	a_4	a_5	a_6	ρ	SE	DW
Quarterly								
CA	.723	.205	^{ab}-.0072	.485	.073	–	.0392	2.08
	(13.83)	(2.90)	(-2.39)	(5.65)	(2.29)			
JA	.830	.053	^{a}-.0026	.173	–	–	.0395	1.84
	(16.51)	(2.64)	(-1.09)	(2.51)				
AU	.634	^{a}.195	-.0024	.651	–	-.243	.0384	1.96
	(4.56)	(2.14)	(-0.82)	(2.59)		(-1.77)		
FR	.282	–	^{a}-.0054	1.941	.404	–	.0291	2.01
	(3.16)		(-4.61)	(8.07)	(4.68)			
GE	.648	.022	-.0018	.622	.035	–	.0268	1.98
	(7.98)	(0.53)	(-1.49)	(3.49)	(1.21)			
IT	.125	.199	–	1.592	.298	–	.0533	2.05
	(1.25)	(4.82)		(7.31)	(3.51)			
NE	.893	^{a}.055	–	.200	–	-.402	.0280	1.78
	(7.75)	(1.37)		(0.82)		(-2.86)		
ST	.867	–	–	-.283	.117	–	.0369	2.14
	(11.72)			(-1.12)	(3.24)			
UK	.565	–	–	.912	.035	–	.0346	1.86
	(7.24)			(5.52)	(1.37)			
FI	.184	^{a}.274	–	.831	.272	–	.0767	2.13
	(1.44)	(2.11)		(4.55)	(2.29)			
AS	.639	.306	–	.996	.100	–	.0459	1.82
	(10.93)	(5.67)		(6.34)	(2.87)			
SO	.765	.213	^{a}-.0073	.638	.101	-.208	.0783	1.96
	(14.85)	(2.77)	(-4.42)	(4.69)	(4.74)	(-2.05)		
KO	.872	.066	–	.193	–	–	.1047	2.01
	(18.12)	(0.83)		(2.48)				
Annual								
BE	.126	.206	–	1.673	–	–	.0257	1.66
	(1.04)	(3.56)		(6.59)				
DE	.212	.219	-.0016	1.866	1.682	–	.0244	2.53
	(2.18)	(2.58)	(-0.57)	(8.73)	(5.82)			
NO	.229	–	^{b}-.0168	.744	.401	–	.0540	2.13
	(1.22)		(-1.49)	(2.87)	(3.18)			
SW	–	.169	–	1.989	–	–	.0422	2.33
		(1.81)		(23.79)				
GR	.253	.282	–	1.274	.516	–	.0830	1.78
	(1.19)	(1.29)		(3.08)	(0.63)			
IR	.303	.180	–	1.137	.282	–	.0556	1.91
	(1.57)	(1.80)		(3.94)	(1.52)			
PO	.758	–	^{b}-.0080	.655	–	–	.1115	1.24
	(5.65)		(-1.25)	(2.32)				
SP	.593	.289	–	1.004	1.166	–	.0574	1.79
	(3.74)	(3.06)		(2.18)	(2.16)			
NZ	.141	.327	–	1.911	.470	–	.0767	2.21
	(0.96)	(3.03)		(6.21)	(1.78)			
SA	.830	–	–	.688	–	–	.1002	1.20
	(23.72)			(5.68)				
VE	.324	.622	–	2.020	.744	–	.1596	1.70
	(2.41)	(2.47)		(3.94)	(2.18)			
CO	.328	.538	–	1.199	.893	–	.0767	2.21
	(2.16)	(1.83)		(4.21)	(2.68)			
JO	.735	.265	–	.273	.960	–	.1043	1.92
	(4.47)	(1.06)		(0.82)	(2.95)			
SY	.250	–	–	.465	.953	–	.2217	2.05
	(1.17)			(1.94)	(1.19)			
ID	.670	–	–	.514	.744	–	.1487	1.90
	(4.22)			(2.01)	(0.80)			
MA	.356	.441	–	1.096	.280	–	.0590	2.21
	(2.25)	(2.70)		(4.92)	(1.70)			
PA	.474	.488	–	.492	–	–	.0661	1.79
	(6.32)	(3.37)		(3.59)				
PH	.478	–	–	.961	.659	–	.1900	1.55
	(2.93)			(2.67)	(1.40)			
TH	.229	.486	–	1.381	1.116	–	.0815	.80
	(1.50)	(3.37)		(5.51)	(3.28)			

^{a} Variable lagged once. ^{b} RB rather than RS.

Table 6.1b
Test Results for Equation 1

	Lags p-val	p^e p-val	log PY p-val	RHO+ p-val	T p-val	Leads p-val	Stability AP (df) λ	Sample
Quarterly								
CA	.094	.095	.315	.926	.289	.357	5.94 (6) 4.25	1966:1–1992:3
JA	.251	.119	.679	.276	.052	.666	5.88 (5) 3.57	1967:3–1992:3
AU	.097	.087	^{a}.008	.286	.113	.375	4.00 (6) 2.21	1971:1–1991:2
FR	.031	.948	–	.398	.269	.537	6.33 (5) 2.03	1971:1–1992:2
GE	.052	.184	.876	.132	.490	.022	*9.03 (6) 1.57	1969:1–1991:4
IT	.007	–	.000	.001	.001	.532	*9.70 (5) 2.00	1972:1–1991:4
NE	.060	–	^{a}.011	.065	.003	.004	*7.83 (5) 1.00	1978:2–1991:4
ST	.004	–	–	.009	.110	.093	*12.88 (4) 2.17	1971:1–1991:4
UK	.325	–	–	.434	.785	.026	5.54 (4) 3.92	1966:1–1992:3
FI	.017	–	^{a}.000	.000	.000	.531	*10.11 (5) 1.00	1976:1–1991:4
AS	.237	–	.406	.177	.545	.320	3.47 (5) 1.69	1971:1–1992:2
SO	.225	.341	.015	.422	.005	.100	*42.02 (7) 4.51	1962:1–1991:2
KO	.521	–	.387	.000	.736	.997	*10.94 (4) 2.03	1964:1–1991:4
Annual								
BE	.365	–	.508	.369	.865	.479	5.73 (4) 1.00	1969–1990
DE	.199	.699	.971	.061	.721	.309	3.06 (6) 1.00	1969–1990
NO	.153	.841	–	.189	.381	.072	3.77 (5) 1.00	1974–1990
SW	.300	–	.858	.427	.790	.391	2.42 (3) 1.00	1969–1990
GR	.884	–	.005	.681	.006	.704	4.94 (5) 1.00	1963–1990
IR	.044	–	.001	.873	.734	.994	*12.71 (5) 1.00	1969–1990
PO	.002	.000	–	.125	.001	.202	*28.35 (4) 1.00	1962–1990
SP	.049	–	.007	.379	.003	.352	*12.22 (5) 1.00	1969–1990
NZ	.588	–	.518	.362	.392	.733	2.07 (5) 1.00	1962–1990
SA	.572	–	–	.002	.230	.794	1.17 (3) 1.00	1970–1989
VE	.805	–	.000	.302	.003	.952	*9.57 (5) 1.00	1963–1991
CO	.381	–	.081	.023	.081	.070	*7.62 (5) 1.00	1972–1991
JO	.434	–	.014	.214	.068	.127	1.48 (5) 1.00	1971–1991
SY	.113	–	–	.654	.206	.066	1.73 (4) 1.00	1965–1990
ID	.363	–	–	.748	.889	.786	6.51 (4) 1.00	1962–1989
MA	.446	–	.721	.285	.653	.054	5.31 (5) 1.00	1972–1987
PA	.145	–	.099	.891	.439	.974	*13.39 (4) 1.00	1972–1991
PH	.150	–	–	.154	.020	.467	5.97 (4) 1.00	1962–1991
TH	.000	–	.806	.014	.000	.204	*18.57 (5) 1.00	1962–1990

^{a} log PY_{-1} used rather than log PY.
*Significant at the one percent level.

value of real per capita assets, and the lagged dependent variable. The variables are in logs except for the interest rates and the asset variable. Equation 2 is similar to the consumption equations in the US model. The two main differences are 1) there is only one category of consumption in the ROW model compared to three in the US model and 2) the income variable is total GDP instead of disposable personal income.

As in Table 6.1a, the estimate of the constant term is not presented in Table 6.2a. The results in Tables 6.2a and 6.2b are of similar quality to the results in Tables 6.1a and 6.1b. The interest rate and asset variables appear in most of the equations in Table 6.2a, and so interest rate and wealth effects on consumption have been picked up as well as the usual income effect.

Most of the tests in Table 6.2b are passed. Eight of the 32 equations fail the lags test, 3 fail the RHO+ test, 5 fail the leads test,[3] and 9 fail the stability

---

[3] Multicollinearity problems prevented the leads test from being computed for the UK.

Table 6.2a

$$\log(C/POP) = a_1 + a_2 \log(C/POP)_{-1} + a_3(RS \, or \, RB)$$
$$+a_4 \log(Y/POP) + a_5[A/(PY \cdot YS)]_{-1}$$

	a_1	a_2	a_3	a_4	a_5	ρ	SE	DW
Quarterly								
CA	-.268	.836	^{ab}-.0017	.189	.026	-.166	.0082	1.97
	(-4.35)	(15.82)	(-4.25)	(3.46)	(4.20)	(-1.65)		
JA	.123	.882	^{b}-.0022	.093	–	-.286	.0101	2.11
	(4.90)	(19.87)	(-3.08)	(2.21)		(-2.87)		
AU	-.622	.254	–	.802	–	–	.0139	1.54
	(-6.58)	(2.76)		(7.91)				
FR	-.098	.853	^{a}-.0007	.160		–	.0069	2.31
	(-1.19)	(9.46)	(-2.65)	(1.55)				
GE	.018	.923	-.0013	.051	.011	-.263	.0060	2.02
	(0.75)	(34.96)	(-5.98)	(1.64)	(3.16)	(-2.54)		
IT	-.340	.821	-.0011	.213	–	.557	.0036	1.85
	(-2.80)	(15.32)	(-4.81)	(3.31)		(5.96)		
NE	-.088	.899	–	.120	–	–	.0085	2.27
	(-2.14)	(12.57)		(2.00)				
ST	.079	.732	-.0029	.164	.017	.404	.0062	1.73
	(0.70)	(8.43)	(-2.98)	(1.85)	(1.85)	(2.89)		
UK	-.359	.895	^{a}-.0017	.151	.021	–	.0112	2.60
	(-3.36)	(22.17)	(-3.68)	(2.99)	(2.52)			
FI	-.127	.689	-.0029	.309	–	–	.0093	2.07
	(-1.43)	(13.75)	(-4.48)	(6.25)				
AS	-.529	.905	-.0010	.157	.013	–	.0078	2.05
	(-2.59)	(21.53)	(-2.36)	(3.27)	(2.21)			
SO	-.518	.975	^{b}-.0019	.102	.016	-.253	.0142	1.92
	(-3.35)	(23.22)	(-2.47)	(2.04)	(4.00)	(-2.68)		
KO	.166	.861	-.0012	.106	.032	–	.0555	2.04
	(1.63)	(18.29)	(-0.94)	(2.61)	(1.91)			
Annual								
BE	-.059	.698	^{b}-.0051	.302	–	–	.0123	2.12
	(-0.34)	(4.39)	(-2.26)	(1.81)				
DE	-.937	.451	^{b}-.0024	.720	.617	–	.0179	1.49
	(-1.64)	(3.37)	(-1.78)	(4.93)	(3.01)			
NO	.593	.243	–	.519	.052	–	.0254	1.34
	(2.62)	(1.05)		(2.63)	(0.92)			
SW	-.113	.467	–	.495	.398	–	.0129	1.50
	(-0.67)	(4.73)		(5.35)	(3.97)			
GR	.013	.540	–	.427		–	.0135	1.48
	(0.13)	(5.39)		(3.99)				
IR	.910	.422	–	.449	.231	–	.0244	1.51
	(1.51)	(2.57)		(4.03)	(2.91)			
PO	-.436	.537	^{b}-.0044	.524	.050	–	.0357	2.22
	(-1.86)	(6.21)	(-1.08)	(5.78)	(1.09)			
SP	-.023	.468	–	.506	.272	–	.0110	1.29
	(-0.19)	(5.68)		(6.12)	(2.43)			
NZ	-.396	.357	^{b}-.0048	.666	.136	–	.0176	1.68
	(-0.69)	(3.07)	(-2.21)	(5.99)	(1.74)			
SA	-.481	.842	–	.196	.190	.396	.1439	1.88
	(-0.42)	(5.42)		(0.59)	(0.70)	(0.92)		
VE	-.198	.965	-.0009	.087	.186	-.227	.0588	1.96
	(-0.48)	(20.57)	(-0.89)	(0.73)	(1.64)	(-1.10)		
CO	–	.464	–	.499	–	–	.0272	1.83
		(2.73)		(3.18)				
JO	-1.233	.568	–	.625	.455	-.337	.0504	2.36
	(-4.70)	(5.70)		(5.11)	(3.44)	(-1.50)		
SY	.980	.634	–	.246	.962	–	.1059	1.87
	(1.24)	(4.36)		(1.78)	(2.45)			
ID	.022	.383	-.0091	.497	.268	-.520	.0266	2.23
	(0.69)	(3.04)	(-3.85)	(5.41)	(2.38)	(-2.77)		
MA	-.910	.354	–	.709	.338	–	.0342	1.75
	(-1.61)	(1.99)		(3.72)	(3.94)			
PA	.100	.842	–	.079	–	-.183	.0319	1.88
	(1.48)	(6.53)		(0.60)		(-2.49)		
PH	.509	.477	–	.257	.159	–	.0313	1.65
	(2.45)	(3.20)		(2.96)	(2.05)			
TH	-.027	.530	–	.454	.297	–	.0248	2.22
	(-0.37)	(5.24)		(5.21)	(3.30)			

^{a} Variable lagged once. ^{b} RB rather than RS.

Table 6.2b
Test Results for Equation 2

	Lags p-val	p^e p-val	RHO+ p-val	T p-val	Leads p-val	Stability AP (df) λ	Sample
Quarterly							
CA	.006	.940	.383	.299	.003	*19.08 (6) 4.248	1966:1–1992.3
JA	.002	.513	.172	.783	.241	4.56 (5) 3.57	1967:3–1992:3
AU	.000	–	.000	.390	.306	3.03 (3) 2.21	1971:1–1991:2
FR	.001	.695	.067	.022	.003	6.61 (4) 2.03	1971:1–1992:2
GE	.085	.773	.047	.941	.015	7.46 (6) 2.66	1969:1–1991:4
IT	.118	.106	.024	.585	.008	3.06 (5) 2.01	1972:1–1991:4
NE	.892	–	.178	.621	.000	3.24 (3) 1.00	1978:2–1991:4
ST	.020	.007	.003	.001	.836	7.03 (6) 2.17	1971:1–1991:4
UK	.021	–	.047	.361	–	*11.39 (6) 3.92	1966:1–1992:3
FI	.048	.317	.139	.708	.909	5.09 (4) 1.00	1976:1–1991:4
AS	.905	.893	.258	.000	.188	*9.99 (5) 1.69	1971:1–1992:2
SO	.001	.007	.507	.002	.003	*13.41 (6) 3.28	1962:1–1991:2
KO	.104	.828	.085	.125	.818	*8.99 (5) 2.03	1964:1–1991:4
Annual							
BE	.288	.968	.892	.150	.241	2.63 (4) 1.00	1969–1990
DE	.077	.357	.398	.590	.048	0.98 (5) 1.00	1969–1990
NO	.005	–	.150	.003	.616	2.59 (4) 1.00	1974–1990
SW	.547	–	.747	.114	.980	1.71 (4) 1.00	1969–1990
GR	.048	–	.698	.000	.331	2.48 (3) 1.00	1963–1990
IR	.839	–	.270	.905	.298	4.18 (4) 1.00	1969–1990
PO	.779	.519	.288	.160	.244	6.28 (5) 1.00	1962–1990
SP	.108	–	.110	.000	.755	*13.26 (4) 1.00	1969–1990
NZ	.292	.304	.218	.659	.033	5.44 (5) 1.00	1962–1990
SA	.205	–	.392	.921	.083	*9.07 (5) 1.00	1970–1989
VE	.106	.030	.872	.006	.578	6.20 (6) 1.00	1963–1991
CO	.786	–	.281	.017	.471	0.98 (2) 1.00	1972–1991
JO	.099	–	.076	.968	.114	3.87 (5) 1.00	1971–1991
SY	.001	–	.000	.000	.886	2.27 (4) 1.00	1965–1990
ID	.119	.070	.193	.755	.189	5.85 (6) 1.00	1962–1989
MA	.448	–	.102	.016	.506	0.75 (4) 1.00	1972–1987
PA	.000	–	.155	.510	.531	*6.35 (3) 1.00	1973–1991
PH	.101	–	.236	.444	.613	2.19 (4) 1.00	1962–1991
TH	.191	–	.292	.209	.324	*13.57 (4) 1.00	1962–1990

*Significant at the one percent level.

test. The led value of the income variable was used for the leads test, and it is significant in only 5 cases. The expected inflation variable is relevant for 16 countries,[4] and it is only significant for 2.

6.4 Equation 3: I: Fixed Investment

Equation 3 explains real fixed investment. It includes as explanatory variables the lagged value of investment, the lagged value of the capital stock, the current

---

[4]Multicollinearity problems also prevented the χ^2 test from being performed for the UK for the p^e case.

Table 6.3a

$$I = a_1 + a_2 I_{-1} + a_3 K_{-1} + a_4 Y + a_5(RS\,or\,RB)$$

	a_2	a_3	a_4	a_5	SE	DW	β	α_1
Quarterly								
CA	.928	-.0019	.042	[ab]-38.10	464.3035	1.38	.041	14.04
	(20.02)	(-1.90)	(4.17)	(-0.75)				
JA	.946	-.0044	.071	[ab]-122.69	343.8421	1.82	.095	13.61
	(34.50)	(-2.13)	(2.17)	(-4.04)				
FR	.799	-.0139	.178	-.23	1.7454	1.87	.084	10.50
	(21.77)	(-5.32)	(5.53)	(-2.52)				
GE	.858	-.0094	.121	-.22	1.3839	1.93	.081	10.50
	(17.66)	(-5.08)	(4.91)	(-3.00)				
IT	.798	-.0089	.117	[b]-85.92	538.3504	1.63	.059	9.84
	(22.18)	(-4.73)	(5.66)	(-4.86)				
UK	.788	-.0086	.115	[a] 50.06	379.5534	2.25	.055	9.77
	(20.66)	(-4.46)	(5.77)	(-2.97)				
SO	.887	-.0032	.096	[ab]-54.80	263.6513	2.57	.043	19.64
	(27.25)	(-1.59)	(3.57)	(-2.21)				
Annual								
BE	.745	-.1083	.329	[b]-8.62	29.1172	2.27	.485	2.66
	(7.52)	(-3.41)	(4.06)	(-1.59)				
DE	.607	-.1122	.271	–	6.8804	1.62	.346	1.99
	(5.39)	(-4.51)	(4.44)					
SW	.786	-.1195	.339	–	4.8812	2.26	.619	2.56
	(7.86)	(-4.30)	(4.72)					
GR	.468	-.1724	.525	–	41.3807	1.96	.384	2.57
	(5.47)	(-5.55)	(5.69)					
IR	.799	-.0976	.267	–	216.9135	2.54	.545	2.44
	(7.46)	(-3.60)	(3.98)					
SA	.688	-.0238	.152	–	9.6964	1.45	.136	3.59
	(4.18)	(-1.56)	(2.54)					
PH	.677	-.0392	.220	-1.83	8.9770	1.52	.182	3.75
	(7.70)	(-2.93)	(4.97)	(-2.95)				

[a] Variable lagged once. [b] RB rather than RS.

value of output, and the short term or long term interest rate. Equation 3 differs from the investment equation 12 for the US model. The use of equations 5.23–5.25 in Chapter 5, which lead to the estimated equation 5.26, did not produce sensible results for most countries. Typically, the coefficient estimate of the current change in output term seemed much too large. Equation 3 instead is based on the following simpler set of equations:

$$K^{**} = \alpha_0 + \alpha_1 Y + \alpha_2 RB \tag{6.1}$$

$$K^* - K_{-1} = \beta(K^{**} - K_{-1}) \tag{6.2}$$

$$I^* = K^* - K_{-1} + \delta K_{-1} \tag{6.3}$$

$$I - I_{-1} = \lambda(I^* - I_{-1}) \tag{6.4}$$

Table 6.3b
Test Results for Equation 3

	Lags p-val	p^e p-val	RHO+ p-val	T p-val	Leads p-val	Stability AP (df) λ	Sample
Quarterly							
CA	.016	.630	.059	.430	.008	*11.59 (6) 4.25	1966:1–1992:3
JA	.000	.026	.368	.155	.005	*32.40 (5) 3.46	1967:3–1992:3
FR	.004	.251	.603	.755	.001	2.74 (5) 2.03	1971:1–1992:2
GE	.000	.842	.014	.012	.005	*8.72 (5) 2.66	1969:1–1991:4
IT	.003	.757	.186	.079	.002	*8.00 (5) 1.98	1972:1–1991:4
UK	.021	.975	.577	.255	.490	4.13 (5) 3.92	1966:1–1992:3
SO	.054	.222	.570	.003	.046	5.63 (5) 3.28	1962:1–1991:2
Annual							
BE	.113	.197	.655	.947	.948	*26.98 (5) 1.00	1969–1990
DE	.000	–	.008	.000	.693	*14.68 (4) 1.00	1969–1990
SW	.328	–	.453	.967	.812	2.69 (4) 1.00	1969–1990
GR	.671	–	.919	.293	.259	6.42 (4) 1.00	1963–1990
IR	.129	–	.948	.883	.320	3.99 (4) 1.00	1969–1990
SA	.205	–	.018	.359	.566	0.60 (4) 1.00	1970–1989
PH	.003	.066	.001	.000	.000	*9.47 (5) 1.00	1962–1991

*Significant at the one percent level.

K^{**} in equation 6.1 is the capital stock that would be desired if there were no adjustment costs of any kind. It is taken to be a function of output and the interest rate. As was the case for the stock of durable goods and the stock of housing in the US model in Chapter 5, two types of partial adjustment are postulated. The first, equation 6.2, is an adjustment of the capital stock, where K^* is the capital stock that would be desired if there were no costs of adjusting gross investment. Given K^*, "desired" gross investment, I^*, is determined by equation 6.3, where δ is the depreciation rate. (As discussed in Chapter 3, δ is .015 for the quarterly countries and .06 for the annual countries.) By definition, $I = K - K_{-1} + \delta K_{-1}$, and equation 6.3 is the same equation for the desired values. The second type of adjustment is an adjustment of gross investment to its desired value, which is equation 6.4.

Combining equations 6.1–6.4 yields:

$$I = (1 - \lambda)I_{-1} + \lambda(\delta - \beta)K_{-1} + \beta\lambda\alpha_0$$

$$+ \beta\lambda\alpha_1 Y + \beta\lambda\alpha_2 RB \tag{6.5}$$

Gross investment is thus a function of its lagged value, the lagged value of the capital stock, current output, and the interest rate. As was the case for durable consumption and housing investment in Chapter 5, the two partial adjustment equations are a way of adding both the lagged dependent variable and the lagged stock to the equation.

Table 6.4a

$$Y = a_1 + a_2 Y_{-1} + a_3 X + a_4 V_{-1}$$

	a_2	a_3	a_4	ρ	SE	DW	α	β
Quarterly								
CA	.305	.724	-.0622	.705	562.66	2.16	.090	.466
	(4.29)	(9.32)	(-1.58)	(7.71)				
JA	.326	.717	-.0645	.198	252.62	1.96	.096	.666
	(5.68)	(12.38)	(-5.78)	(1.78)				
AU	.594	.446	-.0229	–	2.67	1.97	.056	1.750
	(7.39)	(4.96)	(-0.78)					
FR	.667	.442	-.0901	–	3.00	1.85	.271	1.209
	(10.53)	(6.67)	(-5.98)					
GE	.245	.801	-.0822	.731	1.96	2.07	.109	.556
	(3.64)	(11.08)	(-1.91)	(7.50)				
IT	.624	.495	-.0593	.531	1194.83	2.03	.158	2.006
	(5.09)	(3.37)	(-1.60)	(4.50)				
NE	.315	.856	-.3792	.632	.70	2.21	.553	.452
	(7.47)	(12.76)	(-2.16)	(2.89)				
UK	.171	.874	-.0984	.645	544.22	2.01	.119	.461
	(3.95)	(17.15)	(-1.91)	(6.24)				
FI	.628	.410	-.0186	-.002	1148.10	1.95	.050	2.025
	(4.36)	(2.61)	(-1.13)	(-0.01)				
AS	.380	.665	-.0765	.408	417.28	2.06	.123	.585
	(3.99)	(6.47)	(-1.88)	(3.07)				
KO	.284	.725	-.0219	–	390.20	2.03	.031	.408
	(5.88)	(15.17)	(-1.48)					
Annual								
BE	–	1.019	-.2461	–	24.91	1.91	.246	.075
		(59.33)	(-2.50)					
DE	–	1.009	-.2416	–	3.09	1.57	.242	.039
		(50.71)	(-1.60)					
SW	.469	.509	-.1849	–	6.78	1.81	.348	-.118
	(4.20)	(4.80)	(-3.19)					
GR	.428	.722	-.1728	–	53.60	1.71	.302	.871
	(4.39)	(6.78)	(-3.69)					
IR	.261	.871	-.5022	.351	177.33	1.92	.680	.264
	(2.09)	(7.88)	(-1.57)	(0.95)				
SP	.189	.933	-.3838	–	100.34	1.99	.474	.318
	(3.26)	(19.81)	(-6.44)					
SA	.212	.762	-.3826	–	6.57	1.87	.485	-.068
	(3.32)	(10.80)	(-2.28)					
VE	.177	.882	-.1578	.289	13.30	2.05	.192	.373
	(0.82)	(5.04)	(-0.64)	(1.11)				
CO	.319	.765	-.1330	–	36.03	1.76	.195	.636
	(3.08)	(7.80)	(-1.33)					
JO	.083	.966	-.1030	–	17.20	1.84	.112	.480
	(1.74)	(21.89)	(-1.94)					
PA	.126	.955	-.2232	.420	1.38	2.04	.255	.363
	(2.22)	(17.41)	(-1.55)	(1.47)				
PH	–	1.027	-.1560	.888	6.32	1.62	.156	.173
		(13.85)	(-0.12)	(0.72)				
TH	.063	.965	-.0940	–	7.66	1.99	.100	.298
	(0.58)	(10.94)	(-1.01)					

Table 6.4b
Test Results for Equation 4

	Lags p-val	RHO+ p-val	T p-val	Leads p-val	Stability AP (df) λ	Sample
Quarterly						
CA	.016	.141	.217	.001	*21.58 (5) 4.25	1966:1–1992:3
JA	.021	.049	.058	.584	*9.97 (5) 3.57	1967:3–1992:3
AU	.815	.113	.452	.076	4.66 (4) 2.21	1971:1–1991:2
FR	.686	.059	.014	.862	*10.89 (4) 2.03	1971:1–1992:2
GE	.003	.000	.141	.012	5.73 (5) 2.66	1969:1–1991:4
IT	.009	.356	.001	.002	*23.74 (5) 2.00	1972:1–1991:4
NE	.018	.026	.015	.068	4.35 (5) 1.00	1978:2–1991:4
UK	.718	.962	.962	.108	*10.68 (5) 3.92	1966:1–1992:3
FI	.174	.071	.238	.851	*11.56 (5) 1.00	1976:1–1991:4
AS	.500	.303	.026	.751	*11.15 (5) 1.69	1971:1–1992:2
KO	.008	.000	.667	.297	3.47 (4) 2.03	1964:1–1991:4
Annual						
BE	.796	.945	.008	.452	2.53 (3) 1.00	1969–1990
DE	.286	.639	.810	.353	1.39 (3) 1.00	1969–1990
SW	.113	.005	.834	.025	*9.31 (4) 1.00	1969–1990
GR	.340	.639	.121	.686	5.13 (4) 1.00	1963–1990
IR	.492	.929	.540	.023	2.94 (5) 1.00	1969–1990
SP	.027	.566	.331	.748	1.55 (4) 1.00	1969–1990
SA	.004	.063	.481	.082	2.63 (4) 1.00	1970–1989
VE	.149	.130	.806	.024	*8.89 (5) 1.00	1963–1991
CO	.579	.495	.001	.024	0.54 (4) 1.00	1972–1991
JO	.826	.227	.412	.220	*9.15 (4) 1.00	1971–1991
PA	.148	.778	.191	.160	6.42 (5) 1.00	1972–1991
PH	.437	.406	.890	.001	4.87 (4) 1.00	1962–1991
TH	.736	.987	.056	.061	5.04 (4) 1.00	1962–1990

*Significant at the one percent level.

The estimate of the constant term is not presented in Table 6.3a. The estimate of λ is one minus a_2 in the table. Also presented in the table are the implied values of β and α_1. For the quarterly countries λ (i.e., $1 - a_2$) ranges from .054 for JA to .212 for UK and β ranges from .041 for CA to .095 for JA. For the annual countries λ ranges from .201 to .532 and β ranges from .136 to .619.

In Table 6.3b the equation fails the lags test in 6 of the 14 cases, the RHO+ test in 2 cases, the T test in 3 cases, and the leads test in 6 cases. The led value of output was used for the leads test. Equation 3 fails the stability test in 7 of the 14 cases. In none of the 9 relevant cases is the price expectations variable significant. If 4 of the 9 countries for which interest rates were significant, the short term interest rate, RS, gave better results than did the long term rate, and so it was used. In the case of CA both rates gave about the same results and

Table 6.5a

$$\log PY = a_1 + a_2 \log PY_{-1} + a_3 \log PM + a_4 \log W + a_5 ZZ + a_6 JJS$$

	a_2	a_3	a_4	a_5	a_6	ρ	SE	DW
Quarterly								
CA	.762	^{a}.027	.165	–	.259	.591	.0055	2.25
	(14.70)	(2.06)	(4.36)		(3.96)	(6.56)		
JA	.668	.019	.186	–	–	–	.0085	.83
	(13.48)	(5.16)	(6.30)					
AU	.948	^{a}.023	.019	-.115	–	-.449	.0115	2.03
	(25.81)	(1.82)	(.68)	(-1.97)		(-4.34)		
FR	.829	.024	.101	^{a}-.121	–	.300	.0053	1.92
	(23.01)	(2.24)	(3.26)	(-1.54)		(2.68)		
GE	.877	^{a}.010	.071	^{a}-.093	–	–	.0033	1.83
	(33.79)	(2.67)	(4.06)	(-4.67)				
IT	.934	.033	.022	-.184		–	.0075	1.24
	(33.54)	(3.90)	(0.73)	(-4.23)				
NE	.490	.082	.374	–	–	–	.0090	1.72
	(4.41)	(4.34)	(4.19)					
ST	.985	^{a}.006	–	^{a}-.101	^{a}.088	–	.0062	1.89
	(219.73)	(0.69)		(-2.25)	(1.61)			
UK	.821	.076	.088	^{a}-.060	–	.531	.0097	2.26
	(16.78)	(4.98)	(2.32)	(-0.89)		(5.26)		
FI	.847	^{a}.015	.107	–	.140	–	.0066	1.91
	(15.64)	(1.75)	(2.52)		(2.97)			
AS	.962	.025	–	–	.194	–	.0108	1.78
	(74.79)	(2.24)			(2.54)			
SO	.978	.028	–	–	–	–	.0195	2.02
	(48.78)	(1.58)						
KO	.602	.179	.166	^{a}-.266	–	–	.0439	2.20
	(6.81)	(4.89)	(3.53)	(-2.65)				
Annual								
BE	.613	.090	.199	–	.379	.689	.0119	1.97
	(6.19)	(1.55)	(2.33)		(1.36)	(2.12)		
DE	.604	.063	.258	–	–	–	.0086	1.70
	(15.84)	(3.67)	(7.73)					
NO	.501	.583	.029	–	–	–	.0202	1.63
	(4.05)	(4.62)	(0.42)					
SW	.546	.090	.359	–	–	-.339	.0115	2.17
	(12.78)	(5.24)	(8.34)			(-1.42)		
GR	.706	.220	.070	-.296	–	–	.0239	1.87
	(15.99)	(4.38)	(1.58)	(-1.45)				
IR	.493	.086	.327	–	–	–	.0266	1.64
	(5.02)	(1.43)	(2.88)					
PO	.782	.270	–	-.337	–	.455	.0271	2.29
	(18.13)	(5.92)		(-1.79)		(2.39)		
SP	.582	.012	.308	-.125	–	–	.0110	2.30
	(25.16)	(0.52)	(14.27)	(-1.38)				
NZ	.682	.079	.246	–	–	–	.0319	1.67
	(12.54)	(1.59)	(3.42)					
CO	.842	.172	–	–	–	–	.0257	2.10
	(13.32)	(2.73)						
JO	.799	.204	–	–	–	–	.0408	1.79
	(16.39)	(3.62)						
SY	.926	.132	–	–	–	.378	.0761	1.84
	(11.01)	(1.62)				(1.67)		
MA	.905	.061	–	-.856	–	–	.0556	2.01
	(4.29)	(0.34)		(-1.20)				
PA	.699	.217	–	-.066	–	-.390	.0147	2.13
	(28.87)	(10.80)		(-0.36)		(-1.89)		
PH	.802	.181	–	–	–	–	.0629	1.87
	(14.52)	(4.03)						
TH	.638	.251	–	–	–	–	.0428	.90
	(5.40)	(3.17)						

^{a} Variable lagged once.

Table 6.5b
Test Results for Equation 5

	Level p-val	Lags p-val	RHO+ p-val	T p-val	Leads p-val	Chg. p-val	Stability χ^2 (df) λ	Sample
Quarterly								
CA	.470	.074	.117	.836	.398	.000	*16.75 (6) 4.25	1966:1–1992:3
JA	.000	.000	.000	.006	.000	.000	*10.49 (4) 3.57	1967:3–1992:3
AU	.634	.573	.013	.134	.035	.001	5.04 (6) 2.21	1971:1–1991:2
FR	.089	.107	.050	.001	.000	.003	*8.93 (6) 2.03	1971:1–1992:2
GE	.891	.442	.039	.286	.254	.000	6.30 (5) 2.66	1969:1–1991:4
IT	.000	.001	.005	.000	.000	.000	*27.95 (5) 1.98	1972:1–1991:4
NE	.764	.194	.281	.263	.136	.000	2.15 (4) 1.00	1978:2–1991:4
ST	.052	.083	.138	.238	–	.000	4.92 (5) 2.17	1971:1–1991:4
UK	.398	.126	.128	.004	.114	.000	*20.27 (6) 3.92	1966:1–1992:3
FI	.981	.606	.486	.284	.460	.000	*8.50 (5) 1.00	1976:1–1991:4
AS	.423	.747	.263	.214	–	.000	2.98 (4) 1.69	1971:1–1992:2
SO	.088	.236	.028	.000	–	.000	*12.09 (3) 4.51	1962:1–1991:2
KO	.000	.000	.000	.000	.971	.001	*20.66 (5) 2.03	1964:1–1991:4
Annual								
BE	.082	.035	.786	.195	.128	.022	*9.39 (6) 1.00	1969–1990
DE	.787	.870	.091	.562	.116	.000	1.91 (4) 1.00	1969–1990
NO	.146	.023	.918	.587	.036	.000	5.27 (4) 1.00	1974–1990
SW	.076	.206	.078	.394	.290	.000	1.32 (5) 1.00	1969–1990
GR	.150	.001	.088	.322	.292	.000	*18.41 (5) 1.00	1963–1990
IR	.098	.098	.339	.023	.171	.041	*6.98 (4) 1.00	1969–1990
PO	.949	.007	.279	.000	–	.002	*8.93 (5) 1.00	1962–1990
SP	.298	.603	.172	.858	.538	.000	2.90 (5) 1.00	1969–1990
NZ	.001	.002	.627	.992	.173	.000	5.78 (4) 1.00	1962–1990
CO	.256	.534	.219	.006	–	.000	3.23 (3) 1.00	1972–1991
JO	.100	.203	.891	.164	–	.042	0.45 (3) 1.00	1971–1991
SY	.003	.015	.408	.004	–	.046	*7.74 (4) 1.00	1965–1990
MA	.600	.070	.002	.053	–	.935	2.13 (4) 1.00	1972–1987
PA	.036	.057	.382	.276	–	.000	2.42 (5) 1.00	1972–1991
PH	.489	.793	.409	.627	–	.001	*8.34 (3) 1.00	1962–1991
TH	.000	.000	.027	.000	–	.002	1.99 (3) 1.00	1962–1990

*Significant at the one percent level.

both were used.[5]

The reason that equation 3 was estimated for only 14 countries is that the results for the other countries were not good. The main problem, which seemed to exist for any specification tried, is that the coefficient estimate of the current output term is too large. Even though the 2SLS technique is used, there still seems to be a substantial amount of simultaneity bias. The overall results for equation 3 arc thus weak in that the results for over half of the countries did not appear sensible. This is an important area for future work.

[5]The coefficient estimate for RB is presented in Table 6.3a for CA. The coefficient estimate for RS was -38.03, with a t-statistic of -1.03.

The specification of equation 3 that was finally chosen does not use excess capital as an explanatory variable, and so with hindsight the construction of the excess capital variable for each country that was described in Chapter 3 was not needed.

6.5   Equation 4: Y: Production

Equation 4 explains the level of production. It is the same as equation 11 for the US model, which is equation 5.22 in Chapter 5. It includes as explanatory variables the lagged level of production, the current level of sales, and the lagged stock of inventories.

The estimate of the constant term is not presented in Table 6.4a. The estimate of λ is one minus a_2 in the table. Also presented in the table are the implied values of α and β. The parameters λ, α, and β are presented in equations 5.19–5.21. α and λ are adjustment parameters. For the quarterly countries λ (i.e., $1 - a_2$) ranges from .333 to .829 and α ranges from .050 to .553. For the annual countries λ ranges from .531 to .937 and α ranges from .100 to .680. For the United States λ was .707 and α was .473.

Equation 4 does well in the tests in Table 6.4b except for the stability test. Four of the 24 equations fail the lags test, 3 fail the RHO+ test, 3 fail the T test, and 3 fail the leads test. The led value of sales was used for the leads test. The equation fails the stability test in 10 of the 24 cases.

As was the case for equation 11 in the US model, the coefficient estimates of equation 4 are consistent with the view that firms smooth production relative to sales, and so these results add support to the production smoothing hypothesis.

6.6   Equation 5: PY: Price Deflator

Equation 5 explains the GDP price deflator. It is the same as equation 10 for the US model. It includes as explanatory variables the lagged price level, the price of imports, the wage rate, and a demand pressure variable. Data permitting, two demand pressure variables were tried per country. One, denoted ZZ, is the percentage gap between potential and actual output ($(YS - Y)/YS$), and the other, denoted JJS, is the ratio of jobs per capita to its peak to peak interpolation (JJ/JJP). The same tests were performed for equation 5 as were performed for equation 10 in the US model. In particular, the level specification was tested against the more general specification and the change specification was tested against the more general specification.

The estimate of the constant term is not presented in Table 6.5a. The results in the table show that the price of imports is significant in most of the equations. Import prices thus appear to have important effects on domestic prices for most countries. The demand pressure variables were not included in 13 of the 29 cases because they did not have the expected sign. (When a demand pressure variable had the wrong sign, it was almost always insignificant.) The results for the demand pressure variables are thus not as strong as the results for import prices.

Equation 5 does fairly well in the tests in Table 6.5b except for the stability test and possibly the T test. The level specification is rejected over the more general specification in only 6 of the 29 cases. The change specification, on the other hand, is rejected in 24 of the 29 cases, usually with very large χ^2 values. As was the case for the US results, the change specification is strongly rejected by the data.

Seven of the 29 equations fail the lags test, 4 fail the RHO+ test, 10 fail the T test, and 14 fail the stability test. The led value of the wage rate was used for the leads test. The wage rate appears in 18 equations, and of these 18 equations, only 3 fail the leads test.

6.7 Equation 6: $M1$: Money[6]

Equation 6 explains the per capita demand for money. It is the same as equation 9 for the US model. The same nominal versus real adjustment specifications were tested here as were tested for US equation 9 (and for the US equations 17 and 26). Equation 6 includes as explanatory variables one of the two lagged money variables, depending on which adjustment specification won, the short term interest rate, and income.

The estimates in Table 6.6a show that the nominal adjustment specification won in 13 of the 19 cases, and so this hypothesis continues its winning ways. Table 6.6b shows that the equation does well in the tests. Only 1 of the 19 equations fails the lags test, none fail the RHO+ test, 4 fail the T test, and 8 fail the stability test. The nominal versus real (NvsR) test results in the table simply show that adding the lagged money variable that was not chosen for

---

[6]Money demand equations are estimated in Fair (1987) for 27 countries, and the results in this section are essentially an update of these earlier results.

Table 6.6a

$$\log[M1/(POP \cdot PY)] = a_1 + a_2 \log[M1/(POP \cdot PY)]_{-1}$$
$$+a_3 \log[M1_{-1}/(POP_{-1} \cdot PY)] + a_4 RS + a_5 \log(Y/POP)$$

	a_1	a_2	a_3	a_4	a_5	ρ	SE	DW
Quarterly								
CA	-.804	–	.917	-.0055	.112	–	.0238	1.98
	(-4.80)		(53.49)	(-4.70)	(5.10)			
JA	-.211	.930	–	-.0045	.034	-.209	.0220	1.92
	(-1.21)	(37.55)		(-5.05)	(1.35)	(-2.05)		
AU	.344	–	.885	-.0023	.011	.225	.0218	2.08
	(2.65)		(14.80)	(-1.35)	(0.32)	(1.75)		
FR	.915	–	.669	^{a}-.0021	–	–	.0155	1.98
	(4.69)		(9.53)	(-1.89)				
GE	-.161	.845	–	-.0049	.223	.183	.0097	1.98
	(-2.80)	(19.84)		(-8.20)	(3.55)	(1.53)		
IT	-.087	.740	–	^{a}-.0043	.069	.297	.0146	2.08
	(-0.65)	(12.87)		(-6.06)	(3.44)	(2.34)		
NE	-.627	–	.762	-.0067	.559	–	.0168	2.06
	(-2.90)		(10.75)	(-3.74)	(3.20)			
UK	-.379	–	.914	-.0041	.151	-.275	.0262	1.92
	(-3.12)		(55.37)	(-3.69)	(5.47)	(-2.86)		
FI	-1.106	–	.632	^{a}-.0046	.445	-.213	.0314	2.25
	(-2.87)		(6.18)	(-2.65)	(3.62)	(-1.49)		
AS	-.879	–	.900	-.0065	.210	–	.0241	1.77
	(-2.68)		(30.16)	(-4.92)	(4.35)			
SO	-.317	–	.916	–	.129	.265	.0342	2.05
	(-0.84)		(24.48)		(2.57)	(2.67)		
Annual								
BE	.806	.748	–	-.0112	.074	–	.0300	1.27
	(1.06)	(5.66)		(-3.83)	(1.43)			
DE	-1.576	–	.645	-.0118	.620	-.290	.0471	2.23
	(-3.61)		(7.27)	(-3.13)	(4.19)	(-1.28)		
SW	.221	–	.495	-.0049	.399	–	.0357	1.68
	(0.40)		(2.24)	(-1.33)	(1.60)			
PO	.545	.654	–	-.0117	.223	–	.0631	1.95
	(1.53)	(7.89)		(-3.93)	(2.86)			
VE	.074	–	.851	–	.382	–	.1027	1.16
	(0.09)		(12.46)		(1.42)			
ID	-.881	.593	–	-.0010	.573	–	.0472	1.38
	(-3.17)	(4.42)		(-0.22)	(3.17)			
PA	6.069	–	.060	-.0572	.731	–	.0636	1.12
	(9.22)		(0.47)	(-5.74)	(3.75)			
PH	1.840	–	.690	-.0065	.191	–	.0756	2.16
	(2.06)		(5.32)	(-1.68)	(1.95)			

^{a} Variable lagged once.

the final specification does not produce a significant increase in explanatory power.

Table 6.6b
Test Results for Equation 6

	NvsR p-val	Lags p-val	RHO+ p-val	T p-val	Stability AP (df) λ	Sample
Quarterly						
CA	.266	.217	.018	.424	5.44 (4) 3.36	1968:1–1992:3
JA	.154	.001	.017	.000	*17.31 (5) 3.57	1967:3–1992:3
AU	.207	.253	.354	.390	*10.40 (5) 2.21	1971:1–1991:2
FR	.706	.839	.212	.893	2.16 (3) 2.03	1979:1–1992:2
GE	.500	.710	.052	.172	3.76 (5) 2.41	1969:1–1990:4
IT	.066	.199	.093	.139	*11.69 (5) 2.01	1972:1–1991:4
NE	.191	.955	.314	.215	*7.47 (4) 1.00	1978:2–1991:4
UK	.641	.918	.258	.210	5.37 (5) 3.92	1966:1–1992:3
FI	.032	.036	.063	.675	3.52 (5) 1.00	1976:1–1990:4
AS	.080	.874	.281	.055	2.88 (4) 1.69	1971:1–1992:2
SO	.811	.580	.112	.262	*25.99 (4) 4.51	1962:1–1991:2
Annual						
BE	.299	.427	.225	.000	*11.22 (4) 1.00	1969–1990
DE	.295	.212	.041	.048	6.20 (5) 1.00	1969–1990
SW	.189	.011	.079	.302	4.34 (4) 1.00	1971–1990
PO	.970	.664	.379	.002	4.09 (4) 1.00	1962–1990
VE	.013	.376	.059	.001	*7.45 (3) 1.00	1963–1991
ID	.096	.060	.100	.333	*7.48 (4) 1.00	1962–1989
PA	.075	.058	.242	.119	2.87 (4) 1.00	1972–1991
PH	.748	.111	.696	.996	2.17 (4) 1.00	1962–1991

*Significant at the one percent level.

6.8 Equation 7: RS: Short Term Interest Rate

Equation 7 explains the short term (three month) interest rate. It is interpreted as the interest rate reaction function of each country's monetary authority, and it is similar to equation 30 in the US model. The explanatory variables that were tried (as possibly influencing the monetary authority's interest rate decision) are 1) the rate of inflation, 2) the two demand pressure variables, 3) the lagged percentage growth of the money supply, 4) the first two lagged values of the asset variable for the quarterly countries and the current and one year lagged value of the asset variable for the annual countries, and 5) the U.S. short term interest rate. The change in the asset variable is highly correlated with the balance of payments on current account, and so putting in the two asset variables is similar to putting in the balance of payments. The U.S. interest rate was included on the view that some monetary authorities' decisions may be influenced by the Fed's decisions. Similarly, the two asset variables were included on the view that monetary authorities may be influenced in their policy by the status of their balance of payments.

Table 6.7a

$$RS = a_1 + a_2 RS_{-1} + a_3 PCPY + a_4(ZZ \, or \, JJS) + a_5 PCM1_{-1}$$
$$+ a_6[A/(PY \cdot YS)]_{-1} + a_7[A/(PY \cdot YS)]_{-2} + a_8 RSUS$$

	a_2	a_3	a_4	a_6	a_7	a_8	SE	DW
Quarterly								
CA	.262	–	[a]18.58	-8.74	5.09	.857	.7384	2.19
	(3.60)		(1.46)	(-0.68)	(0.38)	(7.51)		
JA	.737	.077	–	-25.52	26.18	.119	.6879	1.99
	(10.55)	(3.13)		(-2.65)	(2.73)	(2.19)		
AU	.748	–	-23.97	-21.43	19.69	.028	.7352	2.05
	(13.15)		(-3.89)	(-4.07)	(3.88)	(0.43)		
FR	.564	.061	–	-31.44	28.61	.345	.8879	1.78
	(3.89)	(1.10)		(-1.92)	(1.85)	(2.62)		
GE	.781	–	-34.00	-8.81	7.79	.154	.7804	2.19
	(17.40)		(-5.92)	(-1.70)	(1.47)	(3.28)		
IT	.534	.143	–	-32.00	24.97	.346	1.0927	2.18
	(5.03)	(2.70)		(-2.96)	(2.39)	(2.92)		
NE	.590	–	-23.76	-12.34	13.67	.406	1.0748	2.13
	(6.59)		(-2.75)	(-1.42)	(1.50)	(3.44)		
ST	.849	–	-13.33	–	–	–	.7961	1.81
	(17.04)		(-3.49)					
UK	.706	–	-13.26	-7.49	6.74	.248	1.2022	1.87
	(9.35)		(-1.95)	(-0.65)	(0.59)	(3.26)		
FI	.836	–	–	-18.94	19.49	.072	.9740	1.68
	(13.93)			(-3.09)	(2.94)	(1.23)		
AS	.786	–	-28.69	-21.68	21.50	.143	1.1976	1.95
	(11.94)		(-3.66)	(-2.18)	(2.16)	(2.20)		
SO	.901	.012	–	–	–	.195	.9518	1.99
	(11.62)	(1.18)				(1.67)		
KO	.951	.024	-8.57	–	–	–	1.1642	2.13
	(25.87)	(3.43)	(-2.56)					
Annual								
BE	.169	.099	–	–	–	.759	1.4647	2.71
	(1.13)	(0.81)				(4.71)		
DE	.171	–	–	-37.83	42.94	.700	2.5174	2.17
	(.72)			(-1.03)	(1.17)	(2.16)		
NO	.774	–	[a]16.62	–	–	.137	1.2926	2.34
	(6.05)		(1.26)			(1.04)		
SW	.756	.035	-30.53	–	–	.494	2.0225	2.71
	(4.67)	(0.86)	(-0.94)			(2.27)		
IR	–	.123	–	-20.81	16.62	.491	2.0081	2.84
	(.00)	(1.35)		(-0.92)	(0.89)	(1.42)		
PO	.713	.292	–	–	–	.332	2.0078	1.89
	(8.76)	(2.98)				(1.53)		
NZ	.555	.266	–	-26.48	5.17	.130	2.8364	1.47
	(2.70)	(1.70)		(-1.31)	(0.22)	(0.47)		
VE	.764	.333	–	-25.43	11.41	.195	5.8892	2.52
	(5.91)	(4.35)		(-1.42)	(0.58)	(0.32)		
PA	.590	.154	–	-17.04	11.21	.120	.8082	1.91
	(4.13)	(3.30)		(-1.51)	(1.01)	(1.28)		
PH	.782	.111	–	–	–	.426	3.1857	1.43
	(4.84)	(1.34)				(1.33)		

[a] JJS rather than ZZ.

$PCPY = 100[(PY/PY_{-1})^4 - 1]$, $PCM1 = 100[(M1/M1_{-1})^4 - 1]$.

Table 6.7b
Test Results for Equation 7

	Lags p-val	RHO+ p-val	T p-val	Stability AP (df) λ	Sample
Quarterly					
CA	.079	.116	.112	*11.90 (7) 1.81	1972:2–1992:3
JA	.019	.373	.851	8.15 (7) 1.81	1972:2–1992:3
AU	.027	.461	.007	*11.34 (6) 1.78	1972:2–1991:2
FR	.040	.046	.999	6.15 (7) 1.65	1972:2–1992:2
GE	.202	.004	.306	2.29 (6) 1.58	1972:2–1991:4
IT	.631	.193	.083	6.51 (8) 1.58	1972:2–1991:4
NE	.110	.010	.331	3.47 (6) 1.00	1978:2–1991:4
ST	.392	.398	.301	1.19 (3) 1.75	1972:2–1991:4
UK	.074	.863	.549	1.96 (6) 1.64	1972:2–1992:3
FI	.550	.060	.567	4.63 (5) 1.00	1976:1–1991:4
AS	.968	.491	.132	4.55 (6) 1.35	1972:2–1992:2
SO	.171	.199	.051	5.56 (5) 1.05	1972:2–1991:2
KO	.309	.023	.767	1.42 (4) 1.00	1972:2–1991:4
Annual					
BE	.100	.011	.151	1.11 (4) 1.00	1972–1990
DE	.957	.998	.571	2.49 (5) 1.00	1972–1990
NO	.561	.122	.075	*8.91 (4) 1.00	1974–1990
SW	.022	.020	.002	3.63 (5) 1.00	1972–1990
IR	.050	.007	.229	3.89 (5) 1.00	1972–1990
PO	.815	.183	.267	2.85 (4) 1.00	1972–1990
NZ	.000	.005	.007	*19.06 (6) 1.00	1972–1990
VE	.697	.173	.612	1.90 (7) 1.00	1972–1991
PA	.000	.049	.396	5.02 (7) 1.00	1972–1991
PH	.043	.771	.067	3.90 (5) 1.00	1972–1991

*Significant at the one percent level.

The estimates of the constant term, the coefficient of the lagged money growth variable, and the serial correlation coefficient are not included in Table 6.7a because of space constraints.[7] The results in Table 6.7a show that the inflation rate is included in 13 of the 23 cases, a demand pressure variable in 10 cases, the asset variables in 15 cases, and the U.S. rate in 21 cases. There is thus evidence that monetary authorities are influenced by inflation, demand pressure, and the balance of payments. The lagged money growth variable, on the other hand, is not significant in any of the 4 cases it is included (see footnote 7), and so there is little evidence in favor of this variable. The monetary authorities of other countries do not appear to be influenced in their setting of interest rates by the lagged growth of the money supply. The signs of the coefficient estimates of the asset variables (negative for the first and

---

[7]Five equations were estimated under the assumption of a first order autoregressive error. The estimates and t-statistics are: CA: .707 (7.07); JA: .339 (2.51); FR: .408 (2.16); IT: .438 (2.66); SO: .644 (4.66). Four equations included the lagged money growth variable. The estimates and t-statistics are: IT: .031 (1.61); VE: .155 (1.33); PA: .056 (1.81); PH: .120 (1.26).

Table 6.8a
$$RB - RS_{-2} = a_1 + a_2(RB_{-1} - RS_{-2}) + a_3(RS - RS_{-2})$$
$$+a_4(RS_{-1} - RS_{-2})$$

	a_1	a_2	a_3	a_4	ρ	SE	R^2	DW
Quarterly								
CA	.108	.898	.470	-.429	–	.4621	0.934	2.17
	(2.10)	(29.42)	(7.75)	(-5.14)				
JA	.009	.901	.535	-.636	-.168	.4322	0.926	2.00
	(.25)	(25.29)	(4.27)	(-3.07)	(-1.33)			
AU	.143	.916	.232	-.090	.340	.2338	0.972	2.01
	(2.21)	(31.32)	(5.48)	(-1.99)	(2.96)			
FR	.101	.840	.332	-.164	.295	.3988	0.934	2.05
	(1.37)	(12.83)	(4.01)	(-1.75)	(2.35)			
GE	.116	.929	.195	-.111	.163	.4154	0.944	1.94
	(1.53)	(25.34)	(2.91)	(-1.49)	(1.28)			
IT	-.108	.813	.287	-.185	.573	.5894	0.947	2.00
	(-.66)	(10.38)	(5.00)	(-2.78)	(4.66)			
NE	.153	.864	.208	-.054	–	.4177	0.918	1.95
	(1.91)	(16.69)	(3.74)	(-0.86)				
ST	.106	.932	.142	-.074	.336	.2500	0.972	2.03
	(1.76)	(32.14)	(2.65)	(-1.36)	(2.84)			
UK	.052	.962	.405	-.376	–	.5498	0.953	1.79
	(.87)	(38.50)	(5.30)	(-4.14)				
AS	.065	.945	.311	-.252	.151	.4599	0.954	1.97
	(.99)	(24.86)	(5.20)	(-3.91)	(1.25)			
SO	.161	.957	.472	-.702	–	.4579	0.971	1.95
	(2.73)	(50.75)	(5.35)	(-4.96)				
Annual[a]								
BE	1.435	.405	.496	–	–	.6368	0.865	1.51
	(4.13)	(2.88)	(7.01)					
DE	.905	.549	.514	–	–	1.3445	0.738	1.51
	(1.98)	(3.11)	(4.72)					
NO	-.344	.204	.646	–	–	.5561	0.781	1.46
	(-1.76)	(0.90)	(5.82)					
SW	.325	.894	.299	–	–	.8289	0.849	2.53
	(1.44)	(6.64)	(3.08)					
IR	.844	.432	.484	–	–	1.3845	0.740	1.32
	(2.29)	(2.71)	(5.18)					
PO	.112	.955	.706	–	–	.6569	0.946	2.67
	(.87)	(14.48)	(11.97)					
NZ	.078	.919	.332	–	–	1.0446	0.843	2.92
	(.29)	(6.91)	(3.55)					
PA	.144	.722	-.085	–	-.410	.7544	0.803	2.25
	(1.20)	(9.91)	(-0.63)		(-1.65)			

[a] For annual countries a_4 is zero and RS_{-1} rather than RS_{-2} is subtracted from the other variables.

positive for the second) suggest that an increase (decrease) in the balance of payments has a negative (positive) effect on the interest rate target of the monetary authority.

Table 6.8b
Test Results for Equation 8

	Restr[a] p-val	Lags p-val	RHO+ p-val	T p-val	Leads p-val	Stability AP (df) λ	Sample
Quarterly							
CA	.028	.048	.474	.042	.093	3.54 (4) 4.25	1966:1–1992:3
JA	.316	.575	.667	.854	.483	2.98 (5) 3.57	1967:3–1992:3
AU	.382	.038	.718	.054	.291	2.49 (5) 2.21	1971:1–1991:2
FR	.303	.066	.070	.144	.987	3.88 (5) 2.03	1971:1–1992:2
GE	.005	.006	.221	.581	.135	6.12 (5) 2.66	1969:1–1991:4
IT	.315	.727	.270	.076	.703	*9.75 (5) 2.03	1972:1–1991:4
NE	.281	.439	.065	.700	.893	0.85 (4) 1.00	1978:2–1991:4
ST	.007	.044	.626	.567	.333	6.15 (5) 2.17	1971:1–1991:4
UK	.396	.247	.805	.007	.391	5.59 (4) 3.92	1966:1–1992:3
AS	.078	.218	.448	.020	.068	3.26 (5) 1.69	1971:1–1992:2
SO	.447	.734	.256	.845	.552	1.78 (4) 2.83	1962:1–1991:2
Annual							
BE	.236	.082	.253	.210	.177	*8.87 (3) 1.00	1969–1990
DE	.714	.364	.761	.011	.924	3.46 (3) 1.00	1969–1990
NO	.693	.970	.341	.732	.033	2.16 (3) 1.00	1974–1990
SW	.079	.551	.018	.429	.427	1.60 (3) 1.00	1969–1990
IR	.774	.386	.093	.000	.705	4.98 (3) 1.00	1969–1990
PO	.015	.061	.264	.638	.013	.84 (3) 1.00	1962–1990
NZ	.308	.000	.000	.853	.656	.19 (3) 1.00	1962–1990
PA	.834	.041	.335	.490	.294	.66 (4) 1.00	1972–1991

[a] RS_{-2} added for quarterly countries, RS_{-1} added for annual countries.
*Significant at the one percent level.

Equation 7 does well in the tests. Two of the 23 equations fail the lags test, 4 fail the RHO=4 test, 3 fail the T test, and 4 fail the stability test.

6.9 Equation 8: RB: Long Term Interest Rate

Equation 8 explains the long term interest rate. It is the same as equations 23 and 24 in the US model. For the quarterly countries the explanatory variables include the lagged dependent variable and the current and two lagged short rates. For the annual countries the explanatory variables include the lagged dependent variable and the current and one lagged short rates. The same restriction was imposed on equation 8 as was imposed on equations 23 and 24, namely that the coefficients on the short rate sum to one in the long run.

The test results in Table 6.8b show that the restriction that the coefficients sum to one in the long run is supported in 17 of the 19 cases. The equation does very well in the other tests. Two of the 19 equations fail the lags test, 1 fails the RHO=4 test, 2 fail the T test, and 2 fail the stability test. The led value of the short term interest rate was used for the leads test, and it is not significant at the one percent level in any of the 19 cases. As noted in Chapter 5, my experience with term structure equations like equation 8 is that they are quite stable and reliable, which the results in Table 6.8b support.

6.10 Equation 9 E: Exchange Rate

Equation 9 explains the country's exchange rate, E. A country's exchange rate is relative to the U.S. dollar, and an increase in E is a *depreciation* of the country's currency relative to the dollar. The theory behind the specification of this equation is discussed in Chapter 2. See in particular the discussion of the experiments in Section 2.2.6 and the discussion of reaction functions in Section 2.2.7. Equation 9 is interpreted as an exchange rate reaction function.

Two types of countries are assumed for the estimation. The first are those countries whose exchange rate is assumed to be at least partly tied to the German exchange rate. Germany is taken to be the leader among the European countries in this respect. The second are those whose exchange rate is assumed not to be tied to the German rate. The first set includes all the European countries. The second set includes Canada, Japan, Australia, South Africa, Korea, New Zealand, Jordan, India, and the Philippines.

Consider first the non European countries. The exchange rate for these countries is based on the following two equations.

$$E^* = e^{\alpha_0}(\frac{1 + RS/100}{1 + RSUS/100})^{.25\alpha_1}(\frac{PY}{PYUS}) \qquad (6.6)$$

$$\frac{E}{E_{-1}} = (\frac{E^*}{E_{-1}})^{\lambda} \qquad (6.7)$$

E is the exchange rate, PY is the country's domestic price deflator, $PYUS$ is the U.S. domestic price deflator (denoted $GDPD$ in the US model), RS is the country's short term interest rate, and $RSUS$ is the U.S. short term interest rate (denoted simply RS in the US model).[8] Equation 6.6 states that the long run exchange rate, E^*, depends on the relative price level, $PY/PYUS$, and the relative interest rate, $(1 + RS/100)/(1 + RSUS/100)$. The coefficient on the relative price level is constrained to be one, which means that in the long run the real exchange rate is assumed merely to fluctuate as the relative interest rate fluctuates. Equation 6.7 is a partial adjustment equation, which

---

[8] RS and $RSUS$ are divided by 100 because they are in percentage points rather than percents. Also, the interest rates are at annual rates, and so α_1 is multiplied by .25 to put the rates at quarterly rates. For the annual countries, the .25 is not used.

says that the actual exchange rate adjusts λ percent of the way to the long run exchange rate each period.

The use of the relative price level in equation 6.6 is consistent with the theoretical model in Chapter 2. In this model a positive price shock led to a depreciation of the exchange rate. (See experiments 3 and 4 in Section 2.2.6.) In other words, there are forces in the theoretical model that put downward pressure on a country's currency when there is a relative increase in the country's price level. Because equation 6.6 is interpreted as an exchange rate reaction function, the use of the relative price level in it is in effect based on the assumption that the monetary authority goes along with the forces on the exchange rate and allows it to change in the long run as the relative price level changes.

Similarly, the use of the relative interest rate in equation 6.6 is consistent with the theoretical model, where a fall in the relative interest rate led to a depreciation. (See experiments 1 and 2 in Section 2.2.6.) Again, the assumption in equation 6.6 is that the monetary authority goes along with the forces on the exchange rate from the relative interest rate change.

Equations 6.6 and 6.7 imply that

$$\log(E/E_{-1}) = \lambda\alpha_0 + \lambda\alpha_1(.25)\log[(1 + RS/100)/(1 + RSUS/100)]$$

$$+ \lambda[\log(PY/PYUS) - \log E_{-1}] \tag{6.8}$$

The restriction that the coefficient of the relative price term is one can be tested by adding $\log E_{-1}$ to equation 6.8. If the coefficient is other than one, this variable should have a nonzero coefficient. This is one of the tests performed in Table 6.9b.

Consider now the European countries (except Germany). The exchange rate for these countries is based on the adjustment equation 6.7 and on the following equation:

$$E^* = e^{\alpha_0}(\frac{1 + RS/100}{1 + RSUS/100})^{.25\alpha_1}(\frac{PY}{PYUS})^{1-\delta}EGE^\delta \tag{6.9}$$

EGE is the German exchange rate. Equation 6.9 differs from equation 6.6 in that the relative price term (with the coefficient of one) is replaced with a weighted average of the relative price term and the German exchange rate, where the weights sum to one. δ is the weight on the German exchange rate. If δ is one, then the exchange rate of the country relative to the German rate fluctuates in the long run merely as the relative interest rate fluctuates. If δ is zero, one is back to the case of the non European countries. For δ less than

Table 6.9a

$$\Delta \log E = a_1 + \lambda[\log(PY/PYUS) - \log E_{-1}] + \lambda\delta[\log EGE - \log(PY/PYUS)]$$
$$+a_4(.25)\log[(1 + RS/100)/(1 + RSUS/100)]$$

	a_1	λ	$\lambda\delta$	a_4	ρ	SE	DW	δ
Quarterly								
CA	.011	.052	–	-.206	.413	.0144	1.96	–
	(1.58)	(1.34)		(-0.29)	(3.51)			
JA	-.093	.047	–	-1.117	.371	.0483	1.94	–
	(-1.11)	(0.95)		(-0.87)	(3.01)			
AU	1.892	.964	.965	-.754	.930	.0051	1.63	1.001
	(22.94)	(50.25)	(75.85)	(-2.60)	(22.41)			
FR	1.033	.846	.821	–	.982	.0213	1.75	.970
	(2.22)	(13.14)	(16.97)		(88.23)			
GE	-.580	.090	–	-2.557	.335	.0514	1.96	–
	(-1.55)	(1.51)		(-1.50)	(2.52)			
IT	4.406	.699	.651	–	.971	.0253	2.23	.932
	(10.40)	(7.89)	(11.71)		(94.22)			
NE	.236	.990	1.010	–	.872	.0052	1.81	1.020
	(2.53)	(60.71)	(69.76)		(17.29)			
ST	-.359	1.003	.973	–	.950	.0259	1.58	.970
	(-0.78)	(14.14)	(15.81)		(41.25)			
UK	3.415	.874	.625	–	.932	.0378	2.00	.715
	(6.32)	(8.03)	(7.35)		(31.98)			
FI	5.073	.758	.626	-1.823	.930	.0241	2.03	.826
	(9.08)	(6.74)	(8.64)	(-1.21)	(23.79)			
AS	.007	.144	–	–	.365	.0422	2.24	–
	(0.98)	(1.67)			(1.91)			
SO	.098	.166	–	–	.191	.0726	1.92	–
	(2.29)	(1.66)			(0.93)			
KO	-.002	.039	–	–	.404	.0270	2.07	–
	(-0.25)	(1.35)			(2.97)			
Annual								
BE	3.664	.880	1.010	–	.940	.0335	1.81	1.147
	(6.83)	(12.06)	(14.56)		(17.07)			
DE	1.770	.955	.975	–	.950	.0293	1.60	1.021
	(3.19)	(14.23)	(15.60)		(28.16)			
NO	.210	.692	.552	-.425	.945	.0302	2.03	.798
	(0.28)	(7.07)	(7.40)	(-0.99)	(14.06)			
SW	1.114	.674	.666	–	.948	.0499	1.88	.989
	(1.09)	(5.16)	(6.57)		(16.11)			
GR	10.936	.606	.607	–	.991	.0436	2.31	1.002
	(0.45)	(4.63)	(7.02)		(42.95)			
IR	5.039	.998	.844	–	.888	.0436	1.71	.846
	(7.63)	(9.70)	(8.68)		(25.23)			
PO	4.707	.514	.633	–	.966	.0757	1.36	1.232
	(1.52)	(2.71)	(4.41)		(27.37)			
SP	3.559	.712	.760	–	.932	.0706	1.92	1.068
	(3.21)	(4.37)	(5.52)		(18.35)			
NZ	.088	.175	–	–	–	.1048	0.92	–
	(1.28)	(0.84)						
JO	-.631	.672	–	–	.856	.0919	1.37	–
	(-2.35)	(2.67)			(4.38)			
ID	-1.154	.272	–	–	.864	.0506	1.72	–
	(-1.23)	(1.21)			(3.13)			
PH	-2.771	.679	–	–	.814	.0685	1.69	–
	(-3.39)	(3.49)			(5.10)			

Table 6.9b
Test Results for Equation 9

	Restr[a] p-val	Lags p-val	RHO+ p-val	T p-val	Stability AP (df) λ	Sample
Quarterly						
CA	.718	.236	.102	.896	0.82 (4) 1.81	1972:2–1992:3
JA	.186	.594	.266	.052	3.16 (4) 1.81	1972:2–1992:3
AU	.461	.039	.772	.587	4.07 (5) 1.78	1972:2–1991:2
FR	.929	.458	.390	.577	*14.58 (4) 1.65	1972:2–1992:2
GE	.654	.654	.396	.976	3.73 (4) 1.58	1972:2–1991:4
IT	.009	.139	.111	.858	*12.00 (4) 1.58	1972:2–1991:4
NE	.011	.059	.001	.017	4.11 (4) 1.00	1978:2–1991:4
ST	.631	.170	.048	.793	2.94 (4) 1.75	1972:2–1991:4
UK	.267	.744	–	.095	3.67 (4) 1.41	1972:2–1992:3
FI	.579	.204	.804	.160	1.40 (5) 1.00	1976:1–1991:4
AS	.299	.369	.466	.279	2.11 (3) 1.35	1972:2–1992:2
SO	.775	.083	.136	.822	1.75 (3) 1.00	1981:1–1991:2
Annual						
BE	.999	.914	.150	.044	3.81 (4) 1.00	1972–1990
DE	.594	.663	.550	.838	5.45 (4) 1.00	1972–1990
NO	.153	.026	.259	.024	2.61 (5) 1.00	1974–1990
SW	.695	.752	.033	.097	2.60 (4) 1.00	1972–1990
GR	.563	.041	.572	.004	1.93 (4) 1.00	1972–1990
IR	.033	.906	.009	.984	0.14 (4) 1.00	1972–1990
PO	.010	.595	.018	.442	3.00 (4) 1.00	1972–1990
SP	.000	.784	.574	.824	3.17 (4) 1.00	1972–1990
NZ	.693	.000	.000	.983	1.99 (2) 1.00	1972–1990
JO	.005	.007	.160	.002	3.85 (3) 1.00	1972–1991
ID	.041	.863	.404	.018	1.96 (3) 1.00	1972–1989
PH	.117	.976	.996	.036	*12.72 (3) 1.00	1972–1991

[a] $\log E_{-1}$ added.
*Significant at the one percent level.

one and greater than zero, the exchange rate fluctuates in the long run as the relative price level, the relative interest rate, and the German rate fluctuate.

The monetary authorities of other European countries may be influenced by the German exchange rate in deciding their own exchange rate targets, and this is the reason for the use of the German rate in equation 6.9. This specification can also be looked upon as an attempt to capture some of the effects of the European Monetary System (EMS). Under the assumption that Germany is the dominant country in the EMS, the German rate will pick up some of the effects of the EMS agreement.

Equations 6.9 and 6.7 imply that

$$\log(E/E_{-1}) = \lambda\alpha_0 + \lambda\alpha_1(.25)\log[(1 + RS/100)/(1 + RSUS/100)]$$

$$+\lambda[\log(PY/PYUS) - \log E_{-1}] + \lambda\delta[\log EGE - \log(PY/PYUS)] \quad (6.10)$$

The restriction that the weights sum to one can be tested by adding $\log E_{-1}$ to equation 6.10. If the weights do not sum to one, this variable should have a nonzero coefficient. This is one of the tests performed in Table 6.9b.

Exchange rate equations were estimated for 25 countries. The implied value of δ is presented in Table 6.9a along with the other results. Consider first the relative interest rate variable. The results do not provide strong support for the use of this variable in the exchange rate equations. It is included for only 6 countries and is only significant for 1 of these (Austria). The variable had the wrong sign (and was almost always insignificant) for the other countries. Two of the countries for which the variable is included are Japan and Germany, which are important countries in the model, and so in this sense the relative interest rate variable is important. It will be seen in Chapter 12 that some of the properties of the model are sensitive to the inclusion of the relative interest rate in the exchange rate equations. Given that the relative interest rate is not significant in either the Japanese or German equation, the properties that are sensitive to the inclusion must be interpreted with considerable caution. This is discussed more in Chapter 12.

Regarding δ, for many countries δ is close to one in Table 6.9a (δ is in fact slightly greater than one in a few cases[9]), and for these countries the exchange rate effectively just follows the German rate in the long run. For many of these countries the estimates of λ are also close to one. This means that the adjustment to the long run value is estimated to be very rapid and thus that the exchange rate follows closely the German rate even in the short run.

For Germany and for most of the non European countries, the estimates of λ are small, which means that it takes considerable time for the exchange rate to adjust to, say, a relative price level change. This is contrary to the case for the European countries (except Germany), where the adjustment to a weighted average of the relative price level and the German exchange rate (with most of the weight on the German rate) is estimated to be quite rapid.

There is considerable first order serial correlation in the error terms in the exchange rate equations for most countries.

Equation 9 does well in the tests. The restriction discussed above that is tested by adding $\log E_{-1}$ to the equation is only rejected in 4 of the 25 cases. Two of the 25 equations fail the lags test, 3 fail the RHO+ test,[10] 2 fail the T test, and 3 fail the stability test. It is encouraging that so few equations fail the

---

[9]δ could have been constrained to be one when its estimate was greater than one, but this was not done here. Doing this would have had little effect on the model because the estimates that are greater than one are in fact quite close to one.

[10]Multicollinearity problems prevented the RHO+ test from being performed for the UK.

stability test. The key German exchange rate equation passes all the tests.

Since equation 9 is in log form, the standard errors are roughly in percentage terms. The standard errors for a number of the European countries are quite low, but this is because of the inclusion of the German rate. A better way of examining how well these equations fit is to solve the overall model, and this is done in Chapter 9. The standard error for Japan, whose rate is not tied to the German rate, is 4.83 percent, and the standard error for Germany is 5.14 percent.

Exchange rate equations are notoriously hard to estimate, and given this, the results in Tables 6.9a and 6.9b do not seem too bad. The test results suggest that most of the dynamics have been captured and that the equations are fairly stable. However, many of the key coefficient estimates have t-statistics that are less than two in absolute value, and there is substantial serial correlation of the error terms.

6.11 Equation 10 F: Forward Rate

Equation 10 explains the country's forward exchange rate, F. This equation is the estimated arbitrage condition, and although it plays no role in the model, it is of interest to see how closely the quarterly data on EE, F, RS, and $USRS$ match the arbitrage condition. The arbitrage condition in this notation is

$$\frac{F}{EE} = (\frac{1 + RS/100}{1 + RSUS/100})^{.25}$$

In equation 10, log F is regressed on log EE and $.25 \log(1 + RS/100)/(1 + RSUS/100)$. If the arbitrage condition were met exactly, the coefficient estimates for both explanatory variables would be one and the fit would be perfect.

The results in Table 6.10a show that the data are generally consistent with the arbitrage condition, especially considering that some of the interest rate data are not exactly the right data to use. Note the t-statistic for France of 5586.14!

Table 6.10a

$$\log F = a_1 \log EE + a_2(.25) \log[(1 + RS/100)/(1 + RSUS/100)]$$

	a_1	a_2	ρ	SE	R^2	DW	Sample
Quarterly							
CA	.9917	.902	.436	.0021	.999	2.08	1972:2–1992:3
	(315.82)	(10.12)	(4.06)				
JA	1.0010	1.323	.392	.0105	.999	1.75	1972:2–1992:3
	(807.43)	(5.31)	(3.79)				
AU	1.0004	1.174	.137	.0064	.999	2.05	1972:2–1991:2
	(4375.14)	(6.61)	(1.17)				
FR	1.0007	.946	–	.0056	.999	2.04	1972:2–1991:1
	(5586.14)	(6.62)					
GE	1.0005	1.168	.618	.0036	.999	2.16	1972:2–1991:4
	(5425.53)	(9.17)	(6.75)				
IT	.9894	1.267	-.148	.0110	.998	2.02	1978:1–1991:4
	(155.45)	(8.60)	(-1.09)				
NE	.9999	1.612	–	.0099	.998	2.05	1978:2–1990:4
	(3268.23)	(4.75)					
ST	1.0003	.889	–	.0071	.999	1.82	1972:2–1991:4
	(5017.04)	(9.52)					
UK	1.0004	1.168	.383	.0063	.999	1.95	1972:2–1984:4
	(363.27)	(4.98)	(2.62)				
FI	.9976	1.479	.616	.0069	.998	2.57	1976:1–1989:3
	(471.03)	(5.54)	(5.77)				
AS	1.0044	1.213	–	.0041	.999	2.21	1977:1–1992:2
	(237.78)	(15.06)					

6.12 Equation 11 PX: Export Price Index

Equation 11 explains the export price index, PX. It provides a link from the
GDP deflator, PY, to the export price index. Export prices are needed when
the countries are linked together (see Table B.4 in Appendix B). If a country
produced only one good, then the export price would be the domestic price
and only one price equation would be needed. In practice, of course, a country
produces many goods, only some of which are exported. If a country is a
price taker with respect to its exports, then its export prices would just be the
world prices of the export goods. To try to capture the in between case where
a country has some effect on its export prices but not complete control over
every price, the following equation is postulated:

$$PX = PY^\lambda (PW\$ \cdot E)^{1-\lambda} \qquad (6.11)$$

$PW\$$ is the world price index in dollars, and so $PW\$ \cdot E$ is the world price index
in local currency. Equation 6.11 thus takes PX to be a weighted average of
PY and the world price index in local currency, where the weights sum to one.
Equation 11 was not estimated for any of the major oil exporting countries,

and so $PW\$$ was constructed to be net of oil prices. (See equations L-4 in Table B.4.)

Equation 6.11 was estimated in the following form:

$$\log PX - \log(PW\$ \cdot E) = \lambda[\log PY - \log(PW\$ \cdot E)] \qquad (6.12)$$

The restriction that the weights sum to one and that $PW\$$ and E have the same coefficient (i.e, that their product enters the equation) can be tested by adding $\log PY$ and $\log E$ to equation 6.12. If this restriction is not met, these variables should be significant. This is one of the tests performed in Table 6.11b.

Some of the estimates of λ in Table 6.11a are close to one (a few are slightly greater than one). For these countries, therefore, there is essentially a one to one link between PY and PX. Equation 11 was estimated under the assumption of a second order autoregressive error, and the estimates of the autoregressive parameters are generally large.

Equation 11 does reasonably well in the tests. The restriction discussed above is rejected in 10 of the 30 cases. The equation fails the RHO+ test in 3 cases. Multicollinearity problems prevented the stability test from being performed for 5 countries (FR, NE, FI, DE, and GR). Of the 25 remaining cases, the equation fails the stability test in 4 of them.

It should be kept in mind that equation 11 is meant only as a rough approximation. If more disaggregated data were available, one would want to estimate separate price equations for each good, where some goods' prices would be strongly influenced by world prices and some would not. This type of disaggregation is beyond the scope of the present work.

6.13 Equation 12: W: Wage Rate

Equation 12 explains the wage rate. It is similar to equation 16 for the US model. It includes as explanatory variables the lagged wage rate, the current price level, the lagged price level, one of three possible measures of labor market tightness (UR, JJS, and ZZ), and a time trend. Equation 16 of the US model included three further lags of the wage rate and price level, which equation 12 does not. Also, equation 16 of the US model does not include any demand pressure variables because none were significant. The same restriction imposed on the price and wage equations in the US model is also imposed here. Given the coefficient estimates of equation 5, the restriction is imposed on the coefficients in equation 12 so that the implied real wage equation does not

Table 6.11a

$$\log PX - \log(PW\$ \cdot E) = \lambda[\log PY - \log(PW\$ \cdot E)]$$

	λ	ρ_1	ρ_2	SE	R^2	DW
Quarterly						
CA	.743	1.307	-.300	.0167	0.975	2.14
	(13.43)	(13.08)	(-2.93)			
JA	.514	.919	.075	.0203	0.892	1.97
	(10.12)	(7.24)	(0.60)			
AU	.661	.817	.179	.0254	0.881	2.03
	(7.74)	(6.90)	(1.52)			
FR	.561	.924	.075	.0105	0.968	1.96
	(17.93)	(8.55)	(0.69)			
GE	.819	1.214	-.215	.0108	0.983	2.03
	(23.24)	(11.59)	(-2.06)			
IT	.458	.864	.135	.0184	0.936	2.00
	(7.11)	(7.62)	(1.19)			
NE	.551	1.476	-.476	.0145	0.884	1.92
	(8.99)	(12.13)	(-3.92)			
ST	.971	.877	.015	.0240	0.974	1.98
	(238.77)	(7.93)	(0.14)			
UK	710	1.199	-.217	.0154	0.972	2.00
	(17.62)	(12.49)	(-2.21)			
FI	.496	.939	.062	.0139	0.970	1.98
.	(7.36)	(7.35)	(0.49)			
AS	.626	1.261	-.267	.0308	0.945	1.95
	(8.38)	(11.64)	(-2.41)			
SO	.695	.866	.140	.0325	0.939	2.05
	(10.88)	(9.44)	(1.49)			
KO	.091	1.167	-.194	.0325	0.869	1.98
	(2.18)	(12.20)	(-2.03)			
Annual						
BE	.963	1.049	-.394	.0479	0.493	1.86
	(92.62)	(4.81)	(-1.84)			
DE	.549	.983	.014	.0188	0.911	1.84
	(9.91)	(4.64)	(0.07)			
NO	.965	1.169	-.453	.0898	0.591	1.74
	(59.86)	(4.85)	(-1.82)			
SW	.988	1.148	-.433	.0444	0.605	1.69
	(139.63)	(5.02)	(-1.83)			
GR	.982	.906	-.129	.0608	0.821	1.81
	(28.66)	(4.07)	(-0.62)			
IR	.422	1.053	-.144	.0294	0.480	1.82
	(4.55)	(4.17)	(-0.57)			
PO	1.026	1.266	-.029	.0356	0.918	1.94
	(63.90)	(6.26)	(-0.11)			
SP	.413	1.277	-.292	.0352	0.906	1.56
	(3.93)	(5.98)	(-1.39)			
NZ	1.007	.846	-.087	.0817	0.584	1.92
	(10.03)	(4.27)	(-0.42)			
CO	1.004	.900	-.275	.1391	0.772	2.06
	(21.71)	(3.87)	(-1.19)			
JO	.380	1.145	-.092	.0361	0.891	1.90
	(3.31)	(4.58)	(-0.35)			
SY	1.179	1.303	-.378	.1812	0.875	2.20
	(7.93)	(6.61)	(-1.79)			
ID	.976	1.187	-.354	.0545	0.795	1.85
	(69.58)	(6.33)	(-1.87)			
MA	.959	.837	-.234	.1378	0.667	1.95
	(11.68)	(3.16)	(-0.88)			
PA	1.014	.601	-.346	.0737	0.636	1.83
	(177.43)	(5.34)	(-3.74)			
PH	1.039	.262	.046	.1828	0.629	1.20
	(85.10)	(1.46)	(0.27)			
TH	1.005	.966	-.468	.0655	0.744	1.84
	(153.42)	(5.62)	(-2.78)			

Table 6.11b
Test Results for Equation 11

	Restr[a] p-val	RHO+ p-val	Stability AP (df) λ	Sample
Quarterly				
CA	.609	.011	3.56 (3) 5.57	1969:1–1992:3
JA	.000	.457	1.21 (3) 3.57	1976:1–1992:3
AU	.000	.001	3.02 (3) 1.05	1971:1–1991:2
FR	.003	.875	–	1971:1–1992:2
GE	.011	.517	1.95 (3) 2.66	1969:1–1991:4
IT	.155	.681	1.89 (3) 1.97	1972:1–1991:4
NE	.286	.839	–	1978:2–1991:4
ST	.144	.885	2.86 (3) 2.17	1971:1–1991:4
UK	.147	.919	4.73 (3) 3.92	1966:1–1992:3
FI	.778	.023	–	1976:1–1991:4
AS	.001	.496	4.07 (3) 1.69	1971:1–1992:2
SO	.008	.044	1.37 (3) 4.51	1962:1–1991:2
KO	.000	.912	*11.75 (3) 2.03	1964:1–1991:4
Annual				
BE	.676	.696	1.61 (3) 1.00	1969–1990
DE	.602	.193	–	1969–1990
NO	.567	.897	1.60 (3) 1.00	1974–1990
SW	.091	.524	3.95 (3) 1.00	1969–1990
GR	.635	.002	–	1965–1990
IR	.522	.430	2.39 (3) 1.00	1969–1990
PO	.957	.006	*17.43 (3) 1.00	1962–1990
SP	.266	.012	1.70 (3) 1.00	1969–1990
NZ	.218	.295	4.69 (3) 1.00	1962–1990
CO	.287	.509	2.09 (3) 1.00	1972–1991
JO	.000	.992	2.44 (3) 1.00	1971–1991
SY	.050	.138	2.95 (3) 1.00	1965–1990
ID	.005	.583	*14.54 (3) 1.00	1962–1989
MA	.329	.677	0.10 (3) 1.00	1972–1987
PA	.009	.069	1.96 (3) 1.00	1972–1991
PH	.001	.944	*5.92 (3) 1.00	1962–1991
TH	.075	.508	1.11 (3) 1.00	1962–1990

[a] log PY and log E added.
*Significant at the one percent level.

have the real wage depend on either the nominal wage rate or the price level separately. (See the discussion of equations 5.35, 5.36, and 5.37 in Section 5.4.)

The estimate of the constant term is not presented in Table 6.12a. The results show that there is a scattering of support for the labor market tightness variables having an effect on the wage rate. One of the variables appears in 12 of the 18 equations, although in half of the 12 the variable is not significant.

The test results in Table 6.12b show that the real wage restriction is rejected in 5 of the 18 cases. Three of the 18 equations fail the lags test, 7 fail the

Table 6.12a

$$\log W = a_1 + a_2 T + a_3 \log W_{-1} + a_4 \log PY$$
$$+ a_5 (U \, Ror \, J \, J \, Sor \, ZZ) + a_6 \log PY_{-1}$$

	a_2	a_3	a_4	a_5	ρ	SE	DW	a_6
Quarterly								
CA	.00009	.955	1.034	–	.108	.0095	1.97	-.986
	(0.62)	(30.20)	(9.07)		(1.03)			
JA	.00032	.916	1.025	–	-.169	.0093	1.86	-.937
	(2.22)	(23.03)	(10.04)		(-1.54)			
AU	.00098	.824	-.425	^{c}.147	–	.0232	2.87	.553
	(3.53)	(13.27)	(-1.36)	(0.89)				
FR	-.00010	1.001	.927	–	–	.0107	1.92	-.933
	(-0.69)	(22.21)	(3.64)					
GE	.00036	.902	1.109	-.069	–	.0110	2.20	-1.004
	(1.79)	(20.37)	(2.19)	(-0.74)				
IT	.00039	.943	.990	^{a}-.377	–	.0135	1.72	-.934
	(1.40)	(25.09)	(4.82)	(-1.80)				
NE	.00157	.552	.153	^{c}-.029	-.241	.0073	1.74	.111
	(7.96)	(7.80)	(1.26)	(-0.55)	(-1.56)			
UK	.00101	.901	.789	–	–	.0117	2.18	-.711
	(3.84)	(26.36)	(12.37)					
FI	.00278	.406	.213	^{a}-.535	–	.0186	2.24	.340
	(4.65)	(3.41)	(0.49)	(-2.41)				
KO	.00786	.582	.809	^{c}-.560	–	.0403	2.02	-.444
	(7.22)	(8.68)	(13.36)	(-3.55)				
Annual								
BE	-.00035	1.147	.793	-1.013	–	.0154	1.54	-.989
	(-0.19)	(15.53)	(3.51)	(-4.34)				
DE	-.00273	1.003	1.290	-.840	-.373	.0179	2.18	-1.239
	(-1.57)	(8.51)	(5.30)	(-4.06)	(-1.52)			
NO	.04361	.477	-.049	^{b}.628	–	.0265	1.72	.064
	(5.45)	(4.45)	(-0.24)	(2.10)				
SW	.00175	-.277	.890	-5.347	.589	.0184	2.14	.371
	(0.49)	(-1.74)	(3.07)	(-4.99)	(4.08)			
GR	.03361	.444	.659	–	.829	.0365	1.89	-.185
	(2.51)	(1.44)	(2.88)		(3.64)			
IR	.00331	1.096	.704	–	–	.0253	1.73	-.879
	(1.17)	(6.81)	(4.63)					
SP	-.01438	.579	.574	-.493	.905	.0143	1.95	-.220
	(-0.24)	(2.08)	(2.87)	(-1.08)	(6.67)			
NZ	.00302	.493	.687	^{c}-.407	.815	.0307	1.46	-.210
	(0.68)	(2.01)	(4.27)	(-1.82)	(4.32)			

^{a}Variable lagged once. ^{b}$J J S$ rather than $U R$. ^{c}ZZ rather than $U R$.

RHO+ test, and 8 fail the stability test. The overall test performance is thus only modest.

Table 6.12b
Test Results for Equation 12

	Restr[a] p-val	Lags p-val	RHO+ p-val	Stability AP (df) λ	Sample
Quarterly					
CA	.850	.824	.000	*29.49 (6) 4.25	1966:1–1992:3
JA	.002	.094	.035	4.63 (5) 2.21	1971:1–1992:3
AU	.067	.000	.000	*21.80 (5) 2.21	1971:1–1991:2
FR	.140	.836	.031	*20.23 (4) 2.03	1971:1–1992:2
GE	.000	.369	.000	*13.95 (5) 2.66	1969:1–1991:4
IT	.297	.241	.002	7.20 (5) 2.01	1972:1–1991:4
NE	.070	.218	.008	6.34 (6) 1.00	1978:2–1991:4
UK	.215	.262	.481	*13.56 (4) 3.92	1966:1–1992:3
FI	.003	.081	.000	*15.33 (5) 1.00	1976:1–1991:4
KO	.000	.004	.000	*31.46 (5) 2.03	1964:1–1991:4
Annual					
BE	.010	.076	.528	4.90 (5) 1.00	1969–1990
DE	.494	.313	.038	3.08 (6) 1.00	1969–1990
NO	.341	.000	.600	7.22 (5) 1.00	1974–1990
SW	.517	.209	.869	7.64 (6) 1.00	1969–1990
GR	.199	.829	.465	6.49 (5) 1.00	1964–1990
IR	.348	.746	.486	*7.11 (4) 1.00	1969–1990
SP	.207	.666	.193	4.26 (6) 1.00	1972–1990
NZ	.744	.077	.041	5.04 (6) 1.00	1962–1990

[a]$\log PY_{-1}$ added.
*Significant at the one percent level.

6.14 Equation 13: J: Employment

Equation 13 explains the change in employment. It is in log form, and it is similar to equation 13 for the US model. It includes as explanatory variables the amount of excess labor on hand, the change in output, the lagged change in output, and a time trend. Equation 13 for the US model does not include the lagged change in output because it was not significant. On the other hand, US equation 13 includes terms designed to pick up a break in the sample period, which equation 13 does not, and it includes the lagged change in employment, which equation 13 does not.

Most of the coefficient estimates for the excess labor variable are significant in Table 6.13a, which is at least indirect support for the theory that firms at times hold excess labor and that the amount of excess labor on hand affects current employment decisions. Most of the change in output terms are also significant. The equation fails the lags test in 4 of the 15 cases. It passes the RHO+ test and the leads test in all cases.[11] The led value of the change in

---

[11]Multicollinearity problems prevented the leads test from being performed for the UK.

Table 6.13a

$$\Delta \log J = a_1 + a_2 T + a_3 \log(J/JMIN)_{-1} + a_4 \Delta \log Y + a_5 \Delta \log Y_{-1}$$

	a_1	a_2	a_3	a_4	a_5	ρ	SE	DW
Quarterly								
CA	.006	-.000023	-.144	.352	.202	.152	.0045	1.92
	(2.03)	(-1.18)	(-3.64)	(4.38)	(3.59)	(1.36)		
JA	–	.000023	-.059	.135	–	-.203	.0041	2.11
	(-0.17)	(1.61)	(-2.47)	(2.54)		(-2.05)		
AU	-.009	.000084	-.046	.124	.072	-.305	.0070	1.96
	(-2.29)	(2.49)	(-1.31)	(1.34)	(1.03)	(-2.72)		
GE	-.006	.000060	-.145	.156	.038	.482	.0021	2.06
	(-2.77)	(3.79)	(-4.50)	(3.67)	(1.01)	(4.99)		
IT	.002	-.000004	-.069	.105	.031	–	.0056	2.25
	(0.50)	(-0.16)	(-1.83)	(0.91)	(0.32)			
ST	-.004	.000067	-.282	.116	–	.739	.0038	2.53
	(-0.46)	(1.01)	(-4.65)	(1.13)		(8.58)		
UK	.004	.000000	-.229	.174	–	.556	.0034	1.89
	(1.41)	(0.00)	(-5.45)	(4.47)		(5.67)		
FI	.035	-.000259	-.160	.210	.145	–	.0056	2.10
	(3.67)	(-3.93)	(-3.47)	(4.11)	(2.83)			
AS	.007	-.000006	-.322	.182	–	.274	.0046	2.03
	(2.04)	(-0.21)	(-6.26)	(2.83)		(2.26)		
Annual								
BE	-.036	.001245	-.274	.372	.065	–	.0098	2.02
	(-3.22)	(2.96)	(-1.40)	(3.26)	(0.53)			
DE	-.001	.000224	-.729	.424	–	–	.0125	1.61
	(-0.05)	(0.51)	(-4.50)	(3.27)				
NO	-.007	.000042	-.715	.381	–	–	.0099	1.28
	(-0.37)	(0.07)	(-4.29)	(2.68)				
SW	-.004	.000299	-.134	.274	.103	.364	.0072	2.08
	(-0.36)	(0.75)	(-0.82)	(2.48)	(0.75)	(1.24)		
IR	-.020	.001236	-.411	.268	–	–	.0129	1.30
	(-1.78)	(2.25)	(-3.02)	(2.05)				
SP	-.085	.002402	-.103	.601	.378	–	.0107	1.91
	(-5.32)	(5.40)	(-0.61)	(3.91)	(2.96)			

output was used for the leads tests. The equation fails the stability test in 4 cases. The overall tests results for equation 13 are thus quite good.

6.15 Equation 14: $L1$: Labor Force—Men; Equation 15: $L2$: Labor Force—Women

Equations 14 and 15 explain the labor force participation rates of men and women, respectively. They are in log form and are similar to equations 5, 6, and 7 in the US model. The explanatory variables include the real wage, the labor constraint variable, a time trend, and the lagged dependent variable.

The labor constraint variable is significant in most cases in Tables 6.14a and 6.15a, which provides support for the discouraged worker effect. There is only very modest support for the real wage. When the real wage appeared

Table 6.13b
Test Results for Equation 13

	Lags p-val	RHO+ p-val	Leads p-val	Stability AP (df) λ	Sample
Quarterly					
CA	.130	.787	.826	8.11 (6) 4.25	1966:1–1992:3
JA	.650	.013	.045	2.08 (5) 3.57	1967:3–1992:3
AU	.114	.648	.860	*8.86 (6) 2.21	1971:1–1991:2
GE	.053	.043	.918	6.64 (6) 2.66	1969:1–1991:4
IT	.627	.028	.093	0.61 (5) 1.98	1972:1–1991:4
ST	.000	.022	.098	*17.19 (5) 2.17	1971:1–1991:4
UK	.000	.823	–	*10.66 (5) 3.92	1966:1–1992:3
FI	.229	.013	.075	*8.48 (5) 1.00	1977:1–1991:4
AS	.066	.469	.380	6.42 (5) 1.69	1971:1–1992:2
Annual					
BE	.973	.023	.274	1.50 (5) 1.00	1969–1990
DE	.295	.371	.421	3.46 (4) 1.00	1969–1990
NO	.002	.034	.543	0.75 (4) 1.00	1974–1990
SW	.011	.775	.313	3.51 (6) 1.00	1969–1990
IR	.000	.859	.725	5.27 (4) 1.00	1969–1990
SP	.051	.393	.027	2.62 (5) 1.00	1969–1990

*Significant at one the percent level.

in the equation, the log of the price level was added to the equation for one of the tests to test the real wage restriction. The log of the price level was significant (and thus the restriction rejected) in 2 of the 7 cases.

Equation 14 fails the lags test in 2 of the 14 cases and the RHO+ in 5 cases. Equation 15 fails no lags tests out of 10 and 3 RHO+ tests. Both equations do poorly in the stability test. Equation 14 fails the test in 11 of the 14 cases, and equation 15 fails in 7 of 10.

6.16   The Trade Share Equations

As discussed in Chapter 3, α_{ij} is the fraction of country i's exports imported by j, where i runs from 1 to 44 and j runs from 1 to 45. The data on α_{ij} are quarterly, with observations for most ij pairs beginning in 1960:1.

One would expect α_{ij} to depend on country i's export price relative to an index of export prices of all the other countries. The empirical work consisted of trying to estimate the effects of relative prices on α_{ij}. A separate equation was estimated for each ij pair. The equation is the following:

$$\alpha_{ijt} = \beta_{ij1} + \beta_{ij2}\alpha_{ijt-1} + \beta_{ij3}\left(\frac{PX\$_{it}}{\sum_{k=1}^{44} \alpha_{kit} PX\$_{kt}}\right) + \mu_{ijt}$$

$$(t = 1, \cdots, T) \tag{6.13}$$

Table 6.14a

$$\log(L1/POP1) = a_1 + a_2 T + a_3 \log(L1/POP1)_{-1}$$
$$+ a_4 \log(W/PY) + a_5 Z$$

	a_1	a_2	a_3	a_4	a_5	ρ	SE	DW
Quarterly								
CA	-.252	-.000315	.764	.050	.097	–	.0035	1.97
	(-3.87)	(-4.20)	(11.69)	(3.59)	(3.34)			
JA	-.012	-.000097	.897	–	.241	–	.0028	2.21
	(-1.69)	(-2.81)	(19.52)		(2.29)			
AU	-.196	-.000559	.830	[a].019	.142	–	.0062	2.00
	(-2.54)	(-2.64)	(12.68)	(1.08)	(1.48)			
GE	.003	0.000016	.972	–	.038	.148	.0016	1.97
	(0.65)	(1.05)	(61.27)		(2.01)	(1.46)		
IT	-.063	-.000729	.578	–	.087	–	.0033	2.01
	(-4.55)	(-4.72)	(6.50)		(1.44)			
ST	-.005	-.000165	.868	–	.109	–	.0039	1.93
	(-1.94)	(-3.46)	(25.43)		(4.18)			
UK	.014	0.000001	.940	–	.009	–	.0029	1.21
	(1.27)	(0.07)	(19.96)		(0.57)			
FI	-.206	-.000766	.044	–	[a].295	–	.0051	1.69
	(-8.06)	(-8.56)	(0.39)		(5.56)			
AS	.045	0.000229	.843	–	.096	–	.0034	2.10
	(3.34)	(2.99)	(16.85)		(3.46)			
Annual								
BE	-.095	-.001298	.858	.014	.150	–	.0045	1.37
	(-0.74)	(-0.50)	(3.15)	(0.73)	(1.89)			
DE	-.053	0.000098	.827	–	–	–	.0077	1.87
	(-1.99)	(0.20)	(6.64)					
NO	-.384	-.002777	.329	.052	.333	–	.0035	2.47
	(-5.46)	(-7.31)	(3.11)	(3.94)	(6.07)			
SW	-.148	-.003189	.352	–	.595	–	.0057	1.13
	(-3.05)	(-2.68)	(1.58)		(2.63)			
SP	-.029	-.004326	.618	–	.064	–	.0121	1.78
	(-2.44)	(-1.36)	(2.53)		(1.08)			

[a] Variable lagged once.

$PX\$_{it}$ is the price index of country i's exports, and $\sum_{k=1}^{44} \alpha_{kit} PX\$_{kt}$ is an index of all countries' export prices, where the weight for a given country k is the share of k's exports to j in the total imports of i. (In this summation $k = i$ is skipped.)

With i running from 1 to 44, j running from 1 to 45, and not counting $i = j$, there are 1936 $(= 44 \times 44)$ ij pairs. There are thus 1936 potential trade share equations to estimate. In fact, only 1560 trade share equations were estimated. Data did not exist for all pairs and all quarters, and if fewer than 26 observations were available for a given pair, the equation was not estimated for that pair. A few other pairs were excluded because at least some of the observations seemed extreme and likely suffering from measurement error. Almost all of these cases were for the smaller countries.

Table 6.14b
Test Results for Equation 14

	Lags p-val	log PY p-val	RHO+ p-val	Stability AP (df) λ	Sample
Quarterly					
CA	.745	.000	.001	*24.85 (5) 3.36	1968:1–1992:3
JA	.038	–	.007	4.13 (4) 3.57	1967:3–1992:3
AU	.738	.292	.113	*24.58 (5) 2.21	1971:1–1991:2
GE	.760	–	.012	*12.50 (5) 2.66	1969:1–1991:4
IT	.263	–	.000	*20.21 (4) 1.98	1972:1–1991:4
ST	.642	–	.000	*23.57 (4) 2.17	1971:1–1991:4
UK	.000	–	.000	*22.31 (4) 4.25	1968:1–1992:3
FI	.755	–	.137	*11.60 (5) 1.00	1976:1–1991:4
AS	.362	–	.614	4.18 (4) 1.69	1971:1–1992:2
Annual					
BE	.513	.008	.713	*10.82 (5) 1.00	1971–1990
DE	.771	–	.255	2.28 (3) 1.00	1969–1990
NO	.731	.015	.284	*13.11 (5) 1.00	1974–1990
SW	.006	–	.231	*7.88 (4) 1.00	1969–1990
SP	.755	–	.957	*8.36 (4) 1.00	1972–1990

*Significant at the one percent level.

Each of the 1560 equations was estimated by ordinary least squares. The main coefficient of interest is β_{ij3}, the coefficient of the relative price variable. Of the 1560 estimates of this coefficient, 83.3 percent (1299) were of the expected negative sign. 44.4 percent had the correct sign and a t-statistic greater than two in absolute value, and 68.1 percent had the correct sign and a t-statistic greater than one in absolute value. 3.2 percent had the wrong sign and a t-statistic greater than two, and 7.5 percent had the wrong sign and a t-statistic greater than one. The overall results are thus quite supportive of the view that relative prices affect trade shares.

The average of the 1299 estimates of β_{ij3} that were of the right sign is $-.0132$. β_{ij3} measures the short run effect of a relative price change on the trade share. The long run effect is $\beta_{ij3}/(1-\beta_{ij2})$, and the average of the 1299 values of this is $-.0580$.

The trade share equations with the wrong sign for β_{ij3} were not used in the solution of the model. The trade shares for these ij pairs were taken to be exogenous.

It should be noted regarding the solution of the model that the predicted values of α_{ijt}, say, $\hat{\alpha}_{ijt}$, do not obey the property that $\sum_{i=1}^{44} \hat{\alpha}_{ijt} = 1$. Unless this property is obeyed, the sum of total world exports will not equal the sum of total world imports. For solution purposes each $\hat{\alpha}_{ijt}$ was divided by $\sum_{i=1}^{44} \hat{\alpha}_{ijt} = 1$, and this adjusted figure was used as the predicted trade share.

Table 6.15a

$$\log(L2/POP2) = a_1 + a_2 T + a_3 \log(L2/POP2)_{-1}$$
$$+ a_4 \log(W/PY) + a_5 Z$$

	a_1	a_2	a_3	a_4	a_5	ρ	SE	DW
Quarterly								
JA	-.053	.000067	.938	–	–	–	.0081	2.28
	(-2.61)	(2.40)	(34.89)					
AU	-.167	-.000157	.876	–	.116	-.276	.0101	1.97
	(-3.19)	(-1.60)	(20.72)		(1.25)	(-2.43)		
IT	-.909	.000988	.551	.065	.558	–	.0111	1.81
	(-3.81)	(3.91)	(5.69)	(2.18)	(2.16)			
ST	-.199	.000207	.779	–	.249	–	.0048	1.35
	(-5.31)	(5.06)	(18.58)		(5.23)			
FI	-.049	-.000015	.904	–	.101	–	.0046	2.47
	(-1.60)	(-0.33)	(18.97)		(2.75)			
AS	-.150	.001040	.846	–	.237	.144	.0079	1.97
	(-2.80)	(2.96)	(16.22)		(3.21)	(1.17)		
Annual								
BE	-.662	.002545	.701	.071	.019	-.492	.0031	2.46
	(-5.05)	(2.30)	(7.96)	(9.86)	(0.40)	(-2.50)		
DE	-.429	.003224	.689	.040	–	–	.0129	1.71
	(-1.40)	(1.20)	(3.72)	(0.69)				
SW	-.035	.000124	.918	–	.712	–	.0057	1.57
	(-0.64)	(0.14)	(14.81)		(3.41)			
SP	-1.467	.012422	–	–	.726	–	.0207	1.77
	(-74.12)	(12.97)			(10.41)			

In other words, the values predicted by the equations in 6.13 were adjusted to satisfy the requirement that the trade shares sum to one.

6.17　Additional Comments

The following are a few general remarks about the results in this chapter.

1. Of the equations explaining the components of GDP—M (equation 1), C (equation 2), I (equation 3), and $V1$ (equation 4)—equation 3 is by far the weakest. It may be that the construction of the capital stock series is too crude to allow good results to be obtained, or it may be that the sample sizes are too small to allow the simultaneity issue to be handled well.

2. The strong rejection of the change form of the price equation in Table 6.5b is an important result. As discussed in point 11 in Section 5.10, this has important implications for the long run properties of the model. The significance of the import price index in the price equations is also

Table 6.15b
Test Results for Equation 15

	Lags p-val	log PY p-val	RHO+ p-val	Stability AP (df) λ	Sample
Quarterly					
JA	.095	–	.242	*14.15 (3) 3.57	1967:3–1992:3
AU	.410	–	.168	*22.28 (5) 2.21	1971:1–1991:2
IT	.645	.692	.000	*9.79 (5) 1.98	1972:1–1991:4
ST	.025	–	.000	*39.17 (4) 2.17	1971:1–1991:4
FI	.156	–	.214	*11.46 (5) 1.00	1976:1–1991:4
AS	.548	–	.501	*21.35 (5) 1.42	1971:1–1992:2
Annual					
BE	.167	.371	.243	3.09 (6) 1.00	1971–1990
DE	.320	.253	.534	4.33 (4) 1.00	1969–1990
SW	.420	–	.000	*8.64 (4) 1.00	1969–1990
SP	.131	–	.888	4.64 (3) 1.00	1972–1990

*Significant at the one percent level.

important. This shows how price levels in different countries affect each other.

3. The results of estimating the demand for money equations in Table 6.6a provide further support for the nominal adjustment hypothesis over the real adjustment hypothesis. See also point 5 in Section 5.10.

4. The U.S. interest rate is significant in 11 of the interest rate reaction functions in Table 6.7a. This is evidence that the Fed influences the economies of other countries by influencing other countries' interest rates. It will be seen in Chapter 12 that this is an important link.

5. A key question for the exchange rate equations in Table 6.9a is whether one can trust the inclusion of the relative interest rate variable in the equations. The verdict is not yet in on this question.

6. The excess labor variable is significant in most of the equations in Table 6.13a, which adds further support to the theory that firms at times hoard labor.

7. As was the case for the US model, the results support the use of nominal interest rates over real interest rates. In very few cases is the inflation expectations variable significant.

8. There is little support for the use of the led values and thus little support for the rational expectations hypothesis. The led values are significant

at the one percent level in only 18 of the 153 cases in which they were tried.

9. The equations in general do well for the lags, T, and RHO+ tests. For the lags test there are 45 failures out of 274 cases; for the T test there are 44 failures out of 217 cases; and for the RHO+ test there are 43 failures out of 304 cases. These results suggest that the dynamic specification of the equations is reasonably good. The results are not as good for the stability test, where there are 105 failures out of 299 cases. More observations are probably needed before much can be done about this problem.

7

Estimating and Testing Complete Models

7.1 Notation

This chapter discusses the estimation and testing of complete models. Some additional notation is needed from that used in Chapter 4 to handle the complete model case. The model will continue to be written as in 4.1. The additional notation is as follows. J_t denotes the $n \times n$ Jacobian whose ij element is $\partial f_i / \partial y_{jt}$, $(i, j = 1, \ldots, n)$. u denotes the $m \cdot T$–dimensional vector $(u_{11}, \ldots, u_{1T}, \ldots, u_{m1}, \ldots, u_{mT})'$. G' denotes the $k \times m \cdot T$ matrix:

$$G' = \begin{bmatrix} G'_1 & 0 & . & . & . & 0 \\ 0 & G'_2 & & & & \\ . & & . & & & \\ . & & & . & & \\ . & & & & . & \\ 0 & & & & & G'_m \end{bmatrix}$$

where G'_i is defined in Section 4.1. Finally, u_t denotes the m–dimensional vector $(u_{1t}, \ldots, u_{mt})$, and Σ denotes the $m \times m$ covariance matrix of u_t.

7.2   3SLS and FIML[1]

Two full information estimation techniques are three stage least squares (3SLS) and full information maximum likelihood (FIML). 3SLS estimates of α are obtained by minimizing

$$S = u'[\hat{\Sigma}^{-1} \otimes Z(Z'Z)^{-1}Z']u = u'Du \tag{7.1}$$

with respect to α, where $\hat{\Sigma}$ is a consistent estimate of Σ and Z is a $T \times K$ matrix of predetermined variables. An estimate of the covariance matrix of the 3SLS coefficient estimates (denoted $\hat{V}_3$) is

$$\hat{V}_3 = (\hat{G}'D\hat{G})^{-1} \tag{7.2}$$

where $\hat{G}$ is G evaluated at the 3SLS estimate of α. Σ is usually estimated from the 2SLS estimated residuals, which is done for the computational work in the next chapter.

Under the assumption that u_t is independently and identically distributed as multivariate normal $N(0, \Sigma)$, FIML estimates of α are obtained by maximizing

$$L = -\frac{T}{2}\log|\Sigma| + \sum_{t=1}^{T}\log|J_t| \tag{7.3}$$

with respect to α. An estimate of the covariance matrix of the FIML coefficient estimates (denoted $\hat{V}_4$) is

$$\hat{V}_4 = -\left(\frac{\partial^2 L}{\partial\alpha\,\partial\alpha'}\right)^{-1} \tag{7.4}$$

where the derivatives are evaluated at the optimum.

7.3   Stochastic Simulation[2]

Some of the methods in this chapter and in Chapter 10 require stochastic simulation, and so it will be useful to give a brief review of it. Stochastic simulation requires that an assumption be made about the distribution of u_t. It is usually assumed that u_t is independently and identically distributed as

---

[1] See Fair (1984), Sections 6.3.3, 6.3.4, 6.5.2, and 6.5.3, for a more detailed discussion of the 3SLS and FIML estimators.

[2] See Fair (1984), Section 7.3, for a more detailed discussion of stochastic simulation.

multivariate normal $N(0, \Sigma)$, although other assumptions can clearly be used. Alternative assumptions simply change the way the error terms are drawn. For the results in this book, the normality assumption has always been used. Stochastic simulation also requires that consistent estimates of α_i be available for all i. Given these estimates, denoted $\hat{\alpha}_i$, consistent estimates of u_{it}, denoted $\hat{u}_{it}$, can be computed as $f_i(y_t, x_t, \hat{\alpha}_i)$. The covariance matrix Σ can then be estimated as $(1/T)\hat{U}\hat{U}'$, where $\hat{U}$ is the $m \times T$ matrix of the values of $\hat{u}_{it}$.

Let u_t^* denote a particular draw of the m error terms for period t from the $N(0, \hat{\Sigma})$ distribution. Given u_t^* and given $\hat{\alpha}_i$ for all i, one can solve the model for period t. This is merely a deterministic simulation for the given values of the error terms and coefficients. Call this simulation a "repetition." Another repetition can be made by drawing a new set of values of u_t^* and solving again. This can be done as many times as desired. From each repetition one obtains a prediction of each endogenous variable. Let y_{it}^j denote the value on the jth repetition of variable i for period t. For J repetitions, the stochastic simulation estimate of the expected value of variable i for period t, denoted $\tilde{\mu}_{it}$, is

$$\tilde{\mu}_{it} = \frac{1}{J} \sum_{j=1}^{J} y_{it}^j \tag{7.5}$$

Let

$$\sigma_{it}^{2j} = (y_{it}^j - \tilde{\mu}_{it})^2 \tag{7.6}$$

The stochastic simulation estimate of the variance of variable i for period t, denoted $\tilde{\sigma}_{it}^2$, is then

$$\tilde{\sigma}_{it}^2 = \frac{1}{J} \sum_{j=1}^{J} \sigma_{it}^{2j} \tag{7.7}$$

Given the data from the repetitions, it is also possible to compute the variances of the stochastic simulation estimates and then to examine the precision of the estimates. The variance of $\tilde{\mu}_{it}$ is simply $\tilde{\sigma}_{it}^2/J$. The variance of $\tilde{\sigma}_{it}^2$, denoted $var(\tilde{\sigma}_{it}^2)$, is

$$var(\tilde{\sigma}_{it}^2) = \left(\frac{1}{J}\right)^2 \sum_{j=1}^{J} (\sigma_{it}^{2j} - \tilde{\sigma}_{it}^2)^2 \tag{7.8}$$

In many applications, one is interested in predicted values more than one period ahead, i.e., in predicted values from dynamic simulations. The above discussion can be easily modified to incorporate this case. One simply draws values for u_t for each period of the simulation. Each repetition is one dynamic simulation over the period of interest. For, say, an eight quarter period, each repetition yields eight predicted values, one per quarter, for each endogenous variable.

It is also possible to draw coefficients for the repetitions. Let $\hat{\alpha}$ denote, say, the 2SLS estimate of all the coefficients in the model, and let $\hat{V}$ denote the estimate of the $k \times k$ covariance matrix of $\hat{\alpha}$. Given $\hat{V}$ and given the normality assumption, an estimate of the distribution of the coefficient estimates is $N(\hat{\alpha}, \hat{V})$. When coefficients are drawn, each repetition consists of a draw of the coefficient vector from $N(\hat{\alpha}, \hat{V})$ and draws of the error terms as above.

An important conclusion that can be drawn from stochastic simulation studies using macroeconometric models is that the values computed from deterministic simulations are quite close to the mean predicted values computed from stochastic simulations. In other words, the bias that results from using deterministic simulation to solve nonlinear models appears to be small.[3]

It may be the case that the forecast means and variances do not exist, although in practice the possible nonexistence of moments is generally ignored. Results in Fair (1984), Section 8.5.5, suggest that the possible nonexistence of moments is not an important problem for macroeconometric models. Alternative measures of dispersion that are robust to the nonexistence problem give very similar results to those obtained using variances.

7.4   Median Unbiased Estimates[4]

The estimator considered in this section will be called the "median unbiased" (MU) estimator. It has been known since the work of Orcutt (1948) and Hurwicz (1950) that least squares estimates of lagged dependent variable (LDV) coefficients are biased even when there are no right hand side endogenous variables. Macroeconometric model builders have generally ignored this problem, perhaps because they feel that the bias is likely to be small for the typical number of observations that are used. Hurwicz's estimates of the bias in an equation with only the LDV as an explanatory variable were small after about 100 observations. For example, for 100 observations the ratio of the expected value of the LDV coefficient estimate to the true value was .9804 (for small values of the coefficient). However, the results in Orcutt and Winokur (1969, Table IV) for 10, 20, and 40 observations show biases larger than those of Hurowitz for the case in which there is a constant term in the equation, suggesting that

---

[3]See Fair (1984), Section 7.3.4, for references.

[4]The material in this section is taken from Fair (1994a).

the bias in this case is also larger for, say, 100 observations. Furthermore, Andrews (1993) has recently shown that the bias is further increased when a time trend is added to the equation. For example, for 100 observations and a true coefficient of .8, the ratio of the median of the LDV coefficient estimate to the true value is .9388 in the equation with the constant term and time trend added.

Typical macroeconomic equations are, of course, more complicated than the equations just discussed. They have more explanatory variables; some of the explanatory variables are likely to be endogenous; the error terms are sometimes serially correlated; and the equations may be nonlinear in both variables and coefficients. It is important to know how the size of the biases for these types of equations compare to those estimated for simpler equations. The following stochastic simulation procedure provides a way of obtaining median unbiased estimates in macroeconometric models. From these estimates the bias for a coefficient, defined as the difference between the base estimates and the MU estimates, can be computed. For the work here the 2SLS estimates will be taken to be the base estimates. This procedure is an extension of Andrews' (1993) idea of computing exact median unbiased estimates in an equation with a constant term, time trend, and lagged dependent variable.

The procedure requires that one coefficient per stochastic equation be singled out for special treatment. The interest here is on the coefficient of the lagged dependent variable, but other coefficients could be considered. Let α_{1i} denote the coefficient of interest in equation i.

The procedure for obtaining median unbiased estimates of the α_{1i} coefficients $(i = 1, \ldots, m)$ using the 2SLS estimator is as follows:

1. Estimate each equation i by 2SLS. Let $\hat{\alpha}_{1i}$ denote the 2SLS estimate of α_{1i}.

2. Guess the bias of $\hat{\alpha}_{1i}$, denoted b_{1i}. Add b_{1i} to $\hat{\alpha}_{1i}$ to obtain a first estimate of the true value of α_{1i}. Let α_{1i}^* denote this estimate: $\alpha_{1i}^* = \hat{\alpha}_{1i} + b_{1i}$. Constrain α_{1i} to be equal to α_{1i}^* and reestimate the other elements of α_i by 2SLS. Let α_i^* denote this estimate of α_i $(i = 1, \ldots, m)$. Use the estimated residuals from these constrained regressions to estimate the covariance matrix Σ. Let Σ^* denote this estimate of Σ.

3. Draw T values of the vector u_t^*, $t = 1, \ldots, T$, from the distribution $N(0, \Sigma^*)$. Use these values and the values α_i^* $(i = 1, \ldots, m)$ to solve the model dynamically for $t = 1, \ldots, T$. This is a dynamic simulation

of the model over the entire estimation period using the drawn values of
the error terms and the coefficient values α_i^*. The lagged endogenous
variable values in x_t in 4.1 are updated in the solution process. After
this solution, update Z_{it} to incorporate the new lagged endogenous
variable values (if lagged endogenous variable values are part of Z_{it}).
Let Z_{it}^*, $t = 1, \ldots, T$, denote this update. Given the new data (i.e., the
solution values of the endogenous and lagged endogenous variables),
estimate each equation by 2SLS, and record the estimate of α_{1i} as $\alpha_{1i}^{(1)}$
($i = 1, \ldots, m$). This is one repetition. Do a second repetition by
drawing another T values of u_t^*, using these values and the values α_i^*
to solve the model, using the new data to estimate each equation by
2SLS, and recording the estimate of α_{1i} as $\alpha_{1i}^{(2)}$ ($i = 1, \ldots, m$). Do
this J times, and then find the median α_{1i}^m of the J values of $\alpha_{1i}^{(j)}$
($j = 1, \ldots, J$), ($i = 1, \ldots, m$).

4. If for each i α_{1i}^m is within a prescribed tolerance level of $\hat{\alpha}_{1i}$, go to step
   6. If this condition is met, it means that for the particular coefficient
   values used to generate the data (the α_i^*'s), the median 2SLS estimates
   are within a prescribed tolerance level of the original estimates based on
   the historical data. If this condition is not met, take the new value of α_{1i}^*
   to be the previous value plus $\hat{\alpha}_{1i} - \alpha_{1i}^m$ for each i. Then constrain α_{1i}
   to be equal to this new value of α_{1i}^* and reestimate the other elements
   of α_i by 2SLS using the historical data. Let α_i^* denote this estimate
   of α_i ($i = 1, \ldots, m$). Again, use the estimated residuals from these
   constrained regressions to estimate the covariance matrix Σ. Let Σ^*
   denote this estimate of Σ. Now repeat step 3 for these new values.

5. Keep doing steps 3 and 4 until convergence is reached and one branches
   to step 6.

6. Take the median unbiased estimate of α_{1i} to be α_{1i}^*, and take the other
   coefficient estimates to be those in α_i^* ($i = 1, \ldots, m$). α_{1i}^* is the median
   unbiased estimate in that it is the value of α_{1i} that generates data that
   lead to the median 2SLS estimate equaling (within a prescribed tolerance
   level) the 2SLS estimate based on the historical data. The estimated bias
   of $\hat{\alpha}_{1i}$ is $\hat{\alpha}_{1i} - \alpha_{1i}^*$.

Confidence intervals for α_{1i}^m can be computed from the final set of values
of $\alpha_{1i}^{(j)}$ ($j = 1, \ldots, J$). For a 90 percent confidence interval, for example,

5 percent of the smallest values and 5 percent of the largest values would be excluded.

As noted above, this procedure does not require the normality assumption. Other distributions could be used to draw the u_t^* values. Also, the basic estimator need not be the 2SLS estimator. Other estimators could be used. The model in 4.1 can also consist of just one equation. In this case Σ is a scalar and the "solution" of the model simply consists of solving the particular equation (dynamically) over the sample period.

The procedure does, however, have two limitations. First, as noted above, it focuses on just one coefficient per equation. No other coefficient estimate in an equation necessarily has the property that its median value in the final set of values is equal to the original estimate. The focus, of course, need not be on the coefficient of the LDV, but it must be on one particular coefficient per equation.

Second, there is no guarantee that the procedure will converge. Remember that overall convergence requires that convergence be reached for each equation, and achieving this much convergence could be a problem. For the results in the next chapter, however, as will be seen, convergence was never a problem.

7.5   Examining the Accuracy of Asymptotic Distributions[5]

It is possible using stochastic simulation and reestimation to examine whether the asymptotic approximations of the distributions of estimators that are used for hypothesis testing are accurate. If some variables are not stationary, the asymptotic approximations may not be very good. In fact, much of the recent literature in time series econometrics has been concerned with the consequences of nonstationary variables.

The procedure proposed here for examining asymptotic distribution accuracy is similar to the procedure of the previous section. Take an estimator, say 2SLS, 3SLS, or FIML, and estimate the model. Take these coefficient estimates, denoted $\hat{\alpha}$, as the base values, and compute $\hat{\Sigma}$ using these estimates. From the $N(0, \hat{\Sigma})$ distribution (assuming the normality assumption is used), draw a vector of the m error terms for each of the T observations. Given these error terms and $\hat{\alpha}$, solve the model for the entire period 1 through T. As in step 3 of the previous section, this is a dynamic simulation of the model over the entire estimation period. The lagged endogenous variable values in 4.1 are

---

[5]As in the previous section, the material in this section is taken from Fair (1994a).

updated in the solution process. Also, the matrices of first stage regressors, Z_{it}, are updated to incorporate the new lagged endogenous variable values if the matrices are used in the estimation, as for 2SLS. The predicted values from this solution form a new data set. Given this data set, estimate the model by the technique in question, and record the set of estimates. This is one repetition. Repeat the draws, solution, and estimation for many repetitions, and record each set of estimates. (Remember that the draws of the errors are always from the $N(0, \hat{\Sigma})$ distribution and that the coefficient vector used in the solution is always $\hat{\alpha}$.)

If J repetitions are done, one has J values of each coefficient estimate, which are likely to be a good approximation of the exact distribution. For ease of exposition, this distribution of the J values will bc called the "exact distribution," although it is only an approximation because Σ is estimated rather than known. The asymptotic distribution can then be compared to this exact distribution to see how close the two distributions are.

There are a number of ways to examine the closeness of the asymptotic distribution to the exact distribution. For the empirical work in the next chapter, the median of the exact distribution for a coefficient was first compared to the coefficient estimate from the technique in question, which is 2SLS in this case. Remember that these coefficient estimates are the ones used to generate the data. One can then examine the bias of a coefficient estimate, defined as the difference between the median and the coefficient estimate. The coefficient estimates of the lagged dependent variables, for example, are likely to be biased downward, as discussed in the previous section.

Next, given the median from the exact distribution and given the estimated standard error of the coefficient estimate from the asymptotic distribution, one can compute the value above which, say, 20 percent of the coefficient estimates should lie if the asymptotic distribution is correct. For 20 percent, this value is the median plus 0.84 times the estimated asymptotic standard error. One can then compute the actual percent of the coefficient estimates from the exact distribution that lie above this value and compare this percent to 20 percent. For the work in the next chapter, this comparison was made for 20, 10, and 5 percent values and for both left and right tails. It will be seen that the exact and asymptotic distributions are generally quite similar regarding their tail properties.

7.6 VAR and AC Models for Comparison Purposes

When testing complete models, it is useful to have benchmark models to use for comparison purposes. Vector autoregressive (VAR) models provide useful benchmarks. As will be seen in the next chapter, however, if the interest is in GDP predictions, "autoregressive components" (AC) models appear to be better benchmarks than VAR models in the sense of being more accurate. An AC model is one in which each component of GDP is regressed on its own lagged values and lagged values of GDP. GDP is then determined from the GDP identity, as the sum of the components. AC models do not have the problem, as VAR models do, of adding large numbers of parameters as the number of variables (components in the AC case) is increased.

Two VAR Models

Two seven variable VAR models are used in the next chapter for comparison with the US model. The seven variables are (in the notation of the variables in the US model) 1) the log of real GDP, $\log GDPR$, 2) the log of the GDP deflator, $\log GDPD$, 3) the log of the wage rate, $\log WF$, 4) the log of the import price deflator, $\log PIM$, 5) the log of the money supply, $\log M1$, 6) the unemployment rate, UR, and 7) the bill rate, RS. These are the same variables used by Sims (1980) with the exception of RS, which has been added here.

For the first VAR model, denoted VAR4, each of the seven variables is taken to be a function of the constant, a time trend, its first four lagged values, and the first four lagged values of each of the other variables. There are thus 30 coefficients to estimate per each of the seven equations. For the second VAR model, denoted VAR5/2, each of the seven variables is taken to be a function of the constant, a time trend, its first five lagged values, and the first two lagged values of each of the other variables, for a total of 19 coefficients per equation.

It is possible to decrease the number of unrestricted coefficients to estimate in VAR models by imposing various priors on the coefficients. For the work in Fair and Shiller (1990) three sets of Bayesian priors were imposed on VAR4. The results using these versions were similar to the results using VAR4, and very little gain seemed to result from the use of the priors in terms of making the VAR models more accurate. Therefore, although no priors were imposed for the work in this book, the results using VAR4 are likely to be close to the results that would be obtained using priors.[6]

---

[6]Sims (1993) considers a nine variable VAR model with five lags and imposes an elab-

The AC Model[7]

There are 19 components of $GDPR$ in the US model (counting the statistical discrepancy $STATP$), and the AC model used in the next chapter consists of estimated equations for each of these components.[8] Each component is taken to be a function of the constant, a time trend, its first five lagged values, and the first two lagged values of $GDPR$. The final equation of the AC model is the $GDPR$ identity.

The results in Fair and Shiller (1990) show that going from a few components to 17 improves the accuracy of the AC model,[9] but that going beyond this does not. The results also show that adding lagged values of $GDPR$ (versus not having $GDPR$ in the equations at all) leads to a slight improvement in accuracy. As with different versions of the VAR model, however, the results are not highly sensitive to different versions of the AC model (i.e., alternative choices of number of components, the length of the lag, and whether or not lagged values of $GDPR$ are included).

7.7 Comparing Predictive Accuracy[10]

As discussed in Section 7.3, stochastic simulation allows one to compute forecast error variances. Let $\tilde{\sigma}^2_{itk}$ denote the stochastic simulation estimate of the variance of the forecast error for a k period ahead forecast of variable i from a simulation beginning in period t. This estimate is presented in equation 7.7 except that a k subscript has been added to denote the length ahead of the forecast. If the estimated variance is based on draws of both the error terms and coefficients, then the uncertainty from both of these sources has been accounted for.

One might think that forecast error variances computed in this way could

---

orate set of priors on the coefficients. In future work it would be interesting to see how well this model does compared to, say, VAR4, but at the present time it would be extremely difficult to try to duplicate Sims' procedures.

[7]AC models were first proposed in Fair and Shiller (1990).

[8]The 19 components in alphabetical order are CD, CN, COG, COS, CS, EX, IHB, IHF, IHH, IKB, IKF, IKG, IKH, IM, IVF, IVH, $PROG$, $PROS$, and $STATP$. $PROG$ and $PROS$ are combined in the US model in such a way that they do not appear as separate variables. They are, however, raw data variables and are defined in Table A.4.

[9]The number of components in the US model at the time of this work was 17, hence 17 instead of 19 components were used.

[10]The method discussed in this section was briefly outlined in Section 1.2, and it is discussed in more detail in Fair (1980a) and in Fair (1984), Chapter 8.

simply be compared across models to see which variances are smaller. There are, however, two additional problems. The first is controlling for different sets of exogenous variables across models (VAR and AC models, for example, have no exogenous variables, whereas a model like the US model has many). This can be done in a variety of ways. One is to estimate autoregressive equations for each exogenous variable and add these equations to the model. The expanded model can then be stochastically simulated to get the variances. The expanded model in effect has no exogenous variables. Another way is to estimate in some manner the forecast error variance for each exogenous variable (perhaps using past errors made by forecasting services in forecasting the variable) and then use these estimates and, say, the normality assumption to draw exogenous variable values for the stochastic simulation.

The second problem is the possibility of data mining. A model may have small estimated variances of the structural error terms and small estimated variances of the coefficient estimates (which leads to small forecast error variances from the stochastic simulation) because it has managed to spuriously fit the sample well. A further step is needed to handle this problem, which is to compare variances estimated from outside sample forecast errors with variances estimated from stochastic simulation. The expected value of the difference between the two estimated variances for a given variable and period is zero for a correctly specified model. The expected value is not in general zero for a misspecified model, and this fact can be used to adjust the forecast error variances for the effects of misspecification.

Let the prediction period begin one period after the end of the estimation period, and call this period s. Consider stochastic simulation with both error terms and coefficients drawn. From a stochastic simulation beginning in period s one obtains an estimate of the variance of the forecast error, $\tilde{\sigma}^2_{isk}$, in equation 7.7, where again k refers to the length ahead of the forecast. From this simulation one also obtains an estimate of the expected value of the k period ahead forecast of variable i, $\tilde{\mu}_{isk}$, in equation 7.5. The difference between this estimate and the actual value, y_{is+k-1}, is the mean forecast error, denoted $\hat{\epsilon}_{isk}$:

$$\hat{\epsilon}_{isk} = y_{is+k-1} - \tilde{\mu}_{isk} \qquad (7.9)$$

If it is assumed that $\tilde{\mu}_{isk}$ exactly equals the true expected value, then $\hat{\epsilon}_{isk}$ in equation 7.9 is a sample draw from a distribution with a known mean of zero and variance σ^2_{isk}, where σ^2_{isk} is the true variance. The square of this error, $\hat{\epsilon}^2_{isk}$, is thus under this assumption an unbiased estimate of σ^2_{isk}. One therefore has two estimates of σ^2_{isk}, one computed from the mean forecast error and one computed by stochastic simulation. Let d_{isk} denote the difference between these two estimates:

$$d_{isk} = \hat{\epsilon}_{isk}^2 - \tilde{\sigma}_{isk}^2 \qquad (7.10)$$

If it is further assumed that $\tilde{\sigma}_{isk}^2$ exactly equals the true value (i.e., $\tilde{\sigma}_{isk}^2 = \sigma_{isk}^2$), then d_{isk} is the difference between the estimated variance based on the mean forecast error and the true variance. Therefore, under the two assumptions of no error in the stochastic simulation estimates, the expected value of d_{isk} is zero for a correctly specified model.

If a model is misspecified, it is not in general true that the expected value of d_{isk} is zero. Misspecification has two effects on d_{isk}. First, if the model is misspecified, the estimated covariance matrices that are used for the stochastic simulation will not in general be unbiased estimates of the true covariance matrices. The estimated variances computed by means of stochastic simulation will thus in general be biased. Second, the estimated variances computed from the forecast errors will in general be biased estimates of the true variances. Since misspecification affects both estimates, the effect on d_{isk} is ambiguous. It is possible for misspecification to affect the two estimates in the same way and thus leave the expected value of the difference between them equal to zero. In general, however, this does not seem likely, and so in general one would not expect the expected value of d_{isk} to be zero for a misspecified model.

Because of the common practice in macroeconometric work of searching for equations that fit the data well (data mining), it seems likely that the estimated means of d_{isk} will be positive in practice for a misspecified model. If the model fits the data well within sample, the stochastic simulation estimates of the variances will be small because they are based on draws from estimated distributions of the error terms and coefficient estimates that have small (in a matrix sense) covariance matrices. If the model, although fitting the data well, is in fact misspecified, this should result in large outside sample forecast errors. The estimated mean of d_{isk} is thus likely to be positive: $\tilde{\sigma}_{isk}^2$ is small because of small estimated covariance matrices, and $\hat{\epsilon}_{isk}^2$ is large because of large outside sample forecast errors.

The procedure described so far uses only one estimation period and one prediction period, where the estimation period ends in period $s - 1$ and the prediction period begins in period s. It results in one value of d_{isk} for each variable i and each length ahead k. Since one observation is obviously not adequate for estimating the mean of d_{isk}, more observations must be generated. This can be done by using successively new estimation periods and new prediction periods. Assume, for example, that one has data from period 1 through period 150. The model can be estimated through, say, period 100, with the prediction beginning with period 101. Stochastic simulation for the prediction period will yield for each i and k a value of $d_{i\,101k}$ in equation 7.10. The model can then be reestimated through period 101, with the prediction period now beginning with period 102. Stochastic simulation for this prediction period will yield for each i and k a value of $d_{i\,102k}$. This process can be repeated through the estimation period ending with period 149. For the one period ahead forecast ($k = 1$) the procedure will yield for each variable i 50 values of d_{is1} ($s = 101, \dots, 150$); for the two period ahead forecast ($k = 2$) it will yield 49 values of d_{is2}, ($s = 101, \dots, 149$); and so on.

The final step in the process is to make an assumption about the mean of d_{isk} that allows the computed values of d_{isk} to be used to estimate the mean. A variety of assumptions are possible, which are discussed in Fair (1984), Chapter 8. The assumption made for the empirical work in the next chapter is that the mean is constant across time. In other words, misspecification is assumed to affect the mean in the same way for all s. Given this assumption, the mean, denoted as $\bar{d}_{ik}$, can be estimated by merely averaging the computed values of d_{isk}. Note that calculating the individual d_{isk} values that are needed to calculate $\bar{d}_{ik}$ is computer intensive in that it requires estimating and stochastic simulating many times.

Given $\bar{d}_{ik}$, it is possible to estimate the total variance of the forecast error. Assume that the period of interest begins in period t, and let $\tilde{\tilde{\sigma}}^2_{itk}$ denote the stochastic simulation estimate of the variance based on draws of error terms, coefficients, and exogenous variables. The total variance, denoted $\hat{\sigma}^2_{itk}$, is the sum of the stochastic simulation estimate plus $\bar{d}_{ik}$:

$$\hat{\sigma}^2_{itk} = \tilde{\tilde{\sigma}}^2_{itk} + \bar{d}_{ik} \tag{7.11}$$

Since the procedure in arriving at $\hat{\sigma}^2_{itk}$ takes into account the four main sources of uncertainty of a forecast, it can be compared across models for a given i, t, and k.

7.8 Comparing Information in Forecasts[11]

Introduction

This section discusses an alternative way of comparing models from the method of comparing variances in the previous section. It focuses on the

---

[11]The material in this section is taken from Fair and Shiller (1990).

information contained in each model's forecast. Econometric models obviously differ in structure and in the data used, and so their forecasts are not perfectly correlated with each other. How should one interpret the differences in forecasts? Does each model have a strength of its own, so that each forecast represents useful information unique to it, or does one model dominate in the sense of incorporating all the information in the other models plus some?

Structural econometric models make use of large information sets in forecasting a given variable. The information set used in a large scale macroeconometric model is typically so large that the number of predetermined variables exceeds the number of observations available for estimating the model. Estimation can proceed effectively only because of the large number of *a priori* restrictions imposed on the model, restrictions that do not work out to be simple exclusion restrictions on the reduced form equation for the variable forecasted.

VAR models are typically much smaller than structural models and in this sense use less information. The above question with respect to VAR models versus structural models is thus whether the information not contained in VAR models (but contained in structural models) is useful for forecasting purposes. In other words, are the *a priori* restrictions of large scale models useful in producing derived reduced forms that depend on so much information, or is most of the information extraneous? The same question can be asked of AC models versus structural models.

One cannot answer this question by doing conventional tests of the restrictions in a structural model. These restrictions might be wrong in important ways and yet the model contain useful information. Even ignoring this point, however, one cannot perform such tests with most large scale models because, as noted above, there are not enough observations to estimate unrestricted reduced forms.

The question whether one model's forecast of a variable, for example, real GDP, carries different information from another's can be examined by regressing the actual change in the variable on the forecasted changes from the two models. This procedure, which is discussed below, is related to the literature on encompassing tests[12] and the literature on the optimal combination of forecasts.[13] This procedure has two advantages over the standard procedure of computing root mean squared errors (RMSEs) to compare alternative forecasts. First, if the RMSEs are close for two forecasts, little can be

---

[12] See, for example, Davidson and MacKinnon (1981), Hendry and Richard (1982), Chong and Hendry (1986), and Mizon and Richard (1986). See also Nelson (1972) and Cooper and Nelson (1975) for an early use of encompassing like tests.

[13] See, for example, Granger and Newbold (1986).

concluded about the relative merits of the two. With the current procedure one can sometimes discriminate more. Second, even if one RMSE is much smaller than the other, it may still be that the forecast with the higher RMSE contains information not in the other forecast. There is no way to test for this using the RMSE framework.

It should be stressed that the current procedure does not allow one to discover whether all the variables in a model contribute useful information for forecasting. If, say, the regression results reveal that a large model contains all the information in smaller models plus some, it may be that the good results for the large model are due to a small subset of it. It can only be said that the large model contains all the information in the smaller models that it has been tested against, not that it contains no extraneous variables.

The procedure requires that forecasts be based only on information available prior to the forecast period. Assume that the beginning of the forecast period is t, so that only information through period $t - 1$ should be used for the forecasts. There are four ways in which future information can creep into a current forecast. The first is if actual values of the exogenous variables for periods after $t - 1$ are used in the forecast. The second is if the coefficients of the model have been estimated over a sample period that includes observations beyond $t - 1$. The third is if information beyond $t - 1$ has been used in the specification of the model even though for purposes of the tests the model is only estimated through period $t - 1$. The fourth is if information beyond period $t - 1$ has been used in the revisions of the data for periods $t - 1$ and back, such as revised seasonal factors and revised benchmark figures.

One way to handle the exogenous variable problem is to estimate, say, an autoregressive equation for each exogenous variable in the model and add these equations to the model. The expanded model effectively has no exogenous variables in it. This method of dealing with exogenous variables in structural models was advocated by Cooper and Nelson (1975) and McNees (1981). McNees, however, noted that the method handicaps the model: "It is easy to think of exogenous variables (policy variables) whose future values can be anticipated or controlled with complete certainty even if the historical values can be represented by covariance stationary processes; to do so introduces superfluous errors into the model solution." (McNees, 1981, p. 404). For the work in the next chapter autoregressive equations have been estimated for each exogenous variable in the US model, although, as McNees notes, this may bias the results against the US model.

The coefficient problem can be handled by doing rolling estimations for each model. For the forecast for period t, for example, the model can be estimated through period $t - 1$; for the forecast for period $t + 1$, the model can be estimated through period t; and so on. By "model" in this case is meant the model inclusive of any exogenous variable equations. If the beginning observation is held fixed for all the regressions, the sample expands by one observation each time a time period elapses. This rolling estimation was followed for the work in the next chapter.

The third problem—the possibility of using information beyond period $t - 1$ in the specification of the model—is more difficult to handle. Models are typically changed through time, and model builders seldom go back to or are interested in "old" versions. For the work in Fair and Shiller (1990), however, a version of the US model was used that existed as of the second quarter of 1976, and all the predictions were for the period after this. For the work in the next chapter the current version of the US model has been used, and so this potential problem has been ignored here. This may bias the results in favor of the US model, although the changes in the model that have been made since 1976 are fairly minor.

The data revision problem is very hard to handle, and almost no one tries. It is extremely difficult to try to purge the data of the possible use of future information. It is not enough simply to use data that existed at any point in time, say period $t - 1$, because data for period t are needed to compare the predicted values to the actual values. To handle the data revision problem one would have to try to construct data for period t that are consistent with the old data for period $t - 1$, and this is not straightforward. For the work in the next chapter nothing has been done about this problem either.

Forecasts that are based only on information prior to the forecast period will be called "quasi ex ante" forecasts. They are not true ex ante forecasts if they were not issued at the time, but they are forecasts that could in principle have been issued had one been making forecasts at the time.

Quasi ex ante forecasts may, of course, have different properties from forecasts made with a model estimated with future data. If the model is misspecified (e.g., parameters change through time), then the rolling estimation forecasts (where estimated parameters vary through time) may carry rather different information from forecasts estimated over the entire sample.[14] The

---

[14]Even if the model is not misspecified, estimated parameters will change through time due to sampling error. If the purpose were to evaluate the forecasting ability of the true model (i.e., the model with the true coefficients), there would be a generated regressor problem. However, the interest here is in the performance of the model *and* its associated estimation procedure. If one were interested in adjusting for generated regressors, the correction discussed in Murphy and Topel (1985) could not be directly applied here because

focus here is on quasi ex ante forecasts.

It should also be noted that some models may use up more degrees of freedom in estimation than others, and with varied estimation procedures it is often very difficult to take formal account of the number of degrees of freedom used up. In the extreme case where there were so many parameters in a model that the degrees of freedom were completely used up when it was estimated (an obviously over parameterized model), it would be the case that the forecast value equals the actual value and there would be a spurious perfect correspondence between the variable forecasted and the forecast. One can guard against this degrees of freedom problem by requiring that no forecasts be within sample forecasts, which is true of quasi ex ante forecasts proposed here.[15]

The Procedure

Let $_{t-s}\hat{Y}_{1t}$ denote a forecast of Y_t made from model 1 using information available at time $t - s$ and using the model's estimation procedure and forecasting method each period. Let $_{t-s}\hat{Y}_{2t}$ denote the same thing for model 2. (In the notation above, these two forecasts should be quasi ex ante forecasts.) The parameter s is the length ahead of the forecast, $s > 0$. Note that the estimation procedure used to estimate a model and the model's forecasting method are considered as part of the model; no account is taken of these procedures here.

The procedure is based on the following regression equation:

$$Y_t - Y_{t-s} = \alpha + \beta(_{t-s}\hat{Y}_{1t} - Y_{t-s}) + \gamma(_{t-s}\hat{Y}_{2t} - Y_{t-s}) + u_t \qquad (7.12)$$

If neither model 1 nor model 2 contains any information useful for s period ahead forecasting of Y_t, then the estimates of β and γ should both be zero. In this case the estimate of the constant term α would be the average s period change in Y. If both models contain independent information[16] for s period ahead forecasting, then β and γ should both be nonzero. If both models contain information, but the information in, say, model 2 is completely contained in

---

the covariance matrix of the coefficient estimates used to generate the forecasts changes through time because of the use of the rolling regressions. Murphy and Topel require a single covariance matrix.

[15]Nelson (1972) and Cooper and Nelson (1975) do not stipulate that the forecasts be based only on information through the previous period.

[16]If both models contain "independent information" in the present terminology, their forecasts will not be perfectly correlated. Lack of perfect correlation can arise either because the models use different data or because they use the same data but impose different restrictions on the reduced form.

model 1 and model 1 contains further relevant information as well, then β but not γ should be nonzero.[17]

The procedure is to estimate equation 7.12 for different models' forecasts and test the hypothesis H_1 that $\beta = 0$ and the hypothesis H_2 that $\gamma = 0$. H_1 is the hypothesis that model 1's forecasts contain no information relevant to forecasting s periods ahead not in the constant term and in model 2, and H_2 is the hypothesis that model 2's forecasts contain no information not in the constant term and in model 1.

As noted above, this procedure bears some relation to encompassing tests, but the setup and interests are somewhat different. For example, it does not make sense in the current setup to constrain β and γ to sum to one, as is usually the case for encompassing tests. If both models' forecasts are just noise, the estimates of both β and γ should be zero. Also, say that the true process generating Y_t is $Y_t = X_t + Z_t$, where X_t and Z_t are independently distributed. Say that model 1 specifies that Y_t is a function of X_t only and that model 2 specifies that Y_t is a function of Z_t only. Both forecasts should thus have coefficients of one in equation 7.12, and so in this case β and γ would sum to two. It also does not make sense in the current setup to constrain the constant term α to be zero. If, for example, both models' forecasts were noise and equation 7.12 were estimated without a constant term, then the estimates of β and γ would not generally be zero when the mean of the dependent variable is nonzero.

It is also not sensible in the current setup to assume that u_t is identically distributed. It is likely that u_t is heteroskedastic. If, for example, $\alpha = 0$, $\beta = 1$, and $\gamma = 0$, u_t is simply the forecast error from model 1, and in general forecast errors are heteroskedastic. Also, if k period ahead forecasts are considered, where $k > 1$, this introduces a $k - 1$ order moving average process to the error term in equation 7.12.[18] Both heteroskedasticity and the moving average process can be corrected for in the estimation of the standard errors of the coefficient estimates. This can be done using the procedure given by Hansen (1982), Cumby, Huizinga, and Obstfeld (1983), and White and Domowitz (1984) for the estimation of asymptotic covariance matrices. Let $\theta = (\alpha\ \beta\ \gamma)'$. Also, define X as the $T \times 3$ matrix of variables, whose row t is $X_t = (1 \quad {}_{t-s}\hat{Y}_{1t} - Y_{t-s} \quad {}_{t-s}\hat{Y}_{2t} - Y_{t-s})$, and let $\hat{u}_t = Y_t - Y_{t-s} - X_t\hat{\theta}$.

---

[17]If both models contain the same information, then the forecasts are perfectly correlated, and β and γ are not separately identified.

[18]The error term in equation 7.12 could, of course, be serially correlated even for the one period ahead forecasts. Such serial correlation, however, does not appear to be a problem for the work in the next chapter, and so it has been assumed to be zero here.

The covariance matrix of $\hat{\theta}$, $V(\hat{\theta})$, is

$$V(\hat{\theta}) = (X'X)^{-1}S(X'X)^{-1} \tag{7.13}$$

where

$$S = \Omega_0 + \sum_{j=1}^{s-1}(\Omega_j + \Omega_j') \tag{7.14}$$

$$\Omega_j = \sum_{t=j+1}^{T} (u_t u_{t-j})\hat{X}_t'\hat{X}_{t-j} \tag{7.15}$$

where $\hat{\theta}$ is the ordinary least squares estimate of θ and s is the forecast horizon. When s equals 1, the second term on the right hand side of 7.14 is zero, and the covariance matrix is simply White's (1980) correction for heteroskedasticity.

Note that as an alternative to equation 7.12 the *level* of Y could be regressed on the forecasted *levels* and a constant. If Y is an integrated process, then any sensible forecast of Y will be cointegrated with Y itself. In the level regression, the sum of β and γ will thus be constrained in effect to one, and one would in effect be estimating one less parameter. If Y is an integrated process, running the levels regression with an additional independent variable Y_{t-1} (thereby estimating β and γ without constraining their sum to one) is essentially equivalent to the differenced regression 7.12. For variables that are not integrated, the levels version of 7.12 can be used.

It should finally be noted that there are cases in which an optimal forecast does not tend to be singled out as best in regressions of the form 7.12, even with many observations. Say the truth is $Y_t - Y_{t-1} = aX_{t-1} + e_t$. Say that model 1 does rolling regressions of $Y_t - Y_{t-1}$ on X_{t-1} and uses these regressions to forecast. Say that model 2 always takes the forecast to be bX_{t-1} where b is some number other than a, so that model 2 remains forever an incorrect model. In equation 7.12 regressions the two forecasts tend to be increasingly collinear as time goes on; essentially they are collinear after the first part of the sample. Thus, the estimates of β and γ tend to be erratic. Adding a large number of observations does not cause the regressions to single out the first model; it only has the effect of enforcing that $\hat{\beta} + (\hat{\gamma}b)/a = 1$. .

7.9 Estimating Event Probabilities[19]

Stochastic simulation can be used to calculate the probability of various events happening. This is straightforward once the stochastic simulation has been set

---

[19]The material in this section is taken from Fair (1993c)

up and the event defined. Consider a five quarter prediction period and the event that within this period there were two consecutive quarters of negative real GDP growth. Assume that 1000 repetitions are taken. For each repetition one can record whether or not this event occurred. If it occurred, say, 150 times out of the 1000 repetitions, its estimated probability would be 15 percent. Many events, of course, can be considered. The only extra work for each extra event is keeping track of how often each event occurs in the repetitions.

Government policy makers and business planners are obviously interested in knowing the probabilities of various economic events happening. Model builders who make forecasts typically do not directly answer probability questions. They typically present a "base" forecast and a few alternative "scenarios." If probabilities are assigned to the scenarios, they are subjective ones of the model builders.[20] An advantage of estimating probabilities from stochastic simulation is that they are objective in the sense that they are based on the use of estimated distributions. They are consistent with the probability structure of the model.

In estimating probabilities by stochastic simulation, it seems best to draw only error terms (not also coefficients). Although coefficient estimates are uncertain, the true coefficients are fixed. In the real world, the reason that economic events are stochastic is because of stochastic shocks (error terms), not because the coefficients are stochastic. (This is assuming, of course, that the true coefficients are fixed, which is the assumption upon which the estimation is based.)[21] For the estimation of probabilities in the next chapter, only error terms are drawn.

This procedure for estimating probabilities can also be used for testing purposes. It is possible for a given event to compute a *series* of probability estimates and compare these estimates to the actual outcomes. Consider an event A_t, such as two consecutive quarters of negative growth out of five for the period beginning in quarter t. Let P_t denote a model's estimate of the probability of A_t occurring, and let R_t denote the actual outcome of A_t, which is 1 if A_t occurred and 0 otherwise. If one computes these probabilities for $t = 1, \ldots, T$, there are T values of P_t and R_t available, where each value of P_t is derived from a separate stochastic simulation.

To see how good a model is at estimating probabilities, P_t can be compared

---

[20]Stock and Watson (1989) do present, however, within the context of their leading indicator approach, estimates of the probability that the economy will be in a recession six months hence.

[21]I am indebted to Gregory Chow for suggesting to me that one may not want to draw coefficients when estimating probabilities.

to R_t for $t = 1, \ldots, T$. Two common measures of the accuracy of probabilities are the quadratic probability score (QPS):

$$QPS = (1/T) \sum_{t=1}^{T} 2(P_t - R_t)^2 \qquad (7.16)$$

and the log probability score (LPS):

$$LPS = -(1/T) \sum_{t=1}^{T} [(1 - R_t) \log(1 - P_t) + R_t \log P_t] \qquad (7.17)$$

where T is the total number of observations.[22] It is also possible simply to compute the mean of P_t (say $\bar{P}$) and the mean of R_t (say $\bar{R}$) and compare the two means. QPS ranges from 0 to 2, with 0 being perfect accuracy, and LPS ranges from 0 to infinity, with 0 being perfect accuracy. Larger errors are penalized more under LPS than under QPS.

The testing procedure is thus simply to define various events and compute QPS and LPS for alternative models for each event. If model 1 has lower values than model 2, this is evidence in favor of model 1.

7.10 Full Information Estimation and Solution of Rational Expectations Models[23]

Introduction

The single equation estimation of equations with rational expectations was discussed in Section 4.3, where Hansen's method was described. It is also possible, however, to use FIML to estimate models with rational expectations. Methods for the solution and FIML estimation of these models were presented in Fair and Taylor (1983) and also discussed in Fair (1984), Chapter 11. The basic solution method, called the "extended path" (EP) method, has come to be widely used for deterministic simulations of rational expectations models,[24]

---

[22] See, for example, Diebold and Rudebusch (1989).

[23] The material in this section is taken from Fair and Taylor (1990).

[24] For example, the extended path method has been programmed as part of the TROLL computer package and is routinely used to solve large scale rational expectations models at the IMF, the Federal Reserve, the Canadian Financial Ministry, and other government agencies. It has also been used for simulation studies such as DeLong and Summers (1986) and King (1988). Other solution methods for rational expectations models are summarized in Taylor and Uhlig (1990). These other methods do not yet appear practical for medium size models and up.

but probably because of the expense, the full information estimation method has not been tried by others. This earlier work discussed a "less expensive" method for obtaining full information estimates, but the preliminary results using the method were mixed. Since this earlier work, however, more experimenting with the less expensive method has been done, and it seems much more promising than was originally thought.

This section has two objectives. The first is to discuss the new results using the less expensive method that have been obtained and to argue that full information estimation now seems feasible for rational expectations models. In the process of doing this some errors in the earlier work regarding the treatment of models with rational expectations and autoregressive errors are corrected. The second objective is to discuss methods for stochastic simulation of rational expectations models, something that was only briefly touched on in the earlier work.

The Solution Method

The notation for the model used here differs somewhat from the notation used in equation 4.1. The lagged values of the endogenous variables are written out explicitly, and x_t is now a vector of only exogenous variables. The model is written as

$$f_i(y_t, y_{t-1}, \ldots, y_{t-p}, E_{t-1}y_t, E_{t-1}y_{t+1}, \ldots, E_{t-1}y_{t+h}, x_t, \alpha_i) = u_{it}$$
$$\tag{7.18}$$
$$u_{it} = \rho_i u_{it-1} + \epsilon_{it}, \quad (i = 1, \ldots, n) \tag{7.19}$$

where y_t is an n–dimensional vector of endogenous variables, x_t is a vector of exogenous variables, E_{t-1} is the conditional expectations operator based on the model and on information through period $t-1$, α_i is a vector of parameters, ρ_i is the serial correlation coefficient for the error term u_{it}, and ϵ_{it} is an error term that may be correlated across equations but not across time. The function f_i may be nonlinear in variables, parameters, and expectations. The following is a brief review of the solution method for this model. More details are presented in Fair and Taylor (1983) and in Fair (1984), Chapter 11. In what follows i is always meant to run from 1 through n.

Case 1: $\rho_i = 0$

Consider solving the model for period s. It is assumed that estimates of α_i are available, that current and expected future values of the exogenous variables are available, and that the current and future values of the error terms have been set to their expected values (which will always be taken to be zero here). If the expectations $E_{s-1}y_s$, $E_{s-1}y_{s+1}$, ..., $E_{s-1}y_{s+h}$ were known, 7.18 could be solved in the usual ways (usually by the Gauss-Seidel technique). The model would be simultaneous, but future predicted values would not affect current predicted values. The EP method iterates over solution *paths*. Values of the expectations through period $s + h + k + h$ are first guessed, where k is a fairly large number relative to h.[25] Given these guesses, the model can be solved for periods s through $s + h + k$ in the usual ways. This solution provides new values for the expectations through period $s + h + k$—the new expectations values are the solution values. Given these new values, the model can be solved again for periods s through $s + h + k$, which provides new expectations values, and so on. This process stops (if it does) when the solution values for one iteration are within a prescribed tolerance criterion of the solution values for the previous iteration for all periods s through $s + h + k$.

So far the guessed values of the expectations for periods $s + h + k + 1$ through $s + h + k + h$ (the h periods beyond the last period solved) have not been changed. If the solution values for periods s through $s + h$ depend in a nontrivial way on these guesses, then overall convergence has not been achieved. To check for this, the entire process above is repeated for k one larger. If increasing k by one has a trivial effect (based on a tolerance criterion) on the solution values for s through $s + h$, then overall convergence has been achieved; otherwise k must continue to be increased until the criterion is met. In practice what is usually done is to experiment to find the value of k that is large enough to make it likely that further increases are unnecessary for any experiment that might be run and then do no further checking using larger values of k.

The expected future values of the exogenous variables (which are needed for the solution) can either be assumed to be the actual values (if available and known by agents) or be projected from an assumed stochastic process. If the expected future values of the exogenous variables are not the actual values, one extra step is needed at the end of the overall solution. In the above process the expected values of the exogenous variables would be used for all the solutions, the expected values of the exogenous variables being chosen ahead of time. This yields values for $E_{s-1}y_s$, $E_{s-1}y_{s+1}$, ..., $E_{s-1}y_{s+h}$. Given these values,

---

[25]Guessed values are usually taken to be the actual values if the solution is within the period for which data exist. Otherwise, the last observed value of a variable can be used for the future values or the variable can be extrapolated in some simple way. Sometimes information on the steady state solution (if there is one) can be used to help form the guesses.

7.18 is then solved for period s using the *actual* value of x_s, which yields the final solution value $\hat{y}_s$. To the extent that the expected value of x_s differs from the actual value, $E_{s-1}y_s$ will differ from $\hat{y}_s$.

Two points about this method should be mentioned. First, no general convergence proofs are available. If convergence is a problem, one can sometimes "damp" the solution values to obtain convergence. In practice convergence is usually not a problem. There may, of course, be more than one set of solution values, and so there is no guarantee that the particular set found is unique. If there is more than one set, the set that the method finds may depend on the guesses used for the expectations for the h periods beyond $s + h + k$.

Second, the method relies on the certainty equivalence assumption even though the model is nonlinear. Since expectations of functions are treated as functions of the expectations in future periods in equation 7.18, the solution is only approximate unless f_i is linear. This assumption is like the linear quadratic approximation to rational expectations models that has been proposed, for example, by Kydland and Prescott (1982). Although the certainty equivalence assumption is widely used, including in the engineering literature, it is, of course, not always a good approximation.

Case 2: $\rho_i \neq 0$ and Data Before $s - 1$ Available

The existence of serial correlation complicates the problem considerably. The error terms for period $t - 1$ ($u_{it-1}, i = 1, \ldots, n$) depend on expectations that were formed at the end of period $t - 2$, and so a new viewpoint date is introduced. This case is discussed in Section 2.2 in Fair and Taylor (1983), but an error was made in the treatment of the second viewpoint date. The following method replaces the method in Section 2.2 of this paper.[26]

Consider again solving for period s. If the values of u_{is-1} were known, one could solve the model as above. The only difference is that the value of an error term like u_{is+r-1} would be $\rho_i^r u_{is-1}$ instead of zero. The overall solution method first uses the EP method to solve for period $s - j$, where $j > 0$, based on the assumption that $u_{is-j-1} = 0$. Once the expectations are solved for, 7.18 is used to solve for u_{is-j}. The actual values of y_{s-j} and x_{s-j} are used for this purpose (although the solution values are used for the expectations) because these are structural errors being estimated, not reduced form errors. Given the values for u_{is-j}, the model is solved for period $s - j + 1$ using the EP method, where an error term like u_{is-j+r} is computed as $\rho_i^r u_{is-j}$. Once

---

[26] The material in Fair and Taylor (1983) is also presented in Fair (1984), Chapter 11, and so the corrections discussed in this section pertain to both sources.

the expectations are solved for, 7.18 is used to solve for u_{is-j+1}, which can be used in the solution for period $s - j + 2$, and so on through the solution for period s.

The solution for period s is based on the assumption that the error terms for period $s - j - 1$ are zero. To see if the solution values for period s are sensitive to this assumption, the entire process is repeated with j increased by 1. If going back one more period has effects on the solution values for period s that are within a prescribed tolerance criterion, then overall convergence has been achieved; otherwise j must continue to be increased. Again, in practice one usually finds a value of j that is large enough to make it likely that further increases are unnecessary for any experiment that might be run and then do no further checking using larger values of j.

It should be noted that once period s is solved for, period $s + 1$ can be solved for without going back again. From the solution for period s, the values of u_{is} can be computed, which can then be used in the solution for period $s + 1$ using the EP method.

Case 3: $\rho_i \neq 0$ and Data Before Period $s - 1$ not Available

This case is based on the assumption that $\epsilon_{is-1} = 0$ when solving for period s. This type of an assumption is usually made when estimating multiple equation models with moving average residuals. The solution problem is to find the values of u_{is-1} that are consistent with this assumption. The overall method begins by guessing values for u_{is-2}. Given these values, the model can be solved for period $s - 1$ using the EP method and the fact that $u_{is+r-2} = \rho_i^r u_{is-2}$. From the solution values for the expectations, 7.18 and 7.19 can be used to solve for ϵ_{is-1}.[27] If the absolute values of these errors are within a prescribed tolerance criterion, convergence has been achieved. Otherwise, the new guess for u_{is-2} is computed as the old guess plus ϵ_{is-1}/ρ_i. The model is solved again for period $s - 1$ using the new guess and the EP method, and so on until convergence is reached.

At the point of convergence u_{is-1} can be computed as $\rho_i u_{is-2}$, where u_{is-2} is the estimated value on the last iteration (the value consistent with ϵ_{is-1} being within a prescribed tolerance criterion of zero). Given the values of u_{is-1}, one can solve for period s using the EP method, and the solution is finished.

---

[27]These are again estimates of the structural error terms, not the reduced form error terms. Step (iii) on page 1176 in Fair and Taylor (1983) is in error in this respect. The errors computed in step (iii) should be the structural error terms.

Computational Costs

The easiest way to think about the computational costs of the solution method is to consider how many times the equations of a model must be "passed" through. Let N_1 be the number of passes through the model that it takes to solve the model for one period, given the expectations. N_1 is usually some number less than 10 when the Gauss-Seidel technique is used. The EP method requires solving the model for $h + k + 1$ periods. Let N_2 be the number of iterations it takes to achieve convergence over these periods. Then the total number of passes for convergence is $N_2 N_1 (h + k + 1)$. If, say, h is 5, k is 30, N_2 is 15, and N_1 is 5, then the total number of passes needed to solve the model for one period is 11,250, which compares to only 5 when there are no expectations. If k is increased by one to check for overall convergence, the total number of passes is slightly more than doubled, although, as noted above, this check is not always done.

For Case 2 above the number of passes is increased by roughly a factor of j if overall convergence is not checked. Checking for overall convergence slightly more than doubles the number of passes. j is usually a number between 5 and 10. If q is the number of iterations it takes to achieve convergence for Case 3 above, the number of passes is increased by a factor of $q + 1$. In practice q seems to be between about 5 and 10. Note for both Cases 2 and 3 that the number of passes is increased relative to the non serial correlation case only for the solution for the first period (period s). If period $s + 1$ is to be solved for, no additional passes are needed over those for the regular case.

FIML Estimation

Assume that the estimation period is 1 through T. The objective function that FIML maximizes (assuming normality) is presented in equation 7.3 above and is repeated here for convenience

$$L = -\frac{T}{2} \log |\Sigma| + \sum_{t=1}^{T} \log |J_t| \qquad (7.20)$$

Σ is the covariance matrix of the error terms and J_t is the Jacobian matrix for period t. Σ is of the dimension of the number of stochastic equations in the model, and J_t is of the dimension of the total number of equations in the model. The ij element of Σ is $(1/T) \sum_{t=1}^{T} \epsilon_{it} \epsilon_{jt}$. Since the expectations have viewpoint date $t - 1$, they are predetermined from the point of view of taking derivatives for the Jacobian, and so no additional problems are involved for the

Jacobian in the rational expectations case. In what follows α will be used to denote the vector of all the coefficients in the model. In the serial correlation case α also includes the ρ_i coefficients.

FIML estimation of moderate to large models is expensive even in the standard case, and some tricks are needed to make the problem computationally feasible. An algorithm that can be used for large scale applications is discussed in Parke (1982), and this algorithm will not be discussed here. Suffice it to say that FIML estimation of large scale models is computationally feasible, and in fact FIML estimates of the US model are presented in the next chapter. What any algorithm needs to do is to evaluate L many times for alternative values of α in the search for the value that maximizes L.

In the standard case computing Σ for a given value of α is fairly inexpensive. One simply solves 7.18 and 7.19 for the ϵ_{it} error terms given the data and the value of α. This is only one pass through the model since it is the structural error terms that are being computed. In the rational expectations case, however, computing the error terms requires knowing the values of the expectations, which themselves depend on α. Therefore, to compute Σ for a given value of α one has to solve for the expectations for each of the T periods. If, say, 11,250 passes through the model are needed to solve the model for one period and if T is 100, then 1,125,000 passes are needed for one evaluation of Σ and thus one evaluation of L. In the 25 coefficient problem below, the Parke algorithm required 2,817 evaluations of L to converge, which would be over 3 trillion passes if done this way.[28]

It should be clear that the straightforward combination of the EP solution method and FIML estimation procedures is not likely to be computationally feasible for most applications. There is, however, a way of cutting the number of times the model has to be solved over the estimation period to roughly the number of estimated coefficients. The trick is to compute numerical derivatives of the expectations with respect to the parameters and use these derivatives to compute Σ (and thus L) each time the algorithm requires a value of L for a given value of α.

Consider the derivative of $E_{t-1}y_{t+r}$ with respect to the first element of α. One can first solve the model for a given value of α and then solve it again for the first element of α changed by a certain percent, both solutions using the EP method. The computed derivative is then the difference in the two solution values of $E_{t-1}y_{t+r}$ divided by the change in the first element of α. To compute

---

[28]Note that these solutions of the error term ϵ_{it} are only approximations when f_i is nonlinear. Hence, the method gives an approximation of the likelihood function.

all the derivatives requires $K + 1$ solutions of the model over the T number of observations, where K is the dimension of α.[29] One solution is for the base values, and the K solutions are for the K changes in α, one coefficient change per solution. From these $K + 1$ solutions, $K \cdot T(h + 1)$ derivatives are computed and stored for each expectations variable, one derivative for each length ahead for each period for each coefficient.[30] Once these derivatives are computed, they can be used in the computation of Σ for a given change in α, and no further solutions of the model are needed. In other words, when the maximization algorithm changes α and wants the corresponding value of L, the derivatives are first used to compute the expectations, which are then used in the computation of Σ. Since one has (from the derivatives) an estimate of how the expectations change when α changes, one does not have to solve the model any more to get the expectations.

Assuming that the solution method in Case 3 above is used for the FIML estimates, derivatives of u_{it-1} with respect to the coefficients are also needed when the errors are serially correlated. These derivatives can also be computed from the $K + 1$ solutions, and so no extra solutions are needed in the serial correlation case.

Once the $K+1$ solutions of the model have been done and the maximization algorithm has found what it considers to be the optimum, the model can be solved again for the T periods using the optimal coefficient values and then L computed. This value of L will in general differ from the value of L computed using the derivatives for the same coefficient values, since the derivatives are only approximations. At this point the new solution values (not computed using the derivatives) can be used as new base values and the problem turned over to the maximization algorithm again. This is the second "iteration" of the overall process. Once the maximization algorithm has found the new optimum, new base values can be computed, a new iteration performed, and so on. Convergence is achieved when the coefficient estimates from one iteration to the next are within a prescribed tolerance criterion of each other. This

---

[29] In the notation presented in Section 7.1 k rather than K is used to denote the dimension of α. K is used in this section since k has already been used in the description of the EP method.

[30] Derivatives computed this way are "one sided." "Two sided" derivatives would require an extra K solutions, where each coefficient would be both increased and decreased by the given percentage. For the work here two sided derivatives seemed unnecessary. For the results below each coefficient was increased by five percent from its base value when computing the derivatives. Five percent seemed to give slightly better results than one percent, although no systematic procedure of trying to find the optimal percentage size was undertaken.

procedure can be modified by recomputing the derivatives at the end of each iteration. This may improve convergence, but it obviously adds considerably to the expense. At a minimum, one might want to recompute the derivatives at the end of overall convergence and then do one more iteration. If the coefficients change substantially on this iteration, then overall convergence has not in fact been achieved.

Table 7.1 reports the results of estimating three models by FIML using the derivatives. The first model, Model 1, is a version of the wage contracting model in Taylor (1980):

$$y_{1t} = \alpha_{11}y_{1t-1} + \alpha_{12}y_{1t-2} + \alpha_{13}E_{t-1}y_{1t+1} + \alpha_{14}E_{t-1}y_{1t+2}$$

$$+ \alpha_{15}E_{t-1}y_{2t} + \alpha_{16}E_{t-1}y_{2t+1} + \alpha_{17}E_{t-1}y_{2t+2} + u_{1t} \tag{7.21}$$

$$y_{2t} = \alpha_{21}y_{1t} + \alpha_{22}y_{1t-1} + \alpha_{23}y_{1t-2} + u_{2t} \tag{7.22}$$

with the restrictions that $\alpha_{11} = \alpha_{13} = 1/3$, $\alpha_{12} = \alpha_{14} = 1/6$, $\alpha_{15} = \alpha_{16} = \alpha_{17}$, and $\alpha_{21} = \alpha_{22} = \alpha_{23}$. There are two free parameters to estimate, α_{15} and α_{21}. Data for this model were generated using normally distributed serially independent errors with zero correlation between equations. Values of α_{15} and α_{21} of .0333333 and $-.333333$ were used for this purpose. Fifty observations were generated.

Because this model is very small and linear, a factorization procedure can be used to evaluate L exactly. This procedure can in turn be used in the maximization of L using an algorithm like DFP. The coefficient estimates computed this way are $\hat{\alpha}_{15} = .0260125$ and $\hat{\alpha}_{21} = -.3916$.

Table 7.1 shows the results using the "derivative" method discussed above. The results for Model 1 show that convergence was essentially achieved after one iteration. Three solutions of the model over the 50 periods were needed for the derivatives for the first iteration, which compares to 61 that would have been needed had the derivatives not been used. The difference between L computed using the derivatives and L computed from the full solution after the first iteration is very small, and so the method worked quite well. The DFP algorithm was used for this problem since the model was not large enough to require the Parke algorithm. The two further iterations for Model 1, which were based on recomputing the derivatives, led to very small changes. The third iteration in particular was unnecessary.

For Model 2 the error term in equation 7.21 is assumed to be serially correlated:

$$u_{1t} = \rho_1 u_{1t-1} + \epsilon_{1t} \tag{7.23}$$

Table 7.1
FIML Results for Three Models

Model 1: Taylor Model, No Serial Correlation

	$\hat{\alpha}_{15}$	$\hat{\alpha}_{21}$	$\hat{L}$ using derivatives	$\hat{L}$ using full solution	No. of func. evals.
Start	.0333333	-.333333		508.6022	
Iteration:					
1	.0252994	-.391662	509.0470	509.0462	61
2	.0260233	-.391609	509.0467	509.0467	50
3	.0260117	-.391612	509.0467	509.0466	37

Model 2: Taylor Model, Serial Correlation

	$\hat{\alpha}_{15}$	$\hat{\rho}_1$	$\hat{\alpha}_{21}$	$\hat{L}$ using derivatives	$\hat{L}$ using full solution	No. of func. evals.
Start	.0200000	.600	-.200000		501.8234	
Iteration:						
1	.0335672	.635	-.210860	505.5016	531.1740	77
2	.0289718	.673	-.321878	532.0178	531.7876	166
3	.0495646	.745	-.321324	532.1676	531.8590	103
4	.0778620	.837	-.322183	532.3424	531.9918	103
5	.0886905	.878	-.322699	532.1248	531.9346	96
6	.0903430	.889	-.322646	531.9557	531.9032	90

Model 3: Six Equation Model, 25 Coefficients

	$\hat{L}$ using derivatives	$\hat{L}$ using full solution	No. of func. evals.
Start		170.3100	
Iteration:			
1	189.1670	184.3381	2817
2	189.2047	189.0098	1103
3	189.0450	189.0297	538
4	189.0784	189.0784	258

The DFP algorithm was used for Models 1 and 2.
The Parke algorithm was used for Model 3.
Derivatives were recomputed after each iteration for
    Models 1 and 2, but not for Model 3.

where ρ_1 was set equal to .7 to generate the data. The coefficient estimates using the factorization routine and the DFP algorithm are $\hat{\alpha}_{15} = .0738367$, $\hat{\rho}_1 = .83545$, and $\hat{\alpha}_{21} = -.32211$. This set of values will be called the "exact"

Table 7.2
Model 3: Six Equations

1. $\log C_t$	cnst, $\log C_{t-1}$, $E_{t-1} \log Y_{t+2}$, R_t
2. $I_t - I_{t-1}$	cnst, $Y_t - Y_{t-1}$, $E_{t-1}(Y_{t+1} - Y_t)$, R_t, t, I_{t-1}
3. $\log(M_t/P_t)$	cnst, $\log(M/P)_{t-1}$, $\log Y_t$, R_t
4. $\log P_t$	cnst, $\log P_{t-1}$, $\log PM_t$, $(YS_t - Y_t)/YS_t$, $E_{t-1}[(YS_{t+1} - Y_{t+1})/YS_{t+1}]$, RHO
5. R_t	cnst, R_{t-1}, $E_{t-1}100[(P_{t+2}/P_{t+1})^4 - 1]$, $100[(Y_t/Y_{t-1})^4 - 1]$, $100[(M_{t-1}/M_{t-2})^4 - 1]$
6. $Y_t =$	$C_t + I_t + Q_t$

answer. The results in Table 7.1 show that the derivative method got close, but not quite, to the exact answer. The largest value of L occurred after the fourth iteration, 531.9918, with coefficient estimates fairly close to the exact answer. On iterations 5 and 6, however, the method moved slightly further away from the answer. The derivatives were computed after each iteration for this problem. The value of L using the exact coefficient estimates (not reported in the table) was 532.0333. The method thus moved from L equal to 501.8234 to L equal to 531.9918, but it could not go the rest of the way to 532.0333. When the method was started off from the exact answer, it moved away from it slightly, like the case for iterations 5 and 6 in Table 1. This basically seems to be a hard computational problem. The likelihood function is fairly flat near the top, especially with respect to α_{15} and ρ_1, and one other local optimum was found in the course of this work.[31]

Model 3 is a simple six equation macroeconomic model with 25 coefficients, one of which is a serial correlation coefficient. The model is meant for computational exercises only; it is not meant to be a good approximation of the economy. The equations are shown in Table 7.2 (C is consumption, I is investment, M is the nominal money supply, P is the GNP deflator, R is the interest rate, Y is GNP, YS is an estimate of potential GNP, PM is the import price deflator, Q is government spending plus net exports, t is the time

---

[31] Also, although not reported in Table 7.1, Model 2 is much harder to solve than Model 1 in requiring a much larger value of k and many more iterations of the solution paths to converge.

trend, RHO means that the error term in the equation is first order serially correlated, and C, I, Y, YS, and Q are in real terms): The exogenous variables in the model are PM_t, YS_t, Q_t, and t. Future expected values are in equations 1, 2, 4, and 5, and the longest lead length is 2.

The equations were first estimated using Hansen's method discussed in Section 4.3. The estimation period was 1954:1–1984:4, for a total of 124 observations. The Hansen estimates were then used as starting values for the FIML calculations.[32]

The results in Table 7.1 for Model 3 are based on only one set of calculations of the derivatives. The model was solved 26 times for the 124 observations to get the derivatives for the 25 coefficients. The Parke algorithm was used for the maximization. It can be seen in Table 7.1 that the use of the derivatives worked quite well. After the first iteration the difference between L computed using the derivatives and L computed from the full model solution is fairly large ($189.1670 - 184.3381$), but the differences are quite small for iterations 2, 3, and 4. Convergence had been achieved after iteration 4.

The good results for Model 3 are encouraging. Model 3 is probably more representative of models likely to be used in practice than is Model 2. Model 2 is probably extreme in the degree to which future predicted values affect current predicted values, and this may be one of the reasons results are not as good for it.

The FIML covariance matrix of the coefficient estimates ($\hat{V}_4$) was estimated for each model using the formula 7.4, where the derivatives are evaluated (numerically) at the optimum. These covariance computations are feasible because the expectations derivatives can be used in calculating the derivatives in 7.4. In other words, no further solutions of the model are needed to compute $\hat{V}_4$ in 7.4. $\hat{V}_4$ for Model 3 is used for the stochastic simulation results discussed next.

Stochastic Simulation

For models with rational expectations one must state very carefully what is meant by a stochastic simulation of the model and what stochastic simulation is to be used for. In the present case stochastic simulation is *not* used to

---

[32]The results for Model 3 in Tables 7.1 and 7.3 are the same as those in Fair and Taylor (1990). They have not been updated for present purposes. Since Model 3 is not part of the US model and is not used for any of the work in the following chapters, there was no need to update. Also, the results for Models 1 and 2 in Table 7.1 are the same as those in Fair and Taylor (1990).

improve on the accuracy of the solutions of the expected values. The expected values are computed exactly as described above—using the EP method. This way of solving for the expected values can be interpreted as assuming that agents at the beginning of period s form their expectations of the endogenous variables for periods s and beyond by 1) forming expectations of the exogenous variables for periods s and beyond, 2) setting the error terms equal to their expected values (say zero) for periods s and beyond, 3) using the existing set of coefficient estimates of the model, and then 4) solving the model for periods s and beyond. These solution values are the agents' expectations.

For present purposes stochastic simulation begins once the expected values have been solved for. Given the expected values for periods s through $s + h$, stochastic simulation is performed for period s. The problem is now no different from the problem for a standard model because the expectations are predetermined. Assume that the errors are distributed $N(0, \hat{\Sigma})$, where $\hat{\Sigma}$ is the FIML estimate of Σ from the last subsection. From this distribution one can draw a vector of error terms for period s. Given these draws (and the expectations), the model can be solved for period s in the usual ways. This is one repetition. Another repetition can be done using a new draw of the vector of error terms, and so on. The means and variances of the forecast values can be computed using equations 7.5 and 7.7 in Section 7.3.

One can also use this approach to analyze the effects of uncertainty in the coefficients by assuming that the coefficients are distributed $N(\hat{\alpha}, \hat{V}_4)$, where $\hat{\alpha}$ is the FIML estimate of α and $\hat{V}_4$ is the estimated covariance matrix of $\hat{\alpha}$. In this case each draw also involves the vector of coefficients.

If u_{it} is serially correlated as in 7.19, then an estimate of u_{is-1} is needed for the solution for period s. This estimate is, however, available from the solution of the model to get the expectations (see Case 2 in the previous subsection), and so no further work is needed. The estimate of u_{is-1} is simply taken as predetermined for all the repetitions, and u_{is} is computed as $\rho_i u_{is-1}$ plus the draw for ϵ_{is}. (Note that the ϵ errors are drawn, not the u errors.)

Stochastic simulation is quite inexpensive if only results for period s are needed because the model only needs to be solved once using the EP method. Once the expectations are obtained, each repetition merely requires solving the model for period s. If, on the other hand, results for more than one period are needed and the simulation is dynamic, the EP method must be used p times for each repetition, where p is the length of the period.

Consider the multiperiod problem. As above, the expectations with viewpoint date $s - 1$ can be solved for and then a vector of error terms and a vector of coefficients drawn to compute the predicted value of y_{is}. This is the first step.

Now go to period $s + 1$. An agent's expectation of, say, y_{is+2} is different with viewpoint date s than with viewpoint date $s - 1$. In particular, the value of y_{is} is in general different from what the agent at the end of period $s - 1$ expected it to be (because of the error terms that were drawn for period s).[33] A new set of expectations must thus be computed with viewpoint date s. Agents are assumed to use the original set of coefficients (not the set that was drawn) and to set the values of the error terms for periods $s + 1$ and beyond equal to zero. Then given the solution value of y_{is} and the actual value of x_s, agents are assumed to solve the model for their expectations for periods $s + 1$ and beyond. This requires a second use of the EP method. Given these expectations, a vector of error terms for period $s + 1$ is drawn and the model is solved for period $s + 1$. If equation i has a serially correlated error, then u_{is+1} is equal to $\rho_i^2 u_{is-1}$ plus the draw for ϵ_{is+1}. Now go to period $s + 2$ and repeat the process, where another use of the EP method is needed to compute the new expectations. The process is repeated through the end of the period of interest. At the end, this is one repetition. The overall process is then repeated for the second repetition, and so on. Note that only one coefficient draw is used per repetition, i.e., per dynamic simulation. After J repetitions one can compute means and variances just as above, where there are now means and variances for each period ahead of the prediction. Also note that agents are always assumed to use the original set of coefficients and to set the current and future error terms to zero. They do not perform stochastic simulation themselves.

Stochastic simulation results for Model 3 are presented in Table 7.3. The FIML estimates of Σ, α, and V_4 from the previous subsection were used for the draws. The length of the prediction was taken to be four, and 100 repetitions were performed. This meant that the number of times the model had to be solved for the expectations was 400. Again, had the length been taken to be one, the number of solutions for the expectations would have been one. The results show, as is common with most macroeconometric models, that the stochastic simulation estimates of the means are quite close to the deterministic simulation estimates. The deterministic simulation estimates are simply based on setting the error terms to zero and solving once for each period (as the agents are assumed to do). The real use of stochastic simulation is to compute standard deviations or variances. The estimated standard deviations are presented in

---

[33] It may also be that the actual value of x_s differs from what the agent expected it to be at the end of $s - 1$.

Table 7.3
Stochastic Simulation Results for Model 3

		1983 1	2	3	4
Consumption	a	2095.4	2111.9	2129.6	2146.5
	b	2094.0	2113.0	2130.8	2149.0
	c	13.1	17.9	23.1	29.4
Investment	a	259.3	264.2	268.2	272.5
	b	259.1	264.1	269.1	274.4
	c	6.7	8.7	9.8	12.3
Money Supply	a	521.5	532.2	543.2	554.5
	b	521.1	533.1	543.8	556.0
	c	5.5	8.4	10.9	11.7
Price Level	a	1.0293	1.0435	1.0587	1.0751
	b	1.0293	1.0437	1.0595	1.0762
	c	.0046	.0083	.0110	.0125
Interest Rate	a	8.39	8.57	8.75	8.94
	b	8.28	8.40	8.74	9.01
	c	.79	.96	1.09	1.21
Real GNP	a	3201.2	3243.9	3273.1	3305.4
	b	3199.6	3244.8	3275.2	3309.8
	c	17.6	23.3	28.1	35.7

a = predicted value from deterministic simulation
b = mean value from stochastic simulation
c = standard deviation from stochastic simulation

The results are based on 100 trials.
Units are billions of 1982 dollars for consumption,
investment, and real GNP; billions of dollars for
the money supply; 1982=1.0 for the price level;
and percentage points for the interest rate.

row c in the table. For real GNP, for example, the estimated standard deviation of the four quarter ahead forecast error is \$35.7 billion, which is about one percent of the mean value of \$3309.8 billion.

Stochastic simulation has also been used to evaluate alternative international monetary systems using the multicountry models in Carloyzi and Taylor (1985) and Taylor (1988). For this work values of ϵ_{it} were drawn, but not values of the coefficients. The vector of coefficients α was taken to be fixed.

It seems that stochastic simulation as defined above is computationally feasible for models with rational expectations. Stochastic simulation is in fact likely to be cheaper than even FIML estimation using the derivatives.

If, for example, the FIML estimation period is 100 observations and there are 25 coefficients to estimate, FIML estimation requires that the model be solved 2600 times using the EP method to get the derivatives. For a stochastic simulation of 8 periods and 100 repetitions, on the other hand, the model has to be solved using the EP method only 800 times.

Conclusion

To conclude, the results in this section are encouraging regarding the use of models with rational expectations. FIML estimation is computationally feasible using the procedure of computing derivatives for the expectations, and stochastic simulation is feasible when done in the manner described above. FIML estimation is particularly important because it takes into account all the nonlinear restrictions implied by the rational expectations hypothesis. It is hoped that the methods discussed in this section will open the way for many more tests of models with rational expectations.

8

Estimating and Testing the US Model

8.1   Introduction

The previous chapter discussed techniques for estimating and testing complete models, and this chapter applies these techniques to the US model. For the work in this chapter the model has been estimated by 2SLAD, 3SLS, and FIML in addition to 2SLS. 2SLAD is discussed in Section 4.4, and 3SLS and FIML are discussed in Section 7.2. Also, median unbiased (MU) estimates have been obtained for 18 lagged dependent variable coefficients using the procedure discussed in Section 7.4, and the 2SLS asymptotic distribution is compared to the exact distribution using the procedure discussed in Section 7.5. Section 8.3 presents the MU estimates; Section 8.4 examines the asymptotic distribution accuracy; and Section 8.5 compares the five sets of estimates.

The rest of this chapter is concerned with testing. In Section 8.6 the total variances discussed in Section 7.7 are computed and compared for the US, VAR5/2, VAR4, and AC models. Section 8.7 uses the procedure discussed in Section 7.8 to examine the information content of the forecasts from these models. Finally, Section 8.8 estimates event probabilities for the models and compares the accuracy of these estimates across the models using the procedure discussed in Section 7.9. A brief summary of the results is presented in Section 8.9.

Some of the tests in this chapter require a version of the US model in which there are no hard to forecast exogenous variables. This version is called US+, and it is discussed in the next section.

219

8.2   US+ Model

The US+ model is the US model with an additional 91 stochastic equations. Each of the additional equations explains an exogenous variable and is an eighth order autoregressive equation with a constant term and time trend added. Equations are estimated for all the exogenous variables in the model except the age variables, the dummy variables, the variables created from peak to peak interpolations, and variables that are constants or nearly constants. All the exogenous variables in the model are listed in Table A.2. Those for which autoregressive equations are *not* estimated are: $AG1$, $AG2$, $AG3$, CDA, $D691$, $D692$, $D714$, $D721$, $D794823$, $D811824$, $D831834$, $DD772$, $DELD$, $DELH$, $DELK$, HFS, HM, $IHHA$, $IKFA$, JJP, LAM, MUH, $P2554$, T, $TAUG$, $TAUS$, TI, $TXCR$, $WLDG$, and $WLDS$. Excluding these variables left 91 variables for which autoregressive equations are estimated. Logs were used for some of the variables. Logs were not used for ratios, for variables that were negative or sometimes negative, and for variables that were sometimes close to zero. The estimation technique was ordinary least squares.

The US+ model thus has no hard to forecast exogenous variables, and in this sense it is comparable to the VAR and AC models discussed in Section 7.6, which have no exogenous variables other than the constant term and time trend. Remember, however, from the discussion in Section 7.8 that this treatment of the exogenous variables may bias the results against the US model. Many of the exogenous variables may not be as uncertain as the autoregressive equations imply.

The covariance matrix of the error terms in the US+ model is 121×121, and for purposes of the stochastic simulation work it was taken to be block diagonal. The first block is the 30×30 covariance matrix of the structural error terms, and the second block is the 91×91 covariance matrix of the exogenous variable error terms. In other words, the error terms in the structural equations were assumed to be uncorrelated with the error terms in the exogenous variable equations. This assumption is consistent with the assumption in the US model that the structural error terms are uncorrelated with the exogenous variables.

8.3 MU Estimates of the US Model[1]

The procedure for obtaining median unbiased (MU) estimates of a model is explained in Section 7.4. This procedure was carried out for the US model, and the results are reported in this section. The starting point was the set of 2SLS estimates in Chapter 5. Starting from these values, median unbiased estimates of the lagged dependent variable (LDV) coefficients were obtained for 18 of the 30 stochastic equations. The estimates for the other 12 equations were fixed at their 2SLS values. The estimation period was 1954:1–1993:2, for a total of 158 observations. The number of repetitions per iteration (i.e., the value of J in step 3 in Section 7.4) was 500. After 3 iterations (i.e., after steps 3 and 4 in Section 7.4 were done 3 times), the largest difference between the successive estimates of any LDV coefficient was less than .001 in absolute value. Convergence thus occurred very quickly.[2]

The results for the LDV coefficient estimates are presented in Table 8.1. The bias for each coefficient estimate, defined as the difference between the 2SLS estimate and the MU estimate, is presented in the table. The "Andrews bias" in the table is the exact bias for an equation with a constant term, time trend, and lagged dependent variable and with the LDV coefficient equal to the 2SLS coefficient estimate presented in the table. These biases are interpolated from Table III in Andrews (1993).

Also presented in Table 8.1 are the 90 percent confidence values. The first 2SLS confidence value for each coefficient is minus 1.645 times the 2SLS estimate of the asymptotic standard error of the LDV coefficient estimate. The second 2SLS confidence value is the absolute value of the first value. The MU values are computed using the coefficient estimates from the 500 repetitions on the last iteration. The first MU confidence value for each coefficient is minus the difference between the median estimate and the estimate at which five percent of the estimates are below it. The second MU confidence value is minus the difference between the median estimate and the estimate at which five percent of the estimates are above it.

---

[1]The material in this section is taken from Fair (1994a). The results in this paper are the same as those in Table 8.1.

[2]To lessen stochastic simulation error, the same draws of the error terms were used for each iteration. The number of errors drawn per iteration is $2{,}370{,}000 = (500 \text{ repetitions}) \times (30 \text{ stochastic equations}) \times (158 \text{ observations})$. The model is solved dynamically over the estimation period for each repetition, and each of the 18 equations is estimated for each repetition.

Table 8.1
Estimated Bias of 2SLS Lagged Dependent Variable
Coefficient Estimates

Eq.	2SLS	Bias	Andrews Bias	90% Confidence Values 2SLS[a]		MU[b]	
1. CS	.943	-.012	-.040	-.052	.052	-.033	.025
2. CN	.620	-.029	-.027	-.070	.070	-.074	.060
3. CD	.575	-.025	-.025	-.104	.104	-.094	.079
4. IHH	.532	-.020	-.025	-.091	.091	-.104	.084
5. L1	.776	-.049	-.031	-.082	.082	-.104	.078
6. L2	.987	-.003	-.051	-.008	.008	-.017	.011
7. L3	.890	-.040	-.036	-.059	.059	-.081	.050
8. LM	.863	-.027	-.034	-.055	.055	-.077	.047
9. MH	.896	-.050	-.036	-.064	.064	-.083	.053
10. PF	.919	-.002	-.036	-.010	.010	-.010	.009
11. Y	.293	-.000	-.020	-.074	.074	-.059	.055
12. IKF	-.040	.000	-.012	-.022	.022	-.020	.017
17. MF	.904	-.027	-.036	-.048	.048	-.067	.042
23. RB	.881	-.002	-.035	-.034	.034	-.035	.027
24. RM	.842	-.003	-.033	-.042	.042	-.048	.034
26. CUR	.957	-.003	-.043	-.018	.018	-.016	.012
27. IM	.872	-.032	-.034	-.054	.054	-.071	.053
30. RS	.892	-.003	-.035	-.031	.031	-.035	.027
Average		-.018	-.033	-.051	.051	-.057	.042

[a] The first number for 2SLS is minus 1.645 times the 2SLS estimate of
the standard error of the LDV coefficient estimate. The second
number for 2SLS is the absolute value of the first number.
[b] The first number for MU is minus the difference between the median
estimate and the estimate at which five percent of the estimates are
below it. The second number for MU is minus the difference between
the median estimate and the estimate at which five percent of
the estimates are above it.

The results in Table 8.1 show that the estimated biases are zero to three
decimal places for 2 of the 18 coefficients and negative for the rest. The
average bias across the 18 estimates is −.018. The average Andrews bias, on
the other hand, is −.033, and so the results suggest that the bias of a typical
macroeconometric equation is on average less than the bias of an equation that
includes only a constant term, time trend, and lagged dependent variable. In
only four cases in the table is the Andrews bias smaller in absolute value—
equations 2, 5, 7, and 9.

The 2SLS and MU confidence values in Table 8.1 are fairly similar. The
average of the left tail values is −.057 for MU and −.051 for 2SLS. The

average of the right tail values is .042 for MU and .051 for 2SLS. It is clear that the MU confidence interval is not symmetric around the median estimate. For all the coefficient estimates the right tail value is less than the left tail value in absolute value. The left tail of the distribution is thus thicker than the right tail, although the differences are fairly minor.

An interesting question is whether the biases in Table 8.1 are quantitatively important regarding the properties of the model. This question is examined in Sections 8.5 and 11.3.5. In Section 8.5 the sensitivity of the predictive accuracy of the model to the use of the MU estimates is examined, and in Section 11.3.5 the sensitivity of the multiplier properties of the model to the use of the estimates is examined. It will be seen that the use of the MU estimates has little effect on the predictive accuracy of the model and on its multiplier properties. These results thus suggest that macroeconometric model builders have not missed much by ignoring the Orcutt and Hurwicz warnings 40 years ago, although work with other models should be done to see if the present results hold up. With hindsight, the present results are perhaps not surprising. What they basically say is that if one changes a LDV coefficient estimate by about half of its estimated standard error and then reestimates the other coefficients in the equation to reflect this change, the fit and properties of the equation do not change very much. This is something that most model builders probably know from experience.

8.4 Asymptotic Distribution Accuracy[3]

The procedure for examining the accuracy of asymptotic distributions was discussed in Section 7.5. It is carried out in this section for the US model. Again, the 2SLS estimates in Chapter 5 were used as the base estimates. For the present results the US model was simulated and estimated 800 times. There are 166 coefficients to estimate in the model, and so the results from this exercise consist of 800 values of 166 coefficients. A summary of these results is presented in Table 8.2. Detailed results are presented for the same 18 coefficients that were examined in Table 8.1, namely the LDV coefficients of the 18 equations, and summary results are presented for all 166 coefficients.

The bias results for the 18 coefficients show, as in Table 8.1, that the 2SLS estimates of the LDV coefficients are biased downwards,[4] with the average

---

[3]The material in this section is also taken from Fair (1994a). The results in this paper are the same as those in Table 8.2.

[4]The bias estimates are slightly different in Table 8.2 than in Table 8.1 because they are

Table 8.2
Asymptotic Distribution Accuracy

Eq.	2SLS	Med.	Med.-2SLS	Left Tail 5	Left Tail 10	Left Tail 20	Right Tail 5	Right Tail 10	Right Tail 20
1. CS	.943	.931	-.012	0.4	1.8	7.9	0.0	0.4	3.3
2. CN	.620	.595	-.025	4.0	10.1	19.5	1.6	4.8	14.6
3. CD	.575	.554	-.021	3.8	8.6	17.6	0.8	4.9	11.1
4. IHH	.532	.516	-.016	8.3	12.5	22.0	1.9	7.5	18.0
5. L1	.776	.731	-.045	8.9	13.6	22.0	5.6	11.6	22.3
6. L2	.987	.984	-.003	13.9	18.5	26.8	8.9	13.8	24.4
7. L3	.890	.856	-.034	9.4	13.8	22.9	1.4	5.8	15.9
8. LM	.863	.839	-.024	9.3	15.6	24.8	2.5	8.1	19.8
9. MH	.896	.850	-.046	9.4	15.1	23.3	2.5	8.3	18.1
10. PF	.919	.919	-.000	6.6	11.5	20.8	2.8	7.5	17.6
11. Y	.293	.292	-.001	2.3	6.0	12.0	1.4	5.0	14.4
12. IKF	-.040	-.039	.001	2.4	6.3	14.4	2.1	5.6	15.0
17. MF	.904	.882	-.022	13.1	18.8	27.1	3.4	9.1	21.1
23. RB	.881	.877	-.004	5.8	10.0	20.1	3.8	8.4	18.5
24. RM	.842	.836	-.006	6.1	11.6	20.3	4.6	8.5	19.0
26. CUR	.957	.954	-.003	4.0	7.5	14.9	1.8	4.4	11.8
27. IM	.872	.846	-.026	10.5	16.4	25.4	4.6	10.8	23.9
30. RS	.892	.889	-.003	6.9	12.4	21.6	3.0	7.4	17.9
MEAN(18)			-.016	5.5	9.9	19.4	4.0	8.1	17.4
MAE(18)				3.3	3.9	4.2	2.5	3.4	4.4
MEAN(166)				5.0	9.3	18.3	4.4	8.7	17.9
MAE(166)				2.8	3.6	4.3	2.4	3.2	4.1

bias being $-.016$. This is as expected.

The main point of Table 8.2 is to compare the left tail and right tail estimated probabilities to the values implied by the asymptotic distribution. Let p_{ik} be the estimated probability for coefficient i for the asymptotic value of k percent. Remember from Section 7.5 how these percentages are computed. Given for a particular coefficient estimate the 2SLS estimate of its asymptotic standard error, one can compute the value above which k percent of the coefficient estimates should lie if the asymptotic standard error is accurate. For k equal to 20, this value is the median plus 0.84 times the estimated asymptotic standard error. For k equal to 10 the multiplier is 1.28, and for k equal to 5 the multiplier is 1.64. From the 800 coefficient estimates one can compute the actual percent of the coefficient estimates that lie above this value. These are the right tail

based on 800 rather than 500 repetitions and because the iterations done for the results in Table 8.1 were not done for the results in Table 8.2.

percents. A similar procedure can be followed for the left tail percents. For each tail and each coefficient i, one can thus compute values of p_{i5}, p_{i10}, and p_{i20}. Values of these probabilities for each tail are presented in Table 8.2 for the 18 LDV coefficient estimates. Also reported in the table are the means of the probabilities across the 18 coefficients and across the 166 coefficients. In addition, the mean absolute errors around the means are presented for the 18 and 166 coefficients. For example, the mean absolute error for the left tail p_{i5} for the 18 coefficients is the sum of $|p_{i5} - 5.5|$ across the 18 coefficients divided by 18, where 5.5 is the mean.

Consider the results for the 166 coefficients in Table 8.2. The means of the 5, 10, and 20 percent left tail values are 5.0, 9.3, and 18.3, with mean absolute errors of 2.8, 3.6, and 4.3, respectively. The corresponding right tail means are 4.4, 8.7, and 17.9, with mean absolute errors of 2.4, 3.2, and 4.1, respectively. These mean values are less than the asymptotic values (except for the equality for the 5 percent left tail value), and so on average the asymptotic distribution has thicker tails than does the exact distribution. These differences are, however, fairly small. In general the asymptotic distribution seems to be a good approximation, although the mean absolute errors reveal that there is some dispersion across the coefficients. The overall results suggest that the use of the asymptotic distribution is not in general likely to give misleading conclusions.

The closeness of the asymptotic distribution to the exact distribution is an important result. If this result holds up for other models, it means that the unit root problems that have received so much attention in the econometric literature are not likely to be of much concern to macro model builders. While the existence of unit roots can in theory cause the asymptotic distributions that are relied on in macroeconometrics to be way off, in practice the asymptotic distributions seem fairly good.

8.5 A Comparison of the Estimates

Section 8.3 examined the closeness of the 2SLS and MU estimates. This section compares the closeness of the 2SLS, 2SLAD, 3SLS, and FIML estimates. It also compares the predictive accuracy of the model for all five sets of estimates.

The first step for the results in this section was to compute the 2SLAD, 3SLS, and FIML estimates. There are some computational tricks that are needed to obtain these estimates. These tricks are discussed in Fair (1984),

Table 8.3
Comparison of 2SLS, 2SLAD, 3SLS, and FIML Estimates

	Number of estimates greater than .5, 1.0, 1.5, 2.0, and 3.0 standard errors away from the 2SLS estimates					Number of sign changes from 2SLS estimates

137 Coefficients:

	.5	1.0	1.5	2.0	3.0	
3SLS	69	22	4	2	0	2
FIML	101	70	51	32	13	6

166 Coefficients:

2SLAD	62	16	4	2	1	3

Average ratio of 2SLS standard error to 3SLS standard error (137 coefficients)	= 1.28
Average ratio of 3SLS standard error to FIML standard error (137 coefficients)	= 0.81

and this discussion will not be repeated here.[5] Of the 166 coefficients, 137 were estimated by 3SLS and FIML, with the remaining coefficients being fixed at their 2SLS values.[6] All 166 coefficients were estimated by 2SLAD. The first stage regressors that were used for 3SLS are listed in Table A.7 in Appendix A.[7] The same first stage regressors were used for 2SLAD as were used for 2SLS, and these are also listed in Table A.7.

A comparison of the four sets of estimates is presented in Table 8.3. The main conclusion from this comparison is that the estimates are fairly close

---

[5]The 2SLAD computational problem is discussed in Section 6.5.4, the 3SLS problem in Section 6.5.3, and the FIML problem in Section 6.5.2 in Fair (1984). The Parke (1982) algorithm was used for the 3SLS and FIML estimates.

[6]The equations whose coefficients were fixed for 3SLS and FIML are 15, 18, 19, 20, 21, 25, 28, and 29. (Remember that the coefficients for equations 19 and 29 were obtained in the manner discussed in Section 5.9 rather than by 2SLS.) In addition, the following other coefficients were fixed: the two autoregressive coefficients in equation 4, the coefficients of T and $DD772 \cdot T$ in equations 13 and 14, and the four dummy variable coefficients in equation 27. These coefficients were fixed to lessen potential collinearity problems. See Fair (1984), Section 6.4, for a discussion of sample size requirements and the estimation of subsets of coefficients.

[7]The choice of first stage regressors for 3SLS is discussed in Fair (1984), Section 6.3.3.

to each other, with the FIML estimates being the farthest apart. Of the 137 3SLS estimates, only 22 were greater than one 2SLS standard error away from the 2SLS estimate, and only 2 were greater than two standard errors. For the FIML estimates, 70 were greater than one standard error away from the 2SLS estimate, and 32 were greater than two standard errors. Of the 166 2SLAD estimates, 16 were greater than one standard error away from the 2SLS estimate, and 2 were greater than two standard errors. There were 2 sign changes for 3SLS, 6 for FIML, and 3 for 2SLAD. The closeness of these estimates is encouraging, since one would not expect for a correctly specified model that the use of different consistent estimators would result in large differences in the estimates.

The second to last result in Table 8.3 shows the efficiency gained from using 3SLS over 2SLS. The average ratio of the 2SLS standard error to the 3SLS standard error across the 137 coefficients is 1.28. In other words, the 2SLS standard errors are on average 28 percent larger than the 3SLS standard errors.

The last result in Table 8.3 shows that the 3SLS standard errors are on average smaller than the FIML standard errors. The average ratio of the 3SLS standard error to the FIML standard error across the 137 coefficients is .81. In other words, the 3SLS standard errors are on average 19 percent smaller than the FIML standard errors. The smaller 3SLS than FIML standard errors is a typical result, and a possible reason for it is discussed in Fair (1984), pp. 245–246. This discussion will not be repeated here.

Another way to compare the different sets of coefficient estimates is to examine the sensitivity of the predictive accuracy of the model to the different sets. This examination is presented in Table 8.4. One, two, three, four, six, and eight quarter ahead RMSEs are presented for four variables for each set of estimates. The prediction period is the same as the estimation period, namely 1954:1–1993:2. These predictions are all within sample predictions.[8] There are 158 one quarter ahead predictions, 157 two quarter ahead predictions, and so on through 151 eight quarter ahead predictions, where each of the 158

---

[8]If different models were being compared, the use of RMSEs in the manner done here would not be appropriate and one should use a method like the one in the next section. The RMSE procedure ignores exogenous variable differences and possible misspecifications. These problems are less serious when it is simply different estimates of the same model being used. There are no exogenous variable differences except for the fact that different coefficients multiply the same exogenous variables across versions. There are also no specification differences, and so misspecification effects differ only to the extent that misspecification is differentially affected by the size of the coefficients across versions.

Table 8.4
RMSEs for Five Sets of Coefficient
Estimates for 1954:1–1993:2
for the US Model

	Number of Quarters Ahead					
	1	2	3	4	6	8
GDPR: Real GDP						
2SLS	0.69	1.05	1.30	1.45	1.55	1.59
2SLAD	0.69	1.07	1.36	1.54	1.72	1.77
3SLS	0.68	1.02	1.27	1.42	1.53	1.58
FIML	0.70	1.02	1.24	1.40	1.56	1.68
MUE	0.68	1.04	1.28	1.42	1.52	1.54
GDPD: GDP Deflator						
2SLS	0.40	0.60	0.78	0.97	1.29	1.52
2SLAD	0.40	0.60	0.78	0.98	1.33	1.60
3SLS	0.40	0.62	0.81	1.00	1.34	1.58
FIML	0.52	0.90	1.28	1.64	2.28	2.80
MUE	0.40	0.60	0.78	0.97	1.29	1.53
UR: Unemployment Rate						
2SLS	0.30	0.56	0.73	0.87	1.02	1.06
2SLAD	0.30	0.57	0.75	0.90	1.09	1.16
3SLS	0.29	0.52	0.68	0.79	0.91	0.95
FIML	0.32	0.58	0.76	0.90	1.03	1.11
MUE	0.30	0.57	0.75	0.89	1.05	1.10
RS: Bill Rate						
2SLS	0.54	1.02	1.20	1.40	1.62	1.72
2SLAD	0.54	1.01	1.20	1.42	1.67	1.78
3SLS	0.55	0.98	1.15	1.33	1.52	1.58
FIML	0.63	1.06	1.28	1.46	1.71	1.82
MUE	0.55	1.03	1.21	1.39	1.61	1.71

Errors are in percentage points.

simulations is based on a different starting point.

The results in Table 8.4 show that the RMSEs are very similar across the five sets of estimates. No one set of estimates dominates the others, and in general the differences are quite small. The largest differences occur for the FIML predictions of the price deflator, which are noticeably less accurate than the others. My experience with the FIML estimation of macroeconometric models is that FIML estimates are the most likely to differ in large ways from other estimates and that when they do differ they generally lead to a poorer fitting model. For example, 3SLS estimates are generally closer to 2SLS estimates than are FIML estimates, and they tend to lead to a better fitting overall model. The 3SLS estimates in Table 8.4 do in fact quite well. They are slightly worse than the 2SLS estimates for the price deflator, but slightly better for the other three variables. Again, however, these differences are small.

The closeness of the results in Table 8.4 is again encouraging, since one would not expect there to be large differences of this sort for a model that is a good approximation of the economy.

The fact that the MU results are similar to the others in Table 8.4 is consistent with the properties of a simple equation with only the lagged dependent variable as an explanatory variable, say $y_t = \alpha y_{t-1} + \epsilon_t$. Malinvaud (1970), p. 554, shows for this equation that the expected value of the prediction error is zero when the distribution of ϵ_t is symmetric even if the estimate of α that is used to make the prediction is biased. The present results show that even for much more complicated models, prediction errors seem to be little affected by coefficient estimation bias.

8.6 Predictive Accuracy

This section uses the method discussed in Section 7.7 to compare the US model to the VAR5/2, VAR4, and AC models. The latter three models are discussed in Section 7.6. The method computes forecast error variances for each variable and period ahead that account for the four main sources of uncertainty of a forecast. The variances can thus be compared across models. The results for the four models are presented in Table 8.5 for four variables: real GDP, the GDP deflator, the unemployment rate, and the bill rate. Standard errors rather than variances are presented in the table because the units are easier to interpret.

There are considerable computations behind the results in Table 8.5, and most of this section is a discussion of this table. Consider the a and b rows for the US model first. The simulation period was 1991:1–1992:4, and 1000 repetitions were made for each row. For the a row, only the structural error terms were drawn, and for the b row, both the structural error terms and the coefficients were drawn. In the notation in Section 7.7, each value in a b row is the square root of $\tilde{\sigma}^2_{itk}$.

The 2SLS estimates in Chapter 5 were used for this work. The estimated covariance matrix of the error terms, $\hat{\Sigma}$, is 30×30. Remember from the discussion at the end of Section 5.9 that equations 19 and 29 are taken to be

Table 8.5
Estimated Standard Errors of Forecasts
for Four Models

| | 1991 | | | | 1992 | | | |
	1	2	3	4	1	2	3	4
GDPR: Real GDP								
US:								
a	.61	.98	1.29	1.49	1.62	1.70	1.78	1.81
b	.63	1.03	1.36	1.58	1.74	1.84	1.93	1.98
c	.72	1.22	1.64	1.95	2.20	2.38	2.48	2.52
d	.86	1.52	2.14	2.56	2.86	2.98	3.05	3.07
VAR5/2:								
a	.80	1.20	1.44	1.55	1.69	1.86	2.04	2.21
b	.83	1.24	1.53	1.77	1.99	2.22	2.42	2.65
d	.96	1.73	2.23	2.62	2.80	2.90	2.93	2.97
VAR4:								
a	.75	1.15	1.40	1.47	1.60	1.74	1.91	2.07
b	.82	1.32	1.57	1.71	1.94	2.12	2.32	2.49
d	1.08	2.01	2.45	2.91	3.35	3.64	3.82	3.89
AC:								
a	.51	.80	.99	1.18	1.34	1.42	1.49	1.53
b	.52	.87	1.15	1.36	1.51	1.64	1.74	1.81
d	.73	1.18	1.61	1.91	2.17	2.39	2.64	2.85
GDPD: GDP Deflator								
US:								
a	.34	.51	.64	.74	.82	.89	.97	1.05
b	.36	.56	.69	.79	.87	.99	1.10	1.18
c	.48	.73	.92	1.08	1.20	1.32	1.41	1.52
d	.43	.70	.92	1.14	1.40	1.70	2.00	2.33
VAR5/2:								
a	.27	.40	.53	.67	.84	1.01	1.17	1.32
b	.27	.44	.60	.78	.97	1.18	1.42	1.64
d	.29	.58	.80	1.05	1.36	1.75	2.14	2.53
VAR4:								
a	.30	.44	.58	.75	.96	1.17	1.36	1.55
b	.31	.49	.65	.88	1.14	1.38	1.64	1.93
d	.33	.62	.86	1.14	1.49	1.89	2.31	2.77

Table 8.5 (continued)

	1991				1992			
	1	2	3	4	1	2	3	4

U R: Unemployment Rate

US:

a	.27	.44	.58	.70	.80	.87	.96	1.03
b	.31	.49	.64	.77	.90	.98	1.07	1.14
c	.31	.52	.70	.87	1.02	1.13	1.21	1.30
d	.27	.55	.79	1.03	1.22	1.30	1.31	1.28

VAR5/2:

a	.24	.44	.58	.66	.71	.76	.83	.90
b	.25	.47	.63	.75	.85	.93	.99	1.07
d	.29	.60	.86	1.08	1.23	1.30	1.30	1.27

VAR4:

a	.23	.42	.54	.62	.65	.69	.75	.81
b	.24	.46	.62	.71	.79	.84	.91	.96
d	.34	.72	1.00	1.24	1.45	1.55	1.59	1.54

R S: Bill Rate

US:

a	.56	.87	1.01	1.11	1.18	1.23	1.30	1.37
b	.54	.89	1.07	1.14	1.24	1.37	1.47	1.53
c	.57	.96	1.17	1.32	1.47	1.60	1.75	1.85
d	.82	1.57	1.88	2.28	2.74	3.03	3.35	3.63

VAR5/2:

a	.67	1.08	1.24	1.35	1.46	1.53	1.63	1.65
b	.66	1.11	1.33	1.53	1.72	1.87	1.95	2.00
d	1.15	2.02	2.46	3.01	3.58	4.02	4.52	4.87

VAR4:

a	.63	1.03	1.21	1.34	1.45	1.52	1.63	1.67
b	.65	1.12	1.37	1.56	1.74	1.91	2.02	2.06
d	1.14	2.11	2.51	3.05	3.77	4.40	4.91	5.31

a = Uncertainty due to error terms.
b = Uncertainty due to error terms and coefficient estimates.
c = Uncertainty due to error terms, coefficient estimates,
    and exogenous variable forecasts.
d = Uncertainty due to error terms, coefficient estimates,
    exogenous variable forecasts, and the possible
    misspecification of the model.
Errors are in percentage points.

stochastic for purposes of computing $\hat{\Sigma}$ even though their coefficients are not estimated in a traditional way. Remember also that equation 19 is divided through by $|AF + 10|$ and that equation 29 is divided through by $|AG|$ before computing the error terms to be used in computing $\hat{\Sigma}$.

The estimation period for $\hat{\Sigma}$ was 1954:1–1993:2. This is the estimation period used for estimating all the equations except 15, which explains HO. The estimation period for equation 15 begins in 1956:1 rather than 1954:1. However, for purposes of computing $\hat{\Sigma}$, the period beginning in 1954:1 was used for equation 15. Data for HO prior to 1956:1 were constructed in the manner discussed in Section 3.2.3.

The estimated covariance matrix of the coefficient estimates, $\hat{V}_2$, is 166×166. The formula for this matrix is given in equation 4.5 in Chapter 4. For purposes of computing $\hat{V}_2$, the coefficients in equations 19 and 29 were taken to be fixed. There are five of these coefficients. Also, four of the coefficients in the wage equation 16 are constrained and thus not freely estimated. There are thus a total of 175 coefficients in the model, but only 166 freely estimated. The dimension of $\hat{V}_2$ is thus 166×166 rather than 175×175.

Consider next the c row for the US model. For this row, structural errors, coefficients, *and* exogenous variable errors were drawn, and again 1000 repetitions were made. The procedure that was used for the exogenous variable errors is the following. First, an eighth order autoregressive equation with a constant and time trend was estimated for each of 91 exogenous variables. These are the same equations that are used for the US+ model discussed in Section 8.2 except that all the equations here are linear whereas many of the equations for US+ are in logs. The estimation period was 1954:1–1993:2. Let $\hat{s}_i$ denote the estimated standard error from the equation for exogenous variable i. Let v_{it} be a normally distributed random variable with mean zero and variance $\hat{s}_i^2 : v_{it} \sim N(0, \hat{s}_i^2)$ for all t. Let x_{it}^a be the actual value of exogenous variable i for period t. Finally, let x_{it}^* be the value of variable i used for a given repetition. Then for prediction period 1 through T, the values for x_{it}^* for a given repetition were taken to be

$$x_{i1}^* = x_{i1}^a + v_{i1}$$

$$x_{i2}^* = x_{i2}^a + v_{i1} + v_{i2}$$

.

.

$$x_{iT}^* = x_{iT}^a + v_{i1} + v_{i2} + \cdots + v_{iT}$$

where each v_{it} $(t = 1, \cdots, T)$ is drawn from the $N(0, \hat{s}_i^2)$ distribution. This treatment implies that the errors are assumed to pertain to *changes* in the exogenous variables. The error v_{i1} is carried along from quarter 1 on, the error v_{i2} is carried along from quarter 2 on, and so forth. Given the way that many exogenous variables are forecast, by extrapolating past trends or taking variables to be unchanged from their last observed values, it may be that any error in forecasting the level of a variable in, say, the first period will persist throughout the forecast period. If this is true, the assumption that the errors pertain to the changes in the variables may be better than the assumption that they pertain to the levels. Given that the simulation period is 8 quarters in length and given that there are 91 exogenous variables, 728 exogenous variable errors are drawn for each repetition.

Turn next to the d row for the US model. This row required by far the most computational work. In the notation in Section 7.7, each value in a d row is the square root of $\hat{\sigma}_{itk}^2$. Put another way, the square of each d row value is equal to the square of the c row value plus $\bar{d}_{ik}$, where $\bar{d}_{ik}$ is the mean of the d_{isk} values discussed in Section 7.7. In computing the d_{isk} values, the model was estimated and stochastically simulated 68 times. All estimation periods began in 1954:1 (except for equation 15, where the beginning was 1956:1). The first estimation period ended in 1976:2, the second in 1976:3, and so on through 1993:1. The estimation technique was 2SLS. For each estimation period the covariance matrix of the structural error terms, Σ, and the covariance matrix of the coefficient estimates, V_2, were estimated along with the coefficients. For this work V_2 was taken to be block diagonal.

Dummy variables whose nonzero values begin after 1976:2 obviously cannot be included in the version of the model estimated only through 1976:2. Dummy variables were thus added when appropriate as the length of the estimation period increased. The variable $D794823 \cdot PCM1_{-1}$ in equation 30 was added for the first time for the estimation period ending in 1979:4. The variable $D811824$ in equation 21 was added for the first time for the period ending in 1981:1, and the variable $D831834$ in the same equation was added for the first time for the period ending in 1983:1. Finally, the variables involving $DD772$ in equations 13 and 14 were added for the first time for the period ending in 1983:1.

Given the 68 sets of estimates, 68 stochastic simulations were run. Each simulation period was of length 8 quarters subject to the restriction that the last quarter for predictions was 1993:2. All simulations were outside the estimation period. The first simulation period began in 1976:3, the second in 1976:4, and so on through 1993:2. Both structural error terms and coefficients were drawn for these simulations (using the appropriate estimates of Σ and V_2), and the number of repetitions per each of the 68 stochastic simulations was 250. For the one quarter ahead prediction ($k = 1$), these calculations allowed 68 values of d_{isk} to be computed for each endogenous variable i, from which the mean $\bar{d}_{ik}$ was computed. For the two quarter ahead prediction, there were 67 values of d_{isk} computed, and so on. Given these means and given the c row values in Table 8.5, the d row values could be computed.

The same procedure was followed for the other three models except that the other models have no exogenous variables and so no c row values are needed. For these models the number of repetitions per stochastic simulation was 1000 even for the 68 stochastic simulations involved in getting the d_{isk} values. The estimation technique was ordinary least squares. As was the case for the US model, the covariance matrices of the coefficient estimates were taken to be block diagonal.

Once these calculations have been done and the d row values computed, one can compare the models. As discussed in Section 7.7, each model is on an equal footing with respect to the d row values in the sense that the four main sources of uncertainty of a forecast have been accounted for. The d row values can thus be compared across models.

Turn now to the d row values in Table 8.5, and consider first the US model versus the two VAR models. For real GDP ($GDPR$) the US model is better than VAR5/2 for the first four quarters and slightly worse for the remaining four. The US model is better than VAR4 for all eight quarters. For the GDP deflator ($GDPD$) the US model is worse than VAR5/2 for the first five quarters and better for the remaining three. The US model is worse than VAR4 for the first three quarters, tied for quarter four, and better for the remaining four quarters. For the unemployment rate (UR) the US model is better than VAR5/2 for the first four quarters and essentially tied for the remaining four. The US model is better than VAR4 for all quarters. For the bill rate (RS) the US model is better than both VAR models for all quarters. Comparing VAR5/2 and VAR4, VAR5/2 is more accurate for all variables and all quarters except for the one quarter ahead prediction of the bill rate, where the two models essentially tie.

Using VAR5/2 as the better of the two VAR models, what conclusion can be drawn about the US model versus VAR5/2? For the first three variables the models are generally quite close, and one might call it a tie. For the fourth variable, the bill rate, the US model does substantially better. The US model may thus have a slight edge over VAR5/2, but only slight. Remember, however, that the present results are based on the use of the autoregressive equations for the 91 exogenous variables. As discussed earlier, these equations may exaggerate the uncertainty of the exogenous variables and thus bias the results against the US model.

Turning next to the AC model, it does very well in the $GDPR$ predictions. It has the smallest d row values in the table. There clearly seems to be predictive power in the lagged components of $GDPR$ that is not captured in the US and VAR models.

Comparing the a and b rows in Table 8.5 shows that coefficient uncertainty contributes much less to the variances than does the uncertainty from the structural error terms. In other words, the a row values are large relative to the difference between the b row and a row values. For the US model the differences between the c row values and the b row values are generally larger than the differences between the b row and a row values, which says that exogenous variable uncertainty (as estimated by the autoregressive equations) generally contributes more to the total variance than does coefficient uncertainty.

The differences between the d row and c row values are measures of the misspecification of the model not already captured in the c row values. On this score, the worst specifications for the models are for the bill rate and the best are for the unemployment rate. Again, the differences between the US model and VAR5/2 regarding misspecification are close except for the bill rate, where the US model is much better.

Outside Sample RMSEs

From the 68 stochastic simulations that are used for the d_{isk} calculations, one has for each endogenous variable i, 68 one quarter ahead outside sample error terms, 67 two quarter ahead outside sample error terms, and so on. (These errors are denoted $\hat{\epsilon}_{isk}$ in Section 7.7.) From these errors one can compute RMSEs, and the results of doing this for four variables are presented in Table 8.6. Remember, however, that comparing RMSEs across models has problems that do not exist when comparing the d row values in Table 8.5 across models. Exogenous variable uncertainty is not accounted for, which affects the comparisons between the US model and the others but not between the other models themselves. Also, the fact that forecast error variances change over time is not accounted for in the RMSE calculations. The RMSEs in Table 8.6 are, however, all outside sample, which is a least a crude way of accounting for misspecification effects.

For what they are worth, the results in Table 8.6 show that the US model is noticeable better than the VAR models for real GDP and the bill rate. The

Table 8.6
RMSEs of Outside Sample Forecasts for
Four Models for 1976:3–1993:2

	Number of Quarters Ahead					
	1	2	3	4	6	8
GDPR: Real GDP						
US	.79	1.39	1.95	2.33	2.64	2.74
VAR5/2	1.07	1.89	2.51	3.06	3.84	4.57
VAR4	1.15	2.05	2.61	3.22	4.33	5.15
AC	.79	1.23	1.64	1.95	2.48	2.99
GDPD: GDP Deflator						
US	.34	.58	.82	1.23	2.32	3.21
VAR5/2	.31	.61	.87	1.18	1.98	2.89
VAR4	.33	.62	.88	1.18	2.01	3.02
UR: Unemployment Rate						
US	.31	.61	.89	1.16	1.51	1.61
VAR5/2	.32	.65	.94	1.20	1.52	1.68
VAR4	.36	.74	1.04	1.29	1.68	1.84
RS: Bill Rate						
US	.80	1.61	1.91	2.29	3.03	3.61
VAR5/2	1.18	2.08	2.52	3.07	4.13	5.10
VAR4	1.17	2.15	2.56	3.12	4.53	5.56

1. The results are based on 68 sets of coefficient
   estimates of each model.
2. Each prediction period began one quarter
   after the end of the estimation period.
3. For UR and RS the erors are in percentage
   points. For $GDPR$ and $GDPD$ the errors
   are expressed as a percent of the forecast
   mean (in percentage points).

results are fairly close for the GDP deflator and the unemployment rate. The
AC model is about the same as the US model and noticeably better than the
VAR models. Therefore, as expected, the US model does better relative to the
other models when exogenous variable uncertainty is not taken into account.

This completes the comparison of the models using the d row values. The
next two sections compare the models in two other ways, and the final section
summarizes the overall comparison results.

8.7 Comparing Information in Forecasts[9]

Section 7.8 discussed a method for comparing the information in various forecasts, and this section uses this method to compare the forecasts from the US, US+, VAR5/2, VAR4, and AC models. The results of comparing the US and US+ models to the other three are presented in Table 8.7, and the results of comparing the AC model to the two VAR models are presented in Table 8.8. The rest of this section is a discussion of these two tables.

When using the method in Section 7.8, the forecasts should be based on information only up to the beginning of the forecast period. In other words, they should be "quasi ex ante" forecasts. The 68 sets of estimates that were used for the results in the previous section are used here to generate the forecasts. As was the case in the previous section, each forecast period begins one quarter after the end of the estimation period. There are 68 one quarter ahead forecasts, 67 two quarter ahead forecasts, and so on. All these forecasts are outside sample, and so they meet one of the requirements of a quasi ex ante forecast.

The other main requirement of a quasi ex ante forecast is that it not be based on exogenous variable values that are unknown at the time of the forecast. The VAR and AC forecasts meet this requirement because the models have no exogenous variables, but the forecasts from the US model do not. The 68 sets of forecasts that were computed for the US model are based on the actual values of the exogenous variables.[10] The US+ model, on the other hand, has no hard to forecast exogenous variables, and so it meets the exogenous variable requirement. Both the US and US+ models were used for the present results to see how sensitive the results for the US model are to the treatment of exogenous variables. For this work the US+ model was also estimated 68 times, including estimation of the 91 exogenous variable equations, and these

---

[9]The material in this section is an updated version of the material in Fair and Shiller (1990) (FS). In FS the US model was compared to six VAR models, eight AC models, and two autoregressive models, whereas for present purposes only two VAR and one AC model are used. In addition, the version of the US model that was used in FS was the version that existed in 1976, whereas the current version of the model is used here. Finally, only the results for real output were discussed in FS, whereas results for the GDP deflator, the unemployment rate, and the bill rate are also discussed here. The forecasts examined in this section are all *quasi* ex ante. The information content of *actual* ex ante forecasts for a number of models is examined in Fair and Shiller (1989) using the present method, but this material is not presented here.

[10]Remember that the actual values of the exogenous variables were used in computing the d_{isk} values in the previous section. Exogenous variable uncertainty was handled through the c row calculations.

Table 8.7
US Model Versus Three Others: Estimates of Equation 7.12

Other Model	One Quarter Ahead Forecast				Four Quarter Ahead Forecast			
	cnst	US β	Other γ	SE	cnst	US β	Other γ	SE
			$GDPR$: Real GDP					
			US Model					
VAR5/2	-.0008	.781	-.051	.00691	-.0025	.753	-.103	.01727
	(0.45)	(5.30)	(0.34)		(0.41)	(4.87)	(0.72)	
VAR4	-.0008	.756	-.003	.00692	-.0021	.767	-.112	.01722
	(0.50)	(5.35)	(0.03)		(0.36)	(4.86)	(0.84)	
AC	-.0020	.620	.324	.00681	-.0101	.505	.578	.01629
	(1.11)	(3.48)	(1.45)		(1.56)	(3.74)	(2.30)	
			US+ Model					
VAR5/2	-.0002	.678	.006	.00825	.0069	.381	.153	.02121
	(0.10)	(3.90)	(0.04)		(0.53)	(1.01)	(0.60)	
VAR4	-.0000	.613	.064	.00823	.0053	.417	.124	.02123
	(0.02)	(3.02)	(0.52)		(0.43)	(1.08)	(0.52)	
AC	-.0020	.289	.758	.00770	-.0116	.335	.911	.01866
	(0.90)	(1.51)	(4.14)		(1.45)	(2.13)	(3.37)	
			$GDPD$: GDP Deflator					
			US Model					
VAR5/2	.0023	.454	.416	.00260	.0079	.519	.341	.01000
	(3.22)	(3.49)	(2.95)		(1.36)	(2.54)	(1.59)	
VAR4	.0027	.461	.387	.00264	.0082	.489	.377	.00981
	(3.71)	(3.49)	(2.67)		(1.54)	(2.39)	(1.89)	
			US+ Model					
VAR5/2	.0024	.394	.454	.00284	.0073	.261	.582	.01050
	(3.08)	(2.26)	(2.41)		(1.10)	(1.02)	(2.41)	
VAR4	.0027	.407	.428	.00282	.0071	.307	.556	.01021
	(3.53)	(2.96)	(2.82)		(1.14)	(1.43)	(2.94)	
			UR: Unemployment Rate					
			US Model					
VAR5/2	.0018	.579	.398	.00278	.0385	.689	-.200	.00909
	(0.97)	(4.25)	(2.84)		(3.96)	(2.82)	(0.85)	
VAR4	.0030	.730	.230	.00288	.0409	.761	-.305	.00892
	(1.68)	(6.23)	(1.89)		(4.89)	(3.20)	(1.48)	
			US+ Model					
VAR5/2	.0011	.595	.392	.00279	.0373	.556	-.071	.00996
	(0.54)	(4.14)	(2.67)		(3.06)	(2.30)	(0.28)	
VAR4	.0021	.748	.225	.00288	.0399	.625	-.176	.00990
	(1.10)	(5.83)	(1.73)		(3.67)	(2.49)	(0.75)	
			RS: Bill Rate					
			US Model					
VAR5/2	-.31	1.069	-.027	.795	1.69	.588	.184	2.180
	(0.88)	(6.55)	(0.20)		(0.92)	(1.74)	(1.21)	
VAR4	-.32	1.097	-.054	.795	1.63	.662	.121	2.209
	(0.94)	(6.82)	(0.37)		(0.86)	(1.83)	(0.75)	
			US+ Model					
VAR5/2	-.35	1.073	-.027	.822	2.28	.501	.186	2.223
	(0.92)	(6.20)	(0.19)		(1.34)	(1.55)	(0.95)	
VAR4	-.36	1.093	-.047	.821	2.22	.575	.123	2.247
	(0.99)	(6.54)	(0.31)		(1.27)	(1.64)	(0.60)	

Table 8.8
AC Versus VAR5/2 and VAR4

Other Model	One Quarter Ahead Forecast				Four Quarter Ahead Forecast			
	cnst	AC β	Other γ	SE	cnst	AC β	Other γ	SE
				GDPR: Real GDP				
VAR5/2	-.0010	.916	.106	.00778	-.0038	.938	.204	.01863
	(0.54)	(5.28)	(0.81)		(0.46)	(3.78)	(2.28)	
VAR4	-.0010	.881	.120	.00774	-.0048	.954	.181	.01873
	(0.54)	(4.81)	(1.18)		(0.60)	(3.79)	(2.22)	

68 sets of estimates were used. All the forecasts for the US+ model were also outside sample. Again, remember from the discussion in Section 7.8 that the treatment of the exogenous variables as in US+ may bias the results against the model. Many of the exogenous variables may not be as uncertain as the autoregressive equations imply.

Both one quarter ahead and four quarter ahead forecasts are examined in Table 8.7. In the estimation of the equations, the standard errors of the coefficient estimates were adjusted in the manner discussed in Section 7.8 to account for heteroskedasticity and (for the four quarter ahead results) a third order moving average process for the error term. Equation 7.12 was used for real GDP and the GDP deflator, where both variables are in logs, and the level version of equation 7.12 was used for the unemployment rate and the bill rate.

Turn now to the results in Table 8.7, and consider the forecasts of real GDP first. Also, ignore for now the results for the AC model. The results show that both US and US+ dominate the VAR models for real GDP. The estimates of the coefficients of the VAR forecasts are never significant, and the estimates of the coefficients of the US and US+ forecasts are significant except for the four quarter ahead forecasts for US+, where the t-statistics are about one. It is thus interesting to note that even though the standard errors of the forecasts in Table 8.5 (the d row values) are fairly close for real GDP for the US and VAR models, the results in Table 8.7 suggest that the VAR forecasts contain no information not already in the US forecasts. In this sense the method used in this section seems better able to discriminate among models.

The results for the GDP deflator show that both the US (and US+) forecasts and the VAR forecasts contain independent information. In most cases both coefficients are significant, the exceptions being US versus the VAR models for the four quarter ahead forecasts, where the VAR forecasts are not quite significant, and US+ versus the VAR models for the four quarter ahead forecasts, where the US+ coefficients are not quite significant.

For the unemployment rate US and US+ dominate the VAR models with the exception of the one quarter ahead forecasts from VAR5/2, which are significant in the US and US+ comparisons, although with t-values smaller than those for the US and US+ forecasts.

The results for the bill rate show that US and US+ dominate the VAR models for the one quarter ahead forecasts. For the four quarter ahead forecasts the US and US+ forecasts have larger coefficient estimates and larger t-values than do the VAR forecasts, although collinearity is such that none of the t-values are greater than two.

The results of these comparisons are thus encouraging for the US model. Only for the GDP deflator is there much evidence that even the US+ forecasts lack information that is contained in the VAR forecasts.

Consider now the AC model, where there are only results for real GDP. The US and US+ comparisons in Table 8.7 suggest that both the US or US+ forecasts and the AC forecasts contain independent information. There clearly seems to be forecasting information in the lagged components of GDP that is not captured in the US model, and this is an interesting area for future research.

The VAR versus AC comparisons in Table 8.8 show that the VAR forecasts appear to contain no independent information for the one quarter ahead forecasts, but at least some slight independent information for the four quarter ahead forecasts. As did the results in the previous section, these results suggest that the AC model may be a better alternative than VAR models for many purposes.[11]

---

[11]With a few exceptions, the results for real GDP here are similar to those in Fair and Shiller (1990) (FS). The US+ version is closest to the version used in FS, and so the following discussion focuses on the US+ results. The one quarter ahead results for US+ in Table 8.7 have the US model dominating the VAR models, which is also true in Table 2 in FS. For the four quarter ahead results neither the US+ nor the VAR forecasts are significant in Table 8.7 and both are significant in Table 2 in FS. However, in both tables the US forecasts have larger coefficient estimates and larger t-values than do the VAR forecasts. Regarding US+ versus AC, the results in Table 8.7 are more favorable for AC than they are in Table 2 in FS. In Table 2 in FS the US model dominates the AC models, whereas in Table 8.7 the AC model has a large and significant coefficient estimate for both the one quarter ahead and four quarter ahead forecasts for US+ versus AC. Finally, the VAR versus AC comparisons in Table 8.8 are similar to those in Table 3 in FS. In both tables the AC forecasts dominate the VAR forecasts for the one quarter ahead results and both forecasts are significant for the four quarter ahead results.

8.8 Estimating Event Probabilities[12]

The use of event probability estimates to compare models was discussed in Section 7.9. This comparison is made in this section for two events and five models. The five models are the US, US+, VAR5/2, VAR4, and AC models. The two events, labelled A and B are:

A = At least two consecutive quarters out of five of negative real GDP growth.

B = At least two quarters out of five of negative real GDP growth.

Event A is a recession as generally defined. Event B allows the two or more quarters of negative growth not to be consecutive.

The first 64 sets of estimates of each model that were used for the results in the previous section were used here. (Only 64 rather than 68 sets of estimates could be used because each forecast here has to be five quarters ahead.) There were 64 five quarter ahead outside sample stochastic simulations performed. The number of repetitions per five quarter forecast was 250 for US and US+ and 1000 for the VAR5/2, VAR4, and AC.

Regarding the US+ model, this is the first time that stochastic simulation of the model is needed. For the results in the previous section only deterministic outside sample forecasts were used. As discussed in Section 8.2, when stochastic simulation was performed using US+, the covariance matrix of all the error terms, which is 121×121, was taken to be block diagonal. For the results in this section this matrix was estimated 64 times, each estimate being used for each of the 64 stochastic simulations. The covariance matrices of the coefficient estimates are not needed for the work in this section because coefficients are not drawn.

From the stochastic simulation work one has five sets of values of P_t $(t = 1, \cdots, 64)$ for each of the two events, one for each model, where P_t is the model's estimate of the probability of the event for the period beginning in quarter t. One also has values of R_t for each event, where R_t is the actual outcome—one if the event occurred and zero otherwise. Given the values

---

[12]The material in this section is an updated and expanded version of the material in Section 3.3 in Fair (1993c). In Fair (1993c) only within sample forecasts were used and the only comparisons were to the constant model and a fourth order autoregressive model. In this section all the forecasts are outside sample and comparisons are made to two VAR models and an AC model in addition to the constant model. Also, no coefficients are drawn for the present results, whereas they were drawn in the earlier work. (See the discussion in Section 7.9 as to why coefficients were not drawn here.)

Table 8.9
Estimates of Probability
Accuracy

	Event A (Actual $\bar{p} = .188$)		
Model	$\bar{p}$	QPS	LPS
Constant	.188	.305	.483
US	.175	.310	.477
US+	.173	.310	.472
VAR5/2	.310	.496	.844
VAR4	.264	.518	.972
AC	.154	.324	.510

	Event B (Actual $\bar{p} = .234$)		
Model	$\bar{p}$	QPS	LPS
Constant	.234	.359	.545
US	.211	.290	.438
US+	.238	.306	.465
VAR5/2	.416	.514	*
VAR4	.358	.521	*
AC	.237	.363	.537

*LPS not computable.

of R_t, another model can be considered, which is the model in which P_t is taken to be equal to $\bar{R}$ for each t, where $\bar{R}$ is the mean of R_t over the 64 observations. This is simply a model in which the estimated probability of the event is constant and equal to the frequency that the event happened historically. This model will be called "Constant." The results for this model are not outside sample because the mean that is used is the mean over the whole sample period.

The summary statistics are presented in Table 8.9. In two cases (both for the VAR models) the LPS measure could not be computed because either P_t was 1 and R_t was 0 or vice versa. This is a limitation of the LPS measure in that in cannot handle extreme errors of this type. It, in effect, gives an infinite loss to this type of error.

The results in Table 8.9 are easy to summarize. Either US or US+ is best for both events for both error measures except the case of the constant model and event A, where the QPS for the constant model is slightly smaller. This is thus strong support for the US model.

The results in Table 8.9 also show that the AC model completely dominates the VAR models. This is in keeping with the results in the previous two sections, which generally show the AC model out performing the VAR models.

Figures 8.1 and 8.2 plot the values of P_t and R_t for the US+ and VAR5/2 models for event A for the 64 observations. It is clear from the plots why US+ has better QPS and LPS values in Table 8.9. VAR5/2 has high probabilities too early in the late 1970s and comes down too fast after the recession started compared to US+. Note that both models do not do well predicting the 1990–1991 recession. No model seems to do well predicting this recession.

8.9 Summary of the Test Results

Overall, the results in Tables 8.5, 8.6, 8.7, and 8.9 are favorable for the US model. Even after correcting for exogenous variable uncertainty that may be biased against the model, the model does well in the tests relative to the VAR and AC models. The GDP deflator results are the weakest for the US model, and this is an area for future work. Also, the results in Table 8.7 show that there is information in the AC forecasts of real GDP not in the US forecasts, which suggests that the US model is not using all the information in the lagged components of GDP. Aside from the GDP deflator forecasts, there does not appear to be much information in the VAR forecasts not in the US forecasts.

The AC model generally does as well as or better than the VAR models. This suggests that there is useful information in the lagged components of GDP that the VAR models are not using. From another perspective, if one wants a simple, non structural model to use for forecasting GDP, an AC model would seem to be a better choice than a VAR model.

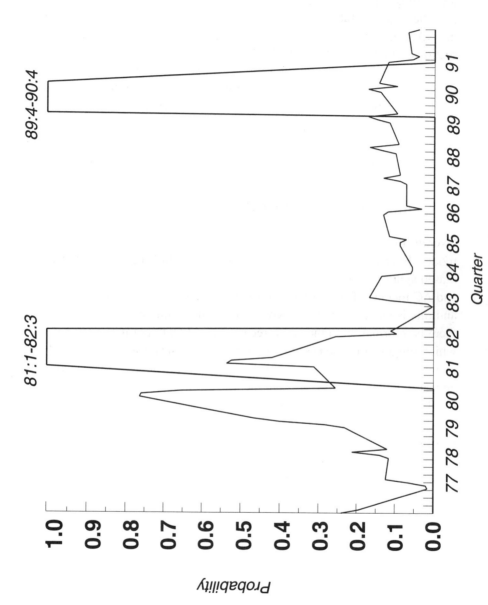

Figure 8.1 Estimated Probabilities for Event A for US+

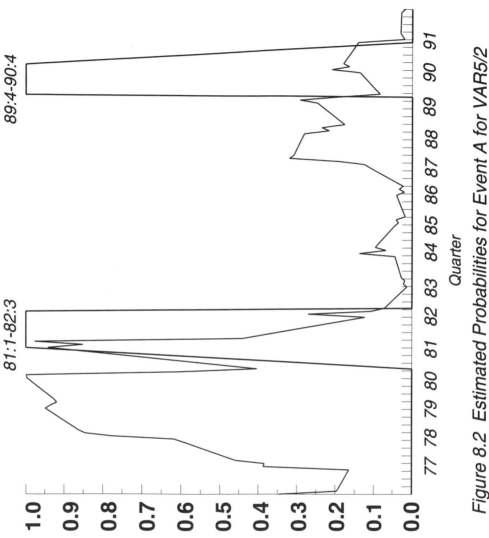

Figure 8.2 Estimated Probabilities for Event A for VAR5/2

9

Testing the MC Model

9.1 Introduction

This chapter is concerned with testing the overall MC model. It is the counterpart of Chapter 8 for the US model. There are, however, many fewer tests in this chapter than there are in Chapter 8. The main problem here is the short length of many of the sample periods. Many of these periods do not begin until the 1970s, which effectively rules out, for example, the successive reestimation that was done in Sections 8.6, 8.7, and 8.8 for the US model. Therefore, the main testing of the MC model must rely on within sample predictions, although some outside sample results are reported in this chapter.

The size of the MC model is discussed in Section 9.2, and the solution of the model is explained. Section 9.3 then presents the model to which the MC model is to be compared. This model, called ARMC, replaces each of the stochastic equations of the ROW model with a fourth order autoregressive equation for the quarterly countries and a second order autoregressive equation for the annual countries. The within sample test results are discussed in Section 9.4, and the outside sample test results are discussed in Section 9.5.

9.2 The Size and Solution of the MC model

The US model, which is part of the MC model, includes 30 stochastic equations plus one more when it is imbedded in the MC model. This additional equation is discussed below. There are 32 countries in the ROW model and up to 15 stochastic equations per country. If each country had all 15 equations, there would be a total of 480 (32×15) stochastic equations in the ROW model. Because of data limitations, however, not all countries have all equations, and there are in fact 315 stochastic equations in the ROW model. Given the 31 stochastic equations in the US model, there are thus 346 stochastic equations in the MC model. There are a total of 1541 unrestricted coefficients in these equations, counting the autoregressive coefficients of the error terms. In addition, as discussed in Section 6.16, there are 1299 estimated trade share equations. Not counting the trade share coefficient estimates, all the coefficient estimates for the US model are presented in Tables 5.1–5.30, and all the coefficient estimates for the ROW model are presented in Tables 6.1a–6.15a. These are the estimates that were used for the within sample results below.

Table B.1 shows that there are in the ROW model 19 variables determined by identities, 4 variables determined when the countries are linked together, and 22 exogenous variables per country. Counting these variables, various transformations of the variables that are needed for the estimation, and the US variables (but not the trade shares), there are about 4000 variables in the MC model.

The way in which the US model is imbedded in the MC model is explained in Table B.5. The two key variables that are exogenous in the US model but become endogenous in the overall MC model are exports, EX, and the price of imports, PIM. EX depends on $X85\$_{US}$, which is determined in Table B.4. PIM depends on PM_{US}, which depends on PMP_{US}, which is also determined in Table B.4.

Feeding into Table B.4 from the US model are PX_{US} and $M85\$A_{US}$. PX_{US} is determined is the same way that PX is determined for the other countries, namely by equation 11. In the US case $\log PX_{US} - \log PW\$_{US}$ is regressed on $\log GDPD - \log PW\$_{US}$. The equation, which is numbered 132 is:

$$\log PX_{US} - \log PW\$_{US} = \lambda(\log GDPD - \log PW\$_{US}) \qquad (132)$$

This equation is estimated under the assumption of a second order autoregressive error for the 1962:1–1992:3 period. The estimate of λ is .956 with a t-statistic of 24.26. The estimates (t-statistics) of the two autoregressive coefficients are 1.50 (19.17) and $-.51$ (-6.55), respectively. The standard error is .0125. Given the predicted value of PX_{US} from equation 132, PEX is determined by the identity listed in Table B.5: $PEX = DEL3 \cdot PX_{US}$. This identity replaces identity 32 in Table A.3 in the US model.

$M85\$A_{US}$, which, as just noted, feeds into Table B.4, depends on M_{US}, which depends on IM. This is shown in Table B.5. IM is determined by equation 27 in the US model. Equation 27 is thus the key equation that determines the U.S. import value that feeds into Table B.4.

The main exogenous variables in the overall MC model are the government spending variables (G). In other words, fiscal policy is exogenous. Monetary policy is not exogenous because of the use of the interest rate and exchange rate reaction functions.

Because some of the countries are annual, the overall MC model is solved a year at a time. A solution period must begin in the first quarter of the year. In the following discussion, assume that year 1 is the first year to be solved. The overall MC model is solved as follows:

1. Given values of $X85\$$, PMP, and $PW\$$ for all four quarters of year 1 for each quarterly country and for year 1 for each annual country, all the stochastic equations and identities are solved. For the annual countries "solved" means that the equations are passed through k_1 times for year 1, where k_1 is determined by experimentation (as discussed below). For the quarterly countries "solved" means that quarter 1 of year 1 is passed through k_1 times, then quarter 2 k_1 times, then quarter 3 k_1 times, and then quarter 4 k_1 times. The solution for the quarterly countries for the four quarters of year 1 is a dynamic simulation in the sense that the predicted values of the endogenous variables from previous quarters are used, when relevant, in the solution for the current quarter.

2. Given from the solution in step 1 values of E, PX, and $M85\$A$ for each country, the calculations in Table B.4 can be performed. Since all the calculations in Table B.4 are quarterly, the annual values of E, PX, and $M85\$A$ from the annual countries have to be converted to quarterly values first. This is done in the manner discussed at the bottom of Table B.4. The procedure in effect takes the distribution of the annual values into the quarterly values to be exogenous. The second task is to compute $PX\$$ using equation L-1. Given the values of $PX\$$, the third task is to compute the values of α_{ij} from the trade share equations—see equation 6.13 in Section 6.16. This solution is also dynamic in the sense that the predicted value of α_{ij} for the previous quarter feeds into the solution for the current quarter. (Remember that the lagged value of α_{ij} is an explanatory variable in the trade share equations.) The fourth task is to compute $X85\$$, PMP, and $PW\$$ for each country using equations L-2, L-3, and L-4. Finally, for the annual countries the quarterly values of these three variables are then converted to annual values by summing in the case of $X85\$$ and averaging in the case of PMP and $PW\$$.

3. Given the new values of $X85\$$, PMP, and $PW\$$ from step 2, repeat step 1 and then step 2. Keep repeating steps 1 and 2 until they have been done k_2 times. At the end of this, declare that the solution for year 1 has been obtained.

4. Repeat steps 1, 2, and 3 for year 2. If the solution is meant to be dynamic, use the predicted values for year 1 for the annual countries and the predicted values for the four quarters of year 1 for the quarterly countries, when relevant, in the solution for year 2. Continue then to year 3, and so on.

I have found that going beyond $k_1 = 4$ and $k_2 = 7$ leads to very little change in the final solution values, and these are the values of k_1 and k_2 that have been used for the results in this chapter and in Chapter 12.

Stochastic Simulation of the MC Model in the Future

Although no stochastic simulation experiments using the MC model were performed for the present work, it should be possible in future work, with a few adjustments, to do so. Since the MC model has 346 stochastic equations and 1541 unrestricted coefficients, the covariance matrix of the error terms is 346×346 and the covariance matrix of the coefficient estimates is 1541×1541. Some of the problems that arise in dealing with these matrices are the following. First, some of the equations are estimated using quarterly data and some using annual data. Second, even if the periodicity of the data were the same, there are not enough observations to estimate the covariance matrix of the error terms unconstrained. Third, the estimation periods generally differ across countries. The best way to handle these problems is probably to take the covariance matrices to be block diagonal, one block per country. In some cases one may also want to take the covariance matrix of the coefficient estimates within a country to be block diagonal, one block per equation.

The computer time needed to solve the MC model once is still large enough to make stochastic simulation costly in time. Even using the block diagonal matrices just discussed, stochastic simulation would not be routine using, say, 486 computers. This computer restriction should, however, be eased considerably with the next generation of chips, and so in a few years it should be possible to perform the same type of calculations for the MC model as were performed in Chapters 8 and 11 for the US model.

9.3 The ARMC Model

In order to decide how good or bad the MC model predicts the data, one needs a basis of comparison. Two VAR models and an AC model were used for this purpose for the US model. A model that has some similarities to the AC model was used as the basis of comparison for the MC model. This model will be called the "ARMC" model. It is simple to describe. Each of the stochastic equations for the quarterly countries (except the US) is replaced with an autoregressive equation in which the left hand side variable is regressed on a constant term, a linear time trend, and the first four lagged values of the variable. For the annual countries only the first two lagged values are used.[1] The MC and ARMC models differ only in this treatment of the stochastic equations. The US model is the same for both models; all the identities arc the same;[2] and the trade share calculations are the same.

The ARMC is like the AC model in that the components of GDP are regressed on their lagged values and the GDP identity is used. It differs from the AC model in that 1) regressions are not performed for components that are not determined by stochastic equations in the MC model, 2) regressions are performed for all the variables determined by stochastic equations, not just the components, and 3) all the identities are used, not just the GDP identity.

Each equation of the ARMC model was estimated over the same sample period as was used for the corresponding equation for the MC model. The model is solved in the same way as the MC model.

---

[1]With the following five exceptions, the left hand side variable for the ARMC model for each equation is the same as that for the MC model. The exceptions are 1) equation 4, where the left hand side variable is $V1$ rather than Y, 2) equation 8, with RB rather than $RB - RS_{-2}$, 3) equation 9, with $\log E$ rather than $\log(E/E_{-1})$, 4) equation 11, with $\log PX$ rather than $\log PX - \log(PW\$ \cdot E)$, and 5) equation 12, with $\log W$ rather than the left hand side variable used to account for the coefficient restriction. Also, because $V1$ is used for the left hand side variable for equation 4, the identity I-4 is changed from $V1 = Y - X$ to $Y = X + V1$.

[2]With the exception noted in the previous footnote.

9.4   Within Sample RMSEs

Given the data availability, the longest period[3] over which the MC model could be solved was 1972–1990. A series of two year (eight quarter) ahead predictions were run over the period. The first prediction began in 1972, the second one in 1973, and so on through 1990. For each endogenous variable this results in 19 one year ahead forecasts and 18 two year ahead forecasts for the annual countries. For the quarterly countries there were 19 one through four quarter ahead forecasts and 18 five through eight quarter ahead forecasts.[4] Given the forecast values, root mean squared errors (RMSEs) were computed. The same forecasts were made using the ARMC model, and RMSEs were computed.

The results from this work are presented in Table 9.1. Presented in the table for each of 17 variables for each country is the ratio of the MC RMSE to the ARMC RMSE. For the quarterly countries ratios are presented for the one quarter ahead, four quarter ahead, and eight quarter ahead RMSEs, and for the annual countries ratios are presented for the one year ahead and two year ahead RMSEs. A ratio less than one means that the MC model is more accurate, and a ratio greater than one means that the ARMC model is more accurate.

Presented at the top of Table 9.1 for each variable is a weighted average of all the results. The weight used for a country is the ratio of its GDP in 1985 in U.S. dollars to the total for all the countries.[5] The first row, labelled I, is the weighted average of the four quarter ahead results for the quarterly countries and the one year ahead results for the annual countries. The second row, labelled II, is the weighted average of the eight quarter ahead results for the quarterly countries and the two year ahead results for the annual countries. These summary results were obtained by taking weighted averages of the individual RMSEs and then computing the ratio of the weighted averages, rather than by taking weighted averages of the individual ratios. The following discussion will concentrate on the weighted averages.

Consider first the results for the exchange rate in Table 9.1. On average

---

[3] In order to use the complete 1972–1990 period, the following countries were dropped in the solution of the model for the following periods: NE: 1972–1976; FI: 1972–1976; NO: 1972–1973; and MA: 1987–1990. Data on some of the variables did not exist for these countries for the respective periods.

[4] Remember that each prediction period begins in the first quarter of the year for the quarterly countries. This is contrary to the case for the US model in Chapter 8, where a new prediction period began each quarter.

[5] GDP in U.S. dollars is $(PY \cdot Y)/E$.

the MC model does not do quite as well as the ARMC model. For the one year ahead results the weighted average ratio is 1.05, and for the two year ahead results it is 1.17. It is well known that structural exchange rate equations have a hard time beating autoregressive equations, and the results in Table 9.1 are examples of this. On average, however, the results are only slightly worse for the structural model. Also, as will be seen in the next section, the outside sample exchange rate results favor MC over ARMC.

Other variables for which the ARMC model is more accurate than the MC model are the price of exports (PX) and the price of imports (PM). The results are mixed for GDP (Y), exports ($X85\$$), and the wage rate (W). For the remaining variables—the price deflator (PY), the interest rate (RS), imports (M), consumption (C), investment (I), the balance of payments (S), and the unemployment rate (UR)—the MC model is more accurate than the ARMC model. On average the result seem reasonably good for the MC model. The model appears to have explanatory power beyond that contained in the lagged values and the time trend.

The results for the United States are presented in Table 9.2. The RMSEs in the rows labelled "MC" are from the same MC solutions used for the results in Table 9.1. The RMSEs in the rows labelled "US" are from the solutions for the US model alone. The same 19 prediction periods were used for the US model alone as were used for the MC model. For the US model alone exports (EX) and the price of imports (PIM) are exogenous.

The results in Table 9.2 show how the accuracy of the US model changes when it is imbedded in the MC model. For real GDP, the RMSE increases between 7 and 27 percent when the US model is imbedded in the MC model. For the GDP deflator the increases (after the first quarter) are between 18 and 66 percent. There is very little change for the unemployment rate and the bill rate. Much of the increase for the GDP deflator is due to the effect of errors made in predicting the price of imports. The RMSE for the price of imports ranges from 2.69 percent for the one quarter ahead forecast to 8.11 percent for the eight quarter ahead forecast. Similarly, much of the increase for real GDP is due to the effect of errors made in predicting exports. The RMSE for exports ranges from 2.29 percent for the one quarter ahead forecast to 6.16 percent for the eight quarter ahead forecast.

Table 9.1
Ratios of Within Sample RMSEs 1972-1990: AC/ARMC

		Y	PY	RS	E	M	C	I	V1/Y	X85$
I	All	.95	.93	.80	1.05	.75	.95	.90	1.08	.94
II	All	1.11	.79	.96	1.17	.75	1.00	.90	1.12	1.04
1	CA	.87	1.20	.96	1.02	.68	.80	.96	1.19	.99
4	CA	1.06	1.18	.93	1.06	.57	.88	1.06	1.04	1.04
8	CA	1.08	.93	.82	1.11	.49	.83	1.08	.97	1.10
1	JA	.91	1.16	1.25	1.00	.78	1.01	.97	1.10	.97
4	JA	1.02	1.02	.69	1.12	.66	.88	.92	.94	.95
8	JA	1.37	.66	.98	1.37	.62	1.10	1.05	.89	1.09
1	AU	.99	1.05	.75	1.03	.82	1.10	–	1.26	1.02
4	AU	1.24	.67	1.11	1.08	.93	1.48	–	1.16	.83
8	AU	1.41	.83	1.35	1.14	1.07	1.54	–	1.36	.96
1	FR	.61	.90	.99	.98	.62	1.14	1.20	1.20	.77
4	FR	.86	.82	.74	1.00	.83	1.21	.92	.99	.83
8	FR	1.20	1.07	.99	1.03	.88	1.41	.91	1.02	1.00
1	GE	.73	.85	.80	1.03	.92	1.11	1.16	1.08	.86
4	GE	.85	.75	.94	1.09	.68	.74	.95	.93	.87
8	GE	.85	.62	.99	1.14	.66	.68	.82	.97	1.00
1	IT	.57	.80	.84	.95	.67	.92	1.12	1.00	1.08
4	IT	1.26	.72	.64	1.02	.91	1.11	.87	1.34	.95
8	IT	1.71	.75	.95	1.00	1.01	1.38	1.12	1.52	1.05
1	NE	.90	1.06	.75	1.01	1.03	1.19	–	1.71	.78
4	NE	.93	.77	.98	1.08	.96	1.02	–	1.02	.81
8	NE	.84	.87	1.03	1.08	.96	.83	–	.98	1.13
1	ST	1.19	.96	.81	1.02	1.09	1.00	–	–	.85
4	ST	1.48	1.11	1.18	1.04	1.15	1.01	–	–	.88
8	ST	1.83	1.41	1.20	1.13	1.31	.95	–	–	.99
1	UK	.89	1.23	.90	.95	1.01	.85	.91	.89	1.02
4	UK	.81	.95	.87	1.01	.68	.76	.76	.91	1.03
8	UK	.79	.65	.86	1.13	.89	.85	.67	.94	1.03
1	FI	.81	.97	.90	.95	.83	.93	–	1.44	1.06
4	FI	.91	.72	1.02	1.06	.76	.89	–	1.00	1.19
8	FI	1.17	.77	1.11	1.12	.82	1.02	–	1.21	2.03
1	AS	.84	.80	1.01	1.07	.80	.96	–	1.01	.96
4	AS	.98	.97	.86	1.10	.71	1.10	–	.84	.76
8	AS	1.27	.78	.90	1.23	.74	1.42	–	.84	.95
1	SO	.99	1.11	1.05	1.06	.76	.91	1.08	–	1.18
4	SO	.86	1.33	1.19	.95	.65	.84	.97	–	.84
8	SO	1.03	1.61	1.41	.96	.82	.95	.95	–	.75
1	KO	.79	.97	1.01	1.02	.98	1.18	–	.87	.95
4	KO	.82	.98	.98	1.13	.92	.93	–	1.18	.93
8	KO	.85	.82	.97	1.18	.92	.93	–	.94	.97
1	BE	.54	.94	.62	.79	.59	.76	.69	.88	.70
2	BE	.48	.94	.73	1.11	.80	.71	.55	.90	.78
1	DE	1.05	.87	.94	.78	.93	1.33	1.01	.97	.80
2	DE	1.08	.63	1.05	1.04	1.16	1.42	.91	.95	1.27
1	NO	1.08	1.05	.88	.74	.65	1.31	–	–	.88
2	NO	1.37	1.24	.81	1.08	.69	1.23	–	–	.92
1	SW	.47	.84	.87	.84	.67	.89	.81	1.70	.69
2	SW	.58	.96	1.05	1.10	.89	.90	.87	1.59	.91
1	GR	.87	.87	–	.82	.86	1.05	1.11	.66	.97
2	GR	.89	.88	–	1.07	.93	.98	1.08	.68	.96
1	IR	.88	.82	.74	.74	1.06	1.07	1.07	1.08	.94
2	IR	.96	.69	.86	1.11	1.33	1.04	1.22	1.16	.98
1	PO	1.66	1.22	1.06	.90	.90	.76	–	–	.85
2	PO	1.86	1.42	1.11	1.13	.97	.78	–	–	1.10
1	SP	1.12	.68	–	.83	.57	.95	–	.64	.84
2	SP	1.41	.63	–	1.06	.49	.83	–	.62	1.25
1	NZ	.82	.97	1.09	1.54	.42	1.22	–	–	.90
2	NZ	1.02	.96	1.30	1.65	.57	.87	–	–	1.28

Table 9.1 (continued)

		P X	*P M*	*S*	*W*	*J*	*L*1	*L*2	*U R*
I	All	1.02	1.05	.87	1.07	.89	1.05	.94	.92
II	All	1.07	1.14	.76	.97	.92	1.23	.96	.89
1	CA	1.17	.98	.78	1.31	1.03	.95	–	1.03
4	CA	1.11	1.04	.67	1.25	.84	1.03	–	.84
8	CA	1.01	1.04	.50	1.18	.85	1.13	–	.86
1	JA	1.06	1.13	.97	1.18	.88	1.15	.95	.81
4	JA	1.08	1.23	1.12	1.22	1.19	1.24	1.01	1.19
8	JA	1.29	1.54	.99	1.04	1.63	1.86	1.02	1.49
1	AU	1.00	1.13	1.00	1.57	1.08	1.02	.98	1.04
4	AU	.95	1.19	.91	1.51	.96	1.03	1.00	1.34
8	AU	1.03	1.09	.62	1.65	1.05	1.05	1.01	1.10
1	FR	1.03	1.02	.69	.93	–	–	–	–
4	FR	.98	.89	.82	1.06	–	–	–	–
8	FR	.92	.87	1.00	1.06	–	–	–	–
1	GE	1.09	1.19	.89	1.09	1.04	1.07	–	1.13
4	GE	1.12	1.12	.90	.75	.88	.90	–	.88
8	GE	1.06	1.18	.92	.69	.80	.93	–	.69
1	IT	.97	1.06	.80	1.06	1.23	1.13	1.17	.90
4	IT	.78	.84	.63	.71	.88	.99	.96	.81
8	IT	.82	.76	.69	.73	1.24	1.08	1.28	.94
1	NE	1.35	1.01	1.10	.97	–	–	–	–
4	NE	1.28	.97	.91	.63	–	–	–	–
8	NE	1.38	.96	1.27	.67	–	–	–	–
1	ST	.98	1.13	1.17	–	1.02	.88	.91	1.62
4	ST	1.03	1.14	1.34	–	1.05	.93	.92	1.46
8	ST	1.15	1.10	1.40	–	.85	1.00	.97	.98
1	UK	.95	1.02	.91	1.24	.83	1.04	–	1.16
4	UK	.79	1.03	1.02	.78	.55	1.03	–	.78
8	UK	.70	1.16	.84	.63	.56	1.02	–	.75
1	FI	1.49	.95	.84	1.15	.65	.86	1.00	.81
4	FI	1.61	.88	.98	1.18	.76	.80	.89	.66
8	FI	1.46	.76	.87	1.04	.57	1.04	.91	.45
1	AS	1.07	1.03	.95	–	.81	1.03	.98	1.16
4	AS	1.27	1.09	1.07	–	.54	.97	.91	.53
8	AS	1.38	1.14	1.09	–	.46	.89	.86	.46
1	SO	1.05	.92	.65	–	–	–	–	–
4	SO	1.15	.74	.50	–	–	–	–	–
8	SO	1.31	.71	.36	–	–	–	–	–
1	KO	1.05	.96	.91	1.95	–	–	–	–
4	KO	.96	1.04	1.11	2.32	–	–	–	–
8	KO	1.03	1.15	.97	1.72	–	–	–	–
1	BE	.91	.61	.45	.88	.87	.78	.57	.81
2	BE	.94	.93	.62	.78	.65	.85	.61	.58
1	DE	.75	.71	.70	.90	.84	1.00	1.04	.85
2	DE	.87	.91	.68	.91	.89	1.01	1.08	.88
1	NO	1.08	.94	.94	1.35	1.69	1.40	–	1.46
2	NO	1.15	1.04	.91	1.56	1.73	1.74	–	1.56
1	SW	1.01	.88	.83	1.20	.95	1.11	1.15	.75
2	SW	1.02	1.10	.95	1.13	.98	1.34	1.26	.66
1	GR	1.04	.77	.85	.97	–	–	–	–
2	GR	1.06	.83	.84	1.09	–	–	–	–
1	IR	.87	.69	.61	1.00	.98	–	–	.96
2	IR	.87	.81	.48	1.15	1.03	–	–	1.01
1	PO	1.12	.93	1.06	–	–	–	–	–
2	PO	1.27	1.11	1.03	–	–	–	–	–
1	SP	.83	.72	.58	1.23	.77	.93	.70	1.13
2	SP	.87	.97	.46	1.27	.58	.86	.49	.99
1	NZ	1.03	1.23	.82	1.03	–	–	–	–
2	NZ	1.00	1.20	.74	1.04	–	–	–	–

Table 9.1 (continued)

		Y	PY	RS	E	M	C	I	V1/Y	X85$	PX	PM	S
1	SA	.82	–	–	–	1.23	.91	.83	1.60	.98	–	1.03	.97
2	SA	.95	–	–	–	1.15	1.00	.61	1.47	.89	–	1.02	.75
1	VE	.83	–	.74	–	.84	.97	–	1.04	1.02	–	1.02	1.08
2	VE	.92	–	.66	–	.76	.99	–	1.13	1.02	–	1.00	.89
1	CO	1.22	1.13	–	–	.56	1.33	–	1.12	1.07	1.08	1.03	.91
2	CO	1.61	1.30	–	–	.62	1.61	–	1.30	1.18	1.13	.99	.58
1	JO	1.10	1.30	–	1.21	.65	.86	–	.96	1.07	1.34	1.16	.79
2	JO	1.18	1.54	–	1.30	.59	.87	–	.97	1.06	1.61	1.12	.73
1	SY	1.04	1.08	–	–	.94	1.01	–	–	1.23	1.14	1.02	.91
2	SY	1.20	1.30	–	–	.77	.75	–	–	1.44	1.29	1.04	.92
1	ID	1.00	–	–	1.08	.97	1.10	–	–	.87	1.00	.94	.99
2	ID	.91	–	–	1.16	.89	.89	–	–	.93	1.31	.82	1.03
1	MA	.71	.90	–	–	.74	.75	–	–	.76	.79	1.05	1.00
2	MA	.69	1.26	–	–	1.21	.69	–	–	.75	.74	1.05	1.00
1	PA	.89	.49	.73	–	1.11	1.04	–	.85	.83	1.14	1.01	.99
2	PA	1.07	.59	.86	–	1.03	1.09	–	1.45	.77	1.28	.98	1.14
1	PH	1.17	1.13	1.13	1.24	.80	1.13	.92	.98	1.06	1.28	1.26	1.65
2	PH	.96	1.15	1.36	1.34	.63	.95	.65	.94	1.27	1.41	1.30	1.49
1	TH	.76	1.40	–	–	.55	.95	–	1.00	1.05	1.05	1.02	.45
2	TH	.95	1.24	–	–	.43	.90	–	1.04	1.12	1.03	1.08	.32

Variables W, J, $L1$, $L2$, and UR are not part of the model for countries SA–TH.
Each number is the ratio of the MC RMSE and the ARMC RMSE.

9.5   Outside Sample RMSEs

As noted at the beginning of this chapter, short sample periods for many countries limit the amount of outside sample work that can be done. The outside sample results in this section are thus very preliminary.

The outside sample results were obtained as follows. First, each of the non US stochastic equations of the MC and ARMC models was estimated through 1986.4 for the quarterly countries and 1986 for the annual countries. These coefficient estimates were then used to predict 1987, 1988, 1989, and 1990. This gave for the annual countries 4 one year ahead forecasts and 3 two year ahead forecast. For the quarterly countries there were 4 one through four quarter ahead forecasts and 3 five through eight quarter ahead forecasts. RMSEs were computed for these forecasts, and the results are presented in Table 9.3. The same weighting scheme was used in Table 9.3 as was used in Table 9.1. When comparing Tables 9.1 and 9.3 remember that, for example, the one year ahead results in Table 9.3 are based on only 4 observations compared to 19 in Table 9.1 and in this sense are less reliable. The following discussion of Table 9.3 will concentrate on the weighted results.

The results in Tables 9.1 and 9.3 differ in that some variables for which the MC model does better in Table 9.1 do worse in Table 9.3 and vice versa. For example, the MC model does much better for the exchange rate in Table 9.3.

Table 9.2
US RMSEs: US Alone Versus US in MC Model

	1	2	3	4	6	8
			GDPR: Real GDP			
Alone	.46	.98	1.04	1.36	1.52	1.52
MC	.54	1.05	1.14	1.46	1.93	1.72
MC÷Alone	1.16	1.07	1.09	1.07	1.27	1.13
			GDPD: GDP Deflator			
Alone	.45	.48	.68	.75	.99	1.15
MC	.44	.57	.82	.96	1.50	1.92
MC÷Alone	.98	1.18	1.20	1.28	1.52	1.66
			UR: Unemployment Rate			
Alone	.22	.41	.45	.54	.76	.77
MC	.22	.39	.38	.52	.85	.77
MC÷Alone	1.01	.95	.86	.95	1.12	1.00
			RS: Bill Rate			
Alone	.50	1.16	1.75	1.33	1.62	1.75
MC	.52	1.13	1.72	1.38	1.71	1,82
MC÷Alone	1.04	.98	.99	1.03	1.05	1.04
			PIM: Import Price Deflator			
MC	2.69	4.14	5.09	5.44	7.66	8.11
			EX: Exports			
MC	2.29	3.20	3.64	4.47	5.17	6.16

Errors are in percentage points.

The ratio is .57 for both the one year ahead and two year ahead results. From the results in Table 9.3 one would conclude that structural exchange rate equations dominate autoregressive ones. On the other hand, the MC model does worse for the interest rate, where the ratios are 1.52 and 1.61. The other variables for which the MC model does worse are consumption, employment, and the unemployment rate. It does better, sometimes considerably better, for the other variables. Overall, the MC model appears to do somewhat better relative to the ARMC model in Table 9.3 than in Table 9.1. This suggests that the ARMC equations may be somewhat more subject to within sample data mining problems than are the MC equations. Again, however, these results are based on only 3 or 4 observations, and so they are very tentative.

This completes the discussion of the RMSE results. One can get from Tables 9.1 and 9.3 an idea of the accuracy of the model for the individual countries, and this is left to the reader. When more data become available in the future, it will be interesting to put the MC model through more tests. In

Table 9.3
Ratios of Outside Sample RMSEs 1987-1990: MC/ARMC

		Y	PY	RS	E	M	C	I	V1/Y	X85$
I	All	.93	1.10	1.52	.57	.86	1.47	.98	.80	.80
II	All	.88	.80	1.61	.57	.81	1.31	.85	.82	.60
1	CA	.43	.89	1.14	.61	.95	1.57	.56	1.02	1.01
4	CA	1.06	.46	1.13	.35	1.79	.29	.74	.85	.48
8	CA	1.01	.41	1.36	.51	.69	.38	.97	.97	.61
1	JA	.69	2.56	5.01	.84	1.21	.52	1.27	3.32	.91
4	JA	1.50	2.82	3.39	.68	.27	1.17	1.29	.27	1.55
8	JA	1.71	2.55	3.36	.73	.56	1.81	1.24	.62	.59
1	AU	1.20	.43	1.14	.95	.80	1.86	–	1.06	.81
4	AU	1.52	.72	2.27	.90	.72	4.53	–	5.18	.54
8	AU	1.06	.80	3.20	.94	1.00	3.70	–	11.21	.43
1	FR	.31	.64	.59	.85	1.15	1.30	.29	.68	.85
4	FR	.17	.95	.37	.67	1.02	2.29	.24	.30	.49
8	FR	.21	.79	.47	.69	.72	2.06	.23	.54	.24
1	GE	.72	.71	2.96	.93	1.69	1.76	.84	1.72	.96
4	GE	.50	.54	3.10	.89	.55	2.28	.42	.64	.73
8	GE	.25	.38	2.51	.90	.49	3.95	.16	.74	.57
1	IT	.52	2.98	.44	.56	.93	2.20	.77	1.89	1.02
4	IT	.95	2.05	.36	.28	.64	1.73	.34	1.00	1.09
8	IT	1.45	1.06	.41	.22	.45	1.70	.30	.94	1.54
1	NE	1.08	.47	.59	.69	.62	1.01	–	2.11	1.74
4	NE	.83	.44	.47	.35	.99	.67	–	.80	.64
8	NE	.33	.20	.57	.27	.81	.55	–	.95	.32
1	ST	1.43	1.31	1.10	.86	1.63	1.94	–	–	.87
4	ST	2.26	1.94	1.41	.98	2.72	1.75	–	–	.74
8	ST	2.30	3.78	1.17	1.33	1.70	.69	–	–	.56
1	UK	1.64	.94	1.35	.66	1.60	2.29	1.67	2.22	.99
4	UK	1.71	.49	2.60	.57	1.97	2.12	1.89	.83	1.07
8	UK	1.33	.30	4.96	.48	1.70	1.52	1.54	.83	1.15
1	FI	.83	2.52	.29	.59	1.15	.86	–	3.90	1.12
4	FI	3.13	2.11	.51	.32	1.53	1.21	–	1.99	2.07
8	FI	2.36	3.56	.50	.26	1.51	1.22	–	1.31	.33
1	AS	1.11	1.04	.61	.55	.61	1.03	–	1.17	.77
4	AS	.71	.73	.76	.55	.53	1.46	–	.72	.58
8	AS	.74	.40	.47	.48	.58	1.67	–	.67	.70
1	SO	.75	1.52	2.49	.28	1.92	.70	.36	–	.60
4	SO	.27	2.11	2.02	.22	1.42	1.52	1.00	–	.29
8	SO	.57	2.46	5.03	.23	1.50	2.32	.43	–	.20
1	KO	.75	2.64	1.06	.57	3.76	2.99	–	1.20	.88
4	KO	.38	4.88	.50	.51	8.98	4.44	–	1.64	.73
8	KO	.60	3.39	.22	.63	15.10	2.18	–	1.05	.62
1	BE	.40	.58	.30	.50	2.71	1.48	.92	.24	.49
2	BE	.20	.69	.45	.60	1.84	.97	.82	.25	.23
1	DE	1.13	.24	2.15	.60	.81	4.09	3.28	1.79	.61
2	DE	.98	.24	2.52	.99	1.31	9.27	3.26	1.66	.38
1	NO	1.39	.89	.30	.64	2.04	.69	–	–	1.07
2	NO	1.21	.69	.22	.96	4.19	.51	–	–	.95
1	SW	.18	.11	.50	.46	.80	1.25	.74	2.24	.57
2	SW	.16	.18	.90	.51	.97	.88	.64	1.45	.38
1	GR	1.64	1.05	–	.85	.66	1.10	5.96	.82	.94
2	GR	1.88	.53	–	.91	.88	.79	6.18	.89	.55
1	IR	2.42	.52	.36	.25	1.19	4.84	3.38	2.35	1.58
2	IR	3.38	.43	.44	.28	2.15	4.94	4.48	1.11	2.02
1	PO	7.13	.64	.06	.54	1.19	4.65	–	–	.93
2	PO	8.48	.58	.05	.63	.62	5.11	–	–	.86
1	SP	.49	.79	–	.46	.49	.33	–	.60	.73
2	SP	1.59	.70	–	.71	.42	.17	–	.30	.51
1	NZ	1.10	.27	1.15	1.15	.90	3.66	–	–	.50
2	NZ	1.01	.21	1.42	1.44	.96	4.59	–	–	.50

Table 9.3 (continued)

		PX	PM	S	W	J	L1	L2	UR
I	All	.65	.55	.58	.65	1.37	1.09	.85	1.39
II	All	.50	.47	.38	.50	1.27	1.39	.82	1.33
1	CA	.94	.44	.69	1.33	.69	1.57	–	1.65
4	CA	.51	.26	.48	1.01	1.12	3.06	–	1.50
8	CA	.42	.45	.14	.88	.97	2.55	–	1.31
1	JA	1.21	1.00	.75	1.09	.96	.48	1.08	1.17
4	JA	1.59	.69	.42	.42	1.70	1.10	1.44	1.59
8	JA	1.60	.66	.18	.32	1.92	2.77	1.52	1.44
1	AU	.67	.77	.61	1.52	.67	1.64	1.47	.88
4	AU	.42	1.09	2.45	3.10	1.61	1.11	2.30	6.97
8	AU	.23	.92	1.75	2.78	.82	.61	3.30	4.98
1	FR	.53	.57	.61	.94	–	–	–	–
4	FR	.21	.73	.60	.69	–	–	–	–
8	FR	.13	.59	.75	.41	–	–	–	–
1	GE	.71	.66	1.16	1.92	1.23	1.07	–	1.61
4	GE	.51	1.50	1.42	.09	1.22	.81	–	1.37
8	GE	.38	1.62	1.23	.13	.57	.68	–	.65
1	IT	.53	.92	1.88	.31	.87	1.00	1.29	.80
4	IT	.17	.20	.21	.23	.61	.99	.28	.41
8	IT	.14	.11	.16	.19	.14	1.16	.25	.11
1	NE	.60	.47	.29	.73	–	–	–	–
4	NE	.29	.19	.09	.16	–	–	–	–
8	NE	.39	.12	.07	.05	–	–	–	–
1	ST	.77	.74	1.34	–	3.82	2.43	5.53	3.46
4	ST	1.01	1.13	1.85	–	4.64	3.50	7.31	1.29
8	ST	1.14	1.40	1.81	–	3.25	4.00	4.70	2.27
1	UK	.93	.42	1.19	1.09	2.25	.82	–	2.21
4	UK	.58	.66	1.43	.57	2.19	.51	–	2.82
8	UK	.42	.37	1.10	.43	2.24	.32	–	2.88
1	FI	1.31	.34	.40	.85	1.60	.87	1.70	.43
4	FI	.67	.23	.15	3.08	.69	.60	1.31	.98
8	FI	.37	.18	.09	5.06	.78	.72	1.17	.73
1	AS	.81	1.13	.60	–	.63	1.02	.89	.78
4	AS	.82	.75	.77	–	.65	1.02	1.06	.84
8	AS	.69	.39	1.92	–	.34	.95	1.03	1.52
1	SO	1.79	.18	.25	–	–	–	–	–
4	SO	2.03	.14	.06	–	–	–	–	–
8	SO	2.54	.14	.15	–	–	–	–	–
1	KO	.56	.52	1.86	4.32	–	–	–	–
4	KO	.32	.53	10.31	3.56	–	–	–	–
8	KO	.34	.68	7.53	3.12	–	–	–	–
1	BE	.33	.31	.46	1.10	2.14	.92	.73	2.05
2	BE	.16	.23	.13	1.97	1.71	.66	.58	1.60
1	DE	.56	.51	.93	.77	1.10	.92	.85	1.34
2	DE	.53	.76	.50	1.06	1.23	.88	.78	1.32
1	NO	1.15	.99	1.13	3.94	.76	1.79	–	.47
2	NO	1.16	.91	1.51	4.65	.65	1.77	–	.41
1	SW	.48	.54	.52	1.05	.77	1.49	1.85	.49
2	SW	.34	.43	.51	.46	.96	2.18	2.84	.15
1	GR	1.69	.41	.78	1.41	–	–	–	–
2	GR	2.17	.19	.42	1.88	–	–	–	–
1	IR	.81	.39	.43	2.06	2.21	–	–	2.16
2	IR	.92	.21	.16	1.52	4.93	–	–	4.85
1	PO	1.69	.83	1.95	–	–	–	–	–
2	PO	1.39	.93	1.46	–	–	–	–	–
1	SP	.33	.40	.18	.75	.67	1.15	.49	.96
2	SP	.31	.61	.07	.74	.33	1.14	.35	2.77
1	NZ	1.94	1.29	1.88	.57	–	–	–	–
2	NZ	2.48	2.94	2.00	.53	–	–	–	–

Table 9.3 (continued)

		Y	PY	RS	E	M	C	I	V1/Y	X85$	PX	PM	S
1	SA	.59	–	–	–	.81	.39	.75	1.03	1.10	–	.74	1.06
2	SA	.48	–	–	–	.25	.26	.59	.42	1.41	–	.78	1.43
1	VE	.54	–	1.22	–	.95	.81	–	2.05	1.10	–	.70	1.31
2	VE	.39	–	1.20	–	.76	.97	–	2.77	1.09	–	.70	1.17
1	CO	1.65	.74	–	–	.52	1.32	–	1.13	1.13	1.37	.77	1.04
2	CO	2.78	.89	–	–	.39	1.63	–	1.23	1.10	2.59	.74	.99
1	JO	2.63	1.04	–	1.12	.31	1.15	–	1.37	.96	1.04	1.01	1.33
2	JO	2.46	.99	–	1.16	.20	.85	–	1.68	.98	1.01	1.07	2.56
1	SY	1.20	1.60	–	–	1.00	2.45	–	–	1.14	7.75	.77	2.83
2	SY	1.11	1.50	–	–	1.32	10.02	–	–	1.55	6.28	.93	2.17
1	ID	1.20	–	–	.69	1.29	1.18	–	–	.68	.68	.63	.87
2	ID	.71	–	–	.66	1.18	.79	–	–	.68	.74	.68	.75
1	MA	1.36	–	–	–	–	–	–	–	.68	–	.89	.14
2	MA	–	–	–	–	–	–	–	–	.58	–	–	–
1	PA	.90	.57	2.51	–	.77	.78	–	4.91	.89	1.07	.79	.95
2	PA	2.85	.50	3.99	–	1.02	1.62	–	3.31	.59	.96	.93	1.29
1	PH	.82	5.58	2.58	1.59	1.04	.72	.62	.94	1.01	3.09	1.04	1.73
2	PH	.71	8.52	3.09	1.97	.66	3.85	.59	.79	.86	1.86	1.13	1.26
1	TH	3.41	1.01	–	–	.67	1.54	–	4.53	.72	.42	.54	.37
2	TH	2.84	.96	–	–	.50	1.43	–	4.48	.75	.25	.60	.17

Variables W, J, $L1$, $L2$, and UR are not part of the model for countries SA–TH.
Each number is the ratio of the MC RMSE and the ARMC RMSE.

particular, it will be interesting to see if the ARMC forecasts contain information not in the MC forecasts, which if true would suggest that the MC model has not handled all the lags right. Other testing techniques will also become available when stochastic simulation of the MC model becomes practical. The possible future use of stochastic simulation of the MC model is discussed in Section 9.2.

10

Analyzing Properties of Models

10.1 Introduction

This chapter discusses various methods for analyzing the properties of macroeconometric models. These methods are then applied in Chapter 11 to the US model and in Chapter 12 to the MC model. The methods discussed here are not tests of models. They are meant to be used after one has some confidence that the model being analyzed is a reasonable approximation of the economy. A model that does not do well in tests is not likely to have properties that accurately reflect the way the economy works.

It is sometimes argued with respect to the testing of models that if a particular model has properties that seem reasonable on *a priori* (i.e., theoretical) grounds, this is evidence in favor of the model. However, because of the back and forth movement between specification and results, including multiplier results, that occurs in macro model building, the final version of a model is likely to have multiplier properties that are similar to what one expects from the theory. Essentially one does not stop until this happens. Therefore, the fact that an econometric model has properties that are consistent with the theory is in no way a confirmation of the model. Models must be tested using methods like those in Chapters 4 and 7, not by examining the "reasonableness" of their multiplier properties.

10.2   Computing Multipliers and Their Standard Errors[1]

A useful way of examining the properties of a model is to consider how the predicted values of the endogenous variables change when one or more exogenous variables are changed. This exercise is usually called multiplier analysis, although the use of the word "multiplier" is somewhat misleading. The output that one examines from this exercise does not have to be the change in the endogenous variables *divided by* the change in the exogenous variable; it can merely be, for example, the change or percentage change in the endogenous variable itself. In fact, if more than one exogenous variable has been changed, there is no obvious thing to divide the change in the endogenous variable by. The form of the output that is examined depends on the nature of the problem, and thus the word "multiplier" should be interpreted in a very general way.

10.2.1   Deterministic Simulation

The procedure that is usually used to compute multipliers is based on deterministic simulation. Let x_t^a denote a "base" set of exogenous variable values for period t, and let x_t^b denote an alternative set. Assume that the prediction period begins in period t and is of length T. Given 1) the initial conditions as of the beginning of period t, 2) the coefficient estimates, 3) a set of exogenous variable values for the entire period, and 4) values of the error terms for the entire period, the predicted values of the endogenous variables can be computed. Let $\hat{y}_{itk}^a$ denote the k period ahead predicted value of endogenous variable i from the simulation that uses x_{t+k-1}^a ($k = 1, \ldots, T$) for the exogenous variable values, and let $\hat{y}_{itk}^b$ denote the predicted value from the simulation that uses x_{t+k-1}^b ($k = 1, \ldots, T$). The difference between the two predicted values, denoted $\hat{\delta}_{itk}$, is an estimate of the effect on the endogenous

---

[1] The original discussion of the procedure discussed in this section is in Fair (1980b). It was also discussed in Fair (1984), Section 9.3. The original procedure required that a stochastic simulation with respect to the error terms be done *within* a stochastic simulation with respect to the coefficients, although the first stochastic simulation could be avoided if one were willing to assume that predicted values from deterministic simulations are close to mean values from stochastic simulations, which is generally the case in practice. In private correspondence in 1984, S.G. Hall pointed out to me that a more straightforward procedure is simply to draw both error terms and coefficients at the same time. This avoids any stochastic simulations within stochastic simulations. The procedure described in the present section uses Hall's suggestion. This section is thus a replacement for Fair (1980b) and Fair (1984), Section 9.3.

variable of changing the exogenous variables:

$$\hat{\delta}_{itk} = \hat{y}^b_{itk} - \hat{y}^a_{itk} \tag{10.1}$$

Obvious values of the error terms to use in the deterministic simulations are their expected values, which are almost always zero. For linear models it makes no difference what values are used as long as the same values are used for both simulations. For nonlinear models the choice does make a difference, and in this case the choice of zero values has some problems. Consider, for example, a model in which inflation responds in a very nonlinear way to the difference between actual and potential output: inflation accelerates as output approaches potential. Consider now a period in which output is close to potential, and consider an experiment in which government spending is increased. This experiment should be quite inflationary, but this will not necessarily be the case if the model is predicting a much lower level of output than actually existed. In other words, if the model is predicting that output is not close to potential when in fact it is, the inflationary consequences of the policy change will not be predicted very well.

There is an easy answer to this problem if the simulation is within the period for which data exist, which is simply to use the actual (historical) values of the error terms rather than zero values. By "actual" in this case is meant the values of the estimated residuals that result from the estimation of the equations. If these values are used and if the actual values of the exogenous variables are used, the simulation will result in a perfect fit. This solution will be called the "perfect tracking" solution. Once the residuals are added to the equations, they are never changed. The same set of values is used for all experiments.

If the actual values of the error terms are used, the problem regarding the response of inflation to output does not exist. With the use of the actual residuals, the model predicts the actual data before any policy change is made. Note that this procedure is not inconsistent with the statistical assumptions of the model, since the error terms are assumed to be uncorrelated with the exogenous variables. The use of the actual values of the error terms has the advantage that only one simulation needs to be performed per policy experiment. $\hat{y}^a_{itk}$ is simply the actual value of the variable, and thus a simulation is only needed to get $\hat{y}^b_{itk}$.

10.2.2 Stochastic Simulation

For nonlinear models $\hat{\delta}_{itk}$ in 10.1 is not an unbiased estimate of the change because the predicted values are not equal to the expected values. This does not, however, seem to be an important problem in practice, since deterministic predictions are generally quite close to the mean values from stochastic simulations, and so if one were only interested in estimates of the changes, it seems unlikely that stochastic simulation would be needed. The main reason for using stochastic simulation is to compute standard errors of $\hat{\delta}_{itk}$.

The stochastic simulation procedure is as follows. The error terms are assumed to be drawn from the $N(0, \hat{\Sigma})$ distribution if the "base" values of the error terms are taken to be zero and from the $N(\hat{u}_t, \hat{\Sigma})$ distribution if the historical values of the error terms are used for the base values, where $\hat{u}_t$ is the vector of historical errors for period t. The coefficients are assumed to be drawn from the $N(\hat{\alpha}, \hat{V})$ distribution, where $\hat{\alpha}$ is the vector of coefficient estimates and $\hat{V}$ is the estimated covariance matrix of $\hat{\alpha}$. .

1. Draw a set of error terms and coefficients and solve the model using the base set of exogenous variables values $(x^a_{t+k-1}, k = 1, \ldots, T)$. Let $\tilde{y}^{aj}_{itk}$ denote the k period ahead predicted value of variable i from this solution.

2. For the same set of error terms and coefficients as in step 1, solve the model again using the alternative set of exogenous variable values $(x^b_{t+k-1}, k = 1, \ldots, T)$. Let $\tilde{y}^{bj}_{itk}$ denote the k period ahead predicted value of variable i from this solution.

3. Compute

$$\tilde{\delta}^j_{itk} = \tilde{y}^{bj}_{itk} - \tilde{y}^{aj}_{itk} \tag{10.2}$$

4. Repeat steps 1 through 3 J times, where J is the desired number of repetitions.

5. Given the values from the J repetitions, compute the mean, denoted $\bar{\delta}_{itk}$, and the variance, denoted $\tilde{s}^2_{itk}$, of $\tilde{\delta}_{itk}$:

$$\bar{\delta}_{itk} = (1/J) \sum_{j=1}^{J} \tilde{\delta}^j_{itk} \tag{10.3}$$

$$\tilde{s}^2_{itk} = (1/J) \sum_{j=1}^{J} (\tilde{\delta}^j_{itk} - \bar{\delta}_{itk})^2 \tag{10.4}$$

$\bar{\delta}_{itk}$ is thus the multiplier, and the square root of $\tilde{s}^2_{itk}$ is its standard error.

10.3   Sources of Economic Fluctuations[2]

There has been considerable discussion in the literature about the ultimate sources of macroeconomic variability. Shiller (1987) surveys this work, where he points out that a number of authors attribute most of output or unemployment variability to only a few sources, sometimes only one. The sources vary from technology shocks for Kydland and Prescott (1982), to unanticipated changes in the money stock for Barro (1977), to "unusual structural shifts," such as changes in the demand for produced goods relative to services, for Lilien (1982), to oil price shocks for Hamilton (1983), to changes in desired consumption for Hall (1986). (See Shiller (1987) for more references.) Although it may be that there are only a few important sources of macroeconomic variability, this is far from obvious. Economies seem complicated, and it may be that there are many important sources. As discussed in this section, it is possible using stochastic simulation to estimate the quantitative importance of various sources of variability from a macroeconometric model.

Macroeconometric models provide an obvious vehicle for estimating the sources of variability of endogenous variables. There are two types of shocks that one needs to consider: shocks to the stochastic equations and shocks to the exogenous variables. Shocks to the stochastic equations can be handled by a straightforward application of stochastic simulation. Shocks to the exogenous variables are less straightforward to handle. Since by definition exogenous variables are not modeled, it is not unambiguous what one means by an exogenous variable shock. One approach is to estimate an autoregressive equation for each exogenous variable in the model and add these equations to the model. Shocks to the exogenous variables can then be handled by stochastic simulation of the expanded model. The US+ model is a model like this, and it is used in the next chapter in the application of the present approach.[3]

Assume, therefore, that one has a model like US+ to work with and assume that the variable of interest is real GDP. As discussed in Section 7.3, given the estimated covariance matrix of the error terms, one can estimate the variance of GDP by means of stochastic simulation. Let $\tilde{\sigma}_{it}^2$ denote the estimated variance of real GDP (endogenous variable i) for period t, where the estimated variance is based on draws of all the error terms in the model, including the error terms in the exogenous variable equations if such equations are added. Now consider

---

[2]The material in this section is taken from Fair (1988a).

[3]When using a model like US+, one may want to take the covariance matrix of the error terms to be block diagonal, as discussed in Section 8.2. This was done for the stochastic simulation work in the next chapter, as it was for the probability calculations in Section 8.8.

fixing one of the error terms at its expected value (usually zero) and computing the variance of GDP again. In this case the stochastic simulation is based on draws of all but one of the error terms. Let $\tilde{\sigma}_{it}^2(k)$ denote the estimated variance of real GDP based on fixing the error term in equation k at its expected value.

The difference between $\tilde{\sigma}_{it}^2$ and $\tilde{\sigma}_{it}^2(k)$ is an estimate of how much the error term in equation k contributes to the variance of GDP.[4] If, say, the variance of GDP falls by 5 percent when the error term for equation k is not drawn, one can say that equation k contributes 5 percent to the variance of GDP.

Another way to estimate this contribution would be to draw *only* the error term for equation k, compute the variance of GDP, and compare this variance to the variance when all the error terms are drawn. If the error term in equation k is correlated with the other error terms in the model, these two procedures are not the same. There is no right or wrong way of estimating this contribution, and because of the correlation, any procedure is somewhat crude. Fortunately, one can examine how sensitive the results are to the effects of the correlation of the error terms across equations to see how to weigh the results. This is done in Section 11.4, where it will be seen that the main conclusions using the US+ model are not sensitive to the effects of the correlation.

In the above discussion k need not refer to just one equation. One can fix the error terms in a subset k of the equations at their expected values and draw from the remaining equations. In this way one can examine the contribution that various sectors make to the variance of GDP. If the error terms across equations are correlated, then fixing, say, two error terms one at a time and summing the two differences is not the same as fixing the two error terms at the same time and computing the one difference. Again, however, one can examine the effects of the error term correlation on the results.

It is important to realize what is and what is not being estimated by this procedure. Consider an exogenous variable shock. What is being estimated is the contribution of the error term in the exogenous variable equation to the variance of GDP. This contribution is *not* the same as the multiplier effect of the exogenous variable on GDP. Two exogenous variables can have the same

---

[4]Regarding the use of this difference as an estimate of an error term's contribution to the variance of GDP, Robert Shiller has informed me that Pigou had the idea first. In the second edition of Industrial Fluctuations, Pigou (1929), after grouping sources of fluctuations into three basic categories, gave his estimate of how much the removal of each source would reduce the amplitude (i.e. the standard deviation) of industrial fluctuations. He thought that the removal of "autonomous monetary causes" would reduce the amplitude by about half. Likewise, the removal of "psychological causes" would reduce the amplitude by about half. Removal of "real causes," such as harvest variations, would reduce the amplitude by about a quarter. See Shiller (1987) for more discussion of this.

multiplier effects and yet make quite different contributions to the variance of GDP. If one exogenous variable fits its autoregressive equation better than does another (in the sense that its equation has a smaller estimated variance), then, other things being equal, it will contribute less to the variance of GDP. It is possible, of course, to use measures of exogenous variable shocks other than error terms from autoregressive equations, but whatever measure is used, it is not likely to be the same as the size of the multiplier.

The notation $\tilde{\sigma}_{it}^2$ will be used to denote the estimated variance of endogenous variable i for period t based on draws of all $m + q$ error terms. The notation $\tilde{\sigma}_{it}^2(k)$ will be used to denote the estimated variance when the error terms in subset k of the equations are fixed at their expected values, where subset k can simply be one equation. Let $\tilde{\delta}_{it}(k)$ be the difference between the two estimated variances:

$$\tilde{\delta}_{it}(k) = \tilde{\sigma}_{it}^2 - \tilde{\sigma}_{it}^2(k) \tag{10.5}$$

In the US application in the next chapter, values of $\tilde{\delta}_{it}(k)$ are computed for the one through eight quarter ahead predictions of real GDP and the private nonfarm price deflator for a number of different choices of k.

Because of the correlation of the error terms across equations, it can turn out that $\tilde{\delta}_{it}(k)$ is negative for some choices of k. Also, as noted above, it is not in general the case that $\tilde{\delta}_{it}(k)$ for, say, k equal to the first and second equations is the same as $\tilde{\delta}_{it}(k)$ for k equal to the first equation plus $\tilde{\delta}_{it}(k)$ for k equal to the second equation.

Computational Issues

For a number of reasons the stochastic simulation estimates of the variances are not exact. First, they are based on the use of estimated coefficients rather than the true values. Second, they are based on the use of an estimated covariance matrix of the error terms rather than the actual matrix. Third, they are based on a finite number of repetitions. Ignoring the first two reasons, it is possible to estimate the precision of the stochastic simulation estimates for a given number of repetitions. In other words, it is possible to estimate the variances of $\tilde{\sigma}_{it}^2$ and $\tilde{\sigma}_{it}^2(k)$. The formula for the variance of $\tilde{\sigma}_{it}^2$ is presented in equation 7.8 in Chapter 7. What is of more concern here, however, is the variance of $\tilde{\delta}_{it}(k)$, and this can also be estimated.

Let

$$\delta_{it}^j(k) = \sigma_{it}^{2j} - \sigma_{it}^{2j}(k) \tag{10.6}$$

where σ_{it}^{2j} is defined in equation 7.6. The estimated mean of $\delta_{it}^{j}(k)$ across the J repetitions is $\tilde{\delta}_{it}(k)$ in equation 10.5:

$$\tilde{\delta}_{it}(k) = \frac{1}{J} \sum_{j=1}^{J} \delta_{it}^{j}(k) \tag{10.7}$$

The estimated variance of $\tilde{\delta}_{it}(k)$, denoted $var[\tilde{\delta}_{it}(k)]$, is then

$$var[\tilde{\delta}_{it}(k)] = (\frac{1}{J})^2 \sum_{j=1}^{J} [\delta_{it}^{j}(k) - \tilde{\delta}_{it}(k)]^2 \tag{10.8}$$

Given values of y_{it}^{j} and $y_{it}^{j}(k)$, $j = 1, \cdots, J$, from the stochastic simulations, all the above values can be computed.

Stochastic simulation error turned out to be a bigger problem than I originally thought it would be. One thousand repetitions was enough to make the variances of $\tilde{\sigma}_{it}^{2}$ and $\tilde{\sigma}_{it}^{2}(k)$ acceptably small, but without any tricks, it was not enough to make the variance of $\tilde{\delta}_{it}(k)$ anywhere close to being acceptably small. Fortunately, there is an easy trick available. The variance of $\tilde{\delta}_{it}(k)$ is equal to the variance of $\tilde{\sigma}_{it}^{2}$ plus the variance of $\tilde{\sigma}_{it}^{2}(k)$ minus twice the covariance. The trick is to make the covariance high, which can be done by using the same draws of the error terms for the computation of both $\tilde{\sigma}_{it}^{2}$ and $\tilde{\sigma}_{it}^{2}(k)$. Any one equation of a model, for example, requires 8000 draws of its error term for 1000 repetitions for a forecast horizon of 8 quarters. If these same 8000 numbers are used to compute both $\tilde{\sigma}_{it}^{2}$ and $\tilde{\sigma}_{it}^{2}(k)$, the covariance between them will be increased. When this trick is used, 1000 repetitions leads to variances of $\tilde{\delta}_{it}(k)$ that are acceptably small. This will be seen in Table 11.10 in the next chapter.

To conclude, estimating sources of economic fluctuations in macroeconometric models is an obvious application of stochastic simulation. The advent of inexpensive computing has made applications like this routine and thus has greatly expanded the questions that can be asked of such models.

10.4   Optimal Choice of Monetary-Policy Instruments[5]

Over twenty years ago today Poole (1970) wrote his classic article on the optimal choice of monetary-policy instruments in a stochastic IS–LM model. Poole assumed that the monetary authority (henceforth called the Fed) can

---

[5]The material in this section is taken from Fair (1988b).

control the interest rate (r) or the money supply (M) exactly. These are the two "instruments" of monetary policy. If the aim is to minimize the squared deviation of real output from its target value, Poole showed that the choice of the optimal instrument depends on the variance of the error term in the IS function, the variance of the error term in the LM function, the covariance of the two error terms, and the size of the parameters in the two functions.

Most people would probably agree that between about October 1979 and October 1982 the Fed put more emphasis on monetary aggregates than it did either before or after. Otherwise, the interest rate has seemed to be the Fed's primary instrument. It is interesting to ask if the use of the interest rate can be justified on the basis of the Poole analysis. Is the economy one in which the variances, covariances, and parameters are such as to lead, a la the Poole analysis, to the optimal instrument being the interest rate?

Stochastic simulation can be used to examine this question using a macroeconometric model. Are the variances, covariances, and parameters in the model such as to favor one instrument over the other, in particular the interest rate over the money supply? The purpose of this section is to show that stochastic simulation can be used to examine Poole like questions in large econometric models. Interestingly enough, Poole's analysis had not been tried on an actual econometric model prior to the work discussed here. The closest study before the present work was that of Tinsley and von zur Muehlen (1983), but they did not analyze the same question that Poole did.[6] Other studies that have extended Poole's work, such as those of Turnovsky (1975) and Yoshikawa (1981), have been primarily theoretical.

Poole also showed that there is a combination policy that is better than either the interest rate policy or the money supply policy. This is the policy where the Fed behaves according to the equation $M = \alpha + \beta r$, where the parameters α and β are chosen optimally.[7] It is possible through repeated

---

[6]In their stochastic simulation experiments, Tinsley and von zur Muehlen always used the interest rate (the Federal Funds rate) as the policy instrument. They used this instrument to target a particular variable, called an "intermediate" target. The intermediate targets they tried are the monetary base, three definitions of the money supply, nominal GNP, and the Federal Funds rate itself. For each of these target choices, they examined how well the choice did in minimizing the squared deviations of the unemployment rate and the inflation rate from their target values. The unemployment rate and the inflation rate are the "ultimate" targets. In the present case the aim is to see how well the interest rate does when it is used as the policy instrument in minimizing the squared deviations of real output from its target value compared to how well the money supply does when it is used as the policy instrument. This is the question that Poole examined.

[7]See also Tobin (1982) for a discussion of this.

stochastic simulation to find the optimal values of α and β for an econometric model, and this procedure is also done in Section 10.4 for the US model.

The Procedure

The procedure is a straightforward application of stochastic simulation. First, fix the interest rate path and perform a stochastic simulation to get the variance of real GDP. Second, fix the money supply path and perform a stochastic simulation to get the variance of real GDP. Finally, compare the two variances. The variance of real GDP for a given period corresponds to Poole's loss function if one takes the target value of GDP for that period to be the mean value from the stochastic simulation. If the variance is smaller when the interest rate is fixed, this is evidence in favor of the interest rate, and vice versa if the variance is smaller when the money supply is fixed.

If the horizon is more than one quarter ahead, then variances are computed for each quarter of the simulation period. The simulations are dynamic, so that, for example, the computed variance for the fourth quarter is the variance of the four quarter ahead prediction error.

Let $\tilde{\sigma}_{it}^2(r)$ denote the stochastic simulation estimate of the variance of endogenous variable i for period t when the interest rate is the policy instrument, and let $\tilde{\sigma}_{it}^2(M)$ denote the same thing when the money supply is the policy instrument. The issue is then to compare $\tilde{\sigma}_{it}^2(r)$ to $\tilde{\sigma}_{it}^2(M)$ for i equal to real GDP to see which is smaller.

10.5 Optimal Control

Optimal control techniques have not been widely used in macroeconometrics. Models may not yet be good enough to warrant the use of such techniques, but if they improve in the future, optimal control techniques are likely to become more popular. The following is a brief discussion of optimal control. A more complete discussion is in Fair (1984), Chapter 10.

The solution of optimal control problems using large scale models turns out to be fairly easy. The first step in setting up a problem is to postulate an objective function. Assume that the period of interest is $t = 1, \ldots, T$. A general specification of the objective function is

$$W = h(y_1, \ldots, y_T, x_1, \ldots, x_T) \tag{10.9}$$

where W, a scalar, is the value of the objective function corresponding to values of the endogenous and exogenous variables for $t = 1, \ldots, T$. In most applications the objective function is assumed to be additive across time, which means that 10.9 can be written

$$W = \sum_{t=1}^{T} h_t(y_t, x_t) \qquad (10.10)$$

where $h_t(y_t, x_t)$ is the value of the objective function for period t. The model can be taken to be the model presented in equation 4.1 in Chapter 4.

Let z_t be a k–dimensional vector of control variables, where z_t is a subset of x_t, and let z be the $k \cdot T$–dimensional vector of all the control values: $z = (z_1, \ldots, z_T)$. Consider first the deterministic case where the error terms in 4.1 are all set to zero. For each value of z one can compute a value of W by first solving the model 4.1 for $y_1, \ldots, y_T$ and then using these values along with the values for $x_1, \ldots, x_T$ to compute W in 10.10. Stated this way, the optimal control problem is choosing variables (the elements of z) to maximize an *unconstrained* nonlinear function. By substitution, the constrained maximization problem is transformed into the problem of maximizing an unconstrained function of the control variables:

$$W = \Phi(z) \qquad (10.11)$$

where Φ stands for the mapping $z \longrightarrow y_1, \ldots, y_T, x_1, \ldots, x_T \longrightarrow W$. For nonlinear models it is generally not possible to express y_t explicitly in terms of x_t, which means that it is generally not possible to write W in 10.11 explicitly as a function of $x_1, \ldots, x_T$. Nevertheless, given values for $x_1, \ldots, x_T$, values of W can be obtained numerically for different values of z.

Given this setup, the problem can be turned over to a nonlinear maximization algorithm like DFP. For each iteration, the derivatives of Φ with respect to the elements of z, which are needed by the algorithm, can be computed numerically. An algorithm like DFP is generally quite good at finding the optimum for a typical control problem.

Consider now the stochastic case, where the error terms in 4.1 are not zero. It is possible to convert this case into the deterministic case by simply setting the error terms to their expected values (usually zero). The problem can then be solved as above. In the nonlinear case this does not lead to the exact answer because the values of W that are computed numerically in the process of solving the problem are not the expected values. In order to compute the expected values correctly, stochastic simulation has to be done. In this case each function evaluation (i.e., each evaluation of the expected value of W for a given value of z) consists of the following:

1. A set of values of the error terms in 4.1 is drawn from an estimated distribution.

2. Given the values of the error terms, the model is solved for $y_1, \ldots, y_T$ and the value of W corresponding to this solution is computed from 10.10. Let $\tilde{W}^j$ denote this value.

3. Steps 1 and 2 are repeated J times, where J is the number of repetitions.

4. Given the J values of $\tilde{W}^j$ ($j = 1, \ldots, J$), the expected value of W is the mean of these values:

$$\bar{W} = (1/J) \sum_{j=1}^{J} \tilde{W}^j \qquad (10.12)$$

This procedure increases the cost of solving control problems by roughly a factor of J, and it is probably not worth the cost for most applications. The bias in predicting the endogenous variables that results from using deterministic rather than stochastic simulation is usually small, and thus the bias in computing the expected value of W using deterministic simulation is likely to be small.

The US model has the following problem regarding the application of optimal control techniques to it. If the aim is to minimize a loss function that has in it squared deviations of output from some target value and inflation from some target value, then the optimal policy for the US model will generally be to achieve the output target almost exactly unless the weight on the inflation loss is very high. The difficulty pertains to the demand pressure variable in the price equation 10, which was discussed in Chapter 5. Reliable estimates of the behavior of the price level at very high output levels cannot be obtained in the sense that the data do not appear to support any nonlinear functional forms. Without some nonlinearity in price behavior at high levels of output, the optimal control solution is likely to correspond to the output target being closely met unless the weight on the inflation loss is very high. In this sense the optimal control exercise is not very interesting because it all hinges on the form of the output variable in the price equation, about which the data tell us little. Because of this problem, no optimal control experiments were performed in the next chapter.

10.6 Counterfactual Multiplier Experiments

It is sometimes of interest to use a model to predict what an economy would have been like had something different happened historically. In Section 11.7, for example, the US model is used to predict what the U.S. economy would have been like in the 1980s had tax rates been higher and interest rates lower than they in fact were. The procedure for doing this is straightforward. One chooses the exogenous variable changes to make and solves the model for these changes. If one wants to use the shocks (error terms) that existed historically, then the estimated residuals are added to the model before solving it. From this base the model can then be solved using either deterministic or stochastic simulation. If stochastic simulation is used, the draws of the error terms are around their estimated historical values. If one is merely interested in the mean paths of the variables, then stochastic simulation is not likely to be necessary because mean values are usually quite close to predicted values from deterministic simulations.

Generating predictions in this manner is a way of answering counterfactual questions. One need not, however, stop with the predicted economies. These economies can be treated like the actual economy, and experiments like multiplier experiments performed. In other words, one can examine the properties of the predicted economies using methods like the ones discussed in this chapter. These properties can then be compared, if desired, to the estimated properties of the actual economy. An example of this is in Section 11.7, where the effectiveness of monetary policy is examined in the predicted economy with higher tax rates and lower interest rates. The monetary-policy properties in this economy are compared to those estimated for the actual economy. These kinds of experiments are useful ways of teaching students macroeconomics.

11

Analyzing Properties
of the US Model

11.1 Introduction

The previous chapter discussed techniques for analyzing the properties of models, and this chapter applies these techniques to the US model. Section 11.2 contains a general discussion of the properties of the model. This is background reading for the multiplier analysis to come. Multipliers and their standard errors are computed in Section 11.3 using the method discussed in Section 10.2. Sections 11.2 and 11.3 are the two main sections in the book to read to get an understanding of the US model. If the model is a reasonable approximation of the actual economy, which the results in Chapter 8 suggest may be the case, then these two sections also provide insights into how the actual economy works.

Section 11.4 examines the sources of economic fluctuations in the US model using the method discussed in Section 10.3. Section 11.5 examines the choice of the optimal monetary-policy instrument in the model using the method discussed in Section 10.4. Section 11.6 examines the sensitivity of the properties of the model to the rational expectations assumption. It uses as an alternative version of the model the equations discussed in Chapter 5 with the values led eight quarters added. Section 11.7 examines the question of whether monetary policy is becoming less effective over time because of the growing size of the federal government debt. The model is first used to predict what the economy would have been like had tax rates been higher and interest rates lower in the 1980s, and then a monetary-policy experiment is performed using this economy. The results of this experiment are then compared to the results of the same experiment performed using the actual economy. Finally, the model is used in Section 11.8 to estimate what the economy would have been like in 1978 and 1990 had the Fed behaved differently. The exercises in Sections 11.7 and 11.8 are examples of counterfactual experiments discussed in Section 10.6.

11.2　A General Discussion of the US Model's Properties

Because the theoretical model in Chapter 2 was used to guide the specification of the US model, the qualitative properties of the two models are similar. Therefore, the discussion of the properties of the theoretical model in Chapter 2 is of relevance here. If there is disequilibrium in the theoretical model in the sense that the labor constraint is binding on households, then an increase in, say, government spending will result in an increase in output. Employment increases, the labor constraint becomes less binding on households, households spend more, employment increases further, and so on. Similarly, if government spending is increased in the US model, output and employment will increase. How much output increases relative to the price level depends on how close actual output (Y) is to potential output (YS). As can be seen from the demand pressure variable in equation 10, the closer is Y to YS, the more will the price level rise for a given change in Y. As Y approaches a value 4 percent greater than YS, the predicted price level approaches infinity, which effectively bounds Y below a value greater than 4 percent of YS.

The main way in which the economy expands in the US model from an increase in, say, government purchases of goods is as follows.

1. The level of sales of the firm sector (X) increases because of the increase in government purchases of goods: Equation 60.

2. The firm sector responds by increasing production (Y): Equation 11.

3. The increase in Y leads to an increase in investment (IKF), jobs (JF), and hours per job (HF): Equations 12, 13, and 14.

4. The increase in jobs and hours per job leads to an increase in disposable income (YD), which leads to an increase in household expenditures: Equations 1, 2, 3, and 4.

5. The increase in investment and household expenditures increases X, which leads to a further increase in Y, and so on.

Fiscal Policy Variables

The main federal government fiscal policy variables in the US model are the following:

COG	Purchases of goods
$D1G$	Personal income tax parameter
$D2G$	Profit tax rate
$D3G$	Indirect business tax rate
$D4G$	Employee social security tax rate
$D5G$	Employer social security tax rate
JG	Number of civilian jobs
JM	Number of military jobs
$TRGH$	Transfer payments to households

Some of these variables appear as explanatory variables in the stochastic equations and thus directly affect the decision variables; others indirectly affect the decision variables by influencing variables (through identities) that in turn influence, directly or indirectly, the decision variables. The effects of changing each of these variables (except JM) in the model are examined below.

Monetary-Policy Options

To see the various monetary-policy options in the model, it will be useful to list a subset of the equations in the US model. These are:

$$MH = f_9(RS, \cdots) \tag{9}$$

$$MF = f_{17}(RS, \cdots) \tag{17}$$

$$CUR = f_{26}(RS, \cdots) \tag{26}$$

$$BO/BR = f_{22}(RS - RD, \cdots) \tag{22}$$

$$BR = -G1 \cdot MB \tag{57}$$

$$0 = \Delta MB + \Delta MH + \Delta MF + \Delta MR + \Delta MG + \Delta MS - \Delta CUR \tag{71}$$

$$0 = SG - \Delta AG - \Delta MG + \Delta CUR + \Delta(BR - BO) - \Delta Q - DISG \tag{77}$$

$$M1 = M1_{-1} + \Delta MH + \Delta MF + \Delta MR + \Delta MS + MDIF \tag{81}$$

The other key equation is the interest rate reaction function, equation 30, which explains RS.

In considering the determination of the variables in the model for the various monetary-policy options, it will be convenient to match variables to equations. Remember, however, that this is done only for expositional convenience. The model is simultaneous, and nearly all the equations are involved in the determination of each endogenous variable.

Consider the matching of variables to equations in the block given above. The demand for money variables, MH, MF, and CUR, can be matched to the stochastic equations that explain them, equations 9, 17, and 26. Bank borrowing, BO, can be matched to its stochastic equation, 22, and total bank reserves, BR, can be matched to its identity, 57. MB can be matched to equation 71, which states that the sum of net demand deposits and currency across all sectors is zero. $M1$ can be matched to its identity, 81. This leaves equation 77, the federal government budget constraint.

The question then is what endogenous variable is to be matched to equation 77. The federal government savings variable, SG, is determined by an identity elsewhere in the model (equation 76), and so it is not a candidate. If equation 30 is included in the model (and thus RS matched to it), the obvious variable to match to equation 77 is AG, the net financial asset variable of the federal government. (AG will be called the "government security" variable. Remember that AG is negative because the federal government is a net debtor.) This means that AG is the variable that adjusts to allow RS to be the value determined by equation 30. In other words, the target bill rate is assumed to be achieved by the purchase or sale of government securities, i.e., by open market operations.

If AG is taken to be endogenous, the following variables in the above block are then exogenous: the discount rate, RD; the reserve requirement ratio, $G1$; demand deposit and currency holdings of the foreign sector, the state and local government sector, and the federal government sector, MR, MS, and MG; gold and foreign exchange holdings of the federal government, Q; the discrepancy term, $DISG$; and the variable that is involved in the definition of $M1$, $MDIF$.

Instead of treating AG as endogenous, one could take it to be exogenous and take either RD or $G1$ to be endogenous and match the one chosen to be endogenous to equation 77. This would mean that the target bill rate was achieved by changing the discount rate or the reserve requirement ratio instead of the amount of government securities outstanding. Since the main instrument of monetary policy in practice is open market operations, it seems better to treat AG as endogenous rather than RD or $G1$.

One can also consider the case in which equation 30 is dropped from the model, but yet both RS and $M1$ remain endogenous. In this case RS is matched to equation 77 and AG is taken to be exogenous. The interest rate is "implicitly" determined in this case: it is the rate needed to clear the asset market given a fixed value of AG. (In the numerical solution of the model in this case, RS is solved using equation 9, MH is solved using equation 71, MB is solved using equation 57, and BR is solved using equation 77.) When equation 30 is dropped, monetary policy is exogenous, and the response of the model to changes in AG can be examined.

In the exogenous monetary-policy case, the main way in which monetary policy affects the economy is by changing interest rates. Changes in AG change interest rates, which in turn change real variables. The main effects of interest rates on the real side of the economy are the direct and indirect effects on household expenditures (equations 1, 2, 3, and 4) and on nonresidential fixed investment of the firm sector (equation 12). The direct effects are from interest rates appearing as explanatory variables in the equations, and the indirect effects are from interest revenue being a part of disposable income and disposable income appearing in the expenditure equations. What this means is that the three instruments of monetary policy—AG, RD, and $G1$— all do the same thing, namely, they affect the economy by affecting interest rates. Using all three instruments is essentially no different from using one with respect to trying to achieve, say, some real output target. It also means in the endogenous monetary-policy case, where AG is endogenous and RD and $G1$ are exogenous, that changes in RD and $G1$ have virtually no effect on the real side of the economy. Any effects that they might have are simply "undone" by changes in AG in the process of achieving the target interest rate implied by equation 30.

It is also possible in the exogenous monetary-policy case to take some variable other than AG to be exogenous. One possible choice is the money supply, $M1$, and another is the level of nonborrowed reserves, $BR - BO$. Both of these are common variables to take as policy variables in monetary-policy experiments. If either of these is taken to be exogenous, AG must be endogenous.[1]

To return to fiscal policy for a moment, it should be obvious that fiscal policy effects are not independent of what one assumes about monetary policy. For a given change in fiscal policy, there are a variety of assumptions that can be made about monetary policy. The main possible assumptions are 1) equation

---

[1]The way in which the model is solved under alternative monetary-policy assumptions is explained in Table A.8 in Appendix A.

30 included in the model and thus monetary policy endogenous, 2) the bill rate exogenous, 3) the money supply exogenous, 4) nonborrowed reserves exogenous, and 5) government securities outstanding, AG, exogenous. In all but assumption 5, AG is endogenous. The sensitivity of fiscal policy effects to the first three of these assumptions is examined below.

Various Relationships

To conclude this general discussion of the model's properties, it will be useful to consider the relationships in the model between certain endogenous variables. Consider first the links from output to the unemployment rate. The first link is that when output increases, the number of jobs increases (equation 13). According to this equation, the initial percentage increase in the number of jobs is less than the percentage increase in output. Although the percentage increase in jobs is less than the percentage increase in output, the relationship between jobs and output is not constant across time. For example, how much the number of jobs changes in any one period depends in part on the amount of excess labor on hand, which varies over time. The second link is that when the number of jobs increases, the number of people holding two jobs increases (equation 8). This means that the number of new people employed increases by less than the number of new jobs (equation 85). How much the number of people holding two jobs changes in any one period depends in part on the value of the labor constraint variable, which also varies over time. The third link is that when the number of jobs increases, the number of people in the labor force increases (equations 5, 6, and 7). This means that the unemployment rate falls less than it otherwise would for a given increase in the number of new people employed (equations 86 and 87). How much the number of people in the labor force changes in any one period also depends on the value of the labor constraint variable.

The size of these links in the model is such that the unemployment rate initially drops less than the percentage change in output. Also, because the links vary in size over time, the relationship between output and the unemployment rate varies over time. At any one time the relationship depends on such things as the amount of excess labor on hand and the value of the labor constraint variable. Because this relationship is not constant, the variables do not obey Okun's law. There is no reason to expect Okun's law to hold in the sense of there being a stable relationship between output and the unemployment rate over time.

The relationship between output and the price level is also not necessarily stable over time in the model. In equation 10 other things affect the price level aside from output, in particular the price of imports, and when these other things change, the price level will change even if output does not. A tight relationship is even less likely to exist between the price level and the unemployment rate because of the many factors that affect the labor force and thus the unemployment rate but not necessarily output.

Consider finally the relationship between output and employment. Productivity defined as output per paid for worker hour, $Y/(JF \cdot HF)$, is procyclical in the model. When Y changes by a certain percentage, $JF \cdot HF$ changes by less than this percentage in the immediate quarter. The buffer for this is the amount of excess labor held: as output falls, excess labor builds up, and vice versa. Other things being equal, excess labor is gradually eliminated because it has a negative effect on the demand for employment and hours. Similar considerations apply to the amount of excess capital held. Excess capital is gradually eliminated because it has a negative effect on investment.

11.3 Computing Multipliers and Their Standard Errors

11.3.1 Fiscal Policy Variables

Multipliers and their standard errors were computed in the manner discussed in Section 10.2. The 2SLS estimates in Chapter 5 were used for these results. The simulation period was 1989:3–1993:2, the last 16 quarters of the sample period. The first set of experiments concerns the fiscal policy variables, where one policy variable was changed per experiment. Eight experiments were performed, and the results are presented in Table 11.1. Results are presented for real GDP, the private nonfarm price deflator, the unemployment rate, the bill rate, and the federal government deficit.[2] The values in the 0 rows are the estimated effects from the deterministic simulations; the values in the a rows are the estimated effects from the stochastic simulations; and the values in the b rows are the estimated standard errors computed from the stochastic simulations. The number of repetitions for each stochastic simulation was 250. For the deterministic simulations the historical errors were added to the equations and treated as exogenous, thus making the base solution the perfect tracking solution. For the stochastic simulations the error terms were drawn from the $N(\hat{u}_t, \hat{\Sigma})$ distribution, where $\hat{u}_t$ is the vector of historical errors for

---

[2]It is easier to discuss the government deficit as a positive number, which is $-SGP$. Consequently, the variable presented in Table 11.1 is $-SGP$. SGP is in nominal terms.

Table 11.1
Estimated Multipliers and Their Standard Errors
for Eight Fiscal Policy Experiments

		Number of Quarters Ahead						
		1	2	3	4	8	12	16
		$GDPR$: Real GDP						
$COG \uparrow$	0	1.11	1.62	1.77	1.75	1.21	.87	.89
	a	1.11	1.63	1.77	1.76	1.17	.84	.87
	b	.07	.09	.11	.15	.29	.30	.31
$D1G \downarrow$	0	.32	.63	.83	.91	.69	.37	.33
	a	.32	.64	.84	.93	.70	.37	.32
	b	.06	.11	.15	.18	.24	.25	.25
$D2G \downarrow$	0	.00	.02	.03	.03	-.05	-.13	-.13
	a	.00	.02	.04	.04	-.05	-.13	-.14
	b	.00	.01	.02	.03	.08	.11	.11
$D3G \downarrow$	0	.59	1.26	1.70	1.89	1.33	.56	.46
	a	.60	1.27	1.72	1.91	1.30	.53	.44
	b	.10	.20	.27	.33	.49	.46	.40
$D4G \downarrow$	0	.33	.69	.91	1.01	.76	.38	.32
	a	.34	.69	.92	1.03	.76	.37	.31
	b	.06	.11	.15	.18	.24	.25	.24
$D5G \downarrow$	0	.01	.04	.07	.11	.20	.21	.22
	a	.01	.04	.07	.11	.20	.21	.22
	b	.00	.01	.02	.03	.04	.06	.09
$JG \uparrow$	0	1.11	1.31	1.32	1.28	.56	.32	.40
	a	1.11	1.31	1.32	1.28	.50	.27	.36
	b	.05	.09	.13	.16	.36	.36	.36
$TRGH \uparrow$	0	.33	.68	.90	1.00	.73	.34	.29
	a	.34	.69	.91	1.01	.73	.34	.29
	b	.06	.11	.15	.18	.23	.24	.22

period t. The coefficients were drawn from the $N(\hat{\alpha}, \hat{V})$ distribution, where $\hat{\alpha}$ is the vector of coefficient estimates and $\hat{V}$ is the estimated covariance matrix of $\hat{\alpha}$. The dimension of $\hat{\Sigma}$ is 30×30, and the dimension of $\hat{V}$ is 166×166.

For the first experiment COG was increased from its historical value each quarter by an amount equal to one percent of the historical value of $GDPR$ in that quarter. The units in Table 11.1 are as follows. For $GDPR$ and PF,

Table 11.1 (continued)

		Number of Quarters Ahead						
		1	2	3	4	8	12	16
		PF: Price Deflator						
COG ↑	0	.00	.11	.28	.44	.80	.82	.82
	a	.00	.12	.30	.49	.92	.90	.92
	b	.00	.04	.10	.18	.41	.33	.40
D1G ↓	0	.00	.03	.09	.16	.36	.38	.37
	a	.00	.03	.10	.18	.42	.43	.43
	b	.00	.01	.04	.07	.19	.18	.31
D2G ↓	0	.00	.00	.00	.01	.01	-.01	-.04
	a	.00	.00	.00	.01	.01	-.01	-.04
	b	.00	.00	.00	.00	.02	.03	.05
D3G ↓	0	.00	.06	.18	.34	.80	.80	.71
	a	.00	.06	.20	.39	.98	.94	.84
	b	.00	.02	.08	.18	.64	.49	.49
D4G ↓	0	.00	.03	.10	.18	.40	.42	.39
	a	.00	.03	.10	.19	.46	.47	.46
	b	.00	.01	.04	.08	.21	.20	.31
D5G ↓	0	-.05	-.10	-.14	-.18	-.29	-.36	-.40
	a	-.05	-.10	-.14	-.18	-.28	-.35	-.37
	b	.01	.01	.02	.02	.04	.06	.17
JG ↑	0	.00	.21	.44	.63	1.02	.99	.99
	a	.00	.22	.47	.70	1.18	1.11	1.11
	b	.00	.07	.17	.27	.57	.43	.50
TRGH ↑	0	.00	.03	.10	.17	.40	.41	.38
	a	.00	.03	.10	.19	.45	.45	.43
	b	.00	.01	.04	.08	.20	.18	.26

a number in the 0 row is $100(\hat{\delta}_{itk}/\hat{y}^a_{itk})$, where $\hat{\delta}_{itk}$ is defined in equation 10.1. The $\hat{y}^a_{itk}$ values are the actual values because the base run is the perfect tracking solution. Since *COG* was changed by one percent of *GDPR*, a number in the 0 row for *GDPR* or *PF* is the percentage change in the variable (in percentage points) that results from an exogenous increase in *GDPR* of one percent. For *UR*, *RS*, and $-SGP$ a number in the 0 row is simply $\hat{\delta}_{itk}$, where the units are in percentage points for *UR* and *RS* and in billions of dollars for $-SGP$.

A number in the a row for *GDPR* and *PF* is the mean of $100(\tilde{\delta}^j_{itk}/\tilde{y}^{aj}_{itk})$ across the *J* repetitions (*J* equals 250 for each experiment), where $\tilde{\delta}^j_{itk}$ is defined in equation 10.2. For *UR*, *RS*, and $-SGP$, a number in the a row

Table 11.1 (continued)

| | | \multicolumn{7}{c}{Number of Quarters Ahead} | | | | | | |
		1	2	3	4	8	12	16
		\multicolumn{7}{c}{UR: Unemployment Rate}						
$COG \uparrow$	0	-.32	-.66	-.93	-1.11	-.89	-.50	-.34
	a	-.32	-.64	-.89	-1.05	-.89	-.50	-.36
	b	.05	.07	.11	.14	.18	.19	.19
$D1G \downarrow$	0	-.06	-.18	-.30	-.40	-.27	.02	.18
	a	-.06	-.17	-.28	-.36	-.30	.00	.17
	b	.02	.05	.08	.12	.16	.14	.14
$D2G \downarrow$	0	.00	-.01	-.01	-.02	.01	.05	.06
	a	.00	-.01	-.01	-.02	.01	.05	.06
	b	.00	.00	.01	.02	.04	.05	.06
$D3G \downarrow$	0	-.13	-.39	-.67	-.90	-.72	-.07	.27
	a	-.12	-.37	-.64	-.85	-.73	-.08	.25
	b	.04	.09	.16	.22	.30	.27	.24
$D4G \downarrow$	0	-.06	-.18	-.32	-.43	-.28	.06	.26
	a	-.06	-.17	-.29	-.39	-.31	.04	.24
	b	.02	.05	.09	.13	.17	.15	.14
$D5G \downarrow$	0	.00	-.01	-.03	-.04	-.09	-.09	-.08
	a	.00	-.01	-.03	-.04	-.10	-.10	-.08
	b	.00	.00	.01	.01	.03	.03	.04
$JG \uparrow$	0	-1.42	-1.52	-1.57	-1.67	-.87	-.39	-.18
	a	-1.41	-1.49	-1.52	-1.59	-.84	-.38	-.20
	b	.02	.05	.09	.13	.20	.22	.22
$TRGH \uparrow$	0	-.10	-.26	-.42	-.56	-.49	-.22	-.08
	a	-.09	-.24	-.40	-.52	-.52	-.23	-.10
	b	.02	.05	.08	.12	.16	.14	.13

is simply the mean of $\tilde{\delta}_{itk}^{j}$, which is denoted $\bar{\delta}_{itk}$ in equation 10.3. A number in the b row for $GDPR$ and PF is the standard deviation of $100(\tilde{\delta}_{itk}^{j}/\tilde{y}_{itk}^{aj})$ from the J repetitions. For UR, RS, and $-SGP$, a number in the b row is the standard deviation of $\tilde{\delta}_{itk}^{j}$, which is the square root of $\tilde{s}_{itk}^{2}$ in equation 10.4.

The changes for the other policy variables in Table 11.1 were made to be comparable to the change in COG with respect to the initial injection of funds into the system. Consider, for example, the change in $D1G$. The aim is to change $D1G$ so that the decrease in personal income taxes in real terms is equal to the change in COG. From equation 47 in the model (see Table A.3), the variable for personal income taxes, THG, is equal to $[D1G + (TAUG \cdot YT)/POP]YT$, where YT is taxable income. Let ΔCOG denote the change

Table 11.1 (continued)

		\multicolumn{7}{c}{Number of Quarters Ahead}					
		1	2	3	4	8	12	16
		\multicolumn{7}{c}{RS: Bill Rate}					
$COG \uparrow$	0	.43	.79	.90	.94	1.12	1.12	1.14
	a	.43	.79	.90	.95	1.11	1.08	1.11
	b	.08	.14	.15	.16	.21	.26	.31
$D1G \downarrow$	0	.12	.29	.41	.48	.59	.55	.53
	a	.12	.30	.42	.49	.60	.55	.53
	b	.03	.08	.10	.13	.18	.21	.24
$D2G \downarrow$	0	.00	-.02	-.03	-.04	-.08	-.10	-.09
	a	.00	-.02	-.03	-.04	-.08	-.10	-.10
	b	.00	.01	.03	.04	.05	.07	.09
$D3G \downarrow$	0	.23	.57	.83	.96	1.15	.98	.87
	a	.23	.58	.84	.99	1.15	.96	.85
	b	.06	.14	.20	.25	.34	.38	.40
$D4G \downarrow$	0	.13	.32	.46	.53	.65	.59	.55
	a	.13	.32	.46	.54	.66	.59	.55
	b	.03	.08	.11	.13	.19	.21	.24
$D5G \downarrow$	0	-.01	-.01	.00	.01	.07	.11	.15
	a	-.01	-.01	.00	.01	.06	.11	.15
	b	.00	.01	.01	.02	.03	.05	.06
$JG \uparrow$	0	.60	1.04	1.16	1.23	1.37	1.35	1.39
	a	.60	1.04	1.16	1.24	1.34	1.31	1.34
	b	.10	.15	.17	.19	.25	.31	.37
$TRGH \uparrow$	0	.13	.32	.45	.52	.63	.57	.52
	a	.13	.32	.46	.53	.64	.57	.52
	b	.03	.08	.11	.13	.18	.20	.23

in COG for a given quarter. The aim is to decrease $D1G$ in such a way that the decrease in THG is equal to $PG \cdot \Delta COG$, where PG is the price deflator for COG. The change in $D1G$ for the given quarter is thus $-(PG \cdot \Delta COG)/YT$. The values that were used for PG and YT for these calculations are the actual values, not the predicted values. The predicted values are, of course, affected by the change in $D1G$. All this procedure does is to change $D1G$ by an amount that would lead personal income taxes to decrease by the historical value of $PG \cdot \Delta COG$ if nothing else happened.

The changes in the other policy variables are similarly done. For $D2G$ the relevant tax variable is TFG, the level of corporate profit taxes, and the relevant equation in Table A.3 is 49. The other matchings are as follows: $D3G$

Table 11.1 (continued)

		Number of Quarters Ahead						
		1	2	3	4	8	12	16
$-SGP$: Federal Government Deficit								
$COG \uparrow$	0	9.8	8.8	8.5	8.6	12.3	15.7	17.9
	a	9.8	8.8	8.4	8.5	12.1	15.5	17.6
	b	.2	.3	.4	.6	.9	1.3	1.8
$D1G \downarrow$	0	12.1	11.7	11.5	11.5	13.7	16.5	18.4
	a	12.0	11.7	11.4	11.4	13.6	16.4	18.3
	b	.2	.3	.4	.6	.8	1.0	1.3
$D2G \downarrow$	0	12.9	13.2	13.6	13.8	15.1	16.5	17.5
	a	12.9	13.1	13.4	13.6	14.6	16.0	17.3
	b	1.5	2.1	2.5	2.7	3.7	3.9	4.5
$D3G \downarrow$	0	11.4	10.1	9.1	8.7	12.1	16.6	19.1
	a	11.4	10.0	9.0	8.5	11.9	16.4	18.7
	b	.3	.5	.8	1.0	1.3	1.5	2.1
$D4G \downarrow$	0	12.0	11.5	11.2	11.2	13.5	16.5	18.4
	a	12.0	11.5	11.2	11.1	13.4	16.4	18.3
	b	.2	.3	.4	.6	.8	1.0	1.3
$D5G \downarrow$	0	9.4	9.8	10.1	10.3	11.4	12.5	13.4
	a	9.4	9.8	10.1	10.3	11.4	12.4	13.3
	b	.1	.1	.2	.3	.5	.6	.8
$JG \uparrow$	0	11.4	11.3	11.3	11.7	15.8	19.3	21.7
	a	11.4	11.2	11.2	11.6	15.6	19.1	21.2
	b	.2	.4	.6	.7	1.2	1.7	2.4
$TRGH \uparrow$	0	12.0	11.5	11.2	11.1	13.4	16.4	18.4
	a	12.0	11.5	11.1	11.0	13.3	16.4	18.2
	b	.2	.3	.4	.6	.7	.9	1.2

0 = Estimated effects from deterministic simulations.
a = Estimated effects from stochastic simulations.
b = Estimated standard errors of a row values.
The units are percentage points except for $-SGP$,
  which are billions of dollars.

to $IBTG$ and equation 51; $D4G$ to $SIHG$ and equation 53; $D5G$ to $SIFG$ and equation 54; JG to $WG \cdot JG \cdot HG$ (no separate equation), and $TRGH$ to itself (no separate equation).[3] To repeat, then, each of the policy variables

---

[3]The tax credit dummy variable, $TXCR$, is also a fiscal policy variable. It appears in the investment equation 12. A multiplier experiment could thus be run in which $TXCR$ was changed. In doing this, however, one would also have to estimate how much profit taxes would be changed by the $TXCR$ change and then adjust $D2G$ accordingly. No attempt was

was changed each quarter by an amount that based on the historical values of the variables in the model led to the same injection of funds into the economy as did the COG increase. In this sense all the experiments in Table 11.1 are of the same size.

Turning now to the results in Table 11.1, it is first immediately clear that the 0 and a rows are very close. Even though macroeconometric models are nonlinear, their predicted values based on deterministic simulations are generally close to the means from stochastic simulations, and this is certainly true for the results in the table. The results of the individual experiments will now be discussed.

COG **Increase**

Table 11.1 shows that the increase in COG leads to an increase in output (real GDP), the price deflator, and the bill rate and to a decrease in the unemployment rate. The government deficit rises. The reasons for the increase in output were discussed above, and this discussion will not be repeated here. The price deflator rises because of the effects of the increase in output on the demand pressure variable in the price equation 10. The Fed responds (equation 30) to the output and price increases by raising the bill rate. The unemployment rate falls because employment rises as a result of the output increase.

The output multiplier reaches a peak of 1.77 in the third quarter and declines after that. Part of the reason for the decline after three quarters is the higher value of the bill rate due to the Fed leaning against the wind.

The table shows that the government deficit $(-SGP)$ rises in response to the COG increase. After four quarters the deficit is \$8.5 billion higher. Although not shown in the table, this increase is less than the increase in nominal government spending $(PG \cdot COG)$. This is because of the endogenous increase in tax revenue as a result of the expanding economy. The deficit increases are, however, considerably higher by the end of the sixteen quarter period. This is due in large part to the increase in government interest payments that results from the higher interest rates. The relationship between government spending changes and changes in the government deficit is examined in more detail in Section 11.3.7 below.

---

made to run a $TXCR$ experiment for the present results. If such an experiment were run, the effects on real GDP would be small because the estimate of the coefficient of $TXCR$ in equation 12 is small.

$D1G$ Decrease

The decrease in $D1G$, the personal income tax parameter, increases disposable income (YD), which has a positive effect on household expenditures. It also increases the after tax interest rates (RSA and RMA), which have a negative effect on household expenditures. Table 11.1 shows that the net effect on the economy is expansionary. The effects of the tax rate decrease are, however, smaller than the effects of the COG increase. This is a standard result. Tax rate decreases generally have smaller effects than government spending increases in models because part of the decrease in tax payments of households is saved.

The decreases in the unemployment rate are much smaller for the $D1G$ decrease than for the COG increase, and in fact by quarter 12 the unemployment rate is higher for the $D1G$ experiment than it was in the base case. This is because the decrease in $D1G$ increases the after tax wage rate (WA), which has a positive effect on the labor supply variables $L2$ and $L3$ and on the number of people holding two jobs (LM). (It also has a negative effect on $L1$, but this is more than offset by the positive effect on $L2$ and $L3$.) Other things being equal, an increase in the labor force leads to an increase in the unemployment rate. The same is true of an increase in LM, since an increase in the number of people holding two jobs means that the total number of people employed rises less than the total number of jobs. These positive effects on the unemployment rate thus offset some of the negative effects from the increase in jobs as a result of the output increase, and in fact, as just noted, by quarter 12 the net effect is positive.

The difference between the unemployment rate effects for the COG and $D1G$ experiments is a good way of seeing why Okun's law is not met in the model. A number of things affect the unemployment rate aside from output.

$D2G$ Decrease

Table 11.1 shows that the decrease in $D2G$, the profit tax rate, has little effect on output. This result, however, is probably not trustworthy. The way in which the profit tax rate affects the economy in the model is the following. When the profit tax rate is decreased, this leads to an increase in after tax profits and thus to an increase in dividends paid by firms. This in turn leads to an increase in disposable income. Also, over time interest payments by firms drop because they need to borrow less due to the higher after tax profits. On the other hand, the government needs to borrow more, other things being equal, because it is receiving less in profit taxes, and so interest payments by the government rise.

The net effect of these interest payment changes on disposable income could thus go either way. Since dividends are slow to respond to after tax profit changes and since the interest payment changes nearly cancel each other out, the net effect on disposable income is small, which leads to only small changes in household expenditures and thus in output.

If the output multipliers from a profit tax rate increase are in fact as low as in Table 11.1, they suggest that a very effective way to decrease the federal government deficit would be to raise the profit tax rate. This would raise revenue and have little negative impact on real output. It is likely, however, that changes in $D2G$ affect the economy in ways that are not captured in the model. For example, it may be that firms pass on an increase in profit tax rates in the form of higher prices, which is not part of the model. I tried adding $D2G$ in various ways to the price equation 10 to see if an effect like this could be picked up, but with no success. It may be that profit tax rates are not changed often enough for reliable results to be obtained. At any rate, the model is probably not trustworthy regarding the effects of $D2G$ changes on the economy.

$D3G$ Decrease

A decrease in $D3G$, the indirect business tax rate, decreases the consumption price deflators PCS, PCN, and PCD (equations 35, 36, and 37), which decreases the overall price deflator for the household sector PH (equation 34). The decrease in PH raises real disposable income, YD/PH, which has a positive effect on household expenditures in equations 1, 2, 3, and 4.

The results in Table 11.1 show that the decrease in $D3G$ has a positive effect on output. After four quarters the output effect is slightly larger than it is for the COG experiment. On the other hand, the fall in the unemployment rate is less for the $D3G$ experiment than it is for the COG experiment. This is because the fall in PH raises the real wage, which has a positive effect on labor force participation. This in turn leads the unemployment rate to fall less than otherwise. In fact, as was the case for the $D1G$ experiment, the unemployment rate is higher than it was in the base case by the end of the 16 quarter period.

$D4G$ Decrease

A decrease in $D4G$, the employee social security tax rate, is similar to a decrease in $D1G$ in that it increases disposable personal income. The results for this experiment are thus similar to those for the $D1G$ experiment. One small difference between the two experiments is that the after tax interest rates RSA and RMA are affected by changes in $D1G$ but not $D4G$ (equations 127 and 128). The social security tax is only a tax on wage income.

$D5G$ **Decrease**

A decrease in $D5G$, the employer social security tax rate, lowers the cost of labor to the firm sector, which has a negative effect on the price level (equation 10). The lower price level leads to an increase in real disposable income, which, among other things, has a positive effect on household expenditures. The overall effect on real GDP is, however, fairly small, and like the $D2G$ experiment, this experiment suggests that an effective way to lower the government deficit would be to increase $D5G$. This would lower the deficit without having much effect on output. Again, these results are probably not trustworthy. There are likely to be other firm responses to a change in $D5G$ that are not captured in the model. In particular, firms may pass on changes in $D5G$ in the form of wage changes, and this is not part of the model.

JG **Increase**

An increase in JG, the number of civilian jobs in the federal government, leads to an increase in employment and thus disposable personal income. This in turn leads to an increase in household expenditures. The output increases for the JG experiment are somewhat below the output increases for the COG experiment (except for the first quarter). On the other hand, the initial decreases in the unemployment rate are larger for the JG experiment. There is a large immediate change in jobs for the JG experiment, whereas for the COG experiment, much of the initial increase in output is produced by firms lowering the amount of excess labor on hand and increasing hours worked per worker rather than increasing jobs.

$TRGH$ **Increase**

An increase in $TRGH$, the level of transfer payments to the household sector, increases disposable personal income, which increases household expenditures. The output effects of this experiment are similar to those of the $D1G$ experiment. The unemployment rate, however, falls less for the $D1G$ experiment than it does for the $TRGH$ experiment. This is because of the labor

Table 11.2
Estimated Multipliers and Their Standard Errors
for a Decrease in RS of One Percentage Point

		Number of Quarters Ahead						
		1	2	3	4	8	12	16
		GDPR: Real GDP						
$RS \downarrow$	0	-.01	.05	.14	.24	.48	.44	.32
	a	-.01	.05	.14	.24	.49	.46	.34
	b	.01	.03	.06	.08	.17	.24	.29
		PF: Price Deflator						
$RS \downarrow$	0	.00	.00	.00	.01	.10	.17	.22
	a	.00	.00	.00	.02	.12	.19	.27
	b	.00	.00	.01	.01	.06	.10	.18
		UR: Unemployment Rate						
$RS \downarrow$	0	.00	-.01	-.05	-.09	-.22	-.22	-.13
	a	.00	-.01	-.04	-.09	-.24	-.24	-.15
	b	.00	.01	.02	.04	.09	.12	.14
		$-SGP$: Federal Government Deficit						
$RS \downarrow$	0	-1.7	-2.0	-2.5	-3.1	-5.0	-6.4	-7.7
	a	-1.7	-2.0	-2.5	-3.1	-5.1	-6.6	-8.0
	b	.1	.1	.2	.3	.7	1.1	1.6

See notes to Table 11.1.

force increase in the $D1G$ experiment caused by the lowering of the tax rate. There is no such tax rate effect at work for the $TRGH$ experiment.

The Estimated Standard Errors

The estimated standard errors (the b row values) in Table 11.1 in general seem fairly small. This result is consistent with the results in Table 8.5, which show that the contribution of the uncertainty of the coefficient estimates to the total uncertainty of the forecast is generally relatively small. Most of the uncertainty of multipliers comes from the uncertainty of the coefficient estimates, and if the effects of coefficient uncertainty are small, multiplier uncertainty will be small.

The results in the b rows in Table 11.1 are thus encouraging regarding the accuracy of the properties of the model, provided that the model is correctly specified. The assumption of correct specification is the key restriction in the present context. Table 8.5 shows that misspecification contributes some to the total variances of the forecasts from the US model, and so it should be taken

into account in the estimation of the standard errors of the multipliers. It is
an open question as to how this can be done. Given that it was not done here,
the present estimates of the standard errors must be interpreted as only lower
bounds.

Another way of trying to get a sense of how much confidence to place on
the multiplier results is to examine their sensitivity to alternative specifications,
where the alternative specifications are supported by the data as much or nearly
as much as the original specification. This is done in Section 11.3.4 below
regarding the specification of the import equation and in Section 11.6 regarding
the use of the rational expectations assumption.

11.3.2   A Monetary-Policy Experiment: RS Decrease

The most straightforward way to examine the effects of monetary policy in
the model is to drop the interest rate reaction function (equation 30), take the
bill rate RS to be exogenous, and then compute multipliers for a change in
RS. The results of doing this are reported in Table 11.2. The experiment is a
sustained decrease in RS of one percentage point, and the simulation period is
the same as that for the fiscal policy experiments: 1989:3–1993:2. The units
in Table 11.2 are the same as those in Table 11.1. Remember from earlier
discussion that a change in RS has both a substitution effect and an income
effect on the economy. The substitution effect from a decrease in the bill rate
is positive, but the income effect is negative.

The results in Table 11.2 show that the overall effect on real GDP from the
one percentage point decrease in RS is moderate. After four quarters the rise in
$GDPR$ is .24 percent, and after eight quarters the rise is .49 percent. After two
years the percentage rise in $GDPR$ is thus about half of the percentage point
decrease in RS. The federal government deficit is $5.1 billion lower after eight
quarters, which is in part because of the lower government interest payments
and in part because of higher tax receipts caused by the more expansionary
economy.

It will be seen in Section 11.7 that the model suggests that the effect on
output of a decrease in RS would be slightly larger if the federal government
debt had not grown so much during the 1980s.

11.3.3 Sensitivity of Fiscal Policy Effects to Assumptions about Monetary Policy

All the experiments in Table 11.1 used the interest rate reaction function as the monetary-policy assumption. It is possible to make other assumptions, and Table 11.3 presents results from making two other assumptions. The results from three experiments are reported in the table. The first experiment is the same as the first experiment in Table 11.1, namely an increase in COG with the interest rate reaction function used. The second experiment is the change in COG with RS held unchanged from its base period values, and the third experiment is the change in COG with $M1$ held unchanged from its base period values. The results for $M1$ are also presented in Table 11.3, along with the results for $GDPR$, PF, UR, RS, and $-SGP$.

In both the first and third experiments the bill rate rises in response to the COG increase, which leads output to increase less for these two experiments than for the second experiment where the bill rate is kept unchanged. After eight quarters the increase in RS is 1.12 percentage points in the first experiment and .40 percentage points in the third experiment. After, say, eight quarters the output differences across the three experiments are modest. This is because, as seen above, the effects of a change in RS on output are modest.

The bill rate rises more in the first experiment than in the third, which results in the first experiment being less expansionary than the third. According to the interest rate reaction function, which is used for the first experiment, the Fed leans against a COG increase by actually having the money supply contract. (See the results for $M1$ for the first experiment in Table 11.3). When the money supply is constrained to be unchanged in the third experiment, the lean in terms of higher interest rates is thus not as great. In other words, the monetary-policy behavior that is reflected in the estimated interest rate reaction function is less accommodating than the behavior of keeping $M1$ unchanged in the wake of an increase in government spending.

11.3.4 Sensitivity of Fiscal Policy Effects to the Specification of the Import Equation

It was seen in the discussion of the import equation in Section 5.7 that the level of nonfarm firm sales dominated disposable income in the equation in the sense of having a higher t-statistic when both variables were included in the equation. Collinearity was such, however, that neither variable was significant. (Disposable income was chosen for the final specification of the equation

Table 11.3
Estimated Multipliers and Their Standard Errors
for an Increase in COG under Three
Monetary Policy Assumptions

		Number of Quarters Ahead						
		1	2	3	4	8	12	16
		GDPR: Real GDP						
$COG \uparrow$ Eq.30	0	1.11	1.62	1.77	1.75	1.21	.87	.89
	a	1.11	1.63	1.77	1.76	1.17	.84	.87
	b	.07	.09	.11	.15	.29	.30	.31
$COG \uparrow R$ Sex.	0	1.10	1.64	1.84	1.90	1.65	1.35	1.26
	a	1.11	1.65	1.85	1.91	1.61	1.31	1.20
	b	.07	.09	.11	.14	.33	.28	.24
$COG \uparrow M1$ex.	0	1.10	1.64	1.82	1.86	1.50	1.18	1.13
	a	1.11	1.65	1.84	1.88	1.46	1.15	1.11
	b	.07	.09	.12	.17	.40	.33	.23
		PF: Price Deflator						
$COG \uparrow$ Eq.30	0	.00	.11	.28	.44	.80	.82	.82
	a	.00	.12	.30	.49	.92	.90	.92
	b	.00	.04	.10	.18	.41	.33	.40
$COG \uparrow R$ Sex.	0	.00	.11	.28	.45	.90	1.00	1.07
	a	.00	.12	.30	.50	1.07	1.13	1.22
	b	.00	.04	.10	.19	.61	.47	.50
$COG \uparrow M1$ex.	0	.00	.11	.28	.45	.87	.94	.99
	a	.00	.11	.29	.53	.99	1.00	1.02
	b	.00	.04	.11	.49	.63	.46	.37
		UR: Unemployment Rate						
$COG \uparrow$ Eq.30	0	-.32	-.66	-.93	-1.11	-.89	-.50	-.34
	a	-.32	-.64	-.89	-1.05	-.89	-.50	-.36
	b	.05	.07	.11	.14	.18	.19	.19
$COG \uparrow R$ Sex.	0	-.32	-.67	-.96	-1.17	-1.11	-.75	-.50
	a	-.32	-.65	-.91	-1.10	-1.11	-.77	-.54
	b	.04	.07	.11	.15	.21	.21	.21
$COG \uparrow M1$ex.	0	-.32	-.67	-.95	-1.16	-1.04	-.67	-.44
	a	-.32	-.65	-.91	-1.09	-1.01	-.65	-.46
	b	.05	.08	.12	.15	.22	.21	.19

because this is consistent with the use of disposable income in the household expenditure equations.) This is thus a case in which the data do not discriminate well between two possible variables, and it is of interest to see how sensitive the properties of the model are to the use of the two variables. The more sensitive the properties are, the less confidence can be placed on them

Table 11.3 (continued)

		\multicolumn{7}{c}{Number of Quarters Ahead}						
		1	2	3	4	8	12	16
\multicolumn{9}{c}{RS: Bill Rate}								
$COG \uparrow$Eq.30	0	.43	.79	.90	.94	1.12	1.12	1.14
	a	.43	.79	.90	.95	1.11	1.08	1.11
	b	.08	.14	.15	.16	.21	.26	.31
$COG \uparrow RS$ex.	0	.00	.00	.00	.00	.00	.00	.00
	a	.00	.00	.00	.00	.00	.00	.00
	b	.00	.00	.00	.00	.00	.00	.00
$COG \uparrow M$1ex.	0	.11	.21	.25	.32	.40	.35	.39
	a	.11	.19	.26	.33	.41	.38	.39
	b	.05	.08	.10	.15	.15	.13	.16
\multicolumn{9}{c}{$-SGP$: Federal Government Deficit}								
$COG \uparrow$Eq.30	0	9.8	8.8	8.5	8.6	12.3	15.7	17.9
	a	9.8	8.8	8.4	8.5	12.1	15.5	17.6
	b	.2	.3	.4	.6	.9	1.3	1.8
$COG \uparrow RS$ex.	0	9.1	7.3	6.4	6.0	7.2	8.6	9.0
	a	9.1	7.3	6.3	5.9	6.9	8.4	8.7
	b	.3	.3	.5	.6	.9	.8	1.1
$COG \uparrow M$1ex.	0	9.3	7.7	7.0	6.9	8.9	10.9	12.0
	a	9.3	7.6	6.9	6.6	8.9	11.0	12.0
	b	.3	.3	.5	1.2	.9	1.1	1.5
\multicolumn{9}{c}{M1: Money Supply}								
$COG \uparrow$Eq.30	0	-.09	-.25	-.43	-.57	-1.13	-1.50	-1.67
	a	-.09	-.25	-.42	-.56	-1.09	-1.43	-1.62
	b	.03	.09	.14	.19	.38	.54	.69
$COG \uparrow RS$ex.	0	.04	.10	.17	.26	.60	.82	.93
	a	.04	.10	.18	.26	.62	.84	.95
	b	.01	.03	.05	.08	.16	.20	.20
$COG \uparrow M$1ex.	0	.00	.00	.00	.00	.00	.00	.00
	a	.00	.00	.00	.00	.00	.00	.00
	b	.00	.00	.00	.00	.00	.00	.00

Eq.30 = Equation 30 used. RSex.= RS exogenous.
M1ex. = M1 exogenous.
See notes to Table 11.1.

because the data do not discriminate between the two variables.

The COG, $D1G$, and $TRGH$ experiments in Table 11.1 were performed with the sales variable replacing the disposable income variable in the import equation. Otherwise, everything else was the same. The results are reported in Table 11.4 for $GDPR$. The results for the first version are the same as those in Table 11.1, and the results for the second version are for the sales variable

Table 11.4
Estimated Multipliers for Three Experiments and
Two Versions of the Import Equation

		Number of Quarters Ahead						
		1	2	3	4	8	12	16
		GDPR: Real GDP						
COG ↑	1	1.11	1.62	1.77	1.75	1.21	.87	.89
	2	1.06	1.53	1.62	1.56	.96	.69	.75
D1G ↓	2	.32	.63	.83	.91	.69	.37	.33
	2	.36	.72	.96	1.08	.90	.62	.63
TRGH ↓	2	.33	.68	.90	1.00	.73	.34	.29
	2	.37	.77	1.03	1.16	.93	.58	.59

1 = Income variable in the import equation (regular version).
2 = Sales variable in the import equation.
Results are from deterministic simulations.

replacing the disposable income variable in the import equation. Only the results from deterministic simulations are presented in Table 11.4.

The results for the COG experiment show that the output multipliers are larger for the first version than for the second. The reason for this is the following. When COG increases, the level of sales directly increases, whereas disposable income only indirectly increases (as income expands due to the expanding economy). Therefore, imports respond more quickly in the second version because they are directly affected by sales. In the first version they respond only as disposable income responds. Since imports respond more in the second version, the output response is less because imports subtract from GDP.

In the other two experiments in Table 11.4 the output response is greater in the second version than in the first, contrary to the case in the first experiment. The reason for this is the following. When $D1G$ or $TRGH$ increase, disposable income directly increases, whereas sales only indirectly increase (as the disposable income increase induces an increase in sales). Therefore, imports respond more quickly in the first version, resulting in a smaller output increase.

The eight quarter ahead multipliers in Table 11.4 are the following for the three experiments: 1.21 versus .96 for the first, .69 versus .90 for the second, and .73 versus .93 for the third. These differences of .25, .21, and .20 compare to the eight quarter ahead estimated standard errors in Table 11.1 of .29, .24, and .23, respectively. The differences are thus slightly less than one standard

Table 11.5
Estimated Multipliers for a COG Increase for Alternative
Sets of Coefficient Estimates

	Number of Quarters Ahead						
	1	2	3	4	8	12	16
	GDPR: Real GDP						
2SLS	1.11	1.62	1.77	1.75	1.21	.87	.89
2SLAD	1.09	1.61	1.81	1.85	1.41	1.02	1.07
3SLS	1.11	1.56	1.67	1.63	1.19	.91	.87
FIML	1.10	1.34	1.38	1.36	1.18	1.07	1.05
MU	1.10	1.62	1.76	1.75	1.19	.81	.82
	PF: Nonfarm Price Deflator						
2SLS	.00	.11	.28	.44	.80	.82	.82
2SLAD	.00	.11	.26	.43	.83	.88	.91
3SLS	.00	.15	.35	.55	.98	1.03	1.06
FIML	.00	.16	.35	.53	.98	1.13	1.30
MU	.00	.11	.28	.44	.80	.81	.80
	RS: Bill Rate						
2SLS	.43	.79	.90	.94	1.12	1.12	1.14
2SLAD	.35	.68	.86	.96	1.27	1.28	1.32
3SLS	.39	.72	.81	.84	1.02	1.04	1.07
FIML	.06	.17	.26	.32	.43	.43	.45
MU	.43	.79	.90	.95	1.13	1.10	1.11
	UR: Unemployment Rate						
2SLS	-.32	-.66	-.93	-1.11	-.89	-.50	-.33
2SLAD	-.34	-.68	-.96	-1.16	-1.07	-.69	-.52
3SLS	-.30	-.59	-.82	-.97	-.82	-.54	-.36
FIML	-.26	-.46	-.61	-.72	-.65	-.53	-.41
MU	-.32	-.66	-.93	-1.11	-.91	-.50	-.29

error. Therefore, if the differences in Table 11.4 were to be taken as estimates of multiplier uncertainty due to possible misspecification of the import
equation, the total multiplier uncertainty would be about double this. This is,
of course, only a very crude way of trying to estimate multiplier uncertainty
due to misspecification, but it may be suggestive of the likely size of this
uncertainty.

11.3.5 Sensitivity of the Multipliers to Alternative
Coefficient Estimates

It is straightforward to compute multipliers for different sets of coefficient
estimates. If quite different multipliers are obtained for different sets of con-

sistent estimates, say 2SLS versus 3SLS, this may be a cause of concern since one does not expect this to be true in a correctly specified model.

Multipliers are presented in Table 11.5 for the five sets of coefficient estimates that have been obtained for the US model—2SLS, 2SLAD, 3SLS, FIML, and MU. The multipliers are for the COG experiment with the interest rate reaction function used. These results are based on deterministic simulations. It can be seen that the multipliers are quite close across the different estimates. The largest difference is for the FIML multipliers for the bill rate, which are less than half the size of the others. As in Section 8.5, the overall FIML results stand out somewhat from the rest. Given that the FIML forecasts are on average not as accurate as the others in Table 8.4, the FIML results in Table 11.5 are probably the least trustworthy. Otherwise, the differences in Table 11.5 are not large enough to have much economic significance. This closeness of the results complements the closeness of the results in Section 8.5 regarding the predictive accuracy of the model.

11.3.6   Multipliers from a Price Shock: PIM Increase

The next experiment examined is an increase in the import price deflator, PIM. It was increased by 10 percent in each of the quarters of the simulation period (from its base period values). The simulation period was the same as in Table 11.1: 1989:3–1993:2. The results are presented in Table 11.6. The units in Table 11.6 are the same as those in Table 11.1.

The results show that an increase in PIM is contractionary and inflationary. When PIM increases, the domestic price level increases (equation 10), which leads to a fall in real disposable income. This in turn leads to a fall in household expenditures. The Fed responds to the initial change in prices by increasing the bill rate, which is another reason for the fall in expenditures. After the second quarter, however, the bill rate is lower, which is the output effect dominating the price effect in the interest rate reaction function (equation 30). After eight quarters output is 1.27 percent lower and the price level is 1.77 percent higher in response to the 10 percent increase in import prices. This experiment is the best example in the model of a situation in which real output and the price level are negatively correlated.

11.3.7   The Deficit Response to Spending and Tax Changes

When the economy expands, tax revenues increase and some government expenditures like unemployment benefits decrease, and when the economy

Table 11.6
Estimated Multipliers and Their Standard Errors
for an Increase in *PIM* of 10 percent

		Number of Quarters Ahead						
		1	2	3	4	8	12	16
GDPR: Real GDP								
PIM ↑	0	-.33	-.75	-1.10	-1.30	-1.24	-.90	-.85
	a	-.33	-.77	-1.12	-1.33	-1.27	-.94	-.87
	b	.06	.14	.20	.26	.38	.40	.41
PF: Price Deflator								
PIM ↑	0	.35	.64	.89	1.09	1.79	2.43	2.93
	a	.35	.65	.90	1.10	1.77	2.42	2.90
	b	.03	.05	.08	.11	.23	.27	.34
UR: Unemployment Rate								
PIM ↑	0	.07	.20	.34	.45	.48	.18	-.07
	a	.06	.20	.37	.51	.56	.24	-.02
	b	.02	.06	.10	.14	.22	.22	.23
RS: Bill Rate								
PIM ↑	0	.35	.26	-.05	-.23	-.45	-.51	-.59
	a	.34	.23	-.07	-.25	-.48	-.54	-.63
	b	.15	.18	.17	.19	.29	.35	.41
−*SGP*: Federal Government Deficit								
PIM ↑	0	1.2	1.9	2.3	2.2	.0	-3.7	-6.9
	a	1.2	1.9	2.3	2.2	.1	-3.7	-6.9
	b	.3	.5	.7	.8	1.1	1.3	1.6

See notes to Table 11.1.

contracts, tax revenues decrease and some government expenditures increase. On this score, then, the government deficit decreases when the economy expands and increases when the economy contracts. Working in the opposite direction, on the other hand, is the fact that the Fed may lower interest rates in contractions and raise them in expansions. As interest rates fall, interest payments of the government fall, which decreases the deficit, and as interest rates rise, interest payments rise, which increases the deficit.

It is of obvious interest to policy makers to know how the deficit responds to changing economic conditions. In particular, if one is contemplating lowering the deficit by decreasing government spending or raising taxes, which will presumably affect the economy, it is important to know how the changes in the economy will affect the deficit. It may be, for example, that to lower the deficit by $10 billion takes more than a $10 billion cut in government spending.

It is easy in a model like the US model to estimate how much the deficit changes as government spending or taxes change, and the purpose of this section is to provide such estimates. These estimates will, of course, depend on what is assumed about monetary policy, since fiscal policy effects in the model depend on the monetary-policy assumption. Of the three assumptions examined in Section 11.3.3—the Fed behaves according to the interest rate reaction function (equation 30), the Fed keeps the bill rate unchanged, and the Fed keeps the money supply unchanged—the one that mitigates the effects of a government spending change or a tax change the most is the use of the reaction function. The results in Table 11.3 show that the bill rate rises the most (in response to the government spending increase) when equation 30 is used. Although not shown in the table, when there is a government spending *decrease*, the bill rate falls the most when equation 30 is used. (The results in Table 11.3 are close to being symmetrical for positive and negative fiscal policy changes.) The least mitigating assumption is when the bill rate is kept unchanged in response to the fiscal policy change.

The estimates in this section were obtained as follows. The simulation period was, as for the multiplier experiments above, 1989:3–1993:2. Also, as above, the residuals from the estimation of the stochastic equations were first added to the stochastic equations, which results in a perfect tracking solution for the model when the actual values of the exogenous variables are used.

Three fiscal policy changes were then made for two monetary-policy assumptions, resulting in six experiments. For the first fiscal policy change, COG was decreased each quarter so as to make the nominal decrease in government spending $(PG \cdot COG)$ $10 billion.[4] For the second fiscal policy change, $D1G$ was increased each quarter so as to make the nominal increase in personal income taxes (THG from equation 47) $10 billion. For the third fiscal policy change, $TRGH$, which is in nominal terms, was decreased by $10 billion each quarter. The two monetary-policy assumptions used were equation 30 and the policy of keeping the bill rate unchanged.

If there were no response of the economy to the fiscal policy changes, the change in the federal government deficit, $-SGP$, would be $-$10 billion in each case. The key question then is how much the changes in $-SGP$ deviate from $-$10 billion. The results for the six experiments are presented in Table 11.7.

---

[4]Since PG is an endogenous variable in the model, COG is in effect an endogenous variable in this experiment (with $PG \cdot COG$ being exogenous). Its value each quarter is whatever is needed to make $PG \cdot COG$ $10 billion less than its base value. A similar situation holds for $D1G$ in the second fiscal policy change.

Table 11.7
Estimated Effects on the Federal Government Deficit of
Six Fiscal Policy Experiments

		Number of Quarters Ahead						
		1	2	3	4	8	12	16
	$-SGP$: Federal Government Deficit							
$COG \downarrow$	Eq.30	-7.7	-6.8	-6.4	-6.5	-9.0	-11.1	-12.2
	RS ex.	-7.2	-5.7	-4.9	-4.6	-5.3	-6.1	-6.2
$D1G \uparrow$	Eq.30	-9.7	-9.5	-9.4	-9.5	-11.4	-13.0	-14.0
	RS ex.	-9.5	-9.0	-8.6	-8.5	-9.3	-10.2	-10.7
$TRGH \downarrow$	Eq.30	-9.5	-8.9	-8.5	-8.4	-10.1	-11.9	-12.8
	RS ex.	-9.3	-8.5	-7.8	-7.5	-8.0	-9.2	-9.7

Eq.30 = Equation 30 used.
*RS*ex. = *RS* exogenous.
Results are from deterministic simulations.
Units are billions of current dollars.

Consider the COG results first. When the bill rate is unchanged, the fall in the deficit is $7.2 billion in the first quarter and $5.7 billion in the second quarter. The fall reaches a low of $4.4 billion in the fifth quarter, and then rises to a little over $6 billion in the fourth year. The government thus loses about 40 cents of each one dollar cut in spending in terms of the impact on the budget if the Fed responds by keeping interest rates unchanged.

The results are much different if the Fed behaves according to equation 30. In this case the decreases in the deficit never fall below $6.4 billion, and by the twelfth quarter the decreases are greater than the $10 billion fall in spending. This is because of the lower interest rates. Although not shown in the table, the fall in RS after a few quarters was a little over .8 percentage points with equation 30 used. By the end of the period the decrease in federal government interest payments ($INTG$) was $6.5 billion. The decrease in GDP was, of course, also less in this case because of the stimulus from the lower interest rates.

The $D1G$ results are presented next in Table 11.7. It is known from Table 11.1 that changes in $D1G$ have smaller impacts on GDP than do changes in COG, and the results in Table 11.7 reflect this. The decreases in the deficit are larger for the $D1G$ increase than for the COG decrease. Even with the bill rate held constant, the decrease in the deficit is greater than $10 billion after 12 quarters. Although not shown in the table, government interest payments are noticeably lower in this case after about two years even with the bill rate held constant because the government debt is lower due to smaller past deficits. For example, by the sixteenth quarter interest payments were $2.4 billion lower. This lower level of interest payments is the primary reason for the deficit reductions greater than $10 billion. The deficit reductions are, of course, even larger when equation 30 is used. In this case the table shows that the fall in the deficit is $14.0 billion by the end of the period. The change in government interest payments caused by various policy changes is now a non trivial part of the overall change in the government deficit. These payments change when interest rates change and when the government debt changes due to current and past deficit changes.

The final results in Table 11.7 are for the $TRGH$ decrease. It can be seen from Table 11.1 that the impact of a change in $TRGH$ on GDP is generally in between the impacts for the COG and $D1G$ changes, although closer to the impacts for the $D1G$ change. Again, the results in Table 11.7 reflect this. The results are in between the COG and $D1G$ results, but close to the $D1G$ results.

To conclude, the present results show that the Fed plays a large role in deficit reduction issues. If the Fed leans against the wind as equation 30 specifies, then a policy of reducing the deficit by contractionary fiscal policies will be much more successful than if the Fed does not allow the interest rate to fall. The results also show that government tax and transfer changes are better tools than government spending changes on goods for lowering the deficit because they have smaller impacts on output. However, although not shown in the table, in all cases for the experiments in Table 11.7 the effects on output were negative, and so deficit reduction is not without some costs even for the most optimistic case in the table. In order to make the output costs zero, the Fed would have to behave in a more expansionary way than that implied by equation 30. One can, of course, never rule out the possibility that the Fed would behave in a more expansionary way in response to some deficit reduction plan than would be implied by its historical behavior. One should thus think about the results in Table 11.7 that use equation 30 as being based on historical Fed behavior.

11.4   Sources of Economic Fluctuations in the US Model[5]

Section 10.3 discussed a procedure for examining the sources of economic fluctuations in macroeconometric models, and this section uses this procedure to examine the sources of economic fluctuations in the US+ model.

Remember that the US+ model is the US model with the addition of 91 autoregressive equations for the exogenous variables. For this model the co-variance matrix of the error terms is 121×121, and it is taken to be block diagonal. The first block is the 30×30 covariance matrix of the structural error terms, and the second block is the 91×91 covariance matrix of the ex-ogenous variable error terms. Only error terms were drawn for the stochastic simulations (not also coefficients). The results for real GDP are presented in Table 11.8, and the results for the price deflator are presented in Table 11.9.

The Results for Real GDP

The results in Table 11.8 are based on 30 stochastic simulations of 1000 rep-etitions each. The first simulation was one in which none of the equations' error terms was fixed. Each of the other 29 simulations consisted of fixing one or more of the error terms in the 121 equations. Each number in Table 11.8 is the difference between the two variances as a percent of the overall variance (in percentage points). In terms of the notation in Section 10.3, each number is $100[\tilde{\delta}_{it}(k)/\tilde{\sigma}_{it}^2]$.

The results in Table 11.8 are divided into five categories: 1) demand shocks, 2) financial shocks, 3) supply shocks, 4) fiscal shocks, and 5) shocks from the interest rate reaction function, which can be interpreted as monetary-policy shocks. This grouping is somewhat arbitrary, but it is useful for orga-nizing the discussion.

Consider the demand shocks first. Nine demand shocks were analyzed: three types of consumption (CS, CN, CD), three types of investment (IHH, IVF, IKF), labor demand (JF, HF, HO), imports (IM), and exports (EX). For each of the nine simulations, one equation's error term was fixed except for the simulation regarding labor demand, where three equations' error terms were fixed. In addition, a tenth simulation was run in which the error terms in all eleven equations were fixed. The first total presented for the demand shocks in Table 11.8 is the value computed from the tenth simulation, and the second total is the sum of the nine individual values. The difference between

---

[5]The material in this section is an updated version of the material in Section IV in Fair (1988a).

Table 11.8
Variance Decomposition for Real GDP

	Number of Quarters Ahead							
	1	2	3	4	5	6	7	8

GDPR: Real GDP

Demand Shocks:

	1	2	3	4	5	6	7	8
CS	5.9	5.8	4.4	5.0	4.8	4.5	4.3	4.3
CN	2.0	2.4	2.5	2.4	1.7	1.5	1.3	1.1
CD	3.4	3.6	3.6	3.1	1.8	1.5	1.5	1.3
IHH	6.3	6.6	6.3	6.3	6.6	6.6	5.5	4.9
IVF (eq. 11)	1.2	-1.5	-.8	-1.0	.8	1.0	.5	.0
IKF	2.1	1.9	1.7	2.1	2.2	1.6	1.8	1.4
JF, HF, HO	.2	-.2	-.2	.5	1.0	.8	1.0	1.2
IM	8.7	7.7	10.9	8.5	4.9	5.0	4.9	4.8
EX	45.9	39.3	37.4	38.5	37.6	35.2	35.2	31.9
Total[a]	81.1	73.2	68.5	64.9	62.6	60.6	57.8	53.7
Total[b]	75.7	65.6	65.8	65.3	61.6	57.7	55.9	51.0

Financial Shocks:

	1	2	3	4	5	6	7	8
MH, MF, CUR	.0	.0	.0	.0	.0	.0	.0	.1
RB, RM	.6	.9	1.1	1.0	1.0	.9	.8	1.0
CG	.0	-.1	.0	.0	.2	.3	.5	.6
Total[a]	.6	.9	1.1	.9	1.0	1.1	1.2	1.5
Total[b]	.6	.9	1.1	1.0	1.1	1.1	1.3	1.7

the two totals is an indication of how much the correlation of the error terms across equations matters. If each of the eleven error terms were uncorrelated with all the other error terms in the model, the two totals would be the same.

The results in the table show that the demand shocks account for between 75.7 and 81.1 percent of the variance of GDP for the first quarter, depending on which total is used. The contribution declines to between 51.0 and 53.7 percent for the eighth quarter. Export shocks contribute by far the most to the total, with import shocks the next most important. The household sector's variables—CS, CN, CD, and IHH—contribute more than do the firm sector's variables—IVF, IKF, JF, HF, and HO—to the variance of GDP. Remember, however, that a result like the one that plant and equipment investment (IKF) shocks have a small effect on the variance of GDP does not mean that plant and equipment investment is unimportant in the model. It simply means that the effects of the shocks to the plant and equipment investment equation are relatively small.

The next type of shocks presented in Table 11.8 are financial shocks. Three

Table 11.8 (continued)

| | \multicolumn{8}{c}{Number of Quarters Ahead} | | | | | | | |
	1	2	3	4	5	6	7	8
Supply Shocks:								
PF	.2	.5	.8	.9	.7	.9	1.0	1.3
WF	.1	.5	-.2	-.5	-.2	-.5	-.6	-.4
PIM	.3	.3	1.1	1.7	3.7	4.6	5.9	7.8
$POP1, 2, 3$	-.1	-.2	-.1	.1	.1	-.1	-.1	-.1
Total[a]	.3	.7	1.3	1.7	4.0	5.2	6.2	8.3
Total[b]	.4	.9	1.6	2.2	4.2	4.9	6.2	8.7
Fiscal Shocks:								
COG	5.6	5.4	4.1	3.0	2.9	1.6	1.5	.8
Fed tax rates	.9	1.0	1.0	.4	.2	.9	1.8	2.6
JG, JM, HG	-.8	-.1	.3	.4	.5	.5	.6	.5
$TRGH$	-2.2	-1.5	-1.4	-.7	-.2	.2	.1	.6
COS	3.7	3.8	2.7	2.7	2.7	2.4	2.4	2.0
S&L tax rates	-.7	-1.2	-1.4	-2.0	-2.2	-2.1	-2.0	-1.9
JS	.4	.1	.3	.2	.2	.2	.8	.9
$TRSH$	6.3	10.6	12.9	12.5	11.5	11.1	10.9	9.1
Total[a]	14.4	21.1	23.1	22.0	20.9	20.3	20.0	19.0
Total[b]	13.3	18.1	18.6	16.5	15.5	14.8	16.0	14.9
Federal Reserve Shocks:								
RS	.0	-.1	-.2	-.4	-.4	.1	.7	.7

[a]Computed from stochastic simulation with all the relevant error terms
set to zero at the same time.
[b]Sum of the individual values.

financial shocks were analyzed: shocks to money demand (MH, MF, CUR),
shocks to long term interest rates (RB, RM), and shocks to stock prices (CG).
The results show that the effects of these shocks are quite small.

The effects of supply shocks are presented next. Four supply shocks were
analyzed: shocks to the aggregate price level (PF), shocks to the aggregate
wage rate (WF), shocks to the price of imports (PIM), and shocks to population ($POP1, POP2, POP3$). The results show that the supply shocks
account for a rising proportion of the variance across the horizon, reaching between 8.3 and 8.7 percent by the eighth quarter. Almost all of this contribution
is from the price of imports.

The effects of fiscal shocks are presented next. Eight fiscal shocks were
analyzed: shocks to federal government purchases of goods (COG), federal

Table 11.9
Variance Decomposition for the Nonfarm Price Deflator

				Number of Quarters Ahead				
	1	2	3	4	5	6	7	8

PF: Price Deflator

Demand Shocks:

	1	2	3	4	5	6	7	8
CS	.0	-.1	-.2	-.3	.7	3.1	1.9	3.1
CN	.0	.0	.1	-1.4	-2.8	-.1	-.8	1.2
CD	.0	.0	.3	.6	1.0	.5	-1.1	.7
IHH	.0	.3	.9	1.6	2.9	6.2	5.0	8.4
IVF (eq. 11)	.0	-.4	-.5	-.5	-.4	-1.6	-2.4	-1.3
IKF	.0	.5	1.0	1.2	.4	3.0	.0	1.3
JF, HF, HO	.0	.1	.2	.4	.5	1.8	.6	.9
IM	.0	.5	.4	.4	1.1	4.5	2.5	9.7
EX	.0	.0	.8	3.3	8.3	14.7	17.7	23.3
Total[a]	.0	1.0	3.0	6.3	12.2	19.0	24.0	31.8
Total[b]	.0	.9	2.8	5.1	11.5	32.1	23.5	47.3

Financial Shocks:

	1	2	3	4	5	6	7	8
MH, MF, CUR	.0	.0	.0	.0	-.2	-.2	-.2	-.6
RB, RM	.0	.0	.1	.2	-1.3	-.5	.4	.9
CG	.0	.0	-.1	-.2	-.3	-1.3	-2.2	-1.1
Total[a]	.0	.0	.0	-.1	-1.8	-1.2	-.9	.8
Total[b]	.0	.0	.0	.0	-1.8	-2.0	-2.1	-.8

tax rates ($D1G, D2G, D3G, D4G, D5G$), federal jobs and hours (JG, JM, HG), federal transfer payments to persons ($TRGH$), state and local government purchases (COS), state and local tax rates ($D1G, D2G, D3G$), state and local jobs (JS), and state and local transfer payments to persons ($TRSH$). The results show that the fiscal shocks are the second largest contributor to the variance of GDP. For the first quarter the contribution is between 13.3 and 14.4 percent, and for the eighth quarter the contribution is between 14.9 and 19.0 percent. The largest contributor to the effects of the fiscal shocks is $TRSH$. The tax rates and labor variables contribute very little.

The effects of the shocks to the interest rate reaction function are presented last in Table 11.8. The results show that these effects are very small.

The overall results for real GDP thus show that demand shocks contribute the most to the variance of real GDP, with fiscal shocks contributing the next most. Supply shocks are of growing importance over the horizon, but still account for less than 10 percent of the variance after eight quarters. The effects of financial shocks and shocks to the interest rate reaction function are

Table 11.9 (continued)

	1	2	3	4	5	6	7	8
	\multicolumn{8}{c}{Number of Quarters Ahead}							

Supply Shocks:								
PF	97.4	91.7	81.5	68.1	50.5	38.0	27.7	20.6
WF	-1.0	-1.5	-2.4	-2.8	-3.9	-3.3	-2.1	-1.6
PIM	1.7	7.1	14.2	23.1	30.9	38.3	36.0	38.2
$POP1, 2, 3$	.0	.0	.0	.0	.1	.1	.0	.2
Total[a]	100.0	99.0	96.2	91.4	81.3	73.6	66.3	60.5
Total[b]	98.0	97.3	93.3	88.4	77.6	73.1	61.5	57.3

Fiscal Shocks:								
COG	.0	-.1	.1	.4	.8	2.1	2.3	3.6
Fed tax rates	.1	.0	-.1	-.1	-1.4	-5.1	-7.9	-3.6
JG, JM, HG	.0	.1	.1	.0	.5	-1.5	-1.9	-.2
$TRGH$	.0	-.1	-.1	-.1	.2	2.4	-3.7	-5.4
COS	.0	.0	.0	.5	-.3	2.0	2.8	4.5
S&L tax rates	.0	.0	.0	-.1	-2.1	-4.2	-5.1	-4.7
JS	.0	.0	.0	.2	.9	1.4	-.5	-.1
$TRSH$	.0	.0	.0	.5	3.1	8.7	8.8	13.2
Total[a]	.1	-.1	.2	1.8	6.4	12.8	15.5	21.8
Total[b]	.1	-.1	.1	1.4	1.6	5.8	-5.4	7.4

Federal Reserve Shocks:								
RS	.0	.0	.0	.1	.4	1.0	.2	1.9

[a] Computed from stochastic simulation with all the relevant error terms
set to zero at the same time.
[b] Sum of the individual values.

very small.[6]

The Results for the Price Deflator

The results for the private nonfarm price deflator are presented in Table 11.9. They are based on the same stochastic simulations as those used for the GDP results. The results show that most of the variability for the first few quarters is due to shocks to the price equation, but after about four quarters other shocks begin to matter. In quarter 8 demand shocks account for between 31.8 and 47.3 percent of the variance, and fiscal shocks account for between 7.4 and 21.8 percent.

---

[6] This general conclusion is the same as the one reached from the results in Table I in Fair (1988a) based on earlier data and estimates.

Within the category of supply shocks, shocks to the price of imports grow in importance over time, contributing 38.2 percent after 8 quarters. There are two reasons for the importance of the shocks to the import price deflator. The first is that the import price deflator has a large effect on the domestic price level in the domestic price equation. The second is that the autoregressive import price equation has a fairly large variance. There are thus large shocks to the import price deflator in the stochastic simulations, which have a large impact on the variance of the GDP deflator through the price equation.[7]

The Effects of the Error Term Correlation Across Equations

The two totals for each type of shock in Table 11.8 are close to each other, and none of the major conclusions from the results depend on which total is used. For example, the eight quarter ahead totals for the demand shocks are 53.7 and 51.0, which are quite close. In this sense the correlation of the error terms across equations is not a problem. The two totals for the demand shocks and fiscal shocks in Table 11.9, on the other hand, are noticeably different for quarters 6, 7, and 8. For example, the eight quarter ahead totals for the demand shocks are 31.8 and 47.3. For these quarters the totals based on summing the individual values are greater than the other totals for the demand shocks and smaller for the fiscal shocks. The "non summation" totals for the demand and fiscal shocks should probably be used in Table 11.9, since these at least take into account the correlation of the error terms within groups. At the same time the estimated effects of the individual components should be discounted somewhat because their sum differs so much from the other total. The two totals for the supply shocks in Table 11.9 are, however, fairly close, and so the estimated effects of the individual supply components are probably more trustworthy.

Comparison with Other Results

The present results can be compared to those of Blanchard and Watson (1986) (BW). Using a four equation model, BW provide estimates of the percent of the variance of GDP[8] due to four shocks: demand, supply, money supply, and

---

[7]Earlier results in Table II in Fair (1988a) for the price deflator attributed less to fiscal shocks and more to supply shocks for quarters 6, 7, and 8 than the results in Table 11.9. Otherwise, the general conclusion from both tables is the same.

[8]BW actually examine the variance of GNP, not GDP, but for ease of exposition GDP will be used in the present discussion.

fiscal.[9] Their demand shocks are probably closest to the first two categories of shocks in Table 11.8 (demand shocks plus financial shocks). (For the following comparisons the first total in Tables 11.8 and 11.9 for each category of shock will be used.) For the one quarter ahead forecast, BW estimate that 74.0 percent of the variance of GDP is due to demand shocks. The relevant number in Table 11.8 is $81.1 + 0.6 = 81.7$ percent. For the four quarter ahead forecast, the BW estimate is 54.0 percent, which compares to $64.9 + 0.9 = 65.8$ in Table 11.8. The supply shocks are 3.0 for BW versus 0.3 in Table 11.8 for the one quarter ahead forecast and 15.0 versus 1.7 for the four quarter ahead forecast. The fiscal shock comparisons are 19.0 versus 14.4 for one quarter ahead and 16.0 versus 22.0 for four quarters ahead. The BW money supply shocks are closest to the shocks to the interest rate reaction function here. The comparisons are 4.0 versus 0.0 for one quarter ahead and 16.0 versus -0.4 for four quarters ahead. The main differences in these results is that four quarters out the US+ model has more contribution from the demand and fiscal shocks and less from the supply and monetary-reaction shocks.

Regarding the variance of the price deflator, BW attribute about three fourths of the variance to supply shocks and about one fourth to demand shocks for one quarter ahead. (The effects of the other shocks are minor.) The values four quarters ahead are two thirds and one third. In Table 11.9 100 percent of the variance is attributed to supply shocks one quarter out and 91.4 percent four quarters out. Four quarters out demand shocks account for 6.3 percent and fiscal shocks 1.8 percent. The present results thus attribute more of the variance to supply shocks. Remember, however, that the total for the supply shocks in Table 11.9 masks important individual differences, in this case the shocks to the domestic price equation versus shocks to the import price deflator. The import price deflator is not a variable in the BW model.

Finally, Bernanke (1986) has employed the BW methodology to estimate a number of small models and then to provide estimates of the decomposition of the variance of output. For the "Money-Credit" model,[10] 53.3 percent of the variance of output is attributed to demand shocks eight quarters out, which compares to 53.7 percent in Table 11.8. Fiscal shocks account for 12.1 percent, compared to 19.0 in Table 11.8, and supply shocks account for 12.4 percent, compared to 8.3 in Table 11.8. These differences are fairly small, with the US+ model attributing slightly more to fiscal shocks and slightly less to supply shocks than does Bernanke's model.

---

[9]The results cited here are taken from Blanchard and Watson (1986), Table 2.3, p. 133.

[10]The results cited here are taken from Bernanke (1986), Table 5, p. 74.

Conclusion

The procedure used in this section allows one to get a good idea of the quantitative contribution of various shocks to the variance of endogenous variables like real GDP and the price deflator. The results for the US+ model show that there are number of important contributors to the overall variance. It is clearly not the case that only one or two shocks dominate. There are thus no simple stories to be told about the sources of output and price variability, at least not within the context of a macroeconometric model like the one used here.

Accuracy of the Stochastic Simulations

Results are presented in Table 11.10 that help give one an idea of the precision of the estimates based on 1000 repetitions. These are the results used for real GDP in Table 11.8. The units are billions of 1987 dollars. The first row in Table 11.10 presents the estimates of the variance of real GDP, and the second row presents the estimated standard errors of the variance estimates. The variance estimates are fairly precise, with estimated standard errors less than 5 percent of the variance estimates. The next two rows pertain to the stochastic simulation in which the error term in the export equation is fixed. The values of the difference are presented in the first of the two rows, and the estimated standard errors of the difference values are presented in the second of the two rows. The same two rows are then presented for the simulation in which the error term in the stock price equation is fixed. The results show that for exports the standard errors are around 10 percent of the difference values, which gives a reasonable amount of precision. For stock prices the differences are small, except perhaps for the predictions seven and eight quarters ahead. For quarters two through six the standard errors are large relative to the differences, although, as just noted, the differences themselves are quite small.

From an examination of results like those in Table 11.10 for all the variables, the standard errors of the difference values in general seemed small enough to allow meaningful comparisons to be made, although they were still fairly far from zero.[11] Remember that these estimates are based on the trick of using the same draws for both simulations. Without this trick, the standard errors are much too large for anything meaningful to be done with the difference values.

---

[11] The results in Table III in Fair (1988a) are similar to those in Table 11.10 except that the differences for the stock price equation fixed are larger both absolutely and relative to their standard errors in Table III than in Table 11.10.

Table 11.10
**Estimated Precision of the Stochastic Simulation Estimates
for Real GDP**

	Number of Quarters Ahead							
	1	2	3	4	5	6	7	8
$\hat{\sigma}^2$	136.1	387.4	693.7	964.9	1208.8	1422.6	1592.4	1688.8
$[var(\hat{\sigma}^2)]^{1/2}$	(6.0)	(17.1)	(31.2)	(44.7)	(54.2)	(64.1)	(72.0)	(71.4)
	Error Term in the Export Equation Fixed							
$\hat{\delta}(k)$	62.5	152.3	259.7	371.5	455.0	500.8	559.9	538.2
$\{var[\hat{\delta}(k)]\}^{1/2}$	(5.0)	(14.0)	(24.4)	(35.7)	(44.0)	(50.8)	(55.5)	(56.1)
	Error Term in the Stock Price Equation Fixed							
$\hat{\delta}(k)$	.028	.35	-.07	.45	-2.13	-3.87	-7.44	-10.35
$\{var[\hat{\delta}(k)]\}^{1/2}$	(.003)	(.38)	(1.11)	(1.98)	(2.79)	(3.60)	(4.21)	(4.90)

Units are billions of 1987 dollars.
Estimates are based on 1000 trials.

11.5 Optimal Choice of Monetary-Policy Instruments in the US Model[12]

Section 10.4 discussed a procedure for comparing the use of different monetary-policy instruments, and this section is an application of this procedure. The procedure requires stochastic simulation, and the US+ model was used for the stochastic simulations. As in the previous section, the covariance matrix of the error terms was taken to be block diagonal, and only error terms were drawn for the repetitions (not also coefficients). As discussed below, equation 30 is dropped from the model for the results in this section, and so the covariance matrix of the error terms is 120×120 rather than 121×121 as in the previous section. The first 29 equations form the first block, and the 91 exogenous variable equations form the second block. The simulation period was 1970:1–1971:4, and the number of repetitions per stochastic simulation was 1000. A similar trick was used here as was used in the previous section for the stochastic simulations, namely the same draws of the error terms were used for the computations of both $\tilde{\sigma}_{it}^2(r)$ and $\tilde{\sigma}_{it}^2(M)$.

When the bill rate (RS) is the policy variable (i.e., exogenous for the stochastic simulation), a path for it is needed. Likewise, when the money supply $(M1)$ is the policy variable,[13] a path for it is needed. The paths were

---

[12]The material in this section is an updated version of the material in Fair (1988b).

[13]When the money supply is the policy instrument, the question arises as to whether it is the nominal or the real money supply that is the instrument. This question does not arise in Poole's analysis because the price level is exogenous. For present purposes the nominal

Table 11.11
Percentage Difference Between the Variance Under
the Money Supply Policy and the Variance Under
the Interest Rate Policy

	Number of Quarters Ahead							
	1	2	3	4	5	6	7	8
$GDPR$	.5	13.3	19.4	21.0	14.7	8.6	2.6	.7
CS	86.8	62.5	46.2	36.7	30.9	19.4	12.2	7.2
CN	.6	26.6	23.7	22.4	16.7	13.6	7.3	4.3
CD	16.8	12.8	9.0	10.3	7.4	5.5	2.3	.5
IHH	27.9	107.5	91.8	76.0	61.5	53.9	40.1	38.7
IKF	.2	.2	2.5	4.1	4.5	4.2	1.6	-1.3
IVF	.0	.7	7.7	14.6	16.1	9.5	9.2	10.4
IM	.8	1.8	1.5	4.4	3.1	3.9	2.8	1.1
CG	219.6	386.8	454.9	413.3	524.2	493.7	399.9	428.7
$PCGDPD$	.9	.7	2.0	1.4	9.7	13.0	2.3	-9.6
UR	.7	5.5	12.2	16.4	14.5	10.9	5.3	2.2
$PIEF$	15.6	9.0	14.6	9.1	13.6	7.1	10.1	2.3

chosen as follows. A dynamic simulation was first run over the eight quarter period with the error terms set to zero and the interest rate reaction function (equation 30) included in the model. The predicted values of the bill rate from this simulation were then taken as the values for the interest rate path. Likewise, the predicted values of the money supply were taken as the values for the money supply path. Once these paths are chosen, equation 30 is then dropped from the model. All the simulations are done without equation 30 in the model.

The percentage differences between the two variances are presented in Table 11.11 for selected variables in the model. In terms of the notation in Section 10.4, each number in the table is $100[\tilde{\sigma}_{it}^2(M) - \tilde{\sigma}_{it}^2(r)]/\tilde{\sigma}_{it}^2(r)$. Remember that for Poole's loss function i is equal to real GDP, and so the results in Table 11.11 for real GDP are the percentage differences between the two loss function values.

The results for real GDP show that the interest rate policy is better for all eight quarters, although for quarters 1, 7, and 8, the differences are very small. The largest difference is four quarters ahead, where the variance under the money supply policy is 21.0 percent larger than the variance under the interest rate policy. The differences for some of the other variables in Table

---

money supply is taken to be the policy instrument.

Table 11.12
Percentage Difference Between the Variance Under
the Money Supply Policy and the Variance Under
the Interest Rate Policy:
No Shocks to the Money Equations

	Number of Quarters Ahead							
	1	2	3	4	5	6	7	8
GDPR	.3	6.6	9.5	8.6	4.5	.9	-5.0	-8.0
CS	42.5	36.0	21.8	13.3	9.8	2.8	-2.8	-6.7
CN	.9	9.1	8.1	5.2	3.9	2.0	-3.1	-5.2
CD	7.4	4.2	4.8	2.9	2.4	2.4	-.7	-2.2
IHH	13.5	43.4	39.3	32.9	25.1	20.7	9.0	8.6
IKF	.1	.2	.8	1.8	1.5	.8	-1.0	-3.6
IVF	.0	.5	2.2	7.6	6.7	4.1	2.7	1.4
IM	.6	.7	.5	2.0	1.8	.9	-.3	-1.1
CG	94.2	173.9	194.7	163.3	226.4	230.4	199.5	202.3
PCGDPD	.4	.3	1.2	1.5	2.2	6.2	.3	-6.2
UR	.3	2.1	5.6	6.7	5.3	3.4	-.3	-4.4
PIEF	5.2	3.3	3.2	.3	1.8	-1.2	-1.9	-5.6

11.11 are quite large. In particular, the differences for CS, IHH, and CG are large and positive, which means that the variances for these three variables are considerably larger under the money supply policy than under the interest rate policy.

An interesting case to consider next is one in which there are no shocks to the money equations. If in Poole's model there are no shocks to the LM function, the money supply policy is better, and it is of interest to see if something similar holds for the US model. This can be done by setting the error terms in the four money equations (equations 9, 17, 22, and 26) to zero across all repetitions and running the stochastic simulations again. The results of doing this are presented in Table 11.12 for real GDP and its components.

The results in Table 11.12 are more favorable for the money supply policy than are the results in Table 11.11, which is as expected. For quarters 7 and 8 the variances of real GDP under the money supply policy are smaller, and for the other six quarters the variances under the money supply policy are closer to the variances under the interest rate policy than they are in Table 11.11. The overall change in results is thus what one would expect from Poole's analysis: the money supply policy does better relative to the interest rate policy when there are no shocks to the money equations.

Table 11.13
Percentage Difference Between the Variance Under
the Optimal Policy and the Variance Under
the Interest Rate Policy

	Number of Quarters Ahead							
	1	2	3	4	5	6	7	8
GDPR	.1	.0	-.1	.0	-.4	-1.4	-2.3	-2.7
CS	-.3	-.6	-1.7	-2.0	-3.0	-4.5	-5.5	-6.2
CN	.0	.6	.4	.1	.0	-.3	-.8	-1.1
CD	.5	.8	.6	.4	.2	-.2	-.4	-.9
IHH	.7	1.2	1.2	1.9	1.7	1.6	.7	.2
IKF	.0	.0	-.2	-.5	-.9	-1.2	-1.8	-2.4
IVF	.0	.1	.1	.2	.5	-.4	-1.0	-.3
IM	-.1	.0	.0	.2	.1	.1	-.1	-.5
CG	4.1	3.8	1.5	3.3	4.9	2.9	2.5	.8
PCGDPD	.0	.0	.1	-.1	.2	.6	-.1	-.8
UR	.1	-.1	-.3	-.1	-.4	-.8	-1.7	-2.4
PIEF	-.7	-1.0	-.7	-1.1	-.9	-1.8	-1.9	-3.0

The Optimal Policy

The optimal policy is defined here to be the policy where the Fed behaves
according to the equation

$$\log M = \log M^* + \beta(r - r^*) \tag{11.1}$$

where M^* and r^* are, respectively, values of the money supply and the interest
rate from the base path (values that do not change from repetition to repetition) and β is the parameter to be determined. The optimal value of β was
determined as follows. Equation 10.9 was added to the model and a particular
value of β was chosen. A stochastic simulation of 1000 repetitions was run,
and the variances of GDP for the eight quarters were recorded. Another value
of β was chosen, and a new stochastic simulation was run. This process was
repeated for a number of values of β, and the value of β that led to the smallest
variances of GDP was taken to be the optimal value. The value that was chosen
as the optimal value was .025. The results using this value of β are presented
in Table 11.13, where the numbers are the percentage differences between
the variance under the optimal policy and the variance under the interest rate
policy.

The main conclusion to be drawn from the results in Table 11.13 is that
the optimal policy is very close to the interest rate policy. The percentage

differences in the table are very small. For example, the eight quarter ahead variance of real GDP under the optimal policy is only 2.7 percent less than under the interest rate policy. Clearly, not much is to be gained by using the optimal policy over the interest rate policy.[14]

11.6 Sensitivity of Multipliers to the Rational Expectations Assumption in the US Model[15]

Section 4.5 discussed how the RE hypothesis can be tested within the context of a macroeconometric model, and Chapter 5 carried out these tests for the US model. This section considers how the economic significance of the RE hypothesis can be examined. How much difference to the properties of a model does the addition of the led values make? Two versions of the US model are examined here. The first version consists of the basic equations in Table 5.1–5.30 in Chapter 5 with three modifications. The three modifications concern the treatment of serial correlation of the error terms. The solution program for models with rational expectations used here can only handle first order autoregressive errors, and so the specification of equation 4 was changed from second to first order and the specification of equation 11 was changed from third to first order. The third modification was that the specification of equation 23 was changed from a first order autoregressive error to no autoregressive error. This was done because collinearity problems prevented the Leads +8 specification from being estimated under the assumption of a first order autoregressive error for equation 23. This version of the model will be called Version 1. It has no led values in it.

With the exception of equations 4, 10, 11, and 23, the second version replaces the basic equations in Tables 5.1–5.30 in Chapter 5 with the equations estimated for the Leads +8 results. These equations have values led 1 through

---

[14]The results in Tables 11.11, 11.12, and 11.13 are similar to those in Tables 1, 2, and 5 in Fair (1988b), respectively. The interest rate policy does a little better in the present results than in the earlier results, and so there is a little more support here for the interest rate policy. The main conclusion about the optimal policy, namely that it is quite close to the interest rate policy, is the same for both sets of results.

In Fair (1988b) two versions of the US model were analyzed that were not analyzed here, one with more interest sensitive expenditures imposed on the model and one with rational expectations in the bond market imposed on the model. In the first version the interest rate policy gains relative to the money supply policy, and in the second version money supply policy gains relative to the interest rate policy.

[15]The material in this section is an updated version of the material in Section 5 in Fair (1993b).

Table 11.14
Estimated Multipliers for the US Model
with Rational Expectations

| | Sustained COG Increase | | | | | |
| | GDPR | | | PF | | |
	1	2	2^a	1	2	2^a
1968:1	–	–	-.21	–	–	.00
1968:2	–	–	-.57	–	–	-.03
1968:3	–	–	-.87	–	–	-.09
1968:4	–	–	-1.01	–	–	-.16
1969:1	–	–	-.90	–	–	-.22
1969:2	–	–	-.54	–	–	-.26
1969:3	–	–	.01	–	–	-.27
1969:4	–	–	.67	–	–	-.25
1970:1	1.19	1.31	2.46	.00	.00	-.19
1970:2	1.59	1.93	3.07	.10	.11	.01
1970:3	1.70	2.11	3.00	.21	.26	.30
1970:4	1.70	2.09	2.63	.32	.41	.59
1971:1	1.69	2.03	2.19	.41	.53	.82
1971:2	1.59	1.87	1.68	.50	.64	.98
1971:3	1.46	1.68	1.19	.58	.74	1.08
1971:4	1.34	1.51	.84	.65	.80	1.10
1972:1	1.21	1.37	.61	.70	.84	1.09
1972:2	1.10	1.30	.55	.75	.88	1.05
1972:3	1.01	1.25	.59	.77	.92	1.01
1972:4	.94	1.24	.70	.79	.96	.98

1 = Non RE Version.

2 = RE Version, unanticipated changes.

2^a = RE Version, anticipated changes.

The COG increase was 1 percent of real GDP.
The increase began in 1970:1.

8 times in them, with the coefficients for each variable constrained to lie on a second degree polynomial with an end point constraint of zero. Equation 11 is an exception because the order of the autoregressive error was dropped from two to one, and equation 23 is an exception because the order was dropped from one to zero. Equation 10 is an exception because the basic equation was used instead of the Leads +8 version. This was done to preserve the restrictions that are imposed on the coefficients in equations 10 and 16. This is not likely to be an important exception because the led values were not significant in equation 10 (see Table 5.10). Finally, equation 4 is an exception because the equation with a first order autoregressive error and Leads +8 did not have sensible coefficient estimates. The equation used in this case is the same as

Table 11.14 (continued)

	Sustained RS Decrease					
	GDPR			PF		
	1	2	2^a	1	2	2^a
1968:1	–	–	.03	–	–	.00
1968:2	–	–	.07	–	–	.00
1968:3	–	–	.10	–	–	.01
1968:4	–	–	.09	–	–	.02
1969:1	–	–	.06	–	–	.03
1969:2	–	–	-.02	–	–	.03
1969:3	–	–	-.14	–	–	.03
1969:4	–	–	-.29	–	–	.02
1970:1	-.00	-.04	-.41	.00	.00	-.00
1970:2	.11	.15	-.27	-.00	-.00	-.02
1970:3	.26	.36	-.06	.01	.01	-.04
1970:4	.41	.54	.15	.02	.03	-.04
1971:1	.53	.65	.32	.05	.06	-.03
1971:2	.62	.71	.45	.08	.10	-.01
1971:3	.69	.73	.53	.11	.13	.02
1971:4	.75	.72	.59	.15	.17	.06
1972:1	.77	.67	.58	.19	.20	.09
1972:2	.77	.60	.55	.24	.23	.12
1972:3	.76	.51	.48	.28	.26	.16
1972:4	.74	.41	.39	.31	.28	.19

1 = Non RE Version.
2 = RE Version, unanticipated changes.
2^a = RE Version, anticipated changes.

The RS decrease was 1 percentage point.
The decrease began in 1970:1.

the one for Version 1, namely the equation with a first order autoregressive error (as opposed to second in Table 5.4) and no led values. This version of the model will be called Version 2.

Any equations in Chapter 5 for which no led values were tried are the same for both versions. Also, the identities are the same for both versions. The estimation period for any equation with led values had to end in 1990:4 rather than 1993:2, and so to make both versions comparable, all the equations for both versions were estimated only through 1990:4. The estimation techniques were 2SLS and Hansen's method. The first stage regressors are the ones listed in Table A.7 except for the equations with led values and a first order autoregressive error (equations 11 and 14), where the first stage regressors are all lagged once.

It should be noted that because of the reestimation only through 1990:4, the coefficient estimates for Version 1 are not the same as the coefficient estimates in Tables 5.1–5.30. The specification is the same (with the three exceptions noted above), but the estimates are not. This shorter estimation period was, however, used for the Leads +8 tests in the tables, and so the results for these tests in the tables are precisely the comparison of the equations of Version 1 versus those of Version 2 (with the three exceptions noted above).

It should also be noted that Version 2 has fewer restrictions imposed on it than are imposed on most RE models. The only restrictions imposed before estimation are that there are eight leads and the coefficients of the led values lie on a second degree polynomial. In many RE models at least some of the coefficients are chosen *a priori* rather than estimated. For example, the RE version of the model in Fair (1979b) simply imposes rational expectations in the bond and stock markets without estimation. It is thus quite possible for Version 2 to have properties similar to those of Version 1 and yet for other, more restricted RE models to have very different properties from those of their non RE versions.

Version 2 is solved under the assumption that expectations are rational in the Muth sense. In particular, it is assumed that agents use the model in solving for their expectations and that their expectations of the exogenous variables are equal to the actual values. These two assumptions imply that agents' expectations of the future values of the endogenous variables are equal to the model's predictions of them. Version 2 is solved using the EP solution method discussed in Section 7.10.

Four policy experiments were performed. The first two are a sustained increase in federal government purchases of goods in real terms (COG) beginning in 1970:1. For experiment 1 the change is unanticipated, and for experiment 2 the change is anticipated as of 1968:1. The second two experiments are a sustained decrease in the bill rate (RS) beginning in 1970:1. For experiment 3 the change is unanticipated, and for experiment 4 the change is anticipated as of 1968:1. For the second two experiments the interest rate reaction function (equation 30) is dropped and the bill rate is taken to be exogenous. The results for real GDP and the private nonfarm price deflator are presented in Table 11.14. Both the anticipated and unanticipated results are the same for Version 1 because future predicted values do not affect current predicted values—Version 1 is not forward looking in this sense.

The results for each experiment were obtained as follows. The version was first solved using the actual values of all exogenous variables. These solution values are the "base" values. The policy variable was then changed and the version was solved again. The difference between the predicted value of a variable from this solution and the predicted value from the first solution is the estimate of the response of the variable to the policy change.

Before discussing the results, it should be noted that the experiments were performed without concern about possible wrong signs of the coefficient estimates of the led values. Although not shown in Tables 5.1–5.30, not all signs for the led values were what one might expect. The aim of the exercise in this section is not to test theories, but to see how much difference the addition of the led values makes to a model's properties, regardless of what their coefficient estimates might be. It may be that other theories would imply different signs, and so this section has remained agnostic about the signs. Likewise, no concern was given as to whether the led values were statistically significant or not. Aside from the exceptions mentioned above, all the equations estimated using Leads +8 in Chapter 5 were used regardless of the significance levels of the led values.

The results are presented in Table 11.14. Consider first the results for the unanticipated government spending increase. For this case Version 2 has slightly higher multipliers than Version 1. The three quarter ahead multiplier is 2.11 for Version 2 versus 1.70 for Version 1. Although not shown in the table, the sum of the output increases over the 12 quarters is $117 billion for Version 1 and $139 billion for Version 2. The effects on real GDP are thus fairly similar for Versions 1 and 2 for the unanticipated case, with Version 2 being slightly more expansionary.

For the anticipated spending increase the changes in real GDP for the first six quarters after the announcement are negative for Version 2, but the changes are noticeably larger than in the unanticipated case once the policy action is taken in 1970:1. Although not shown in the table, the sum of the output increases over the 20 quarters is $115 billion, which is very close to the $117 billion for Version 1. The reason the output increases are negative for the first few quarters after the announcement for Version 2 has to do with the investment equation 12. Although not shown in Table 5.12, the coefficient estimates for the future output changes are negative for the Leads +8 results. The initial changes in investment are thus negative because of the positive future output changes, and this effect is large enough to make the initial changes in output negative. It is not necessarily sensible, of course, for current investment to be a negative function of future output, but, as discussed above, the point of this section is not to worry about signs.

The results for the price deflator for the COG increase parallel fairly closely those for output, which is as expected since output appears in the demand pressure variable in the price equation 10.

The differences between the two versions are also fairly modest for the bill rate decrease. These results are presented in the second half of Table 11.14. Again, the largest differences occur for the anticipated case, where there is about a year's delay after the change in the bill rate is implemented before positive effects on output begin to appear. Also, the output increases are smaller for the rest of the horizon in the anticipated versus unanticipated case.

Overall, the results in Table 11.14 show fairly modest differences in the policy properties of the model from the addition of the led values.[16] This conclusion is perhaps not surprising given the results in Chapter 5. With the exception of three household expenditure equations, most of the led values in Chapter 5 are not significant, and so one would not expect them to contribute in important ways to the properties of the model.

11.7 Is Monetary Policy Becoming Less Effective?[17]

It is well known that the federal government debt as a percent of GDP has risen substantially since 1980. For example, $-AG$, which is the federal government debt variable in the model, rose as a percent of GDP from 16.9 in 1980:1 to 45.5 in 1993:2.[18] (Remember that AG is the value of net financial assets of the federal government. It is negative because the federal government is a net debtor. For ease of exposition, $-AG$ will be referred to as the government debt.) Much of this increase in the government debt was financed by U.S. households, which is an increase in AH in the model.

One consequence of the increasing size of the government debt is that the size of the income effect of interest rate changes on demand is increasing relative to the size of the substitution effect. The larger is the debt, the larger is the change in interest payments of the government ($INTG$) (and thus the interest receipts of those holding the debt) for a given change in interest rates. This means, for example, that household income (YD), which includes interest receipts, is falling more over time for a given fall in interest rates because of

---

[16]The results in Table 11.14 are similar to those in Table 2 in Fair (1993b) based on earlier data and estimates. The main difference is that the differences between Versions 1 and 2 for the bill rate decrease are somewhat larger in Table 2 than in Table 11.14. The same general conclusion, however, is drawn from both sets of results.

[17]The material in this section is taken from Fair (1994b).

[18]For these calculations GDP is taken to be at an annual rate, which means that it is multiplied by four from the variable in the model.

the increasing holdings of government debt by households. A fall in income from a fall in interest rates has a negative effect on demand, which offsets at least some of the positive substitution effect. The ability of the Federal Reserve to, say, stimulate the economy by lowering interest rates may thus be decreasing over time due to the increasing size of the income effect relative to the substitution effect. The purpose of this section is to try to estimate how large this decrease in the effectiveness of monetary policy has been since 1980.

The US model is used to examine this question. The model is first used to estimate what the economy would have been like between 1980 and 1990 had the federal government debt not risen so much. Call this economy the "alternative" economy. The model is then used to run the same monetary-policy experiment for both the actual and alternative economies. The difference in results for the two economies is an estimate of how much the effectiveness has been changed as a result of the rise in the government debt.

An alternative procedure to that followed here would simply be to run the monetary-policy experiment for an earlier period when the government debt was not as large and compare these results to those for a later period. The problem with this procedure, however, is that other things would be different as well between the two periods, and it would not be clear how much of the difference in results to attribute to government debt differences as opposed to other differences. The procedure used here controls better for other differences.

The Alternative Economy

In creating the alternative economy the aim was to raise the personal income tax rate ($D1G$) to generate more tax revenue and thus lower the deficit from its historical path while at the same time lowering the bill rate (RS) to keep real GDP ($GDPR$) roughly unchanged from its historical path. For this work equation 30, the interest rate reaction function, was dropped from the model so that RS could be treated as an exogenous policy variable. The beginning quarter for the changes was 1980:1, and the changes were sustained through 1990:4.

The residuals from the estimation of the stochastic equations were first added to the equations and taken as exogenous.[19] This results in a perfect tracking solution when the actual values of the exogenous variables are used. Then various paths of $D1G$ and RS were tried. It turned out that a sustained

---

[19]Adding the estimated residuals to the equations before solving the model assumes that the shocks that occurred in the actual economy also occur in the alternative economy. The two economies have the same shocks, but different values of $D1G$ and RS.

Table 11.15
Comparison of the Actual and Alternative Economies

Quar.	$-SGP$ Alt.	Act.	Dif.	$-AG$ Alt.	Act.	Dif.	AH Alt.	Act.	Dif.
1980:1	3.9	9.3	-5.4	440.2	446.7	-6.5	2346.9	2312.7	34.2
1980:2	10.0	15.4	-5.5	451.9	464.7	-12.8	2530.5	2496.2	34.3
1980:3	12.5	18.4	-5.9	471.0	489.9	-18.9	2673.1	2634.8	38.3
1980:4	10.3	16.9	-6.6	475.5	501.4	-26.0	2782.9	2743.0	39.9
1981:1	3.1	10.5	-7.5	490.7	524.4	-33.7	2802.7	2763.6	39.1
1981:2	4.4	12.5	-8.1	491.3	533.5	-42.2	2826.5	2789.7	36.8
1981:3	5.1	14.0	-8.9	497.7	549.3	-51.5	2697.5	2664.7	32.8
1981:4	12.1	21.6	-9.5	514.0	575.2	-61.2	2826.6	2799.1	27.5
1982:1	14.7	24.8	-10.0	539.6	611.3	-71.6	2745.6	2724.6	20.9
1982:2	17.5	28.1	-10.6	552.8	635.4	-82.6	2764.3	2750.5	13.9
1982:3	25.7	36.8	-11.1	589.0	682.9	-93.9	2883.0	2877.2	5.7
1982:4	34.6	45.9	-11.3	620.2	725.8	-105.7	3049.5	3052.6	-3.1
1983:1	33.1	44.8	-11.7	670.0	787.4	-117.5	3204.6	3217.1	-12.5
1983:2	30.0	42.2	-12.2	707.3	837.1	-129.8	3388.9	3411.3	-22.4
1983:3	34.0	46.9	-12.9	730.2	873.3	-143.1	3411.8	3444.6	-32.8
1983:4	32.6	46.1	-13.6	743.1	900.1	-157.0	3343.5	3386.9	-43.3
1984:1	26.6	40.9	-14.3	783.8	955.4	-171.6	3315.4	3370.9	-55.5
1984:2	23.5	38.4	-14.9	811.3	997.9	-186.6	3319.7	3386.6	-67.0
1984:3	25.3	40.9	-15.6	850.3	1052.8	-202.5	3440.0	3519.2	-79.2
1984:4	30.5	46.6	-16.2	869.9	1088.9	-218.9	3442.1	3534.4	-92.4
1985:1	21.0	37.5	-16.5	898.4	1134.5	-236.1	3613.7	3719.4	-105.7
1985:2	34.5	51.6	-17.1	933.5	1187.2	-253.8	3726.3	3845.5	-119.2
1985:3	28.1	45.5	-17.4	963.0	1234.2	-271.2	3656.0	3789.8	-133.8
1985:4	28.9	46.8	-17.9	1010.6	1299.9	-289.2	3913.0	4060.8	-147.7
1986:1	27.4	45.8	-18.5	1044.8	1353.1	-308.3	4152.5	4315.1	-162.6
1986:2	37.0	56.0	-18.9	1087.8	1415.3	-327.6	4250.5	4428.7	-178.2
1986:3	35.7	54.9	-19.2	1124.6	1471.8	-347.2	4119.0	4312.4	-193.3
1986:4	24.8	44.4	-19.6	1144.5	1512.0	-367.5	4244.1	4454.2	-210.1
1987:1	27.4	47.4	-20.0	1167.0	1554.5	-387.5	4678.4	4903.2	-224.7
1987:2	12.1	32.5	-20.4	1179.4	1587.3	-407.9	4710.4	4950.6	-240.2
1987:3	12.4	33.6	-21.2	1196.3	1625.7	-429.5	4245.0	4501.0	-256.0
1987:4	16.1	38.2	-22.1	1205.5	1657.1	-451.6	4231.3	4503.6	-272.2
1988:1	17.0	39.4	-22.4	1237.1	1711.3	-474.2	4336.8	4625.6	-288.8
1988:2	10.5	33.6	-23.1	1255.3	1752.9	-497.5	4425.4	4731.4	-306.0
1988:3	6.1	29.9	-23.8	1278.2	1799.7	-521.5	4407.9	4731.0	-323.2
1988:4	9.3	33.8	-24.5	1293.6	1839.7	-546.1	4475.2	4816.0	-340.8
1989:1	2.1	27.5	-25.4	1305.6	1877.2	-571.6	4581.5	4940.6	-359.1
1989:2	1.4	27.4	-26.0	1328.5	1926.5	-598.0	4874.9	5251.7	-376.8
1989:3	5.9	32.0	-26.1	1357.3	1981.2	-624.0	5020.1	5414.9	-394.8
1989:4	8.5	35.4	-26.8	1376.0	2027.1	-651.1	5044.8	5458.3	-413.6
1990:1	14.2	41.6	-27.5	1395.4	2074.4	-679.0	5045.5	5477.8	-432.3
1990:2	9.8	38.0	-28.2	1401.8	2109.5	-707.8	5149.4	5601.7	-452.2
1990:3	7.1	36.2	-29.1	1405.0	2141.9	-737.0	4822.3	5294.8	-472.5
1990:4	18.9	47.8	-28.8	1414.3	2180.5	-766.2	5125.8	5617.4	-491.5

increase in $D1G$ of 1 percentage point and a sustained decrease in RS of 2 percentage points over the 1980:1–1990:4 period led to little change in $GDPR$ from the base path and a substantial decrease in the deficit (and thus the debt).

Table 11.15 (continued)

Quar.	INTG Alt.	INTG Act.	INTG Dif.	SH Alt.	SH Act.	SH Dif.	GDPR Alt.	GDPR Act.	GDPR Dif.
1980:1	11.5	12.5	-1.0	18.6	23.7	-5.1	940.2	942.4	-2.2
1980:2	12.1	13.3	-1.3	29.2	34.5	-5.3	917.5	920.6	-3.0
1980:3	11.6	13.1	-1.5	26.7	32.8	-6.1	919.0	921.4	-2.4
1980:4	12.0	13.8	-1.8	27.0	34.0	-7.0	938.2	939.3	-1.1
1981:1	14.4	16.7	-2.3	23.1	31.0	-7.9	956.7	956.4	.3
1981:2	14.6	17.2	-2.6	25.2	33.8	-8.6	953.5	952.0	1.5
1981:3	15.2	18.3	-3.1	32.2	41.5	-9.3	962.5	960.0	2.5
1981:4	15.9	19.5	-3.6	38.1	48.0	-9.9	950.6	947.5	3.2
1982:1	16.1	20.1	-4.0	38.1	48.4	-10.3	937.4	933.8	3.5
1982:2	16.3	20.9	-4.5	43.3	54.1	-10.8	941.0	937.5	3.6
1982:3	16.8	21.8	-5.0	41.3	52.4	-11.1	933.0	929.6	3.4
1982:4	16.4	21.7	-5.3	37.7	49.1	-11.3	931.9	928.8	3.1
1983:1	16.1	21.8	-5.7	37.2	48.6	-11.4	941.4	938.6	2.8
1983:2	16.2	22.4	-6.2	26.5	38.3	-11.8	964.5	962.0	2.5
1983:3	17.0	23.8	-6.8	24.5	36.6	-12.2	979.2	977.0	2.2
1983:4	17.4	24.8	-7.4	23.3	35.9	-12.6	996.1	994.2	1.9
1984:1	18.3	26.3	-8.0	27.9	40.7	-12.9	1020.2	1018.6	1.6
1984:2	18.4	26.9	-8.5	28.1	41.4	-13.2	1036.3	1034.9	1.4
1984:3	20.0	29.4	-9.4	31.7	45.5	-13.8	1044.2	1043.2	.9
1984:4	20.6	30.6	-10.0	26.8	40.9	-14.1	1048.4	1048.0	.4
1985:1	20.6	31.1	-10.5	16.4	30.3	-14.0	1056.9	1056.9	.0
1985:2	20.9	31.9	-11.0	35.2	49.6	-14.4	1062.9	1063.2	-.2
1985:3	20.4	31.7	-11.3	13.4	27.8	-14.4	1075.9	1076.3	-.4
1985:4	20.5	32.3	-11.8	19.6	34.3	-14.6	1082.3	1082.8	-.4
1986:1	20.4	32.7	-12.3	21.6	36.3	-14.7	1096.2	1096.7	-.5
1986:2	20.3	33.0	-12.7	26.4	41.5	-15.0	1094.8	1095.2	-.4
1986:3	19.6	32.5	-12.9	11.3	26.3	-15.0	1103.1	1103.4	-.3
1986:4	19.4	32.8	-13.3	12.0	27.2	-15.2	1106.1	1106.3	-.2
1987:1	19.3	33.0	-13.7	15.0	30.2	-15.2	1115.4	1115.5	.0
1987:2	19.2	33.4	-14.2	-5.6	9.7	-15.3	1129.7	1129.4	.3
1987:3	19.5	34.4	-14.8	-2.2	13.6	-15.8	1139.3	1138.8	.5
1987:4	20.2	35.8	-15.6	10.1	26.3	-16.3	1156.3	1155.7	.6
1988:1	19.2	34.9	-15.7	9.8	26.0	-16.3	1164.5	1163.8	.6
1988:2	19.8	36.3	-16.4	9.0	25.8	-16.7	1176.8	1176.2	.6
1988:3	20.0	37.0	-17.0	9.8	27.0	-17.2	1184.1	1183.6	.5
1988:4	20.2	37.8	-17.6	10.8	28.3	-17.5	1195.3	1194.9	.4
1989:1	21.3	40.0	-18.6	11.1	29.3	-18.1	1204.4	1204.4	.0
1989:2	22.0	41.5	-19.4	4.2	22.5	-18.3	1209.4	1209.8	-.3
1989:3	21.4	41.1	-19.7	7.9	26.3	-18.4	1209.1	1209.8	-.6
1989:4	21.8	42.2	-20.4	14.0	32.7	-18.7	1213.3	1214.2	-.9
1990:1	21.9	42.9	-21.0	13.6	32.6	-19.0	1223.5	1224.6	-1.1
1990:2	22.4	44.2	-21.8	17.9	37.5	-19.5	1228.0	1229.3	-1.2
1990:3	23.0	45.8	-22.7	17.4	37.2	-19.8	1225.2	1226.6	-1.5
1990:4	21.2	43.6	-22.4	28.4	47.8	-19.4	1215.3	1216.8	-1.5

Units are billions of 1987 dollars for real GDP and billions of current dollars for the others. The flow variables are at quarterly rates.

The actual value of the bill rate ranged between 5.3 and 15.1 percent during this period, and so the lowest value of the bill rate was 3.3 percent for this simulation.[20]

The actual and predicted values of six variables from this simulation are presented in Table 11.15. The six variables are the federal government deficit $(-SGP)$, the federal government debt $(-AG)$, net financial assets of the household sector (AH), interest payments of the federal government $(INTG)$, household saving (SH), and real GDP $(GDPR)$. Remember that the deficit, interest payments, and household saving variables are at quarterly rates in billions of current dollars, and real GDP is at a quarterly rate in billions of 1987 dollars. The variables $-AG$ and AH are stock variables in billions of current dollars.

Table 11.15 shows that by the end of the simulation period the federal debt was $766.2 billion less than the actual (historical) value. The federal deficit was $28.8 billion less at a quarterly rate, which at an annual rate is $115.2 billion. The level of federal interest payments was $22.4 billion less. Household saving was $19.4 billion less, which was caused in part by the lower interest rates. The level of net financial assets of the household sector was $491.5 billion less by the end of the simulation period, which was due to the lower past levels of household saving. Therefore, as expected, raising the personal tax rate and lowering the bill rate led to less government dissaving and less household saving. Note that the real GDP path is similar to the actual path, which was the aim of the simulation.

Although not shown in Table 11.15, nonresidential fixed investment of the firm sector (IKF) is higher in the alternative economy than the actual economy. In equation 12 IKF depends positively on output and negatively on the bond rate. Output is roughly the same in both economies, but the bond rate is lower in the alternative economy, and so investment is higher in the alternative economy. In 1990:4 nonresidential fixed investment was 1.8 percent higher in the alternative economy than the actual economy. More investment means a larger capital stock (KK), and by 1990:4 KK was 3.0 percent higher in the alternative economy. Thus, as expected, lower interest rates with output held constant led to more private investment.

The results in Table 11.15 are interesting in their own right in that they show that a 1 percentage point increase in the average personal income tax rate

---

[20] Although the data used in this book go through 1993:2, the simulation period used in this section was taken to end in 1990:4. By the end of 1992 the actual value of the bill rate was down to 3.0 percent, and a 2 percentage point drop in the bill rate would have lowered it to 1.0 percent, which is extremely low by historical standards. I am reluctant to push the model into values that are too far outside the range used in the estimation, and this is the reason for stopping in 1990:4.

and a 2 percentage point decrease in the bill rate beginning in 1980:1 would have remarkably changed the debt structure of the U.S. economy by the end of the 1980s while having only trivial effects on real GDP.

The Monetary-Policy Experiment

Given the alternative economy, the next step is to run a monetary-policy experiment for the two economies and compare the results. The monetary-policy experiment is a sustained decrease in the bill rate of 1 percentage point beginning in 1987.1. The experiment runs through 1990:4, for a total of 16 quarters.[21] For these experiments the residuals were added to the stochastic equations and taken to be exogenous. This means that when the model is solved using the actual values of the exogenous variables, a perfect tracking solution results. The actual values are thus the "base" values. For the alternative economy the "actual" values of the bill rate and $D1G$ are the values relevant for this economy, and the perfect tracking solution is the solution that reproduces the data for this economy. The residuals are the same for both economies. For each experiment the bill rate was lowered by 1 percentage point in each of the 16 quarters and the model solved.[22] A comparison of the results for the two economies is presented in Table 11.16 for selected variables. The sum of the changes across the 16 quarters is presented for some of the variables, which is a useful summary statistic.

The results in Table 11.16 show that government interest payments fell more in the actual than in the alternative economy—$51.9 billion versus $34.9 billion over the 16 quarters. This resulted in a larger fall in disposable income in the actual economy—$19.4 billion versus $3.6 billion. The (negative) effect from the fall in income is thus larger in the actual economy, which resulted in less household demand and thus smaller real GDP increases. The increase in real GDP over the 16 quarters is $60.1 billion in the actual economy versus $68.1 billion in the alternative economy, a difference of 13.3 percent. It is also the case, however, that the difference between the real GDP increases in Table 11.16 grows larger as the number of quarters ahead increases. By the 16th quarter the change in real GDP from the base value is .35 percent in the alternative economy compared to .27 percent in the actual economy, a difference of 29.6 percent. Note finally from Table 11.16 that the government

---

[21] The smallest value of the bill rate for these experiments was 2.5 percent in 1987:1 for the alternative economy.

[22] The experiment for the actual economy is the same as the one done for the results in Table 11.2 except that the starting quarter here is 1987:1 as opposed to 1989:3 in Table 11.2.

Table 11.16
Estimated Multipliers in the Actual and Alternative
Economies for a Decrease in the Bill Rate of
One Percentage Point

		\multicolumn{8}{c}{Number of Quarters Ahead}

		1	2	3	4	8	12	16	Sum
		\multicolumn{8}{c}{GDPR: Real GDP}							
RS ↓	Act.	-.01	.05	.15	.25	.47	.38	.27	60.1
	Alt.	-.00	.06	.17	.27	.51	.44	.35	68.1
		\multicolumn{8}{c}{PF: Price Deflator}							
RS ↓	Act.	.00	.00	.00	.02	.16	.30	.33	–
	Alt.	.00	.00	.01	.02	.18	.35	.38	–
		\multicolumn{8}{c}{INTG: Federal Government Interest Payments}							
RS ↓	Act.	-1.4	-1.6	-1.7	-1.9	-2.9	-4.2	-5.6	-51.9
	Alt.	-1.1	-1.1	-1.2	-1.3	-2.0	-2.8	-3.6	-34.9
		\multicolumn{8}{c}{YD: Disposable Personal Income}							
RS ↓	Act.	-2.0	-1.9	-1.8	-1.4	-.3	-.9	-2.3	-19.4
	Alt.	-1.7	-1.6	-1.4	-1.0	.5	.5	-.4	-3.6
		\multicolumn{8}{c}{-SGP: Federal Government Deficit}							
RS ↓	Act.	-1.4	-1.6	-2.1	-2.6	-4.4	-5.6	-6.5	-68.9
	Alt.	-1.1	-1.3	-1.8	-2.2	-3.8	-4.7	-5.1	-57.4

Act. = Actual economy.
Alt. = Alternative economy.
Sum = Sum of the effects across the 16 quarters.

Values are percentage changes (in percentage points) from the base values
for $GDPR$ and PF and absolute changes (in billions of current dollars
at a quarterly rate) from the base values for the others.

deficit decreases more in the actual economy than in the alternative economy.
This is primarily due to the larger drop in government interest payments in the
actual economy.

Two Other Alternative Economies

To examine the robustness of the results to the use of different fiscal-policy
tools to generate the alternative economy, two other alternative economies
were generated. For the first the level of transfer payments from the federal
government to households $(TRGH)$ was cut, and for the second the level
of government purchases of goods (COG) was cut. These cuts replaced the
income tax increase. The bill rate change in both cases was as above, namely a
decrease of 2 percentage points in the bill rate from its base value each quarter.

For the first of the two other alternative economies, the level of transfer payments was decreased each quarter from its base value by 1 percent of the historical value of taxable income (YT). This decrease is comparable in size to the 1 percentage point increase in the average personal income tax rate above. The quarterly decreases ranged from $4.8 to $11.6 billion at quarterly rates. As seen in Table 11.1, changing the level of transfer payments in the model has very similar effects to changing the personal income tax rate, and the results using transfer-payment decreases were quite similar to those using tax-rate increases. Real GDP in the alternative economy was little changed from that in the actual economy; the government debt was much less; and the level of net financial assets of the household sector was much less. The results for the monetary-policy experiment were very similar to those in Table 11.16 for the alternative economy. The sum of the real GDP increases across the 16 quarters was $68.5 billion, which compares to $68.1 billion in Table 11.16, and the change in the 16th quarter was .35, which is the same as in Table 11.16. The same conclusions clearly hold when transfer-payment decreases replace tax-rate increases.

For the second of the two other alternative economies, the level of government purchases of goods was decreased each quarter by exactly the amount needed to keep real GDP unchanged from its base value. As also seen in Table 11.1, changing government purchases of goods has more of an impact on GDP in the model than does changing transfer payments or changing personal tax rates. Therefore, the decrease in expenditures on goods needed to keep real GDP unchanged in light of the bill rate decrease was less than the decrease in transfer payments needed or the increase in personal taxes needed. The federal government deficit thus decreased less in this case, and so the government debt decreased less. In 1990:4 the government debt was $593.3 billion lower than in the actual economy, which compares to $766.2 billion in Table 11.15. The level of household net financial assets was $426.6 billion lower than in the actual economy in 1990:4, which compares to $491.5 billion in Table 11.15.

The results for the monetary-policy experiment in this second case were similar to those in Table 11.16 for the alternative economy. The sum of the real GDP increases across the 16 quarters was $67.2 billion. This is 11.8 percent more than in the actual economy, which compares to 13.3 percent more in Table 11.16. The change in the 16th quarter was .33. This is 22.2 percent more than in the actual economy, which compares to 29.6 percent more in Table 11.16. These slightly smaller percentages are as expected, since the alternative economy in the current case has a larger government debt (and a smaller level of household net financial assets) than does the alternative economy used for the results in Table 11.16. The differences are, however, fairly modest, and the same basic conclusion holds here as holds in the other two cases.

Conclusion

The results in Table 11.15 show that the financial asset and liability structure of the U.S. economy would have been considerably different by 1990 had the average personal income tax rate been 1 percentage point higher and the bill rate 2 percentage points lower beginning in 1980. The government would have dissaved less and the household sector would have saved less, resulting in a substantially lower government debt by 1990 and a substantially smaller level of net financial assets of the household sector.

The results in Table 11.16 show that the effectiveness of monetary policy in changing real GDP is between about 13 and 30 percent less, depending on the measure used, in the actual economy than it would be if the economy were instead the alternative economy in Table 11.15. A similar conclusion is reached for two other alternative economies, one generated by cutting transfer payments instead of increasing taxes and one generated by cutting government purchases of goods instead of increasing taxes.

11.8   What if the Fed had Behaved Differently in 1978 and 1990?

As discussed in Section 10.6, one can use a model to ask what the economy would have been like had some government policy been different. For example, an interesting question to consider is what the economy would have been like had the Fed not had such a tight monetary policy during the 1978–1983 period. This question was examined using the US model. The 1978:3–1983:4 period was considered. Equation 30 was dropped from the model, and the estimated residuals were added to the other stochastic equations and taken to be exogenous. The bill rate was then taken to be equal to its 1978:2 value (6.48) for each quarter of the period and the model was solved for this set of values. The solution values from this simulation are estimates of what the economy would have been like had the Fed not tightened and had the same shocks (estimated residuals) occurred. The results are presented in Table 11.17. (The differences for $GDPR$ and PF in the table are percentage differences rather than absolute differences.) The first thing to note from the table is that the bill

Table 11.17
Estimated Economy if the Fed had not Raised Interest
Rates in 1978:3–1983:4

Quar.	RS Est.	RS Act.	RS Dif.	GDPR Est.	GDPR Act.	GDPR Pdif.	PF Est.	PF Act.	PF Pdif.
1978:3	6.48	7.32	-.83	915.7	915.7	.00	.563	.563	.00
1978:4	6.48	8.68	-2.20	928.0	927.4	.06	.575	.575	.00
1979:1	6.48	9.36	-2.88	931.0	928.5	.27	.586	.586	.01
1979:2	6.48	9.37	-2.89	933.5	927.9	.60	.601	.601	.03
1979:3	6.48	9.63	-3.15	944.8	935.9	.95	.616	.616	.08
1979:4	6.48	11.80	-5.32	950.5	938.4	1.28	.628	.627	.17
1980:1	6.48	13.46	-6.98	958.6	942.4	1.72	.647	.645	.28
1980:2	6.48	10.05	-3.57	941.9	920.6	2.32	.662	.659	.43
1980:3	6.48	9.24	-2.75	945.6	921.4	2.63	.675	.671	.55
1980:4	6.48	13.71	-7.23	963.7	939.3	2.60	.690	.685	.68
1981:1	6.48	14.37	-7.89	982.4	956.4	2.71	.708	.702	.83
1981:2	6.48	14.83	-8.35	981.0	952.0	3.05	.723	.716	1.01
1981:3	6.48	15.09	-8.61	992.6	960.0	3.40	.741	.733	1.17
1981:4	6.48	12.02	-5.54	983.1	947.5	3.76	.757	.747	1.36
1982:1	6.48	12.89	-6.41	970.0	933.8	3.87	.769	.757	1.50
1982:2	6.48	12.36	-5.88	972.8	937.5	3.76	.778	.766	1.59
1982:3	6.48	9.71	-3.22	962.8	929.6	3.58	.788	.775	1.67
1982:4	6.48	7.93	-1.45	958.2	928.8	3.17	.797	.784	1.71
1983:1	6.48	8.08	-1.60	961.8	938.6	2.48	.803	.790	1.72
1983:2	6.48	8.42	-1.94	978.2	962.0	1.68	.808	.794	1.70
1983:3	6.48	9.19	-2.71	986.7	977.0	.99	.815	.802	1.67
1983:4	6.48	8.79	-2.31	999.3	994.2	.51	.824	.811	1.60

Quar.	UR Est.	UR Act.	UR Dif.	−SGP Est.	−SGP Act.	−SGP Dif.
1978:3	6.02	6.02	.00	5.1	5.5	-.4
1978:4	5.86	5.88	-.01	3.4	4.5	-1.1
1979:1	5.79	5.87	-.08	.6	2.3	-1.7
1979:2	5.51	5.71	-.20	-.7	1.7	-2.4
1979:3	5.46	5.86	-.40	1.6	4.8	-3.3
1979:4	5.32	5.93	-.61	1.9	6.9	-5.0
1980:1	5.45	6.29	-.84	2.0	9.3	-7.3
1980:2	6.25	7.32	-1.06	8.3	15.4	-7.1
1980:3	6.42	7.68	-1.25	10.4	18.4	-8.0
1980:4	6.06	7.39	-1.33	6.1	16.9	-10.8
1981:1	6.00	7.42	-1.42	-2.3	10.5	-12.8
1981:2	5.84	7.39	-1.55	-1.5	12.5	-14.0
1981:3	5.76	7.41	-1.65	-2.3	14.0	-16.3
1981:4	6.49	8.23	-1.75	5.5	21.6	-16.1
1982:1	7.03	8.84	-1.81	7.2	24.8	-17.5
1982:2	7.59	9.42	-1.83	9.9	28.1	-18.2
1982:3	8.13	9.94	-1.80	19.3	36.8	-17.5
1982:4	9.05	10.67	-1.62	29.8	45.9	-16.1
1983:1	9.07	10.39	-1.32	29.5	44.8	-15.3
1983:2	9.14	10.10	-.96	27.4	42.2	-14.8
1983:3	8.70	9.35	-.66	32.4	46.9	-14.5
1983:4	8.25	8.53	-.28	32.4	46.1	-13.7

Dif. = Est. − Act.
Pdif. = 100[(Est. − Act.)/Act. − 1].

Table 11.18
Estimated Economy if the Fed had Lowered Interest
Rates in 1990:3–1993:2

Quar.	RS Est.	RS Act.	Dif.	GDPR Est.	GDPR Act.	Pdif.	PF Est.	PF Act.	Pdif.
1990:3	3.00	7.49	-4.49	1226.3	1226.6	-.02	1.031	1.031	.00
1990:4	3.00	7.02	-4.02	1219.5	1216.8	.22	1.041	1.041	.00
1991:1	3.00	6.05	-3.05	1217.1	1209.5	.64	1.051	1.051	.01
1991:2	3.00	5.59	-2.59	1226.1	1213.9	1.00	1.059	1.058	.05
1991:3	3.00	5.41	-2.41	1233.3	1218.2	1.24	1.066	1.065	.10
1991:4	3.00	4.58	-1.58	1236.7	1219.9	1.38	1.072	1.071	.16
1992:1	3.00	3.91	-.91	1247.3	1230.5	1.36	1.083	1.080	.23
1992:2	3.00	3.72	-.72	1254.1	1239.1	1.21	1.092	1.089	.29
1992:3	3.00	3.13	-.13	1261.7	1249.5	.97	1.096	1.092	.35
1992:4	3.00	3.08	-.08	1275.6	1267.1	.67	1.105	1.101	.39
1993:1	3.00	2.99	.01	1274.3	1269.5	.37	1.115	1.110	.41
1993:2	3.00	2.98	.02	1276.7	1275.5	.09	1.120	1.116	.41

Quar.	UR Est.	UR Act.	Dif.	−SGP Est.	−SGP Act.	Dif.
1990:3	5.58	5.57	.01	28.1	36.2	-8.1
1990:4	5.94	5.99	-.05	39.1	47.8	-8.7
1991:1	6.32	6.50	-.19	27.3	36.3	-9.0
1991:2	6.38	6.73	-.34	41.4	51.5	-10.1
1991:3	6.26	6.74	-.48	43.0	54.4	-11.5
1991:4	6.41	6.99	-.58	50.1	61.2	-11.1
1992:1	6.62	7.26	-.64	57.1	67.6	-10.5
1992:2	6.85	7.47	-.62	59.8	70.0	-10.2
1992:3	7.00	7.54	-.54	63.9	72.7	-8.7
1992:4	6.90	7.32	-.42	58.0	66.0	-8.1
1993:1	6.74	7.01	-.27	58.8	65.9	-7.1
1993:2	6.85	6.96	-.11	49.3	55.7	-6.4

See notes to Table 11.17.

rate value of 6.48 is much lower than the actual rates that occurred. The actual bill rate peaked at 15.1 percent in 1981:3.

The results in Table 11.17 show, as expected, that output would have been higher, the unemployment rate lower, and the price level higher had the Fed not tightened. By the end of the period the price level would have been 1.6 percent higher. In 1981 and 1982 output would have been over 3 percent higher and the unemployment rate would have been over 1.5 percentage points lower. Whether this is a policy that one thinks should have been followed depends on the weights that one attaches to the price level and output. Is the gain of the added output greater than the loss of a higher price level? Remember that in using the US model to consider this question the data do not discriminate well among alternative forms of the demand pressure variable. At some point the price level is likely to rise rapidly as output increases, and this point cannot be pinned down. Therefore, one has to be cautious in using the model to consider tradeoffs between output and the price level. Having said this, however, the experiment in Table 11.17 does not push the economy into extreme output ranges, and so the tradeoff estimates in this case may not be too bad. If the tradeoff estimates are to be trusted, they suggest that one would really have to hate higher prices not to think that the Fed overdid it a bit during this period.

Another interesting period to consider is the period starting with the recession of 1990–1991, where there was a recession followed by sluggish growth. The question examined here is what this period would have been like had the Fed lowered the bill rate to 3.0 percent right at the beginning of the recession (in 1990:3) and kept it there. This contrasts to its actual behavior, where it lowered the bill rate gradually, only reaching 3.0 percent by the end of 1992. The 1990:3–1993:2 period was considered. Again, equation 30 was dropped from the model, and the estimated residuals were added to the other stochastic equations and taken to be exogenous. The bill rate was then taken to be equal to 3.0 for each quarter of the period and the model was solved for this set of values. The solution values from this simulation are estimates of what the economy would have been like had the Fed kept the bill rate at 3.0 percent and had the same shocks (estimated residuals) occurred. The results are presented in Table 11.18. The format of this table is the same as that of Table 11.17.

Again, as expected, the results show that output would have been higher, the unemployment rate lower, and the price level higher had the bill rate been 3.0 percent. At the peak difference the unemployment rate is .6 percentage points lower and output is 1.4 percent higher. The price level at the end is .4 percent higher. These results thus suggest that had the Fed followed this policy it could not have completely eliminated the sluggish growth that occurred during this period.

12

Analyzing Properties
of the MC Model

12.1 Introduction

The properties of the MC model are examined in this chapter. This chapter is
the counterpart of Chapter 11 for the US model. As was the case with Chapter
8 versus 9, however, this chapter contains fewer different types of experiments
than did Chapter 11. In particular, since no stochastic simulation of the MC
model is done in this study (see the discussion in Section 9.2), none of the
experiments that require stochastic simulation are performed.

Section 12.2 contains a general discussion of the properties of the MC
model. It is similar to Section 11.2 for the US model in that it tries to give
a general idea of the properties of the model before examining the multiplier
experiments. The rest of the chapter is a discussion of multiplier experiments.
The detailed results are presented and discussed in Section 12.3, and a summary
of the major properties of the model is presented in Section 12.4. The main
exogenous variable for each country is the level of government spending. Table
12.1 shows the effects on all the countries of an increase in U.S. government
spending (an increase in COG). Table 12.2 shows how sensitive the properties
of the US model are to its being imbedded in the MC model. Finally, Table 12.3
presents results from 32 multiplier experiments, one per country (except the
United States). The experiment for each country is a change in the country's
government spending. Each experiment is done within the context of the
complete MC model, so that all the effects on and from the other countries
are taken into account. To save space, only the effects on the own country are

presented in Table 12.3. These three tables are discussed in Section 12.3.

12.2   A General Discussion of the MC Model's Properties

The properties of each country's model by itself are similar to the properties of
the US model in the sense that, whenever possible, the specification of the US
equations was used to guide the specification of the other countries' equations.
Much of the discussion of the US model in Section 11.2 is thus relevant here,
and this discussion will not be repeated. Be aware, however, that an important
difference between the US model and the other models is that the other models
do not have an income side. This means that tax and transfer changes cannot
be analyzed in the other models, whereas they can in the US model. Another
difference is that consumption is disaggregated into three categories in the US
model but not in the other models. Also, fixed investment is disaggregated into
residential and non residential in the US model but not in the other models.
While these differences are not trivial, they do not take away from the fact that
the general features of the other models are similar to those of the US model.

The main focus of the discussion in this section is on how the countries
are linked together—how they affect each other. The effects on and of a
country's exchange rate and balance of payments are also discussed. Keep in
mind in the following discussion that because most variables are endogenous
and because the model is simultaneous, a statement like "variable x affects
variable y" is not precise. In general, everything affects everything else, but
it is sometimes helpful to focus on partial effects—effects through only one
channel—in explaining the model's properties. The first link that will be
discussed is the standard trade link.

Trade Links

The MC model has standard trade links. When, for whatever reason, the level
of merchandise imports (M—equation 1) increases, this increases the import
variable that feeds into the trade share calculations ($M85\$A$—equation I-8).
This in turn increases the exports of other countries ($X85\$$—equation L-2),
which increases the export variable that is part of the national income accounts
(EX—equation I-2), which increase sales (X—equation I-3). This in turn
increases production (Y—equation 4), which increases imports, consumption,
and investment (M—equation 1, C—equation 2, I—equation 3). In short
other countries' economies are stimulated by the increase in imports of the
given country.

This is not, of course, the end of the story because the increase in imports of the other countries leads, among other things, to an increase in the given country's exports. This stimulates the given country's economy, which further increases its imports, which increases other countries' exports, and so on. There is thus a "trade feedback effect" in this sense.

Price Links

There are also price links in the model. When, for whatever reason, the domestic price level (PY—equation 5) increases, this increases the country's export price level (PX—equation 11) and the export price variable that feeds into the trade share calculations ($PX\$$—equation L-1). This in turn increases the import prices of other countries (PMP—equation L-3), which increases the import price variable that appears in their domestic price equations (PM— equation I-19), which increases their domestic price level (PY—equation 5). An increase in the given country's domestic price level has thus led to an increase in the other countries' domestic price levels.

This is also not the end of the story because the increase in the other countries' domestic price levels leads, other things being equal, to an increase in the given country's import price level, which then further increases the given country's domestic price level. There is thus a "price feedback effect" in this sense.

U.S. Interest Rate Link

The U.S. short term interest rate (RS) appears as an explanatory variable in most of the interest rate reaction functions of the other countries. Therefore, an increase in the U.S. interest rate increases the other countries' interest rates through these equations. This in turn has a negative effect on demand and output in the countries. Therefore, an increase in the U.S. interest rate, other things being equal, has a negative effect on other countries' output.

German Exchange Rate Link

The German exchange rate appears as an explanatory variable in the exchange rate equations of the other European countries. Therefore, a depreciation of the German exchange rate (relative to the U.S. dollar) leads to depreciations of the other countries' exchange rates through these equations. The German exchange rate equation is important in the model because of the effect that the German exchange rate has on the other European exchange rates.

Effects on Exchange Rates

The two effects on a country's exchange rate through its exchange rate equation are the relative price effect and the relative interest rate effect. For Germany and for countries whose exchange rates are not directly influenced by the German rate, the relative price variable is entered to have a long run coefficient of one, so that in the long run the real exchange rate fluctuates according to fluctuations in the relative interest rate. (For countries whose exchange rates are directly influenced by the German rate, which are the other European countries, the relative price term and the German rate have coefficients that are constrained to sum to one.)

Regarding the relative interest rate variable, it appears in six equations in Table 6.9: the equations for Canada, Japan, Austria, Germany, Finland, and Norway. Because it appears in the Japanese and German equations, it is an important variable in the model. It is not, however, significant in either of these equations, and so the properties of the model that depend on the inclusion of this variable in the equations must be interpreted with considerable caution. Whether or not the relative interest rate is in the exchange rate equations affects the properties of the model in the following way. Say that there is an increase in government spending in the United States that results in an expansion. Assume in this expansion that the U.S. price level rises relative to a particular country's price level and that the U.S. interest rate rises relative to this country's interest rate. If the relative interest rate does not appear in the country's exchange rate equation, but only the relative price variable, then there will be an appreciation of the country's currency relative to the U.S. dollar through the relative price effect. If, on the other hand, the relative interest rate is in the equation, the effect on the exchange rate is ambiguous because, other things being equal, a fall in the country's interest rate relative to the U.S. rate leads to a depreciation of the country's currency. It could thus be that the country's exchange rate depreciates in response to the U.S. expansion if the relative interest rate is in the exchange rate equation.

Exchange Rate Effects on the Economy

A depreciation of a country's currency (an increase in E) leads to an increase in its price of imports (equations L-3 and then I-19). This in turn leads to an increase in its domestic price level (equation 5). A depreciation is thus inflationary. If the increase in the domestic price level is less than the increase in the price of imports, which the domestic price equations imply will be true in this case, then there is a decrease in the demand for imports (equation 1).

Holding the export price index in local currency (PX) constant, a depreciation of a country's currency leads to an increase in the export price index in $ ($PX$$—equation L-1). This in turn leads through the trade share equations for the amount of the imports of other countries that are imported from the given country to rise as a percent of the total imports of the countries. This then leads to an increase in the country's exports ($X85$$—equation L-2).

A depreciation of a country's currency may thus be expansionary since imports fall and exports rise. Offsetting this at least somewhat, however, is the fact that the monetary authority may raise interest rates (through the interest rate reaction function) in response to the increased inflation.

Effects on the Balance of Payments

The balance of payments (S) is determined by equation I-6. The price of exports (PX) and exports ($X85$$) have a positive effect on S and the price of imports (PM) and imports (M) have a negative effect. A depreciation of the exchange rate has a positive effect on exports and a negative effect on imports, which improves the balance of payments. On the other hand, a depreciation has a positive effect on the price of imports, which worsens the balance of payments. The effect of a change in the exchange rate on the balance of payments is thus ambiguous. Depending on the size of the responses and the lags, it may be that a depreciation at first worsens and later improves the balance of payments, which is the J curve effect.

Balance of Payments Effects on the Economy

When S increases, net assets vis-à-vis the rest of the world increase (A—equation I-7). An increase in net assets increases imports and consumption (M—equation 1, C—equation 2). Also, an increase in A leads to a fall in the short term interest rate through the interest rate reaction function (RS—equation 7). In other words, an improving balance of payments leads the monetary authority to lower the short term interest rate, other things being equal.

The Role of the Money Supply

The money supply ($M1$) plays a minor role in the model. The lagged percentage change in the money supply is an explanatory variable in the interest rate reaction functions of only 4 countries, and the only way that the money supply affects other variables in the model is through its effect on the short term interest rate in the reaction functions.

Effects of Oil Price Changes

The oil exporting countries in the MC model are Saudi Arabia, Venezuela, Algeria, Indonesia, Iran, Iraq, Kuwait, Libya, and the United Arab Emirates, where the latter seven are countries with trade share equations only. The export price index (PX) for each of these countries is essentially the price of oil, and PX is taken to be exogenous for each. An increase in the price of oil can thus be modeled by increasing PX for these countries. Doing this increases the price of imports for the other countries (equations L-2 and I-19), which leads to an increase in these other countries' domestic price levels (equation 5). This leads through the price feedback effect to further increases in import prices and domestic prices. An increase in oil prices (or other positive price shocks) can thus lead to a worldwide increase in prices. The key link here is the fact that the price of imports is an explanatory variable in the domestic price equation for each country.

12.3   Computing Multipliers

Change in U.S. Government Spending

For the first experiment U.S. government spending on goods (COG) was increased by one percent of U.S. real GDP for each of the quarters 1984:1–1986:4. A perfect tracking solution was first obtained by adding all the residuals (including the residuals in the trade share equations) to the equations and taking them to be exogenous. COG was then increased. The difference for each variable and period between the solution value from this simulation and the actual value is an estimate of the effect of the change on the variable for the period. The results for selected variables are presented in Table 12.1. Each number in the table is either the percentage change in the variable in percentage points or the absolute change in the variable. The variables for which absolute changes are used are RS, $S/(PY \cdot Y)$, and UR.[1]

As is known from analyzing the US model in Chapter 11, an increase in government spending leads to an increase in output, the price level, and the short term interest rate. This is the case in Table 12.1. The following

---

[1]The absolute changes for $S/(PY \cdot Y)$ and UR were multiplied by 100, since these two variables are in percents rather than percentage points. RS is already in percentage points.

Table 12.1
Multipliers for a U.S. Government Spending Increase

	Y	PY	RS	E	M	C	I	X85$	PX	PM	S^a	UR
1 US	1.12	.07	.46	–	.22	.11	.84	-.02	.06	-.11	-.01	-.28
2 US	1.64	.18	.81	–	.56	.24	1.85	-.10	.16	-.19	-.03	-.55
3 US	1.80	.32	.91	–	.82	.33	2.40	-.22	.29	-.25	-.05	-.73
4 US	1.79	.45	.95	–	1.14	.38	2.81	-.35	.40	-.30	-.07	-.84
8 US	1.21	.89	1.16	–	1.49	.22	1.89	-.91	.81	-.52	-.09	-.94
12 US	.76	.99	1.12	–	1.28	-.03	.43	-1.35	.88	-.74	-.07	-.53
1 CA	.04	.00	.39	.00	.02	.01	.01	.21	-.04	.01	.04	-.01
2 CA	.10	.02	.81	-.01	-.07	.00	-.07	.52	-.06	.05	.12	-.04
3 CA	.17	.05	1.00	-.03	-.24	-.03	-.23	.77	-.06	.10	.21	-.07
4 CA	.22	.08	1.08	-.05	-.40	-.06	-.42	.99	-.05	.15	.29	-.11
8 CA	.24	.28	1.28	-.16	-.86	-.14	-1.12	1.32	-.02	.18	.49	-.15
12 CA	.02	.36	1.14	-.26	-1.08	-.24	-1.85	1.00	-.07	.07	.47	-.04
1 JA	.01	.00	.05	.10	.00	-.01	.00	.10	-.02	.08	.00	.00
2 JA	.02	.01	.14	.26	-.02	-.02	-.01	.28	.01	.24	.01	.00
3 JA	.03	.02	.21	.40	-.07	-.03	-.04	.45	.06	.40	.02	.00
4 JA	.04	.03	.27	.54	-.13	-.05	-.08	.59	.11	.56	.03	-.01
8 JA	-.05	.08	.43	1.04	-.48	-.18	-.40	.88	.22	1.07	.06	.00
12 JA	-.32	.13	.49	1.36	-.90	-.39	-1.01	.79	.25	1.29	.06	.05
1 AU	.00	.00	.01	.29	.00	.00	–	.03	.05	.09	-.01	.00
2 AU	.02	.00	.04	.67	-.02	.01	–	.08	.15	.26	-.02	.00
3 AU	.04	.01	.07	.96	-.05	.04	–	.13	.23	.37	-.01	-.01
4 AU	.07	.03	.10	1.18	-.08	.07	–	.16	.30	.47	.00	-.01
8 AU	.14	.11	.19	1.91	-.13	.14	–	.10	.49	.65	.01	-.04
12 AU	.08	.18	.22	2.41	-.23	.09	–	-.22	.59	.69	-.01	-.05
1 FR	.00	.00	.16	.18	.00	.00	-.02	.02	.01	-.03	.02	–
2 FR	.00	.00	.36	.47	-.07	-.01	-.07	.08	.10	.14	.02	–
3 FR	.01	.00	.51	.74	-.19	-.04	-.13	.14	.20	.30	.04	–
4 FR	.01	.01	.61	.95	-.28	-.07	-.18	.20	.28	.45	.05	–
8 FR	-.07	.05	.82	1.63	-.57	-.22	-.46	.17	.46	.71	.07	–
12 FR	-.28	.02	.81	2.12	-1.00	-.42	-.97	-.14	.52	.74	.10	–
1 GE	.00	.00	.07	.22	-.01	-.01	-.02	.03	.01	.01	.01	.00
2 GE	.01	.00	.18	.54	-.04	-.03	-.05	.10	.06	.22	-.01	.00
3 GE	.01	.00	.29	.82	-.08	-.06	-.11	.18	.11	.41	-.03	.00
4 GE	.01	.01	.38	1.04	-.13	-.11	-.18	.24	.15	.56	-.03	.00
8 GE	-.12	.01	.56	1.73	-.43	-.32	-.65	.28	.22	.82	.00	.04
12 GE	-.33	-.05	.45	2.24	-.77	-.51	-1.17	.04	.22	.99	-.03	.13
1 IT	.00	.00	.16	.14	.00	-.02	-.01	.03	-.01	-.01	.01	.00
2 IT	-.01	.00	.36	.39	-.04	-.06	-.04	.07	.08	.11	.01	.00
3 IT	-.03	.00	.50	.63	-.10	-.11	-.09	.12	.18	.26	.02	.00
4 IT	-.06	.01	.57	.85	-.16	-.16	-.15	.16	.28	.38	.03	.01
8 IT	-.25	-.05	.72	1.49	-.55	-.42	-.61	.12	.43	.68	.06	.03
12 IT	-.57	-.28	.65	1.95	-1.11	-.72	-1.28	-.17	.40	.70	.08	.08
1 NE	.00	.00	.19	.22	.00	.00	–	.01	.04	.03	.01	–
2 NE	.02	.02	.44	.55	.00	.00	–	.04	.16	.26	-.04	–
3 NE	.03	.06	.65	.84	.00	.01	–	.07	.28	.47	-.08	–
4 NE	.06	.09	.79	1.06	-.02	.01	–	.10	.37	.63	-.09	–
8 NE	.03	.19	1.14	1.78	-.11	.01	–	-.04	.60	.97	-.18	–
12 NE	-.14	.25	1.10	2.30	-.29	-.04	–	-.51	.73	1.08	-.29	–
1 ST	.01	.00	.00	.21	.00	.00	–	.04	.00	.03	.00	.00
2 ST	.04	.00	.01	.52	-.01	.01	–	.11	.01	.17	-.04	-.01
3 ST	.08	.01	.02	.79	-.04	.01	–	.18	.02	.35	-.09	-.02
4 ST	.11	.02	.03	.99	-.08	.02	–	.22	.04	.41	-.09	-.03
8 ST	.20	.10	.08	1.65	-.32	.01	–	.20	.12	.59	-.06	-.08
12 ST	.20	.20	.10	2.15	-.58	-.03	–	-.11	.23	.70	-.05	-.11
1 UK	.01	-.01	.11	.12	.01	.00	.01	.04	-.02	-.09	.04	.00
2 UK	.01	-.01	.28	.31	.01	-.02	-.03	.11	.01	.00	.03	.00
3 UK	-.02	.00	.42	.47	-.01	-.07	-.14	.16	.05	.10	.01	.00
4 UK	-.07	.02	.52	.60	-.07	-.14	-.29	.22	.09	.18	.02	.01
8 UK	-.40	.00	.73	.97	-.60	-.60	-1.29	.23	.09	.15	.15	.16
12 UK	-.80	-.10	.63	1.28	-1.38	-1.10	-2.32	-.13	.02	.17	.22	.43

Table 12.1 (continued)

	Y	PY	RS	E	M	C	I	X85$	PX	PM	S^a	UR
1 FI	.00	.00	.03	.30	.00	-.01	–	.05	.08	.06	.02	.00
2 FI	.01	.00	.08	.70	.00	-.03	–	.11	.23	.33	.00	.00
3 FI	.02	.01	.13	.96	-.07	-.05	–	.21	.34	.50	.02	-.01
4 FI	.04	.02	.18	1.15	-.11	-.07	–	.28	.41	.62	.03	-.01
8 FI	-.01	.06	.32	1.74	-.15	-.22	–	.24	.56	.77	.01	.00
12 FI	-.15	.05	.41	2.08	-.24	-.42	–	-.03	.57	.62	.04	.06
1 AS	.00	.00	.06	-.01	.02	-.01	–	.03	-.06	-.09	.01	.00
2 AS	-.01	-.01	.16	-.04	.06	-.02	–	.07	-.11	-.17	.02	.00
3 AS	-.02	-.01	.25	-.08	.09	-.05	–	.08	-.15	-.25	.02	.01
4 AS	-.05	-.02	.31	-.14	.11	-.08	–	.03	-.20	-.33	.02	.01
8 AS	-.19	-.13	.46	-.46	.12	-.27	–	-.16	-.51	-.81	.04	.06
12 AS	-.34	-.36	.40	-.83	-.04	-.48	–	-.45	-.91	-1.22	.02	.12
1 SO	-.01	.00	.09	-.01	.02	-.01	.00	.00	-.05	-.14	.02	–
2 SO	-.03	-.01	.24	-.04	.00	-.03	-.04	.00	-.10	-.29	.05	–
3 SO	-.04	-.02	.39	-.09	-.11	-.05	-.12	-.02	-.14	-.43	.11	–
4 SO	-.05	-.04	.54	-.16	-.27	-.09	-.22	-.04	-.18	-.57	.16	–
8 SO	-.26	-.15	1.10	-.52	-1.23	-.31	-1.02	-.22	-.47	-1.28	.36	–
12 SO	-.75	-.33	1.49	-.90	-2.46	-.69	-2.89	-.68	-.81	-1.95	.51	–
1 KO	.02	-.01	.00	.00	.01	.00	–	.11	-.14	-.06	.00	–
2 KO	.07	-.01	.01	-.01	.03	.01	–	.26	-.23	-.10	.03	–
3 KO	.10	.00	.02	-.02	.05	.02	–	.38	-.30	-.12	.04	–
4 KO	.13	.02	.03	-.04	.08	.03	–	.45	-.35	-.16	.05	–
8 KO	.17	.02	.07	-.14	.22	.06	–	.59	-.74	-.40	-.01	–
12 KO	.06	-.19	.06	-.27	.30	.02	–	.42	-1.16	-.72	-.17	–
1 BE	-.02	.03	.60	.70	-.10	-.16	-.39	.12	.05	.34	-.17	.01
2 BE	-.16	.07	.95	1.67	-.43	-.49	-1.34	.12	.11	.84	-.41	.05
3 BE	-.41	.05	1.03	2.39	-.98	-.91	-2.59	-.14	.10	1.22	-.52	.14
1 DE	.04	.03	.54	.66	-.05	-.04	.07	.12	.19	.24	.03	-.02
2 DE	.02	.09	.86	1.49	-.14	-.11	.06	.11	.45	.53	.03	-.02
3 DE	-.12	.15	.96	2.08	-.41	-.27	-.13	-.23	.60	.72	-.02	.04
1 NO	.09	.13	.11	.61	-.06	.04	–	.15	.14	.22	.03	-.03
2 NO	.12	.29	.25	1.29	-.23	.08	–	.07	.30	.38	.05	-.07
3 NO	.04	.42	.37	1.77	-.51	.04	–	-.37	.43	.47	.04	-.08
1 SW	.02	.01	.39	.44	.04	.01	.04	.13	.01	.05	.02	.00
2 SW	.05	.06	.87	1.13	.07	.04	.12	.17	.06	.27	-.04	.00
3 SW	.04	.10	1.25	1.72	.02	.03	.15	-.07	.11	.45	-.14	.00
1 GR	.01	.02	–	.41	.00	.01	.04	.06	.03	.09	-.01	–
2 GR	.04	.10	–	1.06	-.01	.02	.12	.04	.11	.31	-.06	–
3 GR	.01	.19	–	1.66	-.10	.02	.07	-.35	.20	.48	-.13	–
1 IR	.08	.03	.39	.53	.05	.03	.10	.13	.17	.24	-.01	-.02
2 IR	.09	.07	.58	1.15	.04	.05	.20	.04	.35	.51	-.14	-.04
3 IR	-.13	.12	.63	1.59	-.27	-.06	-.06	-.48	.43	.68	-.31	.00
1 PO	.01	.06	.28	.45	-.15	-.08	–	.08	.05	.19	.00	–
2 PO	.00	.20	.62	1.22	-.46	-.23	–	.03	.19	.58	-.04	–
3 PO	-.05	.38	.89	1.96	-.89	-.43	–	-.36	.37	.89	-.06	–
1 SP	.03	.01	–	.52	-.04	.01	–	.11	.16	.26	.00	-.01
2 SP	.07	.03	–	1.31	-.15	.04	–	.12	.43	.71	-.02	-.03
3 SP	.07	.06	–	1.98	-.29	-.11	–	-.20	.64	.96	-.03	-.04
1 NZ	-.01	-.02	.08	-.05	.05	-.02	–	.06	-.02	-.20	.07	–
2 NZ	-.05	-.07	.13	-.18	.08	-.05	–	.01	-.07	-.50	.15	–
3 NZ	-.15	-.16	.12	-.35	.03	-.11	–	-.26	-.15	-.79	.15	–

Table 12.1 (continued)

	Y	PY	RS	E	M	C	I	X85$	PX	PM	Sᵃ	UR
1 SA	-.02	–	–	–	-.01	.00	-.01	-.06	–	-.22	.12	–
2 SA	-.10	–	–	–	-.08	.00	-.07	-.39	–	-.47	.15	–
3 SA	-.11	–	–	–	-.14	.03	-.11	-.27	–	-.70	.31	–
1 VE	.02	–	.14	–	.06	-.01	–	.16	–	-.02	.04	–
2 VE	.02	–	.32	–	.10	-.03	–	.23	–	.00	.04	–
3 VE	-.02	–	.45	–	.13	-.06	–	.12	–	-.12	.03	–
1 CO	.01	-.01	–	–	.04	.00	–	.14	-.01	-.07	.00	–
2 CO	.02	-.03	–	–	.09	.01	–	.23	-.02	-.09	.00	–
3 CO	-.02	-.05	–	–	.11	.00	–	-.16	-.05	-.19	.00	–
1 JO	-.09	-.10	–	-.24	.08	-.06	–	-.04	-.35	-.48	.19	–
2 JO	-.35	-.33	–	-.79	.37	-.17	–	-.12	-.98	-1.21	.33	–
3 JO	-.72	-.66	–	-1.36	.89	-.33	–	-.25	-1.65	-1.95	.29	–
1 SY	-.07	-.03	–	–	-.03	-.02	–	-.68	.01	-.23	.00	–
2 SY	-.15	-.11	–	–	-.08	-.05	–	-1.75	-.02	-.60	.00	–
3 SY	-.18	-.23	–	–	-.10	-.08	–	-1.59	-.11	-1.01	.04	–
1 ID	.00	–	–	-.07	.00	.00	–	.07	-.01	-.25	.02	–
2 ID	.01	–	–	-.25	.02	.01	–	.06	-.02	-.69	.06	–
3 ID	.01	–	–	-.45	.08	.03	–	-.22	-.03	-1.22	.09	–
1 MA	.00	-.01	–	–	.04	.00	–	.03	-.02	-.10	.05	–
2 MA	-.04	-.05	–	–	.05	-.01	–	-.03	-.07	-.21	.04	–
3 MA	-.09	-.13	–	–	-.01	-.04	–	-.12	.16	-.22	-.02	–
1 PA	-.02	-.03	.09	–	.03	.00	–	-.21	-.02	-.12	.00	–
2 PA	-.06	-.08	.15	–	.08	-.01	–	-.41	-.07	-.26	.00	–
3 PA	-.12	-.18	.19	–	.16	-.01	–	-.86	-.17	-.56	-.03	–
1 PH	-.08	-.05	.32	-.21	-.08	-.02	-.47	.26	-.03	-.26	.13	–
2 PH	-.34	-.18	.68	-.68	-.29	-.08	-2.13	.35	-.14	-.79	.28	–
3 PH	-.67	-.40	.94	-1.15	-.59	-.16	-3.94	.12	-.33	-1.37	.43	–
1 TH	.00	-.04	–	–	.05	.00	–	.06	-.04	-.15	.02	–
2 TH	-.02	-.12	–	–	.14	.00	–	.09	-.12	-.38	.05	–
3 TH	-.08	-.21	–	–	.14	-.02	–	-.19	-.21	-.54	.06	–

ᵃ Variable is $S/(PY \cdot Y)$, not S itself.

discussion will focus on what these changes did to the economies of the other countries.

1. The increase in the U.S. interest rate leads to an increase in the interest rates of other countries (through the other countries' interest rate reaction functions). This, other things being equal, has a contractionary effect on demand and then output in the other countries. Except for Canada, the U.S. interest rate rises more than the other countries' interest rates, and so there is a relative increase in the U.S. rate.

2. The U.S. price level rises not only absolutely but relative to the price levels of the other countries, and so there is a relative increase in the U.S. price level.

3. The relative increase in the U.S. price level has an appreciating effect on the other countries' exchange rates, and the relative increase in the U.S. interest rate has a depreciating effect. As discussed in the previous section, the net effect could go either way. For the non European countries in which the relative interest rate variable is not included in the exchange rate equations, the exchange rates appreciate. These are

Australia, South Africa, Korea, New Zealand, Jordan, India, and the Philippines. This result is, of course, as expected since only the relative price effect is operating. For the other countries except Canada, the exchange rates depreciate, which means that the relative interest rate effect dominates the relative price effect for these countries. (Canada's exchange rate appreciates slightly because of a slight rise in Canada's interest rate relative to the U.S. rate.) The exchange rates of all the European countries depreciate, not just those in which the relative interest rate is an explanatory variable in the exchange rate equations. This is because of the effect of the German exchange rate. The German exchange rate depreciates because the relative interest rate variable is in the German exchange rate equation and this leads to a depreciation of the exchange rates that are influenced by the German exchange rate.

The exchange rate results show that the relative interest rate variable is important. For example, even though it is not significant in the exchange rate equations of Germany and Japan, its inclusion leads to a depreciation of the German and Japanese exchange rates. If the variable were not included, the exchange rates would have appreciated. The depreciation of the exchange rates in Table 12.1 must thus be interpreted with caution. This property is not strongly supported by the data.

4. The net effect on the United States of the exchange rate changes is for the price of imports to fall. In this sense the U.S. dollar on net appreciates. In other words, on net the relative interest rate effect dominates the relative price effect. Again, this property is not strongly supported by the data.

5. U.S. imports increase partly because of the increased demand in the U.S. economy and partly because of the fall in the price of imports relative to the price of domestically produced goods. The increase in U.S. imports leads to an increase in the exports ($X85\$$) of most (but not all) countries. (The reason that exports fall for some countries is discussed in the next item.) U.S. exports, on the other hand, fall, which is primarily because of the net appreciation of the U.S. dollar.

6. The increase in exports of the other countries has a positive effect on their output, but, as noted in item 1, the increase in their interest rates has a negative effect. The net effect could thus go either way, and the net effect does in fact vary across countries. In general, however, there are more negative changes in output than positive ones, and so the interest

Table 12.2
Multipliers for a U.S. Government Spending Increase

	Y	PY	RS	M	C	I	X85$	PX	PM	S	UR
					US Alone						
1 US	1.11	0.08	0.46	0.20	0.10	0.82	0.00	0.08	0.00	-0.01	-0.28
2 US	1.63	0.19	0.82	0.52	0.22	1.81	0.00	0.18	0.00	-0.03	-0.55
3 US	1.79	0.34	0.92	0.75	0.31	2.34	0.00	0.33	0.00	-0.05	-0.73
4 US	1.78	0.47	0.96	1.04	0.34	2.74	0.00	0.45	0.00	-0.06	-0.84
8 US	1.22	0.97	1.19	1.26	0.16	1.84	0.00	0.92	0.00	-0.06	-0.95
12 US	0.79	1.13	1.17	0.87	-0.15	0.38	0.00	1.08	0.00	-0.02	-0.55
					US in MC						
1 US	1.12	0.07	0.46	0.22	0.11	0.84	-0.02	0.06	-0.11	-0.01	-0.28
2 US	1.64	0.18	0.81	0.56	0.24	1.85	-0.10	0.16	-0.19	-0.03	-0.55
3 US	1.80	0.32	0.91	0.82	0.33	2.40	-0.22	0.29	-0.25	-0.05	-0.73
4 US	1.79	0.45	0.95	1.14	0.38	2.81	-0.35	0.40	-0.30	-0.07	-0.84
8 US	1.21	0.89	1.16	1.49	0.22	1.89	-0.91	0.81	-0.52	-0.09	-0.94
12 US	0.76	0.99	1.12	1.28	-0.03	0.43	-1.35	0.88	-0.74	-0.07	-0.53

rate effect on average dominates the export effect. For some countries the level of exports falls, which is due to the drop in import demand from other countries. If a country is one in which exports fall, this can lead to a fall in its output even if there is no interest rate effect operating.

7. The U.S. balance of payments deteriorates, and the balance of payments of most of the other countries improves. The U.S. balance of payments is hurt by the rise in imports and the fall in exports, and it is helped (other things being equal) by the rise in the price of exports and the fall in the price of imports. The net effect is negative.

8. Given the output changes, the effects on employment, the labor force, and the unemployment rate are as discussed in Chapter 11 for the US model, and this discussion will not be repeated here. The unemployment rate generally rises when output falls and vice versa.

Change in U.S. Government Spending in the US Model Alone

It is interesting to see how sensitive the properties of the US model are to being imbedded in the MC model. To examine this, the same experiment just described was done using the US model by itself. The results are presented in Table 12.2. The first set of results is for the US model alone, and the second set is for the US model imbedded in the MC model. The second set is the same as that in Table 12.1. The main differences are:

Table 12.3
Multipliers for Own Government Spending Increases

	Y	PY	RS	E	M	C	I	X85$	PX	PM	S^a	UR
1 US	1.12	.07	.46	–	.22	.11	.84	-.02	.06	-.11	-.01	-.28
2 US	1.64	.18	.81	–	.56	.24	1.85	-.10	.16	-.19	-.03	-.55
3 US	1.80	.32	.91	–	.82	.33	2.40	-.22	.29	-.25	-.05	-.73
4 US	1.79	.45	.95	–	1.14	.38	2.81	-.35	.40	-.30	-.07	-.84
8 US	1.21	.89	1.16	–	1.49	.22	1.89	-.91	.81	-.52	-.09	-.94
12 US	.76	.99	1.12	–	1.28	-.03	.43	-1.35	.88	-.74	-.07	-.53
1 CA	.75	.08	.05	.00	.38	.14	.16	-.01	.06	.00	-.06	-.22
2 CA	1.01	.24	.12	.01	.79	.30	.37	-.02	.18	.01	-.13	-.47
3 CA	1.12	.44	.18	.02	1.15	.45	.55	-.05	.33	.03	-.19	-.58
4 CA	1.18	.65	.22	.05	1.45	.58	.73	-.09	.50	.06	-.21	-.64
8 CA	1.24	1.54	.33	.22	2.15	.89	1.14	-.27	1.21	.26	-.24	-.76
12 CA	1.22	2.37	.39	.50	2.35	.94	1.38	-.46	1.90	.58	-.17	-.79
1 JA	.78	.00	.00	.00	.13	.07	.20	.00	.00	.00	-.03	-.09
2 JA	1.13	.00	.00	.00	.31	.17	.48	.01	.00	.00	-.06	-.15
3 JA	1.35	.00	.01	.00	.49	.27	.79	.01	.00	.00	-.08	-.23
4 JA	1.51	.00	.02	-.01	.66	.38	1.12	.01	.00	.00	-.11	-.31
8 JA	2.11	.00	.06	-.04	1.31	.80	2.49	.02	-.02	-.03	-.17	-.46
12 JA	2.70	.00	.07	-.09	1.92	1.23	3.90	.03	-.04	-.07	-.21	-.67
1 AU	.51	.05	.12	-.02	.30	.41	–	-.01	.03	-.02	-.06	-.06
2 AU	.87	.14	.30	-.06	.70	.80	–	-.03	.08	-.05	-.17	-.16
3 AU	1.12	.25	.50	-.10	1.09	1.10	–	-.06	.13	-.09	-.21	-.25
4 AU	1.25	.37	.71	-.14	1.40	1.28	–	-.10	.20	-.13	-.29	-.33
8 AU	1.35	.79	1.27	-.29	1.96	1.46	–	-.27	.44	-.23	-.33	-.54
12 AU	1.19	1.09	1.38	-.36	1.94	1.29	–	-.47	.62	-.26	-.26	-.68
1 FR	.43	.00	.00	.00	.83	.07	.38	.04	.00	.01	-.16	–
2 FR	.78	.06	.07	-.02	1.69	.18	.99	.04	.03	.01	-.31	–
3 FR	1.08	.16	.16	-.04	2.36	.32	1.73	.04	.08	.00	-.42	–
4 FR	1.33	.28	.27	-.06	2.83	.48	2.49	.03	.15	-.01	-.52	–
8 FR	2.24	1.00	.58	-.25	3.95	1.15	5.38	-.07	.54	-.01	-.61	–
12 FR	2.95	1.90	.73	-.48	4.66	1.85	7.54	-.25	1.05	.05	-.55	–
1 GE	.79	.00	.26	-.15	.44	.01	.41	.01	.00	.04	-.12	-.11
2 GE	.97	.08	.53	-.45	.80	-.01	.83	-.04	.02	-.14	-.16	-.24
3 GE	.98	.17	.75	-.84	.99	-.06	1.11	-.12	.05	-.37	-.15	-.33
4 GE	.93	.26	.91	-1.28	1.06	-.13	1.29	-.23	.06	-.64	-.11	-.38
8 GE	.59	.52	1.06	-2.97	.77	-.46	1.14	-.81	.11	-1.27	.02	-.42
12 GE	.27	.61	.77	-3.82	.37	-.68	.44	-1.21	.12	-1.51	.05	-.30
1 IT	.48	.09	.06	.00	.78	.10	.26	.00	.04	.01	-.14	-.03
2 IT	.83	.24	.18	.00	1.43	.24	.66	.00	.12	.02	-.23	-.08
3 IT	1.10	.43	.32	.00	1.92	.39	1.10	-.02	.21	.02	-.32	-.13
4 IT	1.33	.65	.46	.00	2.29	.56	1.55	-.04	.31	.03	-.38	-.17
8 IT	2.00	1.81	.87	-.04	3.33	1.18	3.23	-.18	.87	.09	-.44	-.34
12 IT	2.35	3.17	1.08	-.12	3.87	1.66	4.11	-.43	1.54	.20	-.33	-.63
1 NE	.86	.00	.20	.00	.17	.10	–	.01	.00	.00	-.11	–
2 NE	1.19	.01	.40	.00	.39	.23	–	.01	.01	.00	-.23	–
3 NE	1.22	.02	.53	-.01	.59	.36	–	.01	.01	.00	-.31	–
4 NE	1.15	.04	.61	-.01	.76	.46	–	.01	.02	.00	-.39	–
8 NE	.99	.07	.66	-.05	1.18	.72	–	.02	.03	-.02	-.52	–
12 NE	1.00	.07	.63	-.09	1.45	.89	–	.04	.03	-.02	-.53	–
1 ST	1.24	.00	.16	.00	-.35	.16	–	.00	.00	.00	.04	-.12
2 ST	1.42	.13	.31	.01	-.68	.26	–	-.03	.13	.01	.14	-.37
3 ST	1.56	.30	.46	.02	-.99	.32	–	-.07	.30	.01	.29	-.54
4 ST	1.67	.52	.61	.03	-1.25	.34	–	-.12	.50	.02	.48	-.66
8 ST	1.55	1.57	.99	.09	-1.42	.22	–	-.50	1.52	.07	.82	-1.16
12 ST	.60	2.50	.94	.12	.04	-.05	–	-1.11	2.43	.11	.63	-1.04
1 UK	.89	.00	.11	.00	.81	.13	.61	.04	.00	.01	-.17	-.14
2 UK	1.07	.05	.22	.01	1.44	.26	1.17	.04	.04	.02	-.31	-.31
3 UK	1.13	.11	.31	.01	1.83	.35	1.59	.04	.09	.03	-.40	-.46
4 UK	1.14	.17	.39	.01	2.05	.42	1.88	.04	.13	.04	-.46	-.58
8 UK	1.21	.37	.59	-.01	2.35	.46	2.41	.04	.29	.11	-.42	-.86
12 UK	1.07	.50	.64	-.06	2.09	.26	2.09	.06	.40	.15	-.34	-.90

Table 12.3 (continued)

	Y	PY	RS	E	M	C	I	X85$	PX	PM	S^a	UR
1 FI	.41	.01	.00	.00	.34	.13	–	.00	.01	.00	-.07	-.08
2 FI	.68	.05	.01	.00	.61	.29	–	.00	.03	.00	-.14	-.21
3 FI	.87	.12	.03	.00	.80	.46	–	-.01	.06	.01	-.17	-.31
4 FI	1.02	.21	.05	.01	.94	.62	–	-.03	.11	.01	-.19	-.39
8 FI	1.33	.76	.09	.07	1.25	1.06	–	-.17	.41	.08	-.16	-.74
12 FI	1.40	1.43	.07	.18	1.41	1.26	–	-.36	.81	.21	-.21	-.81
1 AS	.64	.02	.18	.00	.64	.08	–	.01	.01	.00	-.05	-.09
2 AS	.88	.08	.40	.01	1.30	.17	–	.00	.06	.02	-.12	-.24
3 AS	.95	.18	.60	.04	1.82	.25	–	-.01	.13	.04	-.17	-.35
4 AS	.96	.30	.76	.07	2.17	.30	–	-.02	.21	.08	-.20	-.40
8 AS	.89	.86	1.13	.35	2.61	.32	–	-.06	.67	.36	-.25	-.35
12 AS	.82	1.43	1.18	.76	2.55	.22	–	-.07	1.19	.78	-.23	-.32
1 SO	1.01	.00	.00	.00	.64	.10	.39	.00	.00	.00	-.09	–
2 SO	1.06	.00	.00	.00	1.16	.21	.76	.00	.00	.00	-.21	–
3 SO	1.08	.00	.00	.00	1.54	.30	1.12	.00	.00	.00	-.28	–
4 SO	1.17	.00	.00	.00	1.86	.41	1.45	.00	.00	.00	-.38	–
8 SO	1.66	.00	.00	.00	2.83	.84	3.01	.01	.00	.01	-.60	–
12 SO	2.13	.00	.00	.00	3.41	1.28	5.09	.01	.01	.02	-.67	–
1 KO	.72	.08	.07	.00	.14	.07	–	.00	.01	.00	-.02	–
2 KO	.91	.42	.17	.02	.33	.13	–	-.01	.06	.02	-.07	–
3 KO	.93	.75	.28	.05	.51	.19	–	-.02	.11	.05	-.11	–
4 KO	.92	1.01	.36	.09	.69	.23	–	-.04	.17	.09	-.23	–
8 KO	.73	1.48	.59	.27	1.18	.22	–	-.06	.38	.28	-.42	–
12 KO	.59	1.47	.68	.45	1.33	-.01	–	-.05	.55	.45	-.50	–
1 BE	.61	.13	.02	-.03	1.06	.18	1.28	-.02	.13	-.02	-.59	-.17
2 BE	.63	.36	.03	-.11	1.28	.31	2.11	-.06	.35	-.05	-.48	-.26
3 BE	.60	.62	.03	-.19	1.32	.38	2.36	-.14	.59	-.10	-.23	-.27
1 DE	1.14	.14	.20	-.01	2.14	.80	1.78	-.01	.07	.00	-.55	-.43
2 DE	1.39	.59	.15	-.04	2.25	1.00	2.79	-.07	.31	-.01	-.45	-.96
3 DE	1.47	1.40	-.04	-.09	1.99	.93	2.92	-.24	.75	-.03	-.15	-1.20
1 NO	1.08	-.01	.07	-.03	.73	.56	–	.00	-.01	-.03	-.23	-.31
2 NO	1.17	-.03	.21	-.09	.71	.74	–	-.01	-.04	-.09	-.23	-.80
3 NO	1.27	-.08	.35	-.18	.48	.82	–	-.01	-.09	-.16	-.02	-1.05
1 SW	.52	.14	.18	.00	1.07	.26	.98	-.03	.13	.00	-.25	-.05
2 SW	.90	.41	.46	-.02	1.87	.48	2.23	-.10	.41	.02	-.37	-.12
3 SW	1.19	.35	.69	-.05	2.44	.59	3.54	-.06	.35	.03	-.49	-.03
1 GR	1.07	.32	–	.00	1.45	.45	3.00	-.14	.31	.00	-.22	–
2 GR	1.99	.85	–	-.01	3.06	1.09	6.33	-.32	.83	.00	-.40	–
3 GR	2.82	1.50	–	-.02	4.50	1.79	9.93	-.49	1.48	.00	-.67	–
1 IR	.84	.00	.09	.00	.96	.38	1.06	.01	.00	.00	-.44	-.19
2 IR	1.20	.00	.15	.00	1.54	.60	2.50	.02	.00	.00	-.71	-.47
3 IR	1.33	.00	.16	-.01	1.68	.60	3.62	.03	.00	.00	-.67	-.72
1 PO	1.14	.34	.12	-.04	.67	.56	–	-.10	.35	-.04	-.08	–
2 PO	1.14	.59	.18	-.09	1.16	.84	–	-.16	.61	-.09	-.18	–
3 PO	1.01	.74	.18	-.14	1.43	.91	–	-.21	.77	-.13	-.23	–
1 SP	1.08	.21	–	-.01	1.15	.55	–	-.03	.08	-.01	-.19	-.36
2 SP	1.37	.50	–	-.04	2.06	.91	–	-.06	.19	-.03	-.33	-.67
3 SP	1.33	.77	–	-.09	2.35	.99	–	-.09	.29	-.05	-.31	-.70
1 NZ	.99	.13	.13	.02	1.93	.64	–	-.03	.13	.02	-.28	–
2 NZ	.96	.29	.28	.07	2.03	.77	–	-.05	.30	.07	-.34	–
3 NZ	.98	.48	.39	.14	1.97	.77	–	-.07	.48	.14	-.22	–

Table 12.3 (continued)

	Y	PY	RS	E	M	C	I	X85$	PX	PM	S^a	UR
1 SA	.78	–	–	–	.54	.15	.44	.00	–	.00	-.01	–
2 SA	1.12	–	–	–	1.22	.32	1.04	.01	–	.00	-.14	–
3 SA	1.19	–	–	–	1.83	.42	1.38	.01	–	.01	-.26	–
1 VE	.75	–	.04	–	1.51	.06	–	.00	–	.00	-.24	–
2 VE	.85	–	.17	–	2.10	.09	–	.00	–	.00	-.30	–
3 VE	.86	–	.29	–	2.14	.06	–	.00	–	.00	-.24	–
1 CO	.91	.00	–	–	1.10	.46	–	.00	.00	.00	-.01	–
2 CO	1.41	.00	–	–	1.95	.91	–	.00	.00	.00	-.01	–
3 CO	1.73	.00	–	–	2.47	1.28	–	.00	.00	.00	-.01	–
1 JO	1.61	.00	–	.00	.44	1.00	–	.00	.00	.00	-.13	–
2 JO	2.43	.00	–	.00	.77	1.99	–	.00	.00	.00	-.24	–
3 JO	2.76	.00	–	.00	.74	2.58	–	.00	.00	.00	-.24	–
1 SY	1.11	.00	–	–	.52	.27	–	.00	.00	.00	-.06	–
2 SY	1.14	.00	–	–	.56	.35	–	.00	.00	.00	-.04	–
3 SY	1.15	.00	–	–	.49	.32	–	.00	.00	.00	-.02	–
1 ID	1.43	–	–	.00	.73	.71	–	.00	.00	.00	-.03	–
2 ID	1.64	–	–	.00	1.30	1.07	–	.00	.00	.00	-.05	–
3 ID	1.72	–	–	.00	1.66	1.23	–	.01	.00	.01	-.06	–
1 MA	.70	.61	–	–	1.03	.49	–	-.37	.58	.00	-.17	–
2 MA	.55	1.00	–	–	1.39	.54	–	-.50	.96	.01	-.16	–
3 MA	.44	1.26	–	–	1.50	.47	–	-.36	1.21	.01	.01	–
1 PA	.92	.06	.02	–	.48	.07	–	-.10	.06	.00	-.05	–
2 PA	1.04	.11	.08	–	.79	.14	–	-.12	.11	.00	-.10	–
3 PA	1.05	.14	.07	–	.96	.20	–	-.17	.14	.00	-.12	–
1 PH	1.37	.00	.00	.00	1.31	.35	1.23	.00	.00	.00	-.19	–
2 PH	1.67	.00	.03	.00	2.09	.56	3.23	.00	.00	.00	-.33	–
3 PH	1.76	.00	.05	.00	2.38	.64	4.21	.00	.00	.00	-.45	–
1 TH	.93	.00	–	–	1.28	.42	–	.00	.00	.00	-.02	–
2 TH	1.10	.00	–	–	1.49	.64	–	.00	.00	.00	-.02	–
3 TH	1.19	.00	–	–	1.30	.69	–	.01	.00	.00	-.03	–

^{a} Variable is $S/(PY \cdot Y)$, not S itself.

1. The domestic price level rises more in the U.S. alone case because the price of imports does not fall. This leads to a slightly larger rise in the short term interest rate (through the interest rate reaction function of the Fed). The domestic price level relative to the price of imports rises less in the U.S. alone case.

2. Imports rise less in the U.S. alone case because of the smaller rise in the domestic price level relative to the price of imports. Exports remain unchanged in the U.S. alone case instead of falling as in the other case.

3. The differences in output in the two cases are small. Working in favor of the U.S. alone case in terms of increasing output are the facts that imports rise less and exports do not fall. Working against it are the facts that the interest rate rises more and the price level rises more relative to the nominal wage. These offsetting forces roughly cancel out with respect to the effects on output.

In general the differences in Table 12.2 are fairly small. This means that the results in Chapter 11 for the US model alone would not likely change much if they were done for the US model imbedded in the MC model. The main difference concerns the domestic price level, where the inflationary consequences of spending increases would be at least slightly larger with the US model imbedded in the MC model.

Change in Each Country's Government Spending

As mentioned at the beginning of this chapter, Table 12.3 presents results from 32 multiplier experiments, one per country (except the United States). Government spending (G) for each country was increased by one percent of its real GDP for each of the quarters 1984:1–1986:4 for the quarterly countries and for each of the years 1984–1986 for the annual countries. A perfect tracking solution was first obtained by adding all the residuals (including the residuals in the trade share equations) to the equations and taking them to be exogenous. G was then increased. There were 32 such experiments, all done using the complete MC model. The own results for each country are presented in Table 12.3. Unlike Table 12.1, no results are presented for the non own countries. To do so would have required 32 tables the size of Table 12.1, which is too many tables even for me. Some of the main results in Table 12.3 are the following.

1. In almost every case the domestic price level rises, as does the short term interest rate (if the variables are endogenous).

2. In almost every case the balance of payments worsens.

3. The exchange rate results are mixed. Some exchange rates appreciate and some depreciate. This is as expected since, as discussed above, there are offsetting effects on the exchange rate. The German exchange rate appreciates, so the relative interest rate effect dominates the relative price effect for Germany. The opposite is true for Canada. For Japan the exchange rate changes are very small. The exchange rate changes are also small for many of the European countries, which is due to the fact that their exchange rates are heavily tied to the German exchange rate, which does not change very much as the government spending of the other countries changes.

4. The changes in exports are generally negative, and the changes in imports are generally positive. This is the main reason that the balance of payments changes are generally negative.

5. The changes in the price of imports are generally negative when the exchange rate appreciates and positive when the exchange rate depreciates.

12.4   Common Results Across Countries

One conclusion that emerges from the results in Tables 12.1 and 12.3 is that there are few simple stories. The size and many times the sign of the effects differ across countries. If in practice one were going to use the MC model for policy purposes, to see, say, what the effects on other countries some U.S. policy action would have, the results for each country would have to be examined individually. It is unlikely that a general result across all countries would emerge. Nevertheless, there are a few results that are fairly robust across countries, and this chapter will end by listing them.

A government spending increase in a country generally leads to the following:

1. A rise in the domestic price level.

2. A rise in the short term interest rate.

3. A rise in the demand for imports.

4. A fall in exports.

5. A worsening of the balance of payments.

6. A rise in consumption, investment, employment, and the labor force; a fall in the unemployment rate.

The main effects of a government spending increase that vary across countries are 1) the exchange rate may appreciate or depreciate and 2) because of this, the price of imports may decrease or increase.

13

Conclusion

This book began by arguing for the Cowles Commission approach in dealing with macro data, and the approach was used to construct the US and MC models. Computer technology is now such that much testing and analysis of models can be done that was not practical even a few years ago, and a number of examples of testing and analysis have been presented in this book. The techniques that were used in the book will not be reviewed in this conclusion. Instead, I will review what I think are some of the main theoretical points, what are some of the main macro results that emerge from this work, and where future research seems important.

1. The theoretical model provides an explanation for the existence of disequilibrium within a maximizing context. Households maximize utility and firms maximize profits, but firms do not have enough information to form rational expectations in the Muth sense. In other words, their expectations are not necessarily equal to the model's solution values. Prices and wages may not be set in such a way as always to have the amount of labor that households want to supply at these prices equal to the amount that firms want to employ. If the amount of labor that households want to supply is more than the amount that firms want to employ, a multiplier reaction can take place in the model. Unemployment in the model can be considered to be the difference between the amount of labor that households want to supply at current prices and the amount that firms actually employ. Again, these two amounts can differ in the model because firms may not set prices right because they do not have rational expectations.

2. The Lucas critique is simply handled by arguing that it may be quantitatively of small importance and that if it is not it should be picked up in the various tests. In other words, if the critique is quantitatively important, models that ignore it will be seriously misspecified and should not do well in the tests.

3. Tables 5.10 and 6.5b show that the change form of the price equation is strongly rejected by the data, whereas the level form is generally accepted. This result has very important implications for the long run properties of models and calls into question the widespread use of the inflation rate over the price level as the variable to be explained by price equations.

4. The results in Tables 5.10 and 6.5a provide strong support for the hypothesis that import prices affect prices of domestically produced goods. For almost every country this is so. On the other hand, the data are weak at choosing the functional form of the demand pressure variable. One cannot pin down at what point prices begin to rise very rapidly as output increases. There are too few observations at these points for precise estimates to be made.

5. The results in Tables 5.13, 5.14, and 6.13a support the use of the excess labor variable in explaining employment demand. This is thus support for the theory that firms at times hoard labor, and it provides an explanation for the observed procyclical movements of productivity. The theory is further supported by the survey results of Fay and Medoff (1985) and by the industry results in Fair (1969). The excess capital variable, on the other hand, is not significant in Table 5.12 and did not play a role in the investment equations in the ROW model.

6. The results in Tables 5.11 and 6.4a are consistent with the theory that firms smooth production relative to sales. The theory is further supported by the industry results in Fair (1989).

7. The age distribution variables are significant in Tables 5.1, 5.2, and 5.3. It appears possible to pick up effects of the changing age distribution of the population in at least some macroeconomic equations.

8. The rational expectations hypothesis has a scattering of support in Chapter 5, but very little in Chapter 6. The results in Section 11.6 suggest that the use of the rational expectations assumption has only a minor

effect on the properties of the US model. In this sense it is of minor economic importance. In future work when more data are available, it will be useful to try leads longer than one quarter or one year for the ROW equations in order to provide a stronger test of the rational expectations hypothesis.

9. The results in Section 11.7 suggest that U.S. monetary policy is becoming somewhat less effective over time as the size of the government debt rises.

10. Interest rate and price links are important in the MC model as well as the usual trade links. The U.S. interest rate is estimated as affecting the decisions of the monetary authorities of a number of countries. The result that import prices affect domestic prices provides the main link for prices across countries.

11. The MC model suggests that there are few simple stories that can be told about the effects of one country on another and about the size of the own effects across countries. A few of the robust conclusions than can be drawn from the results are listed in Section 12.4.

In future work with more data and faster computers it should be possible to perform many of the tests and experiments for the MC model that were done in this book for the US model. Faster computers will also ease the computational burden of dealing with the rational expectations assumption, and in the future more work can be done using this assumption. As noted above, there is some scattering of support for the hypothesis, and probably further work is warranted even though in the end the economic importance of the assumption may remain small.

To conclude, I hope that this book will stimulate more work using the Cowles Commission approach. What I have tried to show is that testing can be an important aspect of the approach.

Appendix A
Tables for the US Model

Table A.1

The Six Sectors of the US Model

Sector in the Model	Corresponding Sector(s) in the Flow of Funds Accounts
1. Household (h)	1a. Households and Nonprofit Organizations (H1) 1b. Farm Business (FA) 1c. Nonfarm Noncorporate Business (NN)
2. Firm (f)	2. Nonfarm Nonfinancial Corporate Business (F)
3. Financial (b)	3a. Commercial Banking (B1): (1) U.S. Chartered Commercial Banks (2) Foreign Banking Offices in U.S. (3) Bank Holding Companies (4) Banks in U.S. Affiliated Areas 3b. Private Nonbank Financial Institutions (B2): (1) Funding Corporations (2) Savings Institutions (3) Credit Unions (4) Life Insurance Companies (5) Other Insurance Companies (6) Private Pension Funds (7) State and Local Government Employee Retirement Funds (8) Finance Companies (9) Mortgage Companies (10) Mutual Funds (11) Closed End Funds (12) Money Market Mutual Funds (13) Real Estate Investment Trusts (14) Security Brokers and Dealers (15) Issuers of Asset Backed Securities (ABSs) (16) Bank Personal Trusts
4. Foreign (r)	4. Foreign (R)
5. Fed. Gov. (g)	5a. U.S. Government (US) 5b. Government-Sponsored Enterprises 5c. Federally Related Mortgage Pools 5d. Monetary Authority (MA)
6. S & L Gov. (s)	6. State and Local Governments General Funds (S)

Table A.2

The Variables in the US Model in Alphabetical Order

Variable	Eq.	Description
AA	89	Total net wealth, h, B87$.
AB	73	Net financial assets, b, B$.
AF	70	Net financial assets, f, B$.
AG	77	Net financial assets, g, B$.
$AG1$	Exog.	Percent of 16+ population 26–55 minus percent 16–25.
$AG2$	Exog.	Percent of 16+ population 56–65 minus percent 16–25.
$AG3$	Exog.	Percent of 16+ population 66+ minus percent 16–25.
AH	66	Net financial assets, h, B$.
AR	75	Net financial assets, r, B$.
AS	79	Net financial assets, s, B$.
BF	55	Estimated long term bond issues in the current period, f, B$.
BG	56	Estimated long term bond issues in the current period, g, B$.
BO	22	Bank borrowing from the Fed, B$.
BR	57	Total bank reserves, B$.
CCB	Exog.	Capital consumption, b, B87$.
CCF	21	Capital consumption, f, B$.
CCH	Exog.	Capital consumption, h, B$.
CD	3	Consumer expenditures for durable goods, B87$.
CDA	Exog.	Peak to peak interpolation of CD/POP.
CF	68	Cash flow, f, B$.
CG	25	Capital gains (+) or losses (−) on corporate stocks held by the household sector, B$.
CN	2	Consumer expenditures for nondurable goods, B87$.
COG	Exog.	Purchases of goods, g, B87$.
COS	Exog.	Purchases of goods, s, B87$.
CS	1	Consumer expenditures for services, B87$.
CUR	26	Currency held outside banks, B$.
$D1G$	Exog.	Personal income tax parameter, g.
$D1GM$	90	Marginal personal income tax rate, g.
$D1S$	Exog.	Personal income tax parameter, s.
$D1SM$	91	Marginal personal income tax rate, s.
$D2G$	Exog.	Profit tax rate, g.
$D2S$	Exog.	Profit tax rate, s.
$D3G$	Exog.	Indirect business tax rate, g.
$D3S$	Exog.	Indirect business tax rate, s.
$D4G$	Exog.	Employee social security tax rate, g.
$D5G$	Exog.	Employer social security tax rate, g.
$D691$	Exog.	1 in 1969:1; 0 otherwise.
$D692$	Exog.	1 in 1969:2; 0 otherwise.
$D714$	Exog.	1 in 1971:4; 0 otherwise.
$D721$	Exog.	1 in 1972:1; 0 otherwise.
$D794823$	Exog.	1 from 1979:4 through 1982:3; 0 otherwise.
$D811824$	Exog.	1 from 1981:1 through 1982:4; 0 otherwise.

$D831834$	Exog.	1 from 1983:1 through 1983:4; 0 otherwise.
DB	Exog.	Dividends paid, b, B$.
$DD772$	Exog.	1 from 1977:2 on; 0 otherwise.
$DELD$	Exog.	Physical depreciation rate of the stock of durable goods, rate per quarter.
$DELH$	Exog.	Physical depreciation rate of the stock of housing, rate per quarter.
$DELK$	Exog.	Physical depreciation rate of the stock of capital, rate per quarter.
DF	18	Dividends paid, f, B$.
$DISB$	Exog.	Discrepancy for b, B$.
$DISBA$	Exog.	Discrepancy between NIPA and FFA data on capital consumption, nonfinancial corporate business, B$.
$DISF$	Exog.	Discrepancy for f, B$.
$DISG$	Exog.	Discrepancy for g, B$.
$DISH$	Exog.	Discrepancy for h, B$.
$DISR$	Exog.	Discrepancy for r, B$.
$DISS$	Exog.	Discrepancy for s, B$.
DRS	Exog.	Dividends received by s, B$.
E	85	Total employment, civilian and military, millions.
EX	Exog.	Exports, B87$.
$EXPG$	106	Total expenditures, g, B$.
$EXPS$	113	Total expenditures, s, B$.
FA	Exog.	Farm gross product, B87$.
$FIROW$	Exog.	Payments of factor income to the rest of the world, B$.
$FIROWD$	Exog.	$FIROW$ deflator.
$FIUS$	Exog.	Receipts of factor income from the rest of the world, B$.
$FIUSD$	Exog.	$FIUS$ deflator.
$G1$	Exog.	Reserve requirement ratio.
GDP	82	Gross Domestic Product, B$.
$GDPD$	84	GDP chain price index.
$GDPR$	83	Gross Domestic Product, B87$.
GNP	129	Gross National Product, B$.
$GNPD$	131	GNP chain price index.
$GNPR$	130	Gross National Product, B87$.
HF	14	Average number of hours paid per job, f, hours per quarter.
HFF	100	Deviation of HF from its peak to peak interpolation.
HFS	Exog.	Peak to peak interpolation of HF.
HG	Exog.	Average number of hours paid per civilian job, g, hours per quarter.
HM	Exog.	Average number of hours paid per military job, g, hours per quarter.
HN	62	Average number of non overtime hours paid per job, f, hours per quarter.
HO	15	Average number of overtime hours paid per job, f, hours per quarter.
HS	Exog.	Average number of hours paid per job, s, hours per quarter.
$IBTG$	51	Indirect business taxes, g, B$.
$IBTS$	52	Indirect business taxes, s, B$.
IHB	Exog.	Residential investment, b, B87$.
IHF	Exog.	Residential investment, f, B87$.
IHH	4	Residential investment, h, B87$.
$IHHA$	Exog.	Peak to peak interpolation of IHH/POP.
IKB	Exog.	Nonresidential fixed investment, b, B87$.

IKF	12	Nonresidential fixed investment, f, B87$.
IKFA	Exog.	Peak to peak interpolation of *IKF*.
IKG	Exog.	Nonresidential fixed investment, g, B87$.
IKH	Exog.	Nonresidential fixed investment, h, B87$.
IM	27	Imports, B87$.
INS	Exog.	Insurance credits to households from g, B$.
INTF	19	Net interest payments, f, B$.
INTG	29	Net interest payments, g, B$.
INTOTH	Exog.	Net interest payments, sole proprietorships and partnerships and other private business, B$.
INTROW	88	Net interest receipts, r, B$.
INTS	Exog.	Net interest payments, s, B$.
IVA	20	Inventory valuation adjustment, B$.
IVF	117	Inventory investment, f, B87$.
IVH	Exog.	Inventory investment, h, B87$.
IVVH	Exog.	Inventory investment, h, B$.
JF	13	Number of jobs, f, millions.
JG	Exog.	Number of civilian jobs, g, millions.
JHMIN	94	Number of worker hours required to produce Y, millions.
JJ	95	Ratio of the total number of worker hours paid for to the total population 16 and over.
JJP	Exog.	Potential value of *JJ*.
JJS	96	Ratio of actual to potential *JJ*.
JM	Exog.	Number of military jobs, g, millions.
JS	Exog.	Number of jobs, s, millions.
KD	58	Stock of durable goods, B87$.
KH	59	Stock of housing, h, B87$.
KK	92	Stock of capital, f, B87$.
KKMIN	93	Amount of capital required to produce Y, B87$.
*L*1	5	Labor force of men 25–54, millions.
*L*2	6	Labor force of women 25–54, millions.
*L*3	7	Labor force of all others, 16+, millions.
LAM	Exog.	Amount of output capable of being produced per worker hour.
LM	8	Number of "moonlighters": difference between the total number of jobs (establishment data) and the total number of people employed (household survey data), millions.
*M*1	81	Money supply, end of quarter, B$.
MB	71	Net demand deposits and currency, b, B$.
MDIF	Exog.	Net increase in demand deposits and currency of banks in U.S. possessions plus change in demand deposits and currency of private nonbank financial institutions plus change in demand deposits and currency of federally sponsored credit agencies and mortgage pools minus mail float, U.S. government, B$.
MF	17	Demand deposits and currency, f, B$.
MG	Exog.	Demand deposits and currency, g, B$.
MH	9	Demand deposits and currency, h, B$.
MR	Exog.	Demand deposits and currency, r, B$.
MRS	Exog.	Mineral rights sales, B$.

MS	Exog.	Demand deposits and currency, s, B$.
MUH	Exog.	Amount of output capable of being produced per unit of capital.
$P2554$	Exog.	Percent of 16+ population 25–54.
PCD	37	Price deflator for CD.
$PCGDPD$	122	Percentage change in $GDPD$, annual rate, percentage points.
$PCGDPR$	123	Percentage change in $GDPR$, annual rate, percentage points.
$PCM1$	124	Percentage change in $M1$, annual rate, percentage points.
PCN	36	Price deflator for CN.
PCS	35	Price deflator for CS.
PD	33	Price deflator for $X - EX + IM$ (domestic sales).
PEX	32	Price deflator for EX.
PF	10	Price deflator for $X - FA$.
PFA	Exog.	Price deflator for FA.
PG	40	Price deflator for COG.
PH	34	Price deflator for $CS + CN + CD + IHH$ inclusive of indirect business taxes.
$PIEB$	Exog.	Before tax profits, b, B87$.
$PIEF$	67	Before tax profits, f, B$.
$PIEH$	Exog.	Before tax profits, h, B$.
PIH	38	Price deflator for residential investment.
PIK	39	Price deflator for nonresidential fixed investment.
PIM	Exog.	Price deflator for IM.
PIV	42	Price deflator for inventory investment, adjusted.
POP	120	Noninstitutional population 16+, millions.
$POP1$	Exog.	Noninstitutional population of men 25–54, millions.
$POP2$	Exog.	Noninstitutional population of women 25–54, millions.
$POP3$	Exog.	Noninstitutional population of all others, 16+, millions.
$PROD$	118	Output per paid for worker hour ("productivity").
PS	41	Price deflator for COS.
$PSI1$	Exog.	Ratio of PEX to PX.
$PSI2$	Exog.	Ratio of PCS to $(1 + D3G + D3S)PD$.
$PSI3$	Exog.	Ratio of PCN to $(1 + D3G + D3S)PD$.
$PSI4$	Exog.	Ratio of PCD to $(1 + D3G + D3S)PD$.
$PSI5$	Exog.	Ratio of PIH to PD.
$PSI6$	Exog.	Ratio of PIK to PD.
$PSI7$	Exog.	Ratio of PG to PD.
$PSI8$	Exog.	Ratio of PS to PD.
$PSI9$	Exog.	Ratio of PIV to PD.
$PSI10$	Exog.	Ratio of WG to WF.
$PSI11$	Exog.	Ratio of WM to WF.
$PSI12$	Exog.	Ratio of WS to WF.
$PSI13$	Exog.	Ratio of gross product of g and s to total employee hours of g and s.
$PSI14$	Exog.	Ratio of $INTROW$ to $INTF + INTG$.
PUG	104	Purchases of goods and services, g, B$.
PUS	110	Purchases of goods and services, s, B$.
PX	31	Price deflator for X.
Q	Exog.	Gold and foreign exchange, g, B$.
RB	23	Bond rate, percentage points.

RD	Exog.	Discount rate, percentage points.
$RECG$	105	Total receipts, g, B$.
$RECS$	112	Total receipts, s, B$.
RET	Exog.	Retirement credits to households from s, B$.
RM	24	Mortgage rate, percentage points.
RMA	128	After tax mortgage rate, percentage points.
RNT	Exog.	Rental income, h, B$.
RS	30	Three month Treasury bill rate, percentage points.
RSA	130	After tax bill rate, percentage points.
SB	72	Saving, b, B$.
SF	69	Saving, f, B$.
SG	76	Saving, g, B$.
SGP	107	NIA surplus (+) or deficit (−), g, B$.
SH	65	Saving, h, B$.
$SHRPIE$	121	Ratio of after tax profits to the wage bill net of employer social security taxes.
$SIFG$	54	Employer social insurance contributions, f to g, B$.
$SIFS$	Exog.	Employer social insurance contributions, f to s, B$.
SIG	103	Total employer and employee social insurance contributions to g, B$.
$SIGG$	Exog.	Employer social insurance contributions, g to g, B$.
$SIHG$	53	Employee social insurance contributions, h to g, B$.
$SIHS$	Exog.	Employee social insurance contributions, h to s, B$.
SIS	109	Total employer and employee social insurance contributions to s, B$.
$SISS$	Exog.	Employer social insurance contributions, s to s, B$.
SR	74	Saving, r, B$.
SRZ	116	Saving rate, h.
SS	78	Saving, s, B$.
SSP	114	NIA surplus (+) or deficit (−), s, B$.
$STAT$	Exog.	Statistical discrepancy, B$.
$STATP$	Exog.	Statistical discrepancy relating to the use of chain type price indices, B87$.
$SUBG$	Exog.	Subsidies less current surplus of government enterprises, g, B$.
$SUBS$	Exog.	Subsidies less current surplus of government enterprises, s, B$.
SUR	Exog.	Current surplus of federally sponsored credit agencies and mortgage pools and of the monetary authority, B$.
T	Exog.	1 in 1952:1, 2 in 1952:2, etc.
$TAUG$	Exog.	Progressivity tax parameter in personal income tax equation for g.
$TAUS$	Exog.	Progressivity tax parameter in personal income tax equation for s.
TBG	Exog.	Corporate profit taxes, b to g, B$.
TBS	Exog.	Corporate profit taxes, b to s, B$.
TCG	102	Corporate profit tax receipts, g, B$.
TCS	108	Corporate profit tax receipts, s, B$.
TFA	Exog.	Farm taxes, B$.
TFG	49	Corporate profit taxes, f to g, B$.
TFS	50	Corporate profit taxes, f to s, B$.
THG	47	Personal income taxes, h to g, B$.
THS	48	Personal income taxes, h to s, B$.
TI	Exog.	0 through 1981:2, 1 in 1981:3, 2 in 1981:4, . . . ,40 in 1991:2 and thereafter.

T PG	101	Personal income tax receipts, g, B$.
T RF H	Exog.	Transfer payments, f to h, B$.
T RF R	Exog.	Transfer payments, f to r, B$.
T RGH	Exog.	Transfer payments, g to h, B$.
T RGR	Exog.	Transfer payments, g to r, B$.
T RGS	Exog.	Transfer payments, g to s, B$.
T RHR	Exog.	Transfer payments, h to r, B$.
T RRSH	111	Total transfer payments, s to h, B$.
T RSH	Exog.	Transfer payments, s to h, excluding unemployment insurance benefits, B$.
T XCR	Exog.	Dummy variable for the investment tax credit.
U	86	Number of people unemployed, millions.
U B	28	Unemployment insurance benefits, B$.
U BR	128	Unborrowed reserves, B$.
U R	87	Civilian unemployment rate.
V	63	Stock of inventories, f, B87$.
WA	126	After tax wage rate. (Includes supplements to wages and salaries except employer contributions for social insurance.)
WF	16	Average hourly earnings excluding overtime of workers in f. (Includes supplements to wages and salaries except employer contributions for social insurance.)
WG	44	Average hourly earnings of civilian workers in g. (Includes supplements to wages and salaries including employer contributions for social insurance.)
WH	43	Average hourly earnings excluding overtime of all workers. (Includes supplements to wages and salaries except employer contributions for social insurance.)
WLDG	Exog.	Wage accruals less disbursements, g, B$.
WLDS	Exog.	Wage accruals less disbursements, s, B$.
WM	45	Average hourly earnings of military workers. (Includes supplements to wages and salaries including employer contributions for social insurance.)
WR	119	Real wage rate of workers in f. (Includes supplements to wages and salaries except employer contributions for social insurance.)
WS	46	Average hourly earnings of workers in s. (Includes supplements to wages and salaries including employer contributions for social insurance.)
X	60	Total sales f, B87$.
XX	61	Total sales, f, B$.
Y	11	Production, f, B87$.
YD	115	Disposable income, h, B$.
YNL	99	After tax nonlabor income, h, B$.
YS	98	Potential output of the firm sector.
YT	64	Taxable income, h, B$.
Z	97	Labor constraint variable.

B$ = Billions of dollars,   B87$ = Billions of 1987 dollars.

Table A.3

The Equations of the US Model

STOCHASTIC EQUATIONS

LHS Var.	Explanatory Variables

Household Sector

1. $\log(CS/POP)$

cnst, $AG1$, $AG2$, $AG3$, $\log(CS/POP)_{-1}$, $\log[YD/(POP \cdot PH)]$, RSA
[Consumer expenditures: services]

2. $\log(CN/POP)$

cnst, $AG1$, $AG2$, $AG3$, $\log(CN/POP)_{-1}$, $\Delta \log(CN/POP)_{-1}$,
$\log(AA/POP)_{-1}$, $\log[YD/(POP \cdot PH)]$, RMA
[Consumer expenditures: nondurables]

3. CD/POP

cnst, $AG1$, $AG2$, $AG3$, $(CD/POP)_{-1}$, $(KD/POP)_{-1}$, $YD/(POP \cdot PH)$,
$RMA \cdot CDA$
[Consumer expenditures: durables]

4. IHH/POP

cnst, $(IHH/POP)_{-1}$, $(KH/POP)_{-1}$, $(AA/POP)_{-1}$, $YD/(POP \cdot PH)$,
$RMA_{-1} \cdot IHHA$, $RHO = 2$
[Residential investment—h]

5. $\log(L1/POP1)$

cnst, $\log(L1/POP1)_{-1}$, $\log(WA/PH)$, Z, T
[Labor force—men 25–54]

6. $\log(L2/POP2)$

cnst, $\log(L2/POP2)_{-1}$, $\log(WA/PH)$, Z
[Labor force—women 25–54]

7. $\log(L3/POP3)$

cnst, $\log(L3/POP1)_{-1}$, $\log(WA/PH)$, Z, $\log(AA/POP)_{-1}$, T
[Labor force—all others 16+]

8. $\log(LM/POP)$

cnst, $\log(LM/POP)_{-1}$, $\log(WA/PH)$, Z
[Number of moonlighters]

9. $\log(MH/(POP \cdot PH)$

cnst, $AG1$, $AG2$, $AG3$, $\log[MH_{-1}/(POP_{-1} \cdot PH)]$, $\log[YD/(POP \cdot PH)]$,
RSA, $RHO = 1$
[Demand deposits and currency—h]

Firm Sector

10. $\log PF$

$\log PF_{-1}$, $\log[WF(1 + D5G)]$, cnst, $\log PIM$, $\log[(YS - Y)/YS + .04]_{-1}$,
$RHO = 1$
[Price deflator for $X - FA$]

11. Y

cnst, Y_{-1}, X, V_{-1}, $RHO = 3$
[Production—f]

12. ΔIKF

$(KK - KKMIN)_{-1}$, $IKF_{-1} - DELK \cdot KK_{-1}$, ΔY, ΔY_{-1}, ΔY_{-2}, ΔY_{-3},
ΔY_{-4}, $TXCR \cdot IKFA$, $RB'_{-3} \cdot IKFA$
[Nonresidential fixed investment—f]

13. $\Delta \log JF$

  cnst, $DD772$, $\log(JF/JHMIN)_{-1}$, $DD772 \cdot \log(JF/JHMIN)_{-1}$,
  $\Delta \log JF_{-1}$, $DD772 \cdot \Delta \log JF_{-1}$, T, $DD772 \cdot T$, $\Delta \log Y$
  [Number of jobs—f]

14. $\Delta \log HF$

  cnst, $\log HF_{-1}$, $\log(JF/JHMIN)_{-1}$, T, $\Delta \log Y$, $RHO = 1$
  [Average number of hours paid per job—f]

15. $\log HO$

  cnst, HFF, HFF_{-1}, $RHO = 1$
  [Average number of overtime hours paid per job—f]

16. $\log WF$

  $\log WF_{-1}$, $\log PF$, $\log WF_{-2}$, $\log WF_{-3}$, $\log WF_{-4}$, cnst, T,
  $\log PF_{-1}$, $\log PF_{-2}$, $\log PF_{-3}$, $\log PF_{-4}$, $RHO = 1$
  [Average hourly earnings excluding overtime—f]

17. $\log(MF/PF)$

  cnst, T, $\log(MF_{-1}/PF)$, $\log(X - FA)$, $RS(1 - D2G - D2S)$
  [Demand deposits and currency—f]

18. $\Delta \log DF$

  $\log[(PIEF - TFG - TFS)/DF_{-1}]$
  [Dividends paid—f]

19. $INTF$

  $.41 \cdot TI + \sum_{i=-39}^{0}(\frac{1}{400})RB_i BF_i + (\frac{1}{400})RS \cdot .60 \cdot |AF|$
  [Interest payments—f]

20. IVA

  cnst, $(PX - PX_{-1})V_{-1}$, $RHO = 1$
  [Inventory valuation adjustment]

21. $\Delta \log CCF$

  $\log[(PIK \cdot IKF)/CCF_{-1}]$, $D811824$, $D831834$
  [Capital consumption—f]

Financial Sector

22. BO/BR

  cnst, $(BO/BR)_{-1}$, RS, RD
  [Bank borrowing from the Fed]

23. $RB - RS_{-2}$

  cnst, $RB_{-1} - RS_{-2}$, $RS - RS_{-2}$, $RS_{-1} - RS_{-2}$, $RHO = 1$
  [Bond rate]

24. $RM - RS_{-2}$

  cnst, $RM_{-1} - RS_{-2}$, $RS - RS_{-2}$, $RS_{-1} - RS_{-2}$
  [Mortgage rate]

25. CG

  cnst, ΔRB, $\Delta(CF - TFG - TFS)$
  [Capital gains or losses on corporate stocks held by h]

26. $\log[CUR/(POP \cdot PF)]$

  cnst, $\log[CUR_{-1}/(POP_{-1} \cdot PF)]$, $\log[(X - FA)/POP]$, RSA,
  $RHO = 1$
  [Currency held outside banks]

Import Equation

27. $\log(IM/POP)$

cnst, $\log(IM/POP)_{-1}$, $\log[YD/(POP \cdot PH)]$, $\log(PF/PIM)$, RMA_{-1}, $D691$, $D692$, $D714$, $D721$

[Imports]

Government Sectors

28. $\log UB$

cnst, $\log UB_{-1}$, $\log U$, $\log WF$, $RHO = 1$

[Unemployment insurance benefits]

29. $INTG$

$$\sum_{i=-15}^{0} (\tfrac{1}{400})(RB_i - .4)BG_i + (\tfrac{1}{400})RS \cdot .34 \cdot |AG|$$

[Interest payments—g]

30. RS

cnst, RS_{-1}, $100[(PD/PD_{-1})^4 - 1]$, JJS, $PCGDPR$, $PCM1_{-1}$, $D794823 \cdot PCM1_{-1}$, ΔRS_{-1}, ΔRS_{-2}

[Three month Treasury bill rate]

IDENTITIES

31. $PX =$ $[PF(X - FA) + PFA \cdot FA]/X$

[Price deflator for X]

32. $PEX =$ $PSI1 \cdot PX$

[Price deflator for EX]

33. $PD =$ $(PX \cdot X - PEX \cdot EX + PIM \cdot IM)/(X - EX + IM)$

[Price deflator for domestic sales]

34. $PH =$ $(PCS \cdot CS + PCN \cdot CN + PCD \cdot CD + PIH \cdot IHH + IBTG + IBTS)/(CS + CN + CD + IHH)$

[Price deflator for $(CS + CN + CD + IHH)$ inclusive of indirect business taxes]

35. $PCS =$ $PSI2(1 + D3G + D3S)PD$

[Price deflator for CS]

36. $PCN =$ $PSI3(1 + D3G + D3S)PD$

[Price deflator for CN]

37. $PCD =$ $PSI4(1 + D3G + D3S)PD$

[Price deflator for CD]

38. $PIH =$ $PSI5 \cdot PD$

[Price deflator for residential investment]

39. $PIK =$ $PSI6 \cdot PD$

[Price deflator for nonresidential fixed investment]

40. $PG =$ $PSI7 \cdot PD$

[Price deflator for COG]

41. $PS =$ $PSI8 \cdot PD$

[Price deflator for COS]

42. $PIV =$ $PSI9 \cdot PD$

[Price deflator for inventory investment]

43. $WH =$ $100[(WF \cdot JF(HN + 1.5 \cdot HO) + WG \cdot JG \cdot HG + WM \cdot JM \cdot HM + WS \cdot JS \cdot HS - SIGG - SISS)/(JF(HN + 1.5 \cdot HO) + JG \cdot HG + JM \cdot HM + JS \cdot HS)]$

[Average hourly earnings excluding overtime of all workers]

44. $WG =$ $PSI10 \cdot WF$

[Average hourly earnings of civilian workers—g]

45. $WM =$ $PSI11 \cdot WF$
[Average hourly earnings of military workers]

46. $WS =$ $PSI12 \cdot WF$
[Average hourly earnings of workers—s]

47. $THG =$ $[D1G + ((TAUG \cdot YT)/POP)]YT$
[Personal income taxes—h to g]

48. $THS =$ $[D1S + ((TAUS \cdot YT)/POP)]YT$
[Personal income taxes—h to s]

49. $TFG =$ $D2G(PIEF - TFS)$
[Corporate profits taxes—f to g]

50. $TFS =$ $D2S \cdot PIEF$
[Corporate profits taxes—f to s]

51. $IBTG =$ $[D3G/(1 + D3G)](PCS \cdot CS + PCN \cdot CN + PCD \cdot CD - IBTS)$
[Indirect business taxes—g]

52. $IBTS =$ $[D3S/(1 + D3S)](PCS \cdot CS + PCN \cdot CN + PCD \cdot CD - IBTG)$
[Indirect business taxes—s]

53. $SIHG =$ $D4G[WF \cdot JF(HN + 1.5 \cdot HO)]$
[Employee social insurance contributions—h to g]

54. $SIFG =$ $D5G[WF \cdot JF(HN + 1.5 \cdot HO)]$
[Employer social insurance contributions—f to g]

55. BF $-.40(AF - AF_{-1}) + BF_{-40}$
[Estimated long term bond issues in the current period, f]

56. BG $-.66(AG - AG_{-1}) + BG_{-16}$
[Estimated long term bond issues in the current period, g]

57. $BR =$ $-G1 \cdot MB$
[Total bank reserves]

58. $KD =$ $(1 - DELD)KD_{-1} + CD$
[Stock of durable goods]

59. $KH =$ $(1 - DELH)KH_{-1} + IHH$
[Stock of housing—h]

60. $X =$ $CS + CN + CD + IHH + IKF + EX - IM + COG + COS + IKH + IKB + IKG + IHF + IHB + IVH - PIEB - CCB$
[Total sales—f]

61. $XX =$ $PCS \cdot CS + PCN \cdot CN + PCD \cdot CD + PIH \cdot IHH + PIK \cdot IKF + PEX \cdot EX - PIM \cdot IM + PG \cdot COG + PS \cdot COS + PIK(IKH + IKB + IKG) + PIH(IHF + IHB) + IVVH - PX(PIEB + CCB) - IBTG - IBTS$
[Total nominal sales—f]

62. $HN =$ $HF - HO$
[Average number of non overtime hours paid per job—f]

63. $V =$ $V_{-1} + Y - X$
[Stock of inventories—f]

64. $YT =$ $WF \cdot JF(HN + 1.5 \cdot HO) + WG \cdot JG \cdot HG + WM \cdot JM \cdot HM + WS \cdot JS \cdot HS + DF + DB - DRS + INTF + INTG + INTS + INTOTH - INTROW + RNT + TRFH + PIEH - SIGG - SISS$
[Taxable income—h]

65. $SH =$ $YT + CCH - PCS \cdot CS - PCN \cdot CN - PCD \cdot CD - PIH \cdot IHH - PIK \cdot$
$IKH - IVVH - TRHR - THG - SIHG + TRGH - THS - SIHS +$
$TRSH + UB + INS + RET$
[Saving—h]

66. $0 =$ $SH - \Delta AH - \Delta MH + CG - DISH$
[Budget constraint—h; (determines AH)]

67. $PIEF =$ $XX + PIV(V - V_{-1}) - WF \cdot JF(HN + 1.5 \cdot HO) - RNT - TRFH - TRFR -$
$PIEH - CCH + SUBG + SUBS - INTF - INTOTH + INTROW -$
$CCF - IVA - STAT - SIFG - SIFS + FIUS - FIROW$
[Before tax profits—f]

68. $CF =$ $XX - WF \cdot JF(HN + 1.5 \cdot HO) - RNT - TRFH - TRFR - PIEH -$
$CCH + SUBG + SUBS - INTF - INTOTH + INTROW - PIK \cdot IKF -$
$PIH \cdot IHF - MRS - SIFG - SIFS + FIUS - FIROW$
[Cash flow—f]

69. $SF =$ $CF - TFG - TFS - DF$
[Saving—f]

70. $0 =$ $SF - \Delta AF - \Delta MF - DISF - STAT + DISBA$
[Budget constraint—f; (determines AF)]

71. $0 =$ $\Delta MB + \Delta MH + \Delta MF + \Delta MR + \Delta MG + \Delta MS - \Delta CUR$
[Demand deposit identity; (determines MB)]

72. $SB =$ $PX(PIEB + CCB) - PIK \cdot IKB - PIH \cdot IHB - DB - TBG - TBS - SUR$
[Saving—b]

73. $0 =$ $SB - \Delta AB - \Delta MB - \Delta(BR - BO) - DISB - DISBA$
[Budget constraint—b; (determines AB)]

74. $SR =$ $PIM \cdot IM + TRHR + TRGR + TRFR - PEX \cdot EX + FIROW - FIUS$
[Saving—r]

75. $0 =$ $SR - \Delta AR - \Delta MR + \Delta Q - DISR$
[Budget constraint—r; (determines AR)]

76. $SG =$ $THG + IBTG + TFG + TBG + SUR + SIHG + SIFG + MRS - PG \cdot$
$COG - WG \cdot JG \cdot HG - WM \cdot JM \cdot HM - INTG - TRGR - TRGH -$
$TRGS - SUBG - INS + SIGG - PIK \cdot IKG$
[Saving—g]

77. $0 =$ $SG - \Delta AG - \Delta MG + \Delta CUR + \Delta(BR - BO) - \Delta Q - DISG$
[Budget constraint—g; (determines AG unless AG is exogenous)]

78. $SS =$ $THS + IBTS + TFS + TBS + SIHS + SIFS + TRGS + DRS - PS \cdot$
$COS - WS \cdot JS \cdot HS - INTS - SUBS - TRSH - UB - RET + SISS$
[Saving—s]

79. $0 =$ $SS - \Delta AS - \Delta MS - DISS$
[Budget constraint—s; (determines AS)]

80. $0 =$ $\Delta AH + \Delta AF + \Delta AB + \Delta AG + \Delta AS + \Delta AR - CG + DISH + DISF +$
$DISB + DISG + DISS + DISR + STAT$
[Asset identity (redundant equation)]

81. $M1 =$ $M1_{-1} + \Delta MH + \Delta MF + \Delta MR + \Delta MS + MDIF$
[Money supply]

82. $GDP =$ $XX + PIV(V - V_{-1}) + IBTG + IBTS + WG \cdot JG \cdot HG + WM \cdot JM \cdot$
$HM + WS \cdot JS \cdot HS + WLDG + WLDS + PX(PIEB + CCB)$
[Nominal GDP]

83. $GDPR =$ $Y + PIEB + CCB + PSI13(JG \cdot HG + JM \cdot HM + JS \cdot HS) + STATP$
[Real GDP]

84. $GDPD =$ $GDP/GDPR$
[GDP chain price index]

85. $E =$ $JF + JG + JM + JS - LM$
[Total employment, civilian and military]

86. $U =$ $L1 + L2 + L3 - E$
[Number of people unemployed]

87. $UR =$ $U/(L1 + L2 + L3 - JM)$
[Civilian unemployment rate]

88. $INTROW =$ $PSI14(INTF + INTG)$
[Net interest receipts—r]

89. $AA =$ $(AH + MH)/PH + KH$
[Total net wealth—h]

90. $D1GM =$ $D1G + (2 \cdot TAUG \cdot YT)/POP$
[Marginal personal income tax rate—g]

91. $D1SM =$ $D1S + (2 \cdot TAUS \cdot YT)/POP$
[Marginal personal income tax rate—s]

92. $KK =$ $(1 - DELK)KK_{-1} + IKF$
[Stock of capital—f]

93. $KKMIN =$ Y/MUH
[Amount of capital required to produce Y]

94. $JHMIN =$ Y/LAM
[Number of worker hours required to produce Y]

95. $JJ =$ $(JF \cdot HF + JG \cdot HG + JM \cdot HM + JS \cdot HS)/POP$
[Ratio of the total number of worker hours paid for to the total population 16 and over]

96. $JJS =$ JJ/JJP
[Ratio of actual to potential JJ]

97. $Z =$ $\min(0, 1 - JJP/JJ)$
[Labor constraint variable]

98. $YS =$ $LAM(JJP \cdot POP - JG \cdot HG - JM \cdot HM - JS \cdot HS)$
[Potential output of the firm sector]

99. $YNL =$ $[1 - D1G - D1S - (TAUG + TAUS)(YT/POP)](RNT + DF + DB - DRS + INTF + INTG + INTS + INTOTH - INTROW + TRFH + PIEH) + TRGH + TRSH + UB$
[After-tax nonlabor income—h]

100. $HFF =$ $HF - HFS$
[Deviation of HF from its peak to peak interpolation]

101. $TPG =$ $THG - TFA$
[Personal income tax receipts—g]

102. $TCG =$ $TFG + TFA + TBG$
[Corporate profit tax receipts—g]

103. $SIG =$ $SIHG + SIFG + SIGG$
[Total social insurance contributions to g]

104. $PUG =$ $PG \cdot COG + WG \cdot JG \cdot HG + WM \cdot JM \cdot HM + WLDG$
[Purchases of goods and services—g]

105. $RECG =$ $TPG + TCG + IBTG + SIG$
[Total receipts—g]

106. $EXPG =$ $PUG + TRGH + TRGR + TRGS + INTG + SUBG - WLDG$
[Total expenditures—g]

107. $SGP =$ $RECG - EXPG$
[NIPA surplus or deficit—g]

108. $TCS =$ $TFS + TBS$
[Corporate profit tax receipts—s]

109. $SIS =$ $SIHS + SIFS + SISS$
[Total social insurance contributions to s]

110. $PUS =$ $PS \cdot COS + WS \cdot JS \cdot HS + WLDS$
[Purchases of goods and services—s]

111. $TRRSH =$ $TRSH + UB$
[Total transfer payments—s to h]

112. $RECS =$ $THS + TCS + IBTS + SIS + TRGS$
[Total receipts—s]

113. $EXPS =$ $PUS + TRRSH + INTS - DRS + SUBS - WLDS$
[Total expenditures—s]

114. $SSP =$ $RECS - EXPS$
[NIPA surplus or deficit—s]

115. $YD =$ $WF \cdot JF(HN + 1.5 \cdot HO) + WG \cdot JG \cdot HG + WM \cdot JM \cdot HM + WS \cdot JS \cdot HS + RNT + DF + DB - DRS + INTF + INTG + INTS + INTOTH - INTROW + TRFH + TRGH + TRSH + UB - SIHG - SIHS - THG + TFA - THS - TRHR - SIGG - SISS$
[Disposable income—h]

116. $SRZ =$ $(YD - PCS \cdot CS - PCN \cdot CN - PCD \cdot CD)/YD$
[Saving rate—h]

117. $IVF =$ $V - V_{-1}$
[Inventory investment—f]

118. $PROD =$ $Y/(JF \cdot HF)$
[Output per paid for worker hour: "productivity"]

119. $WR =$ WF/PF
[Real wage rate of workers in f]

120. $POP =$ $POP1 + POP2 + POP3$
[Noninstitutional population 16 and over]

121. $SHRPIE =$ $[(1 - D2G - D2S)PIEF]/[WF \cdot JF(HN + 1.5 \cdot HO)]$
[Ratio of after tax profits to the wage bill net of employer social security taxes]

122. $PCGDPR =$ $100[(GDPR/GDPR_{-1})^4 - 1]$
[Percentage change in $GDPR$]

123. $PCGDPD =$ $100[(GDPD/GDPD_{-1})^4 - 1]$
[Percentage change in $GDPD$]

124. $PCM1 =$ $100[(M1/M1_{-1})^4 - 1]$
[Percentage change in $M1$]

125. $UBR =$ $BR - BO$
[Unborrowed reserves]

126. $WA =$ $100[(1 - D1GM - D1SM - D4G)[WF \cdot JF(HN + 1.5 \cdot HO)] + (1 - D1GM - D1SM)(WG \cdot JG \cdot HG + WM \cdot JM \cdot HM + WS \cdot JS \cdot HS - SIGG - SISS)]/[JF(HN + 1.5 \cdot HO) + JG \cdot HG + JM \cdot HM + JS \cdot HS]$
[After tax wage rate]

127. $RSA =$ $RS(1 - D1GM - D1SM)$
[After tax bill rate]

128. $RMA =$ $RM(1 - D1GM - D1SM)$
[After tax mortgage rate]

129. $GNP =$ $GDP + FIUS - FIROW$
[Nominal GNP]

130. $GNPR =$ $GDPR + FIUS/FIUSD - FIROW/FIROWD$
[Real GNP]

131. $GNPD =$ $GNP/GNPR$
[GNP chain price index]

Sector definitions:

b = financial sector
f = firm sector
g = federal government sector
h = household sector
r = foreign sector
s = state and local government sector

Table A.4

The Raw Data Variables for the US Model

NIPA Data from the Survey of Current Business

Real variables are in 1987 dollars

Variable	Table	Line	Description
R1 GDP	1.1	1	Gross Domestic Product
R2 CDZ	1.1	3	Personal Consumption Expenditures, Durable Goods
R3 CNZ	1.1	4	Personal Consumption Expenditures, Nondurable Goods
R4 CSZ	1.1	5	Personal Consumption Expenditures, Services
R5 IKZ	1.1	8	Nonresidential Fixed Investment
R6 IHZ	1.1	11	Residential Fixed Investment
R7 IVZ	1.1	12	Change in Business Inventories
R8 $IVFAZ$	1.1	14	Change in Farm Business Inventories
R9 EXZ	1.1	16	Exports
R10 IMZ	1.1	17	Imports
R11 $GDPR$ or GDP/PYA	1.2	1	Real Gross Domestic Product
R12 CD or $CDZ/PCDA$	1.2	3	Real Personal Consumption Expenditures, Durable Goods
R13 CN or $CNZ/PCNA$	1.2	4	Real Personal Consumption Expenditures, Nondurable Goods
R14 CS or $CSZ/PCSA$	1.2	5	Real Personal Consumption Expenditures, Services
R15 IK or $IKZ/PIKA$	1.2	8	Real Nonresidential Fixed Investment
R16 IH or $IHZ/PIHA$	1.2	11	Real Residential Fixed Investment
R17 IV	1.2	12	Real Change in Business Inventories
R18 $IVFA$	1.2	14	Real Change in Farm Business Inventories
R19 EX or $EXZ/PEXA$	1.2	16	Real Exports
R20 IM or $IMZ/PIMA$	1.2	17	Real Imports
R21 $PURG$ or $PURGZ/PGA$	1.2	19	Real Federal Government Purchases
R22 $PURS$ or $PURSZ/PSA$	1.2	22	Real State and Local Government Purchases
R23 FAZ	1.7	6	Farm Gross Domestic Product
R24 $PROGZ$	1.7	12	Federal Government Gross Domestic Product
R25 $PROSZ$	1.7	13	State and Local Government Domestic Gross Product
R26 FA	1.8	6	Real Farm Gross Domestic Product
R27 $PROG$	1.8	12	Real Federal Government Gross Domestic Product
R28 $PROS$	1.8	13	Real State and Local Government Gross Domestic Product
R29 $FIUS$	1.9	2	Receipts of Factor Income from the Rest of the World
R30 $FIROW$	1.9	3	Payments of Factor Income to the Rest of the World
R31 CCT	1.9	5	Consumption of Fixed Capital
R32 TRF	1.9	10	Business Transfer Payments
R33 $STAT$	1.9	11	Statistical Discrepancy

R34	*WLDF*	1.9	17	Wage Accruals less Disbursements
R35	*DPER*	1.9	19	Personal Dividend Income
R36	*TRFH*	1.9	21	Business Transfer Payments to Persons
R37	*COMPT*	1.14	2	Compensation of Employees
R38	*SIT*	1.14	7	Employer Contributions for Social Insurance
R39	*DC*	1.14	25	Dividends
R40	*CCCB*	1.16	2	Consumption of Fixed Capital, Corporate Business
R41	*PIECB*	1.16	10	Profits Before Tax, Corporate Business
R42	*DCB*	1.16	13	Dividends, Corporate Business
R43	*IVA*	1.16	15	Inventory Valuation Adjustment, Corporate Business
R44	*CCADCB*	1.16	16	Capital Consumption Adjustment, Corporate Business
R45	*INTF*	1.16	17	Net Interest, Corporate Business
R46	*CCCBN*	1.16	20	Consumption of Fixed Capital, Nonfinancial Corporate Business
R47	*PIECBN*	1.16	28	Profits Before Tax, Nonfinancial Corporate Business
R48	*TCBN*	1.16	29	Profits Tax Liability, Nonfinancial Corporate Business
R49	*DCBN*	1.16	31	Dividends, Nonfinancial Corporate Business
R50	*CCADCBN*	1.16	34	Capital Consumption Adjustment, Nonfinancial Corporate Business
R51	*PRI*	2.1	9	Proprietors' Income with Inventory Valuation and Capital Consumption Adjustments
R52	*RNT*	2.1	12	Rental Income of Persons with Capital Consumption Adjustment
R53	*PII*	2.1	14	Personal Interest Income
R54	*UB*	2.1	17	Government Unemployment Insurance Benefits
R55	*IPP*	2.1	28	Interest Paid by Persons
R56	*TRHR*	2.1	29	Personal Transfer Payments to Rest of the World (net)
R57	*TPG*	3.2	2	Personal Tax and Nontax Receipts, Federal Government (see below for adjustments)
R58	*TCG*	3.2	6	Corporate Profits Tax Accruals, Federal Government
R59	*IBTG*	3.2	9	Indirect Business Tax and Nontax Accruals, Federal Government
R60	*SIG*	3.2	13	Contributions for Social Insurance, Federal Government
R61	*PURGZ*	3.2	15	Purchases, Federal Government
R62	*TRGH*	3.2	19	Transfer Payments (net) to Persons, Federal Government (see below for adjustments)
R63	*TRGR*	3.2	20	Transfer Payments (net) to Rest of the World, Federal Government
R64	*TRGS*	3.2	21	Grants in Aid to State and Local Governments, Federal Government
R65	*INTG*	3.2	22	Net Interest Paid, Federal Government
R66	*SUBG*	3.2	27	Subsidies less Current Surplus of Government Enterprises, Federal Government
R67	*WLDG*	3.2	30	Wage Accruals less Disbursements, Federal Government
R68	*TPS*	3.3	2	Personal Tax and Nontax Receipts, State and Local Government (S&L)
R69	*TCS*	3.3	6	Corporate Profits Tax Accruals, S&L
R70	*IBTS*	3.3	7	Indirect Business Tax and Nontax Accruals, S&L
R71	*SIS*	3.3	11	Contributions for Social Insurance, S&L
R72	*PURSZ*	3.3	14	Purchases of Goods and Services, S&L

R73 *TRRSH*	3.3	17	Transfer Payments to Persons, S&L
R74 *INTS*	3.3	18	Net Interest Paid, S&L
R75 *SUBS*	3.3	22	Subsidies Less Current Surplus of Government Enterprises, S&L
R76 *WLDS*	3.3	25	Wage Accruals less Disbursements, S&L
R77 *COMPMIL*	3.7b	8	Compensation of Employees, Military, Federal Government
R78 *SIHGA*	3.14	3	Personal Contributions for Social Insurance to the Federal Government, annual data only
R79 *SIQGA*	3.14	5	Government Employer Contributions for Social Insurance to the Federal Government, annual data only
R80 *SIFGA*	3.14	6	Other Employer Contributions for Social Insurance to the Federal Government, annual data only
R81 *SIHSA*	3.14	14	Personal Contributions for Social Insurance to the S&L Governments, annual data only
R82 *SIQSA*	3.14	16	Government Employer Contributions for Social Insurance to the S&L Governments, annual data only
R83 *SIFSA*	3.14	17	Other Employer Contributions for Social Insurance to the S&L Governments, annual data only
R84 *PYA*	7.1	6	Chain type Price Index, Gross Domestic Product, data for 1959:3–1987:4
R85 *PCDA*	7.1	22	Chain type Price Index, Personal Consumption Expenditures, Durable Goods, data for 1959:3–1987:4
R86 *PCNA*	7.1	30	Chain type Price Index, Personal Consumption Expenditures, Nondurable Goods, data for 1959:3–1987:4
R87 *PCSA*	7.1	38	Chain type Price Index, Personal Consumption Expenditures, Services, data for 1959:3–1987:4
R88 *PIKA*	7.1	62	Chain type Price Index, Nonresidential Fixed Investment, data for 1959:3–1987:4
R89 *PIHA*	7.1	86	Chain type Price Index, Residential Fixed Investment, data for 1959:3–1987:4
R90 *PEXA*	7.1	94	Chain type Price Index, Exports, data for 1959:3–1987:4
R91 *PIMA*	7.1	102	Chain type Price Index, Imports, data for 1959:3–1987:4
R92 *PGA*	7.1	118	Chain type Price Index, Federal Government Purchases, data for 1959:3–1987:4
R93 *PSA*	7.1	142	Chain type Price Index, State and Local Government Purchases, data for 1959:3–1987:4
R94 *FIUSD*	7.13	2	Implicit Price Deflator for Receipts of Factor Income from the Rest of the World
R95 *FIROWD*	7.13	3	Implicit Price Deflator for Payments of Factor Income to the Rest of the World
R96 *INTROWA*	8.17	61	Net Interest, Rest of the World, annual data only

Flow of Funds Data

Variable	Code	Description
R97 $CDDCF$	103020005	Change in Demand Deposits and Currency, F
R98 $NFIF$	105000005	Net Financial Investment, F
R99 $IHFZ$	105012001	Residential Construction, F
R100 MRS	105030003	Mineral Rights Sales
R101 $PIEF$	106060005	Profits before Tax, F
R102 $CCNF$	106300005	Depreciation Charges, NIPA, F
R103 $DISF1$	107005005	Discrepancy, F
R104 $CDDCNN$	113020003	Change in Demand Deposits and Currency, NN
R105 $NFINN$	115000005	Net Financial Investment, NN
R106 $IKNN$	115013005	Nonresidential Fixed Investment, NN
R107 $IVNN$	115020003	Inventory Investment, NN
R108 $CCNN$	116300005	Capital Consumption, NN. Also, Current Surplus = Gross Saving, NN
R109 $CDDCFA$	133020003	Change in Demand Deposits and Currency, FA
R110 $NFIFA$	135000005	Net Financial Investment, FA
R111 $IKFA$	135013003	Nonresidential Fixed Investment, FA
R112 $PIEFA$	136060005	Corporate Profits, FA
R113 DFA	136120003	Dividends, FA
R114 TFA	136231003	Tax Accruals, FA
R115 $CCFA$	136300103	Capital Consumption, FA
R116 $CCADFA$	136310103	Capital Consumption Adjustment, FA
R117 $CDDCH1$	153020005	Change in Checkable Deposits and Currency, H1
R118 $MVCE, CCE$	153064105	Net Purchases of Corporate Equities of Households, $MVCE$ is the market value of the stock. CCE is the change in the stock excluding capital gains and losses
R119 $NFIH1$	155000005	Net Financial Investment, H1
R120 $IKH1$	155013003	Nonresidential Fixed Investment, Nonprofit Institutions
R121 $DISH1$	157005005	Discrepancy, H1
R122 $NFIS$	205000005	Net Financial Investment, S
R123 $DISS$	207005005	Discrepancy, S
R124 $CDDCS$	213020005	Change in Demand Deposits and Currency, S
R125 RET	224090005	Retirement Credits to Households, S
R126 $CGLDR$	263011005	Change in Gold and SDR's, R
R127 $CDDCR$	263020000	Change in U.S. Demand Deposits, R
R128 $CFXUS$	263111005	Change in U.S. Official Foreign Exchange and Net IMF Position
R129 $NFIR$	265000005	Net Financial Investment, R
R130 $PIEF2$	266060005	Net Corporate Earnings Retained Abroad
R131 $DISR1$	267005005	Discrepancy, R
R132 $CGLDFXUS$	313011005	Change in Gold, SDR's, and Foreign Exchange, US
R133 $CDDCUS$	313020005	Change in Demand Deposits and Currency, US
R134 $NGRR$	313011301	Net Capital Grants from R, US
R135 INS	313154005	Insurance Credits to Households, US
R136 $NFIUS$	315000005	Net Financial Investment, US
R137 $DISUS$	317005005	Discrepancy, US

R138 *CDDCCA*	403020003	Change in Demand Deposits and Currency, CA
R139 *NIACA*	404090005	Net Increase in Financial Assets, CA
R140 *NILCA*	404190005	Net Increase in Liabilities, CA
R141 *IKCAZ*	405013003	Fixed Nonresidential Investment, CA
R142 *GSCA*	406000105	Gross Saving, CA
R143 *DISCA*	407005005	Discrepancy, CA
R144 *NIDDLB2*	493127005	Net Increase in Liabilities in the form of Checkable Deposits, B2
R145 *CBRB2*	443013053	Change in Reserves at Federal Reserve, B2
R146 *IHBZ*	645012205	Residential Construction, Multi Family Units, Reits
R147 *CGD*	656120000	Capital Gains Dividend
R148 *CDDCB2*	693020005	Change in Demand Deposits and Currency, B2
R149 *NIAB2*	694090005	Net Increase in Financial Assets, B2
R150 *NILB2*	694190005	Net Increase in Liabilities, B2
R151 *IKB2Z*	695013005	Nonresidential Fixed Investment, B2
R152 *DISB2*	697005005	Discrepancy, B2
R153 *CGLDFXMA*	713011005	Change in Gold and Foreign Exchange, MA
R154 *CFRLMA*	713068003	Change in Federal Reserve Loans to Domestic Banks, MA
R155 *NILBRMA*	713113000	Change in Member Bank Reserves, MA
R156 *NIDDLRMA*	713122605	Change in Liabilities in the form of Demand Deposits and Currency due to Foreign of the MA
R157 *NIDDLGMA*	713123105	Change in Liabilities in the form of Demand Deposits and Currency due to U.S. Government of the MA
R158 *NILCMA*	713125005	Change in Liabilities in the form of Currency Outside Banks of the MA
R159 *NIAMA*	714090005	Net Increase in Financial Assets, MA
R160 *NILMA*	714190005	Net Increase in Liabilities, MA
R161 *IKMAZ*	715013003	Fixed Nonresidential Investment, MA
R162 *GSMA*	716000105	Gross Savings, MA
R163 *DISMA*	717005005	Discrepancy, MA
R164 *CVCBRB1*	723020005	Change in Vault Cash and Member Bank Reserves, U.S. Chartered Commercial Banks
R165 *NILVCMA*	723025000	Change in Liabilities in the form of Vault Cash of Commercial Banks of the MA
R166 *NIDDAB1*	743020003	Net increase in Financial Assets in the form of Demand Deposits and Currency of Banks in U.S. Possessions
R167 *CBRB1A*	753013003	Change in Reserves at Federal Reserve, Foreign Banking Offices in U.S.
R168 *NIDDLB1*	763120005	Net Increase in Liabilities in the form of Checkable Deposits, B1
R169 *NIAB1*	764090005	Net Increase in Financial Assets, B1
R170 *NILB1*	764190005	Net Increase in Liabilities, B1
R171 *IKB1Z*	765013005	Nonresidential Fixed Investment, B1
R172 *DISB1*	767005005	Discrepancy, B1
R173 *MAILFLT1*	903023105	Mail Float, U.S. Government
R174 *MAILFLT2*	903029205	Mail Float, Private Domestic Nonfinancial

Interest Rate Data

Variable	Description
R175 *RS*	Three Month Treasury Bill Rate (Auction Average), percentage points [FRB, A25. Quarterly average of monthly data.]
R176 *RM*	Mortgage Rate, percentage points. [FRB, A36. FHA mortgages (HUD series), secondary markets. Quarterly average of monthly data. Linear interpolation for missing monthly observations.
R177 *RB*	Aaa Corporate Bond Rate, percentage points. [FRB, A25. Quarterly average of monthly data.]
R178 *RD*	Discount Rate, percentage points. [FRB, A8. Rate at F.R. Bank of N.Y. Quarterly average, inclusive of any surcharge.]

Employment and Population Data

Variable	Description
R179 *CE*	Civilian Employment, SA in millions. [EE, A-33. Quarterly average of monthly data. See below for adjustments.]
R180 *U*	Unemployment, SA in millions. [EE, A-33. Quarterly average of monthly data. See below for adjustments.]
R181 *CL*1	Civilian Labor Force of Males 25–54, SA in millions. [EE, A-36 and A-37. Sum of Employed and Unemployed. Quarterly average of monthly data. See below for adjustments.]
R182 *CL*2	Civilian Labor Force of Females 25–54, SA in millions. [EE, A-36 and A-37. Sum of Employed and Unemployed. Quarterly average of monthly data. See below for adjustments.]
R183 *TL*	Total Labor Force, SA in millions. [BLS, unpublished, "Labor Force Level—Total Noninstitutional Population." Quarterly average of monthly data.]
R184 *AF*1	Armed Forces of Males 25–54, millions. [BLS, unpublished, "Armed Forces, Males 25–54." Quarterly average of monthly data.]
R185 *AF*2	Armed Forces of Females 25–54, millions. [BLS, unpublished, "Armed Forces, Females 25–54." Quarterly average of monthly data.]
R186 *POP*	Total noninstitutional population 16 and over, millions. [BLS, unpublished. Quarterly average of monthly data. See below for adjustments.]
R187 *POP*1	Noninstitutional population of males 25–54, millions. [BLS, unpublished. Quarterly average of monthly data. Sec below for adjustments.]
R188 *POP*2	Noninstitutional population of females 25–54,millions. [BLS, unpublished. Quarterly average of monthly data. See below for adjustments.]
R189 *JF*	Employment, Total Private Sector, All Persons, SA in millions. [BLS, unpublished, "Basic Industry Data for the Economy less General Government, All Persons."]
R190 *HF*	Average Weekly Hours, Total Private Sector, All Persons, SA. [BLS, unpublished, "Basic Industry Data for the Economy less General Government, All Persons."]
R191 *HO*	Average Weekly Overtime Hours in Manufacturing, SA. [EE, C-5. Quarterly average of monthly data.]
R192 *JQ*	Total Government Employment, SA in millions. [EE, B-4. Quarterly average of monthly data.]
R193 *JG*	Federal Government Employment, SA in millions. [EE, B-4. Quarterly average of monthly data.]
R194 *JHQ*	Total Government Employee Hours, SA in millions of hours per quarter. [EE, C-9. Quarterly average of monthly data.]

Adjustments to the Raw Data

R195 $SIHG =$	$[SIHGA/(SIHGA + SIHSA)](SIG + SIS - SIT)$	
	[Employee Contributions for Social Insurance, h to g.]	
R196 $SIHS =$	$SIG + SIS - SIT - SIHG$	
	[Employee Contributions for Social Insurance, h to s.]	
R197 $SIFG =$	$[SIFGA/(SIFGA + SIQGA)](SIG - SIHG)$	
	[Employer Contributions for Social Insurance, f to g.]	
R198 $SIGG =$	$SIG - SIHG - SIFG$	
	[Employer Contributions for Social Insurance, g to g.]	
R199 $SIFS =$	$[SIFSA/(SIFSA + SIQSA)](SIS - SIHS)$	
	[Employer Contributions for Social Insurance, f to s.]	
R200 $SISS =$	$SIS - SIHS - SIFS$	
	[Employer Contributions for Social Insurance, s to s.]	
R201 $TBG =$	$[TCG/(TCG + TCS)](TCG + TCS - TCBN)$	
	[Corporate Profit Tax Accruals, b to g.]	
R202 $TBS =$	$TCG + TCS - TCBN - TBG$	
	[Corporate Profit Tax Accruals, b to s.]	
R203 $INTROW =$	$-[(INTF + INTG)/(INTF \text{ annual} + INTG \text{ annual})]INTROWA$	
	[Net Interest Receipts of r.]	
R57 $TPG =$	TPG from raw data $-TAXADJ$	
R62 $TRGH =$	$TRGH$ from raw data $-TAXADJ$	
	[$TAXADJ$: 1968:3 = 1.525, 1968:4 = 1.775, 1969:1 = 2.675, 1969:2 = 2.725, 1969:3 = 1.775, 1969:4 = 1.825, 1970:1 = 1.25, 1970:2 = 1.25, 1970:3 = 0.1, 1975:2 = −7.8.]	

Multiplication factors (see the discussion in Section 3.2.2.)

Variable	1951:1–1971:4	1952:1–1972:4	1973:1	1952:1–1977:4
POP	1.00547	1.00009	1.00006	-
$POP1$	0.99880	1.00084	1.00056	-
$POP2$	1.00251	1.00042	1.00028	-
$CL1$	0.99878	1.00078	1.00052	1.00014
$CL2$	1.00297	1.00107	1.00071	1.00123
CE	1.00375	1.00069	1.00046	1.00268

Abbreviations:

BLS	Bureau of Labor Statistics
EE	Employment and Earnings, January 1993
FRB	Federal Reserve Bulletin, February 1993
SA	Seasonally Adjusted

Notes:

1. For the construction of variables R195, R197, R199, and R203, the annual observation was used for each quarter of the year.

2. See Table A.1 for abbreviations: B1, B2, CA, F, FA, H1, MA, NN, R, S, US.

The Raw Data Variables in Alphabetical Order

Variable	No.	Variable	No.	Variable	No.	Variable	No.
AF1	R184	DISR1	R131	JQ	R192	PSA	R93
AF2	R185	DISS	R123	MAILFLT1	R173	PURG	R21
CBRB1A	R167	DISUS	R137	MAILFLT2	R174	PURGZ	R61
CBRB2	R145	DPER	R35	MRS	R100	PURS	R22
CCADCB	R44	EX	R19	MVCE	R118	PURSZ	R72
CCADCBN	R50	EXZ	R9	NFIF	R98	PYA	R84
CCADFA	R116	FA	R26	NFIFA	R110	RB	R177
CCCB	R40	FAZ	R23	NFIH1	R119	RD	R178
CCCBN	R46	FIROW	R30	NFINN	R105	RET	R125
CCE	R118	FIROWD	R95	NFIR	R129	RM	R176
CCFA	R115	FIUS	R29	NFIS	R122	RNT	R52
CCNF	R102	FIUSD	R94	NFIUS	R136	RS	R175
CCNN	R108	GDP	R1	NGRR	R134	SIFG	R197
CCT	R31	GDPR	R11	NIAB1	R169	SIFGA	R80
CD	R12	GSCA	R142	NIAB2	R149	SIFS	R199
CDDCB2	R148	GSMA	R162	NIACA	R139	SIFSA	R83
CDDCCA	R138	HF	R190	NIAMA	R159	SIG	R60
CDDCF	R97	HO	R191	NIDDAB1	R166	SIGG	R198
CDDCFA	R109	IBTG	R59	NIDDLB1	R168	SIHG	R195
CDDCH1	R117	IBTS	R70	NIDDLB2	R144	SIHGA	R78
CDDCNN	R104	IH	R16	NIDDLGMA	R157	SIHS	R196
CDDCR	R127	IHBZ	R146	NIDDLRMA	R156	SIHSA	R81
CDDCS	R124	IHFZ	R99	NILBRMA	R155	SIQGA	R79
CDDCUS	R133	IHZ	R6	NILB1	R170	SIQSA	R82
CDZ	R2	IK	R15	NILB2	R150	SIS	R71
CE	R179	IKB1Z	R171	NILCA	R140	SISS	R200
CFRLMA	R154	IKB2Z	R151	NILCMA	R158	SIT	R38
CFXUS	R128	IKCAZ	R141	NILMA	R160	STAT	R33
CGD	R147	IKFA	R111	NILVCMA	R165	SUBG	R66
CGLDFXMA	R153	IKH1	R120	PCDA	R85	SUBS	R75
CGLDFXUS	R132	IKMAZ	R161	PCNA	R86	TBG	R201
CGLDR	R126	IKNN	R106	PCSA	R87	TBS	R202
CL1	R181	IKZ	R5	PEXA	R90	TCBN	R48
CL2	R182	IM	R20	PGA	R92	TCG	R58
CN	R13	IMZ	R10	PIECB	R41	TCS	R69
CNZ	R3	INS	R135	PIECBN	R47	TFA	R114
COMPMIL	R77	INTF	R45	PIEFA	R112	TL	R183
COMPT	R37	INTG	R65	PIEF1	R101	TPG	R57
CS	R14	INTROW	R203	PIEF2	R130	TPS	R68
CSZ	R4	INTROWA	R96	PIHA	R89	TRF	R32
CVCBRB1	R164	INTS	R74	PII	R53	TRFH	R36
DC	R39	IPP	R55	PIKA	R88	TRGH	R62
DCB	R42	IV	R17	PIMA	R91	TRGR	R63
DCBN	R49	IVA	R43	POP	R186	TRGS	R64
DFA	R113	IVFA	R18	POP1	R187	TRHR	R56
DISB1	R172	IVFAZ	R8	POP2	R188	TRRSH	R73
DISB2	R152	IVNN	R107	PRI	R51	U	R180
DISCA	R143	IVZ	R7	PROG	R27	UB	R54
DISF1	R103	JF	R189	PROGZ	R24	WLDF	R34
DISH1	R121	JG	R193	PROS	R28	WLDG	R67
DISMA	R163	JHQ	R194	PROSZ	R25	WLDS	R76

Table A.5

**Links Between the National Income and Product Accounts
and the Flow of Funds Accounts**

Receipts from i to j: $(i, j = h, f, b, r, g, s)$

$hh =$	0
$fh =$	$COMPT - PROGZ - PROSZ - (SIT - SIGG - SISS) - SUBG - SUBS + PRI + RNT + INTF + TRFH + DCBN + DC - DFA - DCB + PIEFA + CCT - CCCB + CCFA + CCADFA - WLDF$
$bh =$	$DCB - DCBN$
$rh =$	0
$gh =$	$PROGZ - SIGG - WLDG + TRGH + INS + INTG + SUBG$
$sh =$	$PROSZ - SISS - WLDS + TRRSH + RET + INTS + DPER - DC + SUBS$
$hf =$	$CSZ + CNZ + CDZ - IBTG - IBTS - IMZ - FIROW - PIECB + PIECBN - CCCB + CCCBN - CCADCB + CCADCBN + IHZ - IHFZ - IHBZ + IKH1 + IKFA + IKNN + IVFAZ + IVNN$
$ff =$	$IHFZ + IKZ - IKH1 - IKFA - IKNN - IKBZ - IKGZ + IVZ - IVFAZ - IVNN$
$bf =$	$IHBZ + IKBZ$
$rf =$	$EXZ + FIUS$
$gf =$	$PURGZ - PROGZ + IKGZ$
$sf =$	$PURSZ - PROSZ$
$hb =$	$PIECB - PIECBN + CCCB - CCCBN + CCADCB - CCADCBN$
$fb =$	0
$bb =$	0
$rb =$	0
$gb =$	0
$sb =$	0
$hr =$	$IMZ + TRHR + FIROW$
$fr =$	$TRFR$
$br =$	0
$rr =$	0
$gr =$	$TRGR$
$sr =$	0
$hg =$	$TPG + TFA + IBTG + SIHG$
$fg =$	$TCG - TFA - TBG + MRS + SIFG$
$bg =$	$TBG + GSCA + GSMA$
$rg =$	0
$gg =$	$SIGG$
$sg =$	0
$hs =$	$TPS + IBTS + SIHS$
$fs =$	$TCS - TBS + SIFS$
$bs =$	TBS
$rs =$	0
$gs =$	$TRGS$
$ss =$	$SISS$

Saving of the Sectors

$SH =$	$fh + bh + gh + sh - (hf + hb + hr + hg + hs)$
$SF =$	$hf + ff + bf + rf + gf + sf - (fh + ff + fg + fs + fr)$
$SB =$	$hb - (bh + bf + bs + bg)$
$SR =$	$hr + gr - rf + fr$
$SG =$	$hg + fg + bg + gg - (gh + gf + gr + gs + gg)$
$SS =$	$hs + fs + bs + gs + ss - (sh + sf + ss)$

Checks

$0 =$	$SH + SF + SB + SR + SG + SS$
$SH =$	$NFIH1 + NFIFA + NFINN + DISH1$
$SF =$	$NFIF + DISF1 + STAT - DISBA + WLDF$
$SB =$	$NIAB1 - NILB1 + NIAB2 - NILB2 + DISB1 + DISB2 + DISBA$
$SR =$	$NFIR + DISR1 + NGRR$
$SG =$	$NFIUS + NIACA - NILCA + NIAMA - NILMA + DISUS + DISCA + DISMA$
$SS =$	$NFIS + DISS$
$0 =$	$-NIDDLB1 + NIDDAB1 + CDDCB2 - NIDDLB2 + CDDCF + MAILFLT1 +$ $MAILFLT2 + CDDCUS + CDDCCA - NIDDLRMA - NIDDLGMA +$ $CDDCH1 + CDDCFA + CDDCNN + CDDCR + CDDCS - NILCMA$
$0 =$	$CVCBRB1 + CBRB1A + CBRB2 - NILBRMA - NILVCMA$
$0 =$	$CGLDR - CFXUS + CGLDFXUS + CGLDFXMA$

See Table A.4 for the definitions of the raw data variables.

Table A.6
Construction of the Variables for the US Model

Variable in US Model	Construction
AA	Def., Eq. 89.
AB	Def., Eq. 73. Base Period=1971:4, Value=244.977
AF	Def., Eq. 70. Base Period=1971:4, Value=−230.421
AG	Def., Eq. 77. Base Period=1971:4, Value=−215.665
AH	Def., Eq. 66. Base Period=1971:4, Value=1926.964
AR	Def., Eq. 75. Base Period=1971:4, Value=−.394
AS	Def., Eq. 79. Base Period=1971:4, Value=−108.310
BF	Def., Eq. 55. Value for 1952.1 taken to be 0.0; values before 1952.1 taken to be the same as the value for 1952.1
BG	Def., Eq. 56. Value for 1952.1 taken to be 7.1; values before 1952.1 taken to be the same as the value for 1952.1
BO	Sum of $CFRLMA$. Base Period=1971:4, Value=.039
BR	Sum of $CVCBRB1 + CBRB1A + CBRB2$. Base Period=1971:4, Value=35.329
CCB	$(CCCB + CCADCB − CCCBN − CCADCBN)/PX$. See below for PX.
CCF	$CCCBN + CCADCBN − CCFA − CCADFA$
CCH	$CCT − CCCB + CCFA + CCADFA$
CD	CD
CDA	Peak to peak interpolation of CD/POP. Peak quarters are 1953:1, 1955:3, 1960:2, 1963:2, 1965:4, 1968:3, 1973:2, 1978:4, 1985:1, 1988:4, and 1993:2.
CF	Def., Eq. 68
CG	$MVCE − MVCE_{-1} − CCE$
CN	CN
COG	$PURG − PROG$
COS	$PURS − PROS$
CS	CS
CUR	Sum of $NILCMA$. Base Period=1971:4, Value=53.521
$D1G$	Def., Eq. 47
$D1GM$	Def., Eq. 90
$D1S$	Def., Eq. 48
$D1SM$	Def., Eq. 91
$D2G$	Def., Eq. 49
$D2S$	Def., Eq. 50
$D3G$	Def., Eq. 51
$D3S$	Def., Eq. 52
$D4G$	Def., Eq. 53
$D5G$	Def., Eq. 55
DB	$DCB − DCBN$
$DELD$	.049511
$DELH$	.006716
$DELK$	.014574 for 1952:1–1970:4, .018428 for 1971:1–1980:4, .023068 for 1981:1–1993:2.
DF	$DC − DFA − (DCB − DCBN)$
$DISB$	$DISB1 + DISB2$
$DISBA$	$CCNF + CCFA − CCCBN$
$DISF$	$DISF1 + WLDF$

$DISG$	$DISUS + DISCA + DISMA$
$DISH$	$DISH1$
$DISR$	$DISR + NGRR$
$DISS$	$DISS$
DRS	$DC - DPER$
E	$TL - U$
EX	EX
$EXPG$	Def., Eq. 106
$EXPS$	Def., Eq. 113
FA	FA
$FIROW$	$FIROW$
$FIROWD$	$FIROWD$
$FIUS$	$FIUS$
$FIUSD$	$FIUSD$
$G1$	Def., Eq. 57
GDP	Def., Eq. 82, or GDP
$GDPD$	Def., Eq. 84
$GDPR$	$GDPR$
GNP	Def., Eq. 129
$GNPD$	Def., Eq. 131
$GNPR$	Def., Eq. 130
HF	$13 \cdot HF$
HFF	Def., Eq. 100
HFS	Peak to peak interpolation of HF. The peaks are 1952:4, 1966:1, 1977:2, and 1989:3.
HG	JHQ/JQ
HM	520
HN	Def., Eq. 62
HO	$13 \cdot HO$. Constructed values for 1952:1–1955:4.
HS	JHQ/JQ
$IBTG$	$IBTG$
$IBTS$	$IBTS$
IHB	$IHBZ/(IHZ/IH)$
IHF	$IHFZ/(IHZ/IH)$
IHH	$(IHZ - IHFZ - IHBZ)/(IHZ/IH)$
$IHHA$	Peak to peak interpolation of IHH/POP. Peak quarters are 1955:2, 1963:4, 1978:3, and 1986:3.
IKB	$(IKB1Z + IKB2Z)/(IKZ/IK)$
IKF	$(IKZ - IKH1 - IKFA - IKNN - IKBZ)/(IKZ/IK)$
$IKFA$	Peak to peak interpolation of IKF. Peak quarters are 1957:3, 1964:3, 1966:1, 1969:3, 1974:1, 1980:1, and 1985:2.
IKG	$((IKCAZ + IKMAZ)/(IKZ/IK)$
IKH	$(IKH1 + IKNN + IKFA)/(IKZ/IK)$
IM	IM
INS	INS
$INTF$	$INTF$
$INTG$	$INTG$
$INTOTH$	$PII - INTF - INTG - INTS - IPP + INTROW$
$INTROW$	$INTROW$
$INTS$	$INTS$

IVA	IVA
IVF	$IV - IVFA - IVNN/PIV$
IVH	$IVFA + IVNN/PIV$
$IVVH$	$IVFAZ + IVNN$
JF	JF
JG	JG
$JHMIN$	Def., Eq. 94
JJ	Def., Eq. 95
JJP	Peak to peak interpolation of JJ. The peaks are 1952:4, 1955:4, 1959:3, 1969:1, 1973:3, 1979:3, 1985:4, and 1990:1. Flat end.
JJS	Def., Eq. 96
JM	$TL - CE - U$
JS	$JQ - JG$
KD	Def., Eq. 58. Base Period=1952:4, Value=313.7, Dep. Rate=$DELD$
KH	Def., Eq. 59. Base Period=1952:4, Value=1270.276, Dep. Rate=$DELH$
KK	Def., Eq. 92. Base Period=1952:4, Value=887.571, Dep. Rate=$DELK$
$KKMIN$	Def., Eq. 93
$L1$	$CL1 + AF1$
$L2$	$CL2 + AF2$
$L3$	Def., Eq. 86
LAM	Peak to peak interpolation of $Y/(JF \cdot HF)$. Peak quarters are 1953:4, 1961:4, 1965:4, 1973:2, 1977:3, and 1992:4.
LM	Def., Eq. 85
$M1$	Def., Eq. 81. Base Period=1971:4, Value=247.219
MB	Def., Eq. 71. Also sum of $-NIDDLB1+NIDDAB1+CDDCB2-NIDDLB2$. Base Period=1971:4, Value=-189.610
$MDIF$	$NIDDAB1 + CDDCB2 + CDDCCA - MAILFLT1$
MF	Sum of $CDDCF + MAILFLT1 + MAILFLT2$, Base Period= 1971:4, Value=64.909
MG	Sum of $CDDCUS + CDDCCA - NIDDLRMA - NIDDLGMA$, Base Period=1971:4, Value=10.526
MH	Sum of $CDDCH1 + CDDCFA + CDDCNN$. Base Period=1971:4, Value=149.079
MR	Sum of $CDDCR$. Base Period=1971:4, Value=6.503
MRS	MRS
MS	Sum of $CDDCS$. Base Period=1971:4, Value=12.114
MUH	Peak to peak interpolation of Y/KK. Peak quarters are 1953:2, 1955:3, 1959:2, 1962:3, 1965:4, 1969:1, 1978:2, 1984:2, 1989:2, and 1992:4. Flat beginning and flat end.
PCD	CDZ/CD
$PCGNPD$	Def., Eq. 122
$PCGNPR$	Def., Eq. 123
$PCM1$	Def., Eq. 124
PCN	CNZ/CN
PCS	CSZ/CS
PD	Def., Eq. 33
PEX	EXZ/EX
PF	Def., Eq. 31
PFA	FAZ/FA

PG	$(PURGZ - PROGZ)/(PURG - PROG)$
PH	Def., Eq. 34
$PIEB$	$(PIECB - PIECBN)/PX$. See below for PX.
$PIEF$	Def., Eq. 67, or $PIEF1 + PIEF2$
$PIEH$	$PIEFA$
PIH	IHZ/IH
PIK	IKZ/IK
PIM	IMZ/IM
PIV	$(IVZ - IVFAZ)/(IV - IVFA)$, with the following adjustments: 1954:4 = .288, 1958:3 = .31, 1959:3 = .355, 1961:2 = .34, 1962:4 = .36, 1970:1 through 1970:4 = .4, 1975:3 and 1975:4 = .6, 1979:3 and 1979:4 = .8, 1980:2 = .8, 1980:4 = .85, 1981:2 = .95, 1982:2 and 1982:3 = 1.0, 1983:2 = .9, 1990:1 = 1.2, 1990:3 = 1.1, 1991:3 = 1.1.
POP	POP
$POP1$	$POP1$
$POP2$	$POP2$
$POP3$	$POP - POP1 - POP2$
$PROD$	Def., Eq. 118
PS	$(PURSZ - PROSZ)/(PURS - PROS)$
$PSI1$	Def., Eq. 32
$PSI2$	Def., Eq. 35
$PSI3$	Def., Eq. 36
$PSI4$	Def., Eq. 37
$PSI5$	Def., Eq. 38
$PSI6$	Def., Eq. 39
$PSI7$	Def., Eq. 40
$PSI8$	Def., Eq. 41
$PSI9$	Def., Eq. 42
$PSI10$	Def., Eq. 44
$PSI11$	Def., Eq. 45
$PSI12$	Def., Eq. 46
$PSI13$	$(PROG + PROS)/(JHQ + 520 \cdot AF)$
$PSI14$	Def., Eq. 88
PUG	Def., Eq. 104 or $PURGZ$
PUS	Def., Eq. 110 or $PURSZ$
PX	$(CDZ + CNZ + CSZ + IHZ + IKZ + PURGZ - PROGZ + PURSZ - PROSZ + EXZ - IMZ - IBTG - IBTS + IVFAZ + IVNN)/(CD + CN + CS + IH + IK + PURG - PROG + PURS - PROS + EX - IM + IVFA + IVNN/PIV)$
Q	Sum of $CGLDFXUS + CGLDFXMA$. Base Period=1971:4, Value=30.867.
RB	RB
RD	RD
$RECG$	Def., Eq. 105
$RECS$	Def., Eq. 112
RET	RET
RM	RM
RMA	Def., Eq. 128
RNT	RNT
RS	RS

RSA	Def., Eq. 130
SB	Def., Eq. 72
SF	Def., Eq. 69
SG	Def., Eq. 76
SGP	Def., Eq. 107
SH	Def., Eq. 65
$SHRPIE$	Def., Eq. 121
$SIFG$	$SIFG$
$SIFS$	$SIFS$
SIG	SIG
$SIGG$	$SIGG$
$SIHG$	$SIHG$
$SIHS$	$SIHS$
SIS	SIS
$SISS$	$SISS$
SR	Def., Eq. 74
SRZ	Def., Eq. 116
SS	Def., Eq. 78
SSP	Def., Eq. 114
$STAT$	$STAT$
$STATP$	Def., Eq. 83
$SUBG$	$SUBG$
$SUBS$	$SUBS$
SUR	$GSCA + GSKA$
$TAUG$	Determined from a regression. See Section 3.2.3.
$TAUS$	Determined from a regression. See Section 3.2.3.
TBG	TBG
TBS	TBS
TCG	TCG
TCS	TCS
TFA	TFA
TFG	Def., Eq. 102
TFS	Def., Eq. 108
THG	Def., Eq. 101
THS	TPS
TI	0 through 1981:2, 1 in 1981:3, 2 in 1981:4, . . . , 40 in 1991:2 and thereafter.
TPG	TPG
$TRFH$	$TRFH$
$TRFR$	$TRF - TRFH$
$TRGH$	$TRGH$
$TRGR$	$TRGR$
$TRGS$	$TRGS$
$TRHR$	$TRHR$
$TRRSH$	$TRRSH$
$TRSH$	Def., Eq. 111
$TXCR$	.5 in 1962:3–1963:4 and 1971:3, 1.0 in 1964:1–1966:3 and 1967:3–1969:1 and 1971:4–1975:1, 1.43 in 1975:2–1986:1, and 0 otherwise
U	U
UB	UB
UBR	Def., Eq. 125

UR	Def., Eq. 87
V	Def., Eq. 117. Base Period=1988:4, Value=870.0
WA	Def., Eq. 126
WF	$[COMPT - PROGZ - PROSZ - (SIT - SIGG - SISS) + PRI]/[JF(HF + .5 \cdot HO)]$
WG	$(PROGZ - COMPMIL - WLDG)/[JG(JHQ/JQ)]$
WH	Def., Eq. 43
$WLDF$	$WLDF$
$WLDG$	$WLDG$
$WLDS$	$WLDS$
WM	$COMPMIL/[520(TL - CE - U)]$
WR	Def., Eq. 119
WS	$(PROSZ - WLDS)/[(JQ - JG)(JHQ/JQ)]$
X	Def., Eq. 60
XX	Def., Eq. 61
Y	Def., Eq. 63
YD	Def., Eq. 115
YNL	Def., Eq. 99
YS	Def., Eq. 98
YT	Def., Eq. 64
Z	Def., Eq. 97

Variables in the model in the first column are defined in terms of the raw data variables in Table A.4 or by the identities in Table A.3.

Table A.7

First Stage Regressors for the US Model for 2SLS and 3SLS

	Basic Sets	
	Linear	Log
1	constant	constant
2	$(AA/POP)_{-1}$	$\log(AA/POP)_{-1}$
3	$COG + COS$	$\log(COG + COS)$
4	$(CD/POP)_{-1}$	$\log(CD/POP)_{-1}$
5	$(CN/POP)_{-1}$	$\log(CN/POP)_{-1}$
6	$(CS/POP)_{-1}$	$\log(CS/POP)_{-1}$
7	$(1 - D1GM - D1SM - D4G)_{-1}$	$\log(1 - D1GM - D1SM - D4G)_{-1}$
8	EX	$\log EX$
9	HF_{-1}	$\log HF_{-1}$
10	$(IHH/POP)_{-1}$	$\log(IHH/POP)_{-1}$
11	$(IM/POP)_{-1}$	$\log(IM/POP)_{-1}$
12	$(JF - JHMIN)_{-1}$	$\log(JF/JHMIN)_{-1}$
13	$(JG \cdot HG + JM \cdot HM + JS \cdot HS)/POP$	$\log[(JG \cdot HG + JM \cdot HM + JS \cdot HS)/POP]$
14	$(KH/POP)_{-1}$	$\log(KH/POP)_{-1}$
15	$(KK - KKMIN)_{-1}$	$\log(KK/KKMIN)_{-1}$
16	$PCM1_{-1}$	$PCM1_{-1}$
17	$100[(PD/PD_{-1})^4 - 1]_{-1}$	$100[(PD/PD_{-1})^4 - 1]_{-1}$
18	PF_{-1}	$\log PF_{-1}$
19	PIM	$\log PIM$
20	RB_{-1}	RB_{-1}
21	RS_{-1}	RS_{-1}
22	RS_{-2}	RS_{-2}
23	T	T
24	$(TRGH + TRSH)/(POP \cdot PH_{-1})$	$\log[(TRGH + TRSH)/(POP \cdot PH_{-1})]$
25	V_{-1}	$\log V_{-1}$
26	WF_{-1}	$\log WF_{-1}$
27	Y_{-1}	$\log Y_{-1}$
28	Y_{-2}	$\log Y_{-2}$
29	Y_{-3}	$\log Y_{-3}$
30	Y_{-4}	$\log Y_{-4}$
31	$[YNL/(POP \cdot PH)]_{-1}$	$\log[YNL/(POP \cdot PH)]_{-1}$
32	Z_{-1}	Z_{-1}
33	UR_{-1}	UR_{-1}

Additional First Stage Regressors for Each Equation

Eq.	Basic Set	Additional
1	log	$\log(WA/PH)_{-1}$, $\log(PCS/PH)_{-1}$, RSA_{-1}, $AG1$, $AG2$, $AG3$, $\log(CS/POP)_{-2}$, $\log[YD/(POP \cdot PH)]_{-1}$, $100[(PD/PD_{-4}) - 1]_{-1}$
2	log	$\log(WA/PH)_{-1}$, $\log(PCN/PH)_{-1}$, RSA_{-1}, RMA_{-1}, $AG1$, $AG2$, $AG3$, $\log(CN/POP)_{-2}$, $\log(CN/POP)_{-3}$, $\log(AA/POP)_{-2}$, $\log[YD/(POP \cdot PH)]_{-1}$, $100[(PD/PD_{-4}) - 1]_{-1}$
3	linear	$(WA/PH)_{-1}$, $(PCD/PH)_{-1}$, $RMA_{-1} \cdot CDA$, $(KD/POP)_{-1}$, $AG1$, $AG2$, $AG3$, $(CD/POP)_{-2}$, $[YD/(POP \cdot PH)]_{-1}$, $100[(PD/PD_{-4}) - 1]_{-1}$
4	linear	$(WA/PH)_{-1}$, $(PIH/PH)_{-1}$, $RMA_{-1} \cdot IHHA$, $(IHH/POP)_{-2}$, $(AA/POP)_{-2}$, $[YD/(POP \cdot PH)]_{-1}$, $[YD/(POP \cdot PH)]_{-2}$, $RMA_{-2} \cdot IHHA_{-1}$, $(KH/POP)_{-2}$, $100[(PD/PD_{-4})-1]_{-1}$, $(IHH/POP)_{-3}$
5	log	$\log(WA_{-1}/PH_{-1})$, $\log(L1/POP1)_{-1}$, $\log(L1/POP1)_{-2}$, $\log(AA/POP)_{-2}$
6	log	$\log(WA_{-1}/PH_{-1})$, $\log(L2/POP2)_{-1}$, $\log(L2/POP2)_{-2}$, $\log(AA/POP)_{-2}$
7	log	$\log(WA_{-1}/PH_{-1})$, $\log(L3/POP3)_{-1}$, $\log(L3/POP1)_{-2}$, $\log(AA/POP)_{-2}$
8	log	$\log(WA_{-1}/PH_{-1})$, $\log(LM/POP)_{-1}$, $\log(LM/POP)_{-2}$, $\log(AA/POP)_{-2}$
9	log	$\log[MH/(POP \cdot PH)]_{-1}$, $\log[YD/(POP \cdot PH)]_{-1}$, $\log[MH_{-1}/(POP_{-1} \cdot PH)]_{-1}$, $AG1$, $AG2$, $AG3$, $AG1_{-1}$, $AG2_{-1}$, $AG3_{-1}$, $\log[YD/(POP \cdot PH)]_{-2}$, RSA_{-2}
10	log	$\log(1+D5G)$, $\log[(YS-Y)/YS+.04]_{-1}$, $\log PF_{-2}$, $\log[(YS-Y)/YS+.04]_{-2}$, $\log(1+D5G)_{-1}$, $\log PIM_{-1}$, $\log PIM_{-2}$, $\log[(YS-Y)/YS+.04]_{-3}$, $\log(1+D5G)_{-2}$, $\log WF_{-2}$, $\log PF_{-3}$
11	linear	V_{-2}, V_{-3}, V_{-4}
12	linear	IKF_{-1}, $DELK \cdot KK_{-1}$, $[RB(1 - D2G - D2S)]_{-1}$, $(KK - KKMIN)_{-2}$, $TXCR \cdot IKFA$, Y_{-5}, $RB'_{-3} \cdot IKFA$, IKF_{-2}
13	log	$\Delta \log JF_{-1}$, $\log(JF/JHMIN)_{-2}$, $\Delta \log JF_{-2}$, $DD772$, $DD772 \cdot T$, $DD772 \cdot \Delta \log JF_{-1}$, $DD772 \cdot \log(JF/JHMIN)_{-1}$, $DD772 \cdot \log(JF/JHMIN)_{-2}$, $DD772_{-1} \cdot \Delta \log JF_{-2}$
14	log	$\log HF_{-2}$, $\log(JF/JHMIN)_{-2}$, $DD772$, $DD772 \cdot T$, $DD772 \cdot \log(JF/JHMIN)_{-1}$, $DD772_{-1} \cdot \log(JF/JHMIN)_{-2}$
16	log	$\log[(YS-Y)/YS+.04]_{-1}$, $\log PF_{-1}$, $\log PF_{-2}$, $\log PF_{-3}$, $\log PF_{-4}$, $\log PF_{-5}$, $\log PF_{-6}$, $\log WF_{-2}$, $\log WF_{-3}$, $\log WF_{-4}$, $\log WF_{-5}$, $\log WF_{-6}$
17	log	$\log(MF/PF)_{-1}$, $1-D2G-D2S$, $RS_{-1}(1-D2G-D2S)_{-1}$, $\log(MF_{-2}/PF_{-1})$, $RS_{-2}(1 - D2G - D2S)_{-2}$
18	log	$\log(PIEF - TFG - TFS)_{-1}$, $\log(D2G + D2S)$, $\log DF_{-1}$, $\log DF_{-2}$
22	linear	$(BO/BR)_{-1}$, RD_{-1}, $(BO/BR)_{-2}$, RD_{-2}
23	linear	RB_{-2}, RB_{-3}, RS_{-3}, RS_{-4}, $100[(PD/PD_{-4}) - 1]_{-1}$
24	linear	RM_{-1}, RM_{-2}, RS_{-3}, $100[(PD/PD_{-4}) - 1]_{-1}$
25	linear	$\Delta(CF - TFG - TFS)_{-1}$, CF_{-1}, $D2G + D2S$, $TFG + TFS$
26	log	$\log[CUR/(POP \cdot PF)]_{-1}$, $\log[(X - FA)/POP]_{-1}$, $\log[CUR_{-2}/(POP_{-2} \cdot PF_{-1})]$
27	log	$D691$, $D692$, $D714$, $D721$, RSA_{-1}, RSA_{-2}, $\log(IM/POP)_{-1}$, $\log(IM/POP)_{-2}$, $100[(PD/PD_{-4}) - 1]_{-1}$, $\log[YD/(POP \cdot PH)]_{-1}$, $\log[YD/(POP \cdot PH)]_{-2}$, $\log(PF/PIM)_{-2}$
28	log	$\log UB_{-1}$, $\log U_{-1}$, $\log U_{-2}$, $\log UB_{-2}$
30	linear	$D794823 \cdot PCM1_{-1}$, JJS_{-1}, RS_{-3}, RS_{-4}, RS_{-5}, RS_{-6}, $100[(PD/PD_{-4}) - 1]_{-1}$

3SLS First Stage Regressors

1	constant	36	$AG2$
2	$(AA/POP)_{-1}$	37	$AG3$
3	$COG + COS$	38	$(KD/POP)_{-1}$
4	$(CD/POP)_{-1}$	39	$\log(CN/POP)_{-2}$
5	$\log(CN/POP)_{-1}$	40	$\log(L1/POP1)_{-1}$
6	$\log(CS/POP)_{-1}$	41	$\log(L2/POP2)_{-1}$
7	$(1 - D1GM - D1SM - D4G)_{-1}$	42	$\log(L3/POP3)_{-1}$
8	EX	43	$\log(LM/POP)_{-1}$
9	$\log HF_{-1}$	44	$\log(WA/PH)_{-1}$
10	$(IHH/POP)_{-1}$	45	$\log(WA/PH)_{-2}$
11	$\log(IM/POP)_{-1}$	46	$\log(WA/PH)_{-3}$
12	$\log(JF/JHMIN)_{-1}$	47	$\log(WA/PH)_{-4}$
13	$(JG \cdot HG + JM \cdot HM + JS \cdot HS)/POP$	48	RM_{-1}
14	$(KH/POP)_{-1}$	49	RM_{-2}
15	$(KK - KKMIN)_{-1}$	50	RS_{-3}
16	$PCM1_{-1}$	51	RS_{-4}
17	$100[(PD/PD_{-1})^4 - 1]_{-1}$	52	RS_{-5}
18	$\log PF_{-1}$	53	RD_{-1}
19	$\log PIM$	54	$(BO/BR)_{-1}$
20	RB_{-1}	55	$\log[MH_{-1}/(POP_{-1} \cdot PH)]$
21	RS_{-1}	56	$\log(MF_{-1}/PF)$
22	RS_{-2}	57	$\log[CUR_{-1}/(POP_{-1} \cdot PF)]$
23	T	58	$D794823 \cdot PMC1_{-1}$
24	$(TRGH + TRSH)/(POP \cdot PH_{-1})$	59	$\log[(YS - Y)/YS + .04]_{-1}$
25	V_{-1}	60	$IKF_{-1} - DELK \cdot KK_{-1}$
26	$\log WF_{-1}$	61	$\log(JF_{-1}/JF_{-2})$
27	Y_{-1}	62	$DD772$
28	Y_{-2}	63	$DD772 \cdot \log(JF/JHMIN)_{-1}$
29	Y_{-3}	64	$DD772 \cdot \Delta \log JF_{-2}$
30	Y_{-4}	65	$DD772 \cdot T$
31	Z_{-1}	66	JJS_{-1}
32	UR_{-1}	67	$(IHH/POP)_{-2}$
33	$\log[YD/(POP \cdot PH)]_{-1}$	68	$TXCR \cdot IKFA$
34	$\log[YD/(POP \cdot PH)]_{-2}$	69	$RB'_{-3} \cdot IKFA$
35	$AG1$		

Table A.8

**Solution of the US Model Under Alternative
Monetary-Policy Assumptions**

There are five possible assumptions that can be made with respect to monetary policy in the US model. In the standard version monetary policy is endogenous; it is explained by equation 30—the interest rate reaction function. Under alternative assumptions, where monetary policy is exogenous, equation 30 is dropped and some of the other equations are rearranged for purposes of solving the model. For example, in the standard version equation 125 is used to solve for the level of nonborrowed reserves (UBR):

$$UBR = BR - BO \tag{125}$$

When, however, the level of nonborrowed reserves is set exogenously, the equation is rearranged and used to solve for total bank reserves (BR):

$$BR = UBR + BO \tag{125}$$

The following shows the arrangement of the equations for each of the five monetary-policy assumptions. The variable listed is the one that is put on the left hand side of the equation and "solved for."

Eq. No.	RS Eq.30	RS Exog.	$M1$ Exog.	UBR Exog.	AG Exog.
9	MH	MH	RSA	RSA	RSA
30	RS	Out	Out	Out	Out
57	BR	BR	BR	MB	MB
71	MB	MB	MB	MH	MH
77	AG	AG	AG	AG	BR
81	$M1$	$M1$	MH	$M1$	$M1$
125	UBR	UBR	UBR	BR	UBR
127	RSA	RSA	RS	RS	RS

Table A.9
Cross-Reference Chart for the US Model

Variable	Eq.	Used in Equation	Variable	Eq.	Used in Equation
AA	89	2, 4, 7	$D794823$	Exog	30
AB	73	80	$D811824$	Exog	21
AF	70	19, 55, 80	$D831834$	Exog	21
AG	77	29, 56, 80	DB	Exog	64, 72, 99, 115
$AG1$	Exog	1, 2, 3, 9	$DD772$	Exog	13, 14
$AG2$	Exog	1, 2, 3, 9	$DELD$	Exog	58
$AG3$	Exog	1, 2, 3, 9	$DELH$	Exog	59
AH	66	80, 89	$DELK$	Exog	12, 92
AR	75	80	DF	18	64, 69, 99, 115
AS	79	80	$DISB$	Exog	73, 80
BF	55	19	$DISBA$	Exog	70, 73
BG	56	29	$DISF$	Exog	70, 80
BO	22	73, 77, 125	$DISG$	Exog	77, 80
BR	57	22, 73, 77, 125	$DISH$	Exog	66, 80
CCB	Exog	60, 61, 72, 82, 83	$DISR$	Exog	75, 80
CCF	21	67	$DISS$	Exog	79, 80
CCH	Exog	65, 67, 68	DRS	Exog	64, 78, 99, 113, 115
CD	3	34, 51, 52, 58, 60, 61, 65, 116	E	85	86
CDA	Exog	3	EX	Exog	33, 60, 61, 74
CF	68	25, 69	$EXPG$	106	107
CG	25	66, 80	$EXPS$	113	114
CN	2	34, 51, 52, 60, 61, 65, 116	FA	Exog	17, 26, 31
COG	Exog	60, 61, 76, 104	$FIROW$	Exog	67, 68, 74, 129, 130
COS	Exog	60, 61, 78, 110	$FIROWD$	Exog	130
CS	1	34, 51, 52, 60, 61, 65, 116	$FIUS$	Exog	67, 68, 74, 129, 130
CUR	26	71, 77	$FIUSD$	Exog	130
$D1G$	Exog	47, 90, 99	$G1$	Exog	57
$D1GM$	90	126, 127, 128	GDP	82	84, 129
$D1S$	Exog	48, 91, 99	$GDPD$	84	123
$D1SM$	91	126, 127, 128	$GDPR$	83	84, 122, 130
$D2G$	Exog	17, 49, 121	GNP	129	131
$D2S$	Exog	17, 50, 121	$GNPD$	131	–
$D3G$	Exog	35, 36, 37, 51	$GNPR$	130	131
$D3S$	Exog	35, 36, 37, 52	HF	14	62, 95, 100, 118
$D4G$	Exog	53, 126	HFF	100	15
$D5G$	Exog	10, 54	HFS	Exog	100
$D691$	Exog	27	HG	Exog	43, 64, 76, 82, 83, 95, 98, 104, 115, 126
$D692$	Exog	27	HM	Exog	43, 64, 76, 82, 83, 95, 98, 104, 115, 126
$D714$	Exog	27	HN	62	43, 53, 54, 64, 67, 68, 115, 121, 126
$D721$	Exog	27	HO	15	43, 53, 54, 62, 64, 67, 68, 115, 121, 126

H S	Exog	43, 64, 78, 82, 83, 95, 98, 110, 115, 126		*M1*	81	124
I B T G	51	34, 52, 61, 76, 82, 105		*M B*	71	57, 73
I B T S	52	34, 51, 61, 78, 82, 112		*M D I F*	Exog	81
I H B	Exog	60, 61, 72		*M F*	17	70, 71, 81
I H F	Exog	60, 61, 68		*M G*	Exog	71, 77
I H H	4	34, 59, 60, 61, 65		*M H*	9	66, 71, 81, 89
I H H A	Exog	4		*M R*	Exog	71, 75, 81
I K B	Exog	60, 61, 72		*M R S*	Exog	68, 76
I K F	12	21, 60, 61, 68, 92		*M S*	Exog	71, 79, 81
I K F A	Exog	12		*M U H*	Exog	93
I K G	Exog	60, 61, 76		*P2554*	Exog	–
I K H	Exog	60, 61, 65		*P C D*	37	34, 51, 52, 61, 65, 116
I M	27	33, 60, 61, 74		*P C G D P D*	122	–
I N S	Exog	65, 76		*P C G D P R*	123	30
I N T F	19	64, 67, 68, 88, 99, 115		*P C M1*	124	30
I N T G	29	64, 76, 88, 99, 106, 115		*P C N*	36	34, 51, 52, 61, 65, 116
I N T O T H	Exog	64, 67, 68, 99, 115		*P C S*	35	34, 51, 52, 61, 65, 116
I N T R O W	88	64, 67, 68, 99, 115		*P D*	33	12, 30, 35, 36, 37, 38, 39, 40, 41, 42
I N T S	Exog	64, 78, 99, 113, 115		*P E X*	32	33, 61, 74
I V A	20	67		*P F*	10	16, 17, 26, 27, 31, 119
I V F	117	–		*P F A*	Exog	31
I V H	Exog	60		*P G*	40	61, 76, 104
I V V H	Exog	61, 65		*P H*	34	1, 2, 3, 4, 5, 6, 7, 8, 9, 27, 89
J F	13	14, 43, 53, 54, 64, 67, 68, 85, 95, 115, 118, 121, 126		*P I E B*	Exog	60, 61, 72, 82, 83
J G	Exog	43, 64, 76, 82, 83, 85, 95, 98, 104, 115, 126		*P I E F*	67	18, 49, 50, 121
J H M I N	94	13, 14		*P I E H*	Exog	64, 67, 68, 99
J J	95	96, 97		*P I H*	38	34, 61, 65, 68, 72
J J P	Exog	96, 97, 98		*P I K*	39	21, 61, 65, 68, 72, 76
J J S	96	30		*P I M*	Exog	10, 27, 33, 61, 74
J M	Exog	43, 64, 76, 82, 83, 85, 87, 95, 98, 104, 115, 126		*P I V*	42	67, 82
J S	Exog	43, 64, 78, 82, 83, 85, 95, 98, 110, 115, 126		*P O P*	120	1, 2, 3, 4, 7, 8, 9, 26, 27, 47, 48, 90, 91, 95, 98, 99
K D	58	3		*P O P1*	Exog	5, 120
K H	59	4, 89		*P O P2*	Exog	6, 120
K K	92	12		*P O P3*	Exog	7, 120
K K M I N	93	12		*P R O D*	118	–
L1	5	86, 87		*P S*	41	61, 78, 110
L2	6	86, 87		*P S I1*	Exog	32
L3	7	86, 87		*P S I2*	Exog	35
L A M	Exog	94, 98		*P S I3*	Exog	36
L M	8	85		*P S I4*	Exog	37

Appendix B

Tables for the ROW Model

Table B.1
The Countries and Variables in the MC Model

Quarterly Countries		Local Currency	Trade Share Equations Only	
1. US	United States	U.S. Dollars (mil.)	34. NI	Nigeria
2. CA	Canada	Can. Dollars (mil.)	35. AL	Algeria
3. JA	Japan	Yen (bil.)	36. IA	Indonesia
4. AU	Austria	Schillings (bil.)	37. IN	Iran
5. FR	France	Fr. Francs (bil.)	38. IQ	Iraq
6. GE	Germany	D. Mark (bil.)	39. KU	Kuwait
7. IT	Italy	Lire (bil.)	40. LI	Libya
8. NE	Netherlands	Guilders (bil.)	41. UA	United Arab Emirates
9. ST	Switzerland	Swill Francs (bil.)	42. IS	Israel
10. UK	United Kingdom	U.K. Pounds (mil.)	43. BA	Bangladish
11. FI	Finland	Markkaa (mil.)	44. SI	Singapore
12. AS	Australia	Aust. Dollars (mil.)	45. AO	All Other
13. SO	South Africa	Rand (mil.)		
14. KO	Korea	Won (bil.)		

Annual Countries

15. BE	Belgium	Bel. Francs (bil.)
16. DE	Denmark	Den. Kroner (bil.)
17. NO	Norway	Nor. Kroner (bil.)
18. SW	Sweden	Swe. Kroner (bil.)
19. GR	Greece	Drachmas (bil.)
20. IR	Ireland	Irish Pounds (mil.)
21. PO	Portugal	Escudos (bil.)
22. SP	Spain	Pesetas (bil.)
23. NZ	New Zealand	N.Z. Dollars (mil.)
24. SA	Saudi Arabia	Riyals (bil.)
25. VE	Venezuela	Bolivares (bil.)
26. CO	Colombia	Col. Pesos (bil.)
27. JO	Jordan	Jor. Dinars (mil.)
28. SY	Syria	Syr. Pounds (mil.)
29. ID	India	Ind. Rupees (bil.)
30. MA	Malaysia	Ringgit (mil.)
31. PA	Pakistan	Pak. Rupees (bil.)
32. PH	Philippines	Phil. Pesos (bil.)
33. TH	Thailand	Baht (bil.)

Table B.1 (continued)

A Brief Listing of the Variables per Country

Variables Determined by Stochastic Equations:

1.	M	Merchandise Imports, 85 lc
2.	C	Consumption, constant lc
3.	I	Fixed Investment, constant lc
4.	Y	Real GDP, constant lc
5.	PY	GDP Deflator, base year = 1.0
6.	$M1$	Money Supply, lc
7.	RS	Three Month Interest Rate, percentage points
8.	RB	Long Term Interest Rate, percentage points
9.	E	Exchange Rate, lc per $
10.	F	Three Month Forward Rate, lc per $
11.	PX	Export Price Index, 1985=1.0
12.	W	Nominal Wage Rate, base year = 1.0
13.	J	Employment, thousands
14.	$L1$	Labor Force—men, thousands
15.	$L2$	Labor Force—women, thousands

Variables Determined by Identities:

I-1.	IM	Total Imports (NIPA), constant lc
I-2.	EX	Total Exports (NIPA), constant lc
I-3.	X	Final Sales, constant lc
I-4.	$V1$	Inventory Investment, constant lc
I-5.	V	Inventory Stock, constant lc
I-6.	S	Balance of Payments, lc
I-7.	A	Net Stock of Foreign Security and Reserve Holdings, lc
I-8.	$M85\$A$	Merchandise Imports from the Trade Share Calculations, 85 $
I-9.	EE	Exchange Rate, end of period, lc per $
I-10.	K	Capital Stock, constant lc
I-11.	$KMIN$	Minimum Required Capital Stock, constant lc
I-12.	UR	Unemployment Rate
I-13.	$JMIN$	Minimum Required Employment, thousands
I-14.	JJ	Employment Population Ratio
I-15.	JJS	Peak to Peak Interpolation of JJ
I-16.	Z	Labor Constraint Variable
I-17.	YS	Potential Y
I-18.	ZZ	Demand Pressure Variable
I-19.	PM	Import Price Index, 1985=1.0

Variables Determined by the Trade Share Calculations:

	α_{ij}	Trade share coefficients from trade share equations
L-1.	$PX\$$	Export Price Index, 1985=1.0
L-2.	$X85\$$	Merchandise Exports from the Trade Share Calculations, 85 $
L-3.	PMP	Import Price Index from the Trade Share Calculations, 1985=1.0
L-4.	$PW\$$	World Price Index, 1985=1.0

Exogenous Variables:

AF	Level of the Armed Forces, thousands
DEL	Depreciation Rate for the Capital Stock
$EXDS$	Export Discrepancy, 85 lc
$E85$	E in 1985, 85 lc per 85 \$
G	Government Expenditures, constant lc
$IMDS$	Import Discrepancy, 85 lc
JJP	Peak to Peak Interpolation of JJ
LAM	Peak to Peak Interpolation of Y/J
MS	Non Merchandise Imports, 85 lc
$M85\$B$	Merchandise Imports from Countries other than the 44 in the Trade Share Matrix, 85 \$
MUH	Peak to Peak Interpolation of Y/K
$PM85$	PM in Base Year divided by PM in 1985
POP	Population, millions
$POP1$	Population of men, thousands
$POP2$	Population of women, thousands
$PSI1$	Ratio of $(EE + EE_{-1})/2$ to E
$PSI2$	Ratio of PM to PMP
$PX85$	PX in Base Year divided by PX in 1985
$STAT$	NIPA Statistical Discrepancy
T	Time Trend
TT	Total Net Transfers, lc
XS	Non Merchandise Exports, 85 lc

Notation:

lc	local currency
85 lc	1985 local currency
constant lc	local currency in the NIPA base year

Table B.2
The Variables for a Given Country in Alphabetical Order

Variable	Eq.No.	Description
A	I-7	Net stock of foreign security and reserve holdings, end of quarter, in lc. $[A_{-1} + S.$ Base value of zero used for the quarter prior to the beginning of the data.]
AF	exog	Level of the armed forces in thousands. [OECD data.]
C	2	Personal consumption in constant lc. [OECD data or IFS96F/CPI.]
CPI	none	Consumer price index, 1985 = 1.0. [(IFS64 or IFS64X)/100.]
DEL	exog	Depreciation rate for the capital stock (K), rate per quarter or year. [.015 per quarter, .060 per year. See Section 3.3.3.]
E	9	Exchange rate, average for the period, lc per \$. [IFSRF.]
EE	I-9	Exchange rate, end of period, lc per \$. [IFSAE.]
EX	I-2	Total exports (NIPA) in constant lc. [OECD data or (IFS90C or IFS90N)/PX.]
$EXDS$	exog	Discrepancy between NIPA export data and other export data in 85 lc. $[EX - PX85(E85 \cdot X85\$ + XS).]$
$E85$	exog	E in 1985, 85 lc per 85 \$. [IFSRF in 1985.]
F	10	Three month forward rate, lc per \$. [IFSB.]
G	exog	Government purchases of goods and services in constant lc. [OECD data or (IFS91F or IFS91FF)/PY.]
I	3	Gross fixed investment in constant lc. [OECD data or IFS93/PY.]
IM	I-1	Total imports (NIPA) in constant lc. [OECD data or IFS98C/PM.]
$IMDS$	exog	Discrepancy between NIPA import data and other import data in 85 lc. $[IM - PM85(M + MS).]$
IP	none	Industrial production index, 1985 = 100. [IFS66 or other 66 options.]
J	13	Total employment in thousands. [OECD data or IFS67.]
JJ	I-14	Employment population ratio. $[J/POP.]$
JJP	exog	Peak to peak interpolation of JJ. [See Section 3.3.3.]
JJS	I-15	Ratio of JJ to JJP. $[JJ/JJP.]$
$JMIN$	I-13	Minimum amount of employment needed to produce Y in thousands. $[Y/LAM.]$
K	I-10	Capital stock in constant lc. [See Section 3.3.3.]
$KMIN$	I-11	Minimum capital stock needed to produce Y in constant lc. $[Y/MUH.]$
LAM	exog	Peak to peak interpolation of Y/J. [See Section 3.3.3.]
$L1$	14	Labor force of men in thousands. [OECD data.]
$L2$	15	Labor force of women in thousands. [OECD data.]
M	1	Total merchandise imports (fob) in 85 lc. [IFS71V/PM.]
MS	exog	Other goods, services, and income (debit) in 85 lc, BOP data. $[(\text{IFS77AED} \cdot E)/PM.]$
$M85\$A$	I-8	Merchandise imports (fob) from the trade share matrix in 85 \$. [See Table B.3.]
$M85\$B$	exog	Difference between total merchandise imports and merchandise imports from the trade share matrix in 85 \$ (i.e., imports from countries other than the 44 in the trade share matrix). $[M/E85 - M85\$A.]$
MUH	exog	Peak to peak interpolation of Y/K. [See Section 3.3.3.]
$M1$	6	Money supply in lc. [IFS34 or IFS34..B.]
PM	I-19	Import price index, 1985 = 1.0. [IFS75/100.]
PMP	L-3	Import price index from DOT data, 1985 = 1.0. [See Table B.3.]

$PM85$	exog	PM in the NIPA base year divided by PM in 1985.
POP	exog	Population in millions. [IFS99Z.]
$POP1$	exog	Population of men in thousands. [OECD data.]
$POP2$	exog	Population of women in thousands. [OECD data.]
$PSI1$	exog	$[[(EE + EE_{-1})/2]/E.]$
$PSI2$	exog	$[PM/PMP.]$
$PW\$$	L-4	World price index, $/85$. [See Table B.4.]
PX	11	Export price index, 1985 = 1.0. [IFS74/100.]
$PX\$$	L-1	Export price index, $/85$, 1985 = 1.0. $[(E85 \cdot PX)/E.]$
$PX85$	exog	PX in the NIPA base year divided by PX in 1985.
PY	5	GDP or GNP deflator, equals 1.0 in the NIPA base year. [OECD data or (IFS99B/IFS99B.P.]
RB	8	Long term interest rate, percentage points. [IFS61 or IFS61A.]
RS	7	Three month interest rate, percentage points. [IFS60 or IFS60B or IFS60C or IFS60X.]
S	I-6	Total net goods, services, and transfers in lc. Balance of payments on current account. Saving of the country. [See Table B.7.]
$STAT$	exog	Statistical discrepancy in constant lc. $[Y - C - I - G - EX + IM - V1.]$
T	exog	Time trend. [For quarterly data, 1 in 1952.1, 2 in 1952.2, etc.; for annual data, 1 in 1952, 2 in 1953, etc.]
TT	exog	Total net transfers in lc. [See Table B.6.]
UR	I-12	Unemployment rate. $[(L1 + L2 - J)/(L1 + L2 - AF).]$
V	I-5	Stock of inventories, end of period, in constant lc. $[V_{-1} + V1.$ Base value of zero was used for the period (quarter or year) prior to the beginning of the data.]
$V1$	I-4	Inventory investment in constant lc. [OECD data or IFS93I/PY.]
W	12	Nominal wage rate. [IFS65 or IFS65EY.]
X	I-3	Final sales in constant lc. $[Y - V1.]$
XS	exog	Other goods, services, and income (credit) in 85 lc. BOP data. $[(IFS77ADD \cdot E)/PX.]$
$X85\$$	L-2	Merchandise exports from the trade share matrix in 85 $. [See Table B.4.]
Y	4	Real GDP or GNP in constant lc. [OECD data or IFS99A.P or IFS99B.P or IFS99A.R or IFS99B.R.]
YS	I-17	Potential value of Y. $[LAM \cdot JJP \cdot POP.]$
Z	I-16	Labor constraint variable. $[\min(0, 1 - JJP/JJ).]$
ZZ	I-18	Demand pressure variable. $[(YS - Y)/YS.]$

lc   = local currency.
NIPA = national income and product accounts.
IFSxx = variable number xx from the IFS data.

Table B.3
The Equations for a Given Country

Stochastic Equations

LHS Var.	Explanatory Variables
1. $\log(M/POP)$	cnst, $\log(M/POP)_{-1}$, $\log(PY/PM)$, RS or RB, $\log(Y/POP)$, $[A/(PY \cdot YS)]_{-1}$
2. $\log(C/POP)$	cnst, $\log(C/POP)_{-1}$, RS or RB, $\log(Y/POP)$, $[A/(PY \cdot YS)]_{-1}$
3. I	cnst, I_{-1}, K_{-1}, Y, RS or RB
4. Y	cnst, Y_{-1}, X, V_{-1}
5. $\log PY$	cnst, $\log PY_{-1}$, $\log PM$, $\log W$, ZZ or JJS
6. $\log(\frac{M1}{POP \cdot PY})$	cnst, $\log[M1/(POP \cdot PY)]_{-1}$ or $\log[M1_{-1}/(POP_{-1} \cdot PY)]$, RS, $\log(Y/POP)$
7. RS	cnst, RS_{-1}, $PCPY$, ZZ or JJS, $PCM1_{-1}$, $[A/(PY \cdot YS)]_{-1}$, $[A/(PY \cdot YS)]_{-2}$, $RSUS$: $PCPY = 100[(PY/PY_{-1})^4 - 1]$ and $PCM1 = 100[(M1/M1_{-1})^4 - 1]$
8. $RB - RS_{-2}$	cnst, $RB_{-1} - RS_{-2}$, $RS - RS_{-2}$, $RS_{-1} - RS_{-2}$
9. $\Delta \log E$	cnst, $\log(PY/PYUS) - \log E_{-1}$, $\log EGE - \log(PY/PYUS)$, $.25 \cdot \log[(1 + RS/100)/(1 + RSUS/100)]$
10. $\log F$	$\log EE$, $.25 \cdot \log[(1 + RS/100)/(1 + RSUS/100)]$
11. $\log(\frac{PX}{PW\$ \cdot E})$	$\log PY - \log(PW\$ \cdot E)$
12. $\log W$	cnst, T, $\log W_{-1}$, $\log PY$, UR or JJS or ZZ, $\log PY_{-1}$,
13. $\Delta \log J$	cnst, T, $\log(J/JMIN)_{-1}$, $\Delta \log Y$, $\Delta \log Y_{-1}$
14. $\log(L1/POP1)$	cnst, T, $\log(L1/POP1)_{-1}$, $\log(W/PY)$, Z
15. $\log(L2/POP2)$	cnst, T, $\log(L2/POP2)_{-1}$, $\log(W/PY)$, Z

Identities

I-1.	$IM = PM85(M + MS) + IMDS$
I-2.	$EX = PX85(E85 \cdot X85\$ + XS) + EXDS$
I-3.	$X = C + I + G + EX - IM + STAT$
I-4.	$V1 = Y - X$
I-5.	$V = V_{-1} + V1$
I-6.	$S = PX(E85 \cdot X85\$ + XS) - PM(M + MS) + TT$
I-7.	$A = A_{-1} + S$
I-8.	$M85\$A = M/E85 - M85\$B$
I-9.	$EE = 2 \cdot PSI1 \cdot E - EE_{-1}$
I-10.	$K = (1 - DEL)K_{-1} + I$
I-11.	$KMIN = Y/MUH$
I-12.	$UR = (L1 + L2 - J)/(L1 + L2 - AF)$
I-13.	$JMIN = Y/LAM$
I-14.	$JJ = J/POP$
I-15.	$JJS = JJ/JJP$
I-16.	$Z = \min(0, 1 - JJP/JJ)$

I-17.	$YS = LAM \cdot JJP \cdot POP$
I-18.	$ZZ = (YS - Y)/YS$
I-19.	$PM = PSI2 \cdot PMP$

Variables Explained When the Countries are Linked Together (Table B.4)

L-1	$PX\$$
L-2.	$X85\$$
L-3.	PMP
L-4.	$PW\$$

Table B.4
Equations that Pertain to the Trade and Price Links Among Countries

L-1. $PX\$_i = (E85_i/E_i)PX_i$, $i = 1, \cdots, 44$

L-2. $X85\$_i = \sum_{j=1}^{45} \alpha_{ij} M85\$A_j$, $i = 1, \cdots, 33$

L-3. $PMP_i = (E_i/E85_i) \sum_{j=1}^{44} \alpha_{ji} PX\$_j$, $i = 1, \cdots, 33$

> An element in this summation is skipped if α_{ji} is missing or $PX\$_j$ is missing. PMP_i is not computed if E_i is missing or $E85_i$ is missing.

L-4. $PW\$_i = (\sum_{j=1}^{33} PX\$_j X85\$_j)/(\sum_{j=1}^{33} X85\$_j)$, $i = 1, \cdots, 33$

> An element in this summation is skipped if $PX\$_j$ is missing or $X85\$_j$ is missing or j=i. This summation also excludes SA and VE, which are the oil exporting countries among the 33.

Construction of α_{ij}:

The raw data are:

$XX\$_{ij}$ Merchandise exports i to j in \$, $i, j = 1, \cdots, 44$ [DOT data.]

$X\$_i$ Total merchandise exports (fob) in \$. $i = 1, \cdots, 33$ [IFS70/E.]

The constructed variables are:

$XX\$_{i45} = X\$_i - \sum_{j=1}^{44} XX\$_{ij}$, $i = 1, \cdots, 33$

$XX85\$_{ij} = XX\$_{ij}/PX\$_i$, $i = 1, \cdots, 44$, $j = 1, \cdots, 45$

> $XX85\$_{ij}$ is missing if $XX\$_{ij}$ is missing or $PX\$_i$ is missing.

$M85\$A_i = \sum_{j=1}^{44} XX85\$_{ji}$, $i = 1, \cdots, 45$

$X85\$_i = \sum_{j=1}^{45} XX85\$_{ij}$, $i = 1, \cdots, 33$

$\alpha_{ij} = XX85\$_{ij}/M85\$A_j$, $i = 1, \cdots, 44$, $j = 1, \cdots, 45$

Linking of the Annual and Quarterly Data

Quarterly data exist for all the trade share calculations, and all these calculations are quarterly. Feeding into these calculations from the annual models are predicted annual values of $PX\$_i$, $M85\$A_i$, and E_i. For each of these three variables the predicted value for a given quarter was taken to be the predicted annual value multiplied by the ratio of the actual quarterly value to the actual annual value. This means in effect that the distribution of an annual value into its quarterly values is taken to be exogenous.

Once the quarterly values have been computed from the trade share calculations, the annual values of $X85\$_i$ that are needed for the annual models are taken to be the sums of the quarterly values. Similarly, the annual values of PMP_i and $PW\$_i$ are taken to be the averages of the quarterly values.

Table B.5
Links Between the US and ROW Models

The data on the variables for the United States that are needed when the US model is imbedded in the MC model were collected as described in Table B.2. These variables are (with the US subscript dropped): $EXDS$, $IMDS$, M, MS, $M85\$A$, $M85\$B$, PM, PMP, $PSI2$, $PW\$$, PX ($= PX\$$), S, TT, XS, and $X85\$$. The PX variable here is not the same as the PX variable in Appendix A.

Variable	Determination
$X85\$_{US}$	Determined in Table B.4
PMP_{US}	Determined in Table B.4
$PW\$_{US}$	Determined in Table B.4
PX_{US}	Determined by equation 132 in the US model. This equation is equivalent to equation 11 for the other countries. See the discussion in Section 9.2.
PEX	$= DEL3 \cdot PX_{US}$. In the US model by itself, PEX is determined as $PSI1 \cdot PX$, which is equation 32 in Table A.2. This equation is dropped when the US model is linked to the ROW model. $DEL3$ is constructed from the data as PEX/PX_{US} and is taken to be exogenous.
PM_{US}	$= PSI2_{US} \cdot PMP_{US}$. This is the same as equation I-19 for the other countries.
PIM	$= DEL4 \cdot PM_{US}$. PIM is an exogenous variable in the US model by itself. $DEL4$ is constructed from the data as PIM/PM_{US} and is taken to be exogenous.
EX	$= (X85\$_{US} + XS_{US} + EXDS_{US})/1000$. This is the same as equation I-2 for the other countries. EX is an exogenous variable in the US model by itself. $EXDS_{US}$ is constructed from the data as $1000 \cdot EX - X85\$_{US} - XS_{US}$ and is taken to be exogenous.
M_{US}	$= 1000 \cdot IM - MS_{US} - IMDS_{US}$. This is the same as equation I-1 for the other countries. $IMDS_{US}$ is constructed from the data as $1000 \cdot IM - M_{US} - MS_{US}$ and is taken to be exogenous.
$M85\$A_{US}$	$= M_{US} - M85\$B_{US}$. This is the same as equation I-8 for the other countries.
S_{US}	$= PX_{US}(X85\$_{US} + XS_{US}) - PM_{US}(M_{US} + MS_{US}) + TT_{US}$. This is the same as equation I-6 for the other countries.

Note:

The new exogenous variables for the US model when it is linked to the ROW model are $DEL3$, $DEL4$, $EXDS_{US}$, $IMDS_{US}$, $M85\$B_{US}$, MS_{US}, $PSI2_{US}$, TT_{US}, and XS_{US}. EX and PIM are exogenous in the US model by itself, but endogenous when the US model is linked to the ROW model.

Table B.6
The Procedure Used to Create Quarterly Data from Annual Data

Let y_t be the (observed) average value of the variable for year t, and let y_{it} be the (unobserved) average value of the variable for quarter i of year t (i = 1, 2, 3, 4). Then:

$$y_{1t} + y_{2t} + y_{3t} + y_{4t} = \lambda y_t \qquad\qquad (i)$$

where

$$\lambda = \{ \begin{array}{l} \text{1 for flow variables (at quarterly rates)} \\ \text{4 for stock variables and price variables} \end{array}$$

Assume that the annual data begin in year 1, and let $\lambda y_1 = a_1, \lambda y_2 = a_2, \lambda y_3 = a_3, \cdots$. The key assumption is that the four quarterly changes within the year are the same:

$$y_{1t} - y_{4t-1} = y_{2t} - y_{1t} = y_{3t} - y_{2t} = y_{4t} - y_{3t} = \{ \begin{array}{l} \delta_2 \text{ for } t = 1, 2 \\ \delta_t \text{ for } t \geq 3 \end{array} \qquad (ii)$$

Given i and ii for $t = 1, 2$, one can solve for y_{40} and δ_2 in terms of a_1 and a_2:

$$y_{40} = (13/32)a_1 - (5/32)a_2$$
$$\delta_2 = (a_2 - a_1)/16$$

Using y_{40} and δ_2, one can then construct quarterly data for years 1 and 2 using ii. Given y_{42} from these calculations and given i and ii for $t = 3$, one can solve for δ_3 in terms of a_3 and y_{42}:

$$\delta_3 = (a_3 - 4y_{42})/10$$

Using y_{42} and δ_3, one can then construct quarterly data for year 3. One can then solve for δ_4 in terms of y_{43} and a_4, and so on.

Note:

The annual population data that were collected for the model are mid year estimates. In order to apply the above procedure to these data, the assumption was made that the average value for the year equals the mid year value.

Table B.7
Construction of the Balance of Payments Data:
Data for S and TT

The relevant raw data variables are:

$M\$'$	Merchandise imports (fob) in \$, BOP data. [IFS77ABD.]
$M\$$	Merchandise imports (fob) in \$. [IFS71V/E.]
$X\$'$	Merchandise exports (fob) in \$, BOP data. [IFS77AAD.]
$X\$$	Merchandise exports (fob) in \$. [IFS70/E.]
$MS\$$	Other goods, services, and income (debit) in \$, BOP data. [IFS77AED.]
$XS\$$	Other goods, services, and income (credit) in \$, BOP data. [IFS77ADD.]
$PT\$$	Private unrequited transfers in \$, BOP data. [IFS77AFD.]
$OT\$$	Official unrequited transfers in \$, BOP data. [IFS77AGD.]

- When quarterly data on all the above variables were available, then $S\$$ and $TT\$$ were constructed as:

$$S\$ = X\$' + XS\$ - M\$' - MS\$ + PT\$ + OT\$ \qquad (i)$$

$$TT\$ = S\$ - X\$ - XS\$ + M\$ + MS\$ \qquad (ii)$$

where $S\$$ is total net goods, services, and transfers in \$ (balance of payments on current account) and $TT\$$ is total net transfers in \$.

- When only annual data on $M\$'$ were available and quarterly data were needed, interpolated quarterly data were constructed using $M\$$. Similarly for $MS\$$.

When only annual data on $X\$'$ were available and quarterly data were needed, interpolated quarterly data were constructed using $X\$$. Similarly for $XS\$$, $PT\$$, and $OT\$$.

When no data on $M\$'$ were available, then $M\$'$ was taken to be $\lambda \cdot M\$$, where λ is the last observed annual value of $M\$'/M\$$. Similarly for $MS\$$ (where λ is the last observed annual value of $MS\$/M\$$.)

When no data on $X\$'$ were available, then $X\$'$ was taken to be $\lambda \cdot X\$$, where λ is the last observed annual value of $X\$'/X\$$. Similarly for $XS\$$ (where λ is the last observed annual value of $XS\$/X\$$), for $PT\$$ (where λ is the last observed annual value of $PT\$/X\$$), and for $OT\$$ (where λ is the last observed annual value of $OT\$/X\$$).

Equations i and ii were then used to construct quarterly data for $S\$$ and $TT\$$.

- After data on $S\$$ and $TT\$$ were constructed, data on S and TT were constructed as:

$$S = E \cdot S\$ \qquad (iii)$$

$$TT = E \cdot TT\$ \qquad (iv)$$

- Note from MS and XS in Table B.2 and from $MS\$$ and $XS\$$ above that

$$MS\$ = (PM \cdot MS)/E \qquad (v)$$

$$XS\$ = (PX \cdot XS)/E \qquad (vi)$$

Note also from Table B.2 that

$$M\$ = (PM \cdot M)/E \qquad (vii)$$

$$X\$ = (E85 \cdot PX \cdot X85\$)/E \qquad (vii)$$

Therefore, from equations ii–vii, the equation for S can be written

$$S = PX(E85 \cdot X85\$ + XS) - PM(M + MS) + TT$$

which is equation I-6 in Table B.3.

Bibliography

Allen, Polly Reynolds, 1973, "A Portfolio Approach to International Capital Flows," *Journal of International Economics*, 3, 135-160.

Almon, Shirley, 1965, "The Distributed Lag Between Capital Appropriations and Expenditures," *Econometrica*, 33, 178-196.

Altug, Sumru, 1989, "Time-to-Build and Aggregate Fluctuations: Some New Evidence," *International Economic Review*, 30, 889-920.

Amemiya, Takeshi, 1982, "The Two Stage Least Absolute Deviations Estimators," *Econometrica*, 50, 689-711.

Andrews, Donald W. K., 1993, "Exactly Median-Unbiased Estimation of First Order Autoregressive/Unit Root Models," *Econometrica*, 61, 139-165.

_____, and Ray C. Fair, 1988, "Inference in Nonlinear Econometric Models with Structural Change," *Review of Economic Studies*, 55, 615-640.

Andrews, Donald W. K., and Werner Ploberger, 1994, "Optimal Tests When a Nuisance Parameter is Present Only Under the Alternative," *Econometrica*, 62.

Arrow, Kenneth, 1991, "Cowles in the History of Economic Thought," in *Cowles Fiftieth Anniversary*, Yale University.

Barro, Robert J., 1977, "Unanticipated Money Growth and Unemployment in the United States," *American Economic Review*, 67, 101-115.

Barro, Robert J., and Herschel I. Grossman, 1971, "A General Disequilibrium Model of Income and Employment," *American Economic Review*, 61, 82-93.

Bernanke, Ben S., 1986, "Alternative Explanations of the Money-Income Correlation," in Karl Brunner and Allan H. Meltzer, eds, *Real Business Cycles, Real Exchange Rates and Actual Policies*, Amsterdam: North-Holland.

Black, Stanley W., 1973, *International Money Markets and Flexible Exchange Rates*, Studies in International Finance, No. 32, Princeton: Princeton University Press.

Blanchard, Olivier J., and Mark W. Watson, 1986, "Are Business Cycles All Alike?" in Robert J. Gordon, ed., *The American Business Cycle: Continuity and Change*, Chicago: University of Chicago Press.

Blinder, Alan, 1981, "Retail Inventory Behavior and Business Fluctuations," *Brookings Papers on Economic Activity*, 443-505.

Branson, William H., 1974, "Stocks and Flows in International Monetary Analysis," in A. Ando, R. Herring, and R. Martson, eds., *International Aspects of Stabilization Policies*, Boston: Federal Reserve Bank of Boston, 27-50.

Canova, F., M. Finn, and A.R. Pagan, 1991, "Econometric Issues in the Analysis of Equilibrium Models," paper given at the Canadian Econometric Study Group meeting, Quebec City, September.

Carloyzi, Nicholas, and John B. Taylor, 1985, "International Capital Mobility in the Coordination of Monetary Policy Rules," in Jagdeep Bandhari, ed., *Exchange Rate Policy under Uncertainty*, Cambridge: M.I.T Press.

Chong, Yock Y., and David F. Hendry, 1986, "Econometric Evaluation of Linear Macro-Econometric Models," *Review of Economic Studies*, 53, 671-690.

Chow, Gregory C., 1991, "Statistical Estimation and Testing of a Real Business Cycle Model," mimeo, August 30.

Christ, Carl F., 1968, "A Simple Macroeconomic Model with a Government Budget Restraint," *Journal of Political Economy*, 76, 53-67.

Christiano, Lawrence J., and Martin Eichenbaum, 1990, "Current Real Business Cycle Theories and Aggregate Labor Market Fluctuations," Discussion Paper 24, Institute for Empirical Macroeconomics.

Clower, Robert W., 1965, "The Keynesian Counterrevolution: A Theoretical Appraisal," in F. H. Hahn and F. P. R. Brechling, eds., *The Theory of Interest Rates*, London: Macmillian.

Cooper, J. Phillip, and Charles R. Nelson, 1975, "The Ex-Ante Prediction Performance of the St. Louis and FRB-MIT-Penn Econometric Models and Some Results on Composite Predictions," *Journal of Money, Credit, and Banking*, 7, 1-32.

Cumby, Robert E., John Huizinga, and Maurice Obstfeld, 1983, "Two-Step Two-Stage Least Squares Estimation in Models with Rational Expectations," *Journal of Econometrics*, 21, 333-355.

Davidson, Russell, and James G. MacKinnon, 1981, "Several Tests of Model Specification in the Presence of Alternative Hypotheses," *Econometrica*, 40, 781-793.

DeLong, J. Bradford and Lawrence H. Summers, 1986, "Is Increased Price Flexibility Stabilizing?", *American Economic Review*, 78, 1031-1043.

Diebold, Francis X., and Glenn D. Rudebusch, 1989, "Scoring the Leading Indicators," *Journal of Business*, 62, 369-391.

Dornbusch, Rudiger, 1976, "Capital Mobility, Flexible Exchange Rates and Macroeconomic Equilibrium," in E. Claassen and P. Salin, eds., *Recent Developments in International Monetary Economics*, Amsterdam: North-Holland, 261-278.

Duesenberry, James S., Gary Fromm, Lawrence R. Klein, and Edwin Kuh, eds., 1965, *The Brookings Quarterly Econometric Model of the United States*, Chicago: Rand McNally & Company.

_____, 1969, *The Brookings Model: Some Further Results*, Chicago: Rand McNally & Company.

Easterlin, Richard A., 1987, *Birth and Fortune: The Impact of Numbers on Personal Welfare*, 2nd ed., Chicago: University of Chicago Press.

Fair, Ray C., 1969, *The Short-Run Demand for Workers and Hours*, North-Holland Publishing Co.

_____, 1974, *A Model of Macroeconomic Activity. Volume I: The Theoretical Model*, Ballinger Publishing Co.

_____, 1976, *A Model of Macroeconomic Activity. Volume II: The Empirical Model*, Ballinger Publishing Co.

_____, 1978, "The Sensitivity of Fiscal-Policy Effects to Assumptions About the Behavior of the Federal Reserve," *Econometrica*, 46, 1165-1179.

_____, 1979a, "A Model of the Balance of Payments," *Journal of International Economics*, 9, 25-46.

_____, 1979b, "An Analysis of a Macro-Econometric Model with Rational Expectations in the Bond and Stock Markets," *The American Economic Review*, 69, 539–552.

_____, 1980a, "Estimating the Expected Predictive Accuracy of Econometric Models," *International Economic Review*, 21, 355-378.

_____, 1980b, "Estimating the Uncertainty of Policy Effects in Nonlinear Econometric Models," *Econometrica*, 48, 1381-1391.

_____, 1984, *Specification, Estimation, and Analysis of Macroeconometric Models*, Cambridge, MA: Harvard University Press.

_____, 1985, "Excess Labor and the Business Cycle," *The American Economic Review*, 75, 239-245.

_____, 1987, "International Evidence on the Demand for Money," *The Review of Economics and Statistics*, 69, 473-480.

_____, 1988a, "Sources of Economic Fluctuations in the United States," *The Quarterly Journal of Economics*, 103, 313-332.

_____, 1988b, "Optimal Choice of Monetary Policy Instruments in a Macroeconometric Model," *Journal of Monetary Economics*, 22, 301-315.

_____, 1989, "The Production Smoothing Model is Alive and Well," *Journal of Monetary Economics*, 23, 353-370.

_____, 1992, "The Cowles Commission Approach, Real Business Cycles Theories, and New Keynesian Economics," in Michael T. Belongia and Michelle R. Garfinkel, eds., *The Business Cycle: Theories and Evidence*, Federal Reserve Bank of St. Louis, 133-147.

_____, 1993a, "Inflationary Expectations and Price Setting Behavior," *The Review of Economics and Statistics*, 75, 8-18.

_____, 1993b, Testing the Rational Expectations Hypothesis in Macroeconometric Models," *Oxford Economic Papers*, 45, 169-190.

_____, 1993c, Estimating Event Probabilities in Macroeconometric Models using Stochastic Simulation," in James H. Stock and Mark W. Watson, eds., *Business Cycles, Indicators, and Forecasting*, Chicago: The University of Chicago Press, 157-176.

_____, 1993d, Testing Macroeconometric Models," *The American Economic Review*, 83, 287-293.

_____, 1994a, "Computing Median Unbiased Estimates and Examining Asymptotic Distribution Accuracy in Macroeconometric Models," mimeo.

_____, 1994b, "Is Monetary Policy Becoming Less Effective?" mimeo.

_____, and Kathryn M. Dominguez, 1991, "Effects of the Changing U.S. Age Distribution on Macroeconomic Equations," *The American Economic Review*, 81, 1276-1294.

Fair, Ray C., and Robert J. Shiller, 1989, "The Informational Content of Ex Ante Forecasts," *The Review of Economics and Statistics*, 71, 325-331.

_____, 1990, "Comparing Information in Forecasts from Econometric Models," *The American Economic Review*, 80, 375-389.

Fair, Ray C., and William R. Parke, 1993, "The Fair-Parke Program for the Estimation and Analysis of Nonlinear Econometric Models," mimeo.

Fair, Ray C., and John B. Taylor, 1983, "Solution and Maximum Likelihood Estimation of Dynamic Rational Expectations Models," *Econometrica*, 51, 1169-1185.

_____, 1990, "Full Information Estimation and Stochastic Simulation of Models with Rational Expectations," *Journal of Applied Econometrics*, 5, 381-392.

Fay, Jon A., and James L. Medoff, 1985, "Labor and Output Over the Business Cycle: Some Direct Evidence," *American Economic Review*, 75, 638-655.

Flow of Funds Coded Tables, 1992, Board of Governors of the Federal Reserve System, January, Washington, D.C., 20551.

Frenkel, Jacob A., and Harry G. Johnson, eds., 1976, *The Monetary Approach to the Balance of Payments*, Toronto: University of Toronto Press.

Frenkel, Jacob A., and Carlos A. Rodrigues, 1975, "Portfolio Equilibrium and the Balance of Payments: A Monetary Approach," *American Economic Review*, 65, 674-688.

Friedman, Benjamin M., and Kenneth N. Kuttner, 1992, "Money, Income, Prices, and Interest Rates," *American Economic Review*, 82, 472-492.

_____, 1993, "Why Does the Paper-Bill Spread Predict Real Economic Activity?" in James H. Stock and Mark W. Watson, eds., *Business Cycles, Indicators, and Forecasting*, Chicago: The University of Chicago Press, 213-249.

Girton, Lance, and Dale W. Henderson, 1976, "Financial Capital Movements and Central Bank Behavior in a Two-Country Portfolio Balance Model," *Journal of Monetary Economics*, 2, 33-61.

Grandmont, Jean-Michel, 1977, "Temporary General Equilibrium Theory," *Econometrica*, 45, 535-572.

Granger, Clive W. J., and Paul Newbold, 1986, *Forecasting Economic Time Series*, 2nd ed., New York: Academic Press.

Hall, Robert E., 1978, "Stochastic Implications of the Life-Cycle Permanent Income Hypothesis: Theory and Evidence," *Journal of Political Economy*, 86, 971-989.

Hall, Robert E., 1986, "The Role of Consumption in Economic Fluctuations," in Robert J. Gordon, ed., *The American Business Cycle: Continuity and Change*, Chicago: University of Chicago Press.

Hamilton, James D., 1983, "Oil and the Macroeconomy since World War II," *Journal of Political Economy*, 91, 228-248.

Hansen, Lars Peter, 1982, "Large Sample Properties of Generalized Method of Moments Estimators," *Econometrica*, 50, 1029-1054.

_____, and Kenneth Singleton, 1982, Generalized Instrumental Variables Estimation of Nonlinear Rational Expectations Models," *Econometrica*, 50, 1269-1286.

Heckman, James J., 1992, "Haavelmo and the Birth of Modern Econometrics: A Review of *The History of Econometric Ideas* by Mary Morgan," *Journal of Economic Literature*, 30, 876-886.

Hendry, David F., 1988, "The Encompassing Implications of Feedback Versus Feedforward Mechanisms in Econometrics," *Oxford Economic Papers*, 40, 132-149.

_____, Adrian R. Pagan, and J. Denis Sargan, 1984, Dynamic Specifications," in Z. Griliches and M. D. Intriligator, eds., *Handbook of Econometrics*, Amsterdam: North-Holland, 1023-1100.

Hendry, David F., and Jean-Francois Richard, 1982, "On the Formulation of Empirical Models in Dynamic Economics," *Journal of Econometrics*, 20, 3-33.

Hurwicz, Leonid, 1950, "Least-Squares Bias in Time Series," in T. C. Koopmans, ed., *Statistical Inference in Dynamic Economic Models*, Cowles Commission Monograph No. 10, New York: John Wiley & Sons, Inc., 365-383.

King, Stephen R., "Is Increased Price Flexibility Stabilizing?: Comment," 1988, *American Economic Review*, 78, 267-272.

Klein, Lawrence R., 1950, *Economic Fluctuations in the United States, 1921-1941*, New York: Wiley, Cowles Monograph No. 11.

_____, and Arthur S. Goldberger, 1955, *An Econometric Model of the United States 1929-1952*, Amsterdam: North-Holland.

Kouri, Penti J. K., 1976, "The Exchange Rate and the Balance of Payments in the Short Run and in the Long Run," *Scandinavian Journal of Economics*, 2, 280-304.

Krane, Spencer D., and Steven N. Braun, 1989, "Production Smoothing Evidence from Physical-Product Data," mimeo.

Kydland, F.E., and E.C. Prescott, 1982, "Time To Build and Aggregate Fluctuations," *Econometrica*, 50, 1342-1370.

Lilien, David M., 1982, "Sectoral Shifts and Cyclical Unemployment," *Journal of Political Economy*, 90, 777-793.

Lucas, Robert E., Jr., 1976, "Econometric Policy Evaluation: A Critique," in K. Brunner and A.H. Meltzer, eds., *The Phillips Curve and Labor Markets*, Amsterdam: North-Holland.

_____, 1987, *Models of Business Cycles*, New York: Blackwell.

Malinvaud, Edmond, 1970, *Statistical Methods of Econometrics*, Amsterdam: North-Holland.

_____, 1991, "Econometric Methodology at the Cowles Commission: Rise and Maturity," in *Cowles Fiftieth Anniversity*, Yale University.

Mankiw, N. Gregory, and David Romer, eds., 1991, *New Keynesian Economics*, Volumes 1 and 2, Cambridge: The MIT Press.

Mankiw, N. Gregory, Julio J. Rotemberg, and Laurence H. Summers, 1985, "Intertemporal Substitution in Macroeconomics," *Quarterly Journal of Economics*, 100, 225-251.

McCallum, B. T., 1976, "Rational Expectations and the Natural Rate Hypothesis: Some Consistent Results," *Econometrica*, 44, 43-52.

McNees, Stephen K., 1981, "The Methodology of Macroeconometric Model Comparisons," in J. Kmenta and J. B. Ramsey, eds., *Large Scale Macroeconometric Models*, Amsterdam: North-Holland, 397-442.

Mizon, Grayham and Richard, Jean-Francois, 1986, "The Encompassing Principle and Its Application to Testing Non-Nested Hypotheses," *Econometrica*, 54, 657-678.

Mortensen, Dale T., 1970, "A Theory of Wage and Employment Dynamics," in E. S. Phelps et al., *Microeconomic Foundations of Employment and Inflation Theory*, New York: Norton, 167-211.

Murphy, Kevin M., and Robert H. Topel, 1985, ""Estimation and Inference in Two-Step Econometric Models," *Journal of Business and Economic Statistics*, 3, 370-379.

Myhrman, Johan, 1976, "Balance-of-Payments Adjustment and Portfolio Theory: A Survey," in E. Claassen and P. Salin, eds., *Recent Developments in International Monetary Economics*, Amsterdam: North-Holland, 203-237.

Nelson, Charles R., 1972, "The Prediction Performance of the FRB-MIT-Penn Model of the U.S. Economy," *American Economic Review*, 62, 902-917.

Okun, Arthur M., 1971, "The Personal Tax Surcharge and Consumer Demand, 1968-70," *Brookings Papers on Economic Activity*, 167-204.

Orcutt, Guy H., 1948, "A Study of the Autoregressive Nature of the Time Series Used for Tinbergen's Model of the Economic System of the United States, 1919-1932," *Journal of the Royal Statistical Society*, Series B, 1-45.

_____, and Herbert S. Winokur, Jr., 1969, "First Order Autoregression: Inference, Estimation, and Prediction," *Econometrica*, 37, 1-14.

Parke, William R., 1982, "An Algorithm for FIML and 3SLS Estimation of Large Nonlinear Models," *Econometrica*, 50, 81-96.

Patinkin, Don, 1956, *Money, Interest, and Prices*, New York: Harper & Row.

Phelps, Edmund S., 1970, "Money Wage Dynamics and Labor Market Equilibrium," in E. S. Phelps et al., *Microeconomic Foundations of Employment and Inflation Theory*, New York: Norton, 124-166.

Phelps, Edmund S., and Sidney G. Winter, Jr., 1970, "Optimal Price Policy Under Atomistic Competition," in E. S. Phelps et al., *Microeconomic Foundations of Employment and Inflation Theory*, New York: Norton, 309-337.

Phelps, Edmund S., et al., 1970, *Microeconomic Foundations of Employment and Inflation Theory*, New York: Norton.

Pigou, Arthur C., 1929, *Industrial Fluctuations*, 2nd ed., London: Macmillian.

Poole, William, 1970, "Optimal Choice of Monetary Policy Instruments in a Simple Stochastic Macro Model," *Quarterly Journal of Economics*, 84, 197-216.

Shiller, Robert J., 1987, "Ultimate Sources of Aggregate Variability," *American Economic Review*, 77, 87-92.

Sims, Christopher A., 1980, "Macroeconomics and Reality," *Econometrica*, 48, 1-48.

_____, 1993, "A Nine-Variable Probabilistic Macroeconomic Forecasting Model," in James H. Stock and Mark W. Watson, eds., *Business Cycles, Indicators, and Forecasting*, Chicago: The University of Chicago Press, 179-204.

Stigler, George J., 1961, "The Economics of Information," *Journal of Political Economy*, 69, 213-225.

Stock, James H., and Mark W. Watson, 1989, "New Indexes of Coincident and Leading Economic Indicators," Discussion Paper No. 178D, John Fitzgerald Kennedy School of Government, Harvard University, April.

Stoker, Thomas M., 1986, "Simple Tests of Distributional Effects on Macroeconomic Equations," *Journal of Political Economy*, 94, 763-795.

Taylor, John B., 1980, "Output and Price Stability: An International Comparison," *Journal of Economic Dynamics and Control*, 2, 109-132.

_____, 1988, "Policy Analysis with a Multicountry Model," NBER Working Paper.

_____, and Harald Uhlig, 1990, "Solving Nonlinear Stochastic Growth Models: A Comparison of Alternative Solution Methods," *Journal of Business and Economic Statistics*, 8, 1-21.

Tinbergen, J., 1939, *Statistical Testing of Business Cycle Theories*, Geneva: League of Nations.

Tinsley, P. A., and P. von zur Muehlen, 1983, "Conditional Intermediate Targeting," Mimeo.

Tobin, James, 1982, "Financial Structure and Monetary Rules," *Geld, Banken und Versicherungen, Band 1 (VVW, Karlsruhe)*.

Triplett, Jack E., 1992, "Economic Theory and BEA's Alternative Quantity and Price Indexes," *Survey of Current Business*, 72, 49-52.

Turnovsky, S., 1975, "Optimal Choice of Monetary Instrument in a Linear Economic Model with Stochastic Coefficients," *Journal of Money, Credit, and Banking*, 7, 51-80.

White, Halbert, 1980, "A Heteroskedasticity Consistent Covariance Matrix Estimator and a Direct Test for Heteroskedasticity," *Econometrica*, 48, 817-838.

White, Halbert, and Ian Domowitz, 1984, "Nonlinear Regression with Dependent Observations," *Econometrica*, 52, 143-161.

Yoshikawa, H., 1981, "Alternative Monetary Policies and Stability in a Stochastic Keynesian Model," *International Economic Review*, 22, 541-565.

Young, Allan H., 1992, "Alternative Measures of Change in Real Output and Prices," *Survey of Current Business*, 72, 32-48.

Index